BESTSELLING
BOOK SERIES

QuickBooks® All-in-One Desk Reference For Dummies® 2nd Edition

Cheat Sheet

W9-BEZ-384

Speedy Keyboard Shortcuts

Shortcut Key Combination	Result
Ctrl+A	Displays the Chart of Accounts window
Ctrl+C	Copies your selection to the clipboard
Ctrl+F	Displays the Find window
Ctrl+G	Goes to the other side of a transfer transaction
Ctrl+I	Displays the Create Invoice window
Ctrl+J	Displays the Customer:Job List window
Ctrl+M	Memorizes a transaction
Ctrl+N	Creates a new *<form>* where *form* is whatever is active at the time
Ctrl+P	Almost always prints the currently active register, list, or form
Ctrl+Q	Creates and displays a QuickReport on the selected transaction
Ctrl+R	Displays the Register window
Crtl+T	Displays the memorized transaction list
Ctrl+V	Pastes the contents of the clipboard
Ctrl+W	Displays the Write Checks window
Ctrl+X	Moves your selection to the clipboard
Ctrl+Z	Undoes your last action — usually
Ctrl+Ins	Inserts a line into a list of items or expenses
Ctrl+Del	Deletes the selected line from a list of items or expenses

How to Perform Common Tasks

To perform a common accounting or bookkeeping task, use these commands. When QuickBooks displays the commands window, you just fill in the boxes and press Enter.

To Do This	Choose This Command
Dealing with Customers	
Invoice a customer	Customers⇨Create Invoices
Record a cash sale	Customers⇨Enter Cash Receipts
Issue a credit memo	Customers⇨Create Credit Memo/Refunds
Record a customer payment	Customers⇨Receive Payments

Copyright © 2005 Wiley Publishing, Inc. All rights reserved.

Item 7662-3.

For more information about Wiley Publishing, call 1-800-762-2974.

For Dummies: Bestselling Book Series for Beginners

QuickBooks® All-in-One Desk Reference For Dummies, 2nd Edition

Cheat Sheet

How to Perform Common Tasks *(continued)*

To Do This	Choose This Command
Banking Activities	
Pay a bill with a check	Banking⇨Write Checks
Buy inventory with a check	Banking⇨Write Checks
Move money between bank accounts	Banking⇨Transfer Funds
Deposit money in a bank account	Banking⇨Make Deposit
See a bank account's transactions	Banking⇨Use Register
Reconcile a bank account	Banking⇨Reconcile
Working with Vendors	
Prepare a purchase order	Vendors⇨Create Purchase Orders
Record when items are received	Vendors⇨Receive Items or Vendors⇨Receive Items and Enter Bill
Record an accounts payable amount	Vendors⇨Enter Bills or Vendors⇨Enter Bills for Received Items
Managing Employees	
Preparing employee payroll	Employees⇨Pay Employees
Paying tax deposits	Employees⇨Pay Liabilities
Updating tax tables	Employees⇨Get Updates⇨Get Updates
Getting Financial Information	
Accounts	Lists⇨Chart of Accounts
Customers	Lists⇨Customer:Job List
Inventory	Lists⇨Item List
Vendors	Lists⇨Vendor List
Employees	Lists⇨Employee List
Managing Employees	
Profit and loss	Reports⇨Company & Financial⇨Profit & Loss Standard or one of the other profit & loss reports on Company & Financial submenu
Net worth	Reports⇨Company & Financial⇨Balance Sheet Standard or one of the other balance sheet reports on the Company & Financial submenu
Managing the QuickBooks System	
Setting up a new company	File⇨New Company
Resetting company information	Company⇨Company Information
Backing up data file	File⇨Back Up
Restoring a data file	File⇨Restore
Customizing QuickBooks	Edit⇨Preferences
Adjusting accounting data	Company⇨Make Journal Entry

For Dummies: Bestselling Book Series for Beginners

QuickBooks®

ALL-IN-ONE DESK REFERENCE

FOR

DUMMIES®

2ND EDITION

QuickBooks®
ALL-IN-ONE DESK REFERENCE

FOR
DUMMIES®
2ND EDITION

by Stephen L. Nelson, MBA, CPA

WILEY

Wiley Publishing, Inc.

QuickBooks® All-in-One Desk Reference For Dummies® 2nd Edition

Published by
Wiley Publishing, Inc.
111 River Street
Hoboken, NJ 07030-5774

WILEY

About the Author

Stephen L. Nelson is a CPA in Redmond, Washington. He provides accounting, business advisory, and tax planning and preparation services to small businesses such as manufacturers, retailers, professional service firms, and startup technology companies. He also teaches CPAs how to help their clients use QuickBooks more effectively and is an Adjunct Professor of Tax at Golden Gate University where he teaches S corporation and LLC tax law.

Curiously enough, Nelson is also the most prolific computer book writer of all time, according to a recent feature in *The Wall Street Journal*. He's also the bestselling author of books about how to use computers to manage one's personal and business finances. In fact, Nelson's 100-plus books have sold more than 4,000,000 copies in English and have been translated into more than a dozen other languages.

Steve holds a BS in accounting, an MBA in finance, and a Master of Science in Taxation. He's been a CPA for more than twenty years. He used to work as a senior consultant with Arthur Andersen & Co. (Yes, *that* Arthur Andersen — but, hey, it was a long time ago.) He also has been the controller and treasurer of a 50-person manufacturing firm and has run his own manufacturing firm. Steve is also the bestselling author of *Quicken 2004 For Dummies* and *QuickBooks 2004 For Dummies* (from Wiley).

Dedication

To the entrepreneurs and small-business people of the world. You folks create most of the new jobs.

Author's Acknowledgments

Okay, I'm not going to make this an Academy Awards-style speech, but let me thank just a few people. First, I want to thank my business school and tax professors at Central Washington University, the University of Washington, and Golden Gate University. Next, thanks to the business clients who've given me the honor of working with them and teaching me about their businesses and industries. Finally, I want to thank all my friends and colleagues at Wiley Publishing, Inc., who gave me the distinct honor of writing not only this book but also *Quicken For Dummies* (14 editions) and *QuickBooks For Dummies* (9 editions). I also want to say a specific thanks to Bob Woerner, my acquisitions editor, Christine Berman, my project editor and copy editor, and David Ringstrom, who performed the technical edit.

Publisher's Acknowledgments

We're proud of this book; please send us your comments through our online registration form located at www.dummies.com/register/.

Some of the people who helped bring this book to market include the following:

Acquisitions, Editorial, and Media Development

Project Editor: Christine Berman

Acquisitions Editor: Bob Woerner

Copy Editor: Christine Berman

Technical Editor: David Ringstrom

Editorial Manager: Carol Sheehan

Media Development Manager: Laura VanWinkle

Media Development Supervisor: Richard Graves

Editorial Assistant: Amanda Foxworth

Cartoons: Rich Tennant (www.the5thwave.com)

Production

Project Coordinator: Emily Wichlinski

Layout and Graphics: Andrea Dahl, Lauren Goddard, Joyce Haughey, Stephanie D. Jumper, Melanee Prendergast, Jacque Roth, Heather Ryan, Julie Trippetti

Proofreaders: Leeann Harney, Jessica Kramer, Linda Quigley

Indexer: Anne Leach

Publishing and Editorial for Technology Dummies

> **Richard Swadley,** Vice President and Executive Group Publisher
>
> **Andy Cummings,** Vice President and Publisher
>
> **Mary Bednarek,** Executive Acquisitions Director
>
> **Mary C. Corder,** Editorial Director

Publishing for Consumer Dummies

> **Diane Graves Steele,** Vice President and Publisher
>
> **Joyce Pepple,** Acquisitions Director

Composition Services

> **Gerry Fahey,** Vice President of Production Services
>
> **Debbie Stailey,** Director of Composition Services

Contents at a Glance

Table of Contents

Introduction

*F*ew people read introductions to reference books, so I'll make this very brief. I just want to tell you which versions of QuickBooks this book works for, what's in the reference, what it assumes about your existing skills, and about the conventions used in the reference.

About This Book

QuickBooks comes in several different flavors, including QuickBooks Basic, QuickBooks Pro, and QuickBooks Premier. This reference talks about QuickBooks 2005 Pro, which is a superset of QuickBooks Basic and a subset of QuickBooks Premium.

However, don't freak out if you're using the simpler version of QuickBooks, QuickBooks Basic, or the more fully featured version of QuickBooks, QuickBooks Premier. And don't freak out if you're using some version of QuickBooks that's very similar to QuickBooks 2005, such as QuickBooks 2003, QuickBooks 2004, or QuickBooks 2006. All the versions of QuickBooks work in roughly the same way. Note, too, that specialty versions of QuickBooks like QuickBooks Accountants Edition and QuickBooks Contractors version also work almost identically to QuickBooks Pro.

If you see some whistle or bell that you really want to use but that isn't available in your version of QuickBooks, you'll know that you should upgrade to the Pro or Premier version of QuickBooks.

Although this reference is about QuickBooks Pro 2005, it also works just fine for the 2001, 2002, and probably 2006 versions of QuickBooks because QuickBooks is a very mature product at this point. The changes from one year to the next are modest. This means that if you're using QuickBooks 2003, stuff may look a little different if you closely compare the images in this book to what you see on your screen, but the information in this reference will still apply to your situation.

The bottom line? Yes, QuickBooks comes in several flavors. Yes, Intuit publishes new editions of these products every year. But you can use this book for any recent version of QuickBooks Basic, QuickBooks Pro, or QuickBooks Premier.

How to Use This Book

This reference combines eight short books, including a book about accounting, one about setting up the QuickBooks system, one for bookkeepers using QuickBooks, one for accountants and managers using QuickBooks, a book about small business financial management, a book about business planning, a book about taking care of a QuickBooks accounting system, and a book of appendixes of further useful information.

I'm not going to go into more detail here about what's available in the book. If you have a specific question about what's covered or where some topic is covered, refer to the Table of Contents in the front of this reference. Remember also that the book provides an index for jumping to the page or pages with the information you need.

While I'm on the subject of what's in this book and how to find information, let me make four tangential points:

✦ You would never read this book from cover to cover unless you're someone with an obsessive-compulsive personality (like me) and many hours to devote to your reading. But that's okay. This reference isn't meant to be read from cover to cover like some Harry Potter page-turner. Instead, chapters within the eight books are organized into largely self-contained descriptions of how you do the things that you need to do. You just read the paragraph, page, or chapter that provides the information you want.

✦ I have not discussed in any detail how to use the QuickBooks Premier features for business planning. The wizard-based approach that QuickBooks Premier provides for business planning is not, in my humble opinion, the right way to do this. Instead, I discuss in detail alternative, superior approaches to business planning and budgeting (using spreadsheets) in Book VI. (Just so you know: The approach I describe and recommend here is the same one that any business school teaches its students.)

✦ At a few points in the book, you'll find me saying things like, "Well, I really don't think you should use this part of the product." I just want to explain here, up front, where I'm coming from on this. First, know that I think QuickBooks is an outstanding product. But not every feature and every command is good. I've already mentioned that the new business planning tools aren't ones that I can recommend. And payroll, very frankly, is another pain-in-the-butt feature that most businesses should avoid. (I do briefly discuss payroll in Book III, Chapter 5.) So, if I think that a particular feature is one that you shouldn't use, I don't use page space (or much page space) describing the feature. I want to rather use that page space to describe other stuff that I believe is going to be valuable to you and other readers.

✦ I should also mention one final thing: Accounting software programs require you to do a certain amount of preparation before you can use them to get real work done. If you haven't started to use QuickBooks yet, I recommend that you skim through Book I and then read Book II to find out what you need to do first.

Hey. There's something else I should tell you. I have fiddled a bit with the Windows display property settings. For example, I've noodled around with the font settings and most of the colors. The benefit is that the pictures in this book are easy to read. And that's good. But the cost of all this is that my pictures look a little bit different than what you see on your screen. In a few places, command buttons get "cut off" on the right side of image, for example. That's not perfect, of course. But in the end, the publisher has found that people are really happier with increased readability. Anyway, I just thought I should mention this here, up front, in case you had any questions about it.

Foolish Assumptions

I'm making only three assumptions about your QuickBooks and accounting skills:

✦ You have a PC with Microsoft Windows 95 or later, or Windows NT 4.0 or higher. (I took pictures of the QuickBooks windows and dialog boxes using Windows XP, in case you're interested.)

✦ You know a little bit about how to work with your computer.

✦ You have or will buy a copy of QuickBooks, QuickBooks Pro, or QuickBooks Premier for each computer on which you want to run the program.

In other words, I don't assume that you're a computer genius or an M.B.A. or super-experienced in the arcane rules of accounting. I assume that QuickBooks and accounting are new subjects to you. But I also assume that you want to learn the subjects because you need to for your job or your business.

Personally, I use QuickBooks Pro, so this book includes some features unique to the Pro and Premier versions. If you're trying to decide which version to buy, I should tell you that QuickBooks Pro and Premier include networking capabilities (which I describe in Book VII, Chapters 1 and 2) and the ability to create estimates and bids (which I describe in Book III, Chapter 1). The standard version of QuickBooks doesn't include these features.

By the way, if you're just starting out with Microsoft Windows, peruse Chapter 1 of the Windows User's Guide or one of the *Windows For Dummies* books on your flavor of Windows, such as *Windows XP For Dummies,* by Andy Rathbone (Wiley Publishing, Inc.).

How This Book Is Organized

This book is organized into eight individual "books." Some of these books give you the skinny on how to powerfully and effectively perform routine tasks with QuickBooks; others focus on general accounting, business planning, or other aspects of managing your operation. All of them, however, deliver the kind of information that savvy business owners need.

Book I: An Accounting Primer

For you non-accountants, Book I covers the basics of general accounting. If you don't know a debit from a credit, this is the place to start.

Book II: Getting Ready to Use QuickBooks

Book II lays the groundwork for using QuickBooks effectively: setting up the program, loading files, and customizing QuickBooks for your purposes.

Book III: Bookkeeping Chores

Book III shows you how to take on those work-a-day tasks in QuickBooks: invoicing customers, paying vendors, and tracking inventory, just to name a few.

Book IV: Accounting Chores

If you really want to get in touch with your inner accountant, this is the part for you. In Book IV, I take on activity-based costing, preparing a budget, and job costing.

Book V: Financial Management

In Book V, I dig into advanced financial management strategies: ratio analysis, EVA, and capital budgeting.

Book VI: Business Plans

Ever wonder what Wal-Mart does so right, while K-Mart continues to flounder? Turn to Book VI to find out how to write a business plan that can help you find your niche.

Book VII: Care and Maintenance

Book VII shows you how to do the things that will keep you working happily and productively in QuickBooks for years to come: setting up a network, protecting your data, and troubleshooting.

Book VIII: Appendixes

QuickBooks is a great program, but it can't do it all. You may find that a spreadsheet program is just the tool you need to supplement QuickBooks. For that reason, in Book VIII, I provide a quick primer on Excel. I also offer an appendix detailing several great online government resources, as well as a glossary of (nearly) every business or accounting term you would ever want to know.

Stuff at My Web site

Oh, here's something I should probably mention. This book has a little bit of companion Web site content that can be found at www.stephenlnelson.com. In a handful of places, I'll provide URLs that you can use to download Excel workbooks discussed in several chapters of this book.

Conventions Used in This Book

To make the best use of your time and energy, you should know about the conventions I use in this book.

When I want you to type something such as **Jennifer**, it's in bold letters.

By the way, except for passwords, you don't have to worry about the case of the stuff you type in QuickBooks. If I tell you to type **Jennifer**, you can type **JENNIFER**. Or you can follow poet e. e. cummings' lead and type **jennifer**.

Whenever I tell you to choose a command from a menu, I say something like, Choose Lists⇨Items, which simply means to first choose the Lists menu and then choose Items. The ⇨ separates one part of the command from the next part.

You can choose menus and commands and select dialog box elements with the mouse. Just click the thing that you want to select.

While I'm on the subject of conventions, let me also mention something about QuickBooks conventions because it turns out there's not really any good place to point this out. QuickBooks doesn't use document windows the same way that other Windows programs do. Instead, it locks the active window into place and then displays a list of windows in its Navigator pane, which is like another little window. To move to a listed window, you click it.

You can tell QuickBooks to use windows like every other program does, however, by choosing View⇨Multiple Windows. You can even remove the Navigator pane by choosing View⇨Open Window List. (You can also move the other locked pane that lists windows and is called the Shortcuts List by choosing View⇨Shortcuts List.)

Special Icons

Like many computer books, this book uses icons, or little pictures, to flag things that don't quite fit into the flow of things:

 Whee, here's a shortcut or pointer to make your life easier!

 This icon is just a friendly reminder to do something.

 And this icon is a friendly reminder not to do something . . . or else.

 This icon points out nerdy technical material that you may want to skip (or read, if you're feeling particularly bright).

Book I

An Accounting Primer

"I bought a software program that should help us monitor and control our spending habits, and while I was there, I picked up a few new games, a couple of screen savers, 4 new mousepads, this nifty pull out keyboard cradle..."

Contents at a Glance

Chapter 1: Principles of Accounting

In This Chapter

- ✔ Figuring out the purpose of accounting
- ✔ Reviewing the common financial statements
- ✔ Understanding the philosophy of accounting
- ✔ Discovering income tax accounting and reporting

A ny discussion of how to use QuickBooks to better manage your business begins with a discussion of the basics of accounting. For this reason, in this chapter and the next two chapters, I attempt to provide the same information that you may receive in an introductory college accounting course. Of course, I tailor the entire discussion to QuickBooks and the small business environment. What you'll read about here and in the next chapters of this book pretty much describes how accounting works in a small business setting using QuickBooks.

If you have had some experience with accounting, if you know how to read an income statement and balance sheet, or if you know how to construct a journal entry, you don't need to read the discussion provided by this chapter or the next. However, if you're new to accounting and business bookkeeping, take the time to carefully read this chapter. The chapter starts by giving a high-level overview of the purpose of accounting. Then, I review the common financial statements that any accounting system worth its salt produces. I also discuss some of the important principles of accounting and the philosophy of accounting. Finally, I talk a little bit about income tax law and tax accounting.

Purpose of Accounting

In the movie *Creator*, Peter O'Toole plays an eccentric professor. At one point, O'Toole's character attempts to talk a young student into working as an unpaid research assistant. When the student protests, noting that he needs 15 credit hours, O'Toole creates a special 15-credit independent study named "Introduction to the Big Picture." In the next section, I describe the "big picture" of accounting, which is really the appropriate place to begin a discussion of accounting. At its very core, accounting makes perfect, logical sense.

The big picture

The most important thing that you need to understand about accounting is that accounting provides financial information to stakeholders. Stakeholders are the people who do business with or interact with a firm; they include managers, employees, investors, banks, vendors, government authorities, and agencies who may tax a firm. Each of these stakeholders and their information requirements deserve a bit more discussion. Why? Because the information needs of these stakeholders determine what an accounting system needs to do.

Managers, investors, and entrepreneurs

The first category of stakeholders is the managers, investors, and entrepreneurs. This group needs financial information to determine whether a business is making money. This group also wants any information that gives insight into whether a business is growing or contracting, and how healthy or sick it is. In order to fulfill its obligations and duties, this group often needs detailed information. For example, a manager or entrepreneur may want to know which customers are particularly profitable — or unprofitable. An active investor may want to know which product lines are growing or contracting.

A related set of information requirements concerns asset and liability record keeping. An *asset* is something that the firm owns, such as cash, inventory, or equipment. A *liability* is some debt or obligation that the firm owes, such as bank loans and accounts payable.

Obviously, someone at a firm — perhaps a manager, bookkeeper, or accountant — needs to have very detailed records of the amount of cash that the firm has in its bank accounts, the inventory that the firm has in its warehouse or on its shelves, and the equipment that the firm owns and uses in its operations.

If you look over the preceding two paragraphs, nothing I've said is particularly surprising regarding the financial information requirements needed by a firm's management. It makes sense, right? Someone who works in a business, manages a business, or actively invests in a business needs good general information about the financial affairs of the firm and, in many cases, very detailed information about important assets (such as cash) and liabilities (such as bank loans).

External creditors

A second category of stakeholders includes outside firms that loan money to a business and credit reporting agencies that supply information to these lenders. For example, banks want to know about the financial affairs and financial condition of a firm before lending money. The accounting system needs to produce the financial information that a bank requires in order to consider a loan request.

What information do lenders want? Lenders want to know that a business is profitable and enjoys a positive cash flow. Profits and positive cash flows allow a business to easily repay debt. In a worst case scenario, a bank or other lender also wants to see assets that can be liquidated to pay a loan — and also other debts that may represent a claim on the firm's assets.

Vendors also typically require financial information from a firm. A vendor often loans a firm money by extending trade credit. What's noteworthy about this is that vendors sometimes require special accounting. For example, one of the categories of vendors that a company such as Wiley Publishing, Inc. deals with is authors. In order to pay an author the royalty that he or she is entitled to, Wiley needs to put in a fair amount of work to calculate royalty-per-unit amounts and then report and remit these amounts to authors.

Other firms sometimes have similar financial reporting requirements for vendors. Franchisees (such as the man or woman who owns and operates the local McDonald's) pay a franchise fee based on revenues. Retailers may need to perform special accounting and reporting in order to enjoy rebates and incentives from the manufacturers of the products that they sell.

Government agencies

Predictable stakeholders requiring financial information from a business are the federal and state government agencies with jurisdiction over the firm. For example, every business in the United States needs to report on its revenues, expenses, and profits so that the firm can correctly calculate income tax due to the federal government and then pay that tax.

Firms with employees must also report to the federal and state government on wages paid to those employees — and pay payroll taxes based on metrics, such as number of employees, wages paid to employees, and unemployment benefits claimed by past employees.

Providing this sort of financial information to government agencies represents a key duty of a firm's accounting system.

Business form generation

In addition to the financial reporting described in the preceding paragraphs, accounting systems typically perform one other key task for businesses: producing business forms. For example, an accounting system almost always produces the checks needed to pay vendors. In addition, an accounting system also prepares the invoices and payroll checks. More sophisticated accounting systems, such as those used by large firms, prepare many other business forms, including purchase orders, monthly customer statements, credit memos to customers, sales receipts, and so forth.

Every accounting function that I have described so far is performed ably by each of the versions of QuickBooks: QuickBooks, QuickBooks Pro, and QuickBooks Premier.

Reviewing the Common Financial Statements

With the background information just provided, I'm ready to talk about some of the common financial statements or accounting reports that an accounting system like QuickBooks produces. If you understand which reports you want your accounting system to produce, you should find it much easier to collect the raw data necessary to prepare these reports.

In the following paragraphs, I describe the three principal financial statements: the income statement, the balance sheet, and the statement of cash flows. I also briefly describe a fourth, catch-all category of accounting reports.

Don't worry — I'll go through this material slowly. You need to understand what financial statements and accounting systems are supposed to provide and what data these financial statements supply.

The income statement

Perhaps the most important financial statement that an accounting system produces is the income statement. The income statement is also known as a profit and loss statement. An income statement summarizes a firm's revenues and expenses for a particular period of time. *Revenues* represent amounts that a business earns by providing goods and services to its customers. *Expenses* represent amounts that a firm spends providing those goods and services. If a business can provide goods or services to customers for revenues that exceed its expenses, the firm earns a profit. If expenses exceed revenues, obviously, the firm suffers a loss.

To show you how this all works — and it's really pretty simple — take a look at Tables 1-1 and 1-2. Table 1-1 summarizes the sales that an imaginary business enjoys. Table 1-2 summarizes the expenses that the same business incurs for the same period of time. These two tables provide all the information necessary to construct an income statement.

Table 1-1	A Sales Journal
Joe	$1,000
Bob	500
Frank	1,000
Abdul	2,000
Yoshio	2,750
Marie	2,250
Jeremy	1,000
Chang	2,500
Total sales	$13,000

Table 1-2	An Expenses Journal
Purchases of dogs and buns	$3,000
Rent	1,000
Wages	4,000
Supplies	1,000
Total supplies	$9,000

Using the information from Tables 1-1 and 1-2, you can construct the simple income statement shown in Table 1-3. Because understanding the details of this income statement is key to your understanding of how accounting works and what accounting tries to do, I want to go into some detail discussing this income statement.

Table 1-3	Simple Income Statement
Sales revenue	$13,000
Less: Cost of goods sold	3,000
Gross margin	$10,000
Operating expenses	
Rent	$1,000
Wages	4,000
Supplies	1,000
Total operating expenses	6,000
Operating profit	$4,000

The first thing to note about the income statement shown in Table 1-3 is the sales revenue figure of $13,000. This sales revenue figure shows the sales generated for a particular period of time. The $13,000 figure shown in Table 1-3 comes directly from the Sales Journal shown in Table 1-1.

One important thing to recognize about accounting for sales revenue is that revenue gets counted when goods or services are provided, and not when a customer pays for the goods or services. If you look at the list of sales shown in Table 1-1, for example, Joe (the first customer listed) may have paid $1,000 in cash, but Bob, Frank, and Abdul (the second, third, and fourth customers) may have paid for their purchases with a credit card. Yoshio, Marie, and Jeremy (the fifth, sixth, and seventh customers listed) may not have even paid for their purchases at the time the goods or services were provided. These customers may have simply promised to pay for the purchases at some later date. However, this timing of the payment for goods or services doesn't matter. Accountants have figured out that you count revenue when goods or services are provided. Information about when customers pay for those goods or services, if you want that information, can come from lists of customer payments. Cost of goods sold and gross margins are two other values that you commonly see on income statements. Before I discuss cost of goods sold and gross margins, however, let me add a little more detail to this example. Suppose, for example, that the financial information shown in Tables 1-1, 1-2, and 1-3 shows the financial results from your business: the hot dog stand that you operate for one day at the major sporting event in the city where you live. Table 1-1 describes sales to customers (now hungry customers). Table 1-2 summarizes the one-day expenses of operating your super-duper hot dog stand.

In this case, the actual items that you sell — hot dogs and buns — are separately shown on the income statement as cost of goods sold. By separately showing the cost of the goods sold, the income statement can show what is called a *gross margin*. The gross margin is the amount of revenue left over after paying for the cost of goods. In Table 1-3, the cost of goods sold shows $3,000 for purchases of dogs and buns. The difference between the $13,000 of sales revenue and the $3,000 of cost of goods sold equals $10,000, which is the gross margin.

Knowing how to calculate gross margin allows you to estimate firm break-even points and also to perform profit, volume, and cost analyses. All of these techniques are extremely useful for thinking about the financial affairs of your business. In fact, Book VI, Chapter 1 describes how you can perform these sorts of analyses.

The operating expenses portion of the simple income statement shown in Table 1-3 repeats the other information listed in the Expenses Journal. The

$1,000 of rent, the $4,000 of wages, and the $1,000 of supplies get totaled. These operating expenses are then subtracted from the gross.

Do you see, then, what an income statement does? An income statement reports on the revenues that a firm has generated. It shows the cost of goods sold and calculates the gross margin. It identifies and shows operating expenses, and finally, shows the profits of the business.

One other important point: Income statements summarize revenues, expenses, and profits for a particular period of time. Some managers and entrepreneurs, for example, may want to prepare income statements on a daily basis. Public companies are required to prepare income statements on a quarterly and annual basis. And taxing authorities, such as the Internal Revenue Service, require preparation both quarterly and annually.

Technically speaking, the quarterly statements required by the Internal Revenue Service don't need to report revenue. The Internal Revenue Service only requires quarterly statements of wages paid to employees. Only the annual income statements required by the Internal Revenue Service report both revenue and expenses. These are the income statements produced to prepare an annual income tax return.

Balance sheet

The second most important financial statement that an accounting system produces is a *balance sheet*. A balance sheet reports on a business's assets, liabilities, and owner contributions of capital at a particular point in time.

+ The assets shown on a balance sheet are those items that are owned by the business, which have value, and for which money was paid.

+ The liabilities shown on a balance sheet are those amounts that a business owes to other people, businesses, and government agencies.

+ The owner's contributions of capital are the amounts that owners, partners, or shareholders have paid into the business in the form of investment or have reinvested in the business by leaving profits inside the company.

As long as you understand what assets and liabilities are, a balance sheet is easy to understand and interpret. Table 1-4, for example, shows a simple balance sheet. Pretend that this balance sheet shows the condition of the hot dog stand at the beginning of the day, before any hot dogs have been sold. The first portion of the balance sheet shows and totals the two assets of the hot dog stand business: the $1,000 of cash that may be in the cash register in a box under the counter, and the $3,000 of hot dogs and buns that you've purchased in order to sell during the day.

Table 1-4	A Simple Balance Sheet
Assets	
Cash	$1,000
Inventory	3,000
Total assets	$4,000
Liabilities	
Accounts payable	$2,000
Loan payable	1,000
Owner's equity	
S. Nelson, capital	1,000
Total liabilities and owner's equity	$4,000

Balance sheets can use several other categories to report assets: accounts receivable (these are amounts that customers owe), investments, fixtures, equipment, and long-term investments. In the case of a small owner-operated business, not all of these asset categories show up. But if you look at the balance sheet of a very large business — say one of the 100 largest businesses in the United States — you will see these sorts of other categories.

The liabilities section of the balance sheet shows the amounts that the firm owes to other people and businesses. For example, the balance sheet in Table 1-4 shows $2,000 of accounts payable and a $1,000 loan payable. Presumably, the $2,000 of accounts payable is the money that you owe to the vendors who have supplied your hot dogs and buns. The $1,000 loan payable represents some loan you've taken out — perhaps from some well-meaning and naive relative.

The owner's equity section shows the amount that the owner, the partners, or shareholders have contributed to the business in the form of original funds invested or profits reinvested. I should make one important point about the balance sheet shown in Table 1-4: This balance sheet shows how owner's equity looks when the business is a sole proprietorship. In the case of a sole proprietor, only one line is reported in the owner's equity section of the balance sheet. This line combines all contributions made by the proprietor — both amounts originally invested and amounts reinvested.

I talk a bit more about owner's equity accounting later in this chapter because the owner's equity sections look different for partnerships and corporations. Before I get into that, however, let me make two important observations about the balance sheet shown in Table 1-4. A balance sheet needs to *balance*. This means that the total assets must equal the total of the liabilities and owner's equity. In the balance sheet shown in Table 1-4, for example, total assets shows as $4,000. Total liabilities and owner's equity also shows as $4,000. This equality is no coincidence. If an accounting system works right and the accountants and bookkeepers entering information into this system do their jobs right, the balance sheet balances.

Another observation worth making is that a balance sheet provides a snapshot of a business's financial condition at a particular point in time. For example, I mention in the introductory remarks related to Table 1-4 that the balance sheet in this table shows the financial condition of the hot dog stand business immediately before beginning the day's business activities. You can prepare a balance sheet for any point in time. It is key that you understand that a balance sheet is prepared for a particular point in time.

By convention, businesses prepare balance sheets to show the financial condition at the end of the period of time for which an income statement is prepared. For example, a business typically prepares an income statement on an annual basis. In this orthodox situation, a firm also prepares a balance sheet at the very end of the year.

At this point, I return to something that I alluded to previously in the chapter — the fact that the owner's equity section of a balance sheet looks different for different types of businesses.

Table 1-5 shows how the owner's equity section of a balance sheet looks for a partnership. In Table 1-5, I show how the owner's equity section of the hot dog stand business may appear if, instead of having a sole proprietor named S. Nelson running the hot dog stand, the business is actually owned and operated by three partners named Tom, Dick, and Harry. In this case, the partners' equity section shows the amounts originally invested and any amounts reinvested by the partners. As is the case with sole proprietorships, each partner's contributions and reinvested profits appear on a single line.

Table 1-5	Owner's Equity for a Partnership
Partners' equity	
Tom, capital	$500
Dick, capital	250
Harry, capital	250
Total partner capital	$1,000

Go ahead and take a look at Table 1-6. It shows how the owner's equity section looks for a corporation.

Table 1-6	Owner's Equity for a Corporation
Shareholders' equity	
Capital stock, 100 shs at $1 par	$100
Contributed capital in excess of par	400
Retained earnings	500
Total shareholder's equity	$1,000

This next part is a little bit weird. For a corporation, the amounts that show in the owner's equity or shareholder's equity section actually fall into two major categories: *retained earnings* and *contributed capital*. Retained earnings represent profits that the shareholders have left in the business. Contributed capital is the money originally contributed by the shareholders to the corporation.

The retained earnings thing makes sense, right? That's just the money — the profits — that investors have reinvested in the business.

The contributed capital thing is more complicated. Here's how it works: If you buy a share of stock in some new corporation — for say, $5 — typically some portion of that price per share is for par value. Now don't ask me to justify par value. It really stems from business practices that were common a century or more ago. Just trust that typically, if you pay some amount — again, say $5 — for a share, some portion of the amount that you pay — maybe 10 cents a share or $1 a share — is for par value.

In the owner's equity section of a corporation's balance sheet, capital that's contributed by original investors is broken down into the amounts paid for this mysterious par value and the amounts paid in excess of this par value. For example, in Table 1-6, you can see that $100 of shareholder's equity or owner's equity represents amounts paid for par value. Another $400 of the amounts contributed by the original investors represents amounts paid in excess of par value. The total shareholder's equity, or total corporate owner's equity, equals the sum of the capital stock par value, the contributed capital and excess of par value, and any retained earnings. So in Table 1-6, the total shareholder's equity equals $1,000.

Statement of cash flows

Now I come to the one tricky financial statement: the statement of cash flows.

Before I begin, I have one comment to make about the statement of cash flows: As an accountant, I've worked with many bright managers and business people. No matter how much handholding and explanation I or other accountants provide, some of these smart people never quite get some of the numbers on the statement of cash flows. In fact, many of the students who major in accounting never (in my opinion, at least) quite get how a statement of cash flows really works.

For this reason, don't spend *too* much time spinning your wheels on this statement or trying to understand what it does. QuickBooks does supply a statement of cash flows, but you don't need to use this statement. In fact, QuickBooks will produce cash basis income statements, which get you almost the same information — and in a more easy-to-understand format.

I think the best way to explain what a statement of cash flows does is to ask you to look again at the balance sheet shown in Table 1-4. This is the balance sheet for the imaginary hot dog stand at the beginning of the day.

Now take a look at Table 1-7, which shows the balance sheet at the end of the day, after operations for the hot dog stand have ended. Notice that at the start of the day, cash equals $1,000, and at the end of the day, cash equals $5,000. The statement of cash flows explains why cash changes from the one number to the other number over a period of time. In other words, a statement of cash flows explains how cash goes from $1,000 at the start of the day to $5,000 at the end of the day.

Table 1-7	Another Simple Balance Sheet
Assets	
Cash	$5,000
Inventory	0
Total assets	$5,000
Liabilities	
Accounts payable	$0
Loan payable	0
Owner's equity	
S. Nelson, capital	5,000
Total liabilities and owner's equity	$5,000

Table 1-8, not coincidentally, shows a statement of cash flows that explains how cash flowed for your imaginary hot dog stand business. You need to understand this statement, presumably, if you're reading this book. I am going to start at the bottom of the statement and work up.

Table 1-8	A Simple Statement of Cash Flows
Operating activities	
Net income	$4,000
Decrease in accounts payable	(2,000)
Adjustment: decrease in inventory	3,000
Net cash provided by operating activities	$5,000
Financing activities	
Decrease in notes payable	(1,000)
Net cash provided (used) by financing activities	(1,000)
Increase in cash	4,000
Cash balance at start of period	1,000
Cash balance at end of period	$5,000

By convention, accountants show negative numbers inside parentheses. These parentheses more clearly flag negative values than a simple minus sign.

The last three lines of the statement of cash flows are all easily understandable. The cash balance at the end of the period, $5,000, shows what cash the business holds at the end of the day. The cash balance at the start of the period, $1,000, shows the cash that the business holds at the beginning of the day. Both the cash balance at the start of the period and the cash balance at the end of the period tie to the cash balance values reported on the two balance sheets. (Look at Table 1-4 and Table 1-7 to corroborate this assertion.) Clearly, if you start the period with $1,000 and end the period with $5,000, cash has increased by $4,000. That's an arithmetic certainty. No question there, right?

The financing activities of the statement of cash flows shows how firm borrowing and firm debt repayment affect the firm cash flow. If the hot dog stand business uses its profits to repay the $1,000 loan payable — and, in this case, this is what happened — this $1,000 cash outflow shows up in the financing activities portion of the statement of cash flows as a negative $1,000.

The top portion of the statement of cash flows is often the trickiest to understand. Note, however, that I've talked about everything else in this statement. So, with a strong push, you'll fight your way through to an understanding of what is going on here.

The operating activities portion of the statement of cash flows essentially shows the cash that comes from the profit. If you look at Table 1-8, for example, you see that the first line in the operating activities portion of the statement of cash flows is net income for $4,000. This is the net income amount reported on the income statement for the period. However, the net income or operating profit reported on the business's income statement isn't necessarily the same thing as cash income or cash profit. A variety of factors need to be adjusted in order to convert this net income amount to what's essentially a cash operating profit amount.

For example, in the case of the hot dog stand business, if you use some of the profits to pay off all of the accounts payable, this payoff uses up some of your cash profit. This is exactly what Table 1-8 shows. You can see that the decrease in the accounts payable from $2,000 to $0 over the day required, quite logically, $2,000 of the net income. Another way to think about this is that essentially, you used up $2,000 of your cash profits to pay off accounts payable. Remember that the accounts payable is the amount that you owed your vendors for hot dogs and buns.

Another adjustment is required for the decrease in inventory. The decrease in inventory from the start of the period to the end of the period produces cash. Basically, you're liquidating inventory. Another way to think about this is that although this inventory — the hot dogs and buns in our example — shows up as an expense for the day's income statement, it isn't purchased during the day. It doesn't consume cash during the day; it was purchased at some point in the past.

When you combine the net income, the accounts payable adjustment, and the inventory adjustment, you get the net cash provided by the operating activities. In Table 1-8, these three amounts combine to $5,000 of cash provided by the operations.

After you understand the details of the financing and operating activities areas of the statement of cash flows, the statement makes sense. Net cash provided by the operating activities equals $5,000. Financing activities reduce cash by $1,000. This means that cash actually increased over the period by $4,000, which explains why cash starts the period at $1,000 and ends the period at $5,000.

Other accounting statements

Thinking back to the discussion at the very start of the chapter, you can probably come up with some examples of several other popular or useful accounting reports. And, not surprising, a good accounting system such as QuickBooks produces most of these reports. For example, one very common report or financial statement that you'll want to see is a list of the amounts that your customers owe you. It's a good idea, for example, to prepare and review such reports on a regular basis to make sure that you don't have customers turning into collection problems.

Table 1-9 shows how the simplest sort of accounts receivable report may look: Each customer is named along with the amount owed.

Table 1-9	An Accounts Receivable Report at End of Day
Customer	*Amount*
W. Churchill	$45.12
G. Patton	34.32
B. Montgomery	12.34
H. Petain	65.87
C. de Gaulle	43.21
Total receivables	$200.86

Table 1-10 shows another common accounting report — an inventory report that the hot dog stand may have at the start of the day. An inventory report like the one shown in Table 1-10 would probably name the various items held for resale, the quantity held, and the amount or value of the inventory item. A report such as this is useful to make sure that you have the appropriate quantities of inventory in stock. (Think of how useful such a report would be if you really were planning to sell thousands of hot dogs at major sporting events in your hometown.)

Table 1-10	An Inventory Report at Start of Day	
Item	*Quantity*	*Amount*
Kielbasa	2000	$900.00
Bratwurst	2000	1,000.00
Plain buns	2000	500.00
Sesame buns	2000	600.00
Total inventory		$3,000.00

Putting it all together

By now, you should understand what an accounting system does. When you boil everything down to its essence, it's straightforward, isn't it? Really, an accounting system just provides you with the financial information that you need to run your business.

Let me add a tangential but important point. QuickBooks supplies all this accounting information. For the most part, preparing these sorts of financial statements in QuickBooks is pretty darn easy. But you have to learn a bit more.

You'll find it helpful to learn about accounting and bookkeeping. However, I will go over that information in the coming chapters. Also, note that the big picture stuff covered in this chapter is the most important knowledge that you need. If you understand the ideas described in this chapter, the battle is more than half won.

Curious about different business forms?

Curious about the differences among a sole proprietorship, a partnership, and a corporation? A *sole proprietorship* is formed automatically in most states and in most industries when an individual decides to go into business. In many jurisdictions, the sole proprietor needs to acquire or apply for a business license from the state or local city government. Other than that modest hurdle, sole proprietorship requires no other special prerequisites.

A *partnership* is formed automatically when two or more people enter into a joint business or investment activity for the purpose of making a profit. As is the case with a sole proprietorship, partnerships typically need to acquire a business license from the state and perhaps the federal government. Partnership formation doesn't necessarily require any additional paperwork or legal maneuvering. However, if you do enter into a partnership, most attorneys (probably all attorneys) will tell you that you do so at a certain amount of risk if you don't have an attorney draw up a partnership agreement that outlines the duties and rights and responsibilities of the partners. However, it is important to note that you can actually form a partnership simply by collaborating in business with someone. The law books are full of stories of people, for example, who have inadvertently created partnerships merely by collaborating on some project, sharing office space, or working together in some activity.

In comparison, most states allow several other business forms, including *corporations,* limited liability companies, and limited liability partnerships. These other business forms require considerably more work to set up, the assistance of a good attorney, and payment of at least several hundred — and possibly several thousand — dollars in legal and licensing fees. The unique feature of most of these other business forms, however, is that the corporation or limited liability company or limited liability partnership becomes a separate legal entity. In many cases, this separate legal entity protects investors from creditors who have a claim on the assets of the business. In comparison, in a sole proprietorship or a partnership, the sole proprietor and the partners are liable for the debts and obligations of the proprietorship or the partnership.

If you have questions about the correct business form in which to operate, talk with a good local attorney. He or she can assist you in choosing the appropriate business form and in considering both the legal and tax aspects of choosing a particular form. As a general rule, more sophisticated business forms such as corporations, limited liability companies, or limited liability partnerships deliver significant legal and tax benefits to investors and managers. Unfortunately, these more sophisticated business forms also require considerably more legal and accounting fiddle-faddling.

The philosophy of accounting

Maybe the phrase "philosophy of accounting" is too strong, but accounting does rest on a rather small set of fundamental assumptions and principles. People often refer to these fundamentals as generally accepted accounting principles.

I want to quickly summarize what these principles are. I find — and I bet you find the same thing — that understanding the principles gives context and makes accounting practices more understandable. With this in mind, let me go through the half dozen or so key accounting principles and assumptions.

Revenue principle

The *revenue principle*, which is also known as the *realization principle*, states that revenue is earned when the sale is made. The sale is made, typically, when goods or services are provided. A key component of the revenue principle, when it comes to the sale of goods, is that revenue is earned when legal ownership of the goods passes from seller to buyer.

On the same token, note that revenue isn't earned when you collect cash for something. It turns out, perhaps counterintuitively, that counting revenue when cash is collected doesn't give the business owner a good idea of what sales really are. Some customers may pay deposits early, before actually receiving the goods or services. Often customers want to use trade credit, paying a firm at some point in the future for goods or services. Because cash flows can fluctuate wildly — even something like a delay in the mail can affect cash flow — you don't want to use cash collection from customers as a measure of sales. Besides that, you can easily track cash collections from customers. So why not have the extra information about when sales actually occur?

Expense principle

The *expense principle* states that an expense occurs when the business uses goods or receives services. In other words, the expense principle is the flip side of the revenue principle. As is the case with the revenue principle, if you receive some goods, simply receiving the goods means that you have incurred the expense of the goods. Similarly, if you received some service — services from your lawyer, for example — you have incurred the expense. It doesn't matter that your lawyer takes a few days or a few weeks to send you the bill. You incur an expense when goods or services are received.

Matching principle

The *matching principle* is related to the revenue and the expense principles. The matching principle states that when you recognize revenue, you should match related expenses with the revenue. The best example of when the matching principle comes into play concerns the case of businesses that resell inventory. In our hot dog stand example, you should count the expense of a hot dog and the expense of a bun on the day when you sell that hot dog and that bun. Don't count the expense when you buy the buns and the dogs. Count the expense when you sell them. In other words, match the expense of the item with the revenue of the item.

Accrual-based accounting, which is a term you have probably heard, is what you get when you apply the revenue principle, the expense principle, and the matching principle. In a nutshell, accrual-based accounting means that you record revenue when a sale is made and record expenses when goods are used or services are received.

Cost principle

The *cost principle* states that amounts in your accounting system should be quantified, or measured, by using historical cost. For example, if you have a business and the business owns a building, that building, according to the cost principle, shows up on your balance sheet at its historical cost. You don't adjust the values in an accounting system for changes in a fair market value. You use the original historical costs.

I should admit that the cost principle is occasionally violated in a couple of ways. The cost principle is adjusted through the application of depreciation, which I discuss in the next chapter. Also, sometimes fair market values are used to value assets, but only when assets are worth less than they cost.

Objectivity principle

The *objectivity principle* states that accounting measurements and accounting reports should use objective, factual, and verifiable data. In other words, accountants, accounting systems, and accounting reports should rely on as little subjectivity as possible.

An accountant will always want to use some data that's objective (even if it's bad) rather than use subjective data (even if the subjective data is arguably better). The idea is that objectivity becomes a protection against the corrupting influence that subjectivity can introduce into a firm's accounting records.

Continuity assumption

The *continuity assumption* — accountants call it an *assumption* rather than a *principle* for reasons unbeknownst to me — states that accounting systems assume that a business will continue to operate. The importance of the continuity assumption becomes most clear if you consider the ramifications of assuming that a business won't continue. If a business won't continue, it becomes very unclear how one should value assets if the assets have no resale value. This sounds like gobbledygook, but think about the implicit continuity assumption built into the balance sheet for the hot dog stand at the beginning of the day. (This is the hot dog stand balance sheet that shows up in Table 1-4.)

Implicit in that balance sheet is the assumption that the $3,000 worth of hot dogs and hot dog buns has some value because they can be sold. If a business won't continue operations, no assurance exists that any of the inventory can be sold. If the inventory can't be sold, what does that say about the owner's equity value shown in the balance sheet?

You can see, I hope, the sorts of accounting problems that one gets into if one can't assume the business will continue to operate.

Unit-of-measure assumption

The *unit-of-measure assumption* assumes that a business's domestic currency is the appropriate unit of measure for the business to use in its accounting. In other words, the unit-of-measure assumption states that it's okay for U.S. businesses to use U.S. dollars in their accounting. And it's okay for U.K. businesses to use pounds sterling as the unit of measure in their accounting system. The unit-of-measure assumption also states, implicitly, that even though inflation and occasionally deflation changes the purchasing power of the unit of measure used in the accounting system, that's still okay. Sure, inflation and deflation foul up some of the numbers in a firm's financial statements. But the unit-of-measure assumption says that's usually okay — especially in light of the fact that no better alternatives exist.

Separate entity assumption

The *separate entity assumption* states that a business entity, like a sole proprietorship, is a separate entity, a separate thing from its business owner. And the separate entity assumption says that a partnership is a separate thing from the partners who own part of the business. The separate entity assumption, therefore, enables one to prepare financial statements just for the sole proprietorship or just for the partnership. As a result, the separate entity assumption also relies on a business being separate and distinct and definable as compared to its business owners.

These are the basic accounting principles that underlie business accounting. Implicit in the earlier discussions in this chapter, and the discussions in the coming chapters of this book, and those of the other books in this all-in-one desk reference, are these principles and assumptions. It is no exaggeration to say that they permeate almost everything about business accounting.

A Few Words about Tax Accounting

I'm not going to talk much about tax accounting or tax preparation in this book. However, one of the key reasons that you do accounting and use a program such as QuickBooks is to make your tax accounting easier. That's obvious. So a fair question is this: How does what I've said so far relate to income tax return preparation?

This is a tough question to answer. Tax laws don't map to generally accepted accounting principles. Generally accepted accounting principles are not the same thing as income tax law.

However, if you use good basic accounting practices as you operate QuickBooks, you get financial information that can usually be used to easily prepare your tax returns, especially if you get some help from your CPA.

If you want, you can also use income tax rules to fine-tune your accounting and bookkeeping. This practice, which is technically known as an *other comprehensive basis of accounting (OCBOA)*, is generally considered an appropriate way to perform accounting for small and medium enterprises.

If you have more specific questions about the right way to prepare a financial statement using generally accepted accounting principles, and for use in preparing an income tax return, consult your CPA or your tax advisor. Applying generally accepted accounting principles or tax laws in specific situations requires an understanding of the specific circumstances and the industry in which a firm operates. Given the one-way nature of the communication in this book — me chattering away at you — I can't provide that sort of detailed commentary here. Sorry, buddy. . . .

Chapter 2: Double-Entry Bookkeeping

In This Chapter

✔ **Checking out the fiddle-faddle method of accounting**

✔ **Grasping how double-entry bookkeeping works**

✔ **Looking at an (almost) real-life example**

✔ **Figuring out how QuickBooks helps**

The preceding chapter describes why businesses create financial statements and how these financial statements can be used. If you've read Book I, Chapter 1, or if you've spent much time managing a business, you probably know what you need to know about financial statements. In truth, financial statements are pretty straightforward. An income statement, for example, shows a firm's revenues, expenses, and profits. A balance sheet itemizes a firm's assets, liabilities, and owner's equity. So far, so good.

Unfortunately, preparing traditional financial statements is more complicated and tedious. The work of preparing financial statements — called *accounting* or *bookkeeping* — either requires a whole bunch of fiddle-faddling with numbers or learning how to use double-entry bookkeeping.

In this chapter, I start by describing the fiddle-faddle method. This is not because I think you should use that method. In fact, I assume that you eventually want to use QuickBooks for your accounting and, by extension, for double-entry bookkeeping. However, by understanding the fiddle-faddle method, you'll see clearly why double-entry bookkeeping is so much better.

After I describe the fiddle-faddle method, I am going to walk you through the steps to using and understanding double-entry bookkeeping. After you see all the anguish and grief that the fiddle-faddle method causes, you'll have no trouble appreciating why double-entry bookkeeping works so much better. And you'll also hopefully commit to the 30 or 40 minutes necessary to learn the basics of double-entry bookkeeping.

The Fiddle-Faddle Method of Accounting

Most small businesses — or at least those small businesses where the owners aren't already trained in accounting — have used the fiddle-faddle method. For example, take a peek at the financial statements shown in Tables 2-1 and 2-2. If you've read or reviewed Book I, Chapter 1, you may recognize these financial statements as those that stem from the imaginary hot dog stand business. Table 2-1 shows the income statement for the one day a year that the imaginary hot dog stand business operates. Table 2-2 shows the balance sheet at the start of the first day of operation.

Table 2-1	A Simple Income Statement for the Hot Dog Stand
Sales revenue	$13,000
Less: Cost of goods sold	3,000
Gross margin	$10,000
Operating expenses	
Rent	$1,000
Wages	4,000
Supplies	1,000
Total operating expenses	6,000
Operating profit	$4,000

Table 2-2	A Simple Balance Sheet for the Hot Dog Stand
Assets	
Cash	$1,000
Inventory	3,000
Total assets	$4,000
Liabilities	
Accounts payable	$2,000
Loan payable	1,000
Owner's equity	
S. Nelson, capital	1,000
Total liabilities and owner's equity	$4,000

With the fiddle-faddle method of accounting, you individually calculate each number shown in the financial statement. For example, the sales revenue figure shown in Table 2-1 equals $13,000. The fiddle-faddle method of accounting requires you to somehow come up with this sales revenue number manually. You may be able to come up with this number by remembering each of the sales that you made over the day. Or, if you prepare invoices or sales receipts, you may be able to come up with this number by adding all of the individual sales. If you have a cash register, you may also be able to come up with this number by looking at the cash register tape.

Other revenue and expense numbers get calculated in the same crude manner. For example, the $1,000 of rent expense gets calculated by either remembering what amount you paid for rent, or by looking in your checkbook register and finding the check that you wrote for rent.

The balance sheet values get produced in roughly the same way. You can deduce the cash balance of $1,000, for example, by looking at the checkbook or, in a worst case scenario, the bank statement. You can deduce the inventory balance of $3,000 by adding the individual inventory item values. You can calculate the liability and owner's equity amounts in similar fashion.

Some of the values shown in an income statement or on a balance sheet get plugged — meaning that they're calculated using other numbers from the financial statement. For example, you don't look up the profit amount in any particular place; instead, you calculate profit by subtracting expenses from revenue. You can also, of course, calculate balance sheet values, such as total assets, owner's equity, and total liability of owner's equity.

Okay, I admit it: The fiddle-faddle method of accounting works reasonably well for a very small business as long as you have a good checkbook. So, for a very small business, you may be able to get away with this crude, piecemeal approach to accounting.

But unfortunately, the fiddle-faddle method suffers from three horrible weaknesses for a firm that doesn't have super-simple finances:

✦ **It's not systematic enough to be automated.** Now, admittedly, you may not care that the fiddle-faddle approach isn't systematic enough for automation. But this point is an important one. A systematic approach like double-entry bookkeeping can be automated, as happens with QuickBooks. This automation means that the task of preparing financial statements requires — oh, I don't know — maybe five mouse clicks. Because the fiddle-faddle approach can't be automated, every time you want to produce financial statements, you or some poor co-worker needs to go to an enormous amount of work to collect the numbers and all of the raw data necessary to produce information like that shown in Table 2-1 and Table 2-2. In reality, of course, with more complicated financial statements, someone goes to much, much more work.

✦ **It's very easy to lose details.** This sounds abstract, but let me give you a good, concrete example. If you look at Table 2-1, you see that the hot dog stand business incurs only three operating expenses: rent, wages, and supplies. If you know the operating expense categories that the business incurs, it is fairly easy to look through the check register and find the check or checks that pay rent, for example. You can use a similar approach with the wages expense. Also, you can use a similar approach with the supplies expense. However, what if you also have an advertising expense category or a business license expense, or some other easy-to-forget category? If you forget a category, you miss expenses. For example, if you forgot that you spent money advertising and, thereby, forgot to tally your advertising expenses, that whole category of operating expense gets omitted from your income statement.

✦ **It doesn't allow rigorous error checking.** This business about error checking seems, perhaps, nit-picky. However, error checking is important with accounting and bookkeeping systems. With all of the numbers and transactions floating around, errors easily creep into the system. I discuss more about error checking later in this chapter, but let me give you an example of the sort of error checking an accounting system can (and should) perform. Take a look at the example of the sales transaction. If you sell an item for $1,000, you can actually check that amount by comparing it to your record of what the customer paid. This makes sense, right? If you sell me an item for $1,000, you actually should be able to compare that $1,000 sale to the amount of cash that I pay you. A $1,000 sale to me should correspond to a $1,000 cash payment from me. The fiddle-faddle method can't make these comparisons. However, double-entry bookkeeping can.

You see where I'm at now, right? I've admitted that you can construct financial statements using the fiddle-faddle method. But I hope I've also convinced you that the fiddle-faddle method suffers from some really debilitating weaknesses. I'm talking about something as important as how you best manage the financial affairs of your business. These weaknesses indicate that you need to use a better tool. Specifically, you need to use double-entry bookkeeping, which I discuss next.

How Double-Entry Bookkeeping Works

After you conclude that the fiddle-faddle method is for the birds, you're ready to absorb the necessary accounting theory and learn the bookkeeping tricks required to employ double-entry bookkeeping. Essentially, you need to do two things in order to work with double-entry bookkeeping. First, you need to understand the accounting model. And second, you need to learn the mechanics of debits and credits. Neither of these things is difficult to deal with. If you flip ahead a few pages, you can see that I am only going to spend a few pages talking about this material. How difficult can anything be that is described in just a few pages? Not very, right?

The accounting model

Here's the first thing you need to understand and internalize in order to use double-entry bookkeeping: Modern accounting uses an accounting model that says assets equal liabilities plus owner's equity. The following formula expresses this in a more conventional, algebraic form:

```
Assets = liabilities + owner's equity
```

If you think about this for a moment and flip back to Table 2-2, you see that this formula summarizes the organization of a business's balance sheet. Conceptually, the formula says that a business owns stuff and that the money or the funds for that stuff come either from creditors (such as the bank or some vendor) or the owners (either in the form of original con- tributed capital or perhaps in reinvested profits). If you understand the bal- ance sheet shown in Table 2-2 and discussed here, you understand the first core principle needed to use double-entry bookkeeping. This isn't that tough so far, is it?

Here's the second thing that you need to understand about the basic account- ing model: Revenues increase owner's equity and expenses decrease owner's equity. Think about that for a minute. That makes intuitive sense. If you receive $1,000 in cash from a customer, you have $1,000 more in the business. If you write a $1,000 check to pay a bill, you have $1,000 less in the business.

Another way to say the same thing is that profits clearly add to the owner's equity. Profits get reinvested in the business and boost owner's equity. Profits are calculated as the difference between revenues and expenses. If revenues exceed expenses, profits exist.

Let me review where I am so far in this discussion about the basic account- ing model. The basic model says that assets equal liabilities plus owner's equity. In other words, the total assets of a firm equal the total of its liabili- ties and owner's equity. Furthermore, revenue increases the owner's equity and expenses decrease the owner's equity.

At this point, you don't have to intuitively get the logic of the accounting model and the way that revenues and expenses plug into the owner's equity of the model. If you do "get it" that's great, but not necessary. However, you do need to memorize or remember the manner in which the basic model works through at least the next few paragraphs.

This may seem like a redundant point, but note that a balance sheet is constructed by using information about a firm's assets, liabilities, and owner's equity. Similarly, note that a firm's income statement is constructed by using information about its revenues and its expenses. Remember that all this discussion, all this tediousness, is really about how you collect the information necessary to produce an income statement and a balance sheet.

Now I come to perhaps the most important point that you need to understand in order to "get" double-entry bookkeeping. Every transaction and every economic event that occurs in the life of a firm produces two effects: An increase in some account shown on the balance sheet or on the income statement, and a decrease in some account shown on the balance sheet or income statement. When something happens, economically speaking, that something affects at least two types of information shown in the financial statement. In the next few paragraphs, I give you some examples so you can really understand this.

Suppose that in your business, you sell $1,000 of an item for $1,000 in cash. In the case of this transaction or economic event, two things occur from the perspective of your financial statements:

+ Your cash increases by $1,000.

+ Your sales revenue increases by $1,000.

Another way to say this same thing is that your $1,000 cash sale affects both your balance sheet (because cash increases) and your income statement (because sales revenue is earned).

See the duality? And you were thinking this might be too complicated for you just a paragraph ago, weren't you?

Here's another common example: Suppose that you buy $1,000 of inventory for cash. In this case, you decrease your cash balance by $1,000, but you increase your inventory balance by $1,000. Note that in this case, both effects of the transaction appear in sort of the same area of your financial statement — the list of assets. Nevertheless, this transaction also affects two accounts.

When I use the word *account*, I simply mean some value that appears on your income statement or on your balance sheet. If you look at Tables 2-1 and 2-2, for example, any value that appears on those financial statements that isn't simply a calculation represents an account. In essence, an account tracks some group of assets, liabilities, owner's equity, contributions, revenues, or expenses. I talk more about accounts in the next section when I get to the actual mechanics of double-entry bookkeeping.

Here's another example that shows this duality of effects in an economic event: Suppose that you spent $1,000 in cash on advertising. In this case, this economic event reduces cash by $1,000 and increases the advertising expense amount by $1,000. This economic event affects both the assets portion of the balance sheet and the operating expenses portion of the income statement.

And now — believe it or not — you're ready to see how the mechanics of double-entry bookkeeping work.

Talking mechanics

Roughly 500 years ago, an Italian monk named Pacioli devised a systematic approach to keeping track of the increases and decreases in account balances. He said that increases in asset and expense accounts should be called *debits*, whereas decreases in asset and expense accounts should be called *credits*. He also said that increases in liabilities, owner's equity, and revenue accounts should be called credits, while decreases in liabilities, owner's equity, and revenue accounts should be called debits.

Table 2-3 summarizes the information that I just shared. Unfortunately — and you can't get around this — you need to memorize this table or dog-ear the page so you can easily refer to it.

Table 2-3	You Must Remember This	
Account	*Debit*	*Credit*
Assets	Increase	Decrease
Expenses	Increase	Decrease
Liabilities	Decrease	Increase
Owner's equity	Decrease	Increase
Revenues	Decrease	Increase

Using Pacioli's debits and credits system, any transaction can be described as a set of balancing debits and credits. Not only does this system work as financial shorthand, but it also provides error checking. To get a better idea of how this works, look at some simple examples.

Take the case of a $1,000 cash sale, for example. Using Pacioli's system, or by using double-entry bookkeeping, you can record this transaction as shown here:

Cash	$1,000	debit
Sales revenue	$1,000	credit

See how that works? The $1,000 cash sale appears as both a debit to cash (which means an increase in cash) and a $1,000 credit to sales (which means a $1,000 increase in sales revenue). Debits equal credits, and that's no accident.

The accounting model and Pacioli's assignment of debits and credits mean that any correctly recorded transaction balances. For a correctly recorded transaction, the transaction's debits equal the transaction's credits.

Although you can show transactions as I've just shown the $1,000 cash sale, you and I may just as well use the more orthodox nomenclature. By convention, accountants and bookkeepers show transactions, or what accountants and bookkeepers call *journal entries*, like this one shown in Table 2-4:

Table 2-4	Journal Entry 1: Recording the Cash Sale	
Account	*Debit*	*Credit*
Cash	1,000	
Sales revenue		1,000

See how that works? Each account that's affected by a transaction appears on a separate line. Debits appear in the left column. Credits appear in the right column.

You actually already understand how this account business works. You have a checkbook. You use it to keep track of both the balance in your checking account and the transactions that change the checking account balance. The rules of double-entry bookkeeping essentially say that you are going to use a similar record-keeping system not only for your cash account, but for every other account you need to prepare your financial statements, too.

Here are a couple of other examples of how this transaction recording works. In the first part of this discussion of how double-entry bookkeeping works, I describe two other transactions: the purchase of $1,000 of inventory for cash, and spending $1,000 in cash on advertising. Table 2-5 shows how the purchase of $1,000 of inventory for cash appears. Table 2-6 shows how spending $1,000 of cash on advertising appears.

Table 2-5	Journal Entry 2: Recording the Inventory Purchase	
Account	*Debit*	*Credit*
Inventory	1,000	
Cash		1,000

Table 2-6	Journal Entry 3: Recording the Advertising Expense	
Account	*Debit*	*Credit*
Advertising	1,000	
Cash		1,000

That darn bank

When I learned about double-entry bookkeeping, I stumbled over the terms *debit* and *credit*. The way I had heard the terms used before didn't agree with the way that double-entry bookkeeping seemed to describe them. This conflict caused a certain amount of confusion for me. Because I don't want you to suffer from the same fate, let me quickly describe my initial confusion.

If you look at Table 2-3, you see that an increase in an asset account is a debit and a decrease in an asset account is a credit. This means that in the case of your cash account, increases to cash are debits and decreases to cash are credits.

However, you've undoubtedly talked at some time to the bank and heard them refer to crediting your bank account — which meant they increased the account balance. And they perhaps talked about debiting your account — which meant they decreased the account balance. So, what's up with that? Am I wrong, and is the bank right?

Actually, both the bank and I are right. And here's why. The bank is talking about debiting and crediting — not a cash account, and not an asset account — but a *liability account*. To them, the money that you've placed in the bank is not cash (an asset) but a liability (money that they owe you). If you look at Table 2-3, you see that increases in a liability are credit amounts and decreases in a liability are debit amounts. Therefore, from the bank's perspective, when they increase the balance in your account, that increase is a credit.

Your assets may represent another firm's liabilities. Your liabilities will represent another firm's assets. Therefore, whenever you hear some other business talking about crediting or debiting your account, what you would do is exactly the opposite. If they credit, you debit. If they debit, you credit.

By tallying the debits and credits to an account, you can calculate the account balance. For example, suppose that before Journal Entries 1, 2, and 3, the cash balance equals $2,000. Journal Entry 1 increases cash by $1,000 (this is the debit). Journal Entries 2 and 3 decrease cash by $1,000 each (these are the $2,000 credits). If you combine all of these entries, you get the new account balance. The following formula shows the calculation:

Beginning balance of cash	$2,000
Plus cash debit from Journal Entry 1	$1,000
Minus cash credit from Journal Entry 2	–$1,000
Minus cash credit from Journal Entry 3	–$1,000
Ending cash balance	$1,000

Do you see how that works? You start with $2,000 as the cash account balance. The first cash debit of $1,000 increases the cash balance to $3,000, and then the cash credit of $1,000 in Journal Entry 2 decreases the cash balance to $2,000. Then, finally, the cash credit of $1,000 in Journal Entry 3 decreases the cash balance to $1,000.

You can calculate the account balance for any account by taking the starting account balance and then adding the debits and credits that have occurred since then. By hand, this arithmetic is a little unwieldy. Your computer (with the help of QuickBooks) does this math easily.

Almost a Real-Life Example

To cement the concepts that I've talked about in the preceding paragraphs of this chapter, I want to quickly step through the journal entries, or book-keeping transactions, that you would record in the case of the hot dog stand business discussed in the preceding chapter. To start, you need to know that the balance sheet shown in Table 2-2 is the balance sheet at the start of the day. This means that the account balances in all of the accounts appear as shown in Table 2-7. This list of account balances is actually called a trial balance. It shows the debit or credit balance for each account.

I am assuming that no year-to-date revenues or expenses exist yet with the hot dog stand business. In other words, the operation is just at a starting period.

Table 2-7	A Trial Balance at the Start of Day	
Account	*Debit*	*Credit*
Cash	1,000	
Inventory		3,000
Accounts payable		2,000
Loan payable		1,000
S. Nelson, capital	____	1,000
Totals	4,000	4,000

You may want to take a quick peek at Table 2-1. It summarizes the business activities of the hot dog stand. The journal entries that follow show how the information necessary for this statement would be recorded.

Rent expense

Suppose that the first transaction that you need to record is a $1,000 check written to pay rent. In this case, the journal entry appears as shown in Table 2-8. In this example, $1,000 is debited to rent expense, and $1,000 is credited to cash.

Table 2-8	Journal Entry 4: Recording the Rent Expense	
Account	*Debit*	*Credit*
Rent	1,000	
Cash		1,000

Wages expense

If you need to record $4,000 of wages expense, you use the journal entry shown in Table 2-9. This journal entry debits wages expense for $4,000 and credits cash for $4,000. In other words, you use $4,000 of cash to pay wages for the hot dog stand business.

Table 2-9	Journal Entry 5: Recording the Wages Expense	
Account	*Debit*	*Credit*
Wages expense	4,000	
Cash		4,000

Supplies expense

To record $1,000 of supplies expense paid for by writing a check, you record the journal entry shown in Table 2-10. This transaction debits supplies expense for $1,000 and credits cash for $1,000.

Table 2-10	Journal Entry 6: Recording the Supplies Expense	
Account	*Debit*	*Credit*
Supplies	1,000	
Cash		1,000

Note that for each of the preceding transactions, debits equal credits. As long as debits equal credits, you know that the transaction is in balance. This balance is one of the ways that double-entry bookkeeping prevents errors.

Recording sales revenue

Suppose that you sell $13,000 worth of hot dogs. To record this transaction in a journal entry, you debit cash for $13,000 and credit sales revenue for $13,000, as is shown in Table 2-11. I should tell you, however, that in the case of the hot dog stand selling hot dogs for a dollar or two a piece, you wouldn't actually be able to use a single journal entry to record sales revenue amounts. If you were selling hot dogs at a dollar a dog, you may actually have 13,000 one-dollar transactions. Each of these transactions would debit cash for a dollar and credit sales revenue for a dollar.

Table 2-11	Journal Entry 7: Recording the Sales Revenue	
Account	*Debit*	*Credit*
Cash	13,000	
Sales revenue		13,000

Recording cost of goods sold

You need to record the expense of the hot dogs and buns that you sell. You also need to record the fact that if you do use up your inventory of hot dogs and buns, your inventory balance has decreased. Table 2-12 shows how you record this. Cost of goods sold gets debited for $3,000, and inventory gets credited for $3,000.

Table 2-12	Journal Entry 8: Recording the Cost of Goods Sold	
Account	*Debit*	*Credit*
Cost of goods sold	3,000	
Inventory		3,000

If you're confused about this cost of goods sold transaction — and it represents the first transaction that doesn't use cash — flip back to Book I, Chapter 1, where I describe the two accounting principles. In short, though, these two principles go like this:

✦ **Expense principle:** This principle says that an expense gets counted when the item gets sold. This means that the inventory isn't counted as cost of goods sold or as an expense when it is purchased. Rather, the expense of the hot dog and bun that you sell gets counted when the item is actually sold to somebody.

✦ **Matching principle:** This principle says that expenses or cost of a sale get matched with the revenue of the sale. This means that you need to recognize the cost of goods sold at the same time that you recognize the sale. Typically, in fact, someone can combine Journal Entry 7 and Journal Entry 8.

Another way to think about the information recorded in Journal Entry 8 is this — rather than "spending" cash to provide customers with hot dogs and buns, you spend inventory.

Recording the payoff of accounts payable

Suppose that one of the things you do at the end of the day is write a check to pay off the accounts payable. The accounts payable are the amounts that you owe vendors — probably the suppliers from whom you purchased the hot dogs and buns. To record the payoff of accounts payable, you debit accounts payable for $2,000 and credit cash for $2,000, as shown in Table 2-13.

Table 2-13	Journal Entry 9: Recording the Payoff of Accounts Payable	
Account	*Debit*	*Credit*
Accounts payable	2,000	
Cash		2,000

Recording the payoff of a loan

Suppose also that you use cash profits from the day to pay off the $1,000 loan that the balance sheet shows (see Table 2-2). To record this transaction, you debit loan payable for $1,000 and credit cash for $1,000, as shown in Table 2-14.

Table 2-14	Journal Entry 10: Recording the Payoff of the Loan	
Account	*Debit*	*Credit*
Loan payable	1,000	
Cash		1,000

Calculating account balance

You may already be able to guess this: If you know an account's starting balance and have a way to add up the debits and the credits to the account, you can easily calculate the ending account balance.

For example, take the case of the cash account balance of the hot dog stand business. If you look at the balance sheet shown in Table 2-2, you see that the beginning balance for cash is $1,000. You can easily construct a little schedule of how the account balance changes — this is called a *T-account* — that calculates the ending balance. In fact, Table 2-15 does just this. If you look closely at Table 2-15, you see that the cash beginning balance is $1,000. Then, on the following lines of the T-account, you see the effects of Journal Entries 4, 5, 6, 7, 9, and 10. Some of these journal entries credit cash. Some of them debit cash. You can calculate the ending cash balance by combining the debit and credit amounts.

Table 2-15	A T-Account of the Cash Account	
	Debit	*Credit*
Beg. balance	1,000	
J.E. #4		1,000
J.E. #5		4,000
J.E. #6		1,000
J.E. #7	13,000	
J.E. #9		2,000
J.E. #10	_____	1,000
End balance	5,000	

The information shown in Table 2-15 should make sense to you. But just in case you're still trying to memorize what debits and credits mean, I'm going to give you a bit more detail. To calculate the ending balance shown in Table 2-15, you add up the debits, add up the credits, and combine the two sums. The net amount in the case of the cash account equals the $5,000 debit. If you recall from the preceding paragraphs, a debit balance in an asset account, such as cash, represents a positive amount. A $5,000 debit balance in the cash account, therefore, indicates that you have $5,000 of cash in the account.

Cash is usually the trickiest account to analyze using a T-account because so many journal entries affect cash. In many cases, however, a T-account analysis of an account balance is much more straightforward. For example, if you look at Table 2-16, you see a T-account analysis of the inventory account. This T-account analysis shows that the beginning inventory account balance equals $3,000. However, when Journal Entry 8 credits inventory for $3,000 — this is the journal entry that records the cost of goods sold — the inventory balance is wiped out.

Table 2-16	A T-Account of the Inventory Account	
	Debit	*Credit*
Beg. balance	3,000	
J.E. #8	_____	3,000
End balance	$ 0	

Paying off the accounts payable and loan payable accounts is similarly straightforward. Table 2-17 shows the T-account analysis of the accounts payable account. Table 2-18 shows the T-account analysis of the loan payable account. In both cases, the T-account analysis shows that the liability accounts start with a credit beginning balance. (Remember that a liability account would have a credit balance if the firm really owed money.) Then, when the payments are recorded to pay off the accounts payable and loan payable in Journal Entries 9 and 10, the liability account is debited. The end result, in the case of both accounts, is that the liability account balance is reduced to zero.

Table 2-17	A T-Account of Accounts Payable	
	Debit	*Credit*
Beg. balance		2,000
J.E. #9	2,000	
End balance	0	

Table 2-18	A T-Account of the Loan Payable Account	
	Debit	*Credit*
Beg. balance		1,000
J.E. #10	1,000	
End balance	0	

I'm not going to show T-account analyses of the other accounts that the preceding journal entries used. In every other case, the only debit or credit to the account comes from the journal entry. This means that the journal entry amount is the account balance. For example, only one journal entry affects the sales revenue account — Journal Entry 7, which credits sales revenue for $13,000. Because there is no beginning balance in the sales revenue account, that $13,000 credit equals the sales revenue account balance. The expense accounts work the same way.

Using T-account analysis results

If you or your accounting program constructs T-accounts for each balance sheet and income statement account, you can easily calculate account balances at a particular point in time by using the T-account analysis results. Table 2-19 shows a trial balance at the end of the day for the hot dog stand business. Each of these account balances can be calculated by using T-account analysis.

Table 2-19	A Trial Balance at End of the Day	
Account	*Debit*	*Credit*
Cash	5,000	
Inventory	0	
Accounts payable		0
Loan payable		0
S. Nelson, capital		1,000
Sales revenue		13,000
Cost of goods sold	3,000	
Rent	1,000	
Wages expense	4,000	
Supplies	1,000	
Totals	14,000	14,000

For example, the first line shown in the trial balance in Table 2-19 is the cash account with the debit balance of $5,000. This debit account balance comes from the T-account analysis shown in Table 2-15. The account balances for inventory, accounts payable, and loan payable also come from the T-account analyses shown previously in this chapter (Table 2-16, Table 2-17, and Table 2-18).

As I noted in the preceding section, you don't need to perform T-account analyses for the other accounts shown in the trial balance provided in Table 2-19. These other accounts showed a single debit or credit.

One final and perhaps already obvious point needs to be made: The information provided in Table 2-19 is the information necessary to construct an income statement for the day, and a balance sheet as of the end of the day. For example, if you take sales revenue, cost of goods sold, rent, wages expense, and supplies expense from the trial balance, you have all the information that you need to construct an income statement for the day. In fact, the information shown in Table 2-19 is the information used to construct the income statement shown in Table 2-1.

Similarly, the asset, liability, and owner's equity balance information shown in the trial balance provided in Table 2-19 supplies the information necessary to construct a balance sheet as of the end of the day.

The end of the day balance sheet won't actually "balance" unless you also include the profits of the day. These profits, either called *retained earnings* or lumped into the owner's capital account, equal $4,000. You can see what this end-of-day balance sheet looks like by turning back to Book I, Chapter 1. In that chapter, Table 1-7 shows the end-of-day balance sheet for the hot dog stand business.

A Few Words about How QuickBooks Works

Before I end this chapter, I want to make just a few comments about how QuickBooks helps you. First of all — and this may be the most important point — QuickBooks makes most of these journal entries for you. For example, in Journal Entry 6, I show you how to record a $1,000 check written to pay supplies. However, you would never have to make this journal entry in QuickBooks yourself. When you use QuickBooks to record a $1,000 check that pays Acme Supplies for some paper products that you purchased, QuickBooks automatically debits supplies expense (as long as you indicate that the check is for supplies) and then credits cash.

Similarly, in the case of Journal Entry 7 and Journal Entry 8, when you produce an invoice that records a sale, QuickBooks would make these journal entries for you. For example, if you sold $13,000 of hot dogs and buns, and those hot dogs and buns actually cost you $3,000, QuickBooks debits cash for $13,000, credits sales revenue for $13,000, debits cost of goods sold for $3,000, and credits inventory for $3,000. In other words, for most of your routine transactions, QuickBooks handles the journal entries for you behind the scenes.

This doesn't mean, however, that you can always avoid working with journal entries. Any transaction that can't be handled through a standard QuickBooks form — such as the invoice form or the write checks form — needs to be recorded by using a journal entry. For example, if you purchase some fixed asset by writing a check, the purchase of the fixed asset gets recorded automatically by QuickBooks. However, the depreciation that will be used to expense the asset over its estimated economic life — something I talk a bit about in the next chapter — needs to get recorded with journal entries that you construct yourself and enter a different way.

One other really important point: I noted in the preceding paragraphs that the trial balance information shown in Table 2-19 provides the raw data that you need to prepare your financial statement. I don't want to leave you with a misunderstanding, however. You don't actually have to take this sort of raw data and prepare your financial statements. Predictably, QuickBooks easily, quickly, and without effort builds your financial statements by using this trial balance information.

Just to put these comments together, then, QuickBooks automatically creates most journal entries for you, builds a trial balance by using journal entry information, and — when asked — produces financial statements. Most of the work of double-entry bookkeeping, then, goes on behind the scenes. You don't need to worry about many journal entries on a day-to-day basis. And if you don't want to ever see a trial balance, you don't have to. In fact, if you just use QuickBooks to produce invoices and to write checks that pay the bills, almost all of the information that you need to prepare your financial statements gets collected automatically. So that's really neat.

However, not all of the information that is necessary for producing good accurate financial statements gets collected automatically. You will encounter a handful of important cases that need to be handled on a special basis through journal entries that either you or your CPA construct and enter.

In the next chapter, I describe some of the most common special cases. However, it is likely that you'll encounter other special cases. With the information in this chapter, you may be able to figure out these journal entries yourself. Or, you may need to pay someone else to help you figure them out. Or, as a sometimes reasonable resort, you may just need to skip the extra precision and accuracy that you can achieve by recording these other journal entries.

Chapter 3: Special Accounting Problems

In This Chapter

✔ **Sorting out accounts receivable and accounts payable**

✔ **Keeping track of inventory**

✔ **Figuring out fixed assets**

✔ **Finding out about asset write-downs**

✔ **Recognizing liability**

✔ **Closing out revenue and expense accounts**

*E*ven if you understand the principles of accounting (which I describe in Book I, Chapter 1) and the basics of double-entry bookkeeping (which I describe in Book I, Chapter 2), you still may not have all the information that you need to keep good records. For example, tracking the amounts that customers owe you and the amounts that you owe vendors can be a bit tricky. Inventory can also present challenging record-keeping problems, a fact that's not surprising to you retailers. And things like fixed assets — oh, don't even get me started.

For these reasons, this chapter describes the most common complexities that business owners confront. You don't need to be an accountant or an experienced bookkeeper to understand the material in this chapter. However, you do need to proceed carefully, take your time, and think a bit about how the material I describe here applies to your specific business situation.

Working with Accounts Receivable

If you read Book I, Chapter 1, you already know that accounting principles state that sales revenue needs to be recognized when a sale is made. And that the sale is made when a business provides goods or services to a customer.

In other words — and this is really an important point — sales revenue doesn't get recorded when you receive payment from a customer. Sales revenue gets recorded when a customer has a legal obligation to pay you because you have (or your business has) provided the customer with the goods or services.

Recording a sale

This requirement to record sales revenue at the time that goods or services are provided means that accounting for sales revenue is slightly more complicated than you may have first guessed. The first transaction, for example, the transaction that records a sale, looks as shown in Table 3-1.

Table 3-1	Journal Entry 1: Recording a Credit Sale	
Account	*Debit*	*Credit*
Accounts receivable	1,000	
Sales revenue		1,000

Journal Entry 1 shows how a $1,000 sale may be recorded. The journal entry shows a $1,000 debit to accounts receivable and a $1,000 credit to sales revenue. To record a $1,000 sale — a credit sale — the journal entry needs to show *both* the $1,000 increase in accounts receivable and the $1,000 increase in sales revenue.

Recording a payment

When the business receives payment from the customer for the $1,000 receivable, the business needs to record a journal entry like that shown in Table 3-2.

Table 3-2	Journal Entry 2: Recording the Customer Payment	
Account	*Debit*	*Credit*
Cash	1,000	
Accounts receivable		1,000

Journal Entry 2 shows a $1,000 debit to cash, which is the $1,000 increase in the cash account that occurs because the customer has just paid you $1,000. Journal Entry 2 also shows a $1,000 credit to accounts receivable. This credit to the accounts receivable asset account reduces the accounts receivable balance.

At the point when you record both Journal Entry 1 and Journal Entry 2, the net effect is a $1,000 debit to cash, showing that the cash has increased by $1,000, and a $1,000 credit to sales revenue, showing that sales revenue has increased by $1,000. The $1,000 debit to accounts receivable and the $1,000 credit to accounts receivable net to zero.

If you think about this accounts receivable business a bit, you should realize that it makes sense. Although the accounts receivable account includes a $1,000 receivable balance, this just means that the customer owes you $1,000. But when the customer finally pays off the $1,000 bill, you need to zero out that receivable.

QuickBooks, by the way, automatically records Journal Entry 1 and Journal Entry 2 for you. Journal Entry 1 gets recorded whenever you issue or create a customer invoice. Therefore, you don't actually need to worry about the debits and credits shown in Journal Entry 1 except for one special occasion: When you set up QuickBooks and QuickBooks items (*items* are things that get included on the invoices), you do specify which account should be credited to track sales revenue. This means that you may not need to worry much about the mechanics of Journal Entry 1. However, you will on occasion still need to understand how this journal entry works — only so that you can set up QuickBooks correctly.

Book II, Chapter 1 describes the mechanics of setting up QuickBooks.

Journal Entry 2 also gets recorded automatically by QuickBooks. QuickBooks records Journal Entry 2 for you whenever you record a cash payment from a customer. You don't need to worry, then, about the debits and credits necessary for recording customer payments. However, I find that it's helpful to understand how this journal entry works and how QuickBooks records this customer payment transaction.

Estimating bad debt expense

One other important journal entry to understand is shown in Table 3-3.

Table 3-3   Journal Entry 3: Recording an Allowance for Uncollectible Accounts

Account	Debit	Credit
Bad debt expense	100	
Allowance for uncollectible A/R		100

Journal Entry 3 records an estimate of the uncollectible portion of accounts receivable. Businesses that don't want to keep accrual-based accounting statements may not need to worry about Journal Entry 3. If you think about it, though, some of the money you bill customers may be uncollectible, unfortunately. Yet Journal Entry 1 records every dollar that you bill your customers as revenue. Therefore, you need a way to offset, or reduce, some of the sales revenue by the amount that ultimately turns out to be uncollectible.

Journal Entry 3 shows a common way of doing this. Journal Entry 3 debits bad debt expense — which is an expense account that you may use to record uncollectible customer receivables. Journal Entry 3 also credits another account shown as allowance for uncollectible A/R. This allowance account is called a *contra-asset* account, which basically reduces the balance reported on the balance sheet of an asset account. In the case of the allowance for uncollectible A/R accounts, for example, this $100 credit would reduce the accounts receivable balance shown on the balance sheet by $100.

Where the bad debt expense shown in Journal Entry 3 appears varies from business to business. Some businesses may report the bad debt expense with the other sales revenue, thereby allowing the income statement to show net sales revenue. Other businesses may report bad debt expense with the other operating expenses. You should report bad debt expense wherever it makes most sense in terms of managing your business.

QuickBooks doesn't automatically record the transaction in Journal Entry 3. You record estimates of bad debt expense yourself by using the QuickBooks Make Journal Entries command.

Removing uncollectible accounts receivable

If you do set up an allowance for uncollectible accounts, you also need to periodically remove the uncollectible accounts from both the accounts receivable balance and the allowance for uncollectible accounts. You don't want to do this while any chance exists for you to collect on the accounts. But at some point, obviously, you may as well clean out the bad receivables from your records. It makes no sense, for example, to have uncollectible receivables from 17 years ago still appearing on your balance sheet. Table 3-4 illustrates how to clean out bad receivables.

Table 3-4	Journal Entry 4: Writing Off an Uncollectible Receivable	
Account	*Debit*	*Credit*
Allowance for uncollectible	100	
Accounts receivable		100

This journal entry debits the allowance from the uncollectible A/R account for $100. The journal entry also credits the accounts receivable account for $100. In combination, these two entries zero out the allowance for the uncollectible A/R account and remove the uncollectible amount from the accounts receivable account.

Writing off an actual, specific uncollectible receivable for invoice should be done on a case-by-case basis. This is what Journal Entry 4 shows.

None of these entries is particularly tricky as long as you understand the logic — something I have hopefully illuminated for you in this discussion. If you do have trouble with these journal entries or with recording the economic events that they attempt to summarize, you may want to consult your CPA. Most likely, you would record these same transactions (of course, with different customers and amounts) many, many times over the year. If you can get a bit of help or a template that shows you how to record these transactions, you should thereafter be able to record them yourself without any outside help.

In order to write off an uncollectible account receivable, you record a credit memo and then apply the credit memo to the uncollectible account. The item shown on your credit memo should cause the allowance for uncollectible accounts to be debited.

Recording Accounts Payable Transactions

Within QuickBooks, you have the option of either working with or without an accounts payable account. If you want to, you can record expenses when you write checks. This means that in order to have a complete list of all your expenses, you must have recorded checks that pay all your expenses. This approach works fine — and, in fact, is the approach that I have always used in my businesses.

QuickBooks also supports a more precise approach of recording expenses. You can set up an accounts payable account (by answering a few questions during the QuickBooks setup process), which is just an account that tracks the amounts that you owe your vendors and other suppliers.

Recording a bill

When you use an accounts payable account, you enter the bills that you receive from vendors when you receive them.

Table 3-5 shows the way this transaction is recorded. Journal Entry 5 automatically debits office supplies expense for $1,000 and credits accounts payable for $1,000. This is the journal entry that would be recorded by QuickBooks if you purchased $1,000 of office supplies and then entered that bill into the QuickBooks system.

Table 3-5	Journal Entry 5: Recording a Credit Purchase	
Account	*Debit*	*Credit*
Office supplies	1,000	
Accounts payable		1,000

Paying a bill

When you later pay that bill, QuickBooks records Journal Entry 6, shown in Table 3-6. In Journal Entry 6, QuickBooks debits accounts payable for $1,000 and credits cash for $1,000. The net effect on accounts payable combining both the purchase and the payment is zero. That makes sense, right? The approach shown in Journal Entries 5 and 6 counts the amount that you owe some vendor or supplier as a liability, accounts payable, only while you owe the money.

Table 3-6	Journal Entry 6: Recording the Payment to Vendor	
Account	*Debit*	*Credit*
Accounts payable	1,000	
Cash		1,000

When you record Journal Entry 5 in QuickBooks, you do need to supply the name of the account that gets debited. QuickBooks obviously knows which account to credit — the accounts payable account. However, QuickBooks also needs to know the expense or asset account to debit.

QuickBooks does need to know which cash account to credit when you pay an accounts payable amount. You identify this when you write the check to pay the bill.

Some other accounts payable pointers

Let me make a couple of additional points about Journal Entries 5 and 6:

+ **The accounts payable method is more accurate.** The accounts payable method, which is what Journal Entries 5 and 6 show, is the best way to record your bills. The accounts payable method means that you record expenses when the expenses actually occur. As you may have already figured out, the accounts payable method is really the mirror image of the accounts receivable approach described in the early paragraphs of this chapter. The big benefit of the accounts payable method, as you may intuit, is that it keeps track of the amounts that you owe vendors and suppliers, and it recognizes expenses as they occur rather than when you pay them (which may be some time later).

✦ **Not every debit is for an expense.** Journal Entry 5 shows the debit going to an office supplies expense account. Many of the accounts payable that you record will be amounts owed for expenses. However, not every accounts payable transaction stems from incurring some expense. You may also need to record the purchase of an asset — such as a piece of equipment. In this case, the debit goes not to an expense account but to an asset account. Other than this minor change, however, the transaction works in the same way. I describe how fixed asset accounting works later in this chapter in the "Accounting for Fixed Assets" section.

Can you guess how an expense or fixed asset purchase gets recorded if you don't use an accounts payable account? In the case where you paid $1,000 for office supplies, QuickBooks debits office supplies expense for $1,000 and credits cash for $1,000 when you write a $1,000 check. As part of writing the check, you identify which expense account to debit.

If you are purchasing a $1,000 piece of equipment, the journal entry looks and works roughly in the same way. When you record the purchase, QuickBooks debits the asset account for $1,000 and credits cash for $1,000. Again, this transaction gets recorded when you write the check to pay for the asset.

Inventory Accounting

Thankfully, most of the inventory accounting that goes on in a business gets handled automatically by QuickBooks. For example, when you purchase an inventory item by writing a check or recording an accounts payable bill, QuickBooks automatically adjusts your inventory accounts both for the dollar value of the inventory and the quantity of the items. When you sell an inventory item to a customer, QuickBooks again automatically adjusts the dollar value of your inventory and adjusts the quantity accounts of the items you sell.

Basically, all this means that QuickBooks maintains a *perpetual inventory* system — an inventory system that lets you know at any time what quantity of items you have in inventory and what value your inventory amounts to. (In the past, smaller firms often needed to use a *periodic inventory* system, which meant that business owners never really knew with any precision the dollar value of their inventory, or the quantity counts for the inventory items that they held.)

Although everything in the preceding paragraph represents good news, several inventory-related headaches do require a bit of accounting magic. Specifically, if your firm carries inventory, you need to know how to deal with obsolete inventory, disposal of obsolete inventory, and inventory shrinkage. I discuss all three accounting gambits in the following paragraphs.

Dealing with obsolete inventory

Obsolete inventory refers to items that you've purchased for sale but turn out not to be saleable. Perhaps customers no longer want it. Perhaps you have too much of the inventory item and will never be able to sell everything that you hold.

In either case, you need to record the fact that your inventory value is actually less than what you purchased it for. And you want to record the fact that, really, the money you spent on the obsolete item is an expense. For example, suppose that you purchased some $100 item that you now realize is obsolete. How do you record this obsolescence? Table 3-7 shows the conventional approach.

Table 3-7	Journal Entry 7: Recording an Allowance for Obsolete Inventory	
Account	*Debit*	*Credit*
Inventory obsolescence	100	
Allowance for obsolete inventory		100

As Journal Entry 7 shows, to record the obsolescence of a $100 inventory item, you first debit an expense account called something like "inventory obsolescence" for $100. Then, you credit a contra-asset account named something like "allowance for obsolete inventory" for $100. As I mention in the discussion of accounts receivable, a contra-asset account gets reported on the balance sheet immediately beneath the asset account to which it relates. The contra-asset account, with its negative credit balance, reduces the net reported value of the asset account. For example, if the inventory account balance was $3,100 and you had an allowance for an obsolete inventory contra-asset account of $100, the net inventory balance shows as $3,000. In other words, the contra-asset account gets subtracted from the related asset account.

QuickBooks makes you record Journal Entry 7 yourself using the Make Journal Entries command.

When you ultimately do dispose of obsolete inventory, you record a journal entry like the one shown in Table 3-8. This journal entry debits the contra-asset account for $100 and credits inventory for $100. In other words, this journal entry removes the value of the obsolete inventory both from the allowance for obsolete inventory account and from the inventory account itself. You record this journal entry when you actually physically dispose of the inventory. This may be, for example, when you pay the junk man to haul away the inventory, or when you toss the inventory out into the large Dumpster behind your office or factory.

Table 3-8	Journal Entry 8: Recording Disposal of Inventory	
Account	*Debit*	*Credit*
Allowance for obsolete inventory	100	
Inventory		100

In general, one of the things you should do every year for tax accounting reasons is deal with your obsolete inventory. The tax rules generally state that you can't write off obsolete inventory unless you actually dispose of it for income purposes. You can, however, typically write down inventory to its liquidation value. Such a write-down works the same way as a write-down for obsolete inventory. A write-down can be a little tricky if you have never done it before, however, so you may want to confer with your tax advisor.

One more really important point about recording disposal of obsolete inventory: Within QuickBooks, you record inventory disposal by adjusting the physical item count of the inventory items. I describe how adjusting the physical inventory accounts works in Book III, Chapter 3. So even though I won't go down that path here, you should know that you don't actually enter a journal entry like the one shown in Journal Entry 8. You adjust the inventory accounts for the obsolete inventory. This adjustment would automatically reduce the inventory account balance. When QuickBooks asks you which account to debit, you specify the allowance for obsolete inventory account.

Dealing with inventory shrinkage

The other chronic inventory headache that many business owners and business managers have to deal with is inventory shrinkage. It's very likely, sometimes for the most innocent reasons, that your inventory records overstate the quantity counts of items. When this happens, you need to adjust your records. Essentially, you want to reduce both the dollar value of your inventory and the quantity counts of your inventory items.

Why not just credit the asset account?

If you are really getting into this double-entry bookkeeping, you may wonder why you don't just credit the inventory account in the case of something like obsolete inventory. Wouldn't that save you time and trouble? Well, yes and no.

Simply crediting the inventory account does make sense. Such an approach saves you the task of having to set up a goofy contra-asset account. However, accountants have concluded over the centuries that it makes sense to keep a record of your obsolete inventory as long as you own it. There are a bunch of different reasons for this, but one reason is that you want to know what inventory you need to get rid of or dispose of.

It's not necessary to set up some sort of separate system for keeping track of obsolete inventory. By using the contra-asset account, you can continue to store information about your inventory in the accounting system without making the balance sheet information and income statement information incorrect.

This logic applies to other contra-asset accounts, too. For example, previously in this chapter, I describe how to set up a contra-asset account for uncollectible accounts receivable. The business about wanting to have some record of your uncollectible accounts receivable — perhaps so you know you don't want to deal with those customers again — means that you may as well keep this information in the accounting system. A contra-asset account allows you to do so and at the same time not have the presence of uncollectible receivables overstate your accounts receivable balance.

Table 3-9 shows the journal entry that QuickBooks makes for you to record this event. This journal entry debits an appropriate expense account — in Journal Entry 9, I call the expense account *shrinkage expense* — for $100. A journal entry also needs to credit the inventory account for $100.

Table 3-9	Journal Entry 9: Recording Inventory Shrinkage	
Account	*Debit*	*Credit*
Shrinkage expense	100	
Inventory		100

Within QuickBooks, as I mentioned, you don't actually record a formal journal entry like the one shown here. You use something called a *physical count worksheet* to adjust the quantities of your inventory item counts to whatever they actually are. When you make this adjustment, QuickBooks automatically credits the inventory account balance and adjusts the quantity counts. QuickBooks also requires you to supply the expense account that it should debit for the shrinkage.

In the old days (by the "old days," I mean a few decades ago), businesses compared their accounting records to the physical counts of inventory items only once a year. In fact, the annual inventory physical count was a painful ritual that many distributors and retailers went through. These days, I think, most businesses have found that it works much better to stage physical inventory counts throughout the year. This approach, called *cycle counting*, means that you're probably comparing your accounting records with physical counts for your most valuable items several times a year. For your moderately valuable items, you're probably comparing your inventory accounting records with physical counts once or twice a year. With your least valuable inventory items, you probably only irregularly compare inventory records with physical counts, and you may accept a degree of imprecision. For example, rather than counting screws in some bin, you may weigh the bin and then make an estimate of the screw count. In any case, you want some system that allows you to compare your accounting records to your physical counts. Inventory shrinkage and inventory obsolescence represent real costs of doing business that won't get recorded in your accounting records in any other way.

Accounting for Fixed Assets

Fixed assets refers to those items that you can't immediately count as an expense when purchased. Fixed assets include such things as vehicles, furniture, equipment, and so forth. Fixed assets are tricky for two reasons: Typically, you must depreciate fixed assets (more on that in a bit), and you need to record the disposal of the fixed asset at some point in the future — for either a gain or for a loss.

Purchasing a fixed asset

Accounting for the purchase of a fixed asset is pretty straightforward. Table 3-10 shows how a fixed asset purchase typically looks:

Table 3-10	Journal Entry 10: Recording Fixed Asset Purchase	
Account	*Debit*	*Credit*
Delivery truck	12,000	
Cash		12,000

If you purchase a $12,000 delivery truck with cash, for example, the journal entry that you use to record this purchase debits delivery truck for $12,000 and credits cash for $12,000.

Within QuickBooks, this journal entry actually gets made when you write the check to pay for the purchase. The one thing that you absolutely must do is set up a fixed asset account for the specific asset. In other words, you don't want to debit a general catch-all fixed asset account. If you buy a delivery truck, you need to set up a fixed asset account for that specific delivery truck. If you buy a computer system, you need to set up a fixed asset account for that particular computer system. In fact, the general rule is that any fixed asset that you would buy individually or dispose of later individually needs its own asset account. The reason for this is that if you don't have individual fixed asset accounts, later on, the job of calculating gains and losses on the disposal of the fixed asset turns into a Herculean task.

Dealing with depreciation

Depreciation is an accounting gimmick to recognize the expense of using a fixed asset over a period of time. Although you may not be all that familiar with the mechanics of depreciation, you probably do understand the logic. For the sake of illustration, suppose that you bought a $12,000 delivery truck. Suppose also that because you know how to do your own repair work and take excellent care of your vehicles, you will be able to use this truck for ten years. Further suppose that at the end of the ten years, the truck will probably have a $2,000 salvage value (your best guess). Depreciation says that if you buy something for $12,000 and that you can later sell it for $2,000, that decrease in value needs to be apportioned to expense. In this case, the $10,000 decrease in value needs to be counted as expense over ten years. That expense is called *depreciation*.

Accountants and tax accounting laws use a variety of methods to apportion the cost of using an asset over the years in which it's used. A common method is called straight-line depreciation. *Straight-line depreciation* divides the decrease in value by the number of years that an asset is used. An asset that decreases $10,000 over ten years, for example, produces $1,000 a year of depreciation expense.

To record depreciation, you use a journal entry like the one shown in Table 3-11.

Table 3-11	Journal Entry 11: Recording Fixed Asset Depreciation	
Account	*Debit*	*Credit*
Depreciation expense	1,000	
Acc. dep. — Delivery truck		1,000

Choosing a depreciation method

Straight-line depreciation, which I've illustrated here, makes for a good example in a book. It's easy to understand and to illustrate. However, most accountants and business owners use more complicated depreciation methods for a variety of reasons. One of the most important reasons is that tax accounting laws generally allow for depreciation methods that accelerate tax deductions.

You need to figure out the annual depreciation according to one of these tax-based depreciation methods with your tax advisor's help. Different rules apply to different types of assets. The rules that you use for a particular asset depend on when you originally purchase the asset. I recommend that you use and record within QuickBooks the asset depreciation that you use for your tax accounting. Depreciation is complicated enough as it is. You don't want to be using one method of depreciation within QuickBooks for your own internal financial management and then another method for your tax returns.

While I am on the subject of depreciation, I should also mention that many small firms have the option of using something called a Section 179 election. (Section 179 is a chunk of law in the Internal Revenue Code.) A Section 179 election allows many businesses to immediately depreciate 100% of the cost of many of their fixed assets at the time of purchase. Despite the fact that a Section 179 election means that you can immediately write off the purchase of, for example, a $24,000 vehicle at the time of purchase, you still want to treat fixed assets expensed via a Section 179 election the way I describe here. The difference is that you'll immediately show the asset as fully depreciated — which means depreciated down to its salvage value or down to zero.

Journal Entry 11 debits an expense account called "depreciation expense" for $1,000. Journal Entry 11 also credits a contra-asset account called "accumulated depreciation — delivery truck" for $1,000. (By convention, because the phrase "accumulated depreciation" is so long, accountants and book-keepers usually abbreviate it as "acc. dep.") Note also that you need to have specific individual accumulated depreciation contra-asset accounts for each specific individual fixed asset account. You don't want to lump all of your accumulated depreciation together into a single catch-all account. That way lies madness and ruin.

Disposing of a fixed asset

The final wrinkle of fixed asset accounting concerns disposal of a fixed asset for a gain or for a loss. When you ultimately sell a fixed asset or trade it in or discard it because it's now junk, you need to record any gain or loss on the disposal of the asset. You also need to remove the fixed asset from your accounting records.

To show you how this works, consider again the example of the $12,000 delivery truck. Suppose that you've owned and operated this truck for two years. Over that time, you've depreciated $2,000 of the truck's original purchase price. Further suppose that you are going to sell the truck for $11,000 in cash. Table 3-12 shows the journal entry that you would need to make in order to record this disposal.

Table 3-12	Journal Entry 12: Recording Fixed Asset Sale for Gain	
Account	*Debit*	*Credit*
Delivery truck		12,000
Cash	11,000	
Acc. dep. — Delivery truck	2,000	
Gain on sale		1,000

The first component of Journal Entry 12 shows the $12,000 credit of the delivery truck asset. This makes sense, right? You need to remove the delivery truck from your fixed asset amounts, which you do by crediting the account for the same amount that you originally debited the account when you purchased the asset.

The next component of the journal entry shows the $11,000 debit to cash. This component, again, is pretty straightforward. It shows the cash that you receive by selling the asset.

The third component of the journal entry backs out the accumulated depreciation. If you depreciated the truck $1,000 a year for two years, the accumulated depreciation contra-asset account for the truck should equal $2,000. To remove this accumulated depreciation from your balance sheet, you need to debit the accumulated depreciation account for $2,000.

The final piece of the disposal journal entry is a plug, a calculated amount. You know the amount and whether that amount is a debit or credit by looking at the other accounts affected. For example, in the case of Journal Entry 12, you know that a $1,000 credit is necessary to balance the journal entry. Debits must equal credits.

A credit is a gain. A credit is essentially revenue, as you may remember from the discussion on double-entry bookkeeping in Book I, Chapter 2.

If the plug was a debit amount, the disposal would produce a loss. This makes sense; a loss is like an expense and expenses are debits.

If you are confused about the gain component of Journal Entry 12, let me make this observation. Over the two years of use, the business depreciated the truck by $2,000. In other words, the business, through the depreciation expense, said that the truck lost $2,000 of value. If, however, the $12,000 delivery truck is sold two years later for $11,000, the loss in value doesn't equal $2,000. The loss in value equals $1,000. The $1,000 gain, essentially, recaptures the unnecessary, extra depreciation that was incorrectly charged.

You can enter both Journal Entries 11 and 12 as journal entries within QuickBooks using the Make Journal Entries command.

Recognizing Liabilities

Liabilities are amounts that a business owes to other parties. For example, if a business owes a bank money because of a loan, that's a liability. If a business owes an employee wages or benefits, that's a liability. If a business owes the federal, state, or local government taxes, those are liabilities.

Borrowing money

Liabilities, fortunately, aren't that tricky to record after you've seen how the journal entries look. Table 3-13, for example, shows how you record money borrowed on a loan. In the case of a $10,000 loan, for example, you would debit cash for $10,000 and credit a loan payable liability account for $10,000.

Table 3-13	Journal Entry 13: Borrowing Money via a Loan	
Account	Debit	Credit
Cash	10,000	
Loan payable		10,000

Sometimes, you may purchase an asset with a loan. Suppose, for example, that you purchased $10,000 of furniture by using a note payable or a loan. Even though there is no immediate cash affect to this entry, you still need to record the transaction. Table 3-14 shows how you record this transaction. A furniture account gets debited for $10,000 and a loan payable account gets credited for $10,000.

Table 3-14	Journal Entry 14: Buying an Asset with a Loan	
Account	Debit	Credit
Furniture	10,000	
Loan payable		10,000

You can record Journal Entry 13 directly into your checkbook when you record the $10,000 cash deposit. You can also record Journal Entry 13, as well as Journal Entry 14, by using the Make Journal Entries command that QuickBooks provides. Journal Entry 14, by the way, can only be recorded by using the Make Journal Entries command.

Making a loan payment

To record the payment on a loan, you or QuickBooks enters a journal entry like the one shown in Table 3-15. For example, suppose that in connection with the loan shown in Journal Entry 13, you need to pay $2,200. Suppose that this amount is for $1,200 of loan interest and $1,000 of principal. In this case, you debit loan payable for $1,000, debit loan interest expense for $1,200, and credit cash for $2,200.

Table 3-15	Journal Entry 15: Paying a Loan Payment	
Account	*Debit*	*Credit*
Loan payable		1,000
Loan interest expense	1,200	
Cash		2,200

Sometimes, the tricky thing about loan payments is breaking the payment amount into its principal and loan components. Hopefully, the lender will provide you with an amortization schedule that breaks down payments into principal and interest.

If a lender doesn't provide such an amortization schedule, you need to calculate the interest expense yourself by using either a spreadsheet or a calculator. Then, after you have calculated the interest expense, you can deduce the principal component by subtracting the interest from the payment amount.

Accruing liabilities

I want to show you one other liability-related journal entry. Very commonly, a business will owe money for some goods or services or taxes that needs to be recorded in the accounting system. For example, if at the end of an accounting period — say at the end of the year — you owe $1,200 of interest on some loan, you really need to record that interest expense in your accounting system. You also need to record the fact that while the loan balance may show as $10,000 in your accounting records, for example, you probably really owe $11,200 because you owe both the $10,000 of principal and $1,200 of accrued interest.

To accrue a liability, you use a journal entry like the one shown in Table 3-16. This journal entry shows the accrual of $1,200 of interest expense on a loan payable.

Table 3-16	Journal Entry 16: Accruing a Liability	
Account	*Debit*	*Credit*
Loan interest expense	1,200	
Loan interest payable		1,200

The journal entry shows a $1,200 debit to loan interest expense and a $1,200 credit to loan interest payable. This journal entry records amounts that you owe as of the end of the accounting period that don't get recorded in some other way.

You need to be careful about using journal entries like the one shown in Journal Entry 16. Typically, you want to use such journal entries when it's very important to count all of your expenses and to accurately measure all of your liabilities.

One common situation in which you would want to be especially careful about making such accruals is if you sell your firm. Any prospective purchaser would want to have not only a very good estimate of your true expenses for the accounting period, but the purchaser would also want a very accurate estimate of liabilities at the point in time that the business is being evaluated.

Liability accruals like the one shown in Journal Entry 16 present the accountant or bookkeeper with a problem, however. To return to the example of the accrued interest shown in Journal Entry 16, suppose that at a later point in time, the business makes a $3,000 payment, which includes the interest accrued in Journal Entry 16. What the accountant or bookkeeper needs to do when he or she later records this loan payment is to remember or recognize the earlier journal entry. You don't want the accountant or bookkeeper to double-count interest expense by again recording the same interest. This makes sense, right?

Because accountants and bookkeepers can't reliably remember these sorts of accrual entries — remember that they may need to recall them months later — they typically back out the effect of the accrual from the first day of the new accounting period.

For example, if Journal Entry 16 were recorded at the end of year 1 to accurately estimate interest expense and liability balances, an accountant or bookkeeper could, on the first day of year 2, enter a *reversing* journal entry. This reversing journal entry would credit loan interest expense for $1,200 and debit loan interest payable for $1,200. In other words, this reversing journal entry reverses the earlier accrual. Because the accrual entry is still in year 1, however, year 1's estimates of interest expense and liability account balances are still correct.

Table 3-17 shows how a reversing entry looks. Again, notice that it's simply the mirror image of Journal Entry 16. The debits and credits are flip-flopped.

Table 3-17	Journal Entry 17: Reversing an Accrual	
Account	*Debit*	*Credit*
Loan interest expense		1,200
Loan interest payable	1,200	

When the actual loan interest payment is made, the journal entry appears as though no accrual or reversal ever existed. Table 3-18 shows this. For example, suppose that at some time in year 2 the business pays $1,800 of interest by making a cash payment. Journal Entry 18 shows how this transaction gets recorded.

Table 3-18	Journal Entry 18: The "Real" Loan Interest Payment	
Account	*Debit*	*Credit*
Loan interest expense	1,800	
Cash		1,800

Let me just quickly summarize what happens with Journal Entries 16, 17, and 18:

✦ Journal Entry 16 enables you to show at the end of year 1 that the business owes $1,200 of interest on a loan — even though that interest hasn't yet been paid. Journal Entry 16 also shows that even though the money wasn't paid, loan interest expense of $1,200 was incurred.

✦ Journal Entries 17 and 18 need to be combined to be understood. Journal Entry 17, for example, reduces the loan interest payable to zero. Remember that the loan interest payable would be a balance sheet liability account. The combination of the $1,200 debit and credit zero this account out. The $1,200 credit to loan interest expense in Journal Entry 17 needs to be combined with the $1,800 debit to loan interest expense in Journal Entry 18. This seems funny because after all, aren't you really paying $1,800 of interest? That's true, but remember, looking back at

Journal Entry 16, you already recorded $1,200 of loan interest expense. That interest expense has been recorded for year 1 in this example. If you have $1,800 of loan interest in total, what's left over for year 2 is the remaining $600. The combination of the $1,200 credit to loan interest expense and the $1,800 debit to loan interest expense produces this $600 of loan interest expense. The only other component of these two journal entries that needs to be mentioned is the $1,800 credit to cash. This credit to cash just represents the actual cash payment that is made to pay the loan interest amount.

You need to be careful when working with accrual entries, reversing entries, and then the real entries that follow and correct everything in the end. These tools can be enormously helpful when it's important to accurately measure expenses and liabilities. However, you must remember to complete the entire sequence of transactions; you can't stop halfway.

One last important point — in Journal Entries 16, 17, and 18, I talk about how to accrue loan interest expense. This accrual technique can be used to recognize any liability, a fact that I want to emphasize here. You can use the technique demonstrated in these journal entries to deal with liabilities for things such as wages owed to employees, taxes owed to the government, and so forth.

Some firms, particularly those with sophisticated accounting systems, can even use this technique to record hard-to-quantify liabilities, such as a warranty liability. (A *warranty* is a promise that you make to a customer; for example, you promise that your product won't break.) These promises create liabilities and expenses. An accurate accounting system requires that you record these expenses as they occur and recognize these liabilities as they come into existence.

Closing Out Revenue and Expense Accounts

You're about to enter the twilight zone of accounting. In this section, I talk about what happens to revenue and expense accounts at the end of the year in traditional manual accounting systems. And then I explain why QuickBooks doesn't quite work that way, and what you need to do about it.

If you want to skip anything in this chapter, this is probably the material. On the other hand, if you're like me and you have a compulsive personality and deem it essential to read everything in this chapter (even stuff that's not particularly exciting), read on.

Book I, Chapters 1 and 2 describe an imaginary hot dog stand business. This is a one-day business that, in my imagination, you operate. (If you've been reading through this chapter and have no questions, you don't even need to worry about those chapters.) Table 3-19 shows the trial balance for this business at the end of the day of operation.

Table 3-19	A Trial Balance at End of the Period	
Account	*Debit*	*Credit*
Cash	5,000	
Inventory	0	
Accounts payable		0
Loan payable		0
S. Nelson, capital		1,000
Sales revenue		13,000
Cost of goods sold	3,000	
Rent	1,000	
Wages expense	4,000	
Supplies	1,000	
Totals	14,000	14,000

The traditional close

As you hopefully already know, revenue and expense accounts count revenue and expenses for a particular period of time. For example, revenue and expense accounts may count for the month, the quarter, or the year.

One of the things that accounting systems traditionally do is zero out the revenue and expense accounts at the end of the year. This makes sense if you think about it a bit. You want your counters reset at the beginning of the year, so counting the new year's revenues and the new year's expenses is easy. In the case of a trial balance like the one shown in Table 3-19, for example, you would typically make the journal entry shown in Table 3-20.

Table 3-20	Journal Entry 19: Closing the Period	
Account	*Debit*	*Credit*
Sales revenue	13,000	
Cost of goods sold		3,000
Rent		1,000
Wages expense		4,000
Supplies		1,000
Owner's equity		4,000

If you look at Journal Entry 19, for example, you see that the first line in the journal entry is a $13,000 debit for sales revenue. If you look back at the trial balance shown in Table 3-19, you see that sales revenue has a $13,000 credit balance. The combination of the account balance shown in Table 3-19 and the closing entry shown in Journal Entry 19 effectively zero out the sales revenue account.

The same sort of accounting magic occurs for each of the other expense accounts shown in the trial balance. The cost of the goods sold balance is equal to a $3,000 debit in Table 3-19, and is zeroed out in Journal Entry 19 with a $3,000 credit. And so it goes.

The QuickBooks close

The sort of accounting taught at local community colleges makes just the sort of closing entry shown in Journal Entry 19. However, you actually don't need or even want to make such a closing entry within QuickBooks.

The closing entry shown in Journal Entry 19 gets made in a manual system so that the revenue and expense accounts can be reset to zero. In comparison, QuickBooks, relying on the power of the computer, doesn't need to have these accounts reset to zero in order to correctly calculate the revenue and expense for the new accounting period. QuickBooks, as you will learn throughout this book, can calculate revenue or sales for any period and for any interval of time by using its report generation tool to summarize revenues and expenses that occur within a particular time interval.

This seemingly missed step doesn't cause any idiosyncratic behavior on the part of QuickBooks. QuickBooks lumps the revenue and expenses from all the previous years into a retained earnings amount reported on the balance sheet. Net income for the current year is also reported in the equity portion of the balance sheet. In addition, if you have a corporation, QuickBooks typically includes a dividends paid account in the equity portion of the balance sheet. I'm getting ahead of myself, however.

The main thing that I want you to know is that this seemingly critical textbook journal entry for closing out revenue and expense accounts isn't made within QuickBooks. This is okay, because QuickBooks doesn't *need* to make the traditional closing entry.

You may want to ask your accountant about this. By convention, however, any dividends paid by a corporation are typically zeroed out or combined with retained earnings at the end of the year. If you want to combine dividends paid for the current year with accumulative retained earnings, you do this with a journal entry. The journal entry credits the dividends paid account and debits retained earnings for the amount of dividends paid for the year. I hesitate to encourage you to make this journal entry willy-nilly, however. I think it's okay to skip making the entry. And before you make it, consult your tax advisor.

One More Thing . . .

In this chapter, I tried to address any of the common, complicated journal entries or accounting transactions that business owners encounter. I know I can't answer every question here, but I do want to provide as thorough a set of instructions as possible. All this is leading up to a special request. If you've read through this chapter and didn't find a discussion of the sort of journal entry or accounting transaction that you need to record, send me an e-mail or write me a letter that tells me what help you hoped to find here . . . but didn't.

I can't promise you that I'll be able to supply an answer. But if you describe a journal entry that I should have included, I'll try to respond to your e-mail with instructions on how to make the journal entry. I'll also include a description of the journal entry in the next edition of this book.

If you want to reach me, you can write me a letter in care of the publisher (the publisher's address is in the front of this book). You can also send me an e-mail message; you can find my e-mail address and other contact information at www.stephenlnelson.com. (Please note that during tax season, I don't respond to reader inquiries as quickly as I do at other times of the year.)

Book II

Getting Ready to Use QuickBooks

The 5th Wave By Rich Tennant

"Since we began online shopping, I just don't know where the money's going."

Contents at a Glance

Chapter 1: Setting Up QuickBooks

In order to use QuickBooks, you need to do two things: install the QuickBooks software and run the setup interview, which is called the EasyStep Interview. This chapter discusses both of these tasks from a bird's-eye view. I also want to spend just a few paragraphs talking about some of the planning that you should do before you set up QuickBooks, and some of the errors created by the EasyStep Interview that you'll have to fix.

Planning Your New QuickBooks System

I'm going to start with a couple of big picture discussions: what accounting does and what accounting systems do. If you understand this big picture stuff from the very start, you'll find that the QuickBooks setup process makes a whole lot more sense.

What accounting does

Let's start with a discussion about what accounting does. People may argue about the little details, but most would agree that accounting does the following four important things:

✦ Measures profits and losses

✦ Reports on a financial condition of a firm (its assets, liabilities, and net worth)

✦ Provides detailed records of the assets, liabilities, and owner's equity accounts

✦ Supplies financial information to stakeholders, especially to management

What accounting systems do

Now take a brief look at what accounting systems — or at least at what small business accounting systems — typically do:

+ Produce financial statements, including income statements, balance sheets, and other accounting reports.

+ Generate business forms, including checks, paychecks, invoices, customer statements, and so forth.

+ Keep detailed records of key accounts, including cash, *accounts receivable* (amounts that customers owe a firm), *accounts payable* (amounts that a firm owes its vendors), inventory items, fixed assets, and so on.

+ Perform specialized information management functions. For example, in the publishing industry, book publishers often pay authors royalties. So royalty accounting is a task that book publisher accounting systems must typically do.

What QuickBooks does

Okay, after you understand what accounting does and what accounting systems typically do, you can see with some perspective what QuickBooks does:

+ Produces financial statements

+ Generates many common business forms, including checks, paychecks, customer invoices, customer statements, credit memos, and purchase orders

+ Keeps detailed records of a handful of key accounts: cash, accounts receivable, accounts payable, inventory in simple settings, and that's about it

Allow me to make an important observation here: QuickBooks does three of the four things that you would expect an accounting system to do. Compare the list that I just provided with the previous list ("What accounting systems do") to see this for yourself. However, I'll save you the time finding the fourth thing; QuickBooks doesn't supply the specialized accounting stuff. For example, QuickBooks doesn't do royalty accounting, as discussed in the earlier example.

And now for the bad news

So, QuickBooks does three of the four things that accounting systems do, but it doesn't do everything. QuickBooks is often an incomplete accounting solution. You need to be careful, therefore, about setting your expectations.

You also typically need to figure out workarounds for some of your special accounting requirements.

QuickBooks gives users and businesses a lot of flexibility. So, returning to the previous example, a book publisher can do much of what it needs to do for royalty accounting in QuickBooks. This royalty accounting work simply requires a certain amount of fiddling as the business is setting up QuickBooks.

However, QuickBooks does suffer from a couple of significant weaknesses:

✦ QuickBooks Basic and Pro don't supply a good way to handle the manufacture of inventory. However, QuickBooks Premier does support simple manufacturing accounting. (QuickBooks helps you account for the process of turning raw materials into finished goods.)

✦ QuickBooks doesn't handle the situation of storing inventory in multiple locations. It will just show, for example, that you have 3,000 widgets. It doesn't let you keep track of the fact that you have 1,000 widgets at the warehouse, 500 widgets at store A, and 1,500 widgets at store B.

In spite of the fact that QuickBooks may be an incomplete solution and the fact that QuickBooks may not handle inventory the way you want or need, QuickBooks is still a very good solution. What QuickBooks does, it does very well. Furthermore, I don't want to suggest that you shouldn't ever use some smaller software company's accounting solution, but consider the fact that QuickBooks will be around for a long, long time.

It's far more likely that an accounting software product with 600 users, for example, will be discontinued than a product like QuickBooks, which has 2,000,000 customers.

Installing QuickBooks

You install QuickBooks in the same way that you install any application program. And how you install an application program depends on which version of Microsoft Windows that you're using. In general, however, recent versions of Microsoft Windows require that you place the QuickBooks CD into your CD-ROM or DVD drive. When you do this, Windows looks at the QuickBooks CD and recognizes it as a CD that includes a new, to-be-installed software program, and starts the process for installing the QuickBooks software.

You don't need to do anything special to install QuickBooks. Simply follow the on-screen instructions. You typically will be prompted to enter the installation key or installation code. This code is available within the QuickBooks packaging — usually on the back of the envelope that the CD or DVD comes in.

The QuickBooks installation process may ask you to answer questions about how you want QuickBooks installed. Almost always, you want to accept the default suggestions. In other words, QuickBooks may ask you whether it can create a new folder in which to install the QuickBooks program files. And in this case, choose yes.

If your version of Microsoft Windows doesn't recognize that you've stuffed the QuickBooks CD into the machine's CD or DVD drive, you have a couple of choices:

✦ **You can wait.** Probably, if you wait, Windows will recognize that you've placed the QuickBooks CD into the CD or DVD drive and, after a short wait (even though it may seem like an eternity), Windows will start the process of installing the QuickBooks program.

✦ **You can manually force the installation of the QuickBooks program.** Windows includes a tool that you can use to add or remove new programs (unsurprisingly named the Add/Remove Programs tool). I don't describe how this Control Panel tool works here, but you can refer to a book such as *Windows XP For Dummies*, by Andy Rathbone (Wiley Publishing, Inc.), or Windows online Help to get this information. In a nutshell, you simply open the Control Panel window, click the Add/Remove Programs tool and follow the on-screen instructions for telling Windows to install a program stored on the CD or DVD in the computer's CD or DVD drive.

QuickBooks works as a multi-user accounting system. This means that several people can use QuickBooks. The QuickBooks data file — the repository of all the QuickBooks information — typically resides on a centrally available computer, or server. People who want to work with the QuickBooks data file simply install the QuickBooks program on their computers and then use the program to access centrally located QuickBooks data files. This multi-user system isn't complicated at all to run; in fact, I talk about it quite a bit in Book VII, Chapter 2. Note that you need to own a separate copy of QuickBooks for each computer on which you install QuickBooks. You can also buy multi-user copies of QuickBooks that let you install the QuickBooks program on up to five computers. I mention this because you don't want to get involved in software piracy — which is a felony — as part of inadvertently setting up QuickBooks in the wrong way. The bottom line: You need a legal copy of QuickBooks for every machine on which you install QuickBooks.

Dealing with the Pre-Interview Jitters

After you install QuickBooks, you run an interview to set up QuickBooks for your firm's accounting. In the next sections, I explain what you need to do before you run the QuickBooks setup interview so that you work in an efficient manner. I also give you an overview of what you'll do as you go through the interview.

Preparing for the interview

In running the interview, you will need to provide quite a bit of information to QuickBooks. As a practical matter, the EasyStep Interview requires that you have the following:

✦ Accurate financial statements as of the conversion-to-QuickBooks date

✦ Detailed records of your accounts payable, accounts receivable, inventory, and fixed assets

✦ A complete or nearly complete list of employees, customers, vendors, and inventory items (if you buy and sell inventory)

Book II
Chapter 1

You want to get all this stuff together before you start the EasyStep Interview because you will be asked about this stuff as part of the interview. Don't try to scurry around, looking for a particular piece of data, while you are running the interview; collect this data up front. Then stack all the necessary paperwork on your desk next to your computer.

**Setting Up
QuickBooks**

Let me also note that you are going to need to make several accounting decisions as you go through the EasyStep Interview. For example, you'll need to decide whether you want to use an accounts payable system. You'll need to tell QuickBooks whether you want to send customers monthly statements. You'll also be asked whether you want to prepare estimates for customers. And you'll be asked whether you want to use classes to further track your income and spending.

In general, when you're asked one of the accounting questions, you can simply accept the default answer. However, you are required by law to be consistent in your accounting for tax purposes. If you want to change your accounting — technically called a *change of accounting method* by the Internal Revenue Service — you need to request permission to make the change from the IRS. How to do this and the ramifications of doing this are beyond the scope of this book, but be forewarned: The IRS insists that you be consistent in your accounting. If you've been treating particular items of income or expense in a certain way, the IRS says, "Hey, dude, you need to continue to treat them that way unless you get permission from us to change."

One final note: You should have your tax return from last year handy because it supplies a bunch of information that you'll need for running the EasyStep Interview. For example, last year's tax return supplies your taxpayer ID number, your legal business name, and your method of accounting.

What happens during the interview

As you walk through the interview, you work with QuickBooks to set up a chart of accounts, to identify your starting trial balance, and to load your key master files. The *chart of accounts*, just so you know, identifies those income, expense, asset, liability, and owner's equity accounts that appear on your financial statement. The *trial balance* identifies your year-to-date income and expense numbers and your asset, liability, and owner's equity numbers as of the conversion date. The *master files* store information that you repeatedly use about customers, vendors, employees, and inventory items. For example, the customer master file stores the customer's name and address, phone number, and the contact person.

In addition, and as noted in the previous paragraphs, you make several accounting decisions during the interview. For example, you decide whether you want to use accounts payable.

Running the EasyStep Interview

After you install the QuickBooks program, the installation program may start QuickBooks automatically and then start the EasyStep Interview. You can also start the EasyStep Interview by starting the QuickBooks program — start QuickBooks the same way you start any program — and by choosing the File⇨New Company command.

The big Welcome

The Welcome portion of the EasyStep Interview requires that you step through roughly half a dozen screens of information. One of the first screens tells you that if this EasyStep Interview is too difficult, you can pay to get help from the QuickBooks certified advisor. (QuickBooks advisors, by the way, are people who have paid $500 to Intuit to get a copy of QuickBooks and be listed on the QuickBooks Web site as a QuickBooks advisor.) The Welcome portion of the EasyStep Interview also gives you some basic information about how to navigate through the interview; you also get some other basic information about the process. Read the screens of information and click the Next button.

No matter how you get to the EasyStep Interview, the first thing you see is the Welcome tab of the EasyStep Interview window, as shown in Figure 1-1.

The EasyStep Interview walks you through a bunch of tabs or screens full of information. To move to the next tab, you click the Next button. To move to the previous tab, you click the Prev button. If you get discouraged and want to give up, you can click the Leave button. But try not to get discouraged.

Figure 1-1:
The
EasyStep
Interview
window
showing the
Welcome
tab.

Supplying company information

The Company Info tab collects several important pieces of information, including your company name and the firm's legal name, your company address, your federal tax ID number, the first month in the income tax year (typically January), the first month in the fiscal year (again, typically January), the type of income tax form that your firm uses to report to the IRS, and the industry or type of company that you are operating (retail, service, and so forth), as shown in Figure 1-2.

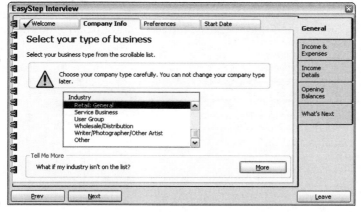

Figure 1-2:
The
Company
Info tab that
asks what
type of
business
you're
running.

As part of the company info process, QuickBooks creates the company data file that stores all of a firm's financial information. QuickBooks suggests a default name or a QuickBooks data file based on the company name (Figure 1-3).

All you need to do is accept the suggested name and the suggested folder location (unless you want to save the data file into the My Documents folder, which isn't a bad idea).

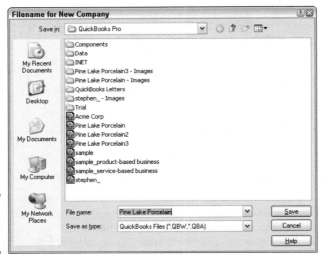

Figure 1-3:
The Save As
dialog box.

Based on the information that you supply about your type of industry and the tax form that you file with the IRS, QuickBooks suggests a starting set of accounts. These accounts are the categories that you'll use to track your income, expenses, assets, and owner's equity. Figure 1-4 shows the Company Info tab that the EasyStep Interview displays for showing you these accounts.

Figure 1-4:
The
Company
Info tab
asks you
which
expense
account you
want.

Choosing your preferences

After you provide high-level company information through the EasyStep Interview, QuickBooks walks you through a bunch of questions about the QuickBooks preferences. Preferences, in effect, give you a way to turn on or off various features about how QuickBooks accounting works, how QuickBooks looks, and so forth, as shown in Figure 1-5. Here are the first questions that the Preferences tab asks:

✦ Does your firm maintain inventory?

✦ Do you want to track the inventory that you buy and sell?

✦ Do you collect sales tax from your customers?

✦ When do you sell items?

✦ What invoice format do you want to use to bill customers?

✦ Do you want to use sales orders to track customer orders and backorders?

✦ Do you want to use QuickBooks to help with your employee payroll?

✦ Do you want to prepare written or verbal estimates for your customers?

✦ Do you ever prepare more than one invoice for one estimate (if you want to do progress billing or partial billing)?

✦ Would you like to track the time that you or your employees spend on jobs or projects for customers?

✦ Do you want to use classes to further segregate income and expense, assets, liabilities, and owner's equity data?

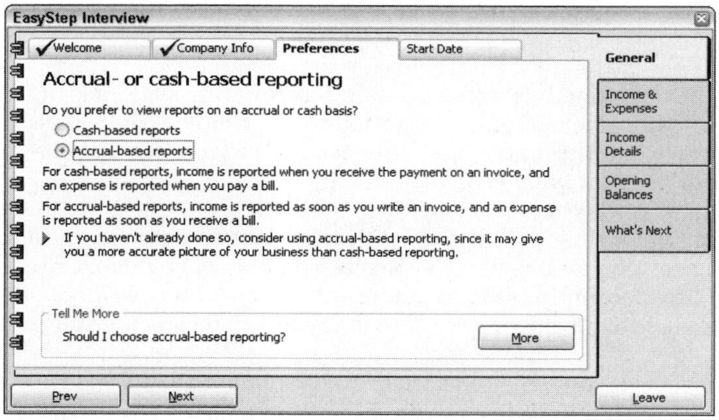

Book II
Chapter 1

Setting Up
QuickBooks

Figure 1-5: The Preferences tab asks whether you want to use accrual- or cash-basis reporting.

✦ How do you want to handle bills and payments (enter the checks directly, or enter the bills first and the payments later)?

✦ How often do you want to see your Reminder List?

✦ Do you prefer to view reports on an accrual or cash basis?

Setting your start date

Perhaps the key decision that you make in setting up any accounting system is the day on which you'll begin using your new system. This is called the *conversion date*. Typically, you want to begin using an accounting system on either the first day of the year or the first day of a new month. QuickBooks uses the Start Date tab of the EasyStep Interview dialog box to explain how important it is to choose an appropriate start date. You'll also be prompted to identify the start date by using the dialog box shown in Figure 1-6.

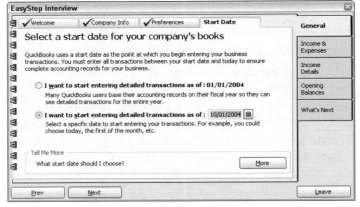

Figure 1-6: The Start Date tab prompts you for your company start date.

The easiest time to start using a new accounting system is at the beginning of the year. The reason? You get to enter a simpler trial balance. At the start of the year, for example, you only need to enter asset, liability, and owner's equity account balances.

At any other time, you also need to enter year-to-date income and year-to-date expense account balances. Typically, you only have this year-to-date income and expense information available at the start of the month. For this reason, the only other feasible start date that you can pick is the start of a month.

In this case, you need to get year-to-date income amounts through the end of the previous month from your previous accounting system. For example, if you've been using Peachtree, you'll need to get year-to-date income and expense amounts from Peachtree. You'll enter all of this trial balance data later in the EasyStep Interview.

After you provide the start date, you have finished with the first general set of interview questions. In other words, you've supplied the basic company information, you've identified most of your accounting preferences, and you've identified the date at which you want to start using QuickBooks.

If you click the Leave button, QuickBooks leaves you in the QuickBooks program, ready to get to work. However, the EasyStep Interview process isn't lost forever; to get back into the interview, just choose EasyStep Interview from the File menu.

Book II
Chapter 1

Setting Up
QuickBooks

Adding income accounts

After you complete the general set of EasyStep Interview questions, QuickBooks asks you to add any income accounts or expense accounts that you'll need for your business. Figure 1-7 shows the Income Accts tab.

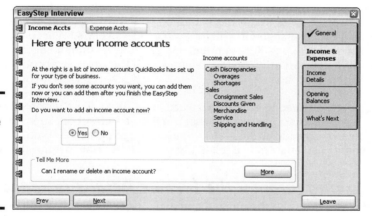

Figure 1-7:
The Income Accts tab of the EasyStep Interview dialog box.

To create a new income account, select the Yes radio button, click Next, and then enter a name for the account into the Account Name box that appears. If you're comfortable, specify on which line of your tax form this account gets reported. For example, if you're entering an account to track gross sales for a sole proprietor, you may enter the account name **Gross Sales** into the Account Name box. Then you can select Income: Gross Receipts or Sales from the Tax Line drop-down list box, as shown in Figure 1-8 (this would end up on the Schedule C tax form).

Figure 1-8:
Creating a new income account.

You can add several accounts for tracking income. To do this, you indicate that you want to add another income account when asked.

After you add the last income account, QuickBooks asks you to review the expense accounts that it has set up on your starting chart of accounts. To add an expense account, you follow a process very similar to that for adding an income account. For example, you give the account an account name. If possible, you identify the tax line on which the expense account gets reported.

You may not need to add expense accounts. Typically, QuickBooks starts with a suggested chart of accounts that provides a rich set of expense accounts. You can easily add additional income and expense accounts to the chart of accounts list later on. In Book II, Chapter 2, I describe just how to do this.

Working through the Income Details introduction

After you describe the income and expense accounts that you need, QuickBooks walks you through a portion of the EasyStep Interview called the Income Details section. The Income Details section asks about how you account for the income that your firm produces. For example, the first question that QuickBooks asks is whether you receive full payment at the time you provide a service or product, as shown in Figure 1-9. QuickBooks also asks whether you want to issue regular monthly statements to customers or simply use invoices to bill customers.

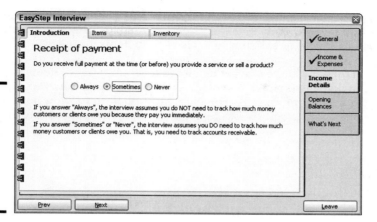

Figure 1-9:
The
EasyStep
Interview
question
about
receipt of
payment.

Identifying your income items

You use the Items tab of the Income Details section to identify the specific things that you sell. In this section, the first question that QuickBooks asks, for example, is whether you want to set up a service item for any work or service that you sell. If you indicate that you do want to set up a service item, QuickBooks displays a dialog box similar to the one shown in Figure 1-10. To set up a service item — or any other item — you need to give the item a name, a description, and a price. You also need to identify which income account should be used to track sales of the item and whether the service item is ever performed by a subcontractor.

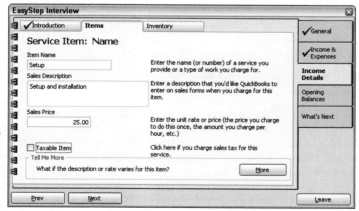

Figure 1-10:
How you set
up a service
item.

QuickBooks also has you set up other types of items. For example, if you sell inventory, you set up inventory items. If you bill customers for other things, such as freight or sales tax, you also set up items for these.

I don't talk about how to set up all the different types of items in this chapter. In Book III, Chapter 3, I go into great detail about how you describe the items that your firm sells. The thing that you need to know here is that you should set up a QuickBooks item for anything that you want to see on an invoice.

If you carry inventory, you will also set up inventory items as part of the EasyStep Interview.

Setting up your inventory balances

The Inventory tab's questions collect information about the inventory items that you buy, hold, and sell. The screen shown in Figure 1-11, for example, lets you name an inventory item, describe the item, and set a sales price.

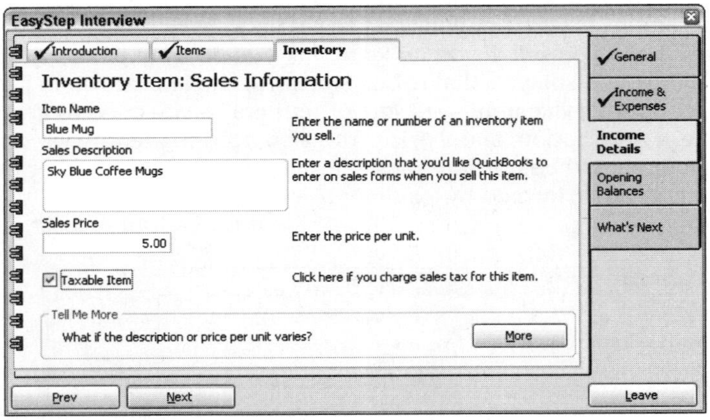

Figure 1-11:
The Inventory tab used to describe an inventory item.

After you identify an inventory item, QuickBooks asks you to specify which income account should be used to track sales of the item. You also need to provide any purchase information that you have. This purchase information includes a description that may go on purchase orders and the estimated cost for each item.

The final bit of inventory item information that you supply concerns your current holdings of the item. You need to enter the number of units that you are holding on your store floor or in the warehouse, the value or cost of that item, and, optionally, the reorder point that you want to use to get reminders from QuickBooks when it's time to reorder. Figure 1-12 shows a version of the Inventory tab that you use to record this important information.

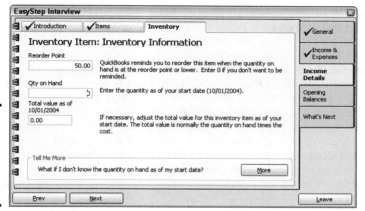

Figure 1-12:
Another
Inventory
tab collects
on-hand
information.

When you identify the quantity and cost of inventory items that you hold, you indirectly set your inventory balances — the same inventory balances that are used on your balance sheet.

If you have a number of inventory items, setting up the inventory item descriptions will take you some time. You need to go through this process where you describe the type of item, and give balance and quantity information for each item that you hold. If you have 20 items to set up in your items list, this process won't take too long. However, if you have 11,000 items in your inventory, you probably won't want to do it.

A suggestion: Before you give up on using a perpetual inventory system (which is what QuickBooks does with its inventory items), talk with your tax advisor or with your accountant. Many retailers do successfully use periodic inventory systems (which means you wouldn't go to the hassle of using the QuickBooks Inventory Items feature). But perpetual inventory systems, which always keep track of how much inventory you have on hand, deliver huge benefits. The biggest benefit is that you'll always know what inventory items are selling well — and what items aren't selling well.

If you have thousands of inventory items, it may be in your best interest to hire some temporary bookkeeping help to enter this information into QuickBooks. Obviously, the best time to hire this temporary person to set up your inventory items file is when you next do a physical inventory count.

Setting up opening balances for customers

The Opening Balances portion of the EasyStep Interview collects information about customers who owe you money, vendors to whom you owe money, and the account balances of all your other balance sheet accounts.

Remember that your start date or conversion date is key here; enter account balances as of the start date.

QuickBooks will ask, as part of setting up your customer opening balance, whether you have any customers who owe you money on your start date. If you indicate in the affirmative, QuickBooks will first ask whether you want to track jobs or projects for your customers. If you do, QuickBooks steps through the process for adding the customer, the job, and the amount owed on the job. If you don't need to track balances by jobs or projects, you simply identify the customer and the amount that the customer owes. Figure 1-13 shows the version of the Customers tab that you use to name a customer and specify the amount that the customer owes. If you select the Has Multiple Jobs check box, QuickBooks forces you to identify the customer job and then the balances owed on various jobs.

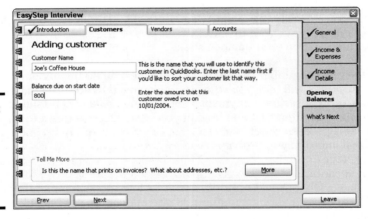

Figure 1-13:
The Customers tab of the EasyStep Interview window.

When you identify the amounts that customers owe you, you indirectly set your accounts receivable balances.

If you want information about tracking amounts that customers owe by job, refer to Book IV, Chapter 5. It describes how you can set up a job costing system.

Providing vendor opening balances

In a manner very similar to that used to provide opening balances for your customers, you also provide opening balances owed to your vendors. QuickBooks will ask you to name a vendor and identify the amount that you owe the vendor. To do this, QuickBooks uses the Vendors tab, as shown in Figure 1-14.

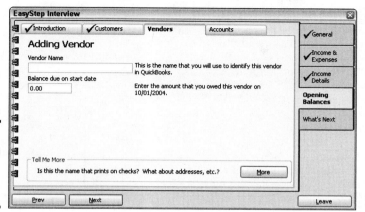

Figure 1-14:
The Vendors
tab of the
EasyStep
Interview.

When you identify the opening balances for your vendors, you indirectly set up your accounts payable account balances.

Setting your other account balances

The Accounts tab of the EasyStep Interview window lets you set account balances for any of the other balance sheet accounts that you use. As part of this section of the EasyStep Interview, for example, QuickBooks asks whether you have a company credit card account on which you charge purchases, lines of credit, open loans and notes, and so forth. If you indicate that the business has a liability, QuickBooks asks you for the account balance at the start date, as shown in Figure 1-15.

After QuickBooks asks about your liability accounts, it asks about your asset accounts. For example, QuickBooks asks if you have a bank account (of course you do), what money you've loaned, what furniture and equipment you possess, any other property that you have, and so forth. As with the liability accounts, if you indicate that you do own a particular asset, QuickBooks asks for the account balance as of the start date.

Figure 1-16 shows the version of the Accounts tab that you use to add an asset account. If you add a fixed asset, QuickBooks also asks whether you need to track depreciation for the asset. If you indicate that you do, QuickBooks asks you to enter both the original cost of the asset and any accumulated depreciation for the asset.

**Book II
Chapter 1**

Setting Up
QuickBooks

Figure 1-15:
Adding a liability account.

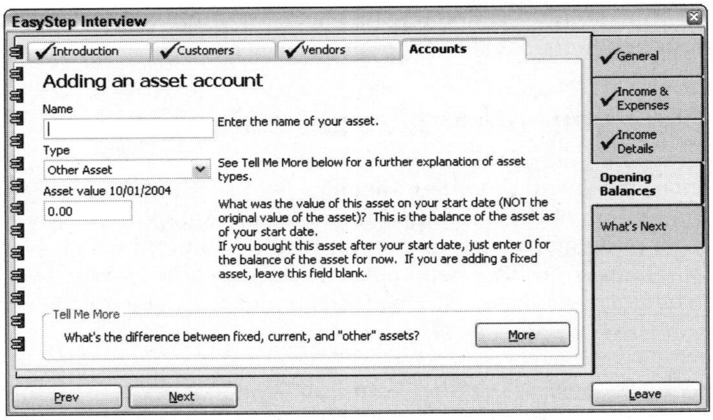

Figure 1-16:
Adding an asset account.

The final set of balance sheet account balances that you need to provide are those for your *equity accounts*. Equity accounts report the money that you originally invested in your business and any profits that you've retained in your business. For sole proprietorships, the equity account stuff is pretty easy. You can put everything into one big account called "Proprietor's Capital" or something like that. Partnerships need to keep track of the capital allocated or held by each partner. In corporations, unfortunately, you need to keep very detailed records of the sources and types of corporate capital that have been contributed by investors.

I talk a little bit about how equity account accounting works in Book I, Chapter 1. If you are a little rough on the accounting, refer there for some introductory information about how owner's equity accounting works.

Owner's equity accounting can be a little tricky — especially if you haven't taken a Principles of Accounting class at the local community college. QuickBooks suggests a list of equity accounts that you'll need based on the business form that you identified earlier in the EasyStep Interview.

Completing the What's Next section of the interview

The What's Next tab of the EasyStep Interview displays a list of tasks that QuickBooks suggests you complete before you begin day-to-day accounting with QuickBooks. For example, it suggests that you make a backup copy of your new QuickBooks data file. QuickBooks also suggests that you enter historical transactions and set up any other users with passwords. QuickBooks also wants you to do some other kinds of nit-picky stuff, such as customizing your forms and signing up for one of the expensive QuickBooks payroll services. (For information about how to back up the QuickBooks data file, refer to Book VII, Chapter 3.)

Book II
Chapter 1

Setting Up
QuickBooks

Looking at the QuickBooks Learning Center window

After you finish with the EasyStep Interview, QuickBooks displays the QuickBooks Learning Center window, , as shown in Figure 1-17. This window provides clickable hyperlinks that you can use to view tutorials that provide a "big picture" overview of how you work with QuickBooks. There's good stuff here, so if you're new to QuickBooks, go ahead: poke around. After you finish poking, click the Begin Using QuickBooks button and the QuickBooks program window appears.

Figure 1-17: The QuickBooks Learning Center window.

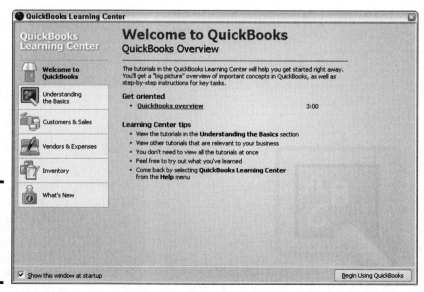

Fixing the EasyStep Interview Errors

Here's an interesting bit of trivia: In spite of all the accounting, tax, and just general financial genius residing at Intuit (the maker of QuickBooks and a bunch of other financial accounting software), the EasyStep Interview almost always leaves you with some errors that need fixing. In a nutshell, QuickBooks simply forgets to ask about or enter the year-to-date income and expense data. Furthermore, QuickBooks muddies the water by incorrectly counting the accounts receivable balance as uncategorized income and the accounts payable balance as uncategorized expense. You need to fix these errors.

In order to record your year-to-date income and expense amounts, you need to record a *journal entry*. The journal entry needs to record the trial balance amounts for all of your income and expense accounts. The *plug*, or difference between your income and expense accounts, needs to be credited or debited to a weird account called Opening Bal Equity, which is a suspense account that QuickBooks uses to attempt to camouflage its bookkeeping madness.

To show you how this works, suppose that you have the trial balances shown in Table 1-1. Note that this is the trial balance used in the discussion in Book I, Chapter 2. The crazy thing about the EasyStep Interview is that only those accounts that appear on the balance sheet end up being set up as part of the EasyStep Interview. This means that the income and expense accounts shown on the trial balance in Table 1-1 don't get set up.

Table 1-1	A Trial Balance	
Account	*Debit*	*Credit*
Cash	5,000	
Inventory	0	
Accounts payable		0
Loan payable		0
S. Nelson, capital		1,000
Sales revenue		13,000
Cost of goods sold	3,000	
Rent	1,000	
Wages expense	4,000	
Supplies	1,000	
Totals	14,000	14,000

Figure 1-18 shows how the General Journal Entries window looks when it records the missing trial balance information from Table 1-1. Note that the plug, or last line of the journal entry, is a debit to Opening Bal Equity. This is the freaky, flaky suspense account that QuickBooks uses to throw stuff into that it doesn't know what to do with. After this journal entry is recorded, the trial balance is correct as of the start date.

For more information about how to record a journal entry by using the General Journal Entry window, you can refer to Book IV, Chapter 1. If you want to try this on your own without any further instruction from me, choose the Company⇨Make Journal Entry command. When QuickBooks displays the General Journal Entries window, as shown in Figure 1-18, use the Account, Debit, and Credit columns to record your journal entry.

**Book II
Chapter 1**

*Setting Up
QuickBooks*

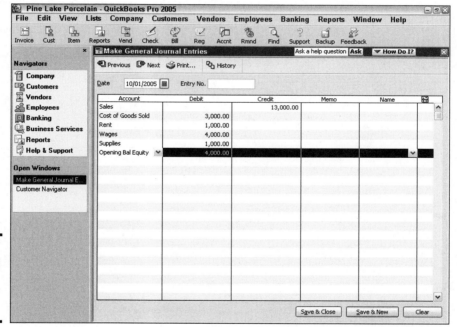

Figure 1-18:
The General Journal Entries window.

Does the idea of making a journal entry terrify the heck out of you? If so, you may find yourself in a bit of a pickle. You need to become comfortable working with double-entry bookkeeping in order to set up QuickBooks at a time other than at the beginning of the year. This means, unfortunately, that if you are setting up QuickBooks sometime during the middle of the year, you need to enter a general journal entry in order to fix the weirdness that the EasyStep Interview creates. If you don't know how double-entry bookkeeping works — if debits and credits aren't your friends — you probably need to get somebody's help. I suggest that you call your CPA or some other friend who truly understands accounting. Get him or her to come over and enter the last part of the trial balance for you by using the General Journal Entry window. Note that this shouldn't be a big project — just in case you decide to call your CPA. If your CPA will come over to your office, and if you have the trial balance ready for her, it should only take a few minutes to enter the general journal entry necessary. Perhaps you can buy her a nice lunch and that will settle the score.

Chapter 2: Loading the Master File Lists

In This Chapter

✔ Setting up the Chart of Accounts List

✔ Setting up the Item List

✔ Setting up the Payroll Item List

✔ Setting up classes

✔ Setting up a Customer List

✔ Setting up the Vendor List

✔ Setting up your employees

✔ Setting up the Profile Lists

Setting up QuickBooks, as a practical matter, requires that you take two steps: Run the EasyStep Interview described in Book II, Chapter 1, and load the master file lists. The master file lists store information that you will use and reuse. For example, one of the master file lists describes each of your customers. And this master file of customer information includes the customer's name and address, contact information, account numbers, and so on.

In this chapter, I walk you through the process of adding information to each of the master files — or *lists*, as QuickBooks calls them — that you'll need to fill (or mostly fill) before you begin using QuickBooks on a day-to-day basis.

One important note: You don't need to completely fill your master files before you start doing anything. If you enter your most important customers into the customer master file, your most important vendors into the vendor master file, and so forth, that amount of information may be all you need to get started. With the master file information you entered through the EasyStep Interview (as described in Book II, Chapter 1) and the addition of a few more entries into key master files, you may be able to add everything else on the fly. QuickBooks enables you to add entries to the various master files as you work with windows and dialog boxes that reference master file information.

Setting Up the Chart of Accounts List

The Chart of Accounts List is a list of accounts that you use to categorize your income, expense, assets, liabilities, and owner's equity amounts. If you want to see a particular line item of financial data on a report, you need an account for that line item. If you want to budget by a particular line item, you need an account for that budget amount. If you want to report some bit of financial information on your tax returns, you need an account to collect that specific data.

Fortunately, the steps for creating new accounts are quite straightforward. To set up a new account within your Chart of Accounts List, follow these steps:

1. Choose the Lists⇨Chart of Accounts command.

When you choose the Lists⇨Chart of Accounts command, QuickBooks displays the Chart of Accounts window shown in Figure 2-1.

2. Click the Account button at the bottom of the window.

QuickBooks displays the Account menu. One of the Account menu options is New, which is the command that you use to add a new account.

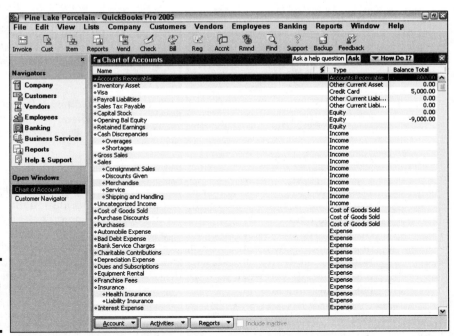

Figure 2-1:
The Chart of
Accounts
window.

3. **Add a new account by choosing the New command from the Account menu.**

QuickBooks displays the New Account dialog box, as shown in Figure 2-2.

4. **Use the Type drop-down list box to identify the type of account that you are adding.**

QuickBooks supplies the following account types: Bank, Accounts Receivable, Other Current Assets, Fixed Assets, Other Assets, Accounts Payable, Credit Card, Other Current Liability, Long Term Liability, Equity, Income, Cost of Goods Sold, Expense, Other Income, and Other Expense. If you have a question about which account type that your new account fits into, you should review Book I, Chapter 1, which describes how financial statements work. These account groups essentially tell QuickBooks in which area of a financial statement account data gets reported.

5. **Use the Name box to give your new account a unique name.**

The name that you give the account will appear on your financial statements.

**Book II
Chapter 2**

Loading the Master
File Lists

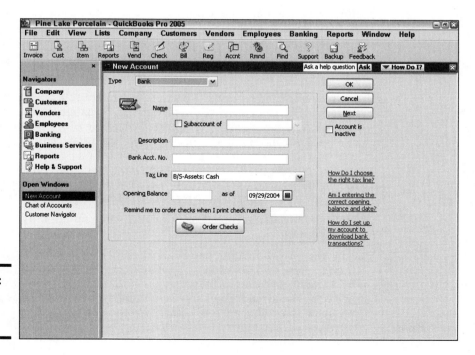

Figure 2-2:
The New
Account
window.

6. **If the account you're adding is a subaccount underneath another parent account, identify the parent account by selecting the Subaccount Of check box.**

   After you select the Subaccount Of check box, name the parent account by using the Subaccount Of drop-down list box.

7. **(Optional) Provide a description for the new account.**

   You don't need to provide a description. Without a description, QuickBooks can still use the account name on financial statements. If you want a more descriptive label placed on accounting reports, however, use the Description box for this purpose.

8. **Provide other account information.**

   The New Account window shown in Figure 2-2 includes a Bank Acct. No. box that lets you record the bank account number for a particular bank account. Other account types may have similar boxes for storing related account information. For example, the credit card account type version of the New Account window lets you store the card number. If you do have another box or two in which to store account information, go ahead and use that, if necessary, to collect the bits and pieces of data that you want to save.

9. **Identify the tax line on which the account information will be reported by selecting a tax form and tax line from the Tax Line drop-down list box.**

   You may not need to assign a particular account to a tax line if that account data isn't reported on the business's tax return. For example, cash account balances aren't reported on a sole proprietor's tax return. So a bank account for a sole proprietor doesn't have any required tax line data. Cash account balances are recorded on a tax return of a corporation, however. So if you were adding a bank account for a corporation, you would use the Tax Line drop-down list box to identify the tax line on which the bank account information gets reported.

10. **(Optional but dangerous) Consider recording an opening balance for the account.**

    Typically, you should not use either the Opening Balance box or the As Of box. These two boxes let you identify an opening account balance for the account at the time you set up the account; this is something you'd rarely do. However, if you know something I don't, you can use these two fields to set the starting balance for the account as of some date. Note that my accounting professors taught me two things that would suggest that this approach to setting account balances is crazy:

    • Debits are supposed to equal credits. (If you're setting the opening balance for an account as part of setting up the new account, you're only recording half of the accounting transaction.)

- Entering the opening balance as part of setting up a new account means no audit trail exists for the transaction. (Rather than having an invoice associated with a transaction or a check, or even a general journal entry, you're just setting balances on the fly. But hey, maybe you know something I don't. . .).

After you describe the new account that you want to set up (as shown in Figure 2-3), you can click the OK button to save the new account to the Chart of Accounts List. You can also click the Next button to save the account information and then redisplay the New Account window so that you can add another account.

If you look closely at Figure 2-3, you will note some boxes and buttons and even a hyperlink that I haven't talked about. QuickBooks does supply other fields for collecting account information. And, occasionally, QuickBooks also provides clickable hyperlinks and buttons that you can use to do special tasks associated with the particular type of account. For example, in the case of a bank account, QuickBooks supplies an Order Checks command button that you can click to start the process of ordering check forms for the new account.

**Book II
Chapter 2**

Loading the Master
File Lists

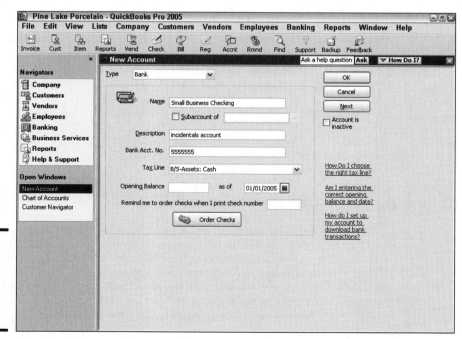

Figure 2-3:
The completed New Account window.

And that's almost everything you need to know about adding accounts. The one other thing I should mention is that the Account menu — this is the menu of commands that QuickBooks displays when you click the Account button available on the Chart of Accounts window — provides several other useful commands for working with accounts. The menu provides a Delete command that you use to delete the selected account (as long as you haven't already used the account). The menu provides an Edit button that you can use to make any changes to the selected account information (by using a window that looks very much like the New Account window shown in Figure 2-2). The Account menu also provides other commands that you can use to work with the Chart of Accounts List. Fortunately, most use self-descriptive command names: Print List, Make Inactive, and so on.

The Activities button, which appears at the bottom of the Chart of Accounts window, displays a menu of commands that you can use to write checks, make deposits, enter credit card charges, transfer funds, make journal entries, reconcile a bank account, and use a register. The Reports button displays a menu of commands that you can use to print out reports that use or show account information.

Setting Up the Item List

If you choose the Lists⇨Item List command, QuickBooks displays the Item List window, as shown in Figure 2-4. The Item List window lists all of the items that you've set up as part of running the EasyStep Interview and items that you've added manually since running the EasyStep Interview.

I don't talk about how you add items to the Item List window here because Book III, Chapter 3 details that. That chapter describes how you add items to the Item List. Note that the Item List is very important! The Item List lets you keep track of what you buy, hold, and sell to your customers.

Working with the Price Level List

The Price Level List lets you create price adjustments that you can use on the fly as you invoice customers, issue credit memos, and so forth. Because the Price Level List directly relates to how you work with and bill for inventory items, I also describe how you work with the Price Level List in Book III, Chapter 3. Rather than repeat information here that will be of interest to only a few people and isn't actually essential for getting started with QuickBooks, I refer you instead to Chapter III, Book 3.

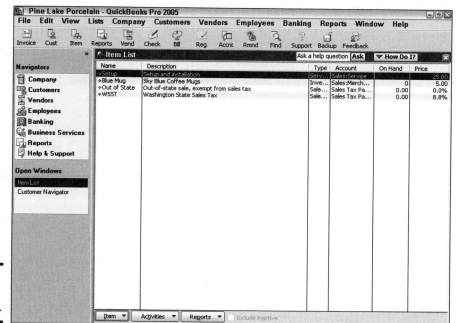

Book II
Chapter 2

Loading the Master
File Lists

Figure 2-4:
The Item
List window.

Using Sales Tax Codes

The Sales Tax Codes List keeps a list of codes, or abbreviations, that you can use to describe items as taxable or nontaxable. If you choose this command, QuickBooks displays a window listing the existing sales tax codes. (Usually, you'll see two existing codes: Tax and Non.) To add a new sales tax code, click the Sales Tax Code button, choose New, and describe the new sales tax.

Setting Up a Payroll Item List

The Payroll Item List identifies items that appear on employee payroll check stubs. If you're using an outside payroll service bureau to handle your payroll — and this is not a bad idea — you don't even need to worry about the Payroll Item List. If you're using either the QuickBooks Deluxe or QuickBooks Premier Payroll Service, again, you don't need to worry about the Payroll Item List. (In either case, the QuickBooks folks will set up the payroll items that you need to use for recording payroll.) And in the case of the QuickBooks Premier Payroll Service, you don't actually even need to track payroll inside QuickBooks because the QuickBooks people will do it at their office location on their computers.

If you do need to add payroll items, follow these steps:

1. **Choose the Lists⇨Payroll Item List command.**

   QuickBooks displays the Payroll Item List window.

2. **To add a new Payroll Item, click the Payroll Item button and then choose New from the Payroll Item menu.**

   QuickBooks displays the Add New Payroll Item dialog box. You can choose to set up a new payroll item either by using the Easy Set Up Method or the Custom Set Up Method. If you want QuickBooks to help you and you're setting up a common payroll item, click the Easy Set Up button and then Next, and simply follow the on-screen instructions.

   If you want to perform a custom setup of a payroll item, click the Custom Set Up button and then Next. QuickBooks then walks you through a multiple screen interview — like the EasyStep Interview discussed in Book II, Chapter 1 — that asks you about the payroll item that you need to set up. For example, the first dialog box that QuickBooks displays asks you to identify the type of payroll item that you want to create. You answer this question by selecting one of the radio buttons, and then clicking Next.

3. **Name the payroll item.**

   After you identify the type of payroll item, you need to name it. QuickBooks provides another version of the Add New Payroll Item dialog box that includes a field you fill in to give the new item a name.

4. **To finish the payroll item setup, click the Next button to move through the remaining payroll items setup questions.**

   You'll need to identify the name of the government agency to which the liability is paid, the taxpayer identification number that uniquely identifies you to the taxing agency, the liability account that you use to track the items, the tax form line that you use to report the item, the rules that QuickBooks should use for calculating the item (such as whether the item is subject to taxes or not), and a couple of other miscellaneous pieces of data. After you supply all this information and click the Finish button (which appears on the last version of the Add New Payroll Item dialog box), QuickBooks adds the new payroll item to the Payroll Item List.

The Payroll Item menu supplies commands that are useful for working with the Payroll Item List. In addition to the commands that you use to add an item to the list, the menu supplies commands for deleting payroll items, renaming payroll items, making payroll items active, and printing the list of payroll items.

Setting Up Classes

QuickBooks lets you use classes to segregate or track financial data in ways that aren't possible by using other bits of accounting information, such as the account number, the customer, the sales rep, the item, and so forth. A firm can use classes, for example, to segregate business units for product lines or geographical territories.

To set up classes, follow these steps:

1. **Choose the Lists⇨Class List command.**

QuickBooks displays the Class List window, as shown in Figure 2-5.

If you don't see the Class List command, Choose Edit⇨Preferences, click the Accounting icon and then the Company Preferences tab, and check the Use Class Tracking box.

2. **To create a new class, click the Class button and choose New from the Class menu.**

QuickBooks displays the New Class window, as shown in Figure 2-6.

**Book II
Chapter 2**

Loading the Master
File Lists

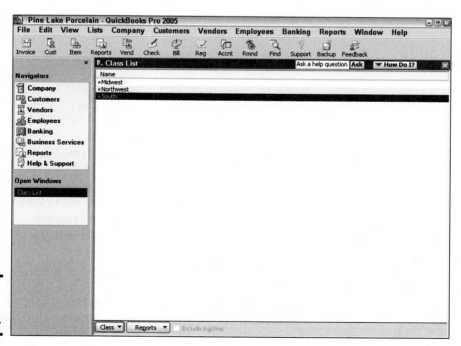

Figure 2-5:
The Class
List window.

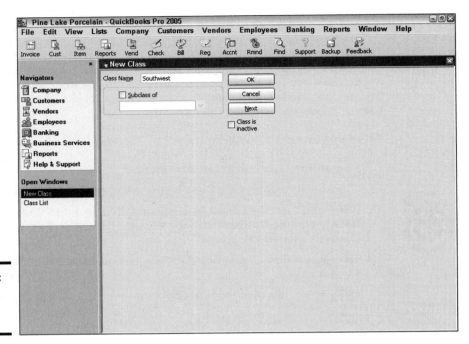

Figure 2-6:
The New
Class
window.

3. **To name the new class, enter a name or abbreviation into the Class Name box.**

Note that you will need to enter the class name whenever you record a transaction that falls into the class. For this reason, you don't want to create lengthy or easy-to-mistype class names. Keep things short, simple, and easy.

4. **If the class that you're setting up is actually a subclass of a parent class, select the Subclass Of check box and then select the parent class from the Subclass Of drop-down list box.**

After you describe the new class, you can click OK to save the class. Alternatively, you can click Cancel to not save the class. Or, you can click the Next button to save the class and redisplay the New Class window.

If you don't want the class to be used any more, you can select the Class Is Inactive check box.

The Class menu, which appears when you click the Class button, also supplies commands for editing the selected classes information, for deleting the selected class, for making the selected class inactive, for printing the list of classes, and several other useful commands as well. These commands are all pretty straightforward to use. Go ahead and experiment with them to find out how they work.

Setting Up a Customer List

A Customer List keeps track of all your customers and your customer information. For example, the Customer List keeps track of billing addresses and shipping addresses for customers.

Follow these steps to add a customer to the Customer List:

1. **Choose the Lists⇨Customer Job List command.**

QuickBooks displays the Customer:Job List window, as shown in Figure 2-7.

The Customer:Job button, besides letting you create new customers, provides a menu of commands for editing customer information, deleting customers, printing a customer list, and so forth.

2. **To add a new customer, click the Customer:Job button and then choose the New command.**

QuickBooks displays the New Customer window, as shown in Figure 2-8.

**Book II
Chapter 2**

Loading the Master
File Lists

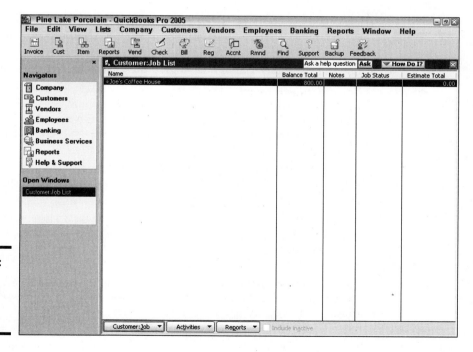

Figure 2-7:
The
Customer:
Job List
window.

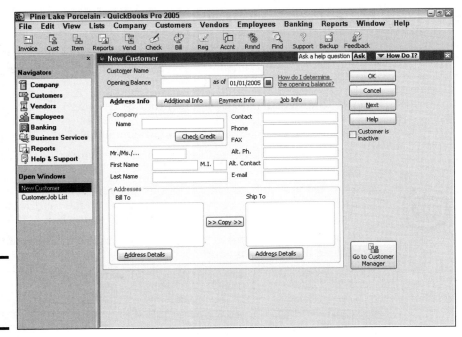

Figure 2-8:
The New
Customer
window.

3. **Use the Customer Name box to give the customer a short name.**

You don't need to enter the customer's full name into the Customer Name box. That information can go into the Company Name box shown on the Address Info tab. You just want some abbreviated version of the customer name that you can use to refer to the customer within the QuickBooks accounting system.

4. **Ignore the Opening Balance and As Of boxes.**

You don't want to set the customer's opening balance by using the Opening Balance and As Of boxes. That's not the right way to set your new customer accounts receivable balance. If you do this, you are essentially setting up the debit part of an entry without the corresponding credit part. Later, you'll have to go in and enter crazy, wacky journal entries in order to fix your incomplete bookkeeping.

5. **Use the boxes of the Address Info tab to supply the company name, including contact information, billing and shipping addresses, contact name, contact phone number, fax number, and so on.**

(I'm not going to tell you that you should enter somebody's first name into the First Name box, or that the phone number of your customer goes into the box labeled Phone. I figure you don't need that kind of help.)

6. **Supply a bit of additional information about the customer.**

If you click the Additional Info tab, shown in Figure 2-9, QuickBooks displays several other boxes that you can use to collect and store customer information. For example, you can use the Type drop-down list box to categorize a customer as fitting into a particular "customer type." (I talk about how to set up a Customer Type List later in this chapter.) Use the Terms drop-down list box to identify the customer's default payment terms. Use the Rep drop-down list box to identify the customer's default sales rep. Finally, use the Preferred Send Method to select the default method for transmitting the customer's invoices and credit memos. You can also record a resale number, specify a default price level, and even click the Define Fields button to specify additional fields that you want to collect and report for the customer.

The Price Level List and how it works is discussed in Book III, Chapter 3.

7. **Click the Payment Info tab to display the set of boxes shown in Figure 2-10. You can record the customer's account number, his or her credit limit, and the preferred payment method.**

Book II
Chapter 2

Loading the Master
File Lists

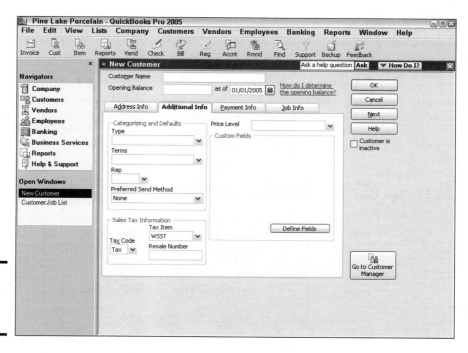

Figure 2-9:
The
Additional
Info tab.

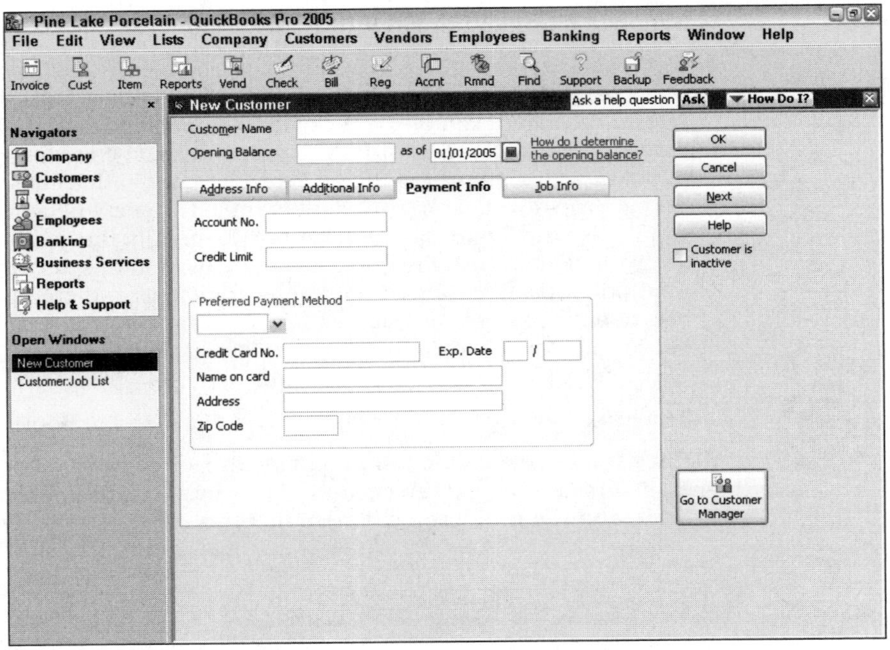

Figure 2-10:
The
Payment
Info tab.

8. **(Optional) Click the Job Info tab to describe the customer job.**

The Job Info tab lets you describe information associated with a particular job being performed for a customer. You use the Job Info tab if you not only set up a customer but also set up a job for that customer. See Book IV, Chapter 5 for more information on how job costing works.

Setting Up the Vendor List

Just as you use a Customer List to keep records on all of your customers, you use a Vendor List to keep records on your vendors. As is the case with a Customer List, the Vendor List lets you collect and record information, such as the vendor's address, the contact person, and so on.

To add a vendor to your Vendor List, follow these steps:

1. **Choose the Lists⇨Vendor List command.**

When you do, QuickBooks displays the Vendor List window, as shown in Figure 2-11.

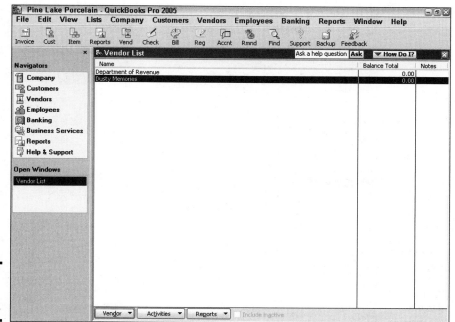

Book II
Chapter 2

Loading the Master
File Lists

Figure 2-11:
The Vendor
List window.

2. To add a new vendor, click the Vendor button and choose New.

QuickBooks displays the New Vendor window, as shown in Figure 2-12.

3. Give the vendor a name in the Vendor Name box.

As is the case with the Customer:Job List, you use this name to refer to the vendor within QuickBooks. For this reason, an abbreviation is fine. You just want something easy to enter and easy to remember.

4. Ignore the Opening Balance and As Of fields.

Don't do anything with the Opening Balance and As Of boxes. People who don't know better use those boxes to enter the opening balance owed a vendor and the date the amount is owed. But this only creates problems later. At some point in the future, this poor soul's accountant will need to find and correct this error.

5. Supply the vendor address information.

The Address Info tab supplies a bunch of easy-to-understand boxes that you use to collect vendor name and address information. You enter, predictably, the vendor's full name into the Company Name box.

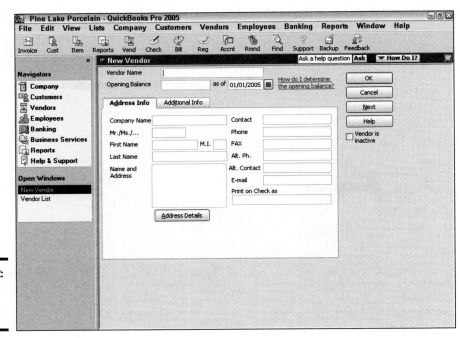

Figure 2-12:
The New
Vendor
window.

You can click the Address Details button to display another dialog box called the Edit Address Information dialog box, which lets you enter the address in typical street address, city, state, and ZIP code format.

6. Supply any additional information necessary.

If you click the Additional Info tab (shown in Figure 2-13), QuickBooks displays a handful of other boxes that you can use to collect and store information, such as your account number with the vendor, the vendor type, the payment terms that you use when paying the vendor, your credit limit, and the vendor's tax ID number. The tax ID number is actually important if you later need to send this vendor a 1099 form to report payments to the vendor.

A good guideline if you're paying a vendor for the first time is to get his or her tax ID number. If somebody won't give you his or her tax ID number — thereby making it impossible for you to report payments that you make to him — it's probably a sign of something a bit amiss.

If you click the Vendor button, you'll note that the menu that QuickBooks displays provides a whole bunch of other commands. Let me just mention here that you can edit vendor information, delete vendors, print a list of vendors, print 1099s for your vendors, and do one or two other things with the menu commands that appear on the Vendor menu.

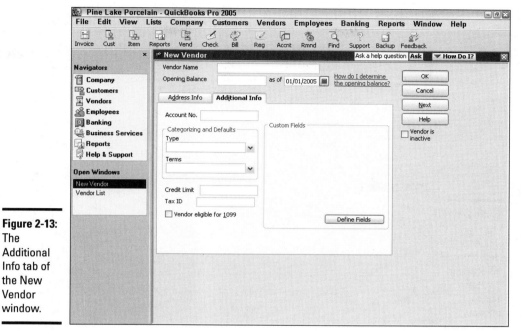

Figure 2-13:
The
Additional
Info tab of
the New
Vendor
window.

Setting Up a Fixed Assets List

If you choose the Lists⇨Fixed Asset Item List command, QuickBooks displays the Fixed Asset Item List window. You can use this window to see a list of the fixed assets — furniture, equipment, machinery, vehicles, and so forth — that you've purchased. Or at least you can after you've click the Item button, chosen New from the menu, and filled in the New Item window for each fixed asset. Figure 2-14 shows the New Item window you use to describe each fixed asset.

Let me make a couple of comments about the QuickBooks Fixed Asset Item List. The Fixed Asset List doesn't really integrate with the QuickBooks general ledger. You record the purchase or disposal of fixed assets using regular old QuickBooks transactions. For example, you might record the purchase of a particular fixed asset simply by entering a check in the usual fashion. And you might record the disposal of a fixed asset by entering a general ledger journal entry.

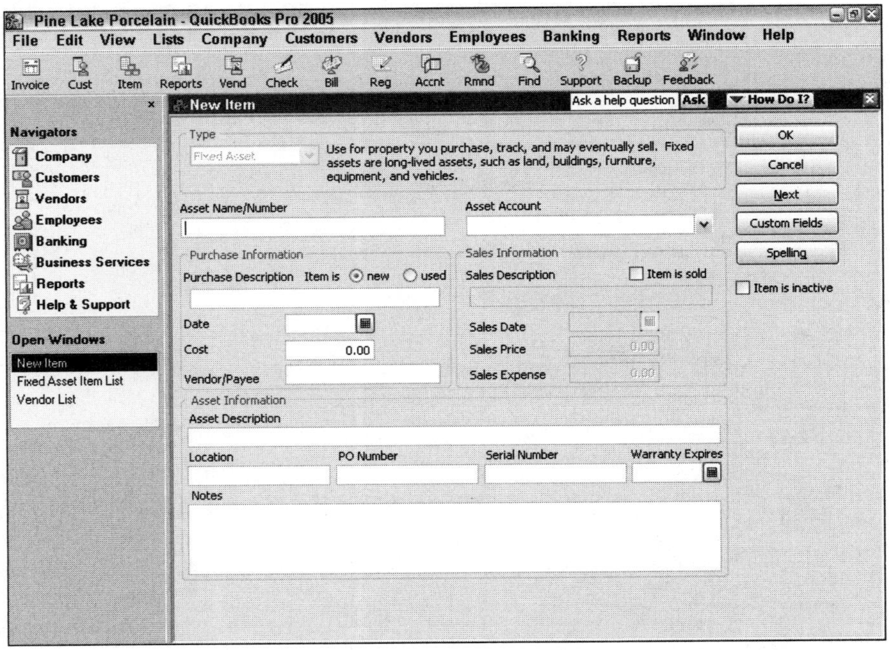

Figure 2-14:
You describe each fixed asset using the New Item window.

The Fixed Assets Item List, then, just acts as a standalone list that lets you keep track of the fixed assets you purchased. Because the list is so standalone-ish, I'm not going to spend much time talking about it in the books of this reference. Let me also say that your CPA probably — no surely — maintains a list of your fixed assets because she needs that list in order to correctly include depreciation on your tax return and in your financial statements (if you get CPA help to prepare those). For this reason, some people — including me — see the fixed asset item list as a little bit redundant.

Setting Up Your Employees

If you choose the Lists⇨Employee List command, QuickBooks displays the Employee List window. You can use this window to see a list of the employees — active or inactive — that you've identified to QuickBooks. You can also click the Employee button and choose New to add employees to the list.

Because I discuss how to add employees to the Employee List in Book III, Chapter 5, I won't repeat that information here.

Setting Up Another Names List

If you choose the Lists⇨Other Names List command, QuickBooks displays the Other Names List window. The Other Names List identifies those businesses or individuals that you pay but don't fall into one of these other standard categories: customers, vendors, and employees. For example, you may use the Other Names List to identify government agencies that you pay.

To add a name to the Other Names List, click the Other Names button, which appears at the bottom of the Other Names window. When QuickBooks displays the Other Names menu, click New. The New Name window that QuickBooks displays after you choose the New command provides boxes for a name, identifying the entity, recording an address, and so on. I don't show this window here because it's just a simplified version of the window that you use to identify and describe a customer, vendor, or employee.

Setting Up the Profile Lists

If you choose the Lists⇨Customer & Vendor Profile List command, QuickBooks displays a submenu of commands that you use to create some of the mini-lists that QuickBooks uses to ease your bookkeeping and accounting. The Profile Lists include lists of sales reps, customer types, vendor types, job types, payment terms, customer messages, payment methods, shipping methods, and vehicles.

Most of the Profile Lists are pretty darn simple to use. For example, if you choose the Sales Rep List command, QuickBooks displays the Sales Rep List window. You then click the Sales Rep button and choose New. QuickBooks displays the New Sales Rep window, as shown in Figure 2-15. I bet you can figure out how to use this window.

In case you're still experiencing a certain amount of accounting anxiety, let me just point out that you enter the name of the sales representative into the Sales Rep Name box. Then, throwing caution to the wind, you enter the sales rep's initials into the Sales Rep Initials box. When you click OK, QuickBooks adds the sales rep to your Sales Rep List.

The other Profile Lists work in the same, simple, scaled-down fashion. You choose the Profile List in the submenu, click the Profile List button, and choose New. When QuickBooks displays a window, you use one or two boxes to describe the new Profile List.

Just to prove to you that this really is as easy as I've said here, take a look at the New Customer Message window shown in Figure 2-16 (accessible from the Customer Message List). This is the window that you use to create a new customer message. You can place customer messages at the bottom of customer invoices and credit memos.

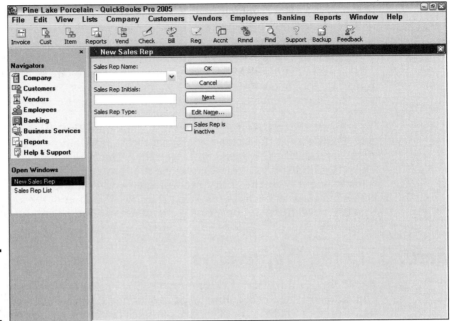

Figure 2-15:
The New
Sales Rep
List window.

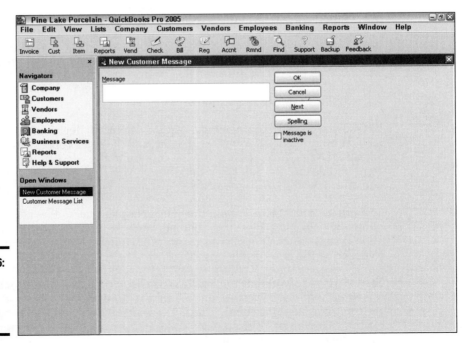

Figure 2-16:
The New
Customer
Message
window.

If you want to track vehicle mileage within QuickBooks — and note that you usually must track business vehicle mileage in order to claim business vehicle expenses as a tax deduction — you can maintain a list of business vehicles using the Vehicle List. This list then lets you easily track your business vehicles — something you do by using the Company➪Enter Vehicle Mileage command.

Chapter 3: Fine-Tuning QuickBooks

In This Chapter

✔ Accessing the Preferences settings

✔ Changing the accounting, checking, and finance charge rules

✔ Setting the desktop view, general, and integrated applications options

✔ Controlling jobs and estimates

✔ Setting up payroll and employees

✔ Setting purchases and vendors preferences

✔ Changing reminders and reports and graphs settings

✔ Dealing with sales, customers, and sales tax

✔ Setting 1099 tax reporting rules

✔ Controlling time tracking

*Y*ou can specify how QuickBooks works for you by setting *preferences*. In fact, just so you know, much of what you do when you run the QuickBooks EasyStep Interview (when you set up QuickBooks) is provide information that QuickBooks uses to set your preferences. For example, if you indicate that you need to charge customers sales tax, the EasyStep Interview describes how sales tax should work for your business by using the sales tax preferences.

Because these preferences have so much effect on how QuickBooks works and on how a particular user works with QuickBooks, I devote this chapter to describing how you change the preferences. None of this material is particularly complicated, but because QuickBooks provides you with a rich set of preferences options, I cover quite a bit of material. Don't worry: You don't have to read this chapter from beginning to end. Simply use it as a reference when you have a question about how to change the way QuickBooks works in a particular area.

Accessing the Preferences Settings

You can set preferences in two ways within QuickBooks:

✦ **During the EasyStep Interview:** You actually set all of the preferences, or at least all of the starting preferences for QuickBooks, when you run the EasyStep Interview. Most of the time, the preferences that the EasyStep Interview sets are correct. The EasyStep Interview is very smart about the way it asks questions and translates your answers into preferences settings. But, if your business changes, or if you make a mistake during the setup interview, or if someone else in your office ran the EasyStep Interview for you, you may still need to check and fiddle-faddle with these preferences.

✦ **By manually changing the preferences:** You can manually change the preferences by choosing the Edit➪Preferences command. QuickBooks displays the Preferences dialog box, as shown in Figure 3-1. QuickBooks groups categories of preferences. For example, QuickBooks groups all of the accounting preferences into an accounting preference set. QuickBooks groups all of the checking account preferences into a checking preference set. If you look closely at Figure 3-1, you see that along the left edge of the Preferences dialog box, QuickBooks displays a list of icons. The first icon is Accounting. The second icon is Checking. To see the preferences within one of these groups, you click that preference's icon.

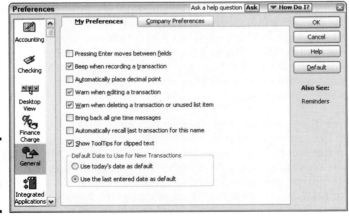

Figure 3-1:
The
Preferences
dialog box.

One other item to note about the Preferences dialog box is that it supplies, in general, two tabs of preferences for each preference set. Preferences that are specific to an individual user appear on the My Preferences tab, shown in Figure 3-1. Preferences that are tied to the company data file appear on the Company Preferences tab, shown in Figure 3-2.

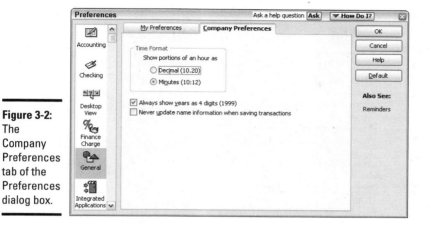

Figure 3-2:
The
Company
Preferences
tab of the
Preferences
dialog box.

Not every My Preferences tab gives you options for changing the way that QuickBooks works. Sometimes a particular set of preferences gives personal options; sometimes it doesn't.

For example, the My Preferences tab of the Accounting set of preferences provides no personalized options. In other words, you can't tell QuickBooks that a firm's accounting works differently for a particular person. This makes sense, right? Accounting needs to work the same way for every user within a firm. However, with other preferences settings, QuickBooks may allow different options for different users. You'll see this as I discuss the various sets of preferences in the remainder of this chapter.

And now, I'm just going to walk you through a discussion of each of these preferences sets. I talk both about the My Preferences option (if available) and the Company Preferences option.

Setting the Accounting Preferences

QuickBooks doesn't give individual users personalized preferences for the way that accounting works within QuickBooks. This makes sense, if you think about it. Accounting for a business needs to work the same way for Jane as it does for Joe and for Susan. However, you do have the option to set company preferences for accounting. This makes sense, again, if you think about it. Different companies need to run their accounting system in different ways. Figure 3-3 shows the Company Preferences tab for the Accounting Preferences set.

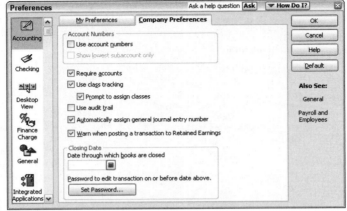

Figure 3-3:
The
Company
Preferences
tab of the
Accounting
Preferences
set.

Using account numbers

By default, QuickBooks lets you use names to identify accounts on the Chart of Accounts or in the accounts list. For example, the account that you use to track wages expense may be known as "wages." However, you can check the Use Account Numbers box to tell QuickBooks that you want to use account numbers rather than account names for identifying accounts. Larger businesses and businesses with very lengthy lists of accounts often use account numbers. Controlling both the ordering of accounts on a financial statement and inserting new accounts into your Chart of Accounts is easier if you're using numbers.

The Show Lowest Subaccount Only check box lets you tell QuickBooks that it should display the lowest subaccount rather than the higher parent account on financial statements. QuickBooks allows you to create subaccounts, which are accounts within accounts (discussed further in Book II, Chapter 2). You can also create sub-sub accounts, which are accounts within subaccounts. You use subaccounts to more finely track assets, liabilities, equity amounts, revenues, and expenses.

General accounting options

The Company Preferences tab provides the following five general accounting check boxes as well as closing date settings. (These check boxes are probably self-explanatory to anybody who has done a bit of accounting with QuickBooks, but for new QuickBooks users, I provide a brief description of what each one does.)

✦ **Use Account Numbers:** The Use Account Numbers check box, if selected, gives you the ability to enter in an account number for a transaction. The associated check box, Show Lowest Subaccount Only, tells QuickBooks to display only the name and account number of a subaccount (if you're using one) instead of the full heritage of the account. If you use a lot of levels of subaccounts, this option can really clean up views, making it easier to tell what account you're looking at.

✦ **Require Accounts:** The Require Accounts check box, if selected, tells QuickBooks that you must specify an account for a transaction. This makes sense. If you aren't using account numbers to track the amounts that flow into and out of the business, you aren't really doing accounting. It would never make sense, in my humble opinion, to deselect the Require Accounts check box.

✦ **Use Class Tracking:** The Use Class Tracking check box lets you tell QuickBooks that you want to use not only accounts to track your financial information but also *classes*. Classes let you split account level information in another way. This sounds complicated, but it's really quite simple. The account list, for example, lets you track revenue and expenses by categories of revenue and expense. You may track expenses by using categories such as wages, rent, and supplies. Classes, therefore, provide you with a way to track this information in another dimension. For example, you can split wages expense into those wages spent for two different locations of your business. A restaurateur with two restaurants may want to do this.

✦ **Use Audit Trail:** The Use Audit Trail check box, if selected, tells QuickBooks to maintain a list of who makes what changes to transactions. If you have more than one person changing the information in QuickBooks — in other words, you have multiple users working with the QuickBooks data file — you want to select the Use Audit Trail check box. If you select the Use Audit Trail check box, QuickBooks slows down a bit. For this degradation in performance, however, you get a good record of who is doing what in QuickBooks. Accountants, by the way, love audit trails. Audit trails enable someone such as your CPA to come in after the fact and figure out why an account balance is what it is.

✦ **Automatically Assign General Journal Entry Number:** This check box tells QuickBooks to assign numbers to the general journal entries that you enter by using the Make Journal Entry command. You want to leave this check box selected. General journal entries, by the way, are typically entered by your CPA or your professional on-staff accountant.

✦ **Closing Date settings:** The Closing Date box lets you identify a date before which your QuickBooks data file can't be changed. In other words, if you set the closing date to December 31, 2004, you're telling QuickBooks that you don't want any changes made to the QuickBooks data file *before* this date. This means that someone can't modify a transaction that is dated before your closing date without getting a scary warning message. It also means that someone can't enter a transaction by using a date before this closing date. You can also click the Set

Password button to display a dialog box that lets you create a password, which is required if someone wants to add an old transaction or modify an old transaction.

Setting the Checking Preferences

If you display the Preferences dialog box and click the Checking icon, QuickBooks displays either the My Preferences tab, shown in Figure 3-4, or the Company Preferences tab, shown in Figure 3-5.

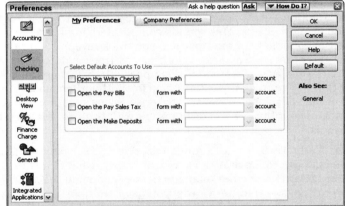

Figure 3-4: The My Preferences tab for Checking Preferences.

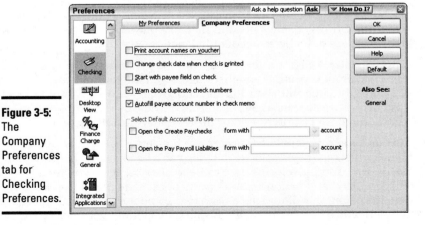

Figure 3-5: The Company Preferences tab for Checking Preferences.

The My Preferences tab for Checking Preferences lets you tell QuickBooks which account it should suggest as a default account when you open particular types of windows within QuickBooks. For example, if you look closely at Figure 3-4, you see the Open the Write Checks check box. This is the first check box on the tab. To the right of the Open the Write Checks check box, you see the Form With Account box. If you check the Open the Write Checks check box, you can select an account from the Form With Account box. This will tell QuickBooks to use or suggest the specified account every time you open the Write Checks window.

The My Preferences tab also includes check boxes that you can use to specify the default account for the Pay Bills window, the Pay Sales Tax window, and the Make Deposits window. If you have multiple checking accounts set up, setting the default accounts using the My Preferences tab is a good idea. Setting these preferences makes it less likely that you'll erroneously write checks on or pay bills from the wrong account.

The Company Preferences tab, as shown in Figure 3-5, provides check boxes that you can use to describe how checks work within QuickBooks:

✦ **Print Account Names On Voucher:** This check box lets you indicate to QuickBooks that it should print account names on the voucher portion of the check.

✦ **Change Check Date When Check Is Printed:** Select this check box to tell QuickBooks to use the current system date as the printed check date.

✦ **Start with Payee Field on Check:** Select this check box to tell QuickBooks to place the insertion point, or text cursor, on the Payee field when you open the Write Checks window.

✦ **Warn about Duplicate Check Numbers:** Selecting this check box tells QuickBooks to alert you to duplicate check numbers. (You want to leave this check box selected, obviously, so that you don't use duplicate or erroneous check numbers.)

✦ **Autofill Payee Account Number in Check Memo:** Select this check box to tell QuickBooks to automatically fill in the payee account number when you write a check. QuickBooks retrieves the account number for a payee from the Vendor List or from the Other Names List.

✦ **Select Default Accounts To Use:** These check boxes let you specify which account QuickBooks suggests when you open the Create Paychecks window or open the Pay Payroll Liabilities window. Essentially, then, these boxes let you tell QuickBooks which checking account you will use to write payroll checks and to pay payroll liabilities, such as federal income tax withholding amounts.

Changing the Desktop View

Figure 3-6 shows the My Preferences tab of the Desktop View Preferences set. The My Preferences tab provides View radio buttons — One Window and Multiple Windows — that let you indicate whether QuickBooks should use one window or multiple windows for displaying all of its information. The Multiple Windows option looks like older versions of Microsoft Windows. With multiple windows, an application such as QuickBooks displays multiple, floating document windows within the application program window. If you have a question about how this works, your best bet is to simply try both view settings.

Figure 3-6:
The My Preferences tab for the Desktop View Preferences.

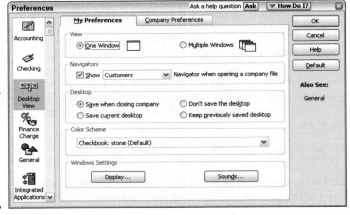

The Navigators check box tells QuickBooks to display the Company Navigator window when you open a company file. (The Company Navigator window, shown in Figure 3-7, provides a sort of home base for your work in QuickBooks.) This is the default setting. You will probably want to keep it.

The Desktop radio buttons (refer to Figure 3-6) let you specify whether and when QuickBooks should save the current appearance, or *view*, of the desktop. You can select the Save When Closing Company radio button to tell QuickBooks that it should save the view of the desktop when you close a company. When you reopen a company, QuickBooks then reuses this desktop view. You can also select the Save Current Desktop radio button to tell QuickBooks to save the current view and then reuse this view when QuickBooks later opens. If you don't want to make changes to the default desktop view, select the Don't Save the Desktop radio button or the Keep Previously Saved Desktop radio button.

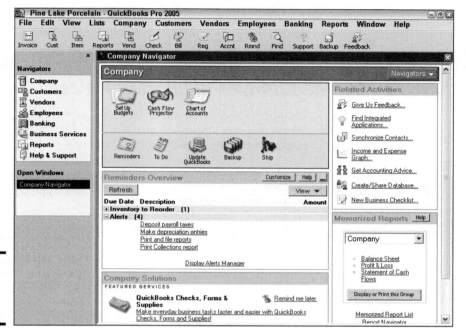

Book II
Chapter 3

Fine-Tuning
QuickBooks

Figure 3-7:
The
Company
Navigator.

The Color Scheme box lets you pick a color set for the QuickBooks program. The default color scheme is the Checkbook: Stone color scheme. QuickBooks provides several other color schemes, including Denim Blue, Desert Isle, Granite Gray, and so on. (If you are wild about color, you can experiment with these other options.) Note that these are My Preferences options, which means that they are personal to you. You can experiment with the settings for color without having anyone else see that you are really into Sea Stone or Summer Linen (two other color options).

The Windows Settings buttons let you access the Windows Display Properties and Windows Sounds Properties settings. Typically, you would make changes to Windows Display Properties and Windows Sounds Properties by using the Control Panel tools. However, you can also make changes from within QuickBooks by using these two buttons. (In actuality, when you click these buttons, QuickBooks just starts the Control Panel tools.)

If you have questions about how the Windows Display Properties or Sounds Properties work, refer to the Windows Help file or to a good book, such as *Windows XP For Dummies*, by Andy Rathbone (Wiley Publishing, Inc.).

No Company Preferences are available for the Desktop view. Desktop views are purely personal. For this reason, you won't find any options or boxes or buttons on a Company Preferences tab.

Setting Finance Charge Calculation Rules

The Finance Charge Preferences settings let you specify how QuickBooks should calculate finance charges on overdue invoices to customers. No My Preferences options are available for finance charges — only Company Preferences. Because I describe how the Company Preferences tab for the Finance Charge Preferences works in Book III, Chapter 1, I won't repeat that information here.

Setting General Preferences

Figure 3-8 shows the My Preferences tab of the General Preferences set. This tab provides check boxes that you can select to tell QuickBooks to do the following:

✦ To move the selection cursor from one field on the window to the next field when you press Enter

✦ To beep when you record a transaction

✦ To automatically place a decimal point two characters from the right end of the number

✦ To warn you when you are editing an existing transaction

✦ To warn you when you are deleting an existing transaction or some item on a list

✦ To bring back all of the one-time Help messages that it shows

✦ To automatically recall the last transaction for a particular name (customer, vendor, employee, and so forth) when you enter a new transaction for the same name

✦ Show ToolTips for clipped text

 If you have specific questions about the My Preferences check boxes that are available for the General Preferences options, click the Help button that appears along the right edge of the Preferences dialog box. QuickBooks provides brief but useful descriptions of how the Preferences options work and what they do.

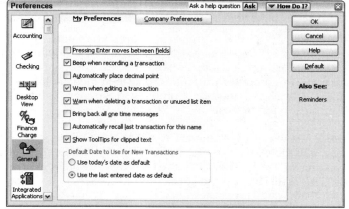

Figure 3-8:
The My
Preferences
tab for
General
Preferences.

Figure 3-9 shows the Company Preferences tab for the General Preferences set. The Time Format radio buttons let you specify whether QuickBooks should show the minutes in an hour as a decimal value or as minutes. The Time Format radio button descriptions include examples of how these two approaches vary, so look closely at the dialog box if you have questions. The Company Preferences tab includes a check box that lets you specify that QuickBooks should always show years using four digits. And the Company Preferences tab includes a check box that you can select to tell QuickBooks that it should not update the name information for a particular customer, vendor, employee, or other name when you are saving a new transaction for that customer, vendor, employee, or other name.

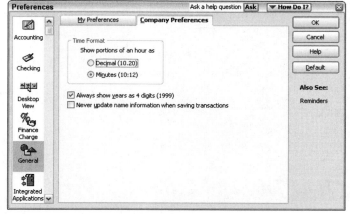

Figure 3-9:
The
Company
Preferences
tab for
General
Preferences.

Controlling Integrated Applications

The Integrated Applications Preferences aren't personal, so no options are available on the My Preferences tab. However, the Company Preferences tab for the Integrated Applications Preferences set does control and track other applications, or computer programs, that open the QuickBooks company data files. Figure 3-10 shows the Company Preferences tab for the Integrated Applications Preferences set.

The Don't Allow Any Applications to Access This Company File check box, if selected, tells QuickBooks that it should not allow other applications to open this company data file. The Notify the User Before Running Any Application Whose Certificate Has Expired check box, if selected, tells QuickBooks that it should not allow any program whose security certificate is out of date to open the QuickBooks company data file without first notifying the user (that's you).

The list box on the Company Preferences tab of the Integrated Applications Preferences set shows the name of the applications that have previously requested to open the QuickBooks company data file. You can remove an application from this list by clicking the application and then the Remove button. You can change the rules or properties that the QuickBooks program applies to access this other application by clicking the application in the list and then clicking the Properties button.

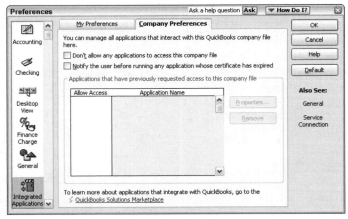

Figure 3-10:
The Company Preferences tab of the Integrated Applications Preferences dialog box.

Controlling How Jobs and Estimates Work

Because no personal preferences are available for Jobs & Estimates preferences, the My Preferences tab for this Preferences set shows no options. However, you have several Company Preferences available regarding jobs and estimates, as shown in Figure 3-11. The Pending text box lets you describe what term or word should be used for jobs that have been submitted but haven't been accepted or rejected. The Awarded box lets you provide a term or description that you want to use within QuickBooks to identify those jobs that customers or clients have accepted. The default description of an awarded job is, cleverly, *awarded*. The In Progress, Closed, and Not Awarded boxes similarly let you describe what term you want to use for jobs that fit into these categories.

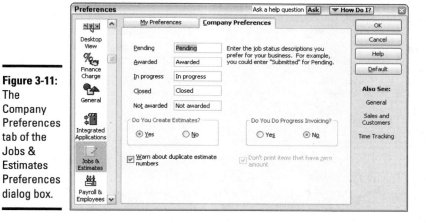

Figure 3-11:
The Company Preferences tab of the Jobs & Estimates Preferences dialog box.

The Do You Create Estimates? radio buttons let you indicate to QuickBooks whether you want to create job estimates for customers. You select the radio button — Yes or No — that answers the question. The Do You Do Progress Invoicing? buttons let you indicate whether you do progress billing for jobs. The Warn About Duplicate Estimate Numbers check box, if selected, tells QuickBooks to warn you about using duplicate estimate numbers. The Don't Print Items That Have Zero Amount check box, if selected, tells QuickBooks not to print estimates that have zero balances.

Book IV, Chapter 5 talks more about setting up jobs and estimates. You may want to refer there if you have questions about how project costing and job costing work within QuickBooks.

Controlling How Payroll Works

The Payroll & Employees Preferences set includes only Company Preferences. The Company Preferences tab is shown in Figure 3-12. The QuickBooks Payroll Features radio buttons let you tell QuickBooks how you want to handle payroll: using an outside payroll service such as Intuit Complete Payroll (select

Complete Payroll Customers in this case), using QuickBooks payroll features (select the Full Payroll radio button), or that you're not using payroll at all (select the No Payroll radio button).

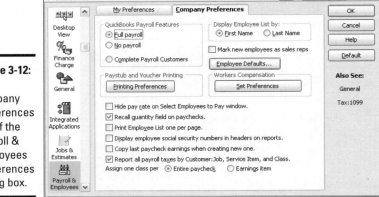

Figure 3-12:
The Company Preferences tab of the Payroll & Employees Preferences dialog box.

The Display Employee List By radio buttons let you specify whether the employee list should be sorted by employees' first names or last names.

The Mark New Employees as Sales Reps check box, if selected, does what you'd expect: It marks new employees that you add to the employee list as sales reps.

If you click the Employee Defaults button, QuickBooks displays a dialog box that you can use to set employee payroll default information, such as deductions for taxes or health insurance.

The Printing check boxes — there are a bunch of these, as you can see from the figure — let you tell QuickBooks what employee information QuickBooks should print on the payroll check: employee address, company address, sick pay information, vacation pay information, and pay period information. You can figure out how this works, right? If you want some bit of information to appear, you select the check box that references that information.

At the bottom of the Company Preferences tab of the Payroll & Employees Preferences set, QuickBooks supplies several other check boxes and radio buttons:

✦ **Hide Pay Rate on Select Employees to Pay window:** QuickBooks hides the pay rate on the Select Employees to Pay window. Duh.

✦ **Recall Quantity Field on Paychecks:** QuickBooks recalls or reuses paycheck quantity information from the last pay period's paychecks. (The

QuickBooks Help File suggests that you use this option when you have a "fixed quantity that occurs from paycheck to paycheck." The Help File uses the example of tiered sales commissions where the commission amount is set for each tier.)

✦ **Print Employee List One Per Page:** QuickBooks prints each employee's payroll information on a separate page when printing the Employee List, making it easier to file payroll information with each employee individually.

✦ **Report All Payroll Taxes by Customer:Job, Service Item, and Class:** QuickBooks segregates payroll tax expense by these other attributes: Customer:Job, Service Item, and Class.

✦ **The Assign One Class Per radio buttons (Entire Paycheck and Earnings Item):** Enables you to break down wages expense into classes more finely. For example, you can indicate that you want to use a different class for each item that appears on an employee's paycheck.

Controlling the Purchasing & Vendors Preferences

The Purchases & Vendors Preferences set doesn't provide personal preferences on the My Preferences tab. The Purchasers & Vendors Preferences set does, however, provide several Company Preferences, as shown in Figure 3-13. The Purchase Orders and Inventory check boxes, for example, let you tell QuickBooks whether you want to use purchase orders. If you do, select the Inventory and Purchase Orders Are Active check box. The two other check boxes, if selected, tell QuickBooks that you want to be warned if you attempt to sell inventory that you don't have in stock or if you attempt to use a duplicate purchase order number.

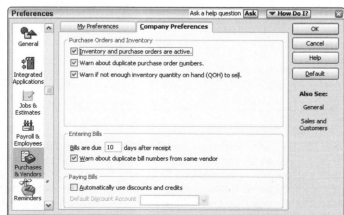

Figure 3-13: The Company Preferences tab of the Purchases & Vendors Preferences set.

The Entering Bills boxes let you specify when bills are due and whether you want QuickBooks to warn you about duplicate bill numbers from the same vendor. The Paying Bills boxes let you tell QuickBooks that it should automatically use purchase discounts and credit memos when you are paying bills and also let you specify what account QuickBooks should use for tracking discounts that you take.

Telling QuickBooks How Reminders Should Work

The My Preferences tab of the Reminders Preferences set consists of just one check box: You can use it to tell QuickBooks that you want to see the Reminders list when you open a company file. Because the My Preferences tab includes only a single check box, I don't show it here as a figure.

The Company Preferences tab, as shown in Figure 3-14, provides a bunch of radio buttons that you can use to specify how QuickBooks should remind you of accounting and bookkeeping tasks that you need to complete: Checks to Print, Paychecks to Print, Invoices/Credit Memos to Print, Overdue Invoices, Sales Receipts to Print, Sales Orders to Print, Inventory to Reorder, Assembly Items to Build, Bills to Pay, Memorized Transactions Due, Money to Deposit, Purchase Orders to Print, and To Do Notes.

Figure 3-14: The Company Preferences tab of the Reminders Preferences set.

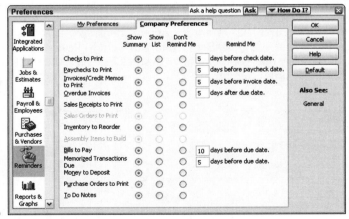

For each of these accounting or bookkeeping tasks, you indicate whether you want to see a reminder for the item in the Summary list that appears in the QuickBooks Company Preferences Reminders list. You can also choose to actually see the List of Tasks — such as the list of Checks to Print — or you can indicate that you don't want to be reminded of some particular category of accounting or bookkeeping. For some of the reminder notes, you need to indicate how many work days in advance you want to be reminded. For example, if you indicate that you want to be reminded to print checks, you must indicate how many days before the check date that you want the reminder to appear. You do this by entering a numeral in one of the Remind Me text boxes.

Specifying Reports & Graphs Preferences

The My Preferences tab of the Reports & Graphs Preferences set is shown in Figure 3-15. This tab provides radio buttons that you can use to indicate how QuickBooks should refresh reports when the information upon which the report is based changes. The default refresh option is Prompt Me to Refresh. If you set refreshing to Prompt Me to Refresh, when QuickBooks needs to update a report for changes in the information, it prompts you via a message box. You can also select the Refresh Automatically radio button to have QuickBooks automatically refresh a report whenever the data changes. You don't want to refresh automatically, however, if you have a large data set and many reports. Refreshing a report can be rather time-consuming. Refreshing many reports based on a large data set takes a long time. You can also select the Don't Refresh radio button if you don't want or don't need to be reminded about refreshing a report.

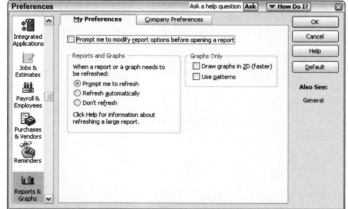

Figure 3-15:
The My Preferences tab of the Reports & Graphs Preferences set.

The Graphs Only check boxes let you control the way QuickBooks graphs report information. You can select the Draw Graphs in 2D check box to tell QuickBooks to draw two-dimensional rather than three-dimensional graphs. (QuickBooks draws two-dimensional graphs much quicker, so you may want to use two-dimensional graphs.) Note also that two-dimensional graphs are visually more precise than three-dimensional graphs. You can also select the Use Patterns check box to tell QuickBooks to draw a graph that uses cross-hatching patterns rather than colors for the different pieces of a chart.

The Prompt Me to Modify Report Options Before Opening a Report check box, if selected, tells QuickBooks to open the Modify Report window whenever you create a report. You can use the Modify Report window to control what information is included in a report (such as what date range the report is based on) and other reporting options as well. If the Prompt Me to Modify Report Options Before Opening a Report check box isn't selected, QuickBooks creates a report by using the default reporting options.

For a complete discussion of the Modify Reports window, refer to the discussion in Book IV, Chapter 2.

Figure 3-16 shows the Company Preferences tab for the Reports & Graphs Preferences set. This Company Preferences tab provides several useful options for default report generation rules. The Summary Reports Basis radio buttons, for example, let you indicate whether the default accounting method used to create a report should be accrual-basis accounting or cash-basis accounting. The Aging Reports radio buttons let you specify how the age of an invoice or bill should be calculated: from the due date or from the transaction date. The Reports-Show Accounts By Option radio buttons let you specify how account information appears on reports: account name only, description only, or both name and description.

Figure 3-16:
The Company Preferences tab of the Reports & Graphs Preferences set.

Two other Company Preference options are especially noteworthy. The Classify Cash button displays a dialog box that lets you indicate whether changes in a particular account balance should appear under the operating, investing, or financing portion of the Statement of Cash Flows. If you're not a professional accountant, you will want to get your CPA's help in making changes to this area of QuickBooks. The rules for presenting a Statement of Cash Flows are quite involved.

The Format button displays the Report Format Preferences dialog box, which lets you customize the report header and footer information. Figure 3-17 shows the Header/Footer tab for the Report Format Preferences dialog box. The Show Header Information check boxes let you specify what information should appear in the report header area. The Show Footer Information check boxes let you make the same specifications for the report footer. The Page Layout Alignment box lets you specify how information should be aligned on the report page.

Book II
Chapter 3

Fine-Tuning
QuickBooks

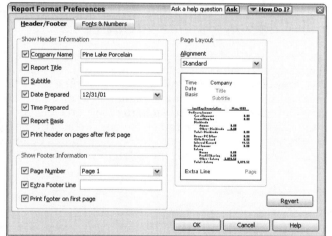

Figure 3-17:
The Header/
Footer of
the Report
Format
Preferences
dialog box.

Figure 3-18 shows the Fonts & Numbers tab of the Report Format Preferences dialog box. This dialog box lets you specify what font and formatting you want to use for bits of report information. For example, if you want to change the font for the reports column labels, click the Column Labels entry in the Change Font For list box. Then click the Change Font button. QuickBooks displays a Font Formatting dialog box that lets you specify the font, font style, point size, and other special effects.

If you're confused about changing report formatting, refer to the discussion in Book IV, Chapter 2. It talks about all this stuff.

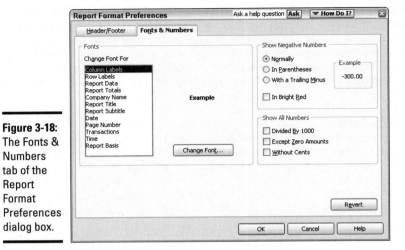

Figure 3-18:
The Fonts &
Numbers
tab of the
Report
Format
Preferences
dialog box.

Setting Sales & Customers Preferences

You can't set personalized preferences for dealing with sales and customers. You can, however, set company preferences for sales and customers. Figure 3-19 shows the Company Preferences tab for the Sales & Customers Preferences set. The Usual Shipping Method box lets you specify the default shipping method. The Default Markup Percentage box lets you specify a default retail markup percentage to use in your pricing (though you should double-check that it's showing up properly on estimates before you count on it). The Usual FOB box lets you set the default FOB, or Free On Board, point.

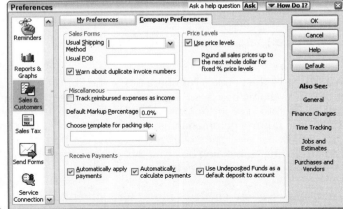

Figure 3-19:
The
Company
Preferences
tab of the
Sales &
Customers
Preferences
set.

The check boxes at the bottom of the Company Preferences tab of the Sales & Customers Preferences set let you indicate that you want to track reimbursed expenses as income, automatically apply payments, warn about duplicate invoice numbers, and use price levels.

Price levels are discussed in more detail in Book III, Chapter 3.

Specifying How Sales Are Taxed

Although no personal preferences are available for sales tax, company preferences do exist. Figure 3-20 shows the Company Preferences tab for the Sales Tax Preferences set. The Do You Charge Sales Tax? radio buttons, which appear near the top of the tab, control whether you can charge sales tax within QuickBooks. You select the radio button — Yes or No — that answers the question.

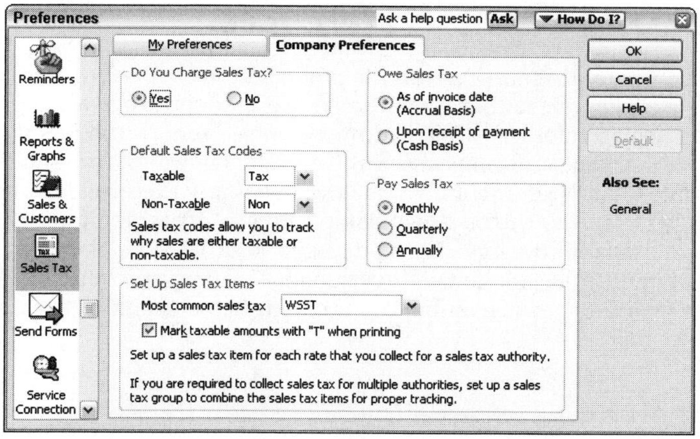

Figure 3-20: The Company Preferences tab of the Sales Tax Preferences set.

The Owe Sales Tax radio buttons let you indicate when the taxing authority says you owe sales tax: as of the invoice date (which means the taxing authority requires accrual-basis accounting) or upon receipt of payment (which means the taxing authority allows cash-basis accounting).

The Default Sales Tax Codes boxes let you define what code QuickBooks should use to identify taxable and non-taxable sales. By default, QuickBooks uses the clever "tax" code for taxable sales and the equally clever "non" code for non-taxable sales. However, you can select the Add New entry from the Taxable drop-down list box or the Non-Taxable drop-down list box and use the dialog box that QuickBooks displays to create your own taxable and non-taxable codes.

The Pay Sales Tax radio buttons (Monthly, Quarterly, and Annually) let you tell QuickBooks how frequently you must remit sales tax amounts. You select the radio button that corresponds to your sales tax payment frequency.

The Set Up Sales Tax Items boxes let you set up an item for the sales tax that you will need to charge on invoices. You can also indicate the default, or most common, sales tax item that you'll want to include by entering this sales tax item name into the Most Common Sales Tax box. To add the sales tax item by using the Most Common Sales Tax box, select the Add New entry from the drop-down list box and complete the dialog box that QuickBooks displays. The New Item dialog box lets you name the sales tax item and identify the sales tax rate. The Mark Taxable Amounts with "T" When Printing check box, if selected, tells QuickBooks to flag taxable amounts on an invoice with the code "T."

Book II, Chapter 2 describes how to set up sales tax items.

Setting the Send Forms Preferences

The Company Preferences tab for the Send Forms Preferences set is shown in Figure 3-21. (Note that no personal preferences are available for these Send Forms Preferences.) The Company Preferences tab lets you specify the default message text, message subject, and salutation for e-mailed invoices, estimates, and statements. To use the Company Preferences tab, you use the Change Default For drop-down list box to specify which type of message text that you want to change. Then you use the other boxes on the Company Preferences tab to make whatever change you want to the default message. To change the message subject, for example, you replace the contents of the Subject text box.

Figure 3-21: The Company Preferences tab of the Send Forms Preferences set.

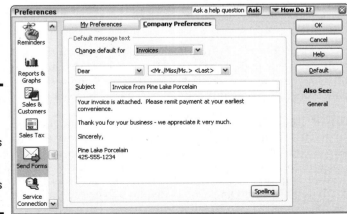

Fine-Tuning the Service Connection

Although no personal preferences exist for the Service Connection Preferences set, several company preferences options are available, as shown in Figure 3-22. You can, for example, indicate whether QuickBooks should automatically connect to QuickBooks Services without asking for a password, or whether it should always ask for a password. To make this decision, you simply select the appropriate radio button. You can also select the Allow Background Downloading of Service Messages check box to tell QuickBooks that background collection of messages is okay. (If you select this check box, QuickBooks downloads new messages during idle times so that it doesn't slow down your other Internet activities.)

Book II
Chapter 3

Fine-Tuning QuickBooks

Figure 3-22:
The Company Preferences tab of the Service Connection Preferences set.

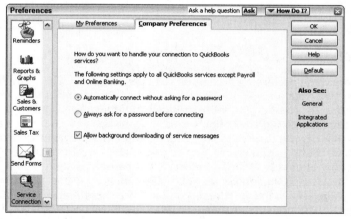

Controlling Spell Checking

No company preferences exist for the Spelling Preferences, but the My Preferences tab (shown in Figure 3-23) provides several options for controlling how spell checking works for you within QuickBooks. You can select the Always Check Spelling Before Printing, Saving, or Sending Supported Forms check box, for example, if you want to have automatic spell checking performed before you actually distribute a document to an outside party, such as a customer or vendor. You can also use the Ignore Words With check boxes to tell QuickBooks not to spell check words or phrases that aren't going to appear correctly spelled because they aren't real words. For example, you can select the Internet Addresses check box to tell QuickBooks that it shouldn't check Internet URL addresses. And you can select the All UPPERCASE Letters check box to tell QuickBooks that it shouldn't attempt to spell check words that are acronyms and abbreviations, such as OK and ASAP.

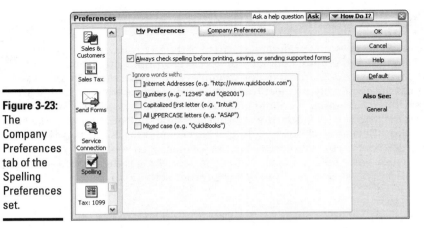

Figure 3-23:
The
Company
Preferences
tab of the
Spelling
Preferences
set.

Controlling How 1099 Tax Reporting Works

No personal preferences exist for 1099 tax reporting. Company preferences, however, exist as indicated by the Company Preferences tab, shown in Figure 3-24. The Company Preferences tab lets you tell QuickBooks when you are required to file 1099-MISC forms. The Company Preferences tab also lets you identify the threshold amounts for the different types of miscellaneous income that you can report. For example, the current threshold amounts for rent that is paid is $600. Therefore, the threshold amount shown for Box 1: Rents on the 1099 appears as $600. You can change this amount by editing the value shown in the Threshold box. Note that different types of 1099 miscellaneous income have different reporting thresholds. For example, if you look down to Box 9: Direct Sales, you see that the reporting threshold is $5,000. Confer with your tax advisor if you have questions about these amounts or visit the IRS Web site at www.irs.gov.

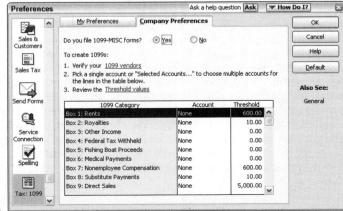

Figure 3-24:
The
Company
Preferences
tab of the
Tax: 1099
Preferences
set.

Setting Time Tracking Preferences

Figure 3-25 shows the Company Preferences tab for the Time Tracking Preferences set. To turn on time tracking within QuickBooks, select Do You Track Time? by selecting the Yes radio button. You can also use the First Day of Work Week box to indicate which day should appear first on the Weekly Time Sheet window. (This is what you will use to describe billable time for the week.) Book III, Chapter 1 talks about billing for time in more detail. You may want to refer there if you have questions about tracking time and billing for that time.

**Book II
Chapter 3**

Figure 3-25:
The
Company
Preferences
tab of the
Time
Tracking
Preferences
set.

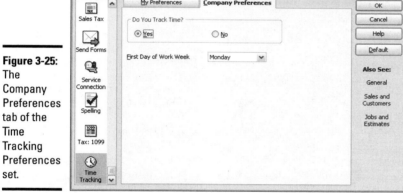

Fine-Tuning
QuickBooks

Book III

Bookkeeping Chores

The 5th Wave   By Rich Tennant

©RICHTENNANT

F. MUTT

"Ms. Lamont, how long have you been sending out bills listing charges for 'Freight', 'Handling', and 'Sales Tax' as 'This', 'That', and 'The Other Thing'?"

Contents at a Glance

Chapter 1: Invoicing Customers

In This Chapter

✓ **Choosing an invoice form**

✓ **Customizing an invoice form**

✓ **Invoicing a customer**

✓ **Billing for time**

✓ **Recording a sales receipt**

✓ **Recording credit memos**

✓ **Receiving customer payments**

✓ **Assessing finance charges**

*Q*uickBooks provides several tools for invoicing your customers. This chapter describes these tools as well as a handful of related tools for recording customer payments and for issuing credit memos.

If you've already been invoicing customers using some manual method — perhaps you've been preparing invoices with a word processor — you'll find QuickBooks to be a godsend. Not only does QuickBooks make invoicing and related tasks easier, but it also collects invoice information, recording this information into the QuickBooks data file. Happily, this means that you get the extra benefit of recording accounting transactions simply by using QuickBooks for invoicing.

Choosing an Invoice Form

QuickBooks allows you to use an invoice form that matches the requirements of your business. For example, businesses that sell products need an invoice that includes descriptions of the product items that are sold. Businesses that sell services — such as a law firm or an architectural firm — need an invoice that appropriately describes these services. Businesses that sell both products and services need a blend of attributes.

Fortunately, QuickBooks lets you choose the invoice form that best matches your business. To choose an invoice form, display the Create Invoices window by choosing the Customers⇨Create Invoices command. When QuickBooks displays the Create Invoices window, use the Form Template drop-down list box, which appears in the top-right portion of the window, to choose the invoice form that you want. This drop-down list box provides a choice for a product invoice, a service invoice, or a professional invoice. Choose the invoice form template that seems to best match your business. QuickBooks redraws the Create Invoices window when you choose a new invoice form template. This means that you can see what an invoice form template looks like simply by choosing an option from the Form Template drop-down list box.

Customizing an Invoice Form

Although you can choose a predefined invoice form template for your invoices, QuickBooks gives you more flexibility than that. You can also customize an existing form template to create an invoice that looks just the way you want. To do this, you can start with one of the basic invoice form templates and then customize it so that it perfectly matches your requirements.

Customizing a predefined form template

To customize a predefined invoice form template, display the Create Invoices window. You can do this by choosing the Customers⇨Create Invoices command. Next, click the Customize button. QuickBooks displays the Customize Template dialog box, shown in Figure 1-1.

The very first time you choose the Create Invoices command, QuickBooks displays a message box asking if you'd like a tutorial about how to enter sales in QuickBooks. I'm going to describe here what you need to know, but if you have the time and feel a little stressed about QuickBooks, it'll probably help to view the tutorial. Hearing the same information more than one time often increases retention.

Figure 1-1:
The
Customize
Template
dialog box.

To customize an existing invoice form template, first select the template that you want to change from the Select a Template list box. For example, if you want to customize the Intuit Professional Invoice form template, you select it from the Select a Template list box. After you select the form template, click the Edit button. QuickBooks displays the Customize Invoice dialog box, shown in Figure 1-2. This window lets you make two simple changes to the form template. The Company tab, shown in Figure 1-2, lets you indicate what information should appear on the form template. You select the check box that corresponds to the bit of information. If you want the company name to appear on the invoice form — this means you aren't using letterhead or preprinted invoice forms — select the Print Company Name check box. You can also use the Company tab to indicate whether to print the company address or to add the company logo.

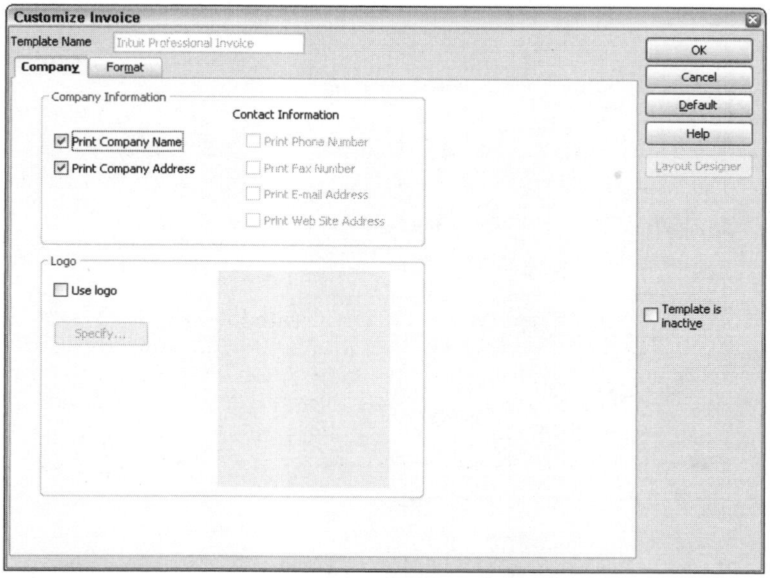

Figure 1-2:
The Customize Invoice dialog box.

The Format tab of the Customize Invoice window lets you change the font used for the pieces of information shown on the invoices. Figure 1-3 shows the Format tab. To change the formatting of a bit of text, first select the text from the Change Font For list box. After you do this, click the Change button. QuickBooks displays the Example dialog box, shown in Figure 1-4. Use its Font, Font Style, and Size boxes to specify what the selected bit of text should look like. The Example dialog box includes a Sample box that shows how your font changes look. When you complete your specification of the font, click OK.

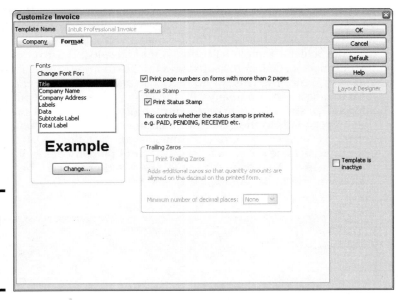

Figure 1-3:
The Format tab of the Customize Invoice dialog box.

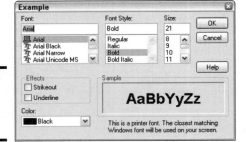

Figure 1-4:
The Example dialog box.

To see a list of all of QuickBooks' form templates, choose the Lists⇨Templates command. You can also create new form templates and customize existing form templates by clicking the Templates button on the Templates List window and choosing the appropriate command.

Creating a new invoice form template

If you can't create invoices that look exactly the way you want by modifying one of the existing predefined form templates, you can also create your own form template from scratch. You can do this because QuickBooks gives you much more flexibility in designing an invoice form template when you start from scratch. To create a new invoice form template, follow these steps:

1. **To indicate that you want to create a new invoice form template, display the Create Invoices window by choosing Customers⇨Create Invoices.**

2. **Click Customize.**

   QuickBooks displays the Customize Template dialog box (refer to Figure 1-1).

3. **Select one of the existing form templates.**

   You will want to select an existing form template that looks closest to the form template that you want to create.

4. **After you select the form template you want to use in the Select a Template list box, click the New button.**

   QuickBooks displays the Customize Invoice dialog box shown in Figure 1-5. This Customize Invoice dialog box resembles the windows shown in Figures 1-2 and 1-3. However, this expanded version of the Customize Invoice dialog box gives you many more options for designing the invoice form template.

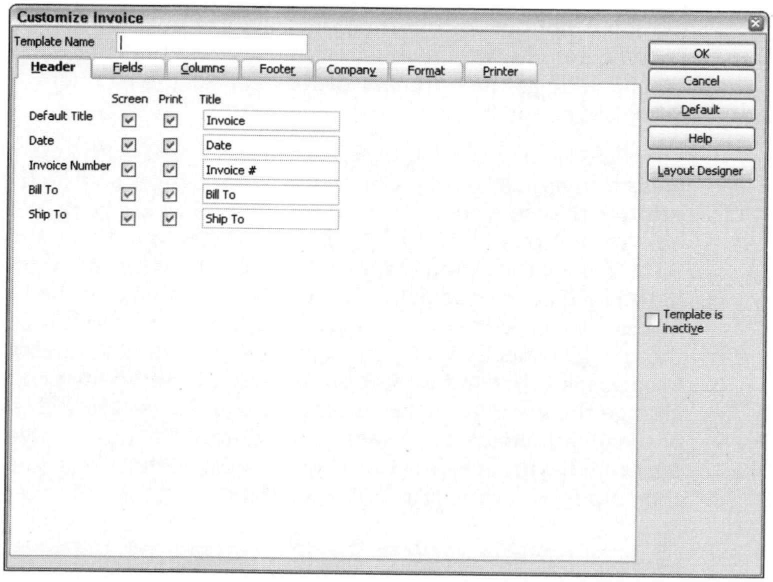

Figure 1-5:
The Header tab of the Customize Invoice window.

5. **Choose which bits of header information appear by selecting or deselecting the check boxes on the Header tab.**

   The Header tab of the Customize Invoice dialog box lets you specify what information goes on the top portion of the Create Invoices window and in the top area of an actual printed invoice form. This information is called the *header* and provides the invoice number, the invoice date, and the billing and shipping information. You can also choose how information is labeled by filling in or editing the contents of the text boxes. For example, the Default Title check boxes let you specify whether the form title should appear on the screen version of the invoice (this would be inside the Create Invoices window) and on the printed version of the invoice. The Default Title text box lets you specify what the form title should be. In a similar fashion, the Date check boxes let you specify whether the date should appear on the screen and print versions of the invoice and what label should be used to describe the invoice date. Figure 1-5, as you can see, uses the clever descriptive text Date for this invoice date information.

If you don't need a particular piece of information on an invoice, leave the Screen and Print check boxes for that bit of data deselected. This tells QuickBooks that it should not include that piece of header information on the window or print version of the invoice form.

6. **Describe the invoice fields, as shown in Figure 1-6.**

The Fields tab allows you to specify what information appears in the middle of the Create Invoices window and the invoice form. Fields information is not header information; also, it is not information about the specific item for which you are billing. Fields information includes bits of data such as the purchase order number, the payment term, the due date, and so forth.

The Fields tab works like the Header tab. If you want some bit of information to appear on the Create Invoices window and on the actual printed invoice, you need to select the Screen check box and Print check box for that bit of information. For example, to indicate that payment term information should appear on both the screen and printed versions of the invoice, you select both the Terms Screen and the Print check boxes. The Fields tab, like the Header tab, also includes Title text boxes that let you specify how you want these bits of data described on the Create Invoices window and on the actual printed invoice form. You can change the descriptive text that QuickBooks uses by editing the content of these text boxes. For example, to change the descriptive text used to describe payment terms from *Terms* to *Payment Terms,* you simply edit the contents of the Terms Title text box.

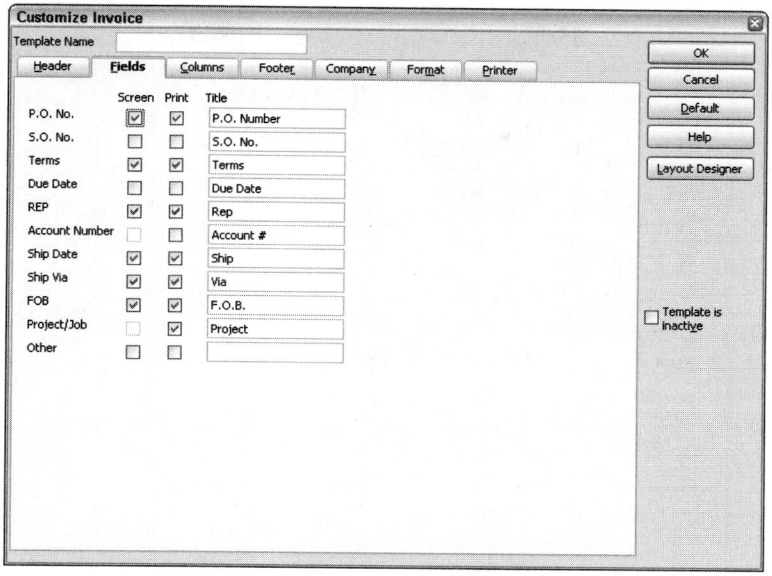

Figure 1-6:
The Fields tab of the Customize Invoice dialog box.

7. Specify the columns of invoice information, as shown in Figure 1-7.

The columns portion of an invoice describes in detail the items for which an invoice bills. For example, product invoice columns describe the specific products, including price and quantity; they also describe the items being invoiced. A service invoice's columns describe the specific services being billed. As you may guess from looking closely at Figure 1-7, the Columns tab of the Customize Invoice dialog box looks like the Header and Fields tabs. You use the Screen and Print check boxes to indicate whether a particular piece of column-level information should appear as a column on the Create Invoices window or on the actual created invoice. Similarly, you use the Title text boxes to provide the descriptive labels that QuickBooks uses on the Create Invoices window and on the printed invoice form. The only unusual option shown on the Columns tab is the Order text boxes (see Figure 1-7). The Order boxes let you indicate in what order (from left to right) the column should appear. If the item number or code should appear in the first column on the left, for example, you enter the value 1 into the Item Order box.

The Header, Fields, and Columns tabs let you make changes to your invoice forms, but don't get too tense about making perfect changes the first time. You can easily see exactly how your changes look simply by clicking OK and then carefully reviewing the new version of the Create Invoices window. If you realize that you've made an error — perhaps you've used the wrong bit of descriptive text or you've incorrectly ordered the columns — you can customize your invoice again and thereby fix your earlier mistakes.

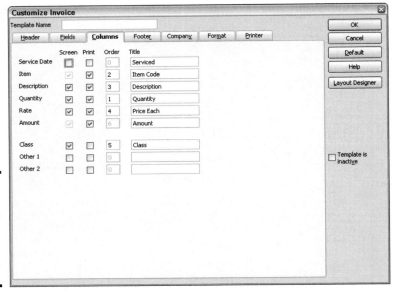

Figure 1-7:
The
Columns tab
of the
Customize
Invoice
dialog box.

Some versions of QuickBooks include a tab for specifying how the columns on a progress billing invoice look and work. This tab, called the Prog Cols tab, looks and works very much like the Columns tab.

8. Describe the invoice footer, as shown in Figure 1-8.

The Footer tab of the Customize Invoice dialog box lets you specify what information appears on the Create Invoices window beneath the columns area and on the actual printed invoice beneath the columns area. As Figure 1-8 indicates, the footer information includes a customer message, the invoice total, payments and credit information, a balance due field, and, optionally, a longer text box. You work with the Footer tab in the same manner as you work with other tabs. If you want some bit of information to appear, select the Screen check box and the Print check box. To change the bit of text that QuickBooks uses, edit the contents of the Title text box.

9. Specify the company information.

The Company tab of the Customize Invoice dialog box lets you specify whether bits of information about your company appear on the invoice. This is the same tab I show earlier in the chapter in Figure 1-2, so I won't show it again. When you customize one of the predefined invoice form templates (described earlier in the chapter), you use check boxes to select what bits of information should appear on the form and whether a logo should appear on the form.

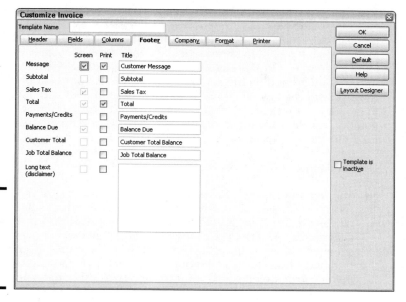

Figure 1-8:
The Footer
tab of the
Customize
Invoice
dialog box.

10. **Specify text formatting.**

The Format tab of the Customize Invoice window (refer to Figure 1-3) lets you specify what font you want to use for invoice text. To specify the font formatting for a particular piece of text, display the Format tab, select the bit of text that you want to format from the Change Font For list box and then click the Change button. When QuickBooks displays the Example dialog box (refer to Figure 1-4), use its boxes to make your choices. Click OK to close the Example box.

11. **Enter the name that you want to use for your new invoice template into the Template Name text box.**

You probably want to use something short and sweet. This name needs to easily fit into the Form Template drop-down list box, which is available on the Create Invoices window.

12. **To save your newly designed invoice form template, click OK.**

Alternatively, if you don't like what you've created and just want to discard your work, click the Cancel button.

You can return all of the customize invoice settings to their default condition by clicking the Default button. When you do this, however, you remove any changes or customizations that you've made.

Working with the Layout Designer tool

If you click the Layout Designer button, which is available in the Customize Invoice dialog box, QuickBooks displays the Layout Designer window, as shown in Figure 1-9. The Layout Designer window lets you move invoice information around on the actual printed invoice. Your best bet for learning to work with the Layout Designer tool is to experiment with it. My recommendation is that you create an example invoice form template — something you don't really care about — and then use this new invoice form template for some goofing around.

Here are some of the things that you may want to try:

✦ **Moving and resizing objects:** You can move and resize objects on the form pretty easily. To move some bit of the form, first select the bit by clicking it. Then use the arrow keys or drag the mouse to move the selected bit. You can resize the selected bit in a similar way. Resize the selected object by dragging the black squares (called *resizing handles*) that show that the selected object is selected. In moving and resizing invoice form objects, you want to keep two additional points in mind:

  • You can select the Show Envelope Window check box to have QuickBooks draw envelope windows on the invoice form to show you where these appear. You will want to have envelope windows shown to make sure that your customized invoice still has its address information showing through.

  • You can click the Grid button to display the Grid and Snap Settings dialog box. This dialog box provides two check boxes that let you indicate whether QuickBooks should use a grid (those are the dots you see) that lets you more accurately line up invoice objects on the form. The Grid and Snap Settings dialog box also includes a Snap to Grid box that lets you tell QuickBooks that it should make gridlines sticky — *sticky* gridlines automatically attract invoice objects so that you can more easily line up the objects against the gridlines. The Grid and Snap Settings dialog box also includes a Grid Spacing box that you can use to specify how wide or narrow QuickBooks should draw gridlines.

✦ **Selecting objects:** You can select multiple objects on the invoice by dragging the mouse. To do so, click at a point above the upper leftmost object that you want to select and drag the mouse to a point that is just below the lower rightmost object that you want to select. As you drag the mouse from one corner to the other, QuickBooks draws a rectangle. Any object that's inside this rectangle when you release the mouse gets selected.

✦ **Resizing multiple objects:** You can change the height, width, and size of multiple selected objects by clicking the Make Same Width, Make Same Height, and Make Same Size buttons. To use these Make Same buttons, you first need to select the objects that you want to make the same.

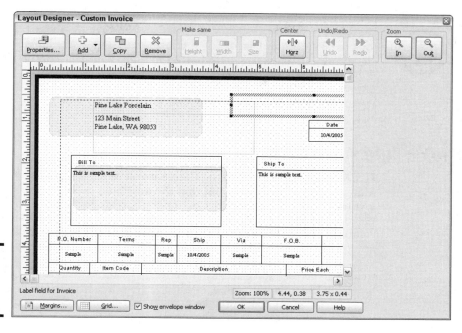

Figure 1-9:
The Layout
Designer
window.

✦ **Changing column widths:** You can change the width of columns in the column area of the invoice form by clicking the Column object. After you do this and QuickBooks selects the columns area, drag the column divider line left or right to resize the column. Note that if you make column 1 narrower, QuickBooks makes column 2 wider to take up the space. Also note that you can resize the entire column area in the manner described in the preceding point.

✦ **Positioning text within fields:** If you click an invoice object and then click the Properties button, QuickBooks displays the Properties dialog box. The Properties dialog box includes a Text tab that lets you specify how text should appear within an invoice object area. The Properties dialog box also includes a Border tab that lets you specify whether QuickBooks should draw a border along the edges of the invoice object.

✦ **Changing fonts:** You can change the font used for the selected object by clicking the Properties button, clicking the Text tab of the Properties dialog box, and then clicking the Font button that appears on this tab. QuickBooks displays the Example dialog box (shown earlier in the chapter in Figure 1-4). The Example dialog box lets you choose a font, font style, a point size, and special effects, such as strikeout, underlining, and color.

✦ **Adjusting margins:** If you click the Margins button, QuickBooks displays the Margins dialog box, which includes a Top, Bottom, Left, and Right text box that you use to specify the margin around the invoice. The default, or initial, margin settings equal half an inch.

Center a selected object on an invoice form by clicking the Center button to activate the Layout Designer. You can click the Zoom In and Zoom Out buttons to see more or less detail. If you want to undo your most recent change, click Undo. Or, click the Redo button to undo your last undo option.

After you use the Layout Designer to make whatever changes are appropriate to your new invoice form template, click OK to save your changes.

Invoicing a Customer

To invoice a customer, use the Create Invoices window to identify the customer and specify the amount that the customer owes. To display the Create Invoices window, choose the Customers⇨Create Invoices command. When you do, QuickBooks displays a Create Invoices window like the one shown in Figure 1-10. Note, however, that the Create Invoices window that you see may not look *exactly* like the one shown in Figure 1-10. As previously described, you can use more than one type of invoice form. You can also choose to customize an invoice form so that it perfectly matches your business requirements. In the following steps, I describe generally how to invoice a customer. The specific steps that you take may be ever-so-slightly different if you're working with a different invoice form template.

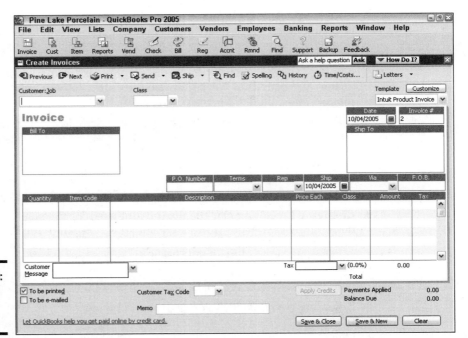

Figure 1-10: The Create Invoices window.

In Figure 1-10, I closed the Open Window List to provide more room for the Create Invoices window. You can close your Open Window List by clicking its close box (the small box marked with an "X" that appears in the upper-right corner of the list. To redisplay the Open Window List after you've closed it, choose View⇨Open Window List.

After you display the Create Invoices window, take the following steps to invoice a customer:

1. **Identify the customer and, if appropriate, the job.**

To do this, select the customer or customer and job combination from the Customer:Job drop-down list box. Don't worry about this "job" business if you aren't familiar with it. I describe how jobs work in Book IV, Chapter 5. You do, however, need to understand how customers work. You need to identify the specific customer that you are invoicing. You do this by selecting the customer from the Customer:Job list box. If the customer is a new customer that you haven't yet invoiced or described in the Customer List, enter a brief name for the customer — like an abbreviation of the customer's business name — into the Customer:Job list box. QuickBooks then indicates that the customer doesn't yet exist on the Customer List and asks whether you want to add the customer; indicate that you do. When prompted, supply the customer information that QuickBooks requests.

For more information about adding customers in QuickBooks, refer to Book II, Chapter 2.

You can also classify an invoice as fitting into a particular category by using the Class drop-down list box. Don't worry at this point about using class tracking. Book IV, Chapter 4 describes how you can use classes to get a better handle on your business's finances.

2. **Confirm or provide new invoice header information.**

After you identify the customer, QuickBooks fills out the Date, Invoice, Bill To, and, possibly, the Ship To fields. You probably don't need to change any of this information. You should review the information shown in these boxes to make sure that it is correct. For example, you wouldn't typically invoice someone unless you have already shipped the product or the service has already been provided. Therefore, you probably should confirm that the invoice date follows the product shipment date or the provision of service date. You may also want to confirm, for example, that the Ship To address is correct.

3. **Provide or confirm the Invoice field information.**

Invoices include field information that records items such as purchase order numbers, payment terms, ship date, and shipping method. You should make sure that whatever QuickBooks shows in these field boxes

**Book III
Chapter 1**

Invoicing Customers

is correct. If a customer has provided you with a purchase order number, for example, enter that purchase order number into the P.O. Number box. Confirm that the payment terms shown in the Terms box are correct. Confirm that the date shown in the Ship field is correct. Not all of these fields need to be filled for every invoice, but you want to supply any information that makes it easier for a customer to pay an invoice, tie an invoice to his or her purchasing records, and figure out how and when an item is being shipped.

4. Describe the items sold.

How the columns area of your invoice looks really depends on whether you are selling products or services. Figure 1-11 shows the columns area for a product. The columns area for a service looks simpler because you don't provide much information when describing service items. In the columns area, you want to describe each item — each product or service — for which an invoice bills. To do this, you use a single row for each item. The first item that you want to bill for, then, goes into row 1 of the columns area. For each item, you enter the quantity ordered, the code for the item, and a price. QuickBooks will retrieve an item description from your Item List and place this data into the description column. QuickBooks will also calculate the amount billed for the item by multiplying the quantity by the price. You can, however, edit both the Description and the Amount fields. If you edit the Amount field, QuickBooks recalculates the Price Each field by dividing the amount by the quantity.

To enter additional items onto the invoice, enter additional rows. Each item that you want to bill for — each item that should appear as a separate charge on the invoice — needs to appear as a row in the columns area. If you want to invoice a customer for some product, one line in the columns area of the invoice needs to be used for that product. If you want to charge a customer for freight, one line of the invoice area needs to describe that freight charge. If you want to bill a customer for sales tax, again, one line or row of the columns area needs to show that sales tax charge.

Discounts represent a tricky line item to include on an invoice. For this reason, I provide an example of how a discount item appears on an invoice. Assume that you want to grant some customer a 25 percent discount. In order to do this, you now know (or should be able to guess) that you need to include a discount line item on your invoice. However, although QuickBooks includes a discount item on its Item List, a discount percentage can only be applied to the previous line item on the invoice. For this reason, QuickBooks also supplies a subtotal line item. You use a subtotal line item to total all of the previous items shown on the invoice. By subtotaling all of the product items shown on the invoice in Figure 1-11, for example, the business can then grant the customer a 25 percent discount on those products.

Click to check spelling.

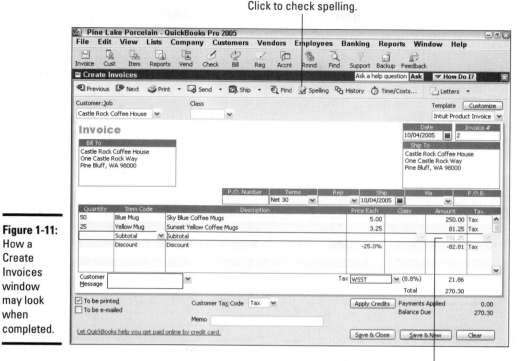

Figure 1-11:
How a
Create
Invoices
window
may look
when
completed.

A Subtotal line enables QuickBooks to calculate a discount.

5. **Use the Customer Message box at the bottom of the Create Invoices window to supply a customer message that will appear at the bottom of the invoice.**

If you've created a custom invoice form template that includes other footer information, these footer boxes will also appear at the bottom of the Create Invoices window. You can use them to collect and transfer additional footer information.

6. **(Optional) Check your spelling.**

If you click the Spelling button, which appears along the top edge of the Create Invoices window, QuickBooks will check the spelling of the words that you've used on the invoice. If QuickBooks finds no spelling errors, QuickBooks displays a message telling you that the spelling check is complete. If QuickBooks finds a spelling error — product code abbreviations often produce spelling errors in QuickBooks — QuickBooks displays the Check Spelling on Form dialog box, shown in Figure 1-12. (In Figure 1-12, I've misspelled the word "Yellow" much to the dismay of my editor.) You can use the Change To box to correct your spelling error — if it actually is a spelling error. You can select one of the suggested replacements from the Suggestions list box by clicking the suggestion and then clicking the Replace button. You can replace all occurrences of the misspelling by clicking the Replace All button. If the word that QuickBooks says is misspelled is actually correctly spelled, you can click the Ignore button to tell QuickBooks to ignore this word or the Ignore All button to tell QuickBooks to ignore all occurrences of this word on the invoice form.

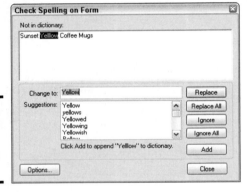

Figure 1-12:
The Check
Spelling on
Form dialog
box.

If you use terms that are always popping up as misspelled words, at least in QuickBooks, you can click the Add button that appears on the Check Spelling on Form dialog box. Clicking the Add button tells QuickBooks to add the word to its spelling dictionary. After you've added a word to the QuickBooks spelling dictionary, QuickBooks doesn't see the word as misspelled. Also note that you can click the Options button to display the Spelling Options dialog box. The Spelling Options dialog box includes check boxes that you can use to turn on or turn off certain types of spell checking logic. For example, the Spelling Options dialog box includes a check box that you can select to tell QuickBooks to always check the spelling of forms before printing, saving, or sending the form. The Spelling Options dialog box also includes check boxes to tell QuickBooks it should ignore certain sorts of words, such as those that use numbers, those that are all uppercase, and those that are mixed case.

7. Click either the Save & Close button or the Save & New button to save your invoice.

Click the Save & Close button if you want to save the invoice and close the Create Invoices window. You use the Save & New button if you want to save the invoice and then enter another invoice into the blank version of the Create Invoices window.

Click the Ship button to display the QuickBooks Shipping Manager window, which lets you automate some of the steps in shipping packages using Federal Express or UPS. If you use Federal Express or UPS, therefore, you may want to experiment with this tool.

One internal control problem within QuickBooks that I hear CPAs complain about over and over is that QuickBooks allows someone to print a form without saving it. This seems innocuous enough, but this little idiosyncrasy can cause serious problems for a business owner. Here is why this "printing without saving" option becomes dangerous: A dishonest employee can create an invoice form, print the invoice form, send the invoice form to a customer, and then not save the invoice form. At this point, a customer has what appears to be a valid invoice from your firm and probably will pay that invoice. If the nefarious employee can intercept the check that pays that invoice, he can then deposit that check into a personal checking account, and you are none the wiser. In order to prevent or at least minimize this opportunity for employee theft, you want to separate the ability to create an invoice form from the ability to print an invoice form. Book VII, Chapter 2 describes how you do this as part of setting up user passwords for segregation of duty. In this scenario, by the way, the people who create invoices (such as sales people or accounting clerks) don't actually print invoices. Somebody else — perhaps even you, the owner — will print the invoices and then arrange to have them distributed. Also note that you can use QuickBooks' e-mail invoices and batch printing to greatly simplify the work of sending out invoices. So you aren't actually creating that much extra work for yourself.

To page through invoices that you've already created, click the Previous and Next buttons. Or, click the Find button and use the Find Invoices dialog box to describe the invoice that you want to locate.

Billing for Time

Most of the time, line items that appear on an invoice will be items that you have described in the item list and then quantify directly on the invoice. However, in some service businesses, you may actually sell many units of the same item. For example, a lawyer may sell hours or partial hours of legal advice. This may be all that she sells. A CPA may sell hours of consulting or accounting or tax preparation work.

In these circumstances, you don't want to have an invoice go out to the customer with one line on it that says, for example, "legal services, 100 hours, $20,000." You instead want an invoice that details each of the tasks that the lawyer performed: the estate planning for 1.5 hours, review of a contract for 4 hours, preparation of a new real estate lease for 2 hours, and so forth. To provide this level of detail — detail that is really beneath the item — you need to use the QuickBooks Time Tracking feature.

QuickBooks supplies two methods for tracking the time spent that will be billed on an invoice as an item. You can use the weekly time sheet or you can time or record individual activities. I briefly describe how both time tracking methods work — neither is difficult. Professional service providers — such as accountants, attorneys, consultants, architects, and so on — will want to consider using one of these features to make sure that they accurately keep good records of the time spent working for a client or customer.

Using a weekly timesheet

To use the weekly timesheet method, choose the Customers⇨Time Tracking⇨ Use Weekly Timesheet command. QuickBooks displays the Weekly Timesheet window, shown in Figure 1-13. To use the Weekly Timesheet window, first use the Name box to identify the employee or vendor or other person performing the service. You should be able to select this person's name from the Name box. If you can't select a person's name from the Name box, enter the person's name into the box, and then, when prompted, tell QuickBooks which list (employee, vendor, or other names) should be added. After you have added the name of the person performing the work, use the columns of the Weekly Timesheet window to describe the customer or job for whom the work has been performed, the service code, a brief description or note, the class (if you are tracking classes), and then the hours spent per day. You can enter as many lines onto the Weekly Timesheet window as you want. Each line separately appears on an invoice. The notes information appears in the description area of the invoice. For this reason, you want to use appropriate and descriptive notes.

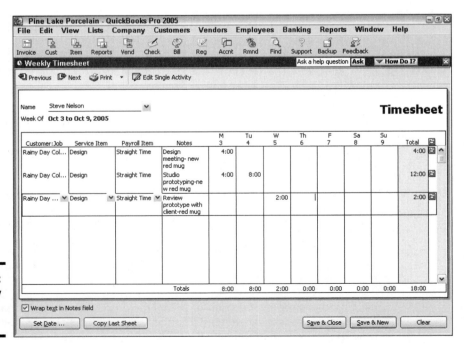

Figure 1-13:
The Weekly Timesheet window.

Timing single activities

If you want to record service activities as they occur, choose the Customers⇨ Time Tracking⇨Time/Enter Single Activity command. QuickBooks displays the Time/Enter Single Activity window, as shown in Figure 1-14.

To time or record a single activity, record the activity date into the Date box. Use the Name box to identify the person performing the service. In the Customer:Job box, identify the customer or the job for which the service is being performed. Select the appropriate service item from the Service Item drop-down list box. If you're tracking classes, predictably, you can also use the Class drop-down list box to classify the activity. The Notes box should be used to record a brief appropriate description of the service. This description appears on the invoice, so be thoughtful about what you write. After describing or providing this general information about the service, you have two ways to record the time spent on the service:

✦ **Manually record time:** You can manually record the time spent on an activity by using the Duration box to enter the time. If you spent 10 minutes, for example, enter **0:10** into the Duration box. If you spent 3 hours and 40 minutes, enter **3:40** into the Duration box.

✦ **Have QuickBooks record the time:** You can also have QuickBooks record the time that you spent on the activity. Just click the Start button in the Duration box when you start the activity, and click the Stop button when you stop the activity. If you want to pause the timer while you take a phone call, for example, click the Pause button.

After you describe the activity you're performing in the Time/Enter Single Activity window, click the Save & New or Save & Close button to save the activity information.

Verify that the Billable check box is selected. The Billable check box appears in the upper-right corner of the Time/Enter Single Activity window. By selecting the Billable box, you tell QuickBooks that it should keep this record of a billable activity for later inclusion on an invoice.

You can use the Previous and Next buttons that appear at the top of the Time/Enter Single Activity window to page back and forth through your records of activity timing. Note, too, that the Spelling button is also available on the Time/Enter Single Activity window. You can, therefore, click the Spelling button to spell check the notes description that you enter — which is a good idea because this information will later appear on an invoice.

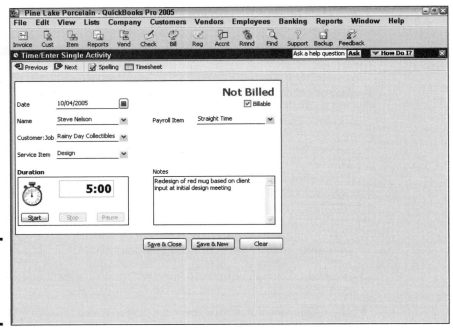

Figure 1-14:
The Time/
Enter Single
Activity
window.

Including billable time on an invoice

To add billable time and cost to an invoice, create the invoice in the usual way, as I describe previously. The only difference when you are adding billable time is that you need to click the Time/Costs button (in the upper right of Figure 1-16). When you do this, QuickBooks displays the Choose Billable Time and Costs dialog box shown in Figure 1-15. The Time tab of the Choose Billable Time and Costs dialog box shows each of the times that you've recorded for a customer. To add these times to the invoice, click the Use column for the time. Or, if you want to select all of the times, click the Select All button. Then click OK. QuickBooks then adds each of these billable times as lines to the invoice. Figure 1-16 shows how billable time information appears on the Create Invoices window.

As Figure 1-15 suggests, you can click the Items, Expenses, or Mileage tabs to see lists of the items, out-of-pocket expenses, or business miles incurred on behalf of a customer. You would add charges to an invoice for these sorts of things in the same was as you add charges for time. I talk about how to record business miles and out-of-pocket expenses you want to later charge to customers in Chapter 2 of this book. By the way, the very last line of the invoice shown in Figure 1-16 bills the client for the out-of-pocket expenses incurred for a luncheon.

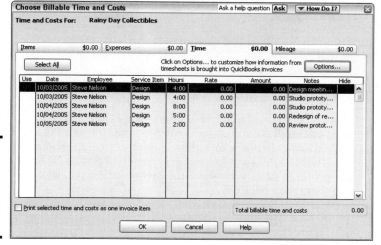

Figure 1-15:
The Choose
Billable
Time and
Costs dialog
box.

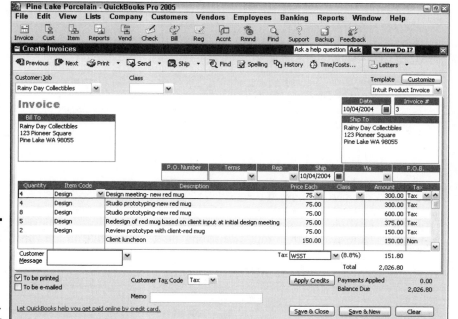

Figure 1-16:
The Create
Invoices
window
billing for
billable time.

Printing Invoices

You can print invoices and then mail the printed invoices in a couple of different ways:

✦ You can print individual invoices by clicking the Print button at the top of the Create Invoices window.

✦ You can also print a batch of invoices by clicking the arrow button next to the Print button, choosing Print Batch from the menu that QuickBooks displays, and then using the Select Invoices to Print dialog box (which QuickBooks displays) to select the To Be Printed Invoices for printing. After you select the invoices that you want to print by clicking them, you click OK.

The menu that QuickBooks displays when you click the Print arrow button includes a Preview command. You can choose the Preview command to see a preview version of the printed invoice.

E-mailing Invoices

You can e-mail an invoice from QuickBooks. To do this, click the E-mail button that appears at the top of the Create Invoice screen. When QuickBooks displays the Send Invoice dialog box, as shown in Figure 1-17, provide the e-mail address and, optionally, a new e-mail message. Then click the Send Now button to send the invoice. Alternatively, you can click the Send Later button to batch your e-mail invoices for later delivery. To send all of your invoices in a batch later, you click the arrow button next to the E-mail button at the top of the Create Invoices window and choose the Send Batch command from the menu that QuickBooks displays.

You can also use the Send Invoice dialog box to send the invoice to QuickBooks and then have the QuickBooks folks mail a paper copy to the customer or client. To do this, mark the Mail through QuickBooks button. QuickBooks then tells you about this extra service and, if you decide to go for it, steps you through the sign-up process.

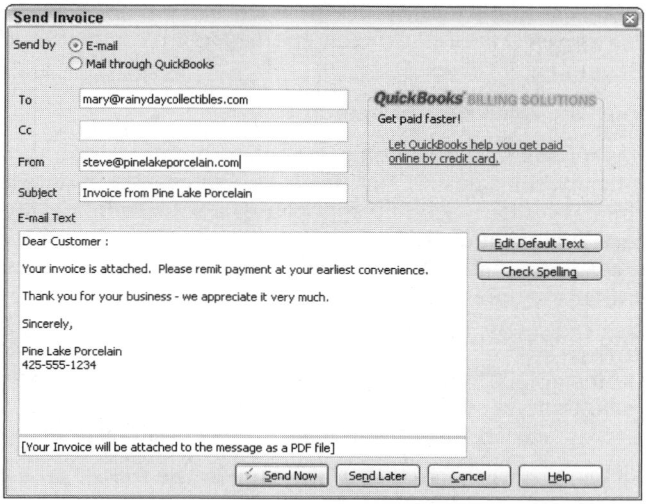

Figure 1-17:
The Send
Invoice
dialog box.

Recording a Sales Receipt

To bill a customer, you create an invoice as I describe earlier in this chapter. To record the fact that you sold the customer some item — presumably this is because the customer simultaneously purchases and pays for the item or service — you don't invoice the customer. Rather, you create a sales receipt. A sales receipt looks very, very similar to an invoice. However, it doesn't include shipping information (because that's irrelevant) and it lets you record the amount that the customer pays.

To record a sales receipt when it is appropriate, choose the Customers➪ Enter Sales Receipts command and then follow these steps:

1. **In the Enter Sales Receipts window, shown in Figure 1-18, use the Customer:Job box to describe the customer or, optionally, the customer and job.**

Use the Class drop-down list box to identify the class if you are performing class tracking.

If you have questions about how the Customer:Job box works or how the Class box works, refer to the discussion on this topic earlier in the chapter.

You can customize a sales receipt in the same basic way that you customize an invoice form. Go back to the section on this topic located at the beginning of this chapter.

2. Provide the sales receipt header info.

A sales receipt, like an invoice, includes some header information. Specifically, the sales receipt includes a sales receipt date and a sales number. The sales receipt also includes a Sold To box, which shows the customer name and address. You should confirm that this information is correct — and it should be if you are recording timely sales receipts and have an up-to-date Customer List.

3. Use the items column to describe the items that you are selling.

The items column on a sales receipt works the exact same way as the items column on an invoice. Therefore, rather than repeat myself, go back to the earlier discussion of how this column works.

4. If you want, enter a customer message in the footer area of the Enter Sales Receipts window.

If you have added other footer information to the Enter Sales Receipts window — this would be because you have customized the sales receipt form template — you can include that information, too.

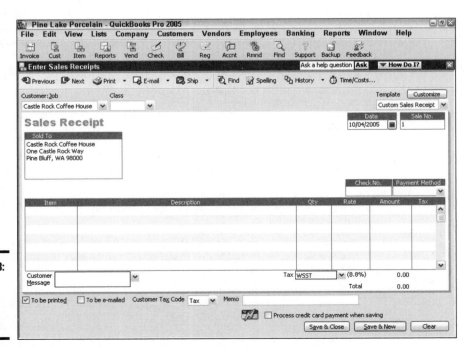

Figure 1-18:
The Enter Sales Receipts window.

5. Describe where the sales proceeds go.

At the bottom-left corner of the Enter Sales Receipts window are two radio buttons: Group with Other Undeposited Funds and Deposit To. Use these radio buttons to indicate what you do with the money that you receive from this sale. If you are going to immediately deposit the amount into a bank account, select the Deposit To radio button and then select the account into which you will deposit the check from the Deposit To box. If you are going to batch this receipt with a bunch of other receipts — maybe you are going to deposit the day's receipts together in one lump sum — select the Group with Other Undeposited Funds radio button.

If you don't see the Group with Other Undeposited Funds and Deposit To boxes, you may have indicated (perhaps even inadvertently) during the setup that you just want QuickBooks to assume funds are deposited into an undeposited funds account. This will probably work just fine. If you do want to specify an account where sales proceeds go when you record the sales receipt, choose the Edit⇔Preferences command, click the Sales and Customers icon, click the Company Preferences tab, and then unmark the Use Undeposited Funds as a default deposit to account.

Book III, Chapter 4 talks about making deposits of undeposited funds.

6. Click the Save & Close or Save & New button to save the sales receipt.

These buttons work the same way for the Enter Sales Receipts window as they do for the Create Invoices window.

7. (Optional) To print a copy of the receipt, click the Print button.

The Previous, Next, Find, Spelling, History, and Time/Cost buttons on the Enter Sales Receipts window work identically to the same buttons on the Create Invoices window.

Both the Create Invoices window (described earlier in the chapter) and the Enter Sales Receipts window (just described) include a To Be Printed check box in the footer area. If you select this check box, QuickBooks adds the invoice or sales receipt to its list of unprinted invoices or sales receipts. You can print invoices and sales receipts that appear on either side of these lists by choosing the File⇔Print Forms command and then either the Invoices or Sales Receipt command. There's also a To Be E-mailed checkbox that you can mark if you want to later e-mail a receipt. (See the earlier discussion, "E-mailing Invoices."

Recording Credit Memos

Credit memos show when a customer no longer owes you money or when you now owe a customer money. Credit memos may occur because your customer returns items that you previously sold to him or her. Credit memos may also occur because you issue a customer a refund for some other good

Book III
Chapter 1

Invoicing Customers

reason — perhaps the product wasn't of the quality that you usually sell, or a service wasn't provided in the manner in which it should have been.

To record a credit memo, first display the Create Credit Memos/Refunds window by choosing Customers⇨Create Credit Memos/Refunds command. Then, follow these steps:

1. Identify the customer or the customer and the job in the Customer:Job box.

Use the Class box for class tracking if you've decided to do that (see Figure 1-19). If you have questions about how either of these boxes works, refer to the earlier discussion about these two boxes. These boxes work the same way for credit memos as they do for invoices.

The Create Credit Memos/Refunds window supplies several buttons that work the same way here as they do on the Create Invoices window: Previous, Next, Print, Find, Spelling, and History. For information about how to use these buttons if you have questions, refer to the earlier chapter section on this topic.

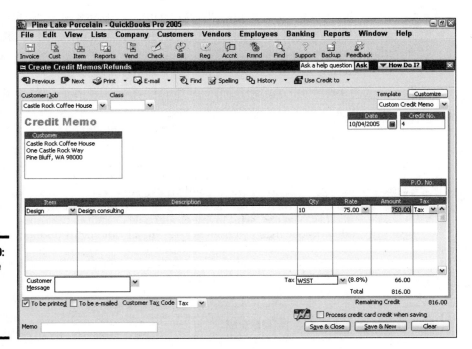

Figure 1-19:
The Create Credit Memos/ Refunds window.

As is the case with invoices, you can create custom credit memo forms. To do this, you click the Customize button. Customizing a credit memo works the same way as customizing an invoice form. Refer to the earlier chapter section on this topic if you have questions about how to customize a credit memo.

2. **Provide the credit memo date, credit memo number, and confirm customer information.**

   Credit memos, like invoices and sales receipts, include a header. This header includes the transaction date and number and the customer information. You should confirm that the credit memo header information is correct on the Create Credit Memos/Refunds window. If it isn't, edit the default information that QuickBooks first uses to fill the Create Credit Memos/Refunds window.

3. **In the columns area of the Create Credit Memos/Refunds window, describe the reason for the credit memo.**

   If the customer returned items, for example, use the columns to describe these items and the original price that you are refunding.

4. **Click either Save & Close or Save & New to save the credit memo.**

5. **Click the Print button to print the credit memo.**

   Note, too, that you can also print credit memos in a batch. Obviously, after you print credit memos, you need to distribute them.

   At the time you save your credit memo, QuickBooks allows you to indicate what you want to do with the credit memo: retain it for later application to a customer invoice, immediately apply it to a customer invoice, or issue a refund check. You apply credit memos to invoices as described in the next section of the chapter. You would write a refund check in the same way as you write other checks. Chapter 4 of Book III describes writing checks.

Receiving Customer Payments

When a customer pays an invoice that you have previously sent, you choose the Customer⇨Receive Payments command to record the payment. To use this command to record a payment, choose the command and then follow these steps:

1. **After QuickBooks displays the Receive Payments window, as shown in Figure 1-20, use the Received From box to identify the customer paying you.**

**Book III
Chapter 1**

Invoicing Customers

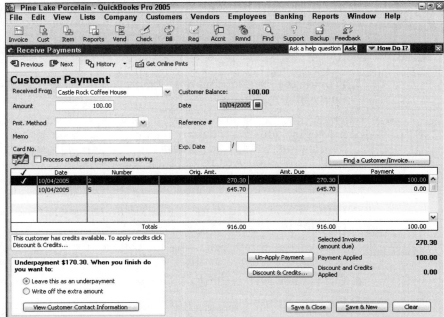

Figure 1-20:
The Receive
Payments
window.

2. **Record the payment information in the Date, Amount, Reference # box,
   Pmt. Method box, and Card No. and Exp. Date boxes (if appropriate).**

3. **Identify the invoice or invoices paid.**

   QuickBooks lists the open invoices for the customer in the columns area
   of the Receive Payments window. You can identify which invoices a customer payment pays by clicking the invoices that you see listed.

4. **Apply any credit memos to open invoices as you apply the payment.**

   Click the Discounts & Credits button. QuickBooks displays the Discounts
   and Credits dialog box, as shown in Figure 1-21. To apply a credit to the
   selected invoices, click the Credits tab and then select credit that you
   want to apply.

5. **Apply any discounts to the open invoices and click Done.**

   Discounts work like credits. In fact, you use the same dialog box
   (see Figure 1-21).

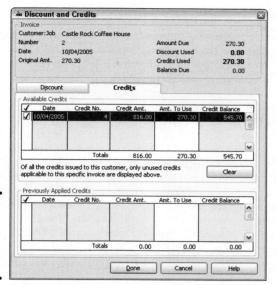

Figure 1-21:
The
Discount
and Credits
dialog box.

6. **Select the Group with Other Undeposited Funds or the Deposit To radio button to indicate whether you are going to immediately deposit the payment or batch the payment with a bunch of other payments that you later deposit.**

   If you have a question about how these buttons work, refer to the earlier discussion of these buttons in the section "Recording a Sales Receipt."

7. **Click the Save & Close or Save & New button to save the customer payment information.**

   Click the Get Online Pmts button to receive online payment information for a customer. The Get Online Pmts button appears only if you are using either online billing or deluxe online billing. The earlier discussion describes how online billing and deluxe online billing work.

   To see a list of the payments that have been applied to an invoice, click the History button.

Assessing Finance Charges

You can tell QuickBooks to assess finance charges on overdue customer invoices. To do this, you first need to set up the finance charge calculation rules. After you've done this, you can easily assess finance charges on overdue amounts by choosing the QuickBooks command.

**Book III
Chapter 1**

Invoicing Customers

Setting up finance charge rules

To set up the finance charge rules, choose the Edit⇨Preferences command. When QuickBooks displays the Preferences dialog box, click the Finance Charge icon and then the Company Preferences tab. The Preferences dialog box at this point should look like the one shown in Figure 1-22. To tell QuickBooks how it should calculate the finance charges, enter the annual interest rate that you'll use for calculating charges into the Annual Interest Rate (%) box. Enter the minimum finance charge amount that you will assess into the Minimum Finance Charge box. If you want to create a grace period, enter the number of grace period days into the Grace Period (Days) box. Use the Finance Charge Account drop-down list box to specify the QuickBooks income account to which finance charge revenue should be credited. Select the Assess Finance Charges on Overdue Finance Charges check box if you want to charge finance charges on finance charges. Finally, use the Calculate Charges From radio buttons — Due Date and Invoice/Billed Date — to specify the date from which finance charges should be calculated. After you've provided this information, you can click OK to save your finance charge calculation rules.

Figure 1-22:
The Company Preferences tab for the Finance Charge Preferences.

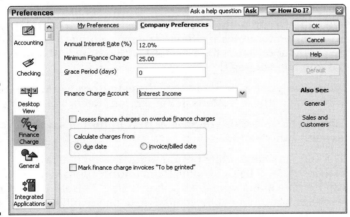

QuickBooks assumes that you don't want to print finance charge invoices. For this reason, the Mark Finance Charge Invoices to Be Printed check box is not selected. Finance charges typically appear only on customer statements.

Calculating finance charges

After you set up the finance charge rules, you can easily assess finance charges on overdue invoices. To do this, choose Customers⇨Assess Finance Charges. QuickBooks displays the Assess Finance Charges window, as shown in Figure 1-23. This window lists all of the overdue invoices that customers owe you and, based on your finance charge calculation rules, calculates a finance charge. To assess the finance charge to a particular customer, click the Assess field for the customer. (By default, QuickBooks assumes that you want to assess finance charges whenever a customer's account is past due.) If you don't want to assess finance charges to a particular customer, remove the check mark from the Assess field by clicking it. After you've identified which customers should be assessed finance charges, click the Assess Charges button. QuickBooks, essentially, creates new invoices for each of these customers. These new invoices charge the customer a finance charge.

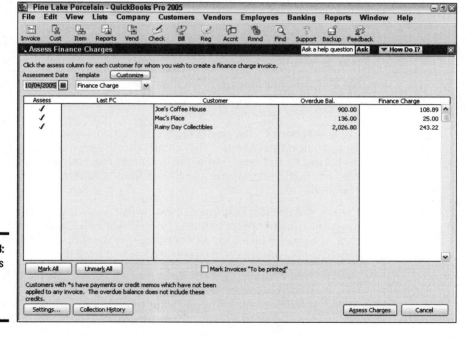

Figure 1-23: The Assess Finance Charges window.

Customer Odds and Ends

In this chapter, I discuss most of the important commands on the Customers menu. However, the Customers menu supplies several other commands that are noteworthy — perhaps even useful — and deserve discussion somewhere in this book. For this reason, I want to briefly describe the other commands available on the Customers menu:

✦ **Customer Navigator:** Displays the Customer Navigator window, which shows a flow chart that explains how the accounting process works for customers. (This includes things such as issuing invoices, issuing credit memos, and accepting payments.) The Customer Navigator window also includes clickable hyperlinks that you can use to do things such as print invoices or add a customer.

✦ **Customer Center:** Displays the Customer Center window, which includes information about your customer list, including the amounts that your customers owe.

✦ **Customer Detail Center:** Displays detailed information about a particular customer, the billing address, contact information, open invoices, and so forth.

✦ **Go To Customer Manager:** Displays a Web page that describes other Intuit products, including the QuickBooks Client Manager and the QuickBooks Customer Manager.

✦ **Enter Statement Charges:** Displays the Accounts Receivable Register. You shouldn't need to use this command. You can, however, use this command to add amounts to the accounts receivable for a particular customer. The amounts would then appear on the customer's next statement.

✦ **Create Statements:** Displays a window that you can use to create a set of monthly statements for customers. Such statements show the amounts that a customer owes, invoices created for the month, credit memos issued for the month, and payments made during the month.

✦ **Credit Card Processing Activities:** Displays a submenu of commands that you can use to deal with credit card payments and credit card billing. QuickBooks, by the way, supports credit card merchant accounts and makes it easy to accept credit cards from customers. This is something you want to do. You should visit the QuickBooks Web site and find out the details.

✦ **Customer Letters with Envelopes:** Displays a submenu of commands that let you prepare customer or client letters for things like thank yous, collection issues, and so forth.

✦ **Customer: Job List:** Displays the Customer:Job list, which is a list of customers, and, if you are using jobs, the jobs associated with particular customers.

✦ **Item List:** Displays the Item List, which shows the items that may be included on the invoice or credit memo.

✦ **Change Item Prices:** Lets you change the prices of a bunch of different items at one time, such as by increasing every price by 5 percent.

✦ **Billing Solutions:** Displays a submenu of commands that explain and, optionally, let you sign up for QuickBooks' online billing.

✦ **Check Credit:** Displays a submenu of commands that lets you either learn more about QuickBooks credit checking services or lets you check the credit of one of your customers.

Chapter 2: Paying Vendors

In This Chapter

*Y*ou can make the process of tracking vendor information as simple or as sophisticated as you like. In this chapter, I assume that you're going for sophisticated. However, you can make vendor management simpler by not using purchase orders and by not using an accounts payable system.

You decide whether to use purchase orders and whether to track accounts payable (amounts that you owe vendors) as part of setting up QuickBooks. You can also later change your decision about using purchase orders and about using account payables. To do this, you choose the Edit➪Preferences command. For more information, refer to Book II, Chapter 3.

Creating a Purchase Order

A purchase order serves a simple purpose: It tells some vendor that you want to purchase some item. In fact, a *purchase order* is a contract to purchase.

Many small businesses don't use purchase orders. But when they grow to a certain size, many businesses decide to use them because purchase orders become permanent records of items that you've ordered. What's more, using purchase orders often formalizes the purchasing process in a company. For example, you may decide that nobody in your firm can purchase anything that costs more than $100 unless they get a purchase order. If only you can issue purchase orders, you've effectively controlled purchasing activities through this procedure.

A real purchase order

To use QuickBooks to create purchase orders, follow these steps:

1. **Tell QuickBooks that you want to create a purchase order by choosing Vendors➪Create Purchase Orders.**

QuickBooks displays the window shown in Figure 2-1.

If the Vendors menu doesn't supply a Create Purchase Orders command, QuickBooks doesn't know that you want to create purchase orders. You'll need to follow the instructions described in Book II, Chapter 3 for turning on the purchase order feature.

2. **Use the Vendors menu drop-down list box to identify the vendor from whom you want to purchase the item.**

The Vendor drop-down list box lists each of the vendors in your Vendor List.

3. **(Optional) Classify the purchase using the Class drop-down list box.**

For more information about how you can use classes, read Book IV, Chapter 4.

Choose the vendor here.

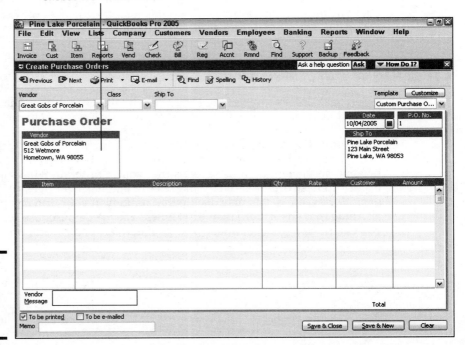

Figure 2-1:
The Create
Purchase
Orders
window.

4. **(Optional) Provide a different Ship To address in the Ship To drop-down list box.**

The Ship To drop-down list box displays a list of all your customers, vendors, and employees. You select the ship to address by selecting one of these other names. After you select an entry from the Ship To list, QuickBooks fills in the Ship To address box with the appropriate information.

The Create Purchase Orders window supplies some standard and, hopefully, familiar buttons and boxes: Previous, Next, Print, Find, Spelling, History, and Template. Because I spend quite a bit of time talking about these buttons and boxes in Book III, Chapter 1, I don't provide a redundant discussion of these buttons and boxes here. If you have questions about what the Previous and Next buttons do, refer to Book III, Chapter 1.

5. **Confirm the purchase order date.**

Initially, QuickBooks puts the current system date into the Date box. You should, however, confirm that the date that QuickBooks enters as the purchase order date is correct. This is the *contract date*. Often, the date sets contractual terms — such as the number of days that the item needs to be shipped within.

6. **Confirm the purchase order number.**

The purchase order number, or *P.O. number*, uniquely identifies the purchase order document. QuickBooks sequentially numbers purchase orders for you and places the next number into the P.O. No. box. The guess that QuickBooks makes about the right purchase order number is usually correct, but if it isn't correct, enter the replacement number.

7. **Confirm the vendor and ship to information.**

The Vendor block and the Ship To block identify the vendor from whom you are purchasing the item and the ship to address to which you want the vendor to send the shipment. This information should be correct if your vendor list is up-to-date and you have correctly used the Ship To drop-down list box to identify, if necessary, an alternative Ship To address. Nevertheless, confirm that the information shown in these two address blocks is correct. If the information isn't correct, of course, fix it. You can edit address block information by selecting the incorrect information and then retyping whatever should be shown.

8. **Describe each item that you want to order.**

You use the columns of the Create Purchase Orders window to describe in detail each item that you want to order as part of the purchase. Each item goes on its own row. To describe an item that you want to purchase from the vendor, you provide the following bits of information:

- **Item:** The Item column lets you record the unique item number for the item that you want to buy. Remember that items need to be entered, or described, in the Item List. Book II, Chapter 2 discusses briefly how you go about setting up the Item List. The next chapter, Book III, Chapter 3, talks in more detail about the Item List. The main thing you need to know about the Item List is that anything that you want to show on the invoice — or, for that matter, on a purchase order — needs to be described in the item file.

- **Description:** The Description column shows the description for the item that you select. You can also edit the Description field so that it makes sense to customers or vendors.

- **Qty:** The Qty column lets you identify the quantity of the item that you want. You enter the number of items that you want in this field, obviously.

- **Rate:** The Rate column lets you enter the price per unit or rate per unit for the item. Note that QuickBooks uses different labels for this column depending on the type of business that you've set up.

- **Customer:** The Customer column lets you identify the customer for whom the item is being purchased.

- **Amount:** The Amount column shows the total expended for the item. QuickBooks will calculate the amount for you by multiplying the quantity by the rate (or price). You can also edit the column amount. In this case, QuickBooks adjusts the rate (or price) so that quantity times rate always equals the amount.

You need to enter a description of each item that should be included on the purchase order. This means, for example, that if you want to order six items from a vendor, your purchase order should include six lines of information.

9. **Print the purchase order.**

You will want to print the purchase order. The purpose of recording a purchase order into QuickBooks is to create a formal record of a purchase. You almost always will want to transmit this purchase order to the vendor. The purchase order tells the vendor exactly what you want to purchase and the price that you are willing to pay. To print the purchase order, you can click the Print button. You can also print purchase orders later in a batch; to do so, save all the purchase orders that you want to create, and then choose the File⇨Print Forms⇨Purchase Orders command.

10. **Save the purchase order.**

To save your purchase order, click either the Save & Close button or the Save & New button. If you click the Save & New button, QuickBooks saves that purchase order and redisplays an empty version of the Create Purchase Orders window so you can record another purchase order.

Purchase order tips and tricks

Even though the last section detailed about all you need to know to create a purchase order, I do need to make a couple of important quick observations:

✦ **Be aware that you can print without saving.** As I note several times throughout this book, QuickBooks allows you to print forms such as purchase orders without actually saving the purchase order. This sometimes creates an internal control risk. For example, someone can invoice a customer or print a check without actually recording the invoice or check in the QuickBooks system. Perhaps the risk isn't quite as great with a purchase order, but still, you definitely don't want to be printing purchase orders, distributing them to vendors, and not saving them. Be aware that you must remember to save your purchase order after you print it.

✦ **Not every purchase deserves a purchase order.** If you're not used to working with purchase orders, it is easy to go overboard when you first start using this handy tool. Nevertheless, keep in mind that not all purchases warrant purchase orders. Typically, businesses use purchase orders as a way to control and document purchases. In fact, many purchases don't really need a purchase order. Amounts that you've agreed to purchase that are documented through standard contracts, such as bills from the telephone company, the gas company, and your landlord, don't need purchase orders, obviously. In addition, modest purchases for things such as office supplies often don't need purchase orders, either. You definitely do need a way to control those expenditures, but purchase orders are probably not the way to go. Other budgetary controls such as "approval from the supervisor" or a simple budget often work just as well.

Recording the Receipt of Items

When you receive items from a vendor, you can record the receipt. You would typically do this when you want to record the receipt of an item even before you receive a bill for the item. For example, in any business with inventory, you want to know exactly how much inventory you have in your warehouse or on your store floor. You don't want to wait to adjust your inventory records for these purchases until you receive the invoice from the vendor. In this scenario, you need to record when you receive items.

To record item receipts, follow these steps:

1. **Choose the Vendors⇨Receive Items command.**

   QuickBooks displays the Create Item Receipts window, as shown in Figure 2-2.

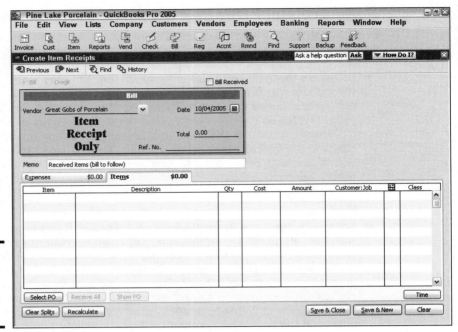

Figure 2-2:
The Create
Item
Receipts
window.

2. **Select the vendor from whom you're receiving items from the Vendor drop-down list box.**

3. **Select any P.O.s that you're receiving items on.**

   If open purchase orders exist for the vendor, QuickBooks displays a Message box. The Message box asks whether you want to receive items against one of the open purchase orders. If the items that you receive are items that you set up on a purchase order, click Yes. When Quick Books displays the Open Purchase Orders dialog box — the dialog box just lists open purchase orders — select the purchase order that ordered the items you are now receiving and then click OK. QuickBooks then fills out the Items tab of the Create Item Receipts window by using the information from the purchase order. This automatic data entry of purchase order information should save you time if the items that you're receiving match those items on the purchase order.

4. **Confirm the receipt date.**

   Use the Date field to confirm the date of receipt. As with the Date field in other places in QuickBooks, enter the date in mm/dd/yyyy format. Or, you can click the Calendar button that appears to the right of the Date field and choose the date from the pop-up calendar that QuickBooks displays.

5. **Use the Total box to identify the total value of the order received, if available.**

   QuickBooks will calculate this total for you by adding up the individual item costs, so you can wait until later.

6. **(Optional) Use a reference number.**

   You can use the Ref. No. field to provide a reference number. For example, you may want to reference the vendor's order number.

7. **(Optional) Provide a memo description.**

8. **Describe the items received.**

   Use the Items tab to identify the items that you've received. The Items tab of the Create Item Receipts window resembles and works like the Items tab of the Create Purchase Order window, as described (briefly) earlier in the chapter and (in some detail) in the preceding chapter. For this reason, I don't discuss how you enter, for example, item codes in the Item column. If you have questions about how the Items tab works, refer to one of the other appropriate chapter sections in this book. For example, you may want to refer to the discussion in Book III, Chapter 1.

9. **Describe any related expenses.**

   The Expenses tab of the Create Item Receipts window works like the Expenses tab of the Write Checks window. If you have questions about how the Expenses tab works, refer to the discussion of writing checks in Book III, Chapter 4.

10. **Click either the Save & Close or Save & New button to save the receipt item.**

    If you click the Save & Close button, QuickBooks saves your item receipt information and closes the Create Item Receipts window. If you click the Save & New button, QuickBooks saves the item receipt information and redisplays a fresh, clean, cleared version of the Create Item Receipts window. You can then use the window to describe the receipts of some other set of items.

That's about all you need to know to work with the Create Item Receipts window. Nevertheless, let me just quickly describe the half-dozen command buttons located at the bottom of the Create Item Receipts window that I haven't referenced in the earlier step discussions:

✦ **Select PO:** This command button displays the Open Purchase Orders dialog box. The Open Purchase Orders dialog box lists the purchase orders open for the selected vendor. By selecting a listed purchase order, you tell QuickBooks to fill out the Item tab with the information from that purchase order or purchase orders.

**Book III
Chapter 2**

Paying Vendors

✦ **Clear Qtys:** This button clears the received quantities shown on the Items tab if you've specified a purchase order. You can use this button to, in effect, start over (when you click this button it changes into the Receive All button, which accepts all items on the purchase order).

✦ **Show P.O.:** This button shows the selected purchase order.

✦ **Clear Splits:** This button erases any expense or item information that you've entered on the Expenses tab or Items tab. In effect, the Clear Splits button lets you start over in recording the receipt of some item or items.

✦ **Recalculate:** This button recalculates the total amount by using the information that you've entered onto the Expenses tab and the Items tab.

✦ **Clear:** This button clears all of the information that you've entered on the Create Item Receipts window, including the Expenses tab information, the Items tab information, and the vendor information shown at the top of the window.

✦ **Time:** This button opens the Select Time Period dialog box, shown in Figure 2-3, which you use to specify the date range of the work for which you're paying.

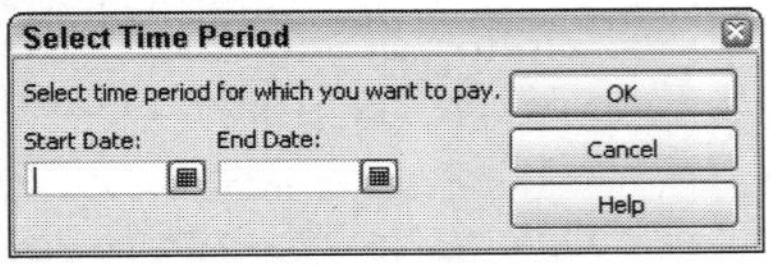

Figure 2-3:
The Select
Time Period
dialog box.

Simultaneously Recording the Receipt and the Bill

You can record a bill for items that you receive at the same time that you record the receipt of the items. You can do this simply by selecting the Bill Received check box that appears near the top of the Create Item Receipts window (as shown in Figure 2-2).

If you know that you're going to record a bill at the same time you record the receipt of items, you can also choose the Vendors➪Receive Items and Enter Bill command. In other words, rather than choosing the Receive Items command from the Vendors menu, you choose the Receive Items and Enter Bill command. When you do this, QuickBooks displays the Enter Bills window, shown in Figure 2-4. Essentially, the Enter Bills window is just another version of the Create Item Receipts window except that the Bill Received check box is already selected. To simultaneously record items that you've received and enter a bill, you follow the same steps as you do to record the receipt of the items.

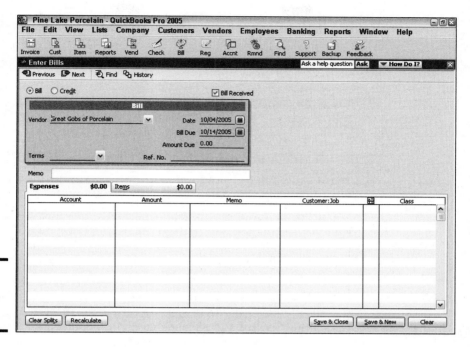

Figure 2-4:
The Enter
Bills
window.

One item worth noting about simultaneously recording bills and the receipt of items, however, is this: When you enter a bill, you probably need to be very precise about the charges of the vendor. For example, in all probability, you won't just pay for the ordered items. You may also pay certain shipping and handling fees. These amounts won't necessarily get recorded on the Items tab. They will probably be recorded on the Expenses tab.

Entering a Bill

If you told QuickBooks during the setup process that you want to track unpaid bills, also known as *accounts payable*, you can enter bills as you receive them. By doing this, QuickBooks keeps track of the unpaid bills that you need to pay.

Good, accurate recordkeeping of unpaid bills, or accounts payable, is essential if you want to do good accrual-basis accounting. As I discuss in Book I, Chapter 1, accrual-basis accounting produces more accurate financial statements.

If you haven't previously recorded item receipt

To enter a bill, you follow one of two sequences of steps. If you are entering a bill and the bill is for items of which you haven't previously recorded the receipt, you follow these steps:

1. **Choose the Vendors⇨Enter Bills command.**

   QuickBooks displays the Enter Bills window, shown in Figure 2-5. You'll use this window to describe the bills that you later need to pay.

2. **Use the Vendor drop-down list box to identify the vendor.**

3. **Use the Date, Bill Due, and Amount Due fields to describe the invoice date, the invoice due date, and the invoice amount.**

   Optionally, use the Terms drop-down list box to identify the payment terms and the Ref. No. box to identify the vendor's reference number. Next, if you want to, go ahead and provide a memo description for the bill by using the Memo box.

4. **Identify the expenses billed.**

   Use the Expenses tab of the Enter Bills window to identify the expenses that the bill represents. To identify expenses, you need to supply the account number that should be debited, the amount, and, optionally, the memo, customer:job, and class information. If you have questions about how the Expenses tab works, refer to the discussion in Book III, Chapter 4 about writing a check. The Expenses tab of the Write Checks window works the same way as the Expenses tab of the Enter Bills window.

5. **Identify the items billed in the Items tab.**

   Use the Items tab of the Enter Bills window to describe any items for which the vendor bills you. For example, use the Item column to identify the thing that you purchased. Then use the Qty, Cost, and Amount columns to identify what the item cost. You can also use the Customer: Job column if you are tracking bills by customers. If you have questions about how to work with the Items tab, know that the Items tab of the Enter Bills window works in the same manner as the Items tab of other QuickBooks windows. You can, for example, refer to the discussion of the Create Invoices window in Book III, Chapter 1.

The buttons at the bottom of the Enter Bills window — Select PO, Receive All, Show PO, Clear Splits, Recalculate, and Clear — work the same way as the similarly titled command buttons located at the bottom of the Create Item Receipts window discussed earlier in the chapter in the section "Recording the Receipt of Items."

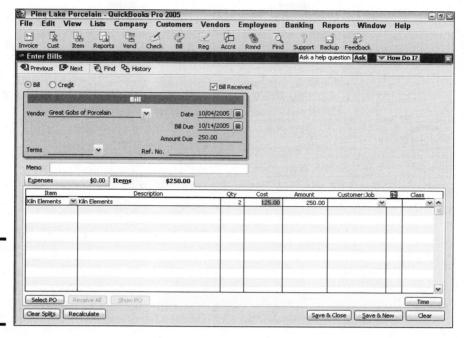

Figure 2-5:
The Enter
Bills
window.
Again.

If you have previously recorded item receipt

To enter a bill when you've already recorded the receipt of the item for
which the bill invoices you, follow these steps:

1. **Choose the Vendors⇨Enter Bill for Received Items command.**

QuickBooks displays the Select Item Receipt window, shown in Figure 2-6.

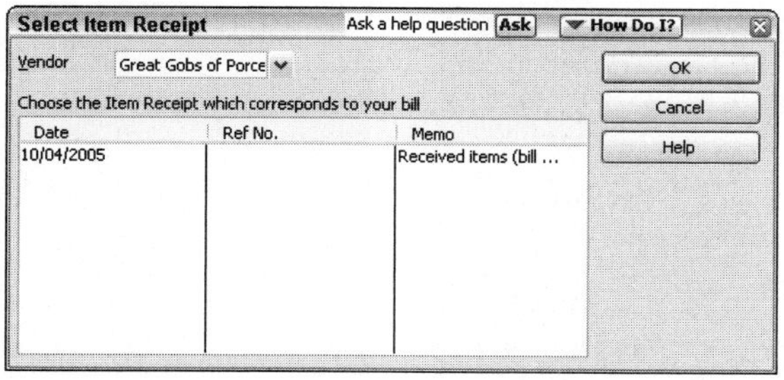

Figure 2-6:
The Select
Item
Receipt
dialog box.

2. **To identify the item receipt for which you are now recording a bill, select the vendor from the Vendor drop-down list box.**

   Then, when QuickBooks displays a list of item receipts for the vendor, click the item receipt that corresponds to your bill. Next, click OK. QuickBooks displays the Enter Bills window for the item. QuickBooks fills out much of the Enter Bills window by using the information from the item receipt, as shown in Figure 2-7.

   You may be able to skip Steps 3, 4, and 5 if your item receipt information correctly and completely fills the Enter Bills window.

3. **Use the Date, Bill Due, and Amount Due fields to describe the invoice date, the invoice due date, and the invoice amount.**

   Optionally, use the Terms drop-down list box to identify the payment terms and the Ref. No. box to identify the vendor's reference number. Next, if you want to, go ahead and provide a memo description for the bill by using the Memo box.

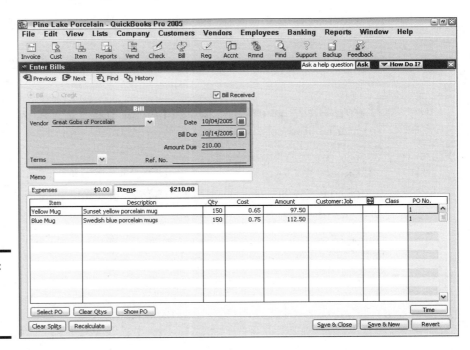

Figure 2-7:
The Enter Bills window. Yet again.

4. **Use the Expenses tab of the Enter Bills window to identify the expenses that the bill represents.**

   To identify expenses, you need to supply the account number that should be debited, the amount, and, optionally, the memo, customer:job, and class information. If you have questions about how the Expenses tab works, refer to the discussion in Book III, Chapter 4 about writing a check. The Expenses tab of the Write Checks window works the same way as the Expenses tab of the Enter Bills window.

5. **Use the Items tab of the Enter Bills window to describe any items for which the vendor bills you.**

   For example, use the Item column to identify the thing that you purchased. Then use the Qty, Cost, and Amount columns to identify what the item cost. You can also use the Customer:Job columns if you are tracking bills by customers. If you have questions about how to work with the Items tab, know that the Items tab of the Enter Bills window works in the same manner as the Items tab of other QuickBooks windows. You can, for example, refer to the discussion of the Create Invoices window in Book III, Chapter 1.

Recording a credit memo

You record credit memos from vendors by using the Enter Bills window, too. The only difference in recording a credit memo is that you mark the Credit button.

Paying Bills

If you use QuickBooks to keep track of the bills that you owe, you don't use the Write Checks window (described in Book III, Chapter 4) to record the bills that you want to pay. Rather, you tell QuickBooks to display a list of these unpaid bills that you've already recorded — and then you pick and choose which bills QuickBooks should pay and which bank account QuickBooks should use to write the check.

Follow these steps to pay bills in this manner:

1. **Choose the Vendors⇨Pay Bills command.**

   QuickBooks displays the Pay Bills window, shown in Figure 2-8. You use the Pay Bills window to describe the payment that you want to make.

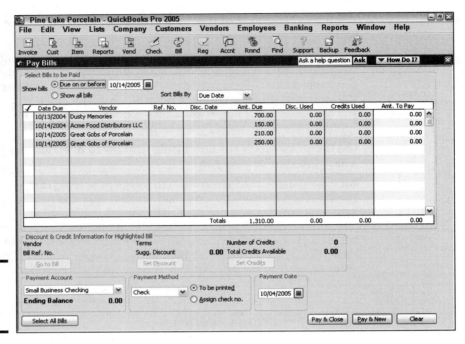

Figure 2-8:
The Pay
Bills
window.

2. Describe which bills you want to pay.

Use the Show Bills radio buttons at the top of the Pay Bills window to identify what you want to see. Select the Due On or Before radio button to only show bills that are due on or before the specified date. To specify the date, enter the date into the Due On or Before date box. To see a list of all the bills that you have to pay, select the Show All Bills radio button.

You can use the Sort Bills By drop-down list box to select the order that QuickBooks uses for listing your bills. For example, you can sort bills by due date, discount date, vendor, and amount due.

3. Select the bills that you want to pay.

To select bills that you want to pay, click the check column. The check column is the leftmost column in the list of unpaid bills — it's headed by a check mark. When you click the check column, QuickBooks marks the bill with a check mark. The check mark tells QuickBooks that you want to pay that bill. To deselect a bill, click the check column again. QuickBooks removes the check mark.

4. (Optional) Review a specific bill.

You can review detailed information about a specific bill by first clicking the bill to highlight it in the list and then by clicking the Go To Bill button. When you do this, QuickBooks displays the Enter Bills window with the bill information. To close the Enter Bills window, click the Close button.

5. Set the discount and credit.

If you click the Set Discount button, QuickBooks displays the Discount tab of the Discount and Credits window, as shown in Figure 2-9. You can use the Discount tab to enter a discount amount for the bill. If you enter a discount amount for the bill, you need to also enter the discount account. This is the account that gets credited for the reduction — the discount — in the amount that you need to pay.

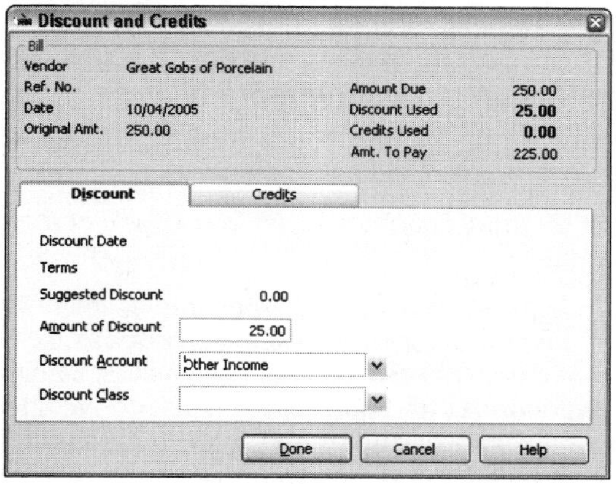

Figure 2-9:
The Discount tab of the Discount and Credits dialog box.

**Book III
Chapter 2**

Paying Vendors

If you click the Set Credits button, QuickBooks displays the Credits tab of the Discount and Credits dialog box, shown in Figure 2-10. The Credit tab lists any credit memos from this vendor. To apply a credit memo to the amount due a vendor, click the Set Credits button. QuickBooks marks applied credits by placing a check mark in the marked column.

When you complete your work with the Discounts and Credits dialog box, click the Done button to close the dialog box and return to the Pay Bills window.

Click the Clear button in the Discount and Credits dialog box to clear the applied credits shown on the Credits tab.

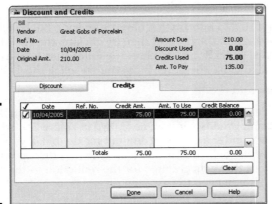

Figure 2-10:
The Credits
tab of the
Discount
and Credits
dialog box.

6. **Use the Payment Account drop-down list box to select the bank account to be used for making payments.**

   The ending balance for the bank account shows the Payment Account drop-down list box.

7. **Use the Payment Method drop-down list box to select the payment method.**

   If you want to pay your bills by check, for example, select Check. Assuming that you will print the checks in QuickBooks, select the To Be Printed radio button (otherwise, select the Assign Check No. radio button to have QuickBooks assign the next consecutive check number). You can also pay bills by other methods, such as by credit card and by online payment (if you are set up for online payment or online banking).

8. **Use the Payment Date drop-down list box to record the payment date that you want.**

   The payment date entry interacts with the payment method entry. The payment date that you set, for example, will affect when an online payment gets made. The payment date also corresponds to the check date that will be shown on printed checks.

9. **After you select the bills that you want to pay and describe how you want to pay them, you can click either the Pay & Close button or the Pay & New button to pay the selected bills.**

   If you click the Pay & Close button, QuickBooks records the payment transactions in the bank account to pay the selected bills. QuickBooks also closes the Pay Bills window. If you click the Pay & New button, QuickBooks does the same thing — but leaves the Pay Bills window open so that you can record another series of bill payments.

10. **Complete your task.**

You still need to print any unprinted checks necessary to pay bills if you are using checks to pay the bills. You also need to transmit any online payment instructions necessary to pay the bills if that's how you've chosen to pay the bills. If you are going to hand-write checks, you obviously need to hand-write the checks and then mail them out. In other words, all QuickBooks does at this point is record in the QuickBooks data file the payment transactions. It hasn't yet affected the transactions. You need to print the checks, send the online payment instructions, or hand-write the checks!

Reviewing the Other Vendor Menu Commands

In the preceding paragraphs of this chapter, I talk about the most important commands on the Vendor menu. Nevertheless, before I wrap up this little dog and pony show, I will quickly review for you the other commands and what they do.

The Vendor Navigator

The first two commands on the Vendors menu, Vendor Navigator and Vendor Detail Center, display windows of vendor-related information. For example, the Vendor Navigator window appears when you choose the Vendors➪Vendor Navigator command. Figure 2-11 shows this window.

The Vendor Navigator window includes a useful flowchart that describes how the various Vendors menu commands work together to record purchase orders, the receipt of items, and the payment of bills. The Vendor Navigator window also provides clickable hyperlinks that you can use to do things such as print checks, add a vendor to the Vendor List, and review the Vendor Detail Center.

If you're just getting started with QuickBooks and you find the whole process a little confusing, and perhaps more than a bit cumbersome, you may want to try working with the Vendor Navigator window. Sometimes, the little vendors flowchart (this appears in the upper-left quarter of the window) amounts to a pretty handy tool. Also, those clickable hyperlinks for doing common tasks can be kind of handy. In any event, the choice is yours.

The Vendor Detail Center

The Vendor Detail Center window, shown in Figure 2-12, displays detailed vendor information for the selected vendor. All you do is select the vendor for which you want to see detailed information from the Vendor Detail drop-down list box. The Vendor Detail Center shows a bunch of information for a vendor. This information all comes from the Vendor List, by the way.

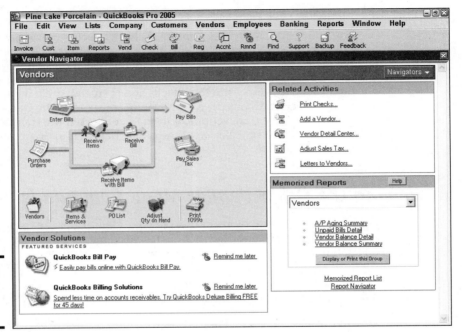

Figure 2-11:
The Vendor
Navigator
window.

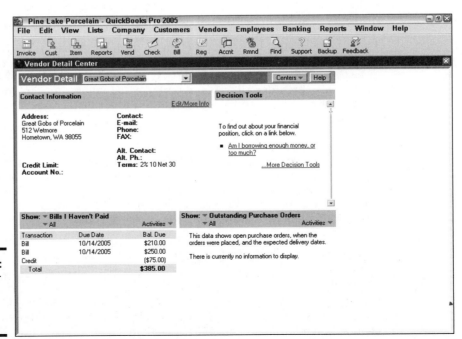

Figure 2-12:
The Vendor
Detail
Center
window.

If you are going to keep records of your vendors, including information such as their telephone numbers, about the best place to store that information in my humble opinion, is in the Vendor List. You have to maintain the Vendor List in order for QuickBooks to work. So why not also go to a little bit extra effort and keep all your vendor information there? If you adopt this approach, the Vendor Detail Center window is the window that you will use to quickly look up things such as the vendor's phone or fax number.

The Sales Tax Menu commands

The Sales Tax command displays a submenu of commands that pay sales tax amounts you've collected to the appropriate tax agency; adjust the sales tax liability due; and produce reports on the sales tax liability you owe, the sales tax revenue you've generated, and the sales tax codes you've set up.

To pay the sales taxes you owe, you simply choose the Vendors⇨Sales Tax⇨ Pay Sales Tax command. When QuickBooks displays the Pay Sales Tax dialog box (which lists the amounts you owe various sales tax collection agencies), you select the agencies you want to pay or click the Pay All Tax button. Quick-Books then records checks into the bank account register (see Chapter 4 of Book III for details about how to work with the bank register) and you print the checks in the usual way.

To adjust the amount that QuickBooks thinks you owe a sales tax collection agency, you can choose the Vendors⇨Sales Tax⇨Adjust Sales Tax Due command. When QuickBooks displays the Sales Tax Adjustment dialog box, select a sales tax agency from the Sales Tax Vendor box, an appropriate expense or income account from the Adjustment Account box, select as appropriate the Increase Sales Tax By or Decrease Sales Tax By buttons, and then enter the adjustment amount into the Amount box.

To print one of the sales tax reports, simply select the command that corresponds with the report. For example, to print the Sales Tax Liability report, choose the Vendors⇨Sales Tax⇨Sales Tax Liability command.

Print 1099s

The Print 1099s command displays the Printing 1099-MISC and 1096 Forms dialog box, shown in Figure 2-13, which lets you print 1099-MISC forms for a selected calendar year. You can select the year for which you need to print 1099 forms by selecting a date range description from the drop-down list box. Initially, for example, the drop-down list box shows Last Calendar Year. Alternatively, you can use the From and To boxes to specify the starting and ending point for the year. After you identify the year for which you want to print 1099 forms, click OK. QuickBooks then creates 1099 forms for any vendors who need them, provided that your 1099 preferences are set up correctly and the vendor is marked as a 1099 recipient in the Vendor List.

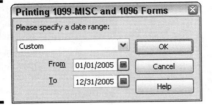

You typically send 1099 forms to vendors to whom you pay more than $600 in a year. You can control the actual threshold amount — it varies from year to year because of inflation and type of payment — by choosing the Edit⇨ Preferences command, clicking the Tax 1099 icon, and then clicking the Company Preferences tab. For more information about how to set tax 1099 preferences, refer to Book II, Chapter 3.

Vendor List

The Vendors⇨Vendor List command displays the Vendor List window, shown in Figure 2-14. The Vendor List window shows a complete list of all the vendors that you have set up. The Vendor List window also provides buttons that you can use to make changes to the Vendor List. Book II, Chapter 2 describes how to set up and work with the Vendor List, also known as the *Vendor Master File.*

Item List

The Vendors⇨Item command displays the Item List window. You can read more about the Item List window in Book III, Chapter 3.

Purchase Orders List

The Vendors⇨Purchase Orders List command displays a list of the open purchase orders. You can use this command to see which purchase orders are open and yet unfilled. Figure 2-15 shows the Purchase Orders List window.

Online Vendor Services

The Vendor Services command displays a submenu with other commands — typically the Purchase Checks and Forms command and Pay Bills Online command. (You may not see both commands on your menu.) The Purchase Checks and Forms command displays the Checks & Supplies window, which describes how you can order check forms and other forms from Intuit. The Pay Bills Online command displays the Pay Bills window, which describes how to pay bills online.

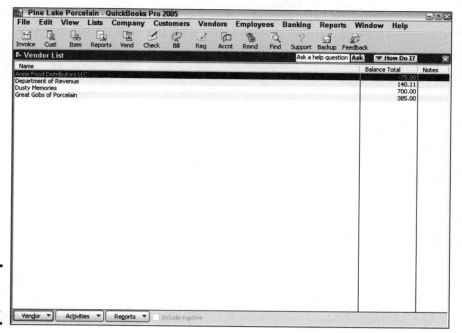

Figure 2-14:
The Vendor List window.

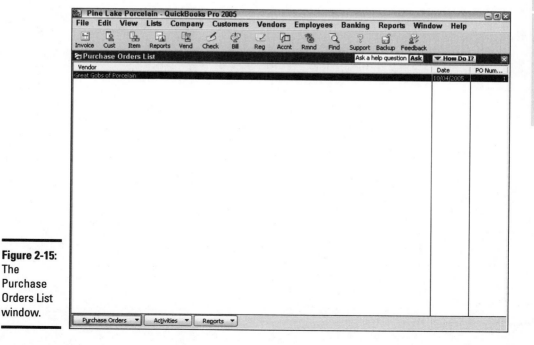

Figure 2-15:
The Purchase Orders List window.

Chapter 3: Tracking Inventory and Items

In This Chapter

✔ **Looking at your Item list**

✔ **Using the Item List window**

✔ **Adding items to the Item list**

✔ **Editing items**

✔ **Adjusting physical counts and inventory values**

✔ **Adjusting prices and price levels**

✔ **Inventory in a manufacturing firm**

*I*f you've worked with QuickBooks, you won't be surprised to hear that the Item list is a key piece of your QuickBooks accounting system. The Item list identifies each of the things that you sell. The Item list also identifies other things that appear on your invoices and — if you use them — on your purchase orders.

In this chapter, I talk about how you work with the QuickBooks Item list: more specifically, how you look at and use the information on the Item list. I explain how to add information to the list and how to edit information already on the list. What's more, I talk about three accounting tasks that are related to your Item list: adjusting physical inventory accounts for inventory shrinkage or spoilage; adjusting price levels of your inventory items; and if you manufacture inventory, how the new version of QuickBooks handles manufactured goods.

Looking at Your Item List

QuickBooks provides a bunch of different ways to see the information that you've stored in your Item list. You may already know some of this stuff if you've worked with QuickBooks a bit. Some of it may be new to you. In any case, the next sections review the half-dozen ways that you can see the items on your Item list.

Using the Item column

The Item column that appears in many of the windows in QuickBooks lets you see a drop-down list of items. Figure 3-1, for example, shows the Item drop-down list box in the Create Invoices window (which is actually defying gravity and "dropping" up). You use the Item column and the individual rows of the Item column to identify the items that appear on an invoice.

One important point to consider as you look at the Item column and Item drop-down list box in Figure 3-1 is space. Note that the Item drop-down list box is pretty narrow. Note also that the Item drop-down list box in Figure 3-1 provides two pieces of information: the item code (the left column) and the item description. The item description — if the description is lengthy — is cut off. You'll want to remember this seemingly trivial but important point as you work with your Item file. You want descriptive item codes and if possible, brief descriptions.

I'm using pretty self-explanatory item codes in this reference, as you can see from Figure 3-1. In real life, your codes may be far more cryptic.

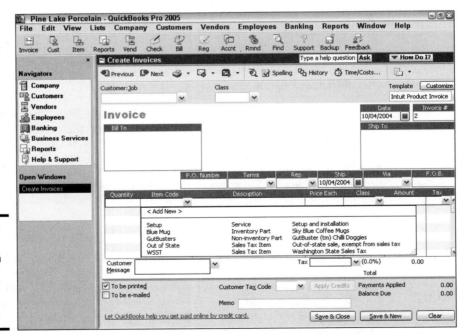

Figure 3-1:
The Item drop-down list box on the Create Invoices window.

Using the Item List window

If you choose the Lists⇨Item List command, QuickBooks displays the Item List window, as shown in Figure 3-2. The Item List window identifies the item code or name, the description, the type of item (I talk more about this in the next section of the chapter), the account that gets credited when you sell some of the items, and inventory stocking and pricing information (if you supply that).

The Item list provides a good way to quickly see what items you can put on invoices and purchase orders. The Item list also provides a quick and convenient way to see the stocking levels and prices.

If you want more information about an item shown in the Item List window, you can double-click the item. When you double-click the item, QuickBooks displays the Edit Item window, as shown in Figure 3-3. Essentially, the Edit Item window displays all of the information available about a particular item. You can use the Edit Item window to change bits of item information. Later in this chapter in the section, "Editing Items," I describe how to do this.

**Book III
Chapter 3**

Tracking Inventory and Items

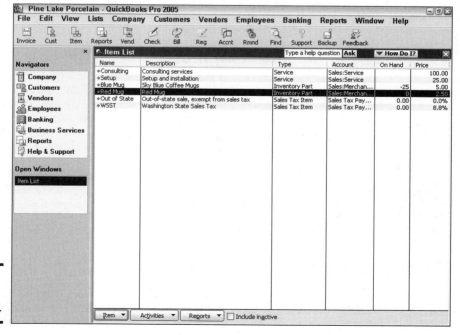

Figure 3-2:
The Item
List window.

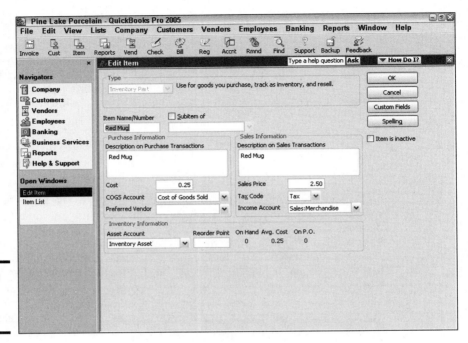

Figure 3-3:
The Edit
Item
window.

Using the inventory reports

I need to mention one other thing because it's so darn useful. As you would expect, QuickBooks supplies several interesting, useful inventory reports. If you choose the Reports➪Inventory command, for example, QuickBooks displays a submenu of inventory reports. The submenu provides a report that gives inventory evaluations, inventory stock levels, and a work sheet that you can use to go out and physically count the inventory on store shelves or in the warehouse.

Book IV, Chapter 2 describes how you produce reports in QuickBooks and how you customize those reports. If you want to find out more about reports and report customization, refer there.

Adding Items to the Item List

You can add a bunch of different types of items to the Item list. Remember that, as noted in the early paragraphs of this chapter, the Item list stores descriptions of anything that you stick on an invoice or purchase order.

If you think about this for a minute, you realize that you have different types of items. For example, if you are a retailer, the inventory that you sell may appear on an invoice. If you provide discounts to different sorts of customers, discounts may appear on an invoice as a line item. If you are in a state that taxes sales, sales tax appears as a line item on an invoice.

Different items look and work differently. For this reason, you describe different items in a different manner. You describe an inventory item that may appear on an invoice differently from a sales tax that you are required to charge.

Given this disparity, I first describe the general process for adding an item to the Item list. After you know the big picture stuff, I talk individually about each of the items that appear on the Item list. Sound okay? I'll get started.

Basic steps for adding an item

To add an item to your Item list, follow these steps:

1. **Choose the Lists⇨Item List command.**

QuickBooks displays the Item List window (an example of which appears in Figure 3-2).

2. **To display the Item menu, click the Item button, which appears in the lower-left corner of the Item List window.**

QuickBooks displays the Item menu.

3. **Choose the New command.**

This tells QuickBooks to display the New Item window, as shown in Figure 3-4.

4. **Use the boxes of the New Item window to describe the item that you want to add.**

Your first step is to identify the type of item that you want to add. Based on the type of item, QuickBooks supplies other boxes that you use to describe the item. (I go into more detail about this in the following paragraphs, so don't get freaked out — yet.)

5. **Save the item.**

After you use the boxes in the New Item window to describe the item that you want to add, click OK. QuickBooks adds the item that you just described to the Item list.

The step-by-step approach described in the preceding paragraphs is the conventional way to add an item, but you can also add items on the fly. For example, if you are in the Create Invoices window or in the Create Purchase Orders window, you can open the Item drop-down list box and select Add New Entry from the list. When you do this, QuickBooks displays the New Item window, as shown in Figure 3-4. You then use the New Item window to add the item in the same manner discussed here.

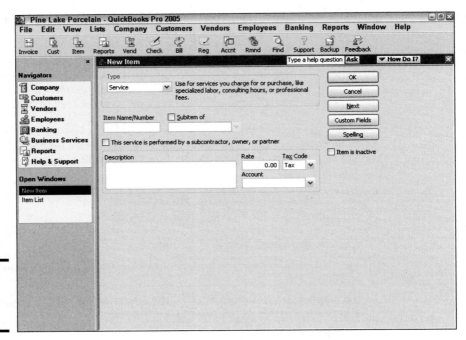

Figure 3-4:
The New
Item
window.

Adding a service item

You use service items to purchase or bill for items that represent service. For example, I am a CPA in Redmond, Washington. One of the things that I do is prepare tax returns for individuals and businesses. When I bill a client for preparing his or her tax return, the line item that appears on the invoice for Tax Return Preparation is a service item.

In your business, you probably have service items, too. For example, a health care provider, such as a dentist or doctor, provides treatment or performs procedures. These activities represent services.

Even retailers and contractors — businesses that you typically think of as selling tangible physical goods — often sell services. For example, a retailer may gift-wrap a purchase, which is a service. A contractor may provide services such as painting or cleanup.

To add a service item, display the New Item window (refer to Figure 3-4). When QuickBooks displays the New Item window, select Service from the Type drop-down list box. Then use the Item Name/Number box to give the service a brief code or name. If the service is a subitem, select the Subitem Of check box and identify the parent item.

Select the This Service Is Performed by a Subcontractor, Owner, or Partner check box if the service is provided by, as the window suggests, a subcontractor, owner, or partner. You indicate which services are performed by subcontractors, owners, and partners because these parties are subject to different tax accounting rules.

Finally, use the Description box to describe the service. Your description appears on invoices and purchase orders, so you want to be thoughtful here. Use the Rate box to describe the price or rate per unit of service. Use the Tax Code box to indicate whether the service is taxable. Finally, use the Account box to identify which Income account should be credited when the item is sold to some customer, client, or patient.

Adding an inventory item

Inventory items are those items that appear on invoices and purchase orders and represent physical goods that you buy, hold, and sell. For example, if you are a retailer, all that stuff that is sitting out on the shelves of your store represents inventory. If you are a manufacturer, the raw materials that you buy and then use to assemble your products represent inventory.

To set up an inventory part, display the New Item window. When QuickBooks displays the window, select Inventory Part from the Type drop-down list box. QuickBooks then displays the Inventory Part version of the New Item window, as shown in Figure 3-5.

Use the Item Name/Number box to provide a descriptive but brief code or name for the item. If the item is a subitem of some other parent item, select the Subitem Of check box and then identify the parent item by using the Subitem Of text box.

The Purchase Information and Sales Information boxes let you describe the information that will appear on purchase orders and invoices. The Description on Purchase Transactions box in the Purchase Information area, for example, lets you provide the text that QuickBooks writes on purchase orders. You can also guess at the purchase cost by using the Cost text box. Specify the Cost of Goods Sold account that should be debited when this item is sold by using the COGS Account drop-down list box and identify the preferred vendor for purchases of this item by using the Preferred Vendor box.

The Sales Information boxes provide the information that QuickBooks needs to correctly include the item on an invoice. The Description On Sales Transactions box provides a space that you can use to supply the description that QuickBooks should use for this item on your invoice. The Sales Price box lets you provide your price for the item. If you're subject to sales tax, you will see (and should use!) the Tax Code drop-down list box to specify whether the item is taxable or non-taxable for sales tax purposes. Finally, the Income Account drop-down list box lets you specify which income account should be credited when this item is sold.

**Book III
Chapter 3**

**Tracking Inventory
and Items**

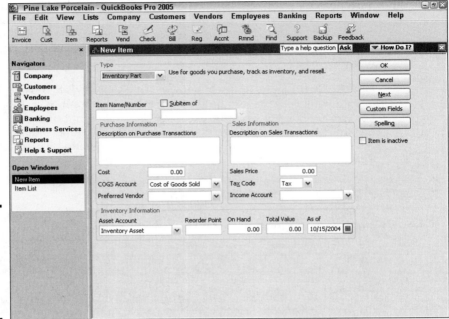

Figure 3-5:
The
Inventory
Part version
of the New
Item
window.

If you're confused about seeing two Account drop-down list boxes on the Inventory Part version of the New Item window, keep in mind that when you sell an item, you need to track the income by crediting an income account and the cost of goods sold by debiting the cost of goods sold account.

Use the Inventory Information boxes to describe how QuickBooks should handle inventory tracking for the item. For example, use the Asset Account drop-down list box to specify which account QuickBooks should use to track the dollar investment in this item. Typically, you use the Inventory Asset account. However, you can conceivably use some other asset account. Use the Reorder Point box to identify the inventory stocking level at which you want QuickBooks to alert you to the need to reorder the item. If you have inventory on hand for this item — and it's very suspicious that you would — enter the quantity that you have on hand and the value that you have on hand by using the On Hand box and the Total Value boxes. You need to also specify the date as of which your quantity and value information is correct by using the As Of box.

You really shouldn't be entering inventory balances for an inventory item when you set it up on the Item list. You should be entering or changing inventory quantities and values when you purchase the inventory (recorded with the Create Purchase Orders window or the Write Checks window) and when you sell the inventory (typically recorded with the Create Invoices window or the Sales Receipts window). If you enter a quantity other than zero or a total value other than zero when using the New Item window, you also need to make a journal entry to record the other half of the transaction. If this "other half" business sounds complicated, just trust me: You should not be entering quantity or value information in this window. If you do understand this "other half" business that I'm referring to, you should know better than to enter quantity or value information in the New Item window!

You can click the Spelling button to check the spelling of words and phrases that you've entered in the New Item window. You can also click the Next button to save the information that you've entered for an item and redisplay the New Item window so you can add another item.

Adding a non-inventory part

To add a non-inventory part — which is a tangible good that you sell but for which you don't track inventory — display the New Item window and select Non-Inventory Part in the Type drop-down list box. When QuickBooks displays the Non-Inventory Part version of the New Item window, as shown in Figure 3-6, give the non-inventory part a name or code by using the Item Name/Number box. If the new item is a subitem, select the Subitem Of check box. Then identify the parent item by using the Subitem Of text box. Use the Description box to provide the description that should go on invoices that bill for this non-inventory part. Obviously, you enter the price into the Price box. Use the Tax Code box to identify whether the item is subject to sales tax. Finally, use the Account drop-down list box to identify the income account that should be credited for sales of this non-inventory part.

Note the check box labeled This Item Is Purchased for and Sold to a Specific Customer:Job. If you select that check box, QuickBooks displays a slightly different version of the Non-Inventory Part window, as shown in Figure 3-7. This version of the Non-Inventory Part New Item window includes Purchase Information and Sales Information areas that work the same way as the Purchase Information and Sales Information areas supplied by the regular Inventory Part version of the New Item window. (Refer to Figure 3-5 and the discussion of Figure 3-5 earlier in the chapter.)

Book III Chapter 3

Tracking Inventory and Items

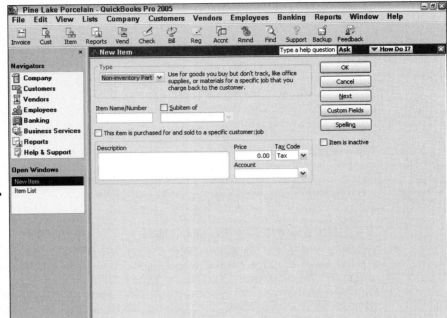

Figure 3-6:
The regular Non-inventory Part version of the New Item window.

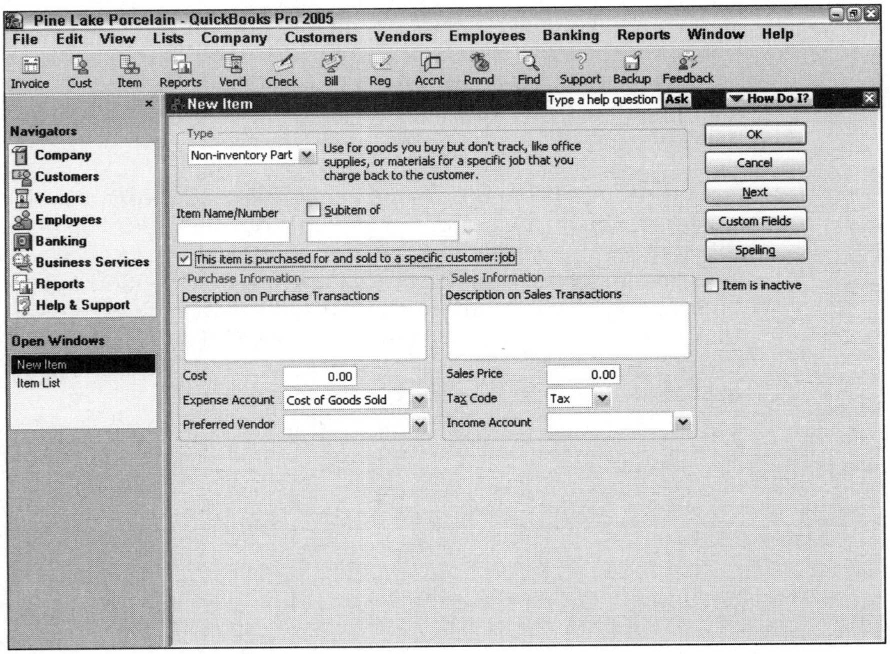

Figure 3-7:
The kooky Non-inventory Part version of the New Item window.

Adding an other charge item

An *other charge item* is an item that you use to purchase or bill for things such as miscellaneous labor or services, materials that you aren't tracking as inventory, and special charges, such as for delivery or setup or rush jobs.

To set up an other charge item, display the New Item window and select Other Charge from the Type drop-down list box. When you do, QuickBooks displays the Other Charge version of the New Item window, as shown in Figure 3-8. To finish setting up your other charge item, give the charge a name or code or abbreviation by using the Item Name/Number box. If the other charge item is a subitem, select the Subitem Of check box and then identify the parent item by using the Subitem Of text box. Obviously, you use the Description box to provide a description of the charge (remember that this description will appear on your invoices). Then use the Amount or % box to identify how the charge gets calculated or billed. Use the Tax Code drop-down list box to identify the charge as subject to sales tax — or not subject to sales tax. Use the Account drop-down list box to identify the income account that should be credited when you bill for this other charge.

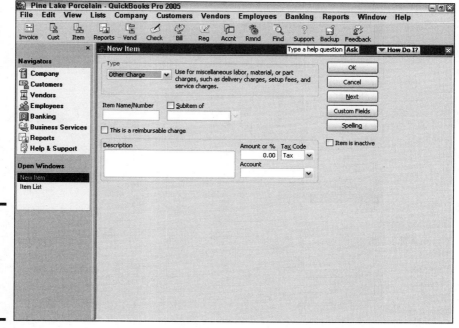

Figure 3-8:
The Other Charge version of the New Item window.

If you select the This Is a Reimbursable Charge check box, QuickBooks adds a second set of boxes to the New Item window. One set of boxes is labeled Purchase Information and provides information that goes on purchase orders or is used to record purchases and purchase orders. The other set of boxes is labeled Sales Information and goes on invoices and sales receipts to record the actual sale or billing for the other charge.

If you want to enter an other charge that should be calculated as a percentage, you must enter the % symbol in the Amount or % box. For example, if you want to include an other charge item on invoices that equals 25 percent of the previous item on the invoice, enter **25%** into the Amount or % box.

Adding a subtotal item

If your purchase order, sales receipt, or invoice will include a subtotal line item, you need to create a subtotal item in your Item list. To do this, display the New Item window and select Subtotal from the drop-down list box. Next, give the subtotal item a name or abbreviation and use the Description box to describe the subtotal. Figure 3-9 shows the Subtotal version of the New Item window.

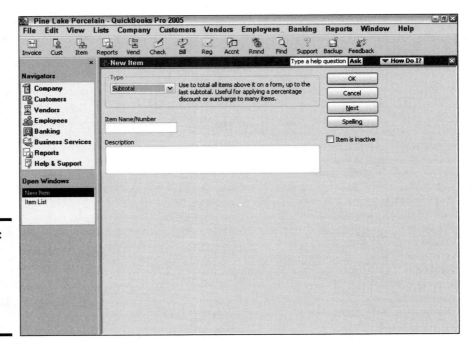

Figure 3-9:
The Subtotal version of the New Item window.

If you're using other charge items that are calculated as a percentage or discount items that are calculated as a percentage, you almost certainly need a subtotal item. An other charge that is calculated as a percentage would typically be calculated as a percentage of a subtotal item. Similarly, a discount item that's calculated as a percentage would be calculated as a percentage of a subtotal item.

Adding a group item

A *group item* lets you more easily invoice customers when, from the customer's perspective, he or she is buying a single item, but from your perspective, you are actually selling several items. This definition sounds curious at first, but let me give you a quick example. Suppose that you are a florist and do a booming business on Valentine's Day. Your best-selling items may be red roses and pretty crystal vases. But you probably don't sell individual roses and individual vases. What you actually sell is a dozen roses and a single vase. Although you want to individually track purchases of dozens of red roses and individual crystal vases on your purchase orders, on your invoices to customers, you want to bill for "a dozen red roses and a crystal vase."

At the end of the chapter, I describe another item type, inventory assembly, that works similarly to the group item type. The inventory assembly item type is for manufacturers.

If that example doesn't make sense, imagine a more complex floral arrangement including the dozen red roses, a crystal vase, baby's breath, flower preservative, tissue paper wrapping, ribbon, a box, and so forth. In this case, do you really want an invoice that shows perhaps twenty different items? Or do you want an invoice that shows a single item: a dozen red roses and a crystal vase? This is why you create group items. A group item lets you create a single item that you use on invoices. However, this group item actually combines a bunch of individual items that you are probably using on your purchase orders.

To create a group item, display the New Item window and select Group from the Type drop-down list box. When QuickBooks displays the group version of the New Item window, use the Group Name/Number box to give the group item a name or code, as shown in Figure 3-10. Use the Description box to give the group item an appropriate description. Use the Item, Description, and Qty columns at the bottom of the Group version of the New Item window to identify the individual items and item quantities that combine to make a group.

Adding a discount item

A *discount item* subtracts either a fixed amount or a percentage from a subtotal. To set up a discount item, display the New Item window. Next, select the Discount entry from the Type drop-down list box. When you do, QuickBooks displays the Discount version of the New Item window, as shown in Figure 3-11.

**Book III
Chapter 3**

**Tracking Inventory
and Items**

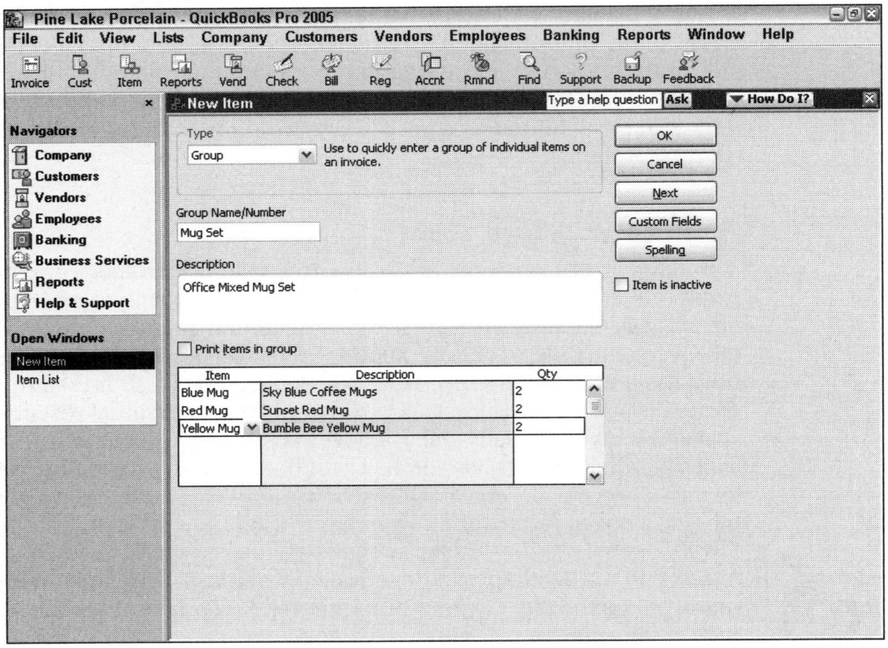

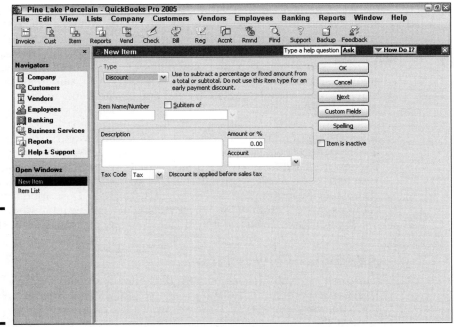

Figure 3-10:
The Group version of the New Item window.

Figure 3-11:
The Discount version of the New Item window.

To set up your discount item, enter a name or abbreviation for the discount into the Item Name/Number box. If the discount item is a subitem, select the Subitem Of check box and then identify the parent item by using the Subitem Of text box. Typically, you will want to describe the discount by using the Description box. Enter the amount of the discount into the Amount or % box as either a dollar amount or as a percentage. If you do enter the discount as a percentage, be sure to include the percentage symbol. Use the Account drop-down list box to specify which account gets debited for the discount. Finally, use the Tax Code drop-down list box to indicate whether the discount is applied before sales tax. (In other words, indicate whether the discount is subject to sales tax.)

If you're going to set up a discount item that calculates the discount as a percentage, you probably also need to have a subtotal item. Then, on your invoices, follow the subtotal item with the discount item. In this manner, you can easily calculate the discount percentage by looking at the subtotal amount.

Adding a payment item

If you sometimes accept payments when you invoice a customer, you can create a payment item and then add the payment item to the bottom of the invoice. By doing this, the invoice and the payment amount and the net amount due all show on the same document. That's pretty cool.

To set up a payment item, display the New Item window and select Payment from the drop-down list box. Use the Item Name/Number box to give the payment item a code or name such as "payment." Use the Description box to provide a nice description for the payment. (No kidding, you may want to include the phrase "thank you" as part of the payment description. For example, how about something such as "Payment . . . thank you!") Use the Payment Method drop-down list box to identify the method of payment: American Express, cash, Discover, Master Card, or Visa — if that's appropriate. Finally, use the radio buttons — Group with Other Undeposited Funds and Deposit To — to identify what happens to the money received as part of the payment. If you indicate that the money is deposited, you should select the correct bank account from the Deposit To drop-down list box. Figure 3-12 shows an example of a Payment version of the New Item window.

**Book III
Chapter 3**

Tracking Inventory and Items

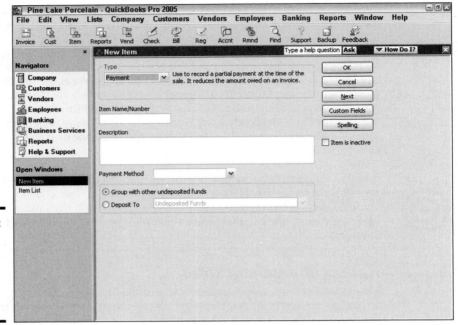

Figure 3-12:
The
Payment
version of
the New
Item
window.

Adding a sales tax item

If you sell items that are subject to sales tax, you need to include line items on your invoices that charge for and track these sales taxes. To do this, you need to create sales tax items. To create a sales tax item, display the New Item window and select Sales Tax Item from the Type drop-down list box. When you do, QuickBooks displays the Sales Tax version of the New Item window, shown in Figure 3-13. Use the Tax Name box to identify or provide an abbreviation for the sales tax. Use the Description box to give the sales tax a description. Finally, use the Tax Rate (%) box to identify the sales tax rate and the Tax Agency box to identify the tax agency that you will pay. For example, Figure 3-13 shows how to set up the Washington state sales tax. This sales tax is 8.8 percent. The tax agency to which sales tax receipts are remitted is the Department of Revenue.

Setting up a sales tax group

In many jurisdictions, although businesses may charge a single sales tax on sales, the sales tax actually gets distributed to several different tax agencies. For example, a firm may be required to charge a 9 percent sales tax. But perhaps 1 percent goes to the local city government. Perhaps another 2 percent goes to the county government. And maybe the remaining 6 percent goes to the state government. In this case, you can set up a sales tax group, which appears as a single line item invoice. However, the sales tax group actually is made up of individual tax items.

To add a sales tax group, display the New Item window and select Sales Tax Group from the Type drop-down list box, as shown in Figure 3-14. Enter a name or an abbreviation for the sales tax into the Group Name/Number box. Provide an appropriate description by using the Description box. Then, use the Tax Item column to identify the individual tax items that comprise the sales tax group. Note that you already need to have set up the tax items that you want to add to the sales tax group.

Adding custom fields to items

If you've worked with the New Item window much or if you've paid particularly close attention to the figures shown in the last few pages of this chapter, you may have noticed the Custom Fields command button that appears on many (although not all) of the New Item windows. (See Figure 3-12.)

The Custom Fields button enables you to add your own custom fields to the Item list. To add a custom field, click the Custom Fields button. When you do, QuickBooks displays a Message box and then a small dialog box labeled Custom Fields for {item}, where {item} actually names the item.

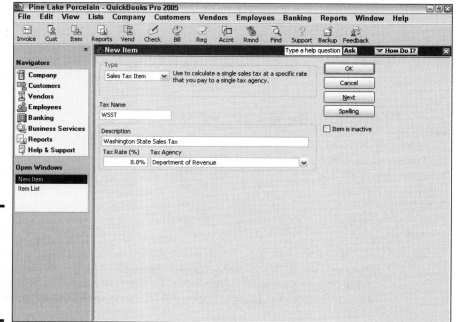

Figure 3-13:
The New Item window for recording a sales tax item.

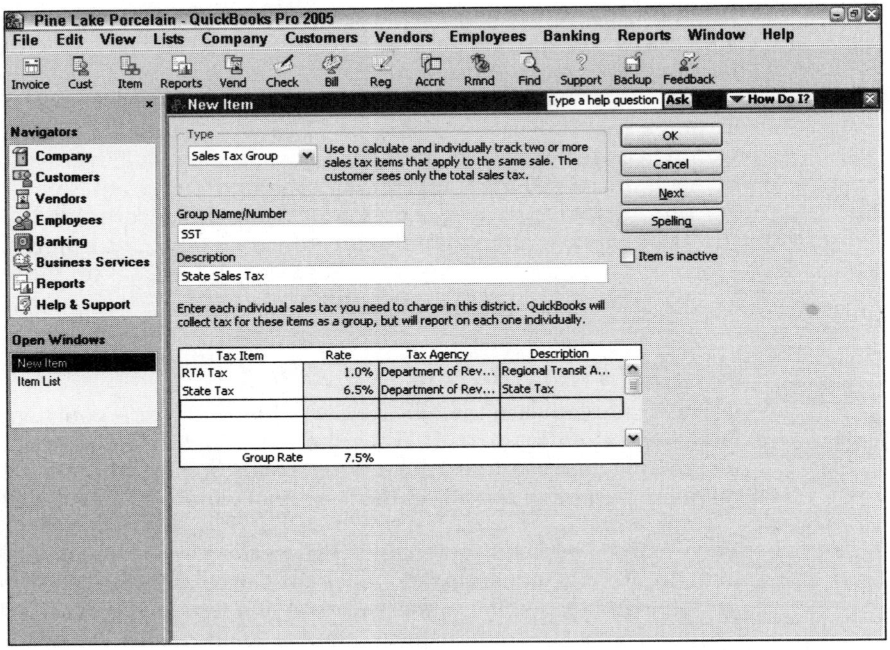

Figure 3-14:
The Sales
Tax Group
item.

When QuickBooks displays the Custom Fields for {item} dialog box, click the
Define Fields button. QuickBooks then displays the Define Custom Fields for
Items dialog box, as shown in Figure 3-15. To add a custom field for the item,
select the Use check box and then use the Label box to give a name to the
field. For example, if you want to add a custom field for Insured Value, you
can select the Use check box and then enter the label **Insured Value**.

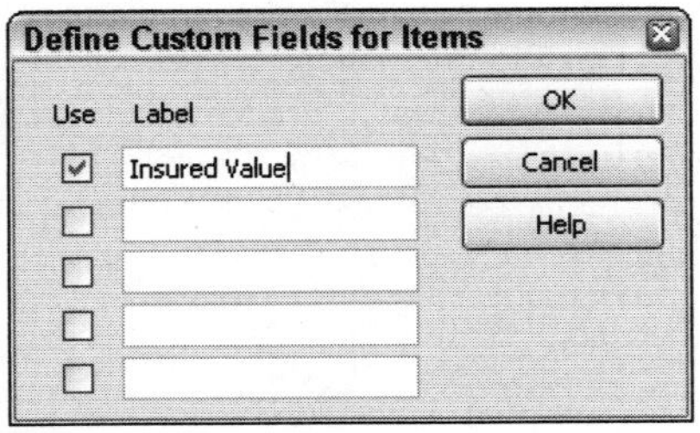

Figure 3-15:
The Define
Custom
Fields for
Items dialog
box.

When you click OK, QuickBooks redisplays the Custom Fields for {item}
dialog box, as shown in Figure 3-16. The Custom Fields for {item} dialog box
now shows the new custom field — in this example, Insured Value.

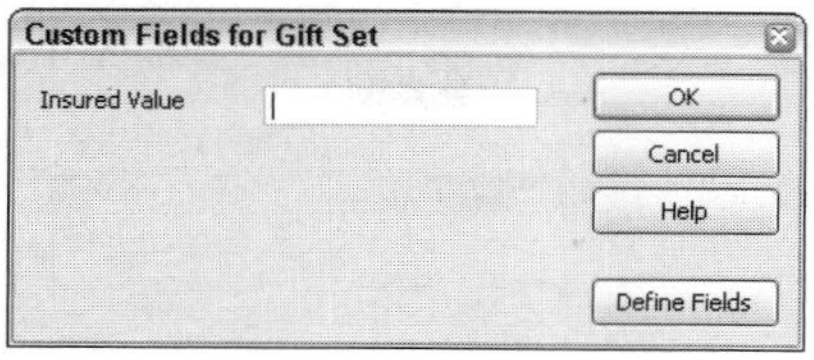

Figure 3-16:
The Custom
Fields for
{item} dialog
box.

Custom Fields for Gift Set

Insured Value		OK
		Cancel
		Help
		Define Fields

Note that custom fields are available for all items. Also note that you see custom fields for items by displaying the item's information in the New Item window or the Edit Item window and then by clicking the Custom Fields button.

Editing Items

You can change item information. To do so, display the Item List window and then double-click the item. When you do this, QuickBooks displays the Edit Item window. The Edit Item window resembles the New Item window. The difference is that the Edit Item window is already filled in with the item information. To change some bit of item information, edit the contents of the field with the information that needs to be updated. Click OK to save your changes.

Adjusting Physical Counts and Inventory Values

Inventory shrinkage, spoilage, and, unfortunately, theft all combine to reduce the inventory that you physically have. In order to record these inventory reductions, you'll periodically need to physically count your inventory and then update your QuickBooks records with the results of your physical counts.

I don't spend any time in this book talking about approaches to providing physical counts; you probably have better ideas than I do about how to do that. You presumably know what works best in your business. However, I can tell you that in order to record your physical count information in Quick-Books, you need to use a special tool. Specifically, you need to use the Adjust Quantity/Value on Hand command. This command is available to you in two different places. If you display the Item list, click the Activities button (which appears at the bottom of the Item List window) and choose the Adjust Quantity/Value on Hand command. You can also choose the Vendors➪ Inventory Activities➪Adjust Quantity/Value on Hand command. Choosing either command displays the Adjust Quantity/Value on Hand window, shown in Figure 3-17.

**Book III
Chapter 3**

**Tracking Inventory
and Items**

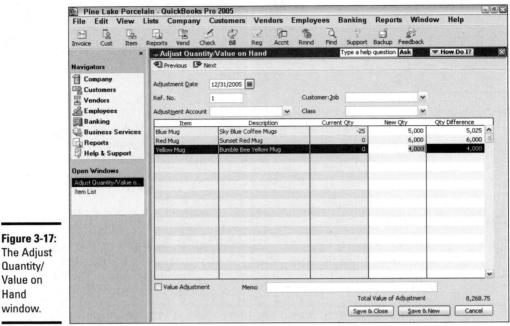

Figure 3-17:
The Adjust
Quantity/
Value on
Hand
window.

To use the Adjust Quantity/Value on Hand window, follow these steps:

1. **Use the Adjustment Date box to record the date of your physical count.**

In other words, you want to adjust your quantities as of the day you took or completed the physical inventory count.

2. **Use the Adjustment Account drop-down list box to identify the expense account that you want to use to track your inventory shrinkage expense.**

3. **(Optional) Identify the customer:job and class.**

If it's appropriate, and in many cases it won't be, use the Customer:Job box to identify the customer:job associated with this inventory shrinkage. In a similar fashion, if appropriate, use the Class box to identify the class that you want to use for tracking this inventory shrinkage.

4. **Supply the correct inventory quantities.**

The Item, Description, and Current Qty columns of the Adjust Quantities/ Value on Hand window identify the inventory items that you are holding and the current quantity counts. Use the New Qty column to provide the correct physical count quantity of the item. After you've entered the new quantity, QuickBooks calculates the quantity difference and shows this value in the Qty Difference column.

You can actually enter a value into either the New Qty column or the Qty Difference column. QuickBooks calculates the other quantity by using the current quantity information that you supply. For example, if you enter the new quantity, QuickBooks calculates the quantity difference by subtracting the new quantity from the current quantity. If you enter the quantity difference, QuickBooks calculates the new quantity by adjusting the current quantity for the quantity difference.

5. **Adjust the value.**

If you select the Value Adjustment check box, QuickBooks displays an expanded version of the Adjust Quantity/Value on Hand window, as shown in Figure 3-18. This window lets you enter both the correct physical count quantity and the updated value for the inventory item. You enter the physical count quantity, obviously, in the New Qty column. You enter the new updated value in the New Value column. You will probably use this version of the Adjust Quantity/Value on Hand window only if you're using a lower-of-cost or market inventory valuation method. For example, both financial accounting standards and tax accounting rules allow you to mark down your inventory to the lower of its original cost or its fair market value. If you were doing this — and how you do this is beyond the scope of this book — you would enter the new inventory value into the New Value column.

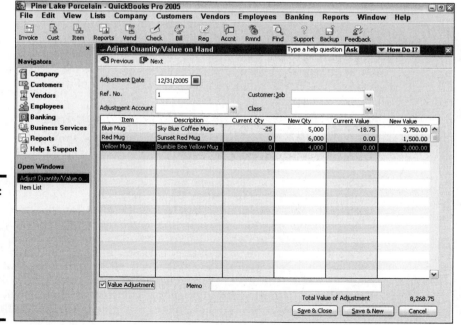

Figure 3-18:
The expanded version of the Adjust Quantity/ Value on Hand window.

Essentially, using the lower-of-cost or market inventory evaluation method just means you do what it says. You keep your inventory valued at either its original cost or, if its value is less than its original cost, at its new value. Obviously, assessing the value of your inventory is a little tricky. But if you have questions, you can ask your CPA for help. One thing to keep in mind, however, is that you can't go changing your accounting methods willy-nilly without permission from the Internal Revenue Service. And changing your inventory valuation method from cost, say, to lower-of-cost or market is a change in accounting method.

6. **Provide a memo description.**

   If you want to further describe the quantity or value adjustment, use the Memo box for this purpose. For example, you may want to reference the physical count worksheets, the people performing the physical count, or the documentation that explains the valuation adjustment.

7. **Save the adjustment.**

   After you have used the Adjust Quantity/Value on Hand window to describe the quantity changes or value changes in your inventory, click either the Save & Close button or the Save & New button to save the adjustment transaction. As you probably know at this point in your life, Save & Close saves the transaction and closes the window. Save & New saves the transaction but leaves the window open in case you want to make additional changes.

Adjusting Prices and Price Levels

QuickBooks provides a couple of handy commands and tools that you can use to change the prices that you charge customers for your products and services. In the following sections, I describe both of these handy aids.

Using the Change Item Prices command

The Change Item Prices command, which appears on the Customers menu, displays the Change Item Prices window, as shown in Figure 3-19. This window lets you change prices of a bunch of different items at one time by an amount or percentage. To use the Change Item Prices command, first mark the items whose prices you want to change. Do this by clicking the Check Mark column. Next use the By (Amount or %) box to specify the dollar amount or the percentage amount by which you want to change the price. For example, if you want to change the price of selected items by $2.00, enter **$2** into the box. If you want to change the price of selected items by 5 percent, enter **5%** into the box. Use the Based On drop-down list box to indicate the base that you want to use for adding the amount of percentage to. After you identify the items that you want to reprice and the way that you want to reprice them, click the Markup button. QuickBooks recalculates the prices and displays this information in the New Price column. If you want to change the prices for the items selected, click OK.

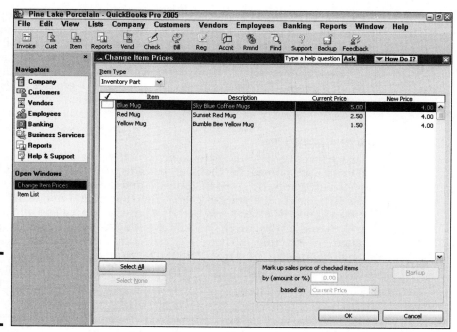

If you don't like the prices listed in the New Price column, you can just keep tinkering with the value in the By (Amount or %) box, clicking the Markup button to refresh the numbers in the New Price column, and clicking OK only when you're satisfied.

Using price levels

Price levels are kind of weird; they let you individually adjust the price of an item up or down. For example, if you have agreed to discount items by 10 percent for a certain customer, you can easily do this by using a price level to knock the price down by 10 percent whenever you're invoicing that customer.

To use price levels, you first have to set up the price levels by using the Price Level list command on the Lists menu. After you set up your price levels, you adjust prices by using prices when you create an invoice. I describe how both tasks work.

Creating a price level

To create a price level, choose the Lists➪Price Level List command. When you do, QuickBooks displays the Price Level List window. To create a price level, click the Price Level button and then choose the New command on the

Price Level menu. QuickBooks displays the New Price Level window, shown in Figure 3-20. Name the price level change by using the Price Level box. Then use the Increase Sales Price By and Reduce Sales Price By radio buttons to indicate that this price level increases or decreases the sales price. Finally, use the Percentage % box to indicate the percentage change. Figure 3-20, for example, shows a price level change that decreases the sales price by 10 percent.

Using a price level

To use a price level, you create an invoice in the usual way. However, click the Price Each column for the item that you want to reprice by using the price level. When you do, QuickBooks turns the Price Each column into a drop-down list box. If you click the arrow button that opens the drop-down list box, QuickBooks displays both the base rate price and any price levels. If you choose a price level, QuickBooks adjusts the price for the price level change. For example, in Figure 3-21, selecting the 10 percent price level change bumps the price from $3.00 to $2.70. In other words, the "ten % down" price level change decreases the default price by 10 percent, from $3.00 to $2.70.

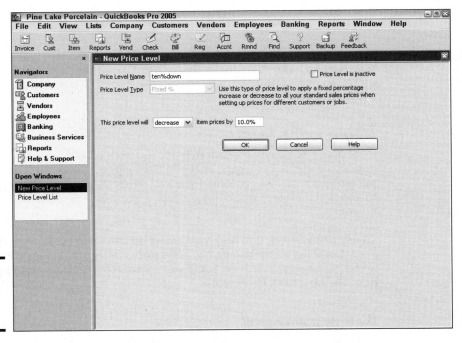

Figure 3-20:
The New
Price Level
window.

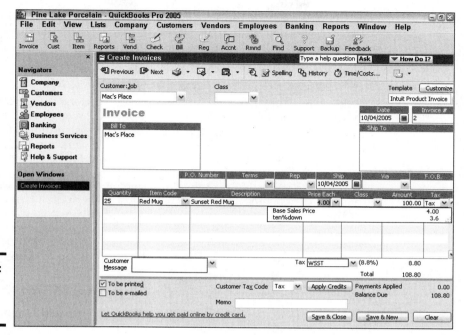

Figure 3-21:
The Create
Invoices
window.

Inventory in a Manufacturing Firm

Tracking inventory in a manufacturing firm is more difficult than in other
types of businesses. When you boil everything down to its essence, the
problem stems from a couple tricky accounting requirements:

✦ **In a manufacturing environment, the manufacturer combines raw
materials items into finished goods items.** This means — and this is the
challenging part — that the manufacturing process reduces the inventory count and value for some items (the raw materials or the components) while at the same time increases the count and value of the other,
finished goods items.

✦ **In a manufacturing environment, the rules say that you don't just
count the value of items in the finished goods item inventory values.**
You also need to count the cost of labor and factory overhead used in
manufacturing the items.

QuickBooks solves the first problem related to manufacturing inventory; however, QuickBooks doesn't solve or address the second problem. Fortunately,
as long as you're a small manufacturer, you probably don't need to worry too

much about the second problem. You should ask your CPA about this. But don't worry — Congress and the Internal Revenue Service have provided a bunch of loopholes for making the accounting easier for the small guys.

Manufactured inventory the simple way

If you're using QuickBooks Pro or some earlier versions of QuickBooks Premier, you don't have the ability to account for the manufacture of inventory in QuickBooks. The best that you can do is to use group items to combine into individual items on a customer's invoice. This approach sounds sloppy, but it isn't quite as bad as you may think at first blush. You can choose to show only the group item on a customer invoice. This means — getting back to the example of the florist selling red roses and vases — that the florist can "manufacture" a crystal vase of a dozen red roses and then show the manufactured item as a group item on the customer's invoice.

The one thing that is problematic about the "just use a group item" approach is that it doesn't give you a way to track the finished goods' inventory values.

Inventory accounting in QuickBooks Premier

To account for the manufacture of inventory in QuickBooks Premier, you add inventory assembly items to the Item list for those items that you manufacture. You also record the manufacture of items as you, well, manufacture them.

For example, suppose that Pine Lake Porcelain mostly just buys and resells coffee mugs and other porcelain doodads. But also suppose that once a year, Pine Lake Porcelain assembles a collection of red coffee mugs into a boxed St. Valentine's Day gift set. In this case, QuickBooks can record the assembly of a boxed gift set that combines, for example, four red coffee mugs, a cardboard box, and some tissue wrapping paper.

Adding inventory assembly items

To describe manufactured items, follow these steps:

1. **Choose Lists⇨Item List.**

   QuickBooks displays the Item List window.

2. **Click the Item button in the Item List window and select New from the drop-down list.**

   QuickBooks displays the New Item window.

3. **Select the Inventory Assembly item from the Type drop-down list box.**

4. Specify the account to use for tracking this item's cost when you sell it.

QuickBooks suggests the Cost of Goods Sold account. If you've created other accounts for your COGS, however, select the other appropriate account.

5. Describe the manufactured item.

Type in a description of the item that you want to appear on documents, such as invoices and so on, that your customers see. (QuickBooks suggests the same description that you used in the Description on Purchase Transactions text box as a default.)

6. Enter the amount that you charge for the item into the Sales Price box.

7. Indicate whether the manufactured item is subject to sales tax using the Tax Code box.

8. Use the Income Account box to specify the account that you want QuickBooks to use for tracking the income from the sale of the item.

9. Identify the components that go into the finished item.

Use the Components Needed list box to identify the individual component items and the quantities needed to make the inventory assembly. Each component item goes on a separate line in the list box. Not to be too redundant, but do note that you both identify the component item and the number of component items needed.

10. Identify the Asset Account.

Specify the other current asset account that you want QuickBooks to use for tracking this inventory item's value.

11. Select a Build Point.

Use the Build Point box to specify the lowest inventory quantity of this item that can remain before you manufacture more. When the inventory level drops to this quantity, QuickBooks adds a Reminder to the Reminders list, notifying you that you need to make more of the item.

12. Ignore the On Hand and the Total Value boxes.

See that On Hand box? Leave it set to zero. To enter a number now is to record an uncategorized transaction, and you don't want to do that. Go ahead and leave the Total Value field set to zero, too. You can also leave the As Of box empty, or you can enter the current date here. It doesn't matter.

Recording manufacture or assembly of items

To build some assembly, choose the Vendors⇨Inventory Activities⇨Build Assemblies command. QuickBooks displays the Build Assemblies window. All you do is select the thing that you want to build from the Assembly Item drop-down list box and then the quantity that you (or some hapless co-worker) have built in the Quantity to Build box. Then you click either the Build & Close or Build & New button. (Click the Build & New button if you want to record the assembly of some other items.)

While I'm on the subject, let me make a handful of observations about the Build Assemblies window and the Build Assemblies command:

✦ In the top-right corner of the window, QuickBooks shows the quantities of the assembly that you have on hand and for which customers have placed orders. That's pretty useful information to have, so, hey, remember that it's there.

✦ The main part of the Build Assemblies window shows you what goes into your product. Not that you care, but this is called a *bill of materials*.

✦ At the bottom of the bill of materials list, QuickBooks shows you the maximum number of assemblies that you can make, given your current inventory holdings.

✦ When you build an item, QuickBooks adjusts the inventory item counts. For example, in the case where you make boxed gift sets, each with four red coffee mugs and two wrapping tissues, QuickBooks reduces the item counts of red coffee mugs and wrapping tissues and increases the item counts of the boxed gift sets when you record building the assembly.

✦ Some of the components used in an assembly may not be inventory items. You can use non-inventory parts in an assembly.

Chapter 4: Managing Cash and Bank Accounts

In This Chapter

✔ **Writing checks**

✔ **Making deposits**

✔ **Transferring money**

✔ **Working with the register**

✔ **Reconciling accounts**

✔ **Reviewing the other banking tools**

*Q*uickBooks provides several tools that make working with your bank accounts easier. For example, QuickBooks gives you a special window for recording the checks you've written. QuickBooks also lets you easily record deposits into accounts. Additionally, QuickBooks includes tools for easily recording transfers between accounts, for reconciling bank accounts, and for performing online banking transactions.

This chapter talks about all these features. Note that if you've used Quick-Books' little brother product, Quicken, much of the information that you see here will be familiar. The QuickBooks banking tools look like the popular Quicken checkbook program. (This is good news for the ten million or so Quicken users.)

Writing Checks

Obviously, any business writes checks — to pay bills and to pay employees. QuickBooks includes a command and a window specifically for the purpose of recording and possibly printing checks.

Recording and printing a check

To record or print checks, choose the Banking⇨Write Checks command. When QuickBooks displays the Write Checks window, as shown in Figure 4-1, take the following steps to write a check:

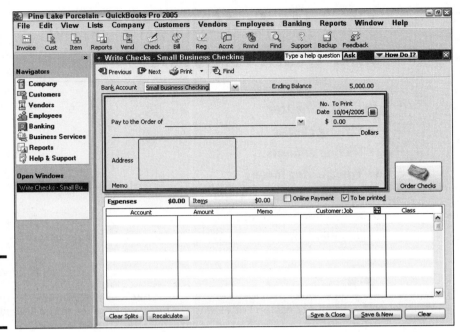

Figure 4-1:
The Write
Checks
window.

1. **Use the Bank Account drop-down list box to select the correct account on which to write a check.**

2. **Use the No., or check number, field to identify the check number.**

   If you don't know the check number yet because you haven't printed the check, leave the No. field blank. Then select the To Be Printed check box, which appears in roughly the middle of the Write Checks window.

   When you select the To Be Printed check box, QuickBooks displays the phrase *To Print* in the No. field.

3. **Use the Date field to record the date that the check is written or will be written.**

   You can enter the check date in mm/dd/yyyy format. Alternatively, you can click the small calendar button that appears to the right of the Date field. When you click the calendar button, QuickBooks displays a pop-up calendar. To select a day shown on the calendar, click the day. The pop-up calendar also includes a pair of buttons that you can click to scroll back and forth through the months.

4. **Use the Pay to the Order Of field to identify the individual or business that you are paying with the check.**

   If the check that you are recording is the first check that you've ever made out to the payee, you must type the payee's name in the Pay to the

Order Of field. If you have previously paid the payee, you can click the arrow button at the right end of the Pay to the Order of field. When you do, QuickBooks displays a list of previous payees. You can select a payee from this list by clicking the name.

5. **Move the selection cursor to the $ (or amount) field and type the check amount.**

   QuickBooks writes out the check amount on the line beneath the Pay to the Order Of field.

6. **(Optional) Provide an address.**

   If you want, you can use the address block to provide the payee's address. Note that QuickBooks writes the payee name on the first line of the address block when you fill in the Pay to the Order Of field. You can add the other lines to the address block manually. Note, though, that if you've previously entered an address for a payee (such as when you last recorded a check to the payee), QuickBooks will reuse this address information for subsequent checks.

   You can edit the address information shown in the Write Checks window.

   You only need to record the address if you are going to print the check and the address will show through the address window, or when you are creating an online payment — something I talk about later in this chapter.

7. **(Optional) Provide a memo description.**

   You can use the Memo field to provide or record additional information. If you're going to print the check, for example, you can use the Memo field to identify your account number or the invoice number that the check pays. If you're simply recording checks and won't be printing checks, you can use the Memo field to record more proprietary or confidential information.

8. **(Optional) Select the Online Payment check box.**

   So here's the deal. If you've told your bank that you want to do the online banking thing and have followed its instructions for setup, you can select the Online Payment check box. This tells QuickBooks to later transmit this check information to your bank along with instructions that the bank make the payment.

   More information on setting up online banking is available later in this chapter.

   To later transmit the payment instructions to the bank, choose Banking➪ Online Banking Center, click Send, and then enter your PIN, or personal identification number, when QuickBooks asks for it.

9. **Distribute the check amount to the appropriate expense or asset accounts.**

If the check pays for a particular expense or purchases a particular asset, click the Expenses tab. Then use the lines or rows of the Expenses tab to identify the account and the amount that the check pays. For example, to record a $50 check that pays supplies expense, use the Account column of the Expenses tab to select the office supplies expense account. Then use the Amount column to identify the amount of the office supplies. Optionally, use the Memo column to provide a memo description of that line of expense detail. And, equally optional, use the Customer:Job column and the Class column to further describe and categorize the line of account detail information. If you do categorize the expense as one incurred for a particular customer or job, you can use the Billable column (marked by an icon) to indicate whether this item should be later billed to the customer (see Figure 4-2).

If a check pays for several different types of expenses, the Expenses tab should show several different lines.

If you write a check to purchase an asset, the Expenses tab doesn't show an expense account; instead, the Expenses tab shows an asset account. For example, if you buy a $5,000 piece of machinery, you may distribute, or categorize, that $5,000 check to an asset account. In this case, the Account column of the Expenses tab shows the asset account name. The Amount column of the Expenses tab shows the amount of the asset purchased.

10. **Describe the items that the check purchases.**

Figure 4-3 shows the Items tab of the Write Checks window. You use the Items tab when you write a check to purchase items shown and described on your Item list. For example, if you write a $1,000 check to buy 1,000 $1 items for inventory, you use the Items tab. To use the Items tab, identify the item being purchased by entering the item code or name into the Item column. Optionally, edit the item description shown in the Description column. Then use the Qty, Cost, and Amount columns to describe the number of items and the total cost of the items purchased. As with the Expenses tab, QuickBooks gives you the option of further classifying an item by using the Customer:Job, Billing, and Class columns.

Book III, Chapter 3 describes how items and the Item list work in QuickBooks. If you are unsure how to work with items, refer to that chapter.

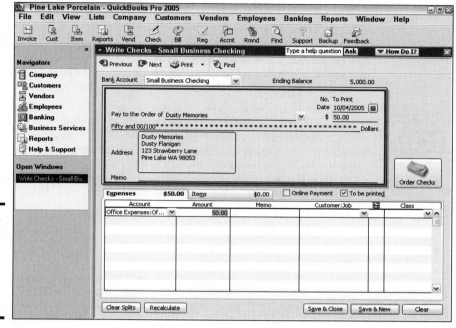

Figure 4-2:
The Write
Checks
window
filled out to
record an
expense.

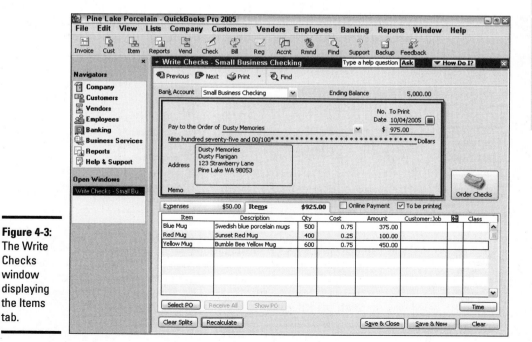

Figure 4-3:
The Write
Checks
window
displaying
the Items
tab.

11. After you describe the check and the reasons for writing the check, click either the Save & Close or the Save & New button.

The Save & Close button saves the check and also closes the Write Checks window. Click the Save & New button to save the check and then redisplay the Write Checks window so that you can record another check. If you don't want to save the check, click the Clear button.

The Write Checks window provides several buttons along its top edge: Previous, Next, Print, and Find. I describe the Print button in the next step, but let me note here that the Previous and Next buttons page back and forth to the checks that you've already written. The Find button displays the Find Checks dialog box, which you can use to describe a check similar to the one you're looking for. After you describe the check you're looking for, click the Find button in the Find Checks dialog box.

12. To print a check, click the Print button.

Alternatively, if you want to print checks in a batch, after you've recorded the very last check that you want to print, click the down arrow to the right of the Print button. When QuickBooks displays the Print menu, choose its Print Batch command. QuickBooks displays the Select Checks to Print dialog box, as shown in Figure 4-4. Select the checks that you want to print by clicking them. Use the First Check Number box to identify the number of the first check form that you will use for printing. If you're using standard or wallet-style checks, you will also need to indicate the number of checks. Then click OK. When QuickBooks displays the Print Checks dialog box, as shown in Figure 4-5, use the Check Style area to identify the type of check forms on which you are printing. Then click the Print button.

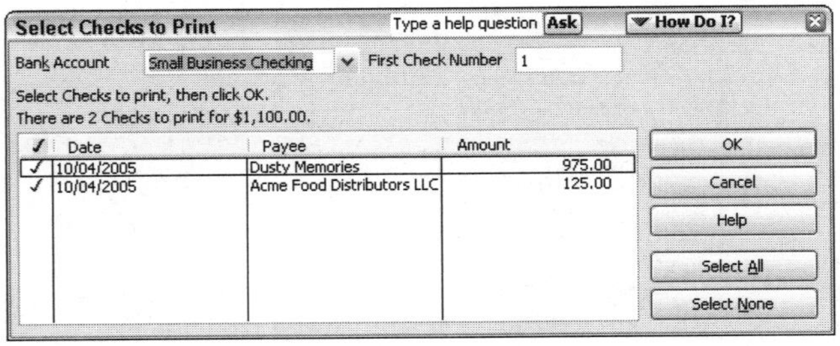

Figure 4-4:
The Select Checks to Print dialog box.

✓	Date	Payee	Amount
✓	10/04/2005	Dusty Memories	975.00
✓	10/04/2005	Acme Food Distributors LLC	125.00

Select Checks to Print

Bank Account: Small Business Checking   First Check Number: 1

Select Checks to print, then click OK.
There are 2 Checks to print for $1,100.00.

OK — Cancel — Help — Select All — Select None

You can also print check forms in a batch by choosing the File➪Print Forms➪Checks command. When you choose this command, QuickBooks displays the Select Checks to Print dialog box. You then identify which checks that you want to print, click OK, and use the Print Checks dialog box to finish printing your checks.

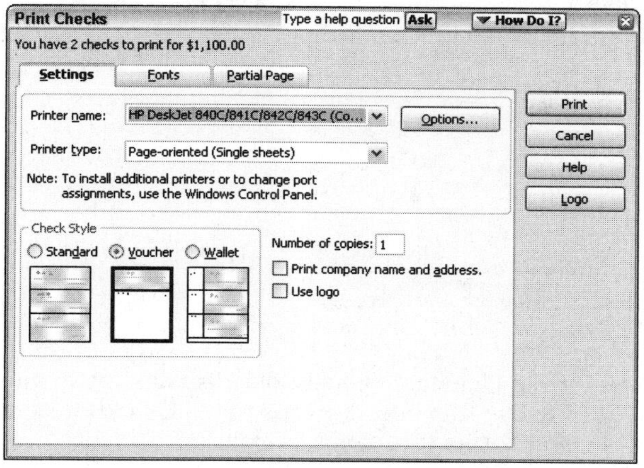

Customizing the check form

While I'm on the subject of printing check forms, let me make a couple of
quick observations. If you click the Fonts tab in the Print Checks dialog box,
QuickBooks displays a couple of buttons you can click to specify what
fonts QuickBooks should use for printing check forms (see Figure 4-6).

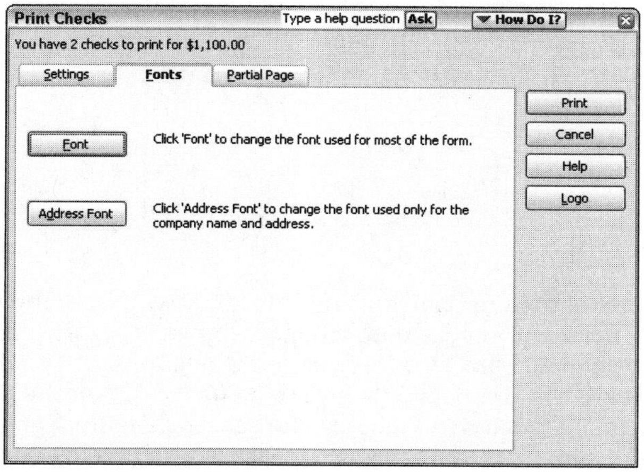

Figure 4-6:
The Fonts
tab of the
Print Checks
dialog box.

If you click the Font button, for example, QuickBooks displays the Select
Font dialog box, shown in Figure 4-7. You select the font you want from
the Font list box, any special type style such as bold or italic from the Font
Style list box, and the point size from the Size list box. You can experiment
with different font settings and see the combined effect in the Sample box.

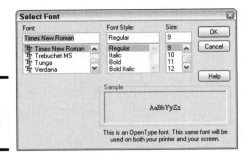

Figure 4-7:
The Select
Font dialog
box.

If you click the Partial Page tab, QuickBooks displays the dialog box tab shown in Figure 4-8. Use this tab's buttons to tell QuickBooks how you feed a partial page of check forms through your printer.

Figure 4-8:
The Partial
Page tab of
the Print
Checks
dialog box.

One final tidbit about customizing check forms. If you click the Logo button (available in the Print Checks dialog box as shown in Figure 4-8), QuickBooks displays a little dialog box that lets you tell QuickBooks it should print a logo on your checks. To print a logo, you need an image file for the logo (perhaps something you've created in Paint or another image editing program). This little dialog box just lets you tell QuickBooks where this logo image file is located.

Making Bank Deposits

QuickBooks also supplies a command and window for recording bank deposits. To record bank deposits, follow these steps:

1. **Choose the Banking⇨Make Deposits command.**

QuickBooks displays the Payments to Deposit window, shown in Figure 4-9.

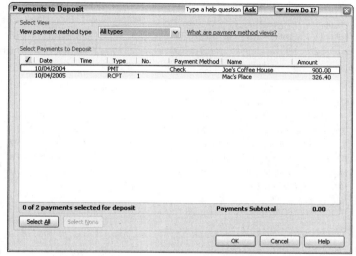

2. **Use the Payments to Deposit window to select the payments you want to deposit.**

You can select all of the payments listed by clicking the Select All button. You can select individual payments by clicking them. QuickBooks marks selected payments with a check mark.

3. **Click OK.**

QuickBooks displays the Make Deposits window, shown in Figure 4-10.

4. **In the Make Deposits window, use the Deposit To box to identify the bank account into which you'll deposit the funds.**

5. **Use the Date box to identify the deposit date.**

You can enter the date in mm/dd/yyyy fashion or you can click the small calendar button to the right of the Date field. On the calendar that appears, click the day that you want the Date field to show.

6. **(Optional) Provide a memo description.**

Initially, QuickBooks uses the Memo field to describe the transaction as a deposit. This is a pretty good description of a deposit transaction, obviously. If you want to change the memo description to something else even more useful — such as "daily cash sales" or something like that — replace the contents of the Memo box.

Perhaps the best use for the box was suggested by the accountant who reviewed this manuscript: You can use this field to further describe any unusual transactions, such as refunds of expenses, rebates, asset sale proceeds, and so forth.

As you may remember from either working with QuickBooks or from the discussion of making sales in Book III, Chapter 1, you have the option of telling QuickBooks (whenever you receive a payment) that the payment be directly deposited to the bank account or lumped with other payments into an "undeposited funds" bucket.

Not all customer payments will appear in the Make Deposits window. As discussed in Book III, Chapter 1, you can also indicate that a customer payment should be deposited into a bank account directly from the Receive Payments window and directly from the Enter Sales Receipts window. These direct-into-the-account payments don't appear in the Make Payments window. You actually record these bank account deposits at the same time that you record the customer payment or the sales receipt.

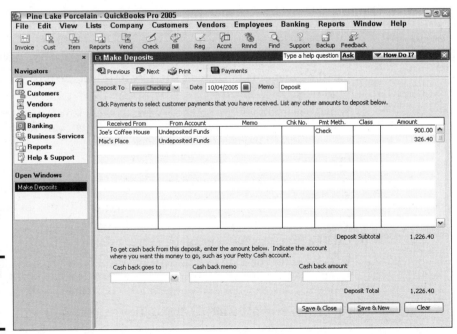

Figure 4-10:
The Make Deposits window.

7. Record any additional deposit amounts.

If you also want to include as part of the deposit some other payment that's not listed initially in the Make Deposits window, you can use the next empty row of the list to describe this payment. To describe the payment, use the Received From column to identify the customer, vendor, or other individual or business making the payment. Use the From Account column to identify the account that should be credited for this payment. In the case of a customer payment that's a sale, for example, your sales revenue account should be the one recorded in the From Account column. Use the other columns of the Make Deposits window — Memo, Chk No., Pmt Meth., Class, and Amount — to provide the other details of the payment.

8. Identify any cash back amount.

If you're making a $1,000 deposit but want to hold $100 of the deposit back as cash, you need to record a cash back amount. To record a cash back amount, use the Cash Back Goes To box to identify the account that should be adjusted for the cash back. Use the Cash Back Memo field to describe the reason for the cash back transaction. Finally, enter the cash back amount into the cleverly titled Cash Back Amount box. For example, if you wanted to hold $100 of cash back for employee bonuses, you may enter **employee bonuses** (pretend this is an expense account) into the Cash Back Goes To box. Then you may use the Cash Back Memo field to describe the occasion for these employee bonuses. Finally, you would enter the cash back amount, **$100**, into the Cash Back Amount box.

9. Save the deposit transaction.

As is the case with other QuickBooks transaction-entry windows, click either the Save & Close or the Save & New button to save your deposit transaction. Note that after you've saved the deposit transaction, QuickBooks records the deposit into the appropriate bank account. This deposit transaction total — which shows at the bottom of the window in the Deposit Total field — is the amount that will appear on your bank statement. It is the amount that will appear on the bank account register. (I talk about bank account registers a little later in the chapter.)

The Make Deposits window also provides Previous and Next buttons that let you page back and forth through your deposit transactions. The Print button in the Make Deposits window lets you print a deposit list. The Payments button lets you redisplay the Payments to Deposit dialog box.

Transferring Money between Bank Accounts

The Banking menu supplies a useful command for transferring money between funds. To transfer money between funds, you can choose the Banking⇨Transfer Funds command. When you do so, QuickBooks displays the Transfer Funds Between Accounts window, as shown in Figure 4-11. To use the Transfer Funds Between Accounts window, follow these steps:

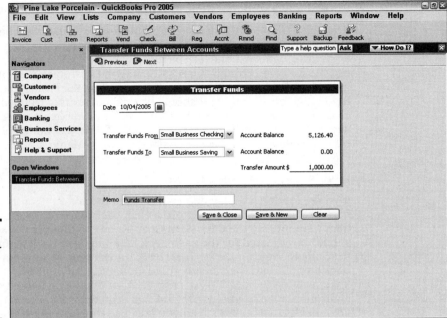

Figure 4-11:
The Transfer
Funds
Between
Accounts
window.

1. **Use the Date field to identify the transfer date.**

You can enter the date in mm/dd/yyyy format, or you can click the small calendar button that appears to the right of the Date field. When QuickBooks displays the calendar, click the day that corresponds to the date you want to enter into the Date field.

2. **Use the Transfer Funds From drop-down list box to select the bank account from which you'll be moving funds.**

You can enter the bank account name into the box or you can click the drop-down arrow at the right end of the box and select a bank account from the list that QuickBooks supplies.

3. **Use the Transfer Funds To drop-down list box to identify the bank account that will receive the transferred funds.**

The Transfer Funds To box works like the Transfer Funds From box.

4. **Use the Transfer Amount box to identify the amount of the transfer.**

For example, if you transfer $100 from your checking to your savings account, the transfer amount is $100.

5. **(Optional) Provide a memo description for the transfer transaction.**

If you want (and this is no big deal), you can use the Memo box to provide some brief memo description of the funds transfer.

6. **Save the transfer transaction.**

To save your transfer transaction, click either the Save & Close or the Save & New button. Alternatively, if you don't want to save the transfer transaction, click the Clear button.

Working with the Register

You can record checks, deposits, and account transfers by using the commands described in the preceding paragraphs of this chapter, but you have another method available, too. You can also use the Register window. The Register window looks like the regular paper register that you may use to keep track of transactions or a bank account. QuickBooks allows you to enter transactions directly into an account register.

Recording register transactions

To enter a bank account transaction directly into an account register, follow these steps:

1. **To display an account register, choose the Banking⇨Use Register command.**

Sometimes, when you choose the Banking⇨Use Register command, QuickBooks displays the Use Register dialog box (see Figure 4-12). Sometimes it displays the actual register (see Figure 4-13). The Use Register dialog box asks you to select the bank account that you want to display in a register. To select the account that you want to use, open the Select Account drop-down list box and select the bank account. QuickBooks then displays the Register window, shown in Figure 4-13.

The Use Register dialog box actually lets you select any account. You can select a non-bank account, too.

Figure 4-12:
The Use
Register
window.

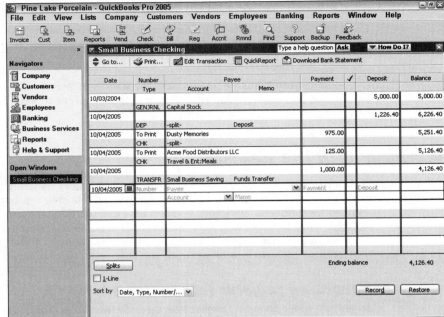

Figure 4-13:
The Register window showing the transactions that have affected the bank account.

2. **Use the Date column of the register to record the date of the deposit, payment, or transfer.**

   You can enter a date by using the mm/dd/yyyy date format. Or you can click the small calendar button at the right end of the Date field to display the month that shows the date and then click the day button that corresponds to the date you want to enter.

3. **(Optional) Assign a transaction number.**

   Use the Number column to uniquely identify the transaction. In the case of check transactions, for example, use the Number field to record the check number. For transfers and deposits, you may not need to record a number.

4. **Use the Payee field to record the payee for a check, the customer paying a deposit, or some other bit of information in the case of a transfer transaction.**

   Note that you can select an existing customer, vendor, or a name from one of the QuickBooks lists by clicking the down-arrow button at the right end of the Payee field. When you do this, QuickBooks displays a list of names. Click the one that you want to select.

5. Provide the transaction amount.

Use the Payment column if you are describing a check transaction or a transfer that moves money from the account. Use the Deposit column if you are describing a deposit into the account or transfer into the account. Enter the amount of the transaction into the appropriate column — Payment or Deposit — by using dollars and cents.

6. Identify the account.

For check transactions, you need to use the Account field to identify the expense that a check pays or the asset that a check purchases. For deposit transactions, you need to use the Account field to identify the sales revenue account that the deposit represents. For Transfer transactions, use the Account field to identify the other bank account involved in the transaction. You can enter the Account name into the Account box or you can open the Account drop-down list box and choose the account that you want by clicking it.

7. (Optional) Provide a memo description.

If you want, use the Memo field to provide a brief description of the payment, deposit, or transfer transaction.

8. (Optional) Split the transaction.

If a transaction needs to be assigned to more than one account, click the Splits button. QuickBooks then displays the Splits area in the register window, shown in Figure 4-14. The Splits area lets you split a transaction among several accounts. For example, a check that pays both office supplies and entertainment expenses can be split between these two expense accounts. Similarly, a deposit transaction that represents both product revenue and service revenue can be split between these two accounts. After you finish with the Splits area, click its Close button.

You can erase the Splits detail by clicking the Clear button. You can also tell QuickBooks to recalculate the payment or deposit amount by using the split transaction data simply by clicking the Recalc button.

The Splits area also lets you do something that isn't possible inside the regular register: You can use the Splits area to record customer:job information, class information, and billing information. To do this, use the Customer:Job column, the Billing column, and the Class column. (The Billing column, by the way, is that column with the funny-looking symbol between the Customer:Job and Class columns in Figure 4-14. I guess that's supposed to be a picture of a bill — go figure.)

9. To record a transaction into the register, click the Record button.

QuickBooks recalculates the account balance and recalculates the ending balance for the new transaction.

Book III
Chapter 4

Managing Cash and
Bank Accounts

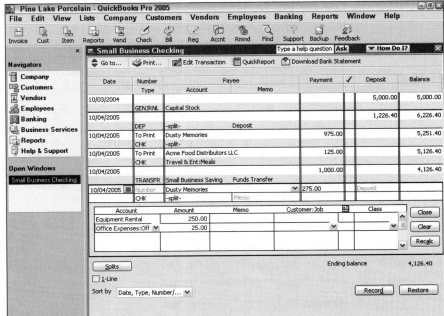

Figure 4-14:
The Register window showing a split transaction.

Using Register window commands and buttons

The Register window provides several buttons and boxes to enable you to more easily work with the Register window and control the way it looks.

The Go To button

Click the Go To button displays the Go To dialog box, as shown in Figure 4-15. The Go To dialog box lets you search for a transaction in the Register window. For example, you can look for a transaction where the Payee/Name uses the name Steve Nelson. You can click the Prev and Next buttons to move to the previous or next transactions that also match the search criteria. To remove the Go To dialog box from the QuickBooks program window, of course, click Cancel.

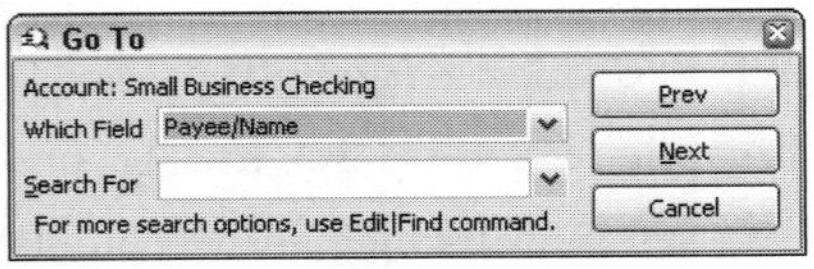

Figure 4-15:
The Go To dialog box.

The Print button

The Print button, when clicked, displays the Print Register dialog box (see Figure 4-16). The Print Register dialog box lets you print a copy of the register for the account. The Print Register dialog box provides Date Range From and Date Range Through boxes, which let you specify the range of dates you want on the printed register. The Print Register dialog box also provides a Print Splits Detail check box, which you can select to tell QuickBooks that you want to see the split transaction detail.

Figure 4-16:
The Print
Register
dialog box.

The Edit Transaction button

The Edit Transaction button, when clicked, tells QuickBooks to display whatever window you used to originally record the selected transaction. Remember that the Register window shows all of the transactions for the bank account. These transactions include, for example, checking account transactions that you recorded when using the Write Checks window. If you click the Edit Transaction button when the selected transaction is one that you originally recorded in the Write Checks window, QuickBooks displays that transaction again in the Write Checks window. You then edit the transaction by using the Write Checks window and click either Save & Close or Save & New to save your changes.

The QuickReport button

Click the QuickReport button to display a report that summarizes register information for the payee or name in the selected transaction. For example, if the selected transaction is a check written to Dusty Memories, clicking QuickReport builds a quick-and-dirty report that summarizes all of the transactions for Dusty Memories (see Figure 4-17).

The 1-Line check box

QuickBooks lets you display either a one-line version of the register or a two-line version of the register (see Figure 4-18). By default, QuickBooks assumes that you want the two-line version of the register. However, you can display a more compact, one-line version of the register by selecting the 1-Line check box.

**Book III
Chapter 4**

**Managing Cash and
Bank Accounts**

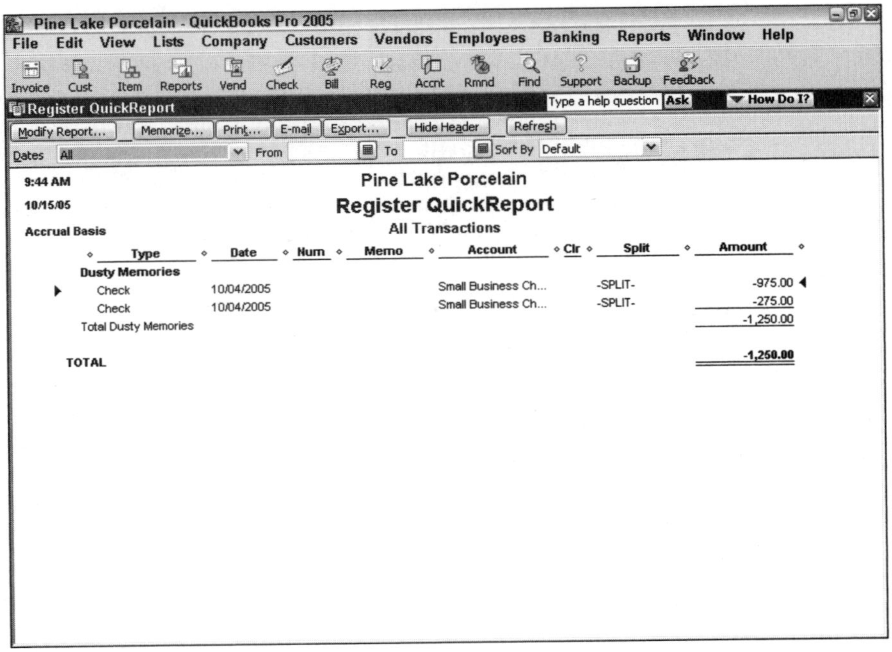

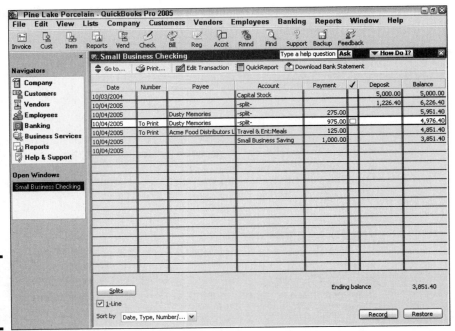

Figure 4-17:
A sample QuickReport.

Figure 4-18:
A 1-line version of the register.

The Sort By box

The Sort By drop-down list box lets you choose how QuickBooks arranges register information. QuickBooks lets you arrange register information by date, by amount, by order entry date, and several other sorting methods as well. To change the way that QuickBooks orders or organizes the information in the register, open the Sort By drop-down list box and choose the ordering sequence that you want.

Using Edit Menu Commands

In the preceding paragraphs of this chapter, I describe how to record check transactions, deposit transactions, transfers between accounts, and how to use the register. You often don't need to know any more than I've already described in order to use the windows discussed and in order to record the transactions described. However, know that the Edit menu (which appears when the Register window is open and active, as shown in Figure 4-19) provides several other useful commands for entering new transactions, editing existing transactions, and for reusing transaction information:

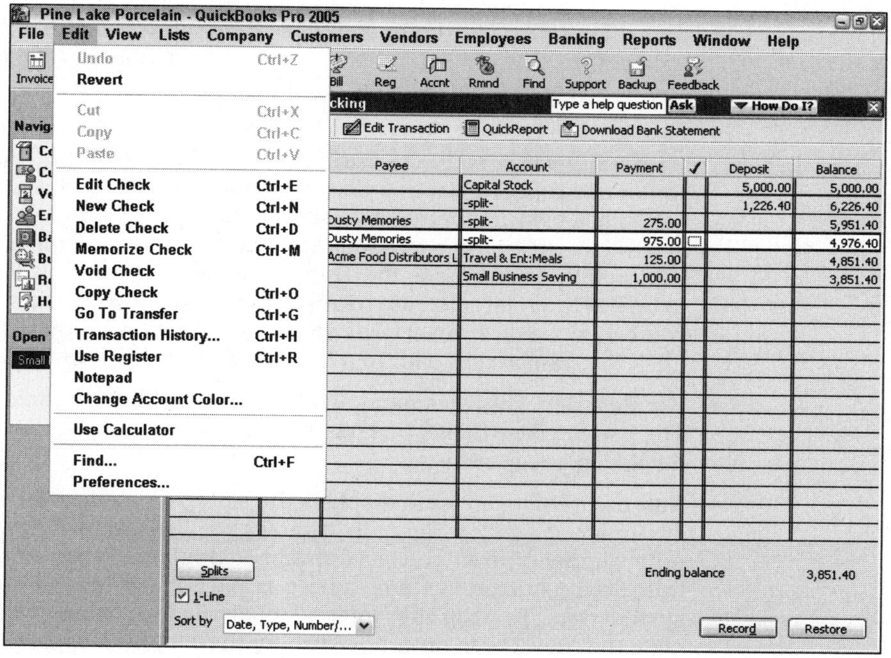

Figure 4-19:
The Edit menu available for the Register window.

✦ **Edit Check/Deposit:** This command is equivalent to the Edit Transaction button (which appears in the Register window). If you choose the Edit Check/Deposit command, QuickBooks displays the Write Checks window so that you can edit the transaction using that tool.

The command name changes depending on the selected transaction. You see the Edit Check command if the selected transaction is a check. You see the Edit Deposit command if the selected transaction is a deposit.

✦ **New Check:** This command displays the Write Checks window so that you can record a new check transaction and record it into the register.

✦ **Delete Check:** The Delete Check command deletes the selected transaction from the register. (The name of this command changes depending on the transaction selected in the register.)

✦ **Memorize Check:** This command memorizes the selected transaction, adds the check information to the memorized transaction list, and thereby allows you to reuse the check information at some point in the future. (If you have a transaction that you record frequently — for example, every month — memorizing the transaction and then reusing it often saves you data entry time.)

✦ **Void Check:** This command lets you void the selected check transaction.

✦ **Go To Transfer:** This command goes to the other side of a transfer transaction. The Go To Transfer command, obviously, only makes sense and only works if the selected transaction is a transfer.

✦ **Transaction History:** This command displays a window that lists all the transactions related to the current selected transaction. Typically, you would use this Transaction History command when the selected transaction is a customer payment. The Transaction History window would, in this case, list all the transactions related to the customer payment transaction. You can use the Transaction History window to go quickly to one of the related transactions. Simply click the transaction listed. You can also edit transactions shown in the Transaction History window. Click the transaction and then the Edit Payment button to do this.

✦ **Use Register:** This command displays the Use Register dialog box. The Use Register dialog box lets you select the account that you want to display in a register.

✦ **Notepad:** This command displays the Notepad window for the selected customer or vendor. Figure 4-20 shows the Notepad window. To enter a note, simply type whatever you want to document. You can click the Date Stamp button to stamp a note or part of a note with the current system date. To print the Notepad, click the Print button. You can also click the New To Do button to display the New To Do dialog box. The New To Do dialog box lets you keep a To Do list for a particular customer or vendor. Figure 4-21 shows the New To Do dialog box.

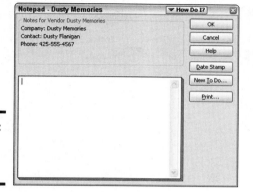

Figure 4-20: The Notepad window.

Figure 4-21: The New To Do window.

✦ **Change Account Color:** This command displays the Change Account Color dialog box. The Change Account Color dialog box lets you choose another color to use as the color of the striping shown in the Register window. To select another color, click the color square that shows the color that you want and then click OK.

✦ **Use Calculator:** This command predictably displays the Windows Calculator. If you have questions about how to work with the Windows Calculator, refer to the Windows documentation, the Window's Help File, or a book such as *Windows XP For Dummies* by Andy Rathbone (Wiley Publishing, Inc.).

✦ **Simple Find:** This command displays the Simple tab of the Find window, as shown in Figure 4-22, which you can use to find transactions. To use the Simple tab, use the Transaction Type, Customer:Job, Date, Invoice #, and Amount boxes to describe the transaction for which you are looking. Enter as much information as you can, but note that if you enter incorrect information, QuickBooks won't (obviously) be able to find the transaction you're looking for. After you describe the transaction in as much detail as you can, click the Find button. QuickBooks displays a list of transactions that match your search criteria (see Figure 4-23). To go to a particular transaction, click the transaction in the list and then click the Go To button.

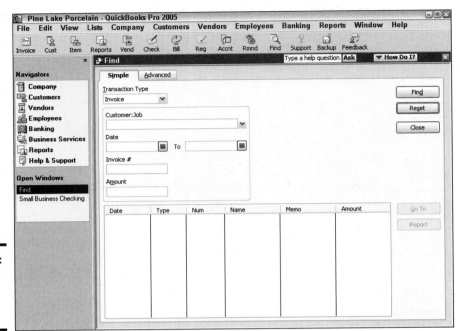

Figure 4-22:
The Simple
tab of the
Find
window.

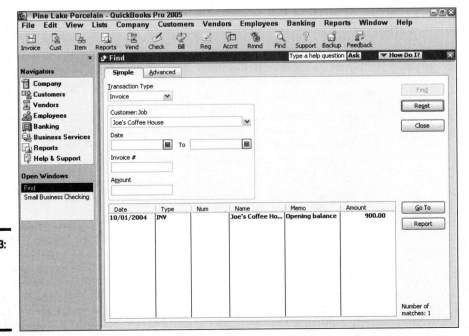

Figure 4-23:
Results of
a simple
search in
the Find
window.

✦ **Advanced Find:** This command displays the Advanced tab of the Find window, as shown in Figure 4-24. The Advanced tab lets you describe a much more precise and complex set of search criteria. Essentially, you can describe in painful detail a filter that QuickBooks should apply to each field that's recorded for a transaction. For example, if you want to filter based on the account, select the account entry from the filter list. Then open the Account drop-down list box and select one of the account groupings that QuickBooks displays. Alternatively, you can click the Select Accounts entry. This displays a dialog box that you can use to select individually the accounts you want to look for. The Include Split Detail button lets you indicate whether you want split detail information. After you describe the filter or filters you want to use, click the Find button. As with the Simple tab of the Find window, QuickBooks displays a list of all the transactions that match your filter. To go to one of the transactions listed, click it and then click the Go To button.

The Report button that appears both on the Simple tab and the Advanced tab creates a report of all the transactions that the Find command has found. You can print this report — QuickBooks displays the report in a regular report window — by choosing the File➪Report command or by clicking the Print button that appears at the top of the Report window. The Simple and the Advanced tabs of the Find window also include a Reset button. I should say someplace that if you want to start your search over by using a new set of search criteria or filtering criteria, you simply need to click the Reset button.

**Book III
Chapter 4**

**Managing Cash and
Bank Accounts**

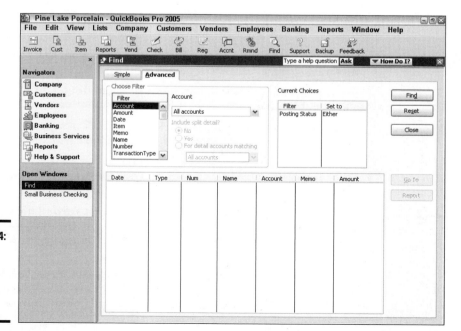

Figure 4-24:
The Advanced tab of the Find window.

✦ **Preferences:** This command enables you to change the way that
QuickBooks works so that it works in a way that best matches your
firm's accounting requirements. Book II, Chapter 3 discusses in detail
the Preferences command.

Reconciling the Bank Account

You can reconcile a bank account with surprising speed in QuickBooks. To
reconcile the bank account, choose the Banking➪Reconcile command. Quick-
Books displays the Begin Reconciliation dialog box, shown in Figure 4-25.

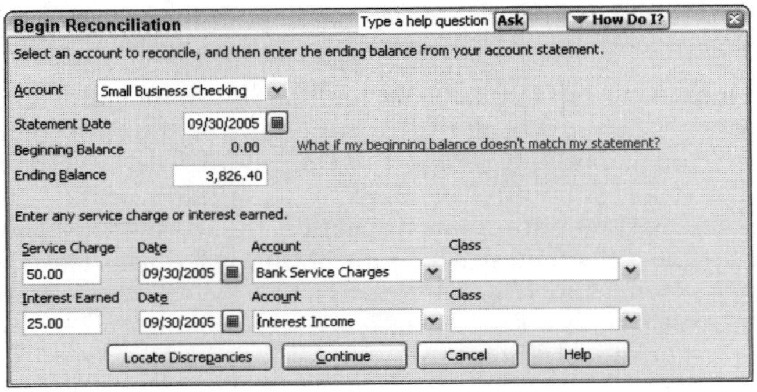

Figure 4-25:
The Begin
Reconcilia-
tion dialog
box.

To begin reconciling your account, follow these steps:

1. **Select the account that you want to reconcile from the Account drop-
down list box.**

2. **Use the Statement Date box to identify the ending date of the bank
statement that you are using in your reconciliation.**

As is always the case with date fields in QuickBooks, you enter the date
in the mm/dd/yyyy date format or you click the calendar button and use
it to select the correct date.

3. **Enter the ending balance shown on your bank account statement into
the Ending Balance box.**

4. **Use the Service Charge boxes and the Interest Earned boxes to identify the amount of any service charge or of any interest, the date of
any such transaction, and the account that you use to track those
charges.**

For example, if your bank statement shows a service charge, enter the
service charge amount into the first Service Charge box. Enter the date of
the service charge transaction into the Service Charge Date box. Finally,

enter an appropriate expense account for tracking service charges into the Service Charge Account drop-down list box. (Bank charges, for example, is a good account to track service charges.)

In a similar fashion, use the Interest Earned boxes to describe any interest earned on a business account.

5. Review the statement information.

After you enter information about the bank account, the statement date, the ending balance, and any service charge or interest earned information, take a moment to review the information and confirm that it is correct. You'll have a whale of a time reconciling an account if the amount that you're trying to reconcile to is incorrect.

6. After you make sure that everything is hunky-dory, click the Continue button.

QuickBooks displays the Reconcile window, as shown in Figure 4-26.

7. To identify checks and payments transactions that have cleared your bank account, click the transactions that have cleared.

The Reconcile window displays two lists of transactions: a list of checks and payments, which appears on the left, and a list of deposits and other credits, which appears on the right. When you click a transaction, QuickBooks marks the transaction with a check. The check indicates that a transaction has cleared. You can mark all of the transactions on a list as cleared by clicking the Mark All button. You can unmark all of the transactions on a list as uncleared by clicking the Unmark All button.

Use the Deposits and Other Credits list to identify those deposit transactions that have cleared the bank account. You identify a cleared deposit transaction in the same way that you identify a cleared check or payment transaction. You can click a transaction, which causes QuickBooks to mark the transaction as cleared. You can also use the Mark All and Unmark All buttons to mark or unmark all of the deposits and other credit transactions at one time.

If you realize that, as part of the reconciliation, you've incorrectly entered the service charge, interest earned, ending balance, or any other information, click the Modify button. QuickBooks redisplays the Begin Reconciliation dialog box (shown earlier in Figure 4-25). Make the necessary changes and click Continue to return to the Reconcile window.

8. Verify that the cleared balance equals the ending balance.

If you have provided correct information in the Begin Reconciliation dialog box (shown in Figure 4-25) and you correctly identified all of the transactions that have cleared your account, the ending balance should equal the cleared balance, as shown in Figure 4-27.

**Book III
Chapter 4**

Managing Cash and Bank Accounts

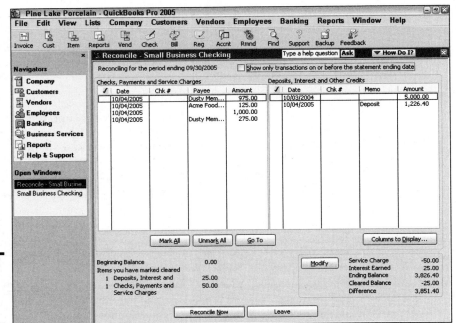

Figure 4-26:
The
Reconcile
window.

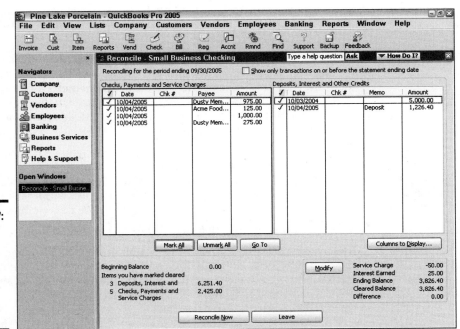

Figure 4-27:
The
Reconcile
window
after the
reconcilia-
tion is
complete.

9. **When the ending balance equals the cleared balance, click the Reconcile Now button.**

   QuickBooks permanently records your cleared transactions as cleared and redisplays the Register window. If you can't reconcile an account, you can click the Leave button. QuickBooks then saves your half-completed reconciliation so that you can come back later and finish it.

 Can I interject a couple of tangential comments here? Good. If you want, you can print a little report that summarizes your reconciliation after you click the Reconcile Now button. (QuickBooks gives you this option in a dialog box that it displays.) You can also click the Previous Reports button to display a dialog box that lets you print other old reconciliation reports. While I'm on the subject of reconciliation reports, I should also mention that you can click the Discrepancy Report button to produce a report that lists transactions that have been edited since you last reconciled the account.

Reviewing the Other Banking Commands

Earlier in this chapter, I describe the most common and useful banking commands. You may not need to use the other commands provided by the Banking menu. Nevertheless, my compulsive personality requires that I describe these other commands.

Banking Navigator command

The Banking Navigator command displays the Banking Navigator window, which displays clickable icons arranged in a flow chart and hyperlinks that you can use to access various Banking commands. For example, the Banking Navigator window includes a Checks icon that you can click to display the Write Checks window. Figure 4-28 shows the Banking Navigator window. Note, too, that the Banking Navigator window includes hyperlinks (see, for example, the Related Activities area in the upper-right corner) that you can use to do banking-type things.

Order Checks & Envelopes command

The Order Checks & Envelopes command displays a submenu of commands you use to order QuickBooks checks and envelopes or to get information about ordering QuickBooks checks and envelopes.

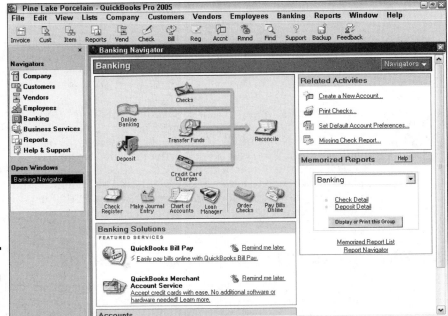

Figure 4-28:
The Banking
Navigator
window.

Record Credit Card Charges command

If you set up a credit card account — this is a credit card account that you or your business would use to charge transactions on — you can choose the Banking⇨Record Credit Card Charges command to display a submenu of credit-card-related commands: Enter Credit Card Charges and Download Credit Card Charges.

If you choose the Enter Credit Card Charges command, the Enter Credit Card Charges window appears (see Figure 4-29). You can figure out how this window works without my help, I'm sure. You identify the credit card account for which you want to record transactions, and you describe the credit card purchase by using the field at the top of the screen. You then use the Expenses and Items tabs — these tabs work the same way as the similar tabs in the Write Checks window — to detail the reasons and the accounts affected by your charge.

If you choose the Download Credit Card Charges command — assuming you've set up credit card accounts that allow for online services — QuickBooks downloads recent credit card transactions directly into the credit card register. Perhaps obviously, for this command to work, several prerequisites must be met:

1. You need a credit card account already set up.

2. You need to have set up the credit card account for online services.

3. You need an Internet connection so QuickBooks can go grab the credit card transactions from the credit card company.

Make Journal Entry command

The Make Journal Entry command really doesn't belong in the Banking window. This command lets you enter a general ledger entry into the QuickBooks data file.

Journal entries should be entered only by people who really understand accounting. Probably, in the case of many small businesses, journal entries should be made only by the outside CPA. If you have questions about how the Make Journal Entry command works, in spite of the warnings I've given you here, refer to Book IV, Chapter 1.

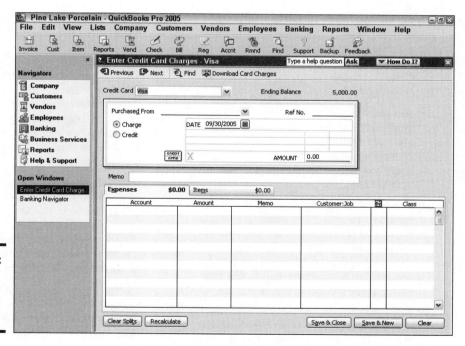

Book III
Chapter 4

Managing Cash and
Bank Accounts

Figure 4-29:
The Enter
Credit Card
Charges
window.

Set Up Online Financial Services command

The Set Up Online Financial Services command displays a submenu of commands that you use to apply for online banking and to see which financial institutions (banks, savings and loans, and credit unions) let you do online banking. If you want to do online banking — this can save businesses a ton of time — call your existing bank and ask whether it provides the service. If it does, ask for a sign-up packet and for specific instructions on how to get going with online banking.

If you don't like the idea of calling your bank directly, choose the Apply For Online Banking command from the Setup Online Financial Services submenu. This command walks you through the process for applying for and setting up online financial services.

When your account won't balance

If your account won't reconcile, the problem stems from one of several conditions. None of the conditions is hard to describe, but they can be pretty hard to fix. Here's a quick overview of what may be causing you trouble and what may be preventing you from reconciling your account:

✔ **Are you working with the right account?** That sounds pretty dumb, doesn't it? But if you have several bank accounts, you may be trying to reconcile the wrong account or using the wrong statement to reconcile your account.

✔ **Are you missing any transactions?** If the bank has recorded transactions that you haven't, this will cause your ending balance to not equal your cleared balance. Look on your statement for any transactions that you are missing or forgot to record, and then record these and mark them as cleared.

✔ **Have you correctly recorded transactions?** This may also sound silly, but if you recorded the transaction and you are a few pennies off or a few dollars off — perhaps you've transposed a couple of numbers — you won't be able to reconcile your account. I commonly find that I've entered a transaction or two wrong per month. (Maybe this is because my fingers are too arthritic to correctly record amounts.) But it's probably very common when you are entering dozens and dozens of transactions to occasionally record a transaction wrong. The occasional errors need to be fixed before you can reconcile an account.

Note that it's quite likely — especially as you are getting started — that you won't be able to successfully reconcile an account because of multiple errors. If you do something like record a transaction erroneously and then forget to record a couple of transactions, you'll need to fix each of these errors in order to reconcile your account.

One final tip: Reconciling an account is much easier if you are using online banking. I talk about how online banking works a little later in this chapter.

Can I close with an editorial comment? Online banking is a real time-saver for business owners. If you're not using online banking, you really should have a pretty darn good reason for not doing so.

Create Online Banking Message command

The Create Online Banking Message command displays a window that you can use to send your bank a message about some online transaction that is causing you problems. Although this command may make you think that online banking is problematic, I've had to use this command only once in the ten or so years that I have been banking online.

Inquire About Online Banking Payment command

The Inquire About Online Banking Payment command displays a window that you use to send a message to your bank about some online payment that has gone amiss. Again, although this command seems to suggest that online banking is problematic, I have not found that to be so. Sure, you'll have the occasional snafu, but online banking is, at least on your end, less problematic than manually writing checks.

Online Banking Center command

The Online Banking Center command displays the Online Banking Center window. You display the Online Banking Center window to transmit online payments and online transactions to your bank. How you use this window is described in the online banking instructions that you get from your bank. In a nutshell, you display the window by choosing a command. You click the Send/Update Account, you provide a PIN, and then you simply watch in admiration as QuickBooks and your bank's computer exchange information. That's really all there is to it.

You can use the Online Banking Center window to record online payments (you can also record online payments by using the Write Checks window described earlier in the chapter), to record online transfers between accounts (you can also use the Transfer Money Between Accounts command described earlier in the chapter), and to send messages. Because you have other ways to do these things, I don't show you how to accomplish these same tasks with the Online Banking Center window. If you do want to use the Online Banking Center window, you can refer to the earlier discussions of the Write Checks window and the Transfer Money Between Accounts window for help about what information goes into what fields and boxes.

Chart of Accounts command

The Chart of Accounts command displays the Chart of Accounts in a window. The Chart of Accounts simply lists all of the accounts that you are using to track assets, liabilities, owner's equity, income, and expense amounts. I don't describe the Chart of Accounts list in this chapter. You should instead refer to Book II, Chapter 2 for information about working with the Chart of Accounts and to Book I, Chapters 1 and 2 for more information about the accounts that make up a business's financial statements.

Other Names list

The Other Names list displays a window that lists all the other names you've used to record transactions. Individuals and businesses that appear on your Other Names list are not customers, vendors, or employees. In other words, the Other Names list includes names that don't neatly fit into one of the standard categories.

Memorized Transactions list

The Memorized Transactions list displays a list of transactions that you've previously memorized. You memorize a transaction by choosing the Edit⇨ Memorize command when the transaction is displayed in a window or the transaction is selected in a Register window. The neat thing about the Memorized Transactions list is that you can select one of the transactions listed and then tell QuickBooks to reuse the transaction as the basis for recording some new transaction. To reuse a memorized transaction in this way, simply double-click the memorized transaction.

Online Banking Services command

The Online Banking Services command displays a submenu command that you can use to access expanded, fee-based banking services: Online Bill Payment, QuickBooks Credit Card, Bank Online, and so forth.

Chapter 5: Paying Employees

In This Chapter

✔ **Setting up Do-it-yourself Payroll**

✔ **Paying employees**

✔ **Editing and voiding checks**

✔ **Paying payroll liabilities**

*Q*uickBooks provides three options for paying employees: "do-it-yourself" Do-it-yourself Payroll (which is called simply "Payroll"), Assisted Payroll, and Complete Payroll. This chapter describes the Do-it-yourself Payroll option. With the Do-it-yourself Payroll option, you do most of the work yourself but you don't pay very much for your payroll processing.

As noted, QuickBooks also supplies an Assisted Payroll option and a Complete Payroll option. With Assisted Payroll, Intuit (the maker of Quick-Books) does payroll for you and then supplies that information to your QuickBooks data file over an Internet connection. The Complete Payroll option is Intuit's alternative to outside payroll services, such as ADP or Paychex. I don't talk about the Assisted Payroll option or the Complete Payroll option in this chapter for a simple reason: If you use either of these options, the QuickBooks folks will help you through the setup process and the payroll processing. You don't need my help. You'll get their help.

 Would you be terribly offended if I offered you a bit of friendly advice? If you're not an accountant, spend the money on Intuit's Complete Payroll service or on one of the equivalent full-service payroll providers such as ADP or Paychex. Having Intuit or ADP or Paychex do your payroll will greatly simplify your payroll accounting work and — in my experience — save you money over time.

Setting Up Do-it-yourself Payroll

To set up Do-it-yourself Payroll, you step through a Web-based interview. To start this interview, choose the Employees⇨Payroll Services⇨Setup Payroll command. QuickBooks displays the Payroll Setup Web page, shown in Figure 5-1. As this Web page indicates, to set up QuickBooks payroll, you go through a six-step process. The first step is choosing a payroll option.

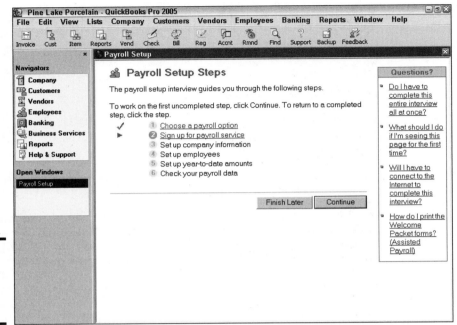

Figure 5-1:
The first
payroll
setup Web
page.

Choosing a payroll option

Even though you have three QuickBooks payroll options, in this chapter, I assume that you want to use the Do-it-yourself Payroll option (shown in Figure 5-2 as QuickBooks Standard or Enhanced Payroll). The Do-it-yourself Payroll option is truly a do-it-yourself solution. You do the work. You need to understand federal and state payroll tax rules. However, you don't have to pay much; in fact, you can do your first payroll for free. After that, you need to keep your payroll tax information up to date by subscribing to a payroll tax service, such as the one that QuickBooks sells.

To choose the Do-it-yourself Payroll option, you click the <u>Choose a Payroll Option</u> hyperlink and select the Standard or Enhanced Payroll radio button when QuickBooks displays the Web page that asks which payroll option you want. Then you click the Continue button. QuickBooks redisplays the Payroll Setup Web page, as shown in Figure 5-1.

Signing up for a payroll service

To sign up for the payroll service after you've selected a particular option, click the <u>Sign Up For Payroll Service</u> hyperlink or simply click the Continue button. QuickBooks next displays the Web page shown in Figure 5-3. You enter your Employer Identification Number, or EIN. Then you click Sign Up Now. QuickBooks then steps you through the process for signup.

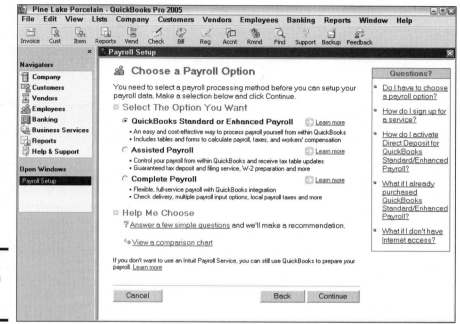

Figure 5-2:
Choosing a payroll option.

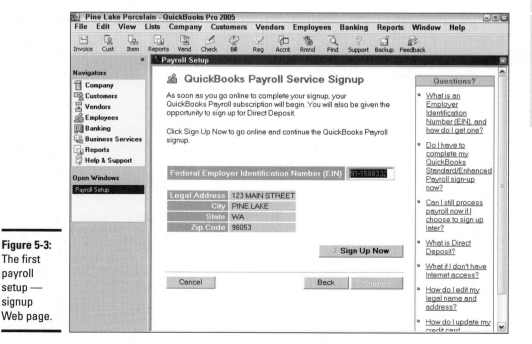

Figure 5-3:
The first payroll setup — signup Web page.

Predictably, during the signup QuickBooks asks you to make additional decisions. For example, the Do-it-yourself Payroll annual fee equals, at this writing, roughly $200 to $300, depending on which additional features, if any, you select.

Setting up company information

After you sign up for and set up the Do-it-yourself Payroll Service, you're ready to set up your company information. To do this, click the <u>Set Up Company Information</u> hyperlink that appears on the Payroll Setup Web page (refer to Figure 5-1).

When you set up your company information for payroll, QuickBooks asks for a bunch of information. I won't repeat the instructions that the Web pages provide, but essentially, you just describe how you pay your employees, to whom you remit deductions, and other stuff like that. You need to carefully read the instructions that QuickBooks provides. This takes some time. If you get into trouble, you may want to get an outside accountant's help to set up the Do-it-yourself Payroll Service.

Setting up employees

After you set up your company information for payroll, you're ready to set up employees for payroll. To do this, click the <u>Set Up Employees</u> hyperlink that appears on the Payroll Setup Web page (refer to Figure 5-1). QuickBooks displays a Web page that includes an Add Employee button. If you click the Add Employee button, QuickBooks displays the New Employee window, shown in Figure 5-4, which lets you describe an employee. You may also access the New Employee window by displaying the Employee List, which you get by choosing the Lists⇨Employee List command, clicking the Employee button, and choosing New.

Describing an employee

To describe an employee, you need to complete the fields supplied on the Personal tab. All this stuff is self-explanatory; you enter the person's first name into the First Name box, the person's middle initial goes into the M.I. box, and so forth.

If you want to collect and store additional information for an employee (such as his bank account number for direct deposit), you can click the Additional Info tab. This tab provides a Define Field button that you can use to collect custom bits of information about an employee. To use the Custom Field option, click the Define Field button, and then use the Define Field dialog box to define the fields that you want to add.

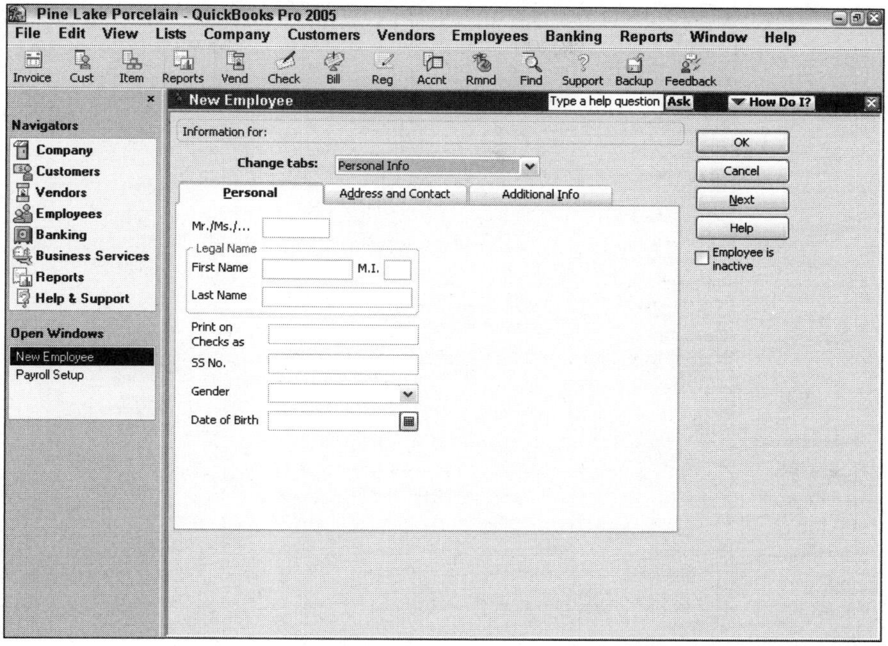

Figure 5-4:
The New
Employee
window.

Providing payroll and tax information

The Payroll and Compensation Info set of tabs lets you describe how an
employee's salary or wages are calculated, as shown in Figure 5-5. You need
to enter the payroll item into the Earnings area. For example, if an employee
earns an annual salary of $30,000, you enter the salary payroll item into the
Item Name column. Then you enter the annual salary of $30,000 into the
Hourly/Annual Rate column. Use the Pay Period drop-down list box to identify the pay period. Optionally, use the Class drop-down list box to classify
payments to this employee.

To describe which taxes an employee pays, click the Taxes button.
QuickBooks displays the Taxes dialog box, shown in Figure 5-6. Use the
Federal tab to identify the employee's filing status, number of allowances
claimed, and any extra withholding specified. In addition, use the Subject To
check boxes to indicate whether this employee is subject to Medicare, Social
Security, or federal unemployment tax, or if the employee is eligible for an
earned income credit. Note that not all employees are subject to Medicare
and Social Security taxes. Consult your tax advisor for more information.

The State tab supplies boxes that you can use to describe state taxes, obviously. I don't show the State tax tab here because the State tax tab varies
depending on the state you're in.

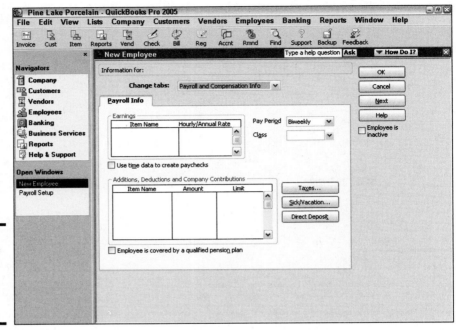

Figure 5-5:
The Payroll
Info tab of
the New
Employee
window.

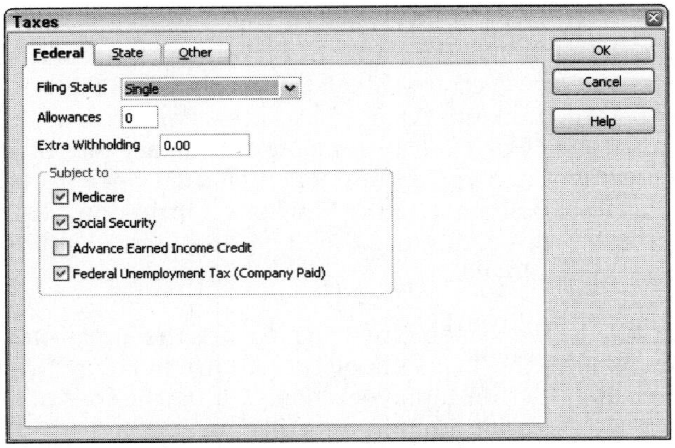

Figure 5-6:
The Federal
tab of the
Taxes dialog
box.

The Other tab lets you describe and store any local tax information, such as
a city income tax. Again, what you see on the Other tab depends on your
locality. For this reason, I don't show it here.

The Sick/Vacation button displays the Sick & Vacation dialog box, shown in
Figure 5-7. This dialog box lets you specify how sick or vacation pay or personal leave time is accrued payroll period by payroll period. You can specify

the number of sick or vacation leave hours at the time you are setting up payroll in the Hours Available As Of text box. You can use the Accrual Period drop-down list box to specify how often sick or vacation pay should be accrued. If sick or vacation pay is accrued, use the Hour Accrued Per box to identify how many hours of sick or vacation time an employee earns each paycheck, hour, or at the beginning of the year. If you have set a maximum number of sick hours or vacation hours that an employee can accumulate, enter this value into the Maximum Number of Hours box. If you want to reset the sick hours and vacation hours to zero at the beginning of each year, select the Reset Hours Each New Year? check box.

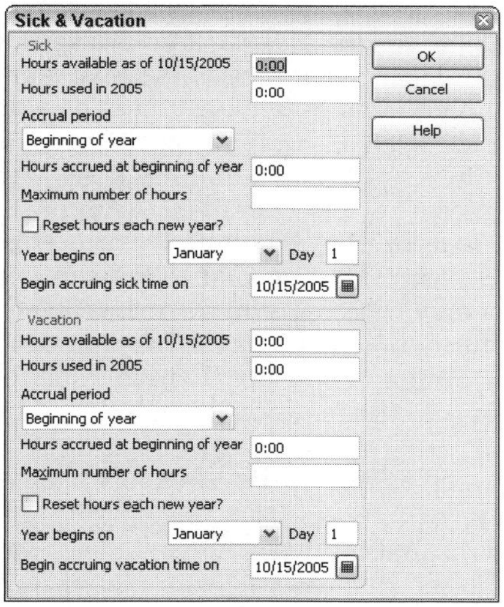

Figure 5-7:
The Sick &
Vacation
dialog box.

**Book III
Chapter 5**

Paying Employees

The Vacation area of the Sick & Vacation dialog box works the same way as the Sick area. For example, enter the number of vacation hours available in the Hours Available As Of box. Use the Accrual drop-down list box to specify how often employees earn vacation time. Use the Hours Accrued Per Paycheck and the Maximum Number of Hours boxes to control how vacation time accrual calculations work. Finally, select the Reset Hours Each New Year? check box to zero out vacation time at the beginning of each new year.

If you've chosen to use the Direct Deposit option — you would have done this when you set up the Do-it-yourself Payroll Service — click the Direct Deposit button on the Payroll Info tab. QuickBooks then prompts you to supply the direct deposit information necessary to do direct deposit checks for employees.

Providing other employment-related information

If you select the Employment Info option from the Change Tabs drop-down list box, QuickBooks displays the Employment tab. The Employment tab lets you store the hire date, fire date, and other similar bits of employment data.

Setting up year-to-date amounts

You can click the Set Up Year-To-Date Amounts hyperlink to tell QuickBooks about year-to-date wages and tax amounts. When you click the Set Up Year-To-Date Amounts hyperlink, QuickBooks displays the Payroll Setup – Year-To-Date Web page. This Web page explains how and why you need to tell QuickBooks what you've already paid employees and what you've already withheld in deductions for employee paychecks. If you're setting up the Do-it-yourself Payroll Service at the very beginning of the business's operation or at the beginning of the year, you don't have to set up any year-to-date amounts. If you're switching to the Do-it-yourself Payroll Service sometime mid-year, you *do* need to set up year-to-date amounts. The Payroll Setup – Year-To-Date Web page provides a Set Up Year-To-Date Amounts button that you click to start the Set Up Year-To-Date Amounts Wizard. This wizard walks you through the process for recording year-to-date amounts. You click the Prev and Next buttons to move through the wizard. When QuickBooks prompts you for pieces of information, such as the point at which you want to begin using the year-to-date amounts for the Do-it-yourself Payroll Service, you enter the answer into the text box provided.

If an outside service bureau such as ADP or Paychex has been doing your payroll processing, the final payroll report from this outside service bureau probably supplies all of the information that you need to set up the Do-it-yourself Payroll Service. If you've been working with a bookkeeper or accountant to get payroll done, you should be able to get this person's help to describe year-to-date payroll amounts.

Checking your payroll data

The sixth and final step is to check your payroll data. If you click the Check Your Payroll Data hyperlink, QuickBooks displays the Payroll Setup – Check Up window. The Payroll Setup – Check Up window provides hyperlinks that you can use to verify that the payroll data that you've set up looks correct and to verify that the payroll tax form information reconciles.

If QuickBooks identifies some suspicious payroll data that doesn't seem right to you — perhaps an employee that you know you've paid shows as having no year-to-date wages — click the Edit button next to the employee's name. Then use the Edit Employee window to correct the incorrect data. Note, however, that the Payroll Setup – Check Up process may identify suspicious payroll data that is, in fact, correct. For example, in the state of Washington (where I live), officers are not subject to state unemployment insurance if they so elect. The Payroll Setup – Check Up Wizard, however, doesn't know this and thus flags officers who are not marked as subject to state unemployment insurance as possible errors.

Again, if you don't feel comfortable answering some of these payroll setup questions, get an accountant's help. Quite frankly, when you have an outside service bureau prepare your payroll checks, what you're really paying for is the expertise and knowledge about how all this payroll processing stuff works. You're not really paying for the computer time and the paper on which the checks are written.

Paying Employees

After you go through the steps required to set up the QuickBooks payroll processing capability, paying employees — thank goodness — is pretty easy.

To pay employees, follow these steps:

1. **Choose Employees⇨Pay Employees.**

   QuickBooks displays the Select Employees to Pay window.

2. **Use the Bank Account drop-down list box to identify the bank account on which you want to write checks.**

   Furthermore, if you are going to print the checks (which is a good idea because it makes the checks easier for your employees to cash), select the To Be Printed check box.

3. **Use the Check Date box to supply the date that you want to appear on payroll checks.**

   Identify the date on which the payroll period ends in the Pay Period Ends box.

4. **Decide whether you want to preview the checks.**

   Next to the Bank Account drop-down list box, QuickBooks supplies a couple of option buttons that you can use to indicate whether you want to preview the checks before they get created. Typically, you want to preview checks, so you should select the Enter Hours and Preview Check Before Creating check box. If you've been using the Do-it-yourself Payroll Service for a long time and you never have any troubles, you can alternatively select the Create Check Without Preview Using Hours Below and Last Quantities check box.

5. **Select the employee whom you want to pay.**

   The Select Employees To Pay window lists the active employees on your Employee List — you add employees to your Employee List as part of setting up the payroll — and from this list, you select the employees whom you want to pay. After doing this, click the check mark column to select the employees who should get paychecks. If you want to pay all the employees, click the Mark All button.

To deselect a selected employee, click the check mark that marks the employee. To deselect all of the selected employees, click the Unmark All button. (The Select Employees To Pay window either shows the Mark All button or the Unmark All button.)

6. Click Create.

QuickBooks calculates the payroll checks and payroll deduction amounts for each of the employees selected. The Preview Paycheck dialog box shows the payroll amount calculated for each employee. To accept the previewed paycheck described or shown in the Preview Paycheck dialog box, click its Create button.

7. Click the Print Paychecks button.

The Print Paychecks command button also appears in the Select Employees To Pay window. When you click this button, QuickBooks displays the Select Paychecks To Print dialog box. You should confirm the bank account from which you want to write the checks. You should also use the First Check Number box to supply the preprinted form number shown on the first payroll check that you'll print. You should also confirm that the employee paychecks listed in the dialog box are those that you want to print. After you confirm that the paycheck printing information is correct, click OK. QuickBooks displays the Print Checks dialog box (the same one you use to print any check) that you use in the usual fashion to print checks.

If you want to deselect a paycheck for printing, click the check column to remove the check mark, and thereby, deselect the paycheck.

8. Distribute the paychecks.

Obviously, after you print the checks, you need to sign and then distribute them. I'll leave you to your own devices here. I am sure you know how to find employees whom you need to pay, and furthermore, how to hand them their paychecks. Heck, they're probably standing beside your desk right now waiting for you to finish the payroll checks anyway.

Editing and Voiding Paychecks

You need to be careful when you want to change payroll check information. Payroll checks are a little trickier than regular checks because the information from the payroll checks affects a bunch of different payroll counters. For example, payroll checks bump up someone's gross wages for the year. Payroll checks also affect the deduction amounts. For this reason, when you want to make a change or void a paycheck that you previously created, you need to choose the Employees➪Edit/Void Paychecks command. When you do this, QuickBooks displays the Edit/Void Paychecks window. This window lists paychecks that you've previously created and printed. To change one of the paychecks listed, double-click the paycheck. When QuickBooks displays the Paychecks window, click the Paycheck Detail button. When QuickBooks displays the Review Paychecks window, use it to make the appropriate change to the paycheck. Note that you can also make changes to other details, such as the name or address, by using the Paycheck window.

To void the paycheck shown in the Paycheck window, choose the Edit➪Void Paycheck command.

After you edit or void a check, you need to click the Save & Close or the Save & New button to save your changes to the paycheck.

Paying Payroll Liabilities

Amounts that you withhold from employees' paychecks become liabilities that you later need to pay. For example, if you withhold federal income tax deductions, you need to remit those to the Internal Revenue Service.

To pay payroll tax liabilities, choose the Employees➪Process Payroll Liabilities➪Pay Payroll Liabilities command. QuickBooks displays the Select Date Range for Liabilities dialog box. It lets you specify the range of dates for which you want to report on payroll liabilities. Use the Show Liabilities From and Through boxes to identify the date range. Then click OK. When you do, QuickBooks displays the Pay Liabilities window.

The Pay Liabilities window identifies the payroll liabilities that you need to pay as of the Show Liabilities Through date. To pay a liability, select the To Be Printed check box, choose the checking account on which you want to write the check from the Checking Account drop-down list box, and enter the payment date into the Payment box.

Identify or select those payroll liabilities that you want to pay by checking the check column of the list. For each payroll liability, QuickBooks identifies the payroll item, the agency to which the payroll item is payable, and the amount. You can choose to pay some amount other than the amount due by editing the values shown in the Amount to Pay column.

After you select which payroll liability amount that you want to pay, you can click the Create button to create checks for paying the liability amounts.

You can select the Create Liability Check Without Reviewing check box to have QuickBooks create a check without any input on your part. Or, what I recommend, you can select the Review Liability Check to Enter Expenses/Penalties check box to have QuickBooks create a liability check but then display the liability check in a dialog box that you can use to check all the numbers.

Book IV

Accounting Chores

The 5th Wave   By Rich Tennant

©RICHTENNANT

"IT'S REALLY QUITE AN ENTERTAINING PIECE OF SOFTWARE. THERE'S ROLLER COASTER ACTION, SUSPENSE AND DRAMA, WHERE SKILL AND STRATEGY ARE MATCHED AGAINST WINNING AND LOSING. AND I THOUGHT MANAGING OUR BUDGET WOULD BE DULL."

Contents at a Glance

Chapter 1: For Accountants Only

In This Chapter

✓ Working with QuickBooks journal entries

✓ Reviewing the Accountant & Taxes reports

✓ Reviewing the Expert Analysis reports

✓ Using the Decision Tools command

✓ Creating an accountant's copy of the QuickBooks data file

In this short chapter, I want to quickly go over stuff that accountants need or will want to know. Because I assume you are an accountant, I go a little faster here than I have in other chapters of this book. I also don't provide blow-by-blow instructions for working with the windows and dialog boxes that this chapter discusses.

If you find yourself just a wee bit frustrated with me at this point — go ahead and peruse the paragraphs of this chapter, keeping in mind that what I discuss in this chapter is pretty advanced accounting stuff. You don't want to do the things that this chapter talks about unless you really know your debits and credits. And if you do know your debits and credits, you should find the information I provide here to be all that you need.

Working with QuickBooks Journal Entries

QuickBooks makes it easy for you — an accountant — to record journal entries. If you've spent any time working with QuickBooks, you may know that most of the journal entries that get recorded into the QuickBooks data file are recorded automatically. If somebody writes a check, for example, QuickBooks records the journal entry for that. When somebody creates an invoice, again, QuickBooks records the journal entry for that.

In some cases, however, somebody — probably you — needs to record a journal entry to get some transaction into the QuickBooks data file. For example, you need to use journal entries to record depreciation, to accrue liabilities, and to record the disposal of assets.

Recording a journal entry

To record the journal entry, choose Company➪Make Journal Entry. Quick-Books displays the General Journal Entry window, as shown in Figure 1-1.

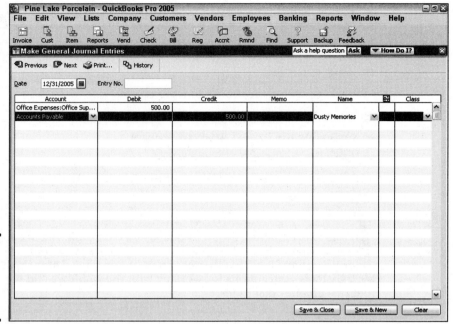

Figure 1-1:
The General
Journal
Entry
window.

You can probably figure out how to use the General Journal Entry window yourself. You enter the general journal entry date into the Date box. You use the Entry No. box to number journal entries or to assign them some meaningful code. After you provide this basic information, you use the columns of the General Journal Entry window to record the journal entry. You don't need me to tell you that the general ledger account number or name goes into the Account column, the debit amount into the Debit column, and the credit amount into the Credit column. You may find it useful, though, to be reminded that you can use the Memo column to enter some description of the debit or credit; you can use the Name column to identify the customer, vendor, employee or other name associated with the credit or debit; and you can use the Class column to classify the debit or credit.

Reversing a journal entry

To reverse a journal entry, first display the General Journal Entries window by choosing the Company⇨Make Journal Entries command. QuickBooks then displays the General Journal Entry window, as shown in Figure 1-1. Use the Previous and Next buttons to page through general journal entries that you've already entered. Found it? Good. How you reverse this entry depends on which version of QuickBooks you're using.

✦ **If you're using QuickBooks Basic or QuickBooks Pro:** Print the general journal entry by clicking the Print button. Then, using the printed journal entry as a reference source, enter a new journal except with the debits and credits reversed. In other words, if the to-be-reversed journal entry debits cash for $500 and credits interest income for $500, you enter a journal entry that credits cash for $500 and debits interest income for $500.

✦ **If you're using QuickBooks Premier:** When you find the journal entry that you want to reverse, click the Reverse button. The Reverse button appears along the top edge of the General Journal Entry window. QuickBooks reverses the general journal entry by entering a transaction into the next accounting month with the debits and credits flip-flopped.

Book I, Chapter 1 discusses the basics of accounting. Chapter 2 in the same book describes basic bookkeeping, including how debits and credits work. Chapter 3 (also in Book I) describes how to do special accounting magic tricks, including how to and why to enter reversing journal entries. If you find yourself in this chapter even though you're not a degreed accountant, you may want to peruse the information from Chapters 1, 2, and 3 of Book I in order to understand what journal entries are and why in the world one would want to reverse one.

Editing journal entries

Typically, you won't want to fool around and later change the journal entries. However, if you do feel the need to make changes, QuickBooks provides an Edit menu with commands that you can use for just this purpose. For example, QuickBooks supplies a Delete General Journal Entry command that you can use to delete the journal entry shown in the General Journal Entry window. QuickBooks also supplies a Void General Journal Entry command that you can use to void the general journal entry shown in the window. Typically — and again you already know this — you don't want to delete general journal entries. Instead, you want to *void* them. Enough said.

Updating Company Information

The Company menu supplies a bunch of other commands in addition to the Make Journal Entry command. Accountants may have occasion to use the Company Information command. The Company Information command enables you to update company name and address information, fiscal and tax year settings, the tax form used to report profits, and taxpayer identification numbers.

**Book IV
Chapter 1**

**For Accountants
Only**

Working with the Memorized Transactions

A quick tip: Most of the transactions that people enter into QuickBooks can be memorized by choosing the Edit➪Memorize command when the transaction shows in the open window. You (or someone else) can later reuse a memorized transaction by choosing the Lists➪Memorized Transaction List command and then, when QuickBooks displays the list of memorized transactions (shown in Figure 1-2), double-clicking the transaction that you want to enter again.

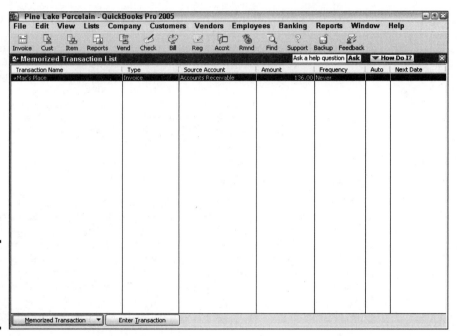

Figure 1-2:
The Memorized Transaction List window.

Reviewing the Accountant & Taxes Reports

The Accountant & Taxes menu appears when you choose the Reports➪ Accountant & Taxes command. Although I don't show pictures of each report that gets displayed by choosing a command from the Accountant & Taxes menu (although I do show the Trial Balance report in Figure 1-3), I want to point out that hidden on this submenu are almost a dozen menu commands and reports that are particularly interesting and useful to accountants. The following list identifies these reports:

✦ **Trial Balance:** The Trial Balance menu command produces, of course, a Trial Balance Report as of a particular date (shown in Figure 1-3).

✦ **General Ledger:** The General Ledger menu command produces a report that simply lists the accounts in your Chart of Accounts and then changes the account for the month or year or whatever accounting period that you specify.

✦ **Transaction Detail by Account:** This menu command produces the report that you would expect: A list of the transactions that affect a particular account.

✦ **Journal:** The Journal menu command produces a report that lists transactions by transaction type and number.

✦ **Audit Trail:** The Audit Trail Report is pretty important for accountants — particularly when an accountant is concerned or worried that transactions have changed when they should *not* have changed. The Audit Trail Report lists transactions by the person entering the transactions. The Audit Trail Report also lists changes to transactions and identifies who made the changes. You need to turn on the Audit Trail feature as described in Book II, Chapter 3. If it's important for you to know who is doing what, the Audit Trail Report provides the answer.

✦ **Closing Date Exception Report:** If you finalize the accounting data for the year (referred to as "closing the books") — and you should — the Closing Date Exception Report identifies changes to closed transactions. Closing the QuickBooks data file is described in Book VII, Chapter 3.

✦ **Transaction List By Date:** The Transaction List By Date Report lists transactions in order of date of entry.

✦ **Account Listing:** The Account Listing Report lists all of the accounts on your Chart of Accounts. The report also gives the account balance and indicates which line on your tax return that the account gets reported on.

✦ **Income Tax Preparation:** The Income Tax Preparation Report shows on which lines of which tax forms that account balances get reported.

✦ **Income Tax Summary:** The Income Tax Summary Report uses your income tax preparation data to show what amounts should be reported on what lines of your tax forms. For example, if you are a sole proprietor filing a Schedule C tax form, QuickBooks looks at all the accounts that you use to track gross receipts or sales. Then it totals the balances in those accounts and shows the actual value that should be reported on the gross receipts or sales line of your Schedule C tax form.

✦ **Income Tax Detail:** The Income Tax Detail Report gives the same information as the Income Tax Summary Report — except that this report shows the individual accounts that get bunched together to produce the tax line total.

**Book IV
Chapter 1**

For Accountants Only

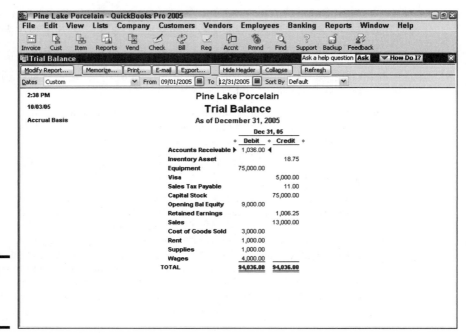

Figure 1-3:
The Trial
Balance
window.

Reviewing the Expert Analysis Reports

While I'm on the subject of the Accountant & Taxes Report, I should also mention that some versions of QuickBooks, such as QuickBooks Premier include a Reports⇨Expert Analysis command. If you choose the Reports⇨Expert Analysis command, QuickBooks displays the Expert Analysis submenu. The Expert Analysis submenu provides another set of menu commands that let you display income statements and balance sheets that compare one month's data to the previous month's data, or one quarter's data to the previous quarter's data, or one year's data to the previous year's data.

I don't discuss the individual Expert Analysis reports here because the menu commands that appear on this submenu are very self-explanatory. However, you should know that these useful reports are there. If you have time and you've already accumulated several months or several years' worth of data, use these reports to make period-to-period comparisons.

A Few Words about the Decision Tools

If you are a professional accountant, you probably don't need to use the Decision Tools command. However, you should know that if you or one of your clients or co-workers chooses the Company⇨Planning & Budgeting⇨ Decision Tools command, QuickBooks displays a submenu that includes commands that start little tutorials of how to manage the finances of a small firm. For example, if someone chooses the Measure Profitability command from the Decision Tools submenu, that person sees first the window shown in Figure 1-4. This Measure Profitability window enables someone to step through a pretty darn cool tutorial about how firms can look at their profit margins and use profit margin data to make better decisions.

Other Decision Tools submenu commands enable a business owner or manager to analyze the financial strength of the firm; compare debt and ownership percentages; learn how to depreciate assets; manage the firm's receivables; figure out whether someone is an employee, an independent contractor, or a temporary employee; and even improve cash flow. All of this stuff is pretty cool.

If you know of a business owner who wants to use QuickBooks for more than just producing forms or getting data ready to file a tax return, be sure that this person knows that the Decision tools are there. Also be sure that this person knows that the Decision tools are written not for accountants — not for people like you and me — but for regular folk who need practical, easy-to-understand discussions of business accounting and financial management.

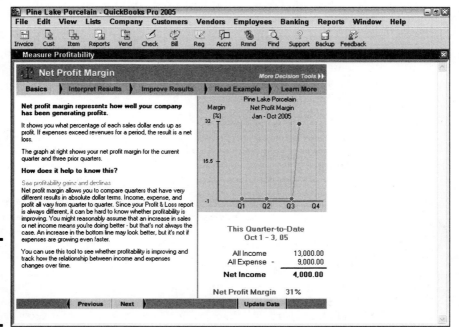

Figure 1-4: The Measure Profitability window.

Book IV
Chapter 1

For Accountants Only

Creating an Accountant's Copy of the QuickBooks Data File

QuickBooks makes it easier for accountants to work with client data files. Consider this scenario: You have a client who needs help finishing up the year's accounting period. You have two choices. First, you can drive over to his or her shop, probably getting stuck in traffic along the way, and find yourself wondering if you can bill the client $150 for your travel time. Second, you can have the client use the Create Accountant's Copy feature in QuickBooks and simply e-mail you or snail-mail you a copy of the QuickBooks data file. You can then review this accountant's copy of the data file, make whatever fixes or changes are appropriate, and then send the changes that need to be made back to the client. The client can then easily import these changes into his or her existing QuickBooks file, and go off on his or her merry way. Pretty neat, right? This is exactly what the accountant's copy lets you do.

Creating an accountant's copy

Your client needs to create the accountant's copy of the QuickBooks data file by using his or her version of QuickBooks and the real data file. Fortunately, the process is very straightforward. Here's what your client needs to do:

1. **Choose the File⇨Accountant's Review⇨Create Accountant's Copy command.**

QuickBooks displays a message telling the client that QuickBooks will need to close all of the windows to create an accountant's copy. QuickBooks may also tell the client to insert a disk. When the client clicks OK, and inserts the disk (if necessary), QuickBooks displays the Save Accountant's Copy to dialog box, shown in Figure 1-5.

2. **Name the accountant's copy.**

Use the File Name box of the Save Accountant's Copy to dialog box to name the accountant's copy of the QuickBooks data file. If necessary, the client can also use the Save In drop-down list box to specify where the accountant's copy of the QuickBooks data file should be saved.

The client needs to remember where the accountant's copy of the file gets saved. This file needs to be given to the accountant — via e-mail, snail-mail, or saved onto a disk that the accountant takes — in order for the accountant to be able to use it.

3. **Create the file.**

After the client names the accountant's copy of the data file and indicates, if necessary, where the accountant's copy should be saved, the client needs to click Save. QuickBooks then saves an accountant's copy of the QuickBooks data file.

This data file then needs to be transmitted to the accountant.

Accountant copies make use of three files types. There's the Accountant Transfer File (with the .qbx file extension), which is what a client creates and gives to the accountant. Then there's the actual Accountant Copy (with the .qba file extension), which is what the accountant works with after he or she opens the Accountant Transfer File. And finally, there's the Accountant Export File (with the .aif file extension), which is discussed later.

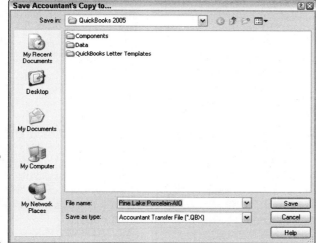

Figure 1-5:
The Save Accountant's Copy to dialog box.

Obviously, it may not actually be your client who takes these steps; you may have to do the dirty work. In either case, though, that's how the process works. Note, however, that the real time savings for the accountant and the cost savings to the client occur when you can get the client to choose the command and work with the dialog box. You can then charge billable time for actually working with QuickBooks data rather than fiddle-faddling with the file.

Using an accountant's copy

You use the accountant's copy by choosing the File⊏>Accountant's Review⊏> Start Using Accountant's Copy command. When you choose this command, QuickBooks displays the Open Accountant's Copy dialog box, shown in Figure 1-6.

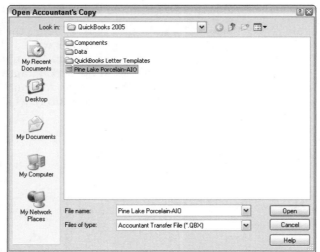

Use the Look In drop-down list box to identify the location of the accountant's copy. If necessary, enter the accountant's copy filename into the File Name box. When you click Open, QuickBooks prompts you to name the accountant's copy and then opens the accountant's copy. Note that you won't be able to make the same changes to an accountant's copy that you can make to a regular QuickBooks data file. QuickBooks limits the sort of changes that you can make in an accountant's copy.

Reusing an accountant's copy

If you've already opened an accountant's copy file once, you can reuse the accountant's copy by choosing the File⇨Accountant's Review⇨Continue Using Accountant's Copy command. When you do this, QuickBooks displays the Open Company dialog box, which works the same way as the Open an Accountant's Copy dialog box. Essentially, you use the Look In drop-down list box to identify the file location and the File Name box to uniquely identify the file. When you click Open, QuickBooks opens the data file so that you can make your changes.

Exporting client changes

After you have used an accountant's copy to correct transactions or to enter new transactions, you export the changes so that they can later be imported into the client's data file. To do this, choose the File⇨Accountant's Review⇨Export Changes for Client command. QuickBooks displays the Save Accountant's Export to dialog box, shown in Figure 1-7. Use the Save In drop-down list box to identify the location of the changes file. Then use the File

Name box to give the file a unique name. When you click Save, QuickBooks saves the changes that you've made into a file. You'll later need to import this file, or have the client import this file, into the QuickBooks data file.

Figure 1-7:
The Save
Account-
ant's Export
to dialog
box.

You don't keep your accountant's copy of the data file. In other words, the accountant's copy is just a temporary copy of the data file that you use to identify and create a set of changes necessary to update or correct client's records. After you make the changes, you export the changes to a changes file. Then the client needs to import those changes (as discussed in the next section). If you need to make changes again some time in the near future, you have the client create a new — a *brand new* — accountant's copy.

To identify when you are working with an accountant's copy, QuickBooks displays the parenthetical phrase (Accountant's Copy) along the top of the QuickBooks program window. QuickBooks also identifies regular QuickBooks data files for which accountant's copies have been created by adding the parenthetical phrase (Accountant's Copy Exists). This phrase only appears on the QuickBooks program window title bar from the point that the client creates the accountant's copy to the point that the client imports changes from the accountant's copy.

Importing accountant's changes

Your clients need to import the changes that you've made in the accountant's copy of the data file into their working copy of the data file. In order to do this, the client needs to choose the File⇨Accountant Review⇨Import Accountant's Changes command.

**Book IV
Chapter 1**

**For Accountants
Only**

QuickBooks prompts the client to back up the QuickBooks data file. I don't describe that process here, but I go into a lot of detail about how to back up a data file in Book VII, Chapter 3.

After the client backs up the data file in the usual manner, QuickBooks displays the Import Changes from Accountant's Copy dialog box, as shown in Figure 1-8. To use the Import Changes from Accountant's Copy dialog box, the client just needs to use the Look In drop-down list box to identify the location of the changes file. After the client identifies the location — this may be the disk with the changes file on it — the client should be able to see the changes file in the middle of the Import Changes from Accountant's Copy dialog box. The accountant can double-click the changes file in order to import the changes into his or her QuickBooks data file.

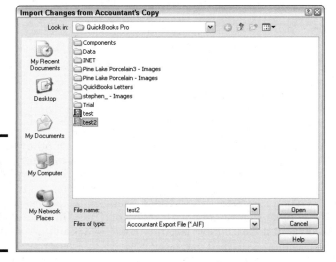

Figure 1-8:
The Import
Changes
from
Account-
ant's Copy
dialog box.

After the client imports the changes, QuickBooks removes the parenthetical phrase (Accountant's Copy Exists) from the QuickBooks program window title bar.

Canceling accountant's changes

Here's a little question for you: What happens if the client gives you an accountant's copy of the QuickBooks data file and then realizes that either you won't be making changes or the client doesn't want to accept the changes? Bummer, right? Well, not really.

In this case, the client needs to cancel the client's changes. When a client creates an accountant's copy of the QuickBooks data file, QuickBooks marks the client's data file as one that can be modified through the accountant's changes. QuickBooks needs to do this in order to later allow the accountant's changes. But if those changes won't be made, the client needs to unmark the data file as available for changes. To do this, the client needs to choose the File⇨Accountant's Review⇨Cancel Accountant's Changes command. When the client chooses this command, QuickBooks displays a message indicating that the client is choosing to cancel out of accountant's copy mode. After the client chooses this command, the client won't be able to import any changes created by using the canceled accountant's copy.

If the client later wants to get changes from his or her accountant, the client needs to create a new accountant's copy by using the procedure described earlier in this chapter.

Chapter 2: Preparing Financial Statements and Reports

In This Chapter

- Producing a report
- Working with the Report window
- Modifying a report
- Processing multiple reports

QuickBooks produces — oh, I don't know — about 100 different financial statements and reports. I tried to count them for purposes of writing this chapter, but lost track after I had counted 90-some reports. I figured that was close enough for my purposes here.

Because QuickBooks contains so many reports, I don't provide individualized descriptions of each report in this chapter. Rather, I talk about some of the stuff that you need to do before you prepare financial statements. Then, after covering those basics, I talk about how you produce and modify reports, and about some of the useful tools that QuickBooks supplies for working with reports.

Some Wise Words Up Front

This is an obvious point, but you should note that the reports you produce in QuickBooks are only as good as the data file. If you have good, rich information in your QuickBooks data file, if they don't contain too many mistakes, and if all of the transactions are entered, your reports should be pretty darn good.

This simple observation has one important ramification: Often, the first step in preparing good financial statements and useful reports is to collect the rest of the data. In other words, you want to make sure that you've entered all of the invoices, purchase orders, checks, and so forth. You also want to make sure that any special accounting transactions, such as for depreciation or asset sales or accruals, have been entered. (Perhaps you need your accountant's help for this.)

The other chapters of this book talk about how to collect and record these other sorts of information, so there's no need to talk more about that here.

But just to beat this thing to death, the first step in producing a good financial statement or a good report is to collect the rest of the information.

Producing a Report

As I mentioned at the beginning of this chapter, QuickBooks provides roughly 100 different financial statements and accounting reports. You get to these reports by opening the Reports menu. The Reports menu, shown in Figure 2-1, arranges reports into roughly a dozen different categories, including Company & Financial, Customers & Receivables, Sales, Jobs & Time, and so forth.

To produce just about any of the reports available through the Reports menu, you first select the Report category. For example, if you want to produce a standard financial statement, such as a profit & loss statement, you choose the Reports⇨Company & Financial command. QuickBooks displays the Company & Financial submenu, as shown in Figure 2-2. This submenu lists the various types of financial statements available.

You pick the submenu command that describes the financial statement that you want. For example, if you want a standard profit & loss financial statement, you choose the Profit & Loss Standard command. After you choose the submenu command, QuickBooks displays the Report window for the report that you selected, as shown in Figure 2-3.

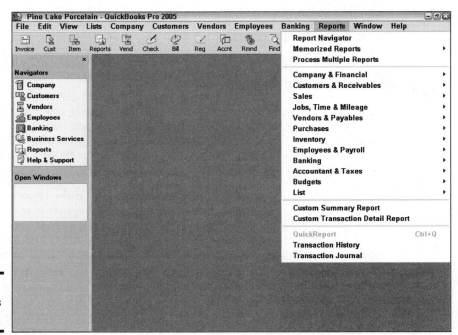

Figure 2-1:
The Reports
menu.

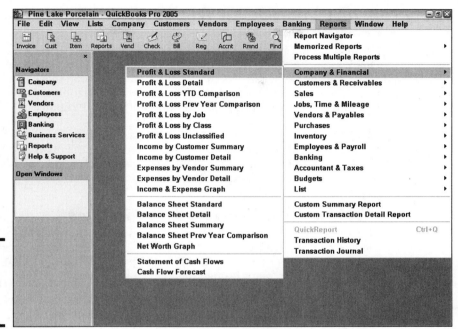

Figure 2-2:
The Company & Financial submenu.

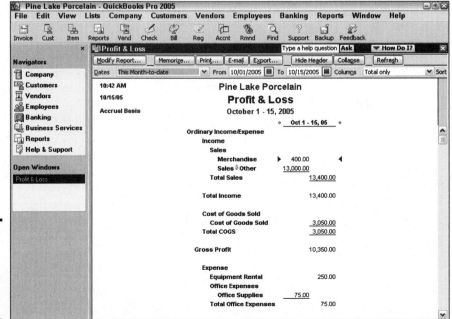

Figure 2-3:
The Report window showing the profit & loss statement.

Working with the Report Window

If you are comfortable working with Microsoft Windows, working with the QuickBooks Report window should be a snap. Typically, a report won't fit within a window because it contains too much data. In this case, however, QuickBooks adds scroll bars, both vertical and horizontal, that you can use to scroll the window around. Pretty straightforward, right?

Along the top edge of the window, QuickBooks displays both buttons and boxes. You use these buttons and boxes to change the display of the Report window and to control the information shown in the Report window. In the next section, I describe each of these buttons and boxes.

Working with Report window buttons

The Report window typically provides seven different buttons: Modify Report, Memorize, Print, Export to Excel, Hide Header, Collapse, and Refresh. You can find out what these command buttons do by experimentation. Or, if you don't have time for that, read through the following sections.

Modify Report

The Modify Report button displays the Modify Report dialog box. I won't go into any detail about this command button here because a later section of this chapter, "Modifying a Report," talks in gritty detail about how you use this command button to customize a report.

Memorize

The Memorize button displays the Memorize Report dialog box, shown in Figure 2-4. The Memorize Report dialog box lets you *memorize*, or permanently save, a particular set of report creation settings. After you memorize these settings, you can later produce the exact same report by choosing the memorized report from the Reports⇨Memorized Reports submenu.

Figure 2-4:
The
Memorize
Report
dialog box.

Not only can you save a memorized report in the Memorized Report Group, but you can also save it in some other report group or category. To do this, select the Save in Memorized Report Group check box. Then use the Save in Memorized Report Group drop-down list box to select the report group in which the memorized report should be saved.

Print

The Print command button enables you to print the report. When you click Print, QuickBooks (sometimes after a bit of annoyance) displays the Print Reports dialog box, as shown in Figure 2-5. The Print Reports dialog box lets you choose how the report should print and where it should print. For example, the Settings tab lets you choose the printer, select a page orientation (either portrait or landscape), specify that you only want to print a range of the report's pages, and control page breaking.

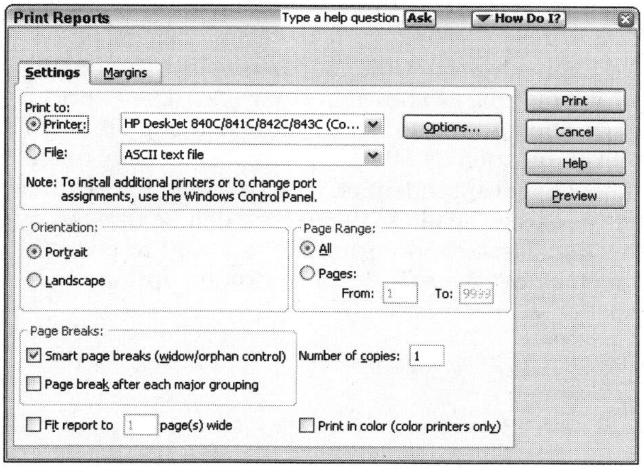

Figure 2-5:
The Settings tab of the Print Reports dialog box.

The Margins tab of the Print Reports menu, shown in Figure 2-6, lets you specify the margins that QuickBooks should use on the printed report pages. You specify the top, right, bottom, and left margins in inches.

Click the Preview button, provided on the Print Reports dialog box, to display the Preview window. The Preview window shows what your printed report pages look like. The Preview window also includes buttons to page to the previous and next pages of the report, to zoom in and out on the report, and to print the report to paper.

After you've used the Settings tab and the Margins tab to specify how QuickBooks should print a report, click Print. QuickBooks sends the report to your printer.

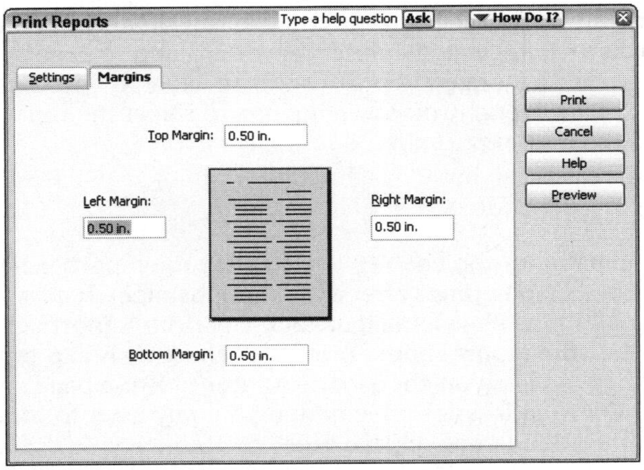

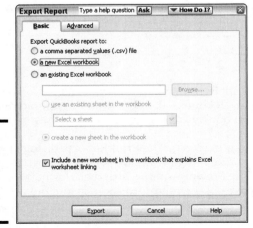

Figure 2-6:
The
Margins tab
of the Print
Reports
dialog box.

Export

If you click the Export button, QuickBooks displays the Basic tab of the Export Report dialog box, as shown in Figure 2-7. The Export Report dialog box lets you take the information in a report and copy it to a file that a spreadsheet program such as Microsoft Excel can easily open. You can send the copy to a new Excel spreadsheet, to an existing Excel spreadsheet, or to a .CSV (comma separated values) file (which can be opened by just about any spreadsheet or database program). If you want to copy the report to a new spreadsheet, select the new Excel workbook option.

Figure 2-7:
The Basic
tab of the
Export
Report
dialog box.

If you want to copy the report to an existing Excel spreadsheet, select the existing Excel workbook option. Then you click the Browse button. When Excel displays the Open Microsoft Excel File dialog box, you use it to identify the specific Excel workbook that you want to open.

If you click the Advanced button in the Export Report dialog box, QuickBooks displays the Advanced tab of the Export Report dialog box, shown in Figure 2-8. This dialog box allows you to control what formatting QuickBooks copies to Excel (do this with the Formatting Options check boxes), to turn on or turn off certain Excel formatting features (do this with the Excel Features check boxes), and to set up some preliminary workbook printing information in Excel (do this with the Printing Options radio buttons). This stuff all relates to how Excel works. If you're comfortable working with Excel, go ahead and make the changes that you want. If you aren't comfortable working with Excel, go ahead and accept QuickBooks' default suggestions. You can change all this stuff later, rather easily, in Excel.

Figure 2-8:
The Advanced tab of the Export Report dialog box.

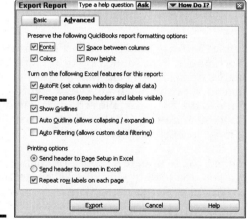

TIP

If you're working with QuickBooks, know that Excel is a wonderful tool for digging deeper into your data. In fact, in several chapters of this book, I assume that you are going to exchange information between Excel and QuickBooks. If you've never done this, or if you haven't yet read those chapters, consider acquiring Excel and then taking the time to learn that powerful spreadsheet product. Also note that next time you buy a PC, you may have the option of getting Microsoft Excel as part of the purchase price. Microsoft Excel often comes with Microsoft Office.

Hide Header

The Hide Header button and the Collapse button change the way the report appears in the Report window and, if printed, on the page.

You click the Hide Header button to remove the header information, such as the company name. If you hide the header, you can click the Hide Header button again to replace the header.

Collapse

The Collapse button collapses detail on a report. QuickBooks doesn't show subaccounts on a collapsed report — only accounts.

To uncollapse a report that you previously collapsed, click the Expand button. QuickBooks replaces the Collapse button with the Expand button when the Report window shows a collapsed report.

Don't spend any time trying to figure out what the Hide Header or Collapse/ Expand buttons do. If you have a question, simply display a report in the Report window and choose the command button about which you have a question. The Report window changes will show you what the command button does.

Refresh

The Refresh button tells QuickBooks to update a report's information for changes in the QuickBooks data file. This sounds crazy at first, but you can actually leave report windows open. This means that a report window may show a profit & loss statement, for example, from a week ago. If you've entered several transactions in the last week, the report data may no longer be correct. By clicking the Refresh button, QuickBooks knows it should update the report for the most recent changes.

QuickBooks typically prompts you to update a report for changes to the QuickBooks data file. If you don't follow QuickBooks' suggestion to update, however, you can later click Refresh to update.

Using the Report window boxes

The Report window provides five boxes: Dates, From, To, Columns, and Sort By. These boxes also enable you to control the information shown in the Report window and the appearance of the information.

Date boxes

The Dates, From, and To boxes, for example, let you tell QuickBooks what reporting interval that you want to show in the report. In other words, you use these boxes to tell QuickBooks for what month, quarter, year, or whatever, that you want the report prepared.

Columns box

The Columns drop-down list box displays a set of column choices. Initially, QuickBooks displays a single total column for a report. However, if you produce, for example, a report that summarizes annual income and expense data, you can use the Columns drop-down list box to tell QuickBooks that you want to see monthly columns. In this situation, QuickBooks would show an annual income statement, but it would also show columns for January, February, March, and so forth. To show you how this works, take a look at Figure 2-9. The profit & loss statement shown in that window is only a Total column.

Now take a look at Figure 2-10; it shows the same profit & loss statement, except this time, the Columns box shows Customer:Job. In this case, QuickBooks shows you a breakdown of your income and expenses by Customer and Job, as well as the total. The Columns drop-down list box gives you a bunch of different column options. Typically, some will make sense for the report that you're working on; others won't. Nevertheless, you should occasionally experiment with this tool. The Columns box often gives you a neat way to further segregate and refine your data.

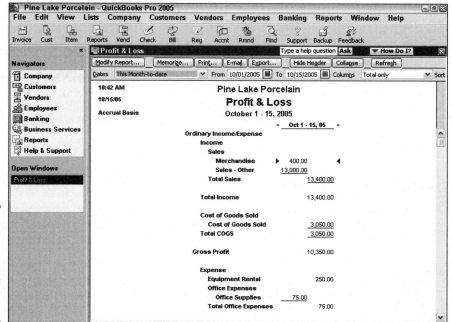

Figure 2-9:
A simple profit & loss statement with a single Total column.

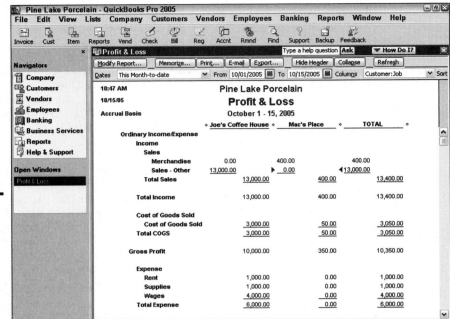

Figure 2-10:
A profit &
loss
statement
with
Customer:-
Job
columns.

Sort By box

The Sort By drop-down list box enables you to choose how information
should be ordered on a report. For many types of reports, the Sort By drop-
down list box doesn't provide any meaningful options. For some types of
reports, however, the Sort By drop-down list box provides handy ways to
organize report information.

Modifying a Report

If you click the Modify Report button, QuickBooks displays the Modify
Report dialog box, which you can use to customize a report. When you customize a report, you change the report's appearance, layout, and the information that it summarizes.

The Modify Report dialog box looks different for different report types.
Nevertheless, if you look past the cosmetic differences, the dialog boxes
pretty much all look and work the same way.

Using the Display tab

The Display tab of the Modify Report dialog box lets you control the report interval date, the report basis, the columns, and some other formatting.

The Report Date Range boxes — Dates, From, and To — do the same thing as the Dates, From, and To boxes on the Report window. These boxes let you control the reporting interval or accounting period. You can choose one of the date descriptions from the Dates box, or you can use the From and To boxes to specify a particular range of dates. The From and To boxes, as shown in Figure 2-11, accept dates in the mm/dd/yyyy format.

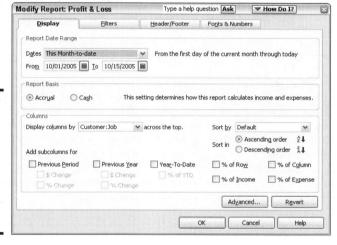

Figure 2-11:
The Display tab of the Modify Report dialog box for a profit & loss statement.

The Report Basis option buttons — accrual and cash — let you specify whether you want QuickBooks to prepare a report on a cash basis or on an accrual basis. Now, quite honestly, you can't simply convert between cash-basis accounting and accrual-basis accounting by clicking these buttons. Cash-basis accounting and accrual-basis accounting are too complicated for QuickBooks to figure out on its own. If you're going to use accrual-basis accounting, for example, you need to be using QuickBooks Accounts Payable feature and you need to be recording revenue and expense transactions when you earn revenue and incur expenses. Nevertheless, these Report Basis buttons enable you to quickly flip between cash-centric profit statements and accrual-like financial statements. And that's pretty handy.

In a nutshell, *cash-basis accounting* counts income and expense when cash moves into and out of a business. *Accrual-basis accounting* counts income when it is earned and counts expense when it is incurred. Chapter 1 of Book I talks in more detail about accounting and the differences between cash-basis accounting and accrual-basis accounting.

The Columns area enables you to control or specify how many columns a report should display. The Display Columns By box is analogous to the Columns box on the Report window. The Columns area also lets you choose a Sort-By option. Again, this is analogous to the Sort By drop-down list box in the Report window.

In addition, the Columns area allows you to add subcolumns (you do this with the Previous Period, Previous Year, and Year-to-Date check boxes) and allows you to add percentages. The neat thing about these percentages is that you are actually adding financial ratios to your financial statement when you do this. I don't talk about financial ratios in this chapter, but I do go into great detail in Book V, Chapter 1 about what financial ratios are and about how they can become powerful tools for assessing and monitoring your financial condition and your financial performance.

To show each line item on an income statement as a percentage of total income, select the % of Income check box.

For more report formatting options, click the Advanced button. QuickBooks displays the Advanced Options dialog box, as shown in Figure 2-12. Use the Display Rows radio buttons to tell QuickBooks when it should or shouldn't display rows of information in a report. Similarly, use the Display Columns radio buttons to tell QuickBooks when it should or shouldn't display columns in a report. You can use the Reporting Calendar radio buttons to select the default annual reporting period. The Default year can be a fiscal year (you set this option when setting up QuickBooks), a calendar year, or an income tax year. Click OK to activate these selections.

Figure 2-12:
The
Advanced
Options
dialog box.

To revert to the Default Display settings, click the Revert button on the Display tab.

Using the Filters tab

The Filters tab is probably the most interesting and useful tab provided by the Modify Report dialog box. The Filters tab enables you to set up filters that you can use to specify what information gets summarized in the report. To use the Filters tab, shown in Figure 2-13, you first select the field on which you want to base a filter from the Filter list box. For example, if you want to filter information based on the account, select Account from the Filter list box.

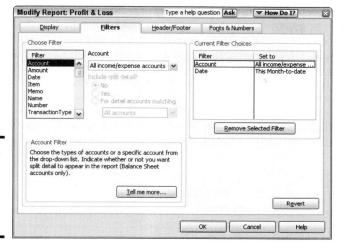

Figure 2-13:
The Filters tab of the Modify Report dialog box.

After you identify the piece of data on which you want to base your filter, open the drop-down list box next to the filter. If you selected an account filter, for example, QuickBooks names this drop-down list box the Account box. When you open the drop-down list box, QuickBooks displays a set of filtering choices. For example, Figure 2-14 shows common filtering choices available when you are creating an account filter: All Income/Expense Accounts, All Ordinary Income/Expense, All Ordinary Income/COGS, and so forth. You can pick a standard account filter from this list.

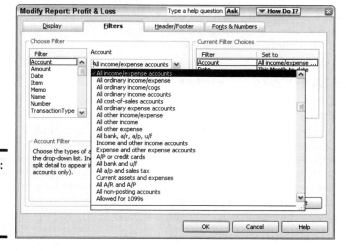

Figure 2-14:
Select a standard account filter.

Alternatively, you can pick the Selected entry from the drop-down list box. If you are creating an account filter, for example, you can pick the Selected Accounts entry from the drop-down list box. In this case, QuickBooks displays the Select Account dialog box, as shown in Figure 2-15. This dialog box lets you select on an individual basis which accounts that you want to appear on the report. For example, if you want to create a report based purely on a checking account, an accounts receivable account, and an inventory asset account, you use the Select Account box to select these accounts. To select the accounts that you want, click them. QuickBooks identifies selected accounts with a check mark.

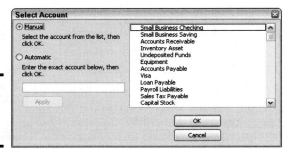

Figure 2-15:
The Select
Account
dialog box.

Other fields and boxes on the Filters tab are probably pretty self-explanatory. The Include Split Detail option buttons, available for account-based filters, let you tell QuickBooks whether it should include split transaction information. The Current Filter Choices box identifies what report filters are used for the report. You can remove a filter by selecting it from the Current Filter Choices list and then clicking the Remove Selected Filter button. You can also revert to the default filter by clicking the Revert button. Note that different boxes appear on the Filters tab for different filters.

Using the Header/Footer tab

The Header/Footer tab, as shown in Figure 2-16, controls what header and footer information appears on your report. You use the Show Header Information boxes to control the report header. For example, if you want your company name to appear at the top of the report, select the Company Name check box. And if you want to change the company name that appears at the top of the report, edit the contents of the company name text box. The other Show Header Information boxes work in the same way. For example, to remove the report title from the report, deselect the Report Title check box. To use a different report title, edit the contents of the Report Title text box.

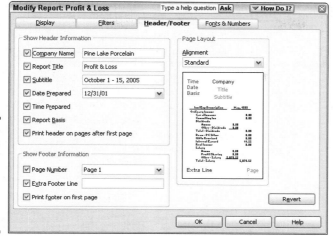

Figure 2-16:
The Header/
Footer tab
of the
Modify
Report
dialog box.

Use the Page Layout area — this provides a single Alignment drop-down list box — to choose a layout for your report. By default, QuickBooks uses a standard alignment. You can also choose a left alignment, right alignment, or a centered alignment. QuickBooks shows you how the report layout changes depending on the alignment selected.

As is the case with the other tabs of the Modify Report dialog box, you can click the Revert button to change back to the default header/footer settings.

Formatting fonts and numbers

The Fonts & Numbers tab, as shown in Figure 2-17, lets you change the font for selected pieces of report information. Use the Change Font For list box to select the bit of report information that you want to change. After this selection, click the Change Font button to display a dialog box like the one shown in Figure 2-18. The Column Labels dialog box appears, for example, when you indicate that you want to change the font for column labels. Use the Font box to select the font for the column labels. Use the Font Style box to select the font style for the column labels. Use the Size box to select the point size for the column labels. Optionally, use the Effects check boxes to add or remove special effects. Or, get really crazy and use the Color box to select the color for the piece of report data. When you're finished, verify that your font formatting choices look right by using the Sample box — and then click OK.

When you click OK to close the dialog box used to change a font (see Figure 2-18), QuickBooks displays a message box, asking if you want to change all of the related fonts. If you do want to change the fonts — and you probably do — click Yes. Note that if you make some change that later turns out to be wrong, you can click the Revert button, which also appears on the Fonts & Numbers tab, to return to the default formatting for fonts and numbers.

**Book IV
Chapter 2**

**Preparing Financial
Statements and
Reports**

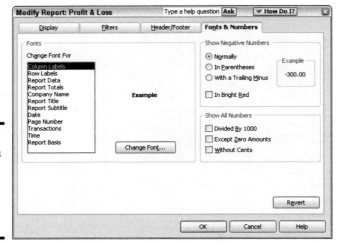

Figure 2-17:
The Fonts &
Numbers
tab of the
Modify
Report
dialog box.

Figure 2-18:
The Column
Labels
version of
the Change
Font dialog
box.

The Show Negative Numbers area provides radio buttons and a check box that you can use to instruct QuickBooks to provide special formatting for negative values. Typically, QuickBooks shows negative values with a minus sign in front of the value. Alternatively, you can tell QuickBooks to place parentheses around the negative values (select the In Parentheses radio button) or with a trailing minus sign (select the With a Trailing Minus radio button). You can also use color to flag negative numbers (select the In Bright Red check box).

The Show All Numbers area provides three check boxes that you can use to clean up and simplify your report. If your business is large enough that your report values are very large, select the Divided By 1,000 check box. In that case, QuickBooks divides all of the report values by 1,000 to make them easier to read. If you select the Except Zero Amounts check box, QuickBooks simplifies your report by not showing zero values. Finally, if you select the Without Cents check box, QuickBooks only shows dollars and not cents.

If you find yourself becoming overwhelmed with the amount of data being presented in a report, the Show All Numbers check boxes provide a handy way to get a somewhat clearer view of the big picture.

Processing Multiple Reports

If you choose the Reports⇨Process Multiple Reports command, QuickBooks displays the Process Multiple Reports dialog box, as shown in Figure 2-19. This dialog box enables you to request at one time a bunch of different reports. To use the Process Multiple Reports dialog box, first select a report group from the Select Memorized Reports From box. Next, select the reports within the report group that you want and check them off the list. If QuickBooks shows a report as selected (indicated with a check mark) that you don't want, click the check mark to remove it. Next, for those reports that you have selected, verify that the From and To boxes show the correct report interval.

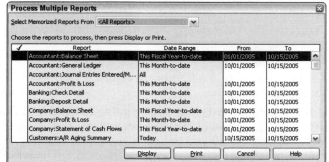

Figure 2-19:
The Process
Multiple
Reports
dialog box.

After you've selected the reports and provided the report interval dates, you can click the Display button to have QuickBooks display the report windows for each of the reports that you've selected. Alternatively, you can click the Print button to have QuickBooks print paper versions of each of the reports that you selected.

A Few Words about Document Retention

People sometimes ask me how long they should keep old reports, copies of invoices, and other bits of accounting information. Unfortunately, I don't really have a one-size-fits-all answer to this. However, I can give you some things to think about.

✦ **Consider whether the other party to a transaction is ever going to want the information.** For example, if you are chronically arguing with a

Book IV
Chapter 2

Preparing Financial
Statements and
Reports

vendor about whether you have paid some bill, it makes sense to hang on to those vendor bills and any records of your payment for as long as the argument may go on. This means that any paperwork that documents vendor bills and payments doesn't necessarily have to be retained if you don't have a problem.

✦ **Consider tax accounting requirements.** By law (a lot of people don't realize this), a business is required to maintain accounting records in order to report its profits, losses, income, and deductions to the Internal Revenue Service. This means that *anything* that you need to calculate your profits or substantiate elements of your calculations should be maintained. However, a statute of limitations exists that typically runs three years from the date you last filed the return. This means that in most cases, you don't need to keep paperwork that's any older than three years past the return that it relates to. In other words, if you have data from the year 2001 and you filed the year 2001 tax return on March 15, 2002, by March 16, 2005, you shouldn't (in most cases) need to keep all of that old paperwork. The statute of limitations dictates that at that point, you should be able to discard the old stuff. A word of caution is in order because a couple of exceptions to this three-year statute of limitations exist:

- If you've been really sloppy and through your sloppiness omitted gross income in excess of 25 percent of what your return shows, the statute of limitations equals six years.

- If no return is filed or a fraudulent return is filed, no statute of limitations exists.

✦ **Consider the old records that you're going to need in the future in order to calculate an item for your tax return.** These need to be retained. For example, if you bought a factory 60 years ago, you need to keep those purchase records until after you sell the factory.

✦ **Consider that in some industries, other document retention rules or regulations exist.** For example, if you're a physician, you need to keep your old patient records — and this may include patient accounting information — for longer than just three years. These other document retention rules vary by industry. Find out what the rules are for your industry.

How do you make sense of these vague suggestions? Come up with a rough guess as to how long you think you should hang on to stuff. In my business, subject to the qualifications listed previously, I hang on to stuff for five years. I'm not doing anything criminal or fraudulent or sloppy, so anything that is over five years old I just toss. By the way, I'm also careful to segregate documents I can throw out by year into boxes. I label the boxes with the year number. I also label the boxes with the note "discard in 2005" just so I know I can toss that stuff out.

You may want to think twice about simply tossing out financial records. (I am a little anal about this because I am a CPA.) I actually don't *toss out* my personal records: I shred the documents first. You may want to do the same thing.

Chapter 3: Preparing a Budget

In This Chapter

✔ Reviewing common budgeting tactics

✔ Following the practical approach to budgeting

✔ Using the Set Up Budgets window

✔ Managing with the budget

Budgets provide business owners and managers with powerful tools for better managing a firm's operation. A budget can give the business owner or manager a way to more easily and more quantifiably manage the people working for the business. A budget can often identify problems or opportunities early. Finally, a budget truly gives the owner or manager a way to plan out the year's operation, think about what's most important, and quantify what the firm should achieve over the year.

For these reasons, this chapter discusses some practical, common-sense approaches to budgeting within QuickBooks. I think you'll be surprised that this process is as straightforward as it is.

Reviewing Common Budgeting Tactics

Before I get into a detailed discussion of how you create a budget and use that budget within QuickBooks, I want to briefly identify and describe three very useful and common budgeting tactics: Top-line budgeting, zero-based budgeting, and benchmarking. None of these three tactics is complicated. You probably know of and understand at least two of them already. You should consider all of these tactics, however, as you construct formal or informal budgets for your business.

Top-line budgeting

A *top-line* budget is the simplest budget technique available. A top-line budget takes last year's numbers or last month's numbers and uses them for this year's budget. Of course, if inflation has occurred, a top-line budget may inflate last year's or last month's numbers by using an inflation factor. Or, conversely, if the business has shrunk a bit or fallen on hard times, the previous year's or month's numbers may be decreased by some amount.

Although top-line budgeting often receives a bad rap from people who don't like the way it perpetuates the past, top-line budgeting offers at least a couple of arguments in its favor.

✦ **Top-line budgeting is easy.** This is something big in its favor. Other budgeting techniques are often much more work.

✦ **Top-line budgeting is based on reality.** The numbers from last year or last month are real. This fact is a unique benefit to top-line budgeting that other budgeting tactics (which I describe in the following paragraphs) don't offer. If you know, for example, that last month you spent $2,000 on rent, the reality of that true, actual number is a very useful starting point for thinking about what you will spend this month.

Top-line budgeting, however, possesses a well-known weakness. Top-line budgeting tends to perpetuate previous bad budgeting decisions. For example, if someone long ago decided to spend $10,000 on an advertisement on some special industry magazine, top-line budgeting may continue to budget that $10,000 annual expense even though it no longer makes sense or may have never made sense.

Zero-based budgeting

Zero-based budgeting is the opposite of top-line budgeting. A zero-based budget works from the bottom up. A zero-based budget starts with individual revenue, expense, asset, liability, and owner's equity accounts. It examines a specific account — postage expense, for example — and then tries to apply common sense and logic for coming up with a good postage expense budget amount. For example, the budgeter may guess that the firm will send out 1,000 letters over the year and that the average postage per letter will equal $0.50. In this case, the zero-based budgeting approach determines that postage expense for the coming year will probably equal $500. The zero-based budgeter calculates this amount by taking 1,000 letters and multiplying this amount by $0.50 postage cost per letter.

The advantage of zero-based budgeting is that it tends to fix poorly figured, previously budgeted amounts. It doesn't simply perpetuate bad budgeting decisions of the past. New budgeted amounts are based on the application of common sense and simple arithmetic; the combination of these two items often produces pretty good numbers. That's really cool.

Another neat feature of zero-based budgeting is that it makes people who benefit from or use some budgeted amount responsible for that budgeted amount. For example, if some manager spent $50,000 on travel expense last year, top-line budgeting states that he or she gets to spend $50,000 this year. Zero-line budgeting, in contrast, makes the manager prove through the application of common sense and simple arithmetic that $50,000 of travel expense is again reasonable for this year.

However, zero-based budgeting isn't perfect; it possesses a weakness in that it's easy for budgeters to forget numbers or make calculation errors. Previously, I used the example of a budgeter guessing that postage expense for the coming year will be $500. That estimate comes from a guess about the number of letters sent for a year (1,000) and an estimate of the average postage expense spent on each letter ($0.50). If either of those numbers is wrong, or if (heaven forbid) the budgeter incorrectly multiplies the one number by the other, the postage expense budget number is wrong. If the budgeter is budgeting hundreds or even thousands of budgeted amounts, he or she will undoubtedly make a few errors in the process. And he or she probably won't be able to fix or find those errors because of the volume of budgeted amounts being guessed.

Benchmarking

One very powerful but unfortunately infrequently used technique is *benchmarking*. Benchmarking compares your actual or your preliminary budgeted numbers to the same numbers of similarly sized businesses in your industry. For example, CPA firms spend money on a tax library. Annual fees for a tax library can run from as little as $15 or $20 a year to roughly $30,000 a year (these amounts are fees for a sole proprietor, by the way). How do you know what number is an appropriate budgeted amount? Well, if you know what other CPA firms or other sole proprietor CPAs are spending on their tax library, that information can probably help you to budget what you should or can spend. The challenge, of course, is getting that comparable information.

Fortunately, getting comparable information is easier than most people realize. You can usually get information about the financial statistics of comparable firms in two different ways:

✦ **Your local library:** You can usually find several good sources of general financial statistical information about businesses of varying sizes and in varying industries. For example, Dun & Bradstreet, the Risk Management Association, Robert Morris & Associates, and a fellow named Troy all publish annual summaries of financial ratios and financial statistics based on several sources. If you trot down to the library and visit the reference desk, you can get the librarian's help in locating one or more of these reference sources. Suddenly, you will have a wealth of information at your fingertips, and you can see how much the average tavern spends on beer and peanuts, for example. You can see how much the average restaurant spends on advertising. In other words, you can see detailed financial information on a business exactly like yours!

✦ **Industry associations:** In addition to the general information available from reference sources commonly stocked at your local library, many industry associations and professional groups collect and publish industry-specific financial information. For example, one of the first jobs I had early in my career was working as the controller of an electronics manufacturing firm. Our firm was a member of the American Electronics Association. That membership meant that we participated in a survey of financial information of member firms in the association. That survey gave us (and other AEA members) good statistics about average salaries spent for different positions, inventory investment, certain administrative expenses, and so forth. Continuing with my example of CPAs buying tax libraries, I should mention that two industry associations — the Texas Society of Certified Public Accountants and the American Institute of Certified Public Accountants — publish statistics for CPA firms. These publications identify what the average sole proprietor spends on his or her tax library. I'll bet you a dill pickle that your industry association — whatever it is — has similar information available.

Putting it all together

Just for the record — you probably already guessed this — you shouldn't use just one approach to build your budget. You may use top-line budgeting for some of your numbers, and you may use zero-based budgeting for other numbers. And for really important or key numbers in your budget, you may go to the work to try to benchmark your numbers against those of similarly sized firms in your industry. Good budgeting, then, combines the budgeting tactics described in this chapter to come up with a budget that makes sense and lets you plan your firm's finances for the year.

Practical Approaches to Budgeting

Business budgeting, unfortunately, isn't simply a matter of listing expected revenue and expense amounts. You also typically need to create a balance sheet. Balance sheet budgeting is too complicated to do on the back of a napkin or sitting at the breakfast table in the morning before the kids get up.

Therefore, to create budgeted numbers for a balance sheet, you need to use a tool and approach like the one described (in some detail) in Book VI, Chapter 2.

If all that you want to budget are revenue amounts and expense amounts, you can do that in a very simplistic, crude fashion. For example, you can just list expected revenue amounts by account on the back of a cocktail napkin.

Using the Set Up Budgets Window

After you've come up with a budget — presumably by using a tool like the one described in Book VI, Chapter 2, and by employing the sorts of budgeting tactics described previously in this chapter — you record your budget in QuickBooks.

Creating a new budget

To create a new budget in QuickBooks, follow these steps:

1. Choose the Company⇨Planning and Budgeting⇨Set Up Budgets command.

QuickBooks displays the Create New Budget window, shown in Figure 3-1. You use this window to record the amount that you expect for each revenue and expense account for each month during the year in which you are budgeting.

Figure 3-1:
The Create New Budget window.

2. Click the Create New Budget button to create a new budget.

This opens the Create New Budget dialog box, which you use to create a new budget (bet you wouldn't have guessed that).

3. Select the fiscal year period.

You need to identify the fiscal year you're budgeting for. To do that, enter the fiscal year in the provided text box, as shown in Figure 3-1. If you are budgeting for fiscal year 2006, for example, you use those buttons to change the year to 2006.

4. **Select the Profit and Loss radio button, or the Balance Sheet radio button, depending on what type of budget you want to create.**

If you're creating a profit and loss budget, click Next. If you're creating a balance sheet budget, click Finish to complete the budget.

Note that you use a different approach for profit and loss budgets and balance sheet budgets. For profit and loss budgets, you budget the amount of revenue or expense expected for the account for the month. For balance sheet budgets, you budget the ending account balance — that's the ending account balance expected for the asset, liability, or owner's equity account at month's end.

5. **Specify additional profit and loss budget criteria and click Next.**

If you chose to create a profit and loss budget, select the Customer:Job radio button to further extend your budget to include Job details, or select the Class radio button to include classes in your budget (see Figure 3-2). Or simply select the No Additional Criteria radio button.

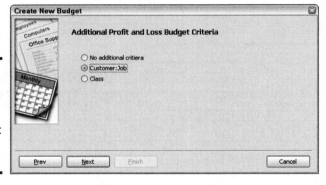

Figure 3-2:
The Additional Profit and Loss Budget Criteria screen.

6. **Choose whether to create the budget from scratch or previous data.**

To create a budget from scratch and start with a clean slate, select the Create Budget from Scratch radio button, shown in Figure 3-3. To create a budget based on your actual data from last year, select the Create Budget from Previous Year's Actual Data radio button. Click Finish when you're done. QuickBooks displays the Set Up Budgets window (see Figure 3-4).

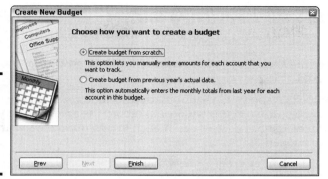

Figure 3-3:
Choosing
whether to
create a
budget from
scratch.

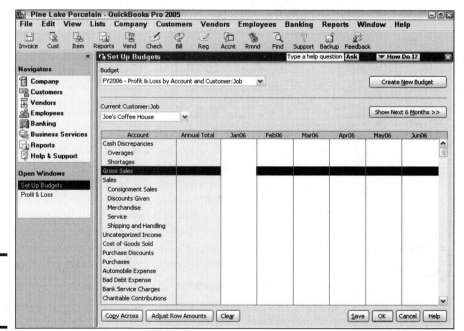

Figure 3-4:
The Set Up
Budgets
window.

**Book IV
Chapter 3**

Preparing a Budget

Working with an existing budget

To edit an existing budget in QuickBooks, follow these steps:

1. **Choose the Company⇨Planning and Budgeting⇨Set Up Budgets command.**

   QuickBooks displays the Set Up Budgets window — the same one shown in Figure 3-4. You use this window to record the amount that you expect for each revenue and expense for each month during the year in which you are budgeting.

2. **Select a budget or create a new one.**

   Select the budget you want to work with from the Budget box at the top of the window. To create a new budget (you can have as many budgets as you want), click the Create New Budget button. For help with creating a new budget, see the previous section.

3. **(Optional) Choose a Customer.**

   You typically budget by account. However, if you want to budget in finer detail by also estimating amounts for customers, jobs, or classes, you can use the Current Customer:Job drop-down list box to identify specific customers from which you'll expect revenue or for whom you will expend costs.

4. **Record the budgeted amounts for each month of the fiscal year.**

   Type the amounts you want to budget for each account in the appropriate month columns. Again, remember that revenue and expense accounts need to be budgeted as the amount expected for the month. Asset, liability, and owner's equity amounts need to be budgeted as the ending account balance expected for the month.

   To copy the budgeted amount for one month into the text boxes for the succeeding months, click the Copy Across button.

5. **(Optional) Adjust row amounts.**

   If you find that the yearly total for an account isn't what you want it to be, you can go back and change the amount for each month, so that it all adds up to the amount. Or, you can click the Adjust Row Amounts button. Clicking this button displays the Adjust Row Amounts dialog box, shown in Figure 3-5. Use the Start At drop-down list box to select which month you want to start with (either the first month or the currently selected month), and then choose whether you want to increase or decrease the amounts, and by how much (enter either a dollar amount or a percentage).

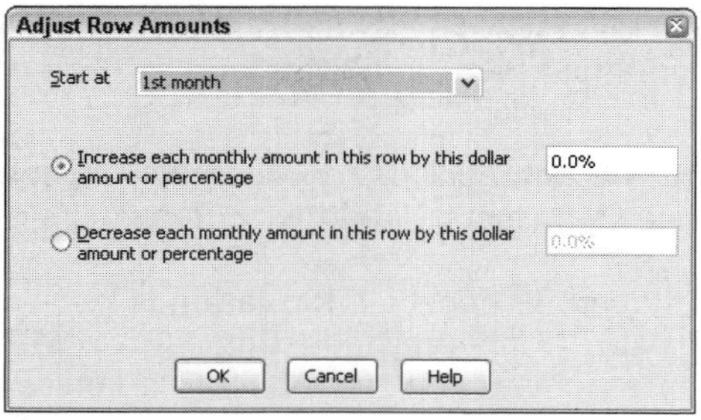

Figure 3-5:
The Adjust
Row
Amounts
dialog box.

6. **Repeat as necessary.**

   You need to repeat Steps 3, 4, and 5 for each of the accounts for which you want to record budgeted amounts.

   Yes, I know, this is a lot of work. Just so you know, in large companies with hundreds of employees, two or three people spend their entire year working on and working with the budgeted data.

Managing with a Budget

After you record your budget in QuickBooks (as described in the previous section, "Using the Set Up Budgets Window"), you can compare your actual financial results to budgeted amounts by choosing commands from the Budget submenu that QuickBooks displays. When you choose the Reports⟩ Budget command, QuickBooks provides several budgeting reports, described in the following list:

+ **Profit & Loss Budget Overview:** This report summarizes your budgeted amounts. You can use it to look at and error-check your budget.

+ **Profit & Loss Budget vs. Actual:** This report lets you compare budgeted income statement information to actual income statement information. The report, therefore, lets you compare your expected revenue and expenses to the actual revenue and expenses.

+ **Profit & Loss Budget by Job Overview:** This report lets you look at your budget by job. You can use this to compare and review your job budgets.

+ **Profit & Loss Budget vs. Actual by Job:** This report lets you look at expected and actual revenue and expense amounts by job.

+ **Budget vs. Actual Graph:** This graph isn't a report. It's a chart that shows budgeted and actual information.

**Book IV
Chapter 3**

Preparing a Budget

✦ **Balance Sheet Budget Overview:** This report shows budgeted amounts for balance sheet accounts: assets, liabilities, and owner's equity accounts.

✦ **Balance Sheet Budget vs. Actual:** This report shows expected and actual account balances for assets, liabilities, and owner's equity.

The way that you use a budgeting report's information is key — and it's also the secret to getting value from your budgeting efforts. With a well-constructed, common-sense budget, you can look for variances between your budget and your actual financial results. You want to use your budget to spot situations in which, for example, an expense item is too low, an asset item is too high, or some revenue number is trailing behind what you expect. Variances between expected results and actual results indicate unexpected results. Unexpected results often suggest either problems . . . or opportunities. Think about the following examples of variance and what the variances may indicate:

✦ **Monthly revenue is $40,000 instead of $50,000.** Monthly revenue that's 20 percent less than expected may indicate problems with your product, problems with your sales force, or problems with your customers. In any case, if sales represent only 80 percent of what you expect, you probably need to implement immediate corrective action.

✦ **Inventory balances are averaging $50,000 at month's end rather than $100,000 at month's end.** Having a lower-than-expected inventory balance may be either good or bad. The ending inventory balance that is half of what you expect may indicate that you are selling products much faster than you expected (and therefore, you should increase your inventory investment and your purchasing of inventory). Having a low inventory investment may also mean, however, that you're simply not getting materials from your vendors as fast as you need them and, as a result, you're at great risk of losing sales because of inadequate stock levels.

✦ **Research and development expenses equal $50,000 a year instead of $25,000 a year.** Research and development expenses that are twice what you expect seems bad. How can it be good to spend twice as much on an expense as you expect? However, doubling your research and development expenditures may be good if you are unexpectedly investing in some promising new product, idea, or technology.

✦ **Sales to a particular class of customer are 50 percent higher.** Suppose that you used classes to track sales to customers inside the country and outside the country. If you see that, quite unexpectedly, sales to customers outside the country are 50 percent above what you expect, that variance may indicate an opportunity to sell even more outside the country. Maybe with more effort and energy, outside-the-country customers can become an even larger part of your business. Sometimes variances identify opportunities that you would otherwise miss.

Some Wrap-Up Comments on Budgeting

Before I leave the subject of budgeting, however, I want to share a handful of final comments:

✦ **Budgeting is an example of the old phrase, "Plan your work, and then work your plan."** Budgets are not handcuffs. Budgets are not straitjackets. Budgets are simply planning tools that you use to thoughtfully make decisions about your firm's financial affairs for the coming year.

✦ **If you aren't getting value from the budgeting process, you shouldn't do it.** Or, at the very least, you need to change the way you're doing it. No kidding, I won't argue that you should budget if you don't get value from the process. I think, however, that most businesses do get value. If you can manage your business without a budget — and I mention an approach that works for doing this in a tip at the end of this chapter — I don't think you should budget. You need to use those tools that deliver the most value to you in managing your firm. For many people, budgeting does just that. If it doesn't for you, skip the work. Time is often the most scarce resource for business owners and managers.

✦ **Budgets can be essential tools for managing people with financially quantifiable responsibilities.** Okay, I know budgets have a bad rap and they aren't perfect, but you know what? If you have people working for you who have responsibilities that you can financially quantify, you can use a budget to manage those people. For example, suppose that you have sales people who should individually sell $25,000 worth of stuff each month. If you budget by sales person (you probably need to set up a class for each sales person or a revenue account for each sales person), you can use a budget to compare actual sales generated by each person to the budgeted sales expected for each person. If you look at Joe every month and see that he has $30,000 in sales predictably, you can use that information in your management of Joe. Probably, Joe's overproducing means he's doing a good job. If you look at Joe's brother Bob, and see that he is doing $20,000 in sales every month when you expect him to do $25,000 in sales, you can probably see a problem and an opportunity for improvement. This all makes sense, right?

✦ **People who like to budget tend to (in my experience) focus on unfavorable variances.** I mention this because, although unfavorable variances often identify problems that need to be corrected, sometimes favorable variances are more interesting and more useful to dissect. Suppose that you have a business in which you expect sales people to generate $25,000 in sales a month. If Julia is generating $75,000 a month in sales, that's pretty darn interesting. Probably, Julia knows something or has skills or an approach that the other sales people don't have. Perhaps, with just a little bit of luck, you can figure out why Julia does so well — and then use this new knowledge to get your other sales people to sell more stuff each month.

✦ **The key budgeting numbers to watch are often a pretty small set.**
Although a budget according to QuickBooks (and, I guess, Steve Nelson) may have hundreds of numbers, you may be able to manage your business just fine by looking at just a handful of numbers. For example, maybe in your business it all gets down to sales. If sales really drive everything else — your expenses and, of course, all of your profit — you may not have much reason to track the amount that you're spending each month on your telephone bill or postage expense. If you can distill your financial plan down to a few numbers that you need to watch, you can make your budgeting and your financial analyses much simpler. All you need to do is identify those key financial statistics that need to be watched — and then regularly watch them.

Financial ratios are often very useful tools for monitoring a firm's financial performance. I know several business owners who successfully manage their businesses without a formal budget by looking at two or three items, including cost of goods sold and gross margin percentages. The *cost of goods sold* includes the cost of the products or items being sold. A *gross margin percentage* is the percentage of sales that are left over after paying for the cost of goods sold. To dig into these terms and find out about working with financial ratios, refer to Book V, Chapter 1.

Chapter 4: Using Activity-Based Costing

In This Chapter

✓ **Revealing traditional overhead allocations**

✓ **Getting a handle on how ABC works**

✓ **Implementing a simple ABC system**

✓ **Working with ABC in QuickBooks**

✓ **Turning on Class Tracking**

Activity-based costing (or, ABC for short) may be the best new accounting idea in the last two decades. No, I must amend that. Activity-based costing *is* the best new idea in accounting in the last two decades.

ABC gives businesses a better way to estimate the profits of products and services, which is more important than you may think. The problem in many businesses is that overhead expenses or operating expenses don't cleanly tie to products or services. Without good allocation of overhead or operating expenses, businesses can't accurately determine which products make money and which don't.

ABC addresses this problem by using the power of the computer (QuickBooks in this example) to directly trace overhead costs to products and services. Surprisingly, ABC accomplishes this task in a pretty straightforward, simple fashion. In this chapter, I show you what I mean.

Revealing Traditional Overhead Allocation

To really understand the contribution that ABC makes, you need to understand how overhead allocation traditionally works. To give you an example, take a look at Table 4-1. This is the same simple income statement that I show in several chapters throughout the book.

Table 4-1	A Simple Income Statement
Sales revenue	$13,000
Less: Cost of goods sold	3,000
Gross margin	$10,000
Operating expenses	
Rent	1,000
Wages	4,000
Supplies	1,000
Total operating expenses	6,000
Operating profit	$4,000

As you may recall, this simple income statement shows the profit for an imaginary hot dog stand business that you operate on opening day of baseball season in your city.

Suppose that in this imaginary business, you sell two different products: a regular hot dog for $2.50, and a super-duper chilidog for $4.00. Suppose also that you sell an even number of both of these products. Therefore, the $13,000 of revenue shown in Table 4-1 actually represents $5,000 in sales of regular hot dogs and $8,000 in sales of chilidogs.

Further suppose that you can break down the cost of goods sold as follows:

✦ **Buns:** Each bun cost you $0.15. This means that you spent $300 on buns for regular dogs and $300 on buns for the chilidogs.

✦ **Dogs:** Each hot dog cost you $0.40. This means that you spent $800 on hot dogs for the regular hot dog product line and another $800 on hot dogs for the chilidog product line.

✦ **Chili:** Each serving of chili for the chilidogs cost you $0.40 (a serving is three heaping tablespoons of chili, as you enjoy telling customers). This means that you spent another $800 on chili for the chilidog product line.

Given this information, you can create an income statement that shows revenues, cost of goods sold, and gross margin by product line, as shown in Table 4-2. Furthermore, note that Table 4-2 does something very traditional — it allocates operating expenses using a simple rule. In Table 4-2, I've simply split the operating expenses right down the middle — allocating $3,000 of operating expenses to the regular hot dog product line and $3,000 of operating expenses to the chilidog product line.

Table 4-2	Traditional Income Statement by Product Line		
	$2.50 Hot Dogs	*$4.00 Chilidogs*	*Total*
Sales revenue			
(2,000 sold in each product line)	5,000	8,000	13,000
Cost of goods sold			
$0.15 buns	300	300	600
$0.40 hot dogs	800	800	1,600
$0.40 of chili for each chilidog	___	800	800
Total cost of goods sold	1,100	1,900	3,000
Gross margin	3,900	6,100	10,000
Operating expenses			
Rent	500	500	1,000
Wages	2,000	2,000	4,000
Supplies	500	500	1,000
Total operating expenses	3,000	3,000	6,000
Net profit	900	3,100	4,000

Stop for a minute and look at the information shown in Table 4-2. When you consider and make decisions based on this information, it becomes much easier to understand traditional overhead allocations.

If you examine the income statement shown in Table 4-2, several pieces of data suggest that there's money in them there chilidogs. For example, look at the sales revenue. The income statement shows that chilidogs generate $8,000 of sales revenue, whereas regular hot dogs only generate $5,000 of sales revenue. Now look at the gross margin. The income statement shows that chilidogs generate $6,100 of gross margin, whereas regular hot dogs generate only $3,900 of gross margin. Finally, look at the net profit. Based on a simple split of overhead or operating expenses, the net profit from the regular hot dog line equals a measly $900 while the net profit from the chilidog product line equals a whopping $3,100.

After reviewing the information shown in Table 4-2, what is your conclusion? It seems pretty clear that you should sell more chilidogs and fewer hot dogs. In fact, you may want to give up on selling regular hot dogs and concentrate on chilidogs. You may also decide that your chilidogs are priced too high — perhaps you could shave the cost a bit on these. You may also decide that the regular hot dogs are priced too low — perhaps the price on these should be bumped up a bit.

Indeed, you can make all sorts of decisions from the collective set of data shown in Table 4-2. You may not realize that the overhead allocation plays an important part in all this. Unfortunately, the overhead allocation shown in Table 4-2, and any of the conclusions I've suggested in the preceding paragraphs, are wrong. This error, however, doesn't show up until you use activity-based costing, and that's why ABC is cool.

How ABC Works

In this section, I tell you how, with ABC, you can create an equivalent income statement for product line profitability. After that, I generalize about the ABC process and define the ABC buzzwords that people usually use to talk about ABC.

The ABC product line income statement

To create an ABC product line income statement, you attempt to trace the overhead cost directly to products or services. For example, suppose that in the case of the imaginary hot dog stand business, the rent expense is necessary because you need an electrical hookup to keep the pot of chili heated. Perhaps you also need an electrical hookup to run the can opener that you use (surreptitiously) to open the cans of chili needed to refill the pot. This means, then, that the rent expense really can't be split between regular hot dogs and chilidogs. It needs to be allocated to chilidogs.

You can treat the supplies expense in a very similar way. For example, suppose that the $1,000 of supplies is really just napkins. Suppose also that based on some observations, you've noted that a regular hot dog customer grabs two napkins for his hot dog, whereas a chilidog customer grabs eight napkins for his chilidog. (You know, to clean up the mess on the front of his shirt when the chili spills.) In this case, you can use this information to better allocate the $1,000 of supplies expense. Consider that this information means that regular hot dog customers use roughly 4,000 napkins. (I calculated this by multiplying the 2,000 hot dogs you've sold by the two napkins used for each regular hot dog customer.) And chilidog customers use 16,000 napkins. (I calculated this by multiplying the 2,000 chilidogs that you've sold by the eight napkins used by each chilidog customer.)

Using this napkin usage information, you can calculate which percentage of the supplies expense is used by regular hot dog customers and chilidog customers. If regular hot dog customers use 4,000 out of a total of 20,000 napkins, 20 percent of the napkins are going to regular hot dog customers (20 percent of the $1,000 of supplies expense equals $200). Therefore, the correct allocation of supplies expense to the regular hot dog line is $200.

You can allocate a portion of the supplies expense for chilidogs by using similar math. If 16,000 of the 20,000 napkins go to chilidog customers, that's 80 percent of the napkins (80 percent of the $1,000 of supplies expense equals $800). Therefore, logically, $800 out of $1,000 of supplies expense should be allocated, or traced, to the chilidog product line.

This all makes sense, right? All you are trying to do is trace overhead costs, or operating expenses, to product lines.

The wages expense of $4,000 probably works in a very similar fashion. Before going further, though, I have to delve into some of the ABC buzzwords. Suppose that all of the $4,000 of wages expense goes to serving customers hot dogs. Furthermore, suppose that the process of serving a regular hot dog to a customer requires two steps:

1. Grab hot dog bun.

2. Place a hot-off-the-grill frankfurter into the bun.

In comparison, the process of serving a chilidog requires five steps:

1. Grab a hot dog bun.

2. Slide a hot-off-the-grill frankfurter into the bun.

3. Ladle a heaping tablespoon of chili into the bun.

4. Ladle another heaping tablespoon of chili into the bun.

5. Ladle a third heaping tablespoon of chili into the bun (yes, you read that correctly).

You may see where I'm going with this. I've actually done something very special — something that business school professors would dress up with a bunch of fancy words in academic business journals. In this example, I've stated that the wages expense actually gets used in an activity called "serving" or "serving customers." I also noted in this example that the process of serving a regular hot dog customer requires two steps, but the process of serving a chilidog customer actually requires five steps.

These steps are known as *cost drivers*. That sounds like something you may not understand right away, but, in fact, the notion of cost drivers is simple common sense. The term *cost drivers* simply suggests that the number of steps an employee takes to serve a customer is a good base on which to allocate the wages expense that comprises the activity of serving.

You may have already guessed how to do this, but I'll tell you anyway. By looking at the total number of steps required to serve regular hot dogs and the total number of steps required to serve chilidogs, you can trace the wages expense to the regular hot dog and chilidog product lines.

For example, if you sell 2,000 regular hot dogs and each hot dog requires two steps, regular hot dogs require 4,000 steps in total. If you sell 2,000 chilidogs and each chilidog requires five steps, the chilidog product line requires 10,000 steps.

You can use these two values — the number of steps for the regular hot dog line and the number of steps for the chilidog line — to allocate the wages expense. For example, to calculate the percentage of the wages expense that goes into preparing regular hot dogs, you can make the following calculation:

> 4,000 (the number of steps required for regular hot dogs) / 14,000 (the total number of steps) x $4,000

This calculation returns the value $1,143.00.

In a similar fashion, you can use the steps information to allocate wages expense to the chilidog product line. Here's how that calculation may work:

> 10,000 (the number of steps to prepare chilidogs) / 14,000 (the total steps) x $4,000

This calculation returns the value $2,857.00.

Now take a look at Table 4-3, which summarizes all of this ABC analysis that I have discussed over the past few paragraphs. The most noteworthy item — and the first item to observe about ABC analysis — is that an ABC approach to product line profitability often produces surprising results.

If you think back to the impressions you had after looking at the income statement shown in Table 4-2, you may have concluded that chilidogs are really a much better product to sell. However, as Table 4-3 shows, when you look at the net profit number, you realize that regular hot dogs make twice as much profit as chilidogs — even though they sell for less money and even though they produce much less gross margin. Only a fair and accurate tracing of overhead expenses shows this fact. Wow. Pass the mustard.

Table 4-3	ABC Income Statement by Product Line		
	$2.50 Hot Dogs	*$4.00 Chilidogs*	*Total*
Sales revenue			
(2000 sold in each product line)	5,000	8,000	13,000
Cost of goods sold			
$.15 buns	300	300	600
$.40 hot dogs	800	800	1,600
$.40 of chili for each chilidog	0	800	800
Total cost of goods sold	1,100	1,900	3,000
Gross margin	3,900	6,100	10,000
Operating expenses			
Rent	0	1,000	1,000
Wages	1,143	2,857	4,000
Supplies	200	800	1,000
Total operating expenses	1,343	4,657	6,000
Net profit	2,557	1,443	4,000

This is all pretty neat, isn't it? If you step away from your imaginary hot dog stand business and look at your real business, you may find yourself asking new and awkward questions, such as "That product generates all that revenue? Maybe a fair accounting of overhead would show it actually loses money . . . "Remember that cheapo product or cheapo service that you never spend much money on — you know the one — and that doesn't generate much gross margin? Well, you may be making a lot more money on it than you thought. Scary, isn't it?

ABC in a small firm

I want to make three important observations about ABC in a small firm. Some of this stuff is obvious, and some of it is redundant. However, I think it's important enough that you hear it at least one more time:

✦ **ABC is most useful when you have lots of overhead and a bunch of different products.** In any environment that doesn't have a lot of overhead, ABC isn't worth the work and won't deliver insights. Likewise, ABC doesn't make sense in any business that sells a single product or that provides a single service, which is usually the case in a small firm. (Keep reading, though, because analysis of cost drivers can provide one unique insight.)

✦ **ABC may not make sense for custom manufacturing environments.** In a custom manufacturing environment — this is any business where you make specific things for specific customers — you can often use job costing to provide good product or service profitability measures. For example, in the case of a single-family home builder, the builder can use job costing to track revenues and expenses by job (single family home). And that job costing may provide the detailed profitability-by-product-line information that is the big benefit of ABC. Remember, ABC is first and foremost a tool for better allocating overhead costs.

✦ **Cost drivers "drive" costs.** For example, in the discussion of the hot dog stand business and the activity labeled "serving a customer," the serving steps were the cost drivers. The number of steps required to serve a customer drove the costs of serving the customer. That may sound really dumb, but sometimes one of the benefits that ABC provides is an insight into how changing the number of cost drivers changes your costs. For example, suppose that instead of spooning three heaping tablespoons of chili onto a chilidog, you purchased one spoon equivalent to three tablespoons; this would change the number of steps from five to three. Recall the original, five-step approach to serving the chilidog customer:

1. Grab a hot dog bun.

2. Slide a hot-off-the-grill frankfurter into the bun.

3. Ladle a heaping tablespoon of chili into the bun.

4. Ladle another heaping tablespoon of chili into the bun.

5. Ladle a third heaping tablespoon of chili into the bun.

This sounds so obvious as to not being worthy of inclusion in this book. However, if you get a three-tablespoon spoon, you can simplify the serving of a chilidog into three steps:

1. Grab a bun.

2. Slide a hot dog into the bun.

3. Heap a three-tablespoon serving of chili on the hot dog.

Changing the number of steps required to serve a customer a chilidog changes the cost of the serving activity for a chilidog. And changing the cost of serving a chilidog changes the profitability (potentially) of serving a chilidog. I say "potentially" because you may not actually be able to reduce your wages expense by buying a three-tablespoon spoon for lathering up your chilidogs with chili, but you get the idea. *Note:* To really save money by reducing the number of steps, you would need to be able to cut your wages expense.

The bottom line concerning ABC is this: ABC lets you better allocate overhead costs and, as an added bonus, ABC also often gives you unique insights into what "drives" your overhead costs. With this information in hand, you can make better decisions about your product and service lines and sometimes you can even change the way you operate your business in a way that reduces your costs.

Implementing a Simple ABC System

I'll admit this right up front: You can make ABC very complicated. Furthermore, if you go out and hire an outside consultant — somebody who wants to charge you thousands or even tens of thousands of dollars to set up one of these systems — you may end up with something that is very, very powerful — and very, very complicated.

That being said, however, ABC systems don't have to be that complicated, particularly if you are really only looking for better allocation of your overhead costs rather than a system to look at the cost drivers or the activities that comprise your overhead costs. ABC can be pretty straightforward. This is especially true in a small- or medium-sized firm. In fact, I think you can probably implement a good, first-rate ABC system by taking the following four steps:

1. **Look at your overhead costs.**

Verify that you have enough overhead to be worrying about. If you are in a business with big fat margins and very low overhead, ABC may not make any sense for you. The incremental value that you achieve by more precisely allocating overhead may be simply a manifestation of an obsessive-compulsive personality disorder rather than good accounting.

2. **Identify the big overhead cost.**

You must do this if you decide that you want to allocate some or a bunch of your overhead via an ABC approach. Don't spend time trying to accurately allocate some penny-ante amount. However, if you want to allocate any simple-to-allocate amounts at the same time, that's also great. Go for the biggest bang you can get for your buck. Create an ABC system that allocates, with a minimal amount of effort, a large chunk of your overhead. Don't get too pedantic.

3. **Identify the principal activities that use up the overhead costs.**

In the simple example of the imaginary hot dog stand business, you only had a single activity — serving a customer. You are certainly going to have more activities than that. However, you don't need to create a list of 80 activities. Identify the big activities that enable you to allocate your overhead. The fewer the activities you can use to do this, the easier your accounting will be. Find a handful of activities that let you fairly and accurately allocate overhead to produce lines. That's the big picture.

4. **Trace the activities to products by using the appropriate measures.**

   After you've identified the handful of activities that let you connect overhead expenses to products, be sure to use the appropriate measure — also known as a cost driver — to tie the overhead expenses to the product lines or service lines. In the example of the hot dog stand business, one overhead cost — rent — didn't even need a cost driver. The supplies expense also didn't need a cost driver because you were able to allocate that cost through simple observation. The wages expense required a more sophisticated textbook approach to allocation. To allocate the wages expense, you needed to create an activity called "serving the customer," and then allocate that activity's cost based on the number of steps that each product line required.

An ABC system is a tool that you can use to manage your overhead costs and the profitability of the products or services that you sell. Practically, you want to focus on the big overhead costs, and, in the end, all you really want is an ABC system that produces useful numbers — numbers that help you more clearly and creatively think about your business.

How QuickBooks Supports ABC

Okay, you are probably saying to yourself, "Steve, this all sounds pretty good. But you're a little short on specifics and a little long on theory. Where's the beef, buddy?"

Oh, that's right. I do need to tell you how an ABC system works in QuickBooks, don't I? No problem, the approach is actually really straightforward if you've already been using QuickBooks. In short, all you need to do to implement a simple ABC system in QuickBooks is to do what you are doing right now. In other words, just keep on tracking your operating expenses by using a good, decent chart of accounts. That's 90 percent of the battle.

You also need to take care of just one or two minor additional items. First, you need to turn on QuickBook's Class Tracking feature. Class Tracking lets you categorize income and expense transactions as falling not just into income and expense accounts — but also as falling into particular classes.

Second, when you record an expense, you need to also identify the class into which the expense falls. By using classes that correspond to your activities — well, you can see that that's all it takes, right?

Turning On Class Tracking

To turn on Class Tracking in QuickBooks, follow these steps:

1. **Choose the Edit menu's Preferences command.**

QuickBooks displays the Preferences dialog box.

2. **Tell QuickBooks you want to work with the accounting preferences.**

To tell QuickBooks that you want to change one of its accounting preferences — Class Tracking, in this case — click the Accounting icon, which appears in the list box along the left edge of the Preferences dialog box. Figure 4-1 shows the Company Preferences tab for the accounting preferences. (If the Company Preferences tab doesn't appear on your screen, simply click the tab.)

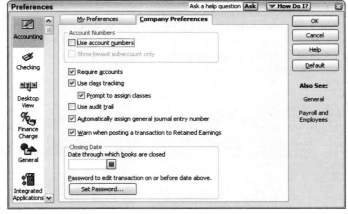

Figure 4-1:
The
Company
Preferences
boxes for
setting your
accounting
preferences.

3. **Select the Use Class Tracking check box to turn on Class Tracking.**

4. **Click OK.**

From this point forward, QuickBooks will add a Class drop-down list box to the Windows dialog box that you use to record revenues and expenses (such as the Create Invoices window, the Write Checks window, the Enter Bills window, and so on). All you need to do is tag transactions as they fit into a particular class.

Using Classes for ABC

After you turn on Class Tracking, using classes is really straightforward. You need to set up classes for the product lines or service lines for which you want to measure profitability. You need to classify transactions as fitting into a particular class either as they're recorded (if you can) or after the fact (if you need to fiddle with the activity and cost driver math).

Setting up your classes

You need to set up a class for each product or service for which you want to measure profitability. In the imaginary hot dog stand business, for example, you set up two classes: one for regular hot dogs and one for chilidogs.

To set up a class, you can just enter the class name into the class box that appears on the window that you use to record invoices, write checks, and make journal entries (these windows are shown later in this section). Alternatively, you can choose the Lists menu's Class List command. When QuickBooks displays the Class List window, click the Class button shown at the bottom of the window and choose New from the menu that QuickBooks displays. Use the New Class window that appears, as shown in Figure 4-2, to describe the new class.

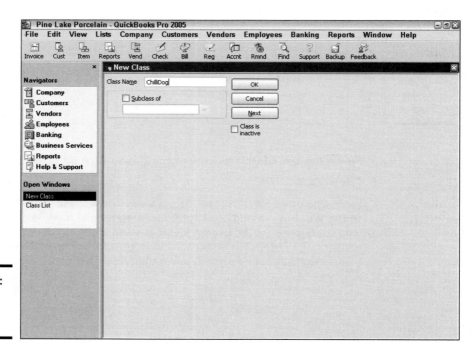

Figure 4-2:
The New
Class
window.

Classifying revenue amounts

To classify revenue as fitting into a particular class, use the Class box that appears on the Create Invoice window and on the Enter Sales Receipt window. (These are the two windows that you use to record sales.) If an invoice records sales of a hot dog, for example, you may record the class as Regular. If a sales receipt records sales of a chilidog, you may record the class as Chilidog. Figure 4-3 shows the Create Invoices window filled out to record the day's regular hot dog sales.

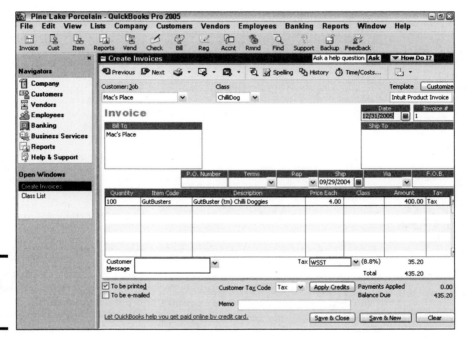

Figure 4-3: The Create Invoices window.

The Class box is in the upper-left corner of the window close to the Customer:Job box.

Classifying expense amounts

To record a check that pays some expense that fits into a particular activity, you also use the Class column — this appears on the Expenses tab as shown in Figure 4-4 — to identify the product line or service into which the expense fits. Figure 4-4 shows how the Write Checks window may appear to record $1,000 of rent expense allocated to the chilidog product line.

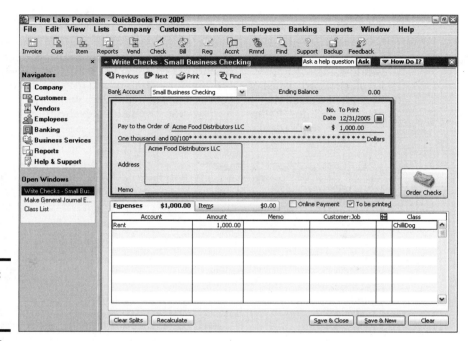

Figure 4-4:
The Write
Checks
window.

The Class column is located along the right edge of the Expense tab.

After-the-fact classifications

In some cases, you won't be able to classify an expense or revenue amount at the time the initial transaction is recorded. For example, in the hot dog stand example, you probably wouldn't be able to figure out how to split the wages expense between regular hot dogs and chilidogs until after you'd paid the employees. The same thing would be true of the supplies expense. In both cases, you need to know how many regular hot dogs and how many chilidogs you sell before you can allocate, or trace, supplies and wages.

In these sorts of cases, you use the Make General Journal Entries window to classify previously unclassified expenses. Figure 4-5, for example, shows you how to take $4,000 of previously unclassified wages expense and allocate the amount to the regular and chilidog product lines.

The Class column is located along the right edge of the General Journal Entry window.

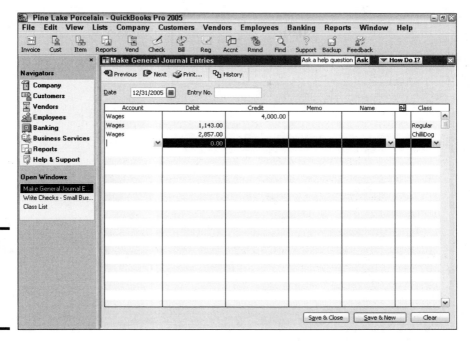

Figure 4-5:
The Make
General
Journal
Entries
window.

Producing ABC reports

After you allocate as much overhead as you can to the product or service lines, you can prepare a profit and loss statement by class that shows the profitability-by-product-line data. Chapter 2 of Book IV explains and discusses QuickBooks reports. Note that if you used the example data discussed in this chapter, you could produce a QuickBooks report that looked almost identical to the income statement shown previously in this chapter in Table 4-3.

To produce a profit and loss statement by class, choose the Reports➪ Company & Financial➪Profit & Loss by Class command.

Chapter 5: Setting Up Project and Job Costing Systems

In This Chapter

✔ Setting up jobs and projects

✔ Accounting for job and project costs

✔ Finding alternative ways to do job costing

✔ Using estimates

✔ Figuring out progress billing

Many businesses work on projects or jobs. For example, one way to look at a home builder's business is as a series of home construction projects. A manufacturer, such as a commercial printer, may print books, brochures, or posters for their customers. Each of those items represents jobs that are performed for specific customers.

Accounting works a bit differently when a firm organizes its work into projects or jobs. Essentially, a firm needs to track revenues and expenses — not just by a standard chart of accounts — but also by jobs or projects. Fortunately, QuickBooks makes job costing, or project costing, pretty darn easy. In this chapter, I talk about the tools that QuickBooks provides.

Setting Up a QuickBooks Job

To set up a QuickBooks job, choose the Lists⇨Customer:Job List command. QuickBooks displays the Customer:Job List window, shown in Figure 5-1.

To set up a job for a particular customer, click the customer, and then click the Customer:Job button at the bottom of the window and choose the Add Job Menu command. When you do so, QuickBooks displays the New Job window, shown in Figure 5-2.

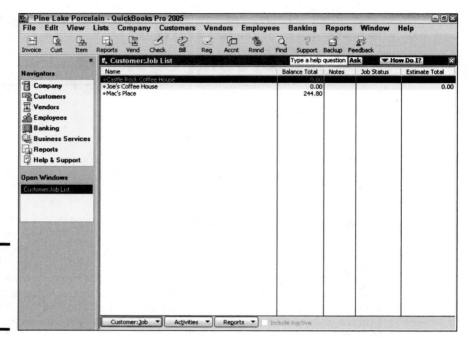

Figure 5-1:
The
Customer:
Job List
window.

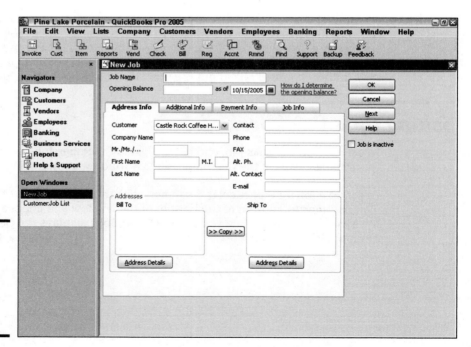

Figure 5-2:
The
Address
Info tab of
the New
Job
window.

To set up a job for a customer, use the Job Name box to give the job or project a name. For example, a home builder may use the address of the home as the job (perhaps just the street address would suffice).

Optionally, you can also use the Address Info, Additional Info, Payment Info (shown in Figure 5-3), and Job Info tabs to provide additional information about the job. Figure 5-4 shows the Job Info tab of the New Job window. This tab provides drop-down list boxes that you can use to identify the job status or the job type. The tab also provides text boxes that you can use to enter the job start date, projected end date, and actual end date. If a job is inactive and you no longer want it to appear in the Customer:Job List window, you can also select the Job Is Inactive check box.

And that, my friend, is that. Essentially, all you need to do to begin tracking jobs is to add jobs to the Customer:Job List. Sweet, right?

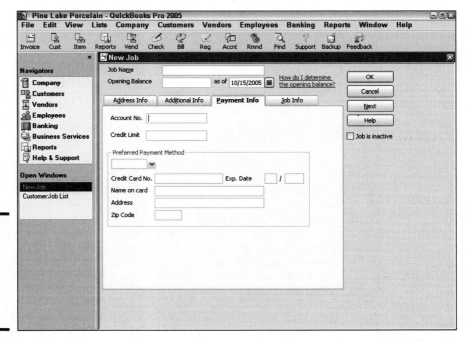

Figure 5-3:
The Payment Info tab of the New Job window.

Book IV
Chapter 5

Setting Up Project
and Job Costing
Systems

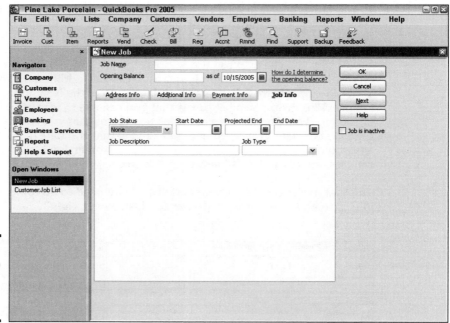

Figure 5-4:
The Job Info
tab of the
New Job
window.

Tracking Job or Project Costs

After you set up a job on the Customer:Job List, you track the income and expenses associated with the job. To do this, you enter the customer and job name in the Customer:Job box (rather than just the customer). For example, if you take a quick look at Figure 5-5, you can see the Create Invoices window (I go into more detail about the Create Invoices window in Book III, Chapter 1). Note that the Customer:Job box can show both the customer and job name. If an invoice is associated with a particular job, you want to identify both the customer and the job by using the Customer:Job box. (You can't see the full Customer:Job name combination, unfortunately, but it is there.) And that's really all it takes.

Other windows that you use to record income and expenses also provide Customer:Job boxes. For example, if you look at the Time/Enter Single Activity window, shown in Figure 5-6, you can see that QuickBooks supplies the Customer:Job box for recording the time that you've worked on a particular customer's project or job. (Book III, Chapter 1 also talks about billing for time.) Again, all you need to do to track the time associated with a particular job is to identify both the customer and the job by using the Customer:Job box.

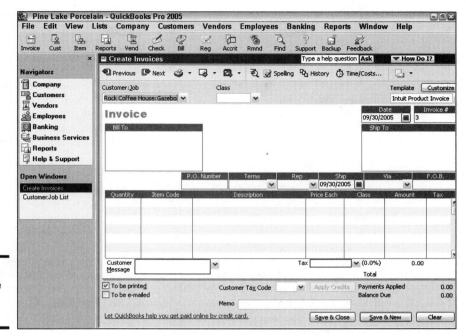

Figure 5-5:
The Create Invoices window.

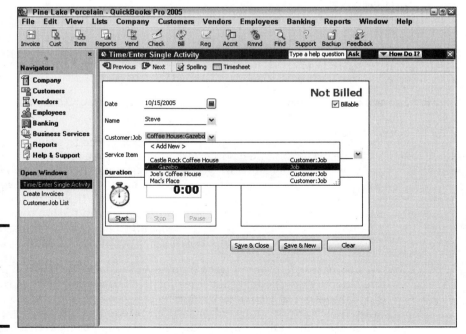

Figure 5-6:
The Time/Enter Single Activity window.

Alternatives to traditional job costing

Because QuickBooks' job-costing approach may not work for everybody — and may even be more than some users need — let me point out that you can do some simple job costing or project costing without using the Customer:Job box. Here are two options:

✔ You can also use classes to segregate costs. Classes work as a very reasonable way to track income and expense transactions for particular jobs if they are associated. I think that the traditional Customer:Job box provides a more convenient way to do this. But, if you have your heart set on it, you can also use the Class box. The Class box or Class column typically appears next to the Customer:Job box or the Customer:Job column. You work with the Class box in the same way that you work with the Customer:Job box. Note that the Class box or column only appears if you enable class tracking using the Preferences dialog box.

✔ You can also construct a very detailed chart of accounts, including accounts, subaccounts, and sub-subaccounts. With a very detailed chart of accounts, you can use collections of accounts to track expenses that are associated with particular projects or jobs. If jobs take a very long time to complete and you're only working on a few jobs, for example, the chart of accounts approach works just fine.

If you use an alternative job costing approach with QuickBooks, unfortunately, you won't be able to rely on QuickBooks' job costing reports. QuickBooks, as I discuss in the next section of this chapter, "Job Cost Reporting," provides a bunch of handy job costing reports. QuickBooks expects that you will use the Customer:Job box to collect job cost information. If you don't use the Customer:Job box, you'll need to make sure that you have a good way to track the costs associated with a particular job or customer.

Another problem with both alternative approaches to job costing — classes or lots of subaccounts — is that you may later want to use classes and subaccounts in some way that's incompatible with using them for job costing. Jobs are, very frankly, best accounted for by using the QuickBooks' job feature.

Just because I have a compulsive personality, I need to point out one more example of the Customer:Job box. If you take a look at the Write Checks window, shown in Figure 5-7, you see that one of the columns shown on the Expenses tab is the Customer:Job column. This column lets you tag any expense amount as being associated with a particular customer's job. All you need to do is identify both the customer and the job by using the Customer:Job column. You won't be surprised to hear that if you happen to click the Items tab, you'll note that it also supplies a Customer:Job column.

To summarize, in order to track income and expense by job, you need to not only identify the account that some income transaction or expense transaction falls into, you also need to identify the customer and job associated with the income or expense transaction. You do this by entering the customer name and job name into the Customer:Job box. And that's all you have to do. You just need to remember to fill in that box.

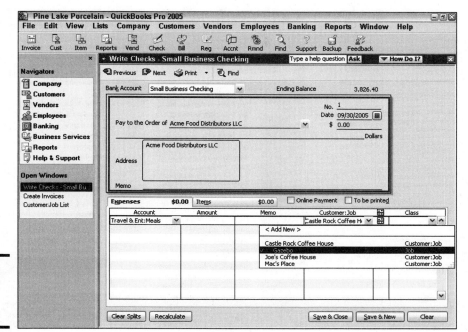

Figure 5-7:
The Write
Checks
window.

Job Cost Reporting

Other chapters in other books of this reference talk about QuickBooks reports. For example, Book IV, Chapter 2 talks about how you can easily pre-pare QuickBooks financial statements and reports. Because I have already talked about QuickBooks reports in some detail, including how you print and customize reports, I don't talk about that stuff here. However, I do want to point out that if you choose the Reports⇨Jobs, Time & Mileage command, QuickBooks displays a submenu, shown in Figure 5-8, of about a dozen differ-ent reports that supply job costing information. The report titles are pretty self-explanatory. Some reports give job profitability, such as the Job Profitability Summary report, shown in Figure 5-9. Some reports identify the estimates associated with a particular job. Other reports compare job esti-mates with actual job costs. You get the picture.

Obviously, you'll want to experiment with these reports if you do begin to use job costing. These reports let you slice and dice your job accounting data in a bunch of different ways. You should be able to use these reports (albeit with perhaps some modifications) to supply most of the information that you need to make good job costing decisions and to manage job costs.

**Book IV
Chapter 5**

**Setting Up Project
and Job Costing
Systems**

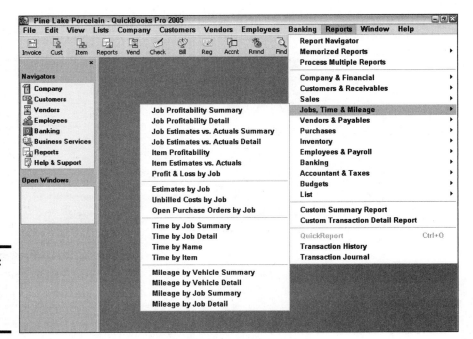

Figure 5-8:
The Jobs,
Time &
Mileage
submenu.

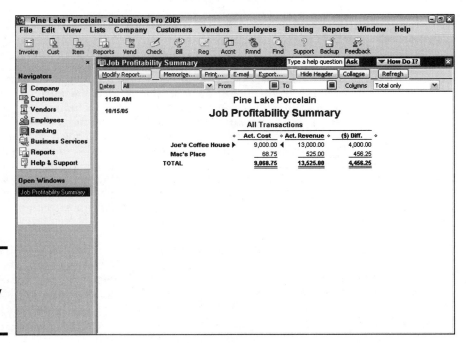

Figure 5-9:
The Job
Profitability
Summary
window.

Using Job Estimates

If you've told QuickBooks that you want to create estimates — you do this during the QuickBooks setup — you can create job estimates of amounts you'll later invoice.

To create a job estimate, choose the Customers⇨Create Estimates command. QuickBooks displays the Create Estimates window, as shown in Figure 5-10. I don't describe how to fill in the fields of this window because this window mirrors the Create Invoices window, which is described in detail in Book III, Chapter 1. In a nutshell, you fill out the Create Estimates window the same way you fill out the Create Invoices window. This makes sense. An estimate is just an example or guess at the future invoice for a job. Predictably, you need to collect and supply the same information, and you fill the fields in the same way.

If you have questions about how to work with a particular field or box on the Create Estimates window, refer to Book III, Chapter 1. Find the description of the related field on the Create Invoices window. Whatever you do with that field in the Create Invoices window is the same thing you do in the Create Estimates window.

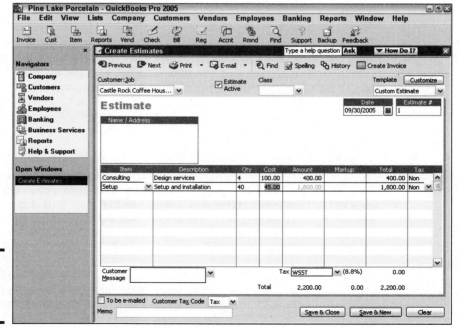

Figure 5-10:
The Create
Estimates
window.

If you didn't originally turn on Estimates when you set up QuickBooks, you can do so after the fact. Choose the Edit⇨Preferences command, click the Jobs & Estimates icon, click the Company Preferences tab, shown in Figure 5-11, and then select the Yes radio button next to Do You Create Estimates?. You may also want to select the Yes radio button next to Do You Do Progress Invoicing?, if you do progress invoicing. (I talk about progress invoicing or progress billing in the next section of this chapter.)

Figure 5-11:
The Company Preferences tab in the Preferences window.

If you use estimates to create invoices, you actually create another way to track job costs. You can ask QuickBooks to prepare reports that compare, item by item, the estimated amounts for a job with the invoiced amounts for job. To produce this report, you choose the Item Estimates vs. Actual command from the Jobs, Time & Mileage submenu.

Progress Billing

Progress billing occurs when you actually invoice, or bill, a customer for a portion of an amount that you've previously estimated. For example, take a peek at the Create Estimates window shown in Figure 5-10. Suppose that this window records an estimate that a client has asked you to supply. Further suppose, just for purposes of this discussion, that the estimate is for a consulting job that you are doing.

If you wanted to later bill the consulting client for the actual work, you click the Create Invoice button that appears along the top edge of the Create Estimates window. QuickBooks displays the Create Progress Invoice Based on Estimate dialog box, as shown in Figure 5-12. This dialog box lets you create an invoice by using the estimate information.

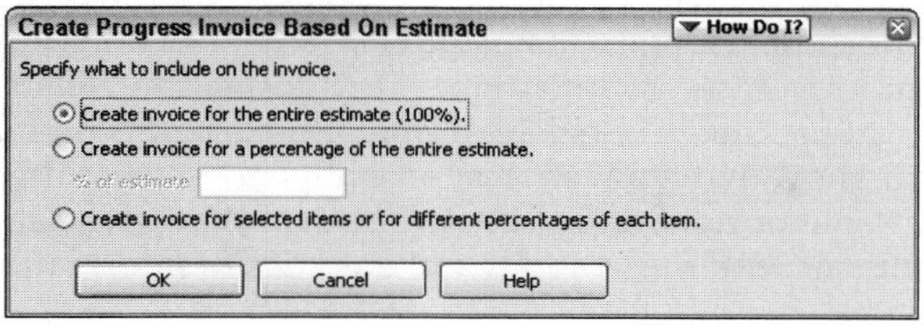

Figure 5-12:
The Create Progress Invoice Based on Estimate dialog box.

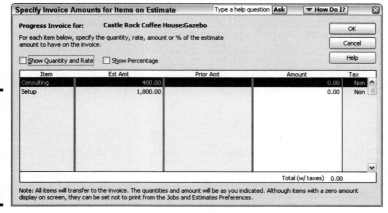

If you select Create an Invoice for the Entire Estimate, QuickBooks creates one invoice that uses all of the information from the Create Estimates window. Alternatively, you can select one of the other option buttons to bill only a portion of the estimate. For example, you can select the Create Invoice for a Percentage of the Entire Estimate radio button and then enter the percentage into the % of Estimate box. In this case, QuickBooks will bill the customer for some specified percentage of the estimate. Alternatively, you can also select the Create Invoice for Selected Items or for Different Percentages of Each Item radio button. In this case, QuickBooks lets you specify that different percentages of the items shown on the estimate should be billed.

When you click OK, QuickBooks either creates the invoice by using the estimate information, or, if you indicated that you wanted to specify different percentages for different items on the invoice, QuickBooks displays the Specify Invoice Amounts for Items on Estimate dialog box, as shown in Figure 5-13. You use the Amount column to specify a portion of the estimated amount that you want to bill on the progress invoice.

Figure 5-13:
The Specify Invoice Amounts for Items on Estimate dialog box.

If you select the Show Quantity and Rate check box on the Specify Invoice Amounts for Items on Estimate dialog box, QuickBooks adds columns to the dialog box that let you see quantity and rate information. Similarly, if you select the Show Percentage check box, QuickBooks adds columns to the dialog box that show percentages. You probably don't need this extra information, but if it's important to be very precise on your invoice, you may want to experiment with these additional columns of information.

Book V

Financial Management

The 5th Wave   By Rich Tennant

"This isn't a quantitative or a qualitative estimate of the job. This is a 'wish-upon-a-star' estimate of the project."

Contents at a Glance

Chapter 1: Ratio Analysis

In This Chapter

✔ Examples of and caveats about ratio analysis

✔ Liquidity ratios

✔ Leverage ratios

✔ Activity ratios

✔ Profitability ratios

Numbers from your financial statements make more sense when you can compare them with other numbers and to other external benchmarks. In this chapter, I talk about how you can perform this sort of analysis, which is called *ratio analysis*. Even if you're not a numbers person, you can use ratio analysis to your benefit. Ratio analysis is easy to apply, and by using it, even non-quantitative types can better understand the information in financial statements.

Let me give you a quick example of ratio analysis. One particularly useful ratio is the *gross margin percentage*, which is your gross margin divided by your total sales. Although this ratio may not seem useful at first blush, it can be very valuable.

For example, if you compare your gross margin percentage for this year with last year and see a decline, you know that this isn't good. Less gross margin means less money for operating expenses, interest expenses, and profits. On the other hand, if you compare your declining gross margin percentage with a competitor and see that your competitor's gross margin percentage is declining even more rapidly than yours, well, you know that's good. This comparison shows that you may actually be in pretty good shape: At least you aren't hurting like your competitor.

These are the sorts of insights that ratio analysis can provide. They enable you to put numbers from your income statement and balance sheet into context.

This chapter steps through the formulas, provides examples, and gives useful guidelines for 16 common financial ratios. I group the ratios into four categories: liquidity ratios, leverage (or debt) ratios, activity ratios, and profitability ratios.

Some Caveats about Ratio Analysis

Before you go any further in using ratio analysis to draw conclusions, consider these two warnings about it:

✦ **The ratios are only as good as your inputs.** Obviously, the more accurate your QuickBooks accounting records, the more accurate any ratios that you calculate by using the numbers from your QuickBooks financial statements. This makes sense, right? Garbage in — garbage out. Even if your financial records are garbage free, if they contain something just slightly wacky, such as an unusually large transaction that skews all the numbers, your financial ratios aren't as good as they can be.

✦ **Ratios become relevant through comparison.** Your financial ratios become most relevant — I already hinted at this — by comparing your numbers with those of your competitors, the numbers that you had a year ago, and the numbers that a bank loan agreement specifies are necessary for you to continue achieving in order to be in the good graces of the bank. A comparison with other ratios is crucial because your numbers are often only just numbers if they can't be compared with external benchmarks.

Industries commonly prepare reports that summarize financial ratio information of other firms in the industry. For example, early in my career, I was the controller of an electronics manufacturing firm. Our industry group, the American Electronics Association, prepared a financial ratio survey. With this financial ratio survey, I was able to easily compare the financial ratios of the firm I worked at with the financial ratios of other firms. Currently, as a CPA, I find it very useful that the Texas Society of CPAs prepares an annual financial study that shows financial ratios for CPA firms around the United States. You probably also operate in an industry that has a professional association. Keep your eyes and ears open to the possibility that this group or association prepares and distributes reports that include financial ratios. Such a report can be a useful tool to you as you manage your firm.

Note: When you compare yourself with other firms by using financial ratios, you need to compare yourself with firms of a similar size. It usually doesn't make sense to compare, for example, a million-dollar business with a billion-dollar business.

Some of the QuickBooks financial statements provide simple financial ratios automatically. For example, you can add the gross margin percentage (and other percentage measures) to the standard income statement and to the standard balance sheet. For more information about how to work with any of these simple financial ratios, refer to Book IV, Chapter 2.

Liquidity Ratios

Liquidity ratios measure how easily and comfortably a firm can pay its immediate financial obligations and exploit immediate short-term financial opportunities. For example, everything else being equal, the firm that is sitting on a large hoard of cash can more easily pay its bills and can take advantage of great opportunities that pop up. (For example, if a competitor gets into trouble and wants to sell valuable assets at fire sale prices, a very liquid firm with great gobs of cash can more easily exploit such an opportunity.)

Current ratio

The *current ratio* liquidity measure compares a firm's current assets with its current liabilities. A firm's current assets include cash, inventory, accounts receivable, and any other asset that can or will be quickly turned into cash. Most small businesses don't have much in the way of other current assets, although some do have some, such as short-term investments. Current liabilities include bills that must be paid in the coming year: accounts payable, wages payable, taxes payable, and — if you are borrowing money on a long-term basis (such as through bank loans) — the principal portions of the coming year's payment on a loan.

The following is the exact formula used to calculate the current ratio:

```
current assets/current liabilities
```

The simple balance sheet shown in Table 1-1 gives you an example of how this current ratio formula works. As Table 1-1 shows, this firm's current assets equal $50,000. The firm's only current liability is $20,000 of accounts payable. (For purposes of this discussion, I'm assuming that this firm has no other current liabilities.) To calculate the current ratio of the firm described by the balance sheet in Table 1-1, you use the following formula:

```
$50,000/$20,000
```

This formula returns the value 2.5. Therefore, the value 2.5 is this firm's current ratio.

Here is a general guideline concerning current ratios: A firm's current ratio should be a value of 2 or higher. In other words, the firm's current assets should be double or more than double the firm's current liabilities.

Table 1-1	A Simple Balance Sheet
Assets	
Cash	$25,000
Inventory	25,000
Current assets	$50,000
Fixed assets (net)	270,000
Total assets	$320,000
Liabilities	
Accounts payable	$20,000
Loan payable	100,000
Owner's equity	
S. Nelson, capital	200,000
Total liabilities and owner's equity	$320,000

Acid test ratio

Also known as the *quick* ratio, the *acid test* ratio is a more severe measure of a firm's liquidity. However, it serves the same general purpose as the current ratio. The acid test ratio indicates how easily a firm can meet its current financial obligations and exploit any financial opportunities that pop up.

The following formula is used for calculating the acid test ratio:

```
(current assets-inventory)/current liabilities
```

For example, in the case of the business described by the balance sheet shown in Table 1-1, you use the following formula to calculate the acid test ratio:

```
$25,000/$20,000
```

This formula returns the value 1.25. Therefore, the value of 1.25 is this firm's acid test ratio.

Here is a guideline for acid test ratio: A firm's acid test ratio should be a value of 1 or higher. In other words, the current assets after you subtract out the inventory should provide enough money to pay the current liabilities.

Leverage Ratios

Leverage ratios measure how much debt a firm carries and how easily a firm pays the interest expenses of carrying that debt. Leverage ratios are important for an obvious reason. Typically, a firm mostly financed with debt needs to continue to borrow in order to stay in business. (If this doesn't make sense, think about what happens if a bank won't extend a loan or won't refinance a mortgage to a firm that's heavily dependent on debt!)

What's more, a firm that carries a lot of debt typically also spends a lot of money on interest expense. The heavy interest expense means that it is especially important for such a firm to have adequate operating income. *Operating income* is the income available to pay interest and other profits. A firm with a lot of operating income, relative to its interest expense, doesn't really have much of a problem paying the interest — and this will be true even if operating income declines or decreases. In contrast, a firm with only very modest operating income relative to its interest expense quickly gets into trouble if the operating income decreases.

Debt ratio

The *debt* ratio simply shows the firm's debt as a percentage of its capital structure. The term *capital structure* refers to the total liabilities and owner's equity amount. For example, in the case of the balance sheet shown in Table 1-1, the capital structure totals $320,000. Not coincidentally, the total liability and owner's equity amount, $320,000, equals the total assets amount, $320,000. This makes sense if you think about it a bit. A firm funds its assets with its capital. Therefore, the total assets always equal the total capital structure.

The formula for calculating the debt ratio is a simple one:

```
total debt/total assets
```

Using numbers from the simple balance sheet shown in Table 1-1, for example, the debt ratio can be calculated as follows:

```
$120,000/$320,000
```

This formula returns the debt ratio of .375. This indicates that 37.5 percent of the firm's capital comes from debt.

No guideline exists for debt ratio. Appropriate debt ratios vary by industry and by the size of the firm in an industry. In general, small firms that use QuickBooks probably want to show lower debt ratios than larger firms. Small firms, in my experience, see their operating income fluctuate more wildly than large firms. Because of that fluctuation, carrying and servicing such debt is more problematic. Lower debt, therefore, is probably better. This makes sense, of course, so I'm not telling you anything that you don't already know.

Debt equity ratio

A *debt equity* ratio compares a firm's long-term debt with a stockholder's equity or owner's equity. Essentially, the debt equity ratio expresses a firm's long-term debt as a percentage of its owner's equity.

Stockholder's equity is synonymous with *owner's equity* and, in the case of a sole proprietorship, with a sole proprietor's capital account.

The following is the formula used to calculate a debt equity ratio:

```
long-term debt/stockholder's equity
```

By using the example balance sheet shown in Table 1-1, you can calculate the debt equity ratio by using this formula:

```
$100,000/$200,000
```

This formula returns the debt equity ratio of 0.5. Therefore, this firm's long-term debt equals 0.5, or 50 percent of its owner's equity.

I can't really give you a guideline for a debt equity ratio. You simply need to compare your debt equity ratio with the debt equity ratios of other, similar-sized firms in your industry. As is the case with the debt ratio previously described, the less long-term debt you carry, the better — all other things being equal.

Times interest earned ratio

The *times interest earned* ratio indicates how easily a firm pays interest expenses incurred on its debt. In order to calculate the times interest earned ratio, you need an income statement that shows both operating income and interest expense. Table 1-2 provides this information.

Table 1-2	A Simple Income Statement
Sales revenue	$150,000
Less: Cost of goods sold	30,000
Gross margin	$120,000
Rent	5,000
Wages	50,000
Supplies	5,000
Total operating expenses	60,000
Operating income	60,000
Interest expense	(10,000)
Net income	$50,000

The following formula is used for calculating the times interest earned ratio:

```
operating income/interest expense
```

If you look at the income statement shown in Table 1-2, you see that operating income, which is the income that a firm has *before* paying its interest expense, equals $60,000. Interest expense shows up as $10,000. Therefore, you calculate the times interest earned ratio by using this formula:

```
$60,000/$10,000
```

This formula returns the times interest earned ratio of 6. Therefore, the firm's operating profits pay the interest expense six times over.

No standard guideline exists for the times interest earned ratio. Obviously, however, the times interest earned ratio should indicate that a firm can easily pay its interest expense. It would be sort of scary, if you think about it, for the operating income to only be a little bit greater than the firm's interest expense. Such a situation would indicate that a modest drop in operating income would make paying interest expense impossible.

Fixed-charges coverage ratio

The *fixed-charges coverage* ratio resembles the times interest earned ratio. The fixed-charges coverage ratio calculates how easily a firm pays not only its interest expenses but also any principal payments on loans and any other obligations for which a firm is legally obligated to pay.

The fixed-charges coverage ratio uses the following formula:

```
income available for fixed charges/fixed charges
```

Returning to the example business described by the balance sheet shown in Table 1-1 and the income statement shown in Table 1-2, suppose that the $5,000 of rent shown in the income statement is actually a fixed charge because the firm is renting space on a long-term lease. Further suppose for the purpose of this ratio, although it doesn't show up on the income statement, that the $100,000 loan that shows up on the balance sheet requires annual $5,000 principal payments.

In this case, this firm is obligated to pay fixed charges as summarized in Table 1-3. In total, then, fixed charges for this firm equal $20,000 a year.

Table 1-3	Fixed Charges Calculation
Interest (as shown in Table 1-2)	$10,000
Rent (as shown in Table 1-2)	5,000
Principal (as mentioned in text)	5,000
Fixed charges	$20,000

The other input needed to calculate the fixed-charges coverage ratio is the income available for these fixed charges. Table 1-4 shows you how to calculate the income available for fixed charges. You start with the operating income, which equals $60,000, as shown in Table 1-2. (Remember that the operating income is the income before paying interest expense.) You must add to the operating income any fixed charges included in the income statement. In this case, the rent turns out to be a fixed charge. Therefore, the $5,000 of rent needs to be added to the operating income in order to get income available for fixed charges. As Table 1-4 shows, the income available for fixed charges equals $65,000.

Table 1-4	Income Available for Fixed Charges
Operating income	$60,000
Add back of rent	5,000
Fixed charges	$65,000

With the two needed inputs, you can calculate the fixed-charges coverage ratio by using this formula:

`$65,000/$20,000`

This formula returns a fixed-charges coverage ratio of 3.25, which indicates that the firm generates slightly more than three times as much income as needed to pay its fixed charges.

No guideline exists to specify what your fixed-charges coverage ratio should be. In fact, it is particularly difficult to get the information necessary to think about fixed-charge coverage ratios because fixed charges don't clearly appear in the standard set of simple financial statements. One of the things that make financial statements (that are prepared in accordance with generally accepted accounting principles) so useful is that the fixed-charges information is usually disclosed in little footnotes that appear at the end of the financial statements.

Activity Ratios

Activity ratios provide an indication of how efficiently a firm runs its operations. For example (all other factors being equal), a firm that keeps a very modest amount of inventory is in better shape than a firm that has to keep (store, manage, warehouse, insure, and so forth) a bunch of inventory. That makes sense, right?

Dell Computer, as you may know, keeps only a few days' worth of inventory on hand. In other words, it sells out its current inventory holdings every few days. Other computer manufacturers — especially in the past — kept weeks and even months worth of inventory. Comparing the two examples, which is more efficiently and more leanly managing its inventory? Which has the minimal investment tied up? Which isn't suffering or paying the price of warehousing all that extra, quickly obsolete inventory? The answer is Dell, obviously. So, predictably, Dell's activity ratios look really good compared with its competitors.

Activity ratios, in essence, measure how well a firm uses its assets. If a firm makes super-efficient use of its factory, for example, that efficiency will show up in its activity ratios. And if a firm runs lean and mean, that leanness and meanness will show up in its activity ratios.

Inventory turnover ratio

The *inventory turnover* ratio measures how many times in an accounting period the inventory balance sells out. The formula is as follows:

```
cost of goods sold/average inventory
```

In the example business described by the balance sheet in Table 1-1 and the income statement in Table 1-2, you can use the following formula to calculate the inventory turnover:

```
$30,000/$25,000
```

This formula returns the inventory turnover ratio of 1.2.

Technically, you shouldn't use just an ending inventory balance, which is what appears in Table 1-1. You should use an *average inventory balance.* You can calculate an average inventory balance in all the usual, common-sense ways. For example, you can use the inventory balance both from this year's balance sheet and the previous year's balance sheet and then average them.

The inventory turnover period, as you may have noticed, depends on the period measured in the income statement. If the income statement is an annual statement, and therefore the cost of goods sold amount is an annual cost of goods sold amount, an inventory turnover ratio of 1.2 means that a firm sells 120 percent of its inventory balance in a year. If the inventory turnover ratio uses the cost of goods sold amount reported in a monthly income statement, then the inventory turnover period is a month. For example, with a monthly cost of goods sold amount, a firm with a 1.2 inventory ratio sells 120 percent of its inventory in a month.

No guideline exists for inventory turnover ratios. A good inventory turnover ratio depends on what your competitors are doing within your industry. If you want to stay competitive, you want an inventory turnover ratio that at least comes close to your competitor's ratio. Dell's competitors, to make a long, sad story short, found out the hard way not to compete with someone who turns around inventory much more quickly than they could. (Imagine soft, sad violin music playing in the background. . . .)

Days of inventory ratio

The *days of inventory* ratio resembles the inventory turnover financial ratio; it estimates how many days of inventory that a firm is storing. The ratio uses the following formula:

```
average inventory/(annual cost of goods sold/365)
```

For example, the simple balance sheet shown in Table 1-1 shows inventory equal to $25,000. Assume that this also equals the average inventory that the firm carries. In order to calculate the daily sales, you need to take the cost of goods sold number reported in the annual income statement shown in Table 1-2 and divide it by 365 (the number of days in a year). Putting these numbers together in the form of the formula just introduced, the math looks like this:

$25,000/($30,000/365)

This formula returns the value 304 (roughly). This value means that this firm is carrying roughly 304 days of inventory. Stated another way, this firm would require 304 days of sales to sell its entire inventory.

As is the case with the inventory turnover ratio, you don't see generalized rules for what is an acceptable number for days of inventory. The general rule is that you need to be turning your inventory around just as quickly as your competitor does.

I return to the case of Dell Computer because it's so instructive — even if scary — to most of us. Dell sells out its inventory in a few days. Dell's competitors were taking months to sell out their inventory. In an industry where inventory was quickly becoming obsolete and was very expensive to start with, think of the competitive disadvantage that Dell's competitors suffered by having to carry inventory for months longer than Dell did. Is it any wonder that many of Dell's competitors got into trouble? The lesson of Dell applies to many of us who run or advise businesses that carry inventory. Inventory turnover and days of inventory ratios need to be watched carefully and be compared to other firms of the same size in the same industry.

Average collection period ratio

The *average collection period* ratio shows how long it takes for a firm to collect on its receivables. You can think about this ratio as a measure of the quality of a firm's credit and collection procedures. In other words, this ratio shows how smart a firm is at deciding to whom to extend credit. This ratio also shows how effective a firm is in collecting from customers.

The average collection period ratio formula looks like this:

```
average accounts receivable/average credit sales per day
```

The balance sheet shown in Table 1-1 doesn't show an average accounts receivable balance. The income statement shown in Table 1-2 also doesn't break out sales into credit and cash components. Therefore, let me introduce another example into the text. Suppose that in the business you run, the average accounts receivable is $60,000. Further suppose that your average credit daily sales equal $1,000. Using the formula just given, you can calculate the average collection period as follows:

```
$60,000/$1,000
```

This formula returns the value 60. In this case, your business has 60 days of sales in accounts receivable.

The guideline about the average collection period is that it should tie to your payment terms. If your average number of days of credit sales in accounts receivable equals 60, for example, your payment terms should probably be something like net 60 days (which means customers are supposed to pay you in 60 days or less). Your average collection period, in other words, should show that most of your customers are paying on time. Remember that some of your customers will pay early, and obviously, some of your customers will pay a bit late. Hopefully, on average, customers pay on time.

Fixed asset turnover ratio

The *fixed asset turnover* ratio quantifies how efficiently a firm employs its fixed assets. Predictably, this financial ratio is most useful when a firm has a lot of fixed assets: real estate, equipment, and so forth.

The fixed asset turnover ratio uses the following formula:

```
sales/fixed assets
```

Based on the numbers supplied by the balance sheet shown in Table 1-1 and the income statement shown in Table 1-2, you can calculate the following fixed asset turnover ratio:

```
$150,000/$270,000
```

This formula returns the value of 0.556. In a nutshell, this ratio says that this firm requires $270,000 of fixed assets to produce $150,000 of sales. Or, more specifically, that the firm produces sales equal to roughly 56 percent of its fixed assets.

As is the case with many of these financial ratios, no guideline exists that you can use to determine a good fixed asset turnover ratio. You need to compare your fixed asset turnover ratio with firms of a similar size in your industry.

Total assets turnover ratio

The *total assets turnover* ratio also measures how efficiently you're employing your assets. This ratio is probably more appropriate in the situation where a firm doesn't have a lot of fixed assets, but the firm still wins or loses at the game of business based on how well the firm manages its assets.

The total assets turnover ratio formula is as follows:

```
sales/total assets
```

Here's the formula that calculates the ratio by using the financial data from Tables 1-1 and 1-2. If the total sales equal $150,000 and the total assets equal $320,000, the following formula makes the calculation:

```
$150,000/$320,000
```

This formula returns the ratio of 0.469, which means that the firm generates sales equal to roughly 47 percent of its total assets.

The total assets turnover ratio that you calculate for your business can't be compared with some external benchmark or standardized rule. You need to compare your ratio with the same ratio of similarly sized businesses in your industry. Obviously, your main consideration is whether you're efficiently using your assets to produce sales relative to your competitors. The more sales you can produce with a given level of assets, the better off your business is.

Profitability Ratios

The profitability ratios analyze a firm's profitability. In a sense, these profitability ratios are the most important ratios that you can calculate. They typically provide terribly useful insights into how profitable a firm is and why.

For example, one particularly important profitability ratio is the gross margin percentage, which expresses gross margin as a percent of sales. As discussed in Book VI, Chapter 1, you can calculate a firm's break-even point simply by dividing the firm's fixed costs by its gross margin percentage.

Gross margin percentage

Also known as the *gross profit margin* ratio, the gross margin percentage shows how much a firm has left over after paying its cost of goods sold. The gross margin is what pays the operating expenses, financing expenses (interest), and, of course, the profits.

The gross margin percentage ratio uses the following formula:

```
gross margin/sales
```

For example, using the data from Table 1-2, you can calculate gross margin percentage as follows:

```
$120,000/$150,000
```

This formula returns the value of 0.8, meaning that gross margin equals 80 percent of the firm's sales.

No guideline exists for what a gross margin percentage should be. Some firms enjoy very high gross margins. Other firms make good money even though the gross margin percentages are very low. In general, of course, the higher the gross margin percentage, the better.

I need to make one cautionary statement here: In my humble opinion, small businesses should enjoy high gross margin percentages. I think it is common to assume that a small business can get away with a lower gross margin percentage than some large competitors can. However, in my experience, that isn't really true. Gross margin percentages should be higher for small businesses because small businesses often can't get the economies of scale that large businesses can get. A low gross margin percentage may work just fine for a Wal-Mart, for example. However, it's tough for a small retailer to work with such a small gross margin percentage.

Operating income/sales

In the case of the business shown in Table 1-2, where operating income equals $60,000 and sales equal $150,000, you calculate the net operating margin percentage by using this formula:

```
$60,000/$150,000
```

This formula returns the value 0.4. A 0.4 operating margin percentage, which is equivalent to 40 percent, indicates that a firm's operating income equals 40 percent of its sales.

No guideline exists for what a net operating margin percentage should be. Your main consideration, as you will probably find yourself repeating in your sleep after hearing me say it so much, is that *you want to be competitive*. You want your operating margin percentage to be close to or better than what your competitors' net operating margin percentages are. That parity (or superiority) enables you to stay competitive.

Profit margin percentage

The *profit margin percentage* works like the net operating margin percentage; it expresses the firm's net income as a percentage of sales, as shown in the following formula:

```
net income/sales
```

In the case of the business described by the income statement shown in Table 1-2, the net income equals $50,000, and sales equal $150,000. This firm's profit margin percentage, therefore, can be calculated with the following formula:

```
$50,000/$150,000
```

This formula returns a financial ratio of 0.33. This indicates that the firm's net income equals roughly 33 percent of its sales.

Return on assets

The *return on assets* shows the return that the firm delivers to stockholders and the interest that the firm pays to lenders as the percentage of the firm's assets. Some businesses use return on assets to evaluate the business's profitability. (Banks do this, for example.)

The actual formula is

```
(net income + interest)/total assets
```

In the case of the example business described in Tables 1-1 and 1-2, the net income equals $50,000. Interest expense equals $10,000. Total assets equal $320,000. The formula to calculate this firm's return on assets is

```
($50,000 + $10,000)/$320,000
```

This formula returns the value 0.188. This value indicates that the firm's return (including both net income and interest) on its assets is roughly 19 percent.

No guideline exists for what a return on assets ratio should be. The main consideration is, predictably, that the return on assets needs to exceed the capital charges on the assets.

In Book V, Chapter 2, I talk more about capital charges and how they relate to something called *economic value added analysis*. Capital charges aren't complicated to understand. The bottom line is that a firm needs to deliver a return on its assets that exceeds the funding sources cost for those assets. In other words, if (on average) the creditor and shareholders providing money to a firm want something less than, for example, 19 percent and the firm can earn 19 percent as its return on assets, that's really good. If, on the other hand, the return on assets percentage is 18.8 percent, but the funding sources for those assets cost 20 percent, well, that's not so good. That firm is in trouble.

The term *capital charge* just equals the sum of the minimum profit that shareholders require to invest their money in a firm and the interest charges that lenders require for the money that they've loaned to the firm.

Return on equity

The *return on equity* financial ratio expresses a firm's net income as a percentage of its owner's equity, or shareholder's equity (shareholder's and owner's equity are the same thing).

The formula, which is deceptively simple, is as follows:

```
net income/owner's equity
```

In the case of the example business described in Tables 1-1 and 1-2, the net income equals $50,000, and the owner's equity equals $200,000. This firm's return on equity, therefore, can be calculated by using the following formula:

```
$50,000/$200,000
```

This formula returns the value of 0.25, which means that this firm's return on equity is 25 percent — a number that's probably pretty good.

No guideline exists for what is and is not an acceptable return on equity. However, I can make two useful observations about how you should interpret the return on equity ratio that you calculate:

+ **The return on equity ratio that you calculate needs to be at least as good as you deserve.** Okay, that sounds circular. So think about it this way: If you are investing money in your business, you deserve a return on that money. And that return needs to be reasonable compared with your other alternatives. If you can go out and invest money in a stock market mutual fund and get 10 percent, you shouldn't be investing in things that deliver a return of less than 10 percent. That makes sense, right? Therefore, if you want to earn a 20 percent return on the money that you've invested in your own firm (by the way, a 20 percent return is a very reasonable return for a small business), you want to make sure that your return on equity (after you get going) exceeds this minimum return.

+ **The return on equity ratio hints at the sustainable growth rate that your firm can manage.** This sounds complicated. However, you need to understand what sustainable growth is and how it ties back to the return on equity ratio. *Sustainable growth* is the growth rate that your business can sustain over a long period of time: three years, five years, ten years, and so on. If you don't take money out of the business (other than your salary) and you reinvest the return on equity that the business generates, the return on equity ratio equals your sustainable growth. In other words, the example business described in Tables 1-1 and 1-2 can grow on a sustained basis as fast as 25 percent.

Alternatively, suppose that the owners of the imaginary firm previously described in the financial statements take half of the equity money out of the business. Perhaps half of the $50,000 net income is distributed as a dividend to shareholders, for example. In this case, because only half of the return on equity is reinvested, sustainable growth only equals half of the return on equity percentage. If the return on equity percentage equals 25 percent but the owners withdraw half of the return (12.5 percent), the reinvested half of the return on equity percentage (12.5 percent) equals the sustainable growth rate. In other words, this business can grow on a sustained basis at 12.5 percent annually.

In my experience, this sustainable growth business makes intuitive sense to some people, but it just leads to head-scratching for other people. In case you're in the head-scratching group, consider a couple more comments:

✦ **Growing sales and profits also requires growing your capital structure.** The idea of a sustainable growth rate (which was pioneered by Hewlett-Packard, interestingly enough) is based on an intuitively understandable proposition: To grow your sales and your profits over the long run, you need to grow your assets. If you're going to double your sales and your profits, for example, you're probably going to have to double your assets. And if you double your assets, you're going to need to double your funding of those assets. Doubled funding of your assets means that you need to double your borrowing and your owner's equity. Assuming that you can get creditors to loan you more money — that should be possible if you're growing not only sales but profits — you're still going to need to double your owner's equity. And the way that you usually double or grow your owner's equity in a small business is by reinvesting the return on the equity.

Large businesses also have another way to grow owner's equity. A large business, such as Hewlett-Packard, can go out into the capital markets and raise money by issuing stock. In fact, the real reason for making a company public isn't to make the owners rich but to access the public's capital markets. Those markets provide a firm with access to almost unlimited amounts of capital. (That is, unless you pull an Enron or WorldCom by proving that you don't really deserve access to the capital markets.) In the case where a firm can tap these capital markets for cash or funding, the sustainable growth rate formula gets more complicated. These capital markets provide another way to grow owner's equity.

✦ **If you don't grow owner's equity as your business grows, watch out.** You'll have big problems if you ignore the sustainable growth rate if your business grows fast. If you don't grow your owner's equity at least as fast as your business grows, your debt percentage ratio skyrockets (perhaps) without you even realizing it. Just think about this logically: If your sales double, your assets probably double. And if your owner's equity doesn't double, creditors have to make up the difference. Exploding debt means that it becomes all the more important for you to refinance that debt and refinance even larger amounts of that debt. And exploding debt means that your interest expense is growing all the time because your debt levels are rising.

I've seen more businesses fail because they ignored the sustainable growth concept than for any other reason. In the case where a successful business — defined as one that has been making a reasonable profit and is chugging along merrily — gets into trouble as the firm grows, the problem almost invariably is that the firm has grown too fast. The firm has grown faster than its capital base can grow. And that only leads to trouble. The symptoms often make the situation look like something other than a problem of growing too fast. However, when you boil everything down to its essence, in my experience, the successful business that fails or gets into trouble as it grows has simply ignored the realities of sustainable growth.

Chapter 2: Economic Value Added Analysis

In This Chapter

✓ Introducing the logic of EVA

✓ A simple example of EVA in action

✓ Some important points about EVA

✓ A more complicated EVA example with debt

*H*ere's a curious fact: Even if your QuickBooks income statement shows a profit, you may not actually be making any money. How can this be? Ah, to really answer this question you need to use a tool called *Economic Value Added analysis (EVA)*, which was developed by (and is a trademark of) Stern Stewart & Co., a management consulting firm.

In this chapter, I discuss what Economic Value Added analysis does and how you can use the information that you create with QuickBooks to perform the EVA analysis. This is neat stuff but a bit theoretical. Fortunately, when you boil EVA down to its very essence, it's quite practical.

Introducing the Logic of EVA

Economic Value Added analysis states in a formula something you already know in your gut: If you are a business owner and you can make more money by selling your business and reinvesting the proceeds, then hey — you're not doing yourself or your family any favors by running your own business.

Let me walk you through an example to show you mathematically why this is the case. Suppose that after paying yourself a fair salary, your firm makes $20,000 in additional profits. Further suppose that you can sell your firm to a competitor for $200,000. If you did, you could probably invest the money in a stock mutual fund and earn about $20,000 a year in profits, right? (And yes, I know that the stock market doesn't promise 10 percent annual returns, but neither does your business. So just suppose that these numbers are right for the purposes of this discussion.)

In this simple example, running your own business doesn't really make sense. Sure, you're making a salary. And, sure, you're earning a return on the money that you and your family have invested. But you aren't getting anything more than that. You may as well just sell your firm, reinvest the money in the stock market (just one option), and get a job working for the phone company.

Don't get all bummed out on me here — I'm not trying to talk you into selling your business. I just want to explain how to use a powerful tool, EVA, to better manage your business.

EVA in Action

EVA analysis has two variations; I explain the simple version first. By starting with the simple version, you'll understand all the little nuances and subtleties of the EVA model from the very start. After you're finished with the simple version of EVA analysis — called an *equity-based* EVA — you'll be ready to move on to the more complicated EVA model.

In order to proceed with this discussion, you need to take a gander at a couple of financial statements. Table 2-1 shows a simple income statement, and Table 2-2 shows a simple balance sheet. These two financial statements provide much — and maybe most — of the information that you would need to perform EVA analysis for your business. In fact, just go ahead and suppose that these two financial statements describe your business.

If you're uncomfortable interpreting either income statements or balance sheet financial statements, you may want to review the material covered in Book I, Chapter 1. In that chapter, I describe how financial statements work.

If you're not sure how to produce a financial statement by using QuickBooks, refer to Book IV, Chapter 2. In that chapter, I describe how to prepare QuickBooks financial statements, including income statements (also known as *profit & loss statements*) and balance sheets.

Essentially, EVA includes a *charge* for the capital that you've invested in a business. To see whether you are actually making money, you deduct this charge from your net income. A positive EVA amount indicates that your business truly produces an economic profit; in other words, a positive EVA amount indicates that even after your firm pays wages to employees, interest to lenders, and a return to shareholders, some money is still left over. This leftover money is the *economic profit*.

Table 2-1	A Simple Income Statement
Sales revenue	$150,000
Less: Cost of goods sold	30,000
Gross margin	$120,000
Rent	5,000
Wages	50,000
Supplies	5,000
Total operating expenses	60,000
Operating income	60,000
Interest expense	(10,000)
Net income	$50,000

Table 2-2	A Simple Balance Sheet
Assets	
Cash	$25,000
Inventory	25,000
Current assets	$50,000
Fixed assets (net)	270,000
Total assets	$320,000
Liabilities	
Accounts payable	$20,000
Loan payable	100,000
Owner's equity	
S. Nelson, capital	200,000
Total liabilities and owner's equity	$320,000

The capital charge equals the cost of the capital (specified as an interest rate or annual return percentage) multiplied by the capital invested in the business period. The capital invested in your business equals, essentially, your owner's equity. The cost of capital return percentage equals the return that you could earn in a similarly risky investment in something else.

An example of EVA

From the example data in Tables 2-1 and 2-2, calculate each of these amounts by using the following steps:

1. **Calculate the capital charge.**

For the sake of illustration, suppose that you earn a 20 percent return on the money that you have invested in the business described in Tables 2-1 and 2-2. To calculate an EVA in this situation, use the following formula:

```
capital charge = 20% × $200,000 (of owner's equity)
```

The result of this formula is a capital charge of $40,000. That's the amount that should be returned to the shareholder. (In the case of a small business owned and operated by an entrepreneur, the shareholder is the owner/entrepreneur.)

2. **Subtract the capital charge from the net income.**

In Table 2-1, the net income equals $50,000. To calculate the EVA, use the following formula:

```
net income ($50,000) - capital charge ($40,000) = EVA
```

The result — $10,000 — equals the EVA.

Therefore, by using the data from the example business detailed in Tables 2-1 and 2-2 and assuming a 20 percent cost of capital, this business delivers an economic profit. After paying each stakeholder his or her fair share, the firm also has leftover money — an economic profit — of $10,000.

Another example of EVA

To continue this example, suppose that the capital charge is really $50,000 (calculated by multiplying a 25 percent cost of capital percentage by the $200,000 of capital or owner's equity). In this case, what does the EVA equal? The answer is zero. In other words, if the business makes $50,000 of profit (as shown in Table 2-1) but the shareholders require a $50,000 return on their investment (calculated as 25 percent multiplied by $200,000), the business produces no EVA.

Does the preceding scenario make sense to you? The math may seem a little unwieldy, but don't get too tangled up in the computations. My guess is that you understand in your gut what EVA analysis does. If you really did own a business like the one summarized in Table 2-1 and Table 2-2, you know that you should be earning a fair return on the money that you and your family have invested. And if you're only earning the same amount of money that you could earn in any other business — say a stock mutual fund — then you're not really getting ahead.

That's all EVA analysis really does. It makes sure that you're getting at least, or ideally more than, a fair return on your investment.

Some Important Points about EVA

The purpose of EVA analysis is simple: You want to see whether you're earning an economic profit by owning your own business.

To make sure that you're on track with your analysis, you typically want to consider several things:

+ **How good are the numbers?** This is an important point. Do your income statement and balance sheet values really describe your profit (one of the numbers used in your calculation) and the value that you may be able to sell for and then reinvest (another important value used in your calculation)? You are always going to have to accept some imprecision in your numbers. That's a fact of life. But a *lot* of imprecision in those two numbers corrupts the results.

You should compare your owner's equity value with what you think you would get if you sold your business. If your owner's equity value (the amount shown on your balance sheet) is wildly different than the cash-out value, you should probably use the cash-out value in your EVA analysis rather than the owner's equity value.

+ **How good is the cost of capital percentage?** The capital charge calculation relies heavily on the cost of capital value. This is a tough number to come up with, quite frankly. If you owned a billion-dollar business, you would probably need a team of Ph.D.s to come up with a number for you (and clearly this isn't feasible for a small business). Therefore, I recommend that you use a range of values. Many people think that a small business (any business with sales less than, say, $50,000,000 dollars) should produce returns annually of 20 to 25 percent. That seems to be a good range of values to use in EVA analysis. You may also be interested to know that for a large company, the cost of capital rates run from approximately 10 to 12 percent. So you clearly don't want to be that low. Finally, note that venture capital returns — those returns delivered by the most successful, fastest growing small businesses — often run 35 to 45 percent annually. It seems, therefore, that cost of capital rates used in your EVA analysis should be considerably less than this. Or at least for most businesses, the cost of capital rates should be considerably less than 35 to 45 percent.

Try a range of rates when you perform EVA analysis. For example, try 15 percent as your cost of capital, then 20 percent, 25 percent, and 30 percent. The calculations, after you have the profit number and the owner's equity number, are pretty simple after all. It's not really difficult to calculate several estimates of EVA.

+ **What about psychological income?** In the case of an owner-managed business, I think it's okay to factor in psychological income. You can't ignore the economy. A viable healthy business — especially if it's yours — should deliver a nice profit over time and pay for the capital that it uses. Having said that, however, if you really love your work, I'm the last guy to say that you should sell your winery and go to work for the local big box retailer. (Not that there's anything wrong with wearing an orange vest and spending all day on concrete floors.) My point is that, in my opinion, owning your own business is about more than just an economic profit.

+ **Have fluctuations occurred?** Another important point is that in many small businesses (and in all the small businesses that I've owned and managed), profits fluctuate. You can't, therefore, look at just a single, perhaps terribly bad year and decide it's time to pack up. Similarly, you also shouldn't look at just a single blowout year and decide it's time to buy the villa in the south of France. EVA analysis works when the inputs reflect the general condition of the business — the general level of profits, the general amount for which you could cash out, the general cost of capital estimate, and so on. If something screwy happens one year to push one of these inputs way out of whack, the results returned by your EVA analysis become pretty undependable, in my opinion.

+ **Is your business in a special situation?** Everybody admits that EVA analysis is really tricky and may be impossible in certain situations. For example, most people who love EVA analysis readily admit that EVA analysis doesn't work very well in a start-up business situation. Most of these people also admit that EVA analysis doesn't work very well when a firm is growing very quickly. In both of these cases, the problem is that the income statement just doesn't produce an accurate measure of the value being created by the company. As a result, it's impossible to really figure out what sort of economic profit the business has created. Again, this should make intuitive sense. You may very well expect that in the first year or two, the business produces a loss or very meager profits. And that is totally okay.

Your EVA calculation is only as good as your inputs and assumptions. The trend or pattern in EVA values is probably more important than a particular value. And that's especially true for business owners. In the end, you can't lose sight of the big picture, which is answering the question, "Am I really making money by running my own business?"

Using EVA When Your Business Has Debt

In very large businesses, EVA analysis gets really computationally burdensome. Although I don't go into great detail about potential problems in this chapter, you do need to be familiar with one common complication: debt.

Here's the deal. If a business can restructure its debt, bank loans, credit lines, mortgages, and so forth, that borrowing can be used to boost EVA. Accordingly, and quite helpfully, another EVA model, which is slightly more complicated, enables you to recognize this extra wrinkle. In the next sections, I provide a couple of examples of how this slightly more sophisticated EVA model works.

The first example of the modified EVA formula

If your firm can freely restructure its debts, you may want to make two adjustments to the EVA analysis. First, you may need to use an all-encompassing cost of capital. An *all-encompassing cost of capital* considers both the cost of equity (this is what I did earlier in the first part of this chapter) and the cost of any debt. Second, you need to use an adjusted net income number that includes not only the amounts paid to the shareholders but also the amounts paid to lenders.

Calculating an all-encompassing cost of capital is the first step. For the sake of illustration, suppose that a business uses capital from three sources: trade vendors, a bank (which loans money at 10 percent), and the owner's equity. Table 2-3 shows an approach to estimating the capital charge that needs to be compared with the net income when this other debt is considered.

Table 2-3	Estimating the All-Encompassing Capital Charge
Trade vendors ($20,000 @ 0 percent)	$0
Bank loan ($100,000 @ 10 percent)	10,000
Owner's equity ($200,000 @ 20 percent)	40,000
Adjusted capital charge	$50,000

Let me walk you through the numbers in Table 2-3, although none of them are difficult to figure out:

✦ **Trade vendors:** The trade vendors provide debt — $20,000 in the balance sheet shown in Table 2-2 — but the firm doesn't have to pay a charge to those creditors. In effect, any implicit charge that the firm pays to trade vendors is already counted in the amount that you pay those vendors for the products or services that they supply. So, that portion of the capital charge is zero.

✦ **Bank loan:** This $100,000 bank loan charges 10 percent. That bank loan, then, carries a $10,000 capital charge. In other words, in order to use the bank's capital, the business pays $10,000 a year.

✦ **Owner's equity:** This final component of the capital charge is what the business owes the owners. In Table 2-3, the owner's equity capital charge is shown as $40,000. (This is the same $40,000 capital charge discussed earlier in the chapter.) This capital charge is calculated by multiplying a cost of capital percentage, 20 percent, times the owner's equity (20 percent of $200,000 equals $40,000). The adjusted capital charge, therefore, equals $50,000

Okay. So far, so good. The second step in working with this slightly more complicated EVA model is to add back the interest charges paid to lenders in order to achieve an adjusted income number. Think about this for a minute. The business made $50,000 in income (as shown in Table 2-1), but this amount has already been adjusted for $10,000 of interest expense. Therefore, if you want to compare the funds that the business generated and that are available to pay capital sources, you need to add back the $10,000 of interest expense. In other words, when you are looking at paying all the capital sources of return (whether in the form of interest or dividends), you not only have the $50,000 of net income, you also have the $10,000 of interest expense. Does that make sense?

Finally, there's a pot of money left over at the end to pay creditors and owners. And the pot of money, as shown on the income statement in Table 2-1, includes both the $10,000 of interest expense and the $50,000 of net income.

After you've figured out an all-encompassing cost of capital and an adjusted income amount, you can calculate the EVA in the usual way. In this example, you use the following formula:

```
adjusted income ($60,000) - the weighted cost of
      capital charge ($50,000)
```

The result equals $10,000, which is the EVA amount.

It's no coincidence that the simple EVA formula and the more complicated EVA formula return the same result. EVA shouldn't change because you use a more complicated formula — as long as both the simple and complicated formulas are correct. (They are.) So what's up? The more complicated formula lets you see how changes in your debt affect the EVA.

Another EVA with debt example

Here's another example of the modified EVA approach. Suppose that you, the business owner, go down to the bank and take out another $100,000 loan. Then suppose that the business pays this amount out to the business owner (you) in the form of a dividend. If this were done at the beginning of the year, you get the income statement and balance sheet shown in Table 2-4 and Table 2-5 (reflecting the additional loan).

Table 2-4	A Simple Income Statement
Sales revenue	$150,000
Less: Cost of goods sold	30,000
Gross margin	$120,000
Operating expenses	
Rent	5,000
Wages	50,000
Supplies	5,000
Total operating expenses	60,000
Operating income	60,000
Interest expense	(20,000)
Net income	$40,000

Table 2-5	A Simple Balance Sheet
Assets	
Cash	$25,000
Inventory	25,000
Current assets	$50,000
Fixed assets (net)	270,000
Total assets	$320,000
Liabilities	
Accounts payable	$20,000
Loan payable	200,000
Owner's equity	
S. Nelson, capital	100,000
Total liabilities and owner's equity	$320,000

In other words, the only difference between the business described in the first two tables and in the second two tables is that the firm has $100,000 more debt and $100,000 less owner's equity, and the extra debt produces another $10,000 a year of interest expense. That's pretty straightforward, right? All I've really talked about is using more debt and less owner's equity.

Table 2-6 estimates the capital charge for this new, more highly leveraged firm. Once again, let me walk you through the components of the capital charge. The trade vendors, who supply $20,000 of trade credit in the form of accounts payable, don't really charge anything, so there is no capital charge for their contribution to the firm's capital structure. In the new, more highly leveraged firm, the bank loan charge has gone way up. Now the firm is carrying a $200,000 loan. With 10 percent interest, the capital charge on the loan rises to $20,000 annually.

Table 2-6	Estimating the New Capital Charge
Trade vendors ($20,000 @ 0 percent)	$0
Bank loan ($200,000 @ 10 percent)	20,000
Owner's equity ($100,000 @ 20 percent)	20,000
Adjusted capital charge	$40,000

The final owner's equity capital charge also changes — it drops. With the decrease in owner's equity to just $100,000, the 20 percent capital charge decreases to $20,000 a year.

When you add up all the bits and pieces, you come up with an adjusted capital charge of $40,000. Remember that this is the capital charge for the new, more highly leveraged business.

For this new, more highly leveraged business, the EVA changes. The adjusted income for the business is $60,000 (calculated as the $40,000 of net income plus $20,000 of interest expense). You can calculate the EVA by subtracting the $40,000 capital charge from the $60,000 of adjusted income. The result equals $20,000 of EVA. The EVA doubles, obviously, by more highly leveraging the business.

This second example shows why the more complicated EVA formula can be useful. The example recognizes more explicitly how EVA results when a firm produces income in excess of the capital charges.

Two Final Pointers

I want to share two final pointers with business owners who may want to use EVA analysis to think about the economics of their businesses. (My first point is pretty basic, but I think it's probably the most important thing to take away from this chapter.)

✦ **EVA analysis is most useful to business owners and managers — or at least to small- and medium-sized firms — as a thinking tool.** In other words, even if you don't scratch out the numbers on the back of an envelope, EVA makes sense as a way to think about how you should run your business and whether it makes sense to make changes. Just knowing that you should compare your firm's net income with the amount that you could earn by selling and then reinvesting the capital elsewhere is a useful idea to keep in mind.

I have a literary agent friend who likes to say, "Listen to the universe." I think that his suggestion, especially as it relates to the economics of running a business, is pretty darn good. You should listen to the economy when you think about your business, and EVA provides a tool for you to do that. In order for a business to make sense, it needs to return a fair share to each of its stakeholders: wages to employees, interest and debt service payments to lenders, a return to shareholders who invested capital, and then, as a practical matter, a little something left over for you, the owner. Indeed, in order for a business to make sense, it needs to pay more than just its capital charge.

✦ **Although you can use EVA analysis to evaluate a business in its entirety, EVA analysis isn't limited to that application.** You can use EVA analysis, with a little bit of fiddle-faddling, to evaluate a business unit, a particular product line, your managers, and so forth.

This is really neat if you think about it. You can use EVA analysis to break down your business into different profit activities. By using EVA analysis to look at the economic profit of these different profit activities, you can probably find those activities that should be emphasized because they produce an economic profit, and you can identify those activities that should be discontinued (perhaps) because they don't produce an economic profit. You can also evaluate customers and managers in the same way.

If you want to do this more granular EVA analysis, work with a chart of accounts that supports more detailed income statements and balance sheets. In other words, if you're going to break down your business into two different business units, you need to use a chart of accounts that lets you easily see the income statement for each business unit. In a similar fashion, you need to use a chart of accounts for your balance sheet that lets you see the capital investment for both business units. Remember that any line item that you want to appear on an income statement or balance sheet needs its own account in the chart of accounts. Book II, Chapter 1 describes how to create your QuickBooks Chart of Accounts. This chapter can also address any questions that you may have about how to set up additional income statement accounts and balance sheet accounts.

And Now a Word to My Critics

I may as well admit something here: Some people, hopefully only a few, aren't going to like my simplistic approach to EVA.

The following are the points that I simplified, but you can take this information and delve deeper into EVA analysis:

+ **More work is involved in this process, per the textbook theory of EVA, than what I've described here.** In a perfect world, you should take the net income number off the QuickBooks income statement and fiddle-faddle with it so that you get a better, more accurate, more cash-flow-centric measure of income.

+ **Owner's equity isn't the world's greatest measure of the fair market value of the capital invested in a firm.** It would be great if a firm could follow the textbook approach described by the creators of EVA analysis (Stern Stewart & Co.) and work with good estimates of the market values of a firm's equity and debt. But you know what? That's a lot of work for an often-modest increase in precision, especially if you need to pay some consultant the big bucks to come up with better market values for your equity and debt.

+ **My rough-and-tumble approach to the capital charge of the owner's equity (my suggestion that you simply use a range of values from 15 to 30 percent) is sort of financial heresy.** M.B.A.s and Ph.D.s would probably be much more comfortable using something complicated, such as the capital asset pricing model. Unfortunately, that's a complicated statistical model that, quite truthfully, scares me half to death. And yes, you probably could come up with a more precise rate of return percentage — if you put in a lot more effort.

So, I'm guilty. I admit that I've made several simplifications to the EVA model. Before the judge passes sentence, however, I want to suggest two extenuating circumstances that the judge should consider:

+ **Small business EVA works differently than big business EVA.** Remember that EVA is a tool to help managers think like shareholders. However, in the case of a small business owner using QuickBooks, the manager and the shareholder are one person. The dual role implies that this person can more loosely apply the EVA model — and still get the benefits of EVA-type thinking. Some of the machinations involved in very sophisticated EVA analysis stem from the fact that management is independent of shareholders. This is simply not the case with a $1,000,000 manufacturing business or a $10,000,000 distribution business.

✦ **Precision costs money.** Employing someone who's very sophisticated in the wizardry of finance may not be worth the additional cost. Think about the typical small business owner using QuickBooks as his or her accounting tool. For example, a firm that produces $10,000 of EVA (as in the examples used in this chapter) shouldn't spend $10,000 or $20,000 on consultants to get a super-precise measure of income or the perfect cost of capital measurement. In my opinion, a firm that produces $100,000 in EVA also shouldn't have this expenditure.

I rest my case and throw myself on the mercy of the court.

Chapter 3: Capital Budgeting in a Nutshell

In This Chapter

✔ **Introducing the theory of capital budgeting**

✔ **Putting it all together**

✔ **Calculating the rate of return on capital**

✔ **Measuring liquidity**

✔ **Thinking about risk**

✔ **Relating capital budgeting to QuickBooks**

The challenge for any business is allocating *capital*, or money. Although you have limited amounts of capital, your ideas and opportunities are often unlimited.

Capital budgeting, in a nutshell, helps you to sift through all of these ideas and opportunities. Capital budgeting lets you answer questions like the following: Should I replace that key piece of machinery that we use in the factory or get a new delivery truck? Should we buy the building our offices are in? Or should we purchase that competitor's operation because it's for sale?

Introducing the Theory of Capital Budgeting

Capital budgeting boils down to the idea that you should look at capital investments (machinery, vehicles, real estate, entire businesses, yard art, and so on) like you look at the CDs (certificates of deposits) that a bank offers.

Don't worry — you actually already know how to do this. When you buy a bank CD, you essentially look at one big thing and then a couple of small things in order to decide whether a CD makes sense. The big thing is the interest rate. The two small things are the CD maturity and the risk. In the next couple of sections, I talk a bit about all three things because they apply so neatly to the problem and challenge of capital budgeting.

The big thing is the return

The big thing, as I just mentioned, is the interest rate that a CD pays. You want to earn the highest return possible on your money. Therefore, you want a CD that pays a high interest rate! An 8 percent interest rate is better than a 6 percent interest rate. And a 12 percent interest rate is way better than a 6 percent interest rate.

You can also look at the interest rates earned on capital investments. Before I go any further, though, you should know that interest rates don't typically go by that name in capital investing. For some strange reason, the interest rate that a capital investment (like a piece of machinery, vehicle, or real estate) earns is called a *return on investment*, or a *rate of return*. But it's the same thing. The rate of return or return on investment (or ROI) is really just the interest rate that a capital investment or capital expenditure pays.

The return is important because it shows the profitability of the investment, albeit as a percentage of your investment. But the first thing that you need to know about the theory of capital budgeting is that the big thing that matters is the return.

One little thing is maturity

The first little thing that you also look at in the case of a certificate of deposit is the maturity. The *maturity* simply refers to the amount of time that your money gets tied up in the investment. For example, you may not want a one-month CD. That short maturity means you have to roll over or reinvest the CD at a new, perhaps lower, rate of return in a month. On the other hand, you may also want to avoid tying up your money for a long period, such as 40 years. Tying up your money for a very long time period means that you won't be able to get to the money if a new, better opportunity comes along. You probably would see very few opportunities that are so good, so surefire, so long term that they warrant tying up your money for decades and decades, right?

In the case of capital investments, you don't actually use the word *maturity* in most situations. Instead, you should use a term called *liquidity*, which simply means how close an investment is to cash or how quickly an investment returns or pays back the cash that you've invested.

You can measure liquidity in a bunch of different ways. A little later in the chapter, I talk about one simple approach to measuring liquidity — the payback period. The key thing to remember about liquidity is this: Liquidity isn't as important as the return on investment. Remember, the return shows profitability. Nevertheless, you do want to think about the liquidity of a capital investment. What you think depends on your circumstances. In different circumstances, you will prefer capital investments with different degrees of liquidity.

Another little thing is risk

With CDs, government insurance programs such as Federal Deposit Insurance Corporation (FDIC) reduce the risk of investing. But the risks still matter, right? If you are over the limits of insurance coverage, you don't put all your money in the same bank. Even if you are under the FDIC insurance limits, you don't put money into a bank that is at risk of going under. Do that and you'll have the hassle of getting your money back.

You also typically carefully select CD-like investments, such as debentures, which some finance companies offer to CD investors. Again, that makes sense. *Risk* — the chance that maybe you won't be repaid, or maybe not all of your interest will be repaid — is one of the things that you want to consider when you talk about CDs.

In the same way that risk matters to CDs, risk matters to capital investments. In fact, risk probably matters more in the latter case. No government agency guarantees that some capital investment will deliver the returns that you plan on. For this reason, you must consider the risk of capital investments. You can consider risk both *quantitatively* (which means using measurements that produce values that measure the risk) and *qualitatively* (which means relying on your gut).

Putting It All Together

The bottom line is this: You actually already know the theory of capital budgeting — that it works like picking a CD down at the local bank. You want to look at the profitability of the investment by somehow measuring the return on the investment, or the interest rate. However, profitability isn't the only consideration. If you look at a capital expenditure, you also need to consider the liquidity of the investment. Likewise, you also need to consider the risk of the investment.

Stated a slightly different way, when you make capital investments, you want to invest in things that pay the highest return. But you also want to recognize the importance of liquidity, not to mention the risk. You get the theory, now, right?

The difference with capital budgeting, then, is that you (rather than the bank issuing the CD) need to calculate the return, quantify or measure the liquidity, and think carefully about the risks. That's really it. You just do those three additional things, which — surprise, surprise — I discuss in the next sections of this chapter.

Calculating the Rate of Return on Capital

I need to tell you right up front that calculating the rate of return on a capital investment is a little bit tricky. In almost every case, you either need a financial calculator (a good one) or a spreadsheet program, such as Microsoft Excel. For the purpose of this discussion, I assume that you have (or have access to) Microsoft Excel. If you don't have Excel, you should still be able to read through almost all the following discussion and then translate what I talk about into the instructions that you need in order to use a financial calculator or some other spreadsheet program. Note that the spreadsheet mechanics that I describe aren't very difficult.

If you aren't all that comfortable with the notion of using Microsoft Excel — even though it's already installed on your computer — you may want to think about picking up a copy of *Excel For Dummies* by Greg Harvey (Wiley Publishing, Inc.). Just make sure you pick up the version of *Excel For Dummies* that talks about your specific version of Excel. For example, if you're running Excel 2003, make sure you get *Excel 2003 For Dummies*.

Calculating a rate of return on a capital expenditure requires three steps:

1. **Calculate the investment amount.**

2. **Estimate the net cash flows paid by the investment.**

3. **Use either a financial calculator, such as one of those fancy Hewlett-Packard calculators, or a spreadsheet program, such as Microsoft Excel, to calculate the rate of return measure.**

In the next sections, I explain each of these steps.

If you can, use a spreadsheet program rather than going the fancy-calculator route — such calculators can be less than user-friendly. Twenty years ago, when I was graduating with an M.B.A. in Finance from the University of Washington, the joke among many young M.B.A.s was that the ability to calculate the rate of return measures on a Hewlett-Packard 12C calculator was worth $40,000 a year. The slogan, in fact, was "40G for a 12C."

Calculate the investment amount

The first step in calculating a return is estimating the amount that you need to invest. This is the amount that's similar to the check you write to a bank in order to buy a CD.

For example, suppose that you are considering the purchase of a new office building. Just to keep everything really simple, suppose also that you can buy a building that would house your offices for $350,000. Further suppose that you can finance $300,000 of this purchase with a mortgage from your friendly local bank. However, you will also need to pay closing costs that equal $15,000.

Table 3-1 shows the initial investment that you must make in order to invest in a new office building. The bottom line amount is $65,000. The table shows how this amount gets calculated. The formula is pretty simple: The building costs $350,000, and you need to pay $15,000 in closing costs. That totals $365,000. The bank, however, will finance $300,000 of this amount. This means that you need to come up with $65,000 out of your own pocket.

Make sure that you understand why the initial investment, or the first check that you need to write, is $65,000. This is the investment that you make in the building.

Table 3-1	Calculating the Investment
Price of building	$350,000
Less: Mortgage	300,000
Down payment	50,000
Add: Closing costs	15,000
Total initial investment	$65,000

Estimate the net cash flows

The process of estimating the net cash flows from the investment requires a bit more work than the previous exercise did. You need to sit down and think carefully about any additional revenues and any additional costs that the investment produces. Obviously, you hope that the net effect of the investment will save you cash. However, certain amounts of the invest-ment will cost you. On the other hand, you will also receive savings that the investment returns.

You want to construct a little schedule — this can be written on the back of a cocktail napkin or typed into a spreadsheet program like Excel — and use the schedule to carefully estimate and calculate cash flows.

Suppose, in the case of the office building, that the following two items determine the net cash flows.

✦ **The new mortgage requires an annual $21,000 interest payment.** To keep things simple (don't worry about principal amortization just yet), suppose that this is an interest-only mortgage. Further suppose that you need to pay the entire mortgage balance in 20 years as part of a balloon payment. In the meantime, however, you'll pay $21,000 at the end of every year.

✦ **Because you own your own building, you save $20,000 in rent the first year.** This amount, however, will increase every year. If the rent that you've been paying has increased every year by 3 percent because of inflation, you may want to assume that your rent savings, in order to be accurately forecasted, need to be inflated by 3 percent every year as well. For example, you may want to assume that in the second year, your rent savings equal 103 percent of $20,000. In the third year, your rent savings equal 103 percent of $20,600 (which is the second year's rent savings).

Does this business of rent savings make sense? With capital expenditure investment, the capital investment often saves you money in some way. Therefore, you need to estimate those savings over the years that you will use the capital investment. In this case, the rent savings should be equal to the current rent savings plus inflation for each year. Another way to look at the rent savings amount is to say that the rent savings equals the rent that you won't have to pay if you own the building.

Table 3-2 summarizes the cash flows that you enjoy by investing in this building. The table has a column for each year number (the schedule shows 20 years of rent savings and mortgage payments). The schedule also includes three columns, which report on the rent savings, the annual mortgage interest payment, and the net cash flow amount. The net cash flow amount equals the rent savings minus the mortgage interest payment. Notice that in the first two years, the mortgage interest payment exceeds the rent savings. However, in year 3 and beyond, the rent savings exceeds the mortgage payment.

Table 3-2	Summary of Building Cash Flows		
Year	*Rent Savings*	*Mortgage Payment*	*Net Cash Flows*
1	20,000	21,000	-1,000
2	20,600	21,000	-400
3	21,218	21,000	218
4	21,855	21,000	855
5	22,511	21,000	1,511
6	23,186	21,000	2,186
7	23,882	21,000	2,882
8	24,598	21,000	3,598
9	25,336	21,000	4,336
10	26,096	21,000	5,096
11	26,879	21,000	5,879
12	27,685	21,000	6,685

Year	Rent Savings	Mortgage Payment	Net Cash Flows
13	28,516	21,000	7,516
14	29,371	21,000	8,371
15	30,252	21,000	9,252
16	31,160	21,000	10,160
17	32,095	21,000	11,095
18	33,058	21,000	12,058
19	34,050	21,000	13,050
20	35,072	21,000	14,072

Just to make sure you understand the information shown in Table 3-2, take a peek at the information estimated for year 17. What does it mean? For year 17, the schedule shows that the rent savings equal $32,095. In other words, this schedule estimates that in year 17 of building ownership, you save $32,095 by owning the building. This is the amount that you are guessing you would have had to pay in rent to a landlord had you not purchased the building. You will also have to pay $21,000 in interest on that $300,000 mortgage in year 17. The net savings that you accrue, which is the net cash flow in year 17, equals $11,095. This is simply the net amount left over from the rent savings after paying the mortgage interest.

I need to add one other important wrinkle to the information shown in Table 3-2. When you look at the cash flows that stem from a capital investment, you need to make some assumption about what happens at the end of the investment's life. In the case of the building investment, for example, you probably need to show that the mortgage is paid off. You also may want to show the sale of the building at some point.

To show you how this works, suppose that at the end of year 20, you pay off the mortgage (which will still be $300,000 because you have only been paying interest) and suppose that you will sell the building for $630,000 — this amount is an estimate. To come up with this estimate, I took the original $350,000 purchase price and then annually inflated that amount by 3 percent over 20 years. Doing so produces an estimated sale price in year 20 of $630,000. You'll also pay selling costs that total $30,000.

Table 3-3 shows how these numbers produce a final, liquidation cash flow. The gross sales price equals $630,000, as mentioned earlier. Then you have to pay the $300,000 mortgage. Then you also have $30,000 of selling costs. If you subtract the mortgage and the selling costs from the gross sales price, the final cash flow, then, equals $300,000. This makes sense, right? The gross sales price of $630,000 minus $300,000 for the mortgage payment minus $30,000 for selling costs equals $300,000.

Table 3-3	Estimating the Liquidation Cash Flow
Gross sale price	$630,000
Less: Mortgage	300,000
Less: Selling costs	30,000
Final cash flow from sale	$300,000

The final step is to combine the information shown in Tables 3-2 and 3-3. Table 3-4 does this. The net cash flows column summarizes the net cash flows from Table 3-2. The liquidation cash flow column shows 0 during the first 19 years. Then in year 20, however, the liquidation cash flow shows as $300,000. The real deal combines the net cash flows and the liquidation cash flow.

Table 3-4	Combining All Cash Flows		
Year	Net Cash Flows	Liquidation Cash Flow	The Real Deal
1	−1,000	0	−1,000
2	−400	0	−400
3	218	0	218
4	855	0	855
5	1,511	0	1,511
6	2,186	0	2,186
7	2,882	0	2,882
8	3,598	0	3,598
9	4,336	0	4,336
10	5,096	0	5,096
11	5,879	0	5,879
12	6,685	0	6,685
13	7,516	0	7,516
14	8,371	0	8,371
15	9,252	0	9,252
16	10,160	0	10,160
17	11,095	0	11,095
18	12,058	0	12,058
19	13,050	0	13,050
20	14,072	300,000	314,072

Just to make sure that you understand the real deal column's numbers, I will go into detail about a couple of them. Start by looking at year 5. For year 5, the table shows a net cash flow of $1,511, no liquidation cash flow, and an actual cash flow to you, the business owner, of $1,511. If this building weren't a building but was really a CD, this is the amount of interest that the CD would pay you for year 5.

In year 20, things look a bit different. The net cash flow equals $14,072 when you combine both the rent savings and the mortgage interest. The sale of the building at the end of the year also produces a $300,000 cash flow. This is actually the amount that you would receive from the escrow company after the sale of the building closed. The net or final cash flow that you receive, then, combines these two amounts: the $14,072 of net cash flow and the $300,000 of liquidation cash flow. This cash flow is like the accrued interest being paid back by the bank on a CD.

And now the hard part is done. You essentially turned your building investment into just another set of cash flows. These cash flows look to a financial calculator or spreadsheet program like just another investment. In fact, these cash flows could describe some crazy 20-year CD investment. In this case, of course, they describe an imaginary building investment. But they could be the cash flows from any investment — a new piece of machinery, a corporate jet, or a new delivery truck.

Calculating the return

As I mention previously in this chapter, I'm going to show you the two basic ways that you can calculate a return by using Microsoft Excel. (I use Excel because it's so ubiquitous.) You can, however, use another spreadsheet program, such as Lotus 1-2-3, or any high-powered financial business calculator. Basically, if you understand the logic of the stuff described here, you should be able to translate what I say into Lotus-1-2-3-speak, or Hewlett-Packard-Business-Calculator-speak.

In order to calculate a rate of return with Microsoft Excel, you first enter the cash flows produced by the investment. In Figure 3-1, I've created a simple Excel worksheet that does just this. Even if you've never used Excel before, you may be able to construct this — all you have to do is start Excel (the same way you start any other Windows program). Then you need to enter the cash flows shown for the building investment. Actually, you only need to enter the values shown in cells B2, B3, B4, B5, and so on, through cell B22. These values are the cash flow numbers calculated and summarized in Table 3-4. (Flip back and look at Table 3-4 if you don't see this clearly.)

Microsoft Excel - Book1

File   Edit   View   Insert   Format   Tools   Data   Window   Help   Type a question for help

Arial   ▾ 10 ▾

Reply with Changes... End Review...

G4   ▾   *fx* =+IRR(B2:B22,0.1)

	A	B	C	D	E	F	G	H	I	J	K
1	Year	Net Cash Flows									
2	0	-65000									
3	1	-1000									
4	2	-400		Internal Rate of Return			11%				
5	3	218									
6	4	855		Net Present Value			$9,821.71				
7	5	1511									
8	6	2186									
9	7	2882									
10	8	3598									
11	9	4336									
12	10	5096									
13	11	5879									
14	12	6685									
15	13	7516									
16	14	8371									
17	15	9252									
18	16	10160									
19	17	11095									
20	18	12058									
21	19	13050									
22	20	314072									
23											
24											
25											

Sheet1 / Sheet2 / Sheet3 /

Ready   NUM

Figure 3-1:
A simple
Excel
worksheet
that shows
investment
cash flows.

By the way, in case you are new to Excel, all you need to do to enter one of these values is click the box (technically called a *cell*) and then type the value. For example, to enter the initial investment required to buy the building — $65,000 — you click the B2 cell and then type **-65000**. After you type this number, press Enter. You enter each of the other net cash flow values in the same manner in order to make the rate of return calculations.

I also put in values to label the years and then a little bit of text in A1 and B1 to identify what the labels are. However, you don't have to enter those extraneous bits of information.

After you provide the cash flow values of the investment, you tell Excel the rate of return that you want calculated. In Figure 3-1, I actually calculate two rates of return. In Cell G4, for example, I calculate an internal rate of return. An *internal rate of return* is truly the interest rate that the investment delivers. For example, a CD that pays an 11 percent interest rate pays an 11 percent internal rate of return. To calculate an internal rate of return, you enter an internal rate of return function formula into a worksheet cell. In the case of the worksheet shown in Figure 3-1, for example, you click cell G4 and then type the following:

```
=IRR(B2:B22)
```

If you've never seen an Excel function before, this probably looks like Greek. But all this function does is tell Excel to calculate the internal rate of return for the cash flows stored in the *range*, or block of cells, that go from cell B2 to cell B22. The office building cash flows, it turns out, produce an internal rate of return equal to 11 percent. This means that, essentially, the office building delivers an 11 percent interest rate annually on the amounts invested in the office building.

Another common rate of return measure is something called a *net present value*, which essentially specifies by what dollar amount the rate of return on a business exceeds a benchmark rate of return. For example, the worksheet shown in Figure 3-1 shows the net present value equal to $9,821.71. In other words, this investment exceeds a benchmark rate of return by $9,821.71. You can't see it — it's buried in the formula — but the benchmark rate of return equals 10 percent. So, this rate of return essentially is $9,821.71 better than a 10 percent rate of return.

To calculate the net present value by using Excel, you use another function. In the case of the worksheet shown in Figure 3-1, for example, you click cell G6 and type the following formula:

```
=NPV(0.1,B3:B22)+B2
```

This formula looks at the cash flows for years 1 through 20, discounts these cash flows by using a 10 percent rate of return, and then compares these discounted cash flows with the initial investment amount, which is the value stored in cell B2.

This all may sound a bit tricky, but essentially, this is what's going on: The net present value formula looks at the cash flows stored in the worksheet and calculates the present value amount by which these cash flows exceed a 10 percent rate of return.

The discount rate equals the rate of return that you expect on your capital investments. I should also note that the discount rate is the rate at which you can reinvest any money you get from the capital investment's cash flows.

One final comment about the information shown in Figure 3-1 (this is actually also true of the information from Table 3-4): In this figure, I've described how to calculate pre-tax cash flows and, therefore, how to calculate a pre-tax rate of return measure. In some situations, however, you may want to calculate an after-tax set of cash flows and an after-tax rate of return. If taxes are a significant factor and if you are considering alternative capital investments that deliver different tax benefits, you can get more precise and sometimes different results by looking at after-tax cash flows and after-tax rates of return. If you do want to look at after-tax cash flows and profitability measures, you probably need the help of your tax advisor.

An important thing to know about pre-tax cash flows and returns versus after-tax cash flows and returns: Make sure that you're using apples-to-apples comparisons. It's often fine to work with pre-tax cash flows; just make sure that you're comparing pre-tax cash flows with other pre-tax cash flows. You don't want to compare pre-tax returns with after-tax returns. That's an apples-to-oranges comparison. Predictably, it doesn't work.

Some problems with the IRR measurement

I kind of like the internal rate of return (IRR) measurement because it makes a lot of intuitive sense. Capital budgeting is burdensome enough without being weighed down further by some tricky, abstract, theoretical capital budgeting tool such as the net present value.

You should know, however, that the internal rate of return has some practical weaknesses, which is why people with M.B.A.s and Ph.D.s in business and finance greatly prefer the net present value measure. In this sidebar, I identify these weaknesses for you. Knowing about the weaknesses enables you to more safely use the IRR tool. On the other hand, knowing about the weaknesses may also make you choose to just bear with the abstractness of the net present value model and use it instead. Anyway, here are the weaknesses:

✔ The IRR measure doesn't always identify the best investment. In other words, you sometimes can't pick the investment with the highest IRR and get the most profitable investment. As an extreme example of this, suppose that you have $100,000 to invest. Would you rather invest only $10,000 of your money in something earning 20 percent annually or look at something earning 18 percent annually but in which you can invest the entire $100,000? Do you see the difference? Twenty percent of $10,000 isn't going to be as good as 18 percent of $100,000. Unfortunately, the IRR measure — by focusing on the percentage return — sometimes causes people to lose sight of the dollars of profit, which is obviously what you really want to maximize. In comparison, the net present value *does* calculate a straight dollar profit amount. By picking an investment with the highest net present value, you're picking the investment that delivers the most dollars and profits.

✔ The IRR measure doesn't recognize reinvestment risk very well. This sounds like another mumble-jumble problem, but it's actually a pretty important one. For example, suppose that you have a million dollars to invest. Would you rather pick a 1-year investment (Option A) that earns 30 percent or a 20-year investment (Option B) that earns 20 percent? At first blush, a 30 percent investment seems like a pretty good one. Obviously, 30 percent is a lot more than 20 percent. However, here's what you have to consider: Into what are you going to invest the money from Option A one year from now when that investment liquidates? The key is that you have to be able to invest the 1.3 million dollars (this is what you get from Option A one year from now) in something that beats the Option B investment. In other words, you have to think about that reinvestment risk for your investments. The IRR doesn't really do this. In comparison, the net present value *does*. Implicitly, the net present value assumes that you can reinvest money at the discount rate used in the calculation. In essence, the discount rate is the going rate that you can earn on your other capital investments, so it automatically factors in reinvestment.

✔ The IRR measure doesn't always produce a solution (or, that is, a unique solution). The IRR formula isn't solvable, for example, when the cash flows don't really look like investment cash flows. If you have an investment that only generates cash because there is no initial cash outlay, you can't calculate an internal rate of return. But such an investment, obviously, is a very good deal and should be selected. Another related problem is that sometimes the IRR formula can't be uniquely solved. This business about no unique solution stems from a little bit of mathematical weirdness. (The problem is that technically, an IRR formula is an nth root polynomial equation with up to nth possible solutions!) This multiple solutions weirdness pops up when you have the cash flow signs changing over the years that the investment is held. In the case of the office building investment, only one sign change exists. In year 2, the cash flow is negative. And in year 3, the cash flow becomes positive and stays positive. This means that the building has only one single internal rate of return. If in some years, the cash flow were positive and in some years, the cash flow were negative, however, each of these flips from negative to positive cash value or vice versa indicates another solution to the IRR formula. I won't go into any more detail, but the important point is with the net present value formula, you always know that a solution exists and that a single unique solution exists, given a particular discount rate.

Measuring Liquidity

In large businesses, people don't worry or talk as much about liquidity — at least when it comes to capital investments. Liquidity as a criterion for looking at capital investments is downplayed. The logic behind this is that in most cases, very large firms have almost unlimited access to capital through the capital markets (either the stock markets or the debt markets or even just big-time borrowing from enormous banks). For many smaller businesses, however, liquidity is important. You have only a limited number of investments that you can make. Additionally, you have a limited amount of capital — less than you like, almost always. New opportunities and ways to invest your money continually arrive. For these reasons, you typically want to look at the liquidity of your capital investments.

One easy way to measure liquidity is with a *payback period*, which measures what it takes for an investment to pay back its original investment. The office building example doesn't work very well for this sort of calculation, so to make things a little easier, suppose that you are considering a $10,000 investment that produces $2,000 a year in net cash flows. In this case, you can calculate the payback period with the following formula:

```
Payback period = initial investment/annual cash flow
```

In the case of the $10,000 investment described here, the actual formula is

```
$10,000/$2,000 = 5
```

This means that the $10,000 investment, through its $2,000 per year cash flows, takes five years to pay back.

Again, you don't want to focus on liquidity. Liquidity is almost never as important as profitability. And even though profitability is paramount, liquidity is often something that you want to consider. At times, you are going to want investments that pay back more quickly rather than those that pay back less quickly. When the investments do pay off, you'll have other good reinvestment opportunities.

Thinking about Risk

Obviously, risk matters. Risk is an issue even with simple investments like those made in bank CDs. But with capital investments, no government agency is looking out for your interest and picking up the pieces if things do a Humpty Dumpty and come crashing down.

So think for a minute about risk management and assessment in the case of capital expenditures. Here are three important comments that I can share:

✦ **Be very careful and thoughtful in coming up with cash flows.** The better job that you do thinking about and estimating the cash flows from a capital expenditure, the more reliable and useful your results are. Good cash flow estimates produce good rate of return measurements. Look back to the examples shown in Tables 3-1, 3-2, 3-3, and 3-4.

✦ **Experiment.** You absolutely need to experiment with your assumptions. Make changes and see how those changes impact both the cash flow and rate of return measurements. Looking back at the cash flow information shown in Tables 3-3 and 3-4, for example, you can see that the single biggest cash flow in the building investment is the resale amount in year 20. It would be very interesting to see what effect a lower inflation, or appreciation, rate has on the ultimate rate of return. A 2 percent inflation rate would dramatically change the cash flows and the rate of return measurement for this investment. Similarly, an inflation rate of 5 percent or 6 percent over those 20 years would also dramatically change things. In the former case, things get ugly, quickly. In the latter case, well, we all remember how good a leveraged real estate investment can be when given high, continued inflation rates, right?

✦ **Think about the discount rate that you use.** I didn't spend a lot of time talking about the discount rate, but it should implicitly take into consideration the risk that an investment makes you face. My finance professor always said, "Your discount rate should equal the rate of return that similarly risky investments produce." There is tremendous wisdom in this simple guideline. (Thanks, Professor Schall!) In other words, if you're looking at a very risky investment, that investment should be compared with the hopefully higher rates of return that other similarly risky investments deliver. You would never pick an investment that, given its risk level, delivered an inferior rate of return. At the same time, if you're looking at lower risk investments, you want to use a lower discount rate. A relatively low risk investment in something like an office building, for example, shouldn't be evaluated with a discount rate that's maybe appropriate to some super-risky investment in some new bit of leading-edge technology. Another related point is that maybe you want to try some different discount rates. By experimenting not only with your cash flow numbers but also with your discount rates, you can see how the quality of an investment changes when you use different discount rates (and implicitly make different assumptions about the investment's risk).

What Does All This Have to Do with QuickBooks?

So here's a question: What does all this capital budgeting stuff have to do with QuickBooks?

Well, quite honestly, capital budgeting doesn't really directly relate to using QuickBooks. In some ways, capital budgeting is about a financial management task that is critically important and that you need to think about . . . but a task that QuickBooks doesn't directly support.

That said, do note that much of the data that you've collected with QuickBooks is often extremely useful in getting good estimates of the savings and costs associated with some capital expenditure.

In looking at the example of investing in an office building, for example, knowing what you have been paying in rent and what you may be able to save by buying your own building is exactly the sort of information that you need — and exactly the sort of information that the rich financial database of QuickBooks supplies. In truth, your estimates of cash flows will typically be much more involved than what I've shown in this chapter. If you did have a building investment under consideration, you would need to consider all sorts of expenses related to repairing and maintaining the building. If you've been leasing space in someone else's building, you'd have to consider all sorts of expenses associated with that, including special insurance that the landlord makes you buy, special amounts that you spend because the space doesn't quite meet your requirements, and so on. QuickBooks helps you with this type of information.

Book VI

Business Plans

"Oh, we're doing just great. Philip and I are selling decorative jelly jars on the Web. I run the Web site and Philip sort of controls the inventory."

Contents at a Glance

Chapter 1: Profit-Volume-Cost Analysis

In This Chapter

- Understanding how profit-volume-cost analysis works
- Calculating breakeven points
- Using real QuickBooks data for profit-volume-cost analysis
- Dealing with some minor conundrums
- Using the Profit-Volume-Cost Analysis workbook
- Dealing with vary-with-profit costs

Profit-volume-cost analysis is a powerful tool that estimates how a business's profits change as the sales volumes change as well as breakeven points. (A *breakeven point* is the sales revenue level that produces zero profits.)

Profit-volume-cost analysis often produces surprising results. Typically, the analysis shows that small changes in a business's sales volume produce big changes in profits.

Hotels and airlines are types of businesses that often see surprising fluctuations in their profits based on relatively modest changes in their sales revenue. Indeed, now that you know this, you'll probably notice that investment analysts often use small changes in hotel occupancy and in airline load factors (the percentage of seats filled on a plane) to explain big changes in profits.

The first part of this chapter talks about the theory of profit-volume-cost analysis. Understanding this theory may be all you need in order to apply the tool to your specific setting. At the end of the chapter, I describe an Excel workbook that you can use for more sophisticated profit-volume-cost analysis. That workbook is available to download from my Web site at www.stephenlnelson.com/pvc,xls. (You can also visit my Web site; click on the Business Consulting link and then click on the pvc,xls link.)

How Profit-Volume-Cost Analysis Works

Profit-volume-cost analysis uses three pieces of information to show how your profits change as sales revenues change: estimates of your sales revenue, your gross margin percentage, and your fixed costs. Usually, all three items of data are easy to come by.

For example, suppose that you are a builder of high-end racing sailboats that sell for $100,000 each. Further suppose that each boat costs you $40,000 in labor and material and that your shop costs $160,000 a year to keep open.

You can calculate your gross margin percentage by using the following formula:

```
(boat sales price - direct labor and material costs) ÷
    (boat sales cost)
```

Or you can use the actual numbers from my example:

```
($100,000 - $40,000) ÷ ($100,000)
```

This formula returns the result 0.6, or 60 percent. In this case, your fixed cost amount equals $160,000.

With the fixed cost and gross margin percentage information, you can calculate the profits that different sales revenues produce. To make this calculation, you use the following formula:

```
profits = (sales x gross margin percentage) - fixed cost
```

Table 1-1 shows some examples of how you can use this formula to estimate the profits at different sales volume levels. At $200,000 in annual sales, for example, the business suffers a $40,000 loss. At $300,000 in sales, the business earns a $20,000 profit. At $400,000 in sales, the business earns an $80,000 profit. Table 1-1 also shows the formula used to estimate profits.

Table 1-1	Applying the Profit-Volume-Cost Formula	
Sales	*Formula*	*Result*
$200,000	($200,000 x 0.60) – $160,000	$40,000; a loss
$300,000	($300,000 x 0.60) – $160,000	$20,000; a little profit
$400,000	($400,000 x 0.60) – $160,000	$80,000; a nice profit

The really interesting thing about the information shown in Table 1-1 — and I don't want to beat a dead horse here — is that profits often change more significantly than revenues change. Look at Table 1-1 and examine what happens when revenues increase from $300,000 to $400,000 — roughly a 33 percent increase. You see that profits quadruple from $20,000 to $80,000.

Here's another way to look at the estimated profits at the $300,000 and $400,000 sales levels: If sales drop by 25 percent from $400,000 to $300,000, profits decrease by 75 percent from $80,000 to $20,000.

The information shown in Table 1-1 is commonly the case with businesses. Relatively modest changes in sales revenue produce large — sometimes stunningly large — changes in profits. The reason that you perform profit-volume-cost analysis, therefore, is to understand how sensitive your business profits are to changes in sales volume. With this information, you can understand how important it is to prevent decreases in sales and you can reap the rewards of increasing sales.

I need to make one final point about the information shown in Table 1-1: You can calculate this same information almost in a longhand fashion by using miniature income statements. Table 1-2, for example, shows some miniature income statements that calculate profits at various sales levels.

Table 1-2	Miniature Income Statements		
Boats sold	2	3	4
Sales revenue	$200,000	$300,000	$400,000
Variable costs	($80,000)	($120,000)	($160,000)
Gross margin	120,000	180,000	240,000
Fixed costs	(160,000)	(160,000)	(160,000)
Profits	$40,000	$20,000	$80,000

It's no coincidence that the miniature income statements shown in Table 1-2 produce the same estimates of profit as the formulas shown in Table 1-1. The difference — and the advantage of the information approach illustrated in Table 1-1 — is that the formula makes it possible to quickly calculate estimates of profits at any sales level. Constructing even a miniature income statement like the one shown in Table 1-2 is typically more work than the approach shown in Table 1-1.

Calculating Breakeven Points

Here's another important piece of information that belongs between your ears: A common application of the formula used in Table 1-1 is to calculate a breakeven point. A *breakeven point*, as noted previously, shows the sales revenue volume that produces zero profit and zero loss.

Remember the formula for performing profit-volume-cost analysis? It goes like this:

```
profits = (sales revenue x gross margin percentage) -
    fixed costs
```

Rather than calculate profits based on the other three variables (sales revenue, gross margin percentage, and fixed costs), you can calculate a sales revenue amount based on the other three variables (profits, gross margin percentage, and fixed costs).

The formula for making such a breakeven calculation, based on algebraic manipulation of the profit-volume-cost analysis formula, looks like this:

```
breakeven point (in sales revenue) = fixed costs ÷
    gross margin percentage
```

To calculate the breakeven point in sales revenue for the example boat-building business, you make the following calculation:

```
$160,000 ÷ 40 percent
```

which produces the result:

```
$266,667
```

Accordingly, the boat-building business needs $266,667 of revenue to break even.

The breakeven point formula described in the preceding paragraphs estimates a breakeven point in revenue. However, such a revenue-based breakeven point often doesn't make complete sense. For example, in the case of the boat-building business in which you sell boats for $100,000 each, there's no practical way to get $266,667 of revenue. You can't sell two-thirds of a boat. The correct way to interpret a breakeven point in revenue in this example, then, is to interpret it as a *rough* breakeven point. As a practical matter in the boat-building business, the breakeven point is slightly less than three boats per year.

Confused about the breakeven point formula?

The formula for calculating the breakeven point seems pretty different from the formula for calculating profit-volume-cost information — or at least it does at first blush. However, the second formula is derived from the first. Because some compulsive readers may want to know how this variation works, I show it to you in this section.

Here's the fixed base formula:

```
profits = (sales revenue x
    gross margin percentage) -
    fixed costs
```

If I subtract the fixed costs from both sides of the formula, I get the following:

```
profits - fixed costs = sales
    revenue x gross margin
    percentage
```

Because profits equal zero at the breakeven point, I can simplify this formula further by just scratching out the profits variable, as shown here:

```
-fixed costs = sales revenue x
    gross margin percentage
```

If I divide both sides of the equation by the gross margin percentage, I get the basic breakeven point formula, as shown here:

```
-fixed costs x gross margin
    percentage = sales revenue
```

And that's the way the formula gets created. Essentially, all you have to do is divide the fixed costs amount by the gross margin percentage. The result shows the sales revenue at which a firm breaks even.

If, in this example, you were working with boats that cost $1,000 each or $100 each, the precision of the breakeven point would be much closer. For example, if you manufactured day sailor boats that were $1,000 apiece, you would know that the breakeven point is somewhere between 266 and 267 boats (calculated by dividing the $266,667 of revenue by $1,000). If the boats cost $100 each — perhaps they are model boats — you know that the breakeven point is between 2,666 model boats and 2,667 model boats (calculated by dividing the revenue amount by $100).

In either case, you see that the smaller the revenue per unit, the more precision you get in the breakeven point in units.

You can also see from this example that the process of converting a breakeven point in revenue to a breakeven point in units is simply a matter of dividing the breakeven point in revenue by the unit price.

Using Real QuickBooks Data for Profit-Volume-Cost Analysis

As noted previously, you need three items of data in order to perform profit-volume-cost analysis: sales revenue, gross margin percentage, and fixed cost. Typically, these items of data aren't difficult to find if you have been using QuickBooks. Nevertheless, this data doesn't map perfectly to line items that appear on a QuickBooks income statement. For this reason, I briefly discuss how you come up with these pieces of information.

Sales revenue

The sales revenue levels that you use in the formula are the sales revenue levels that you want to experiment with. They probably represent possible or maybe even likely sales revenue levels that you may experience. Accordingly, the sales revenue levels don't really come from QuickBooks. Of course, you may want to look at past income statements in order to determine reasonable or likely sales revenue levels. However, the formula inputs will probably just be rough estimates; they don't actually come from a QuickBooks income statement.

Gross margin percentage

The gross margin percentage, as illustrated previously, is calculated by subtracting your variable costs from your sales revenue and then by dividing that result (which is the gross margin) by the sales revenue. The variable costs include the costs of the items that you sell: inventory, commissions, shipping, and similar costs.

Because calculating the gross margin percentage can be a little bit confusing the first few times, here are a couple of examples to review:

✦ If you sell $100,000 boats, but the material, labor, and commissions expenses for those boats total $40,000, you can calculate the gross margin percentage by using the formula: ($100,000 – $40,000) ÷ $100,000. That formula returns 0.6, or 60 percent, which is the gross margin percentage of the boat-building business.

✦ For another example, assume that you are running a personal service business in which you prepare tax returns for a living. Further assume that you charge $200 for a small business tax return and that the only variable cost is a $40 fee that you have to pay to the tax software company for the return. In this case, you calculate the gross margin percentage by using the formula ($200 – $40) ÷ $200. This formula returns the value 0.8, or 80 percent. In this case, 80 percent is the gross margin percentage for your tax return preparation business.

The key point is that variable costs vary with the sales revenue. If a sale occurs, the sale produces variable costs. If no sale occurs, no variable costs are incurred.

So what does all this mean? Well, typically, the variable costs equal the cost of goods sold number that's shown on your QuickBooks income statement. This cost of goods sold number probably includes the inventory items that you sell (if you are in a business in which you resell inventory) and other items, such as freight and sales commissions. You can, therefore, get most or all the variable cost information right off the QuickBooks income statement.

You may need to fiddle with the cost of goods sold amount reported on the QuickBooks income statement. Remember that variable costs are those costs that vary with sales, and, as a result, some of the costs that you've included in the cost of goods sold section of your income statement may not be variable. Some of the costs reported in the regular operating expenses portion of your income statement are actually variable.

Book VI Chapter 1

Profit-Volume-Cost Analysis

Therefore, you may want to think about the costs reported in the cost of goods sold section and in the operating expenses section of your income statement. If you realize that the cost of goods sold value isn't a good estimate of variable costs, make some adjustments. A fixed cost that's included in the cost of goods sold number should be subtracted, obviously. And a variable cost that is included with the other operating expenses may need to be added to the cost of goods sold.

Fixed costs

Fixed costs include all your other non-variable costs. In a nutshell, fixed costs are fixed because they don't change with sales volume. Fixed costs include items such as rent paid on an office or factory, salaries paid to permanent employees, overhead for insurance, and so forth.

To see how fixed costs work and get calculated, return to the examples of the boat-building business and the tax return preparation service:

✦ In the boat-building business, the firm carries an overhead of over $160,000. This amount may include $80,000 for the shop in which you build your boats and $80,000 for the salaries that you pay to two craftsmen whom you continue to employ whether or not you have boats to build. In this case, then, these overhead costs constitute your $160,000 of fixed costs. These fixed costs don't change based on changes in sales volume.

✦ In the tax return service, your only fixed expenses are $100 a month for Yellow Pages advertisements and $700 a month to rent a small office. In this case, then, your fixed costs equal $800 a month. Again, these fixed costs don't change based on changes in sales volume.

The Downside of the Profit-Volume-Cost Model

Okay, this stuff all sounds fine and good, but what happens when little reservations start to pop up? Annoying little problems? Minor weaknesses that turn into irritations?

Here's the problem: Like any abstract explanation of reality, the profit-volume-cost model isn't perfect. If you want to get nit-picky — and you should for a moment — several practical problems creep into the calculations of the profit-volume-cost formula and its application to your real-life business affairs. I discuss these problems in the following list, but I don't think that having such problems means that you shouldn't use the model. They only change the way that you should work with the model.

✦ **Any assumptions that you make about variable costs and fixed costs typically apply only over a range of sales revenues.** In the boat-building business, for example, the numbers used in the preceding sections don't apply if the boat builder scales up and builds 500 boats a year. That's obvious, right? It may be that the range of sales revenues valid for a 60 percent gross margin percentage — and therefore, $160,000 of fixed costs — are really somewhere between zero boats per year and eight boats per year. Move to a sales revenue level above eight boats a year and, very likely, either the gross margin percentage or the fixed cost amount changes.

✦ **In the super-long run, as a practical matter, there is no such thing as a fixed cost.** Essentially, every cost is variable. In the boat-building business, for example, you could — in the long run — lay off two craftsmen and move to a smaller shop. Perhaps you could even build boats in your back yard. Fixed costs, in other words, are fixed only for a particular period of time. If you move beyond that period of time, the fixed costs are no longer fixed. This seems like an obvious point, but it is important to recognize.

✦ **In the super-short term, there is no such thing as a variable cost.** (Or at least there aren't very many variable costs.) For example, in the boat-building business, even if you pay your laborers an hourly wage for building the boats, you probably can't send the laborers home early just because work for the day is done. You can't tell your laborers at the end of Tuesday not to come in for Wednesday, Thursday, or Friday just because you have no work for them. Other variable costs may work the same way — not always, but sometimes. In any case, you need to recognize that some costs may vary over a month or year but not over a day or a week. In other words, in the super-short term, variable costs often aren't very variable.

The three preceding conundrums indicate that profit-volume-cost analysis suffers from some limits. You can't use a gross margin percentage and a fixed cost amount for *any* sales revenue estimates — you need to use those two items of data for a carefully considered range of sales revenue volumes. Furthermore, you can't use profit-volume-cost analysis for super-short time frames. Variable costs in that case aren't really variable. And you can't use profit-volume-cost analysis for super-long time frames because in the long run, no fixed cost stays fixed.

To generalize, the profit-volume-cost analysis tool provides rough measurements. These rough measurements can be very useful to you, but they are still really just rough measurements. Always apply common sense when using profit-volume-cost analysis.

Maybe it's only a little game I play with myself, but sometimes I don't think about fixed costs and variable costs. Instead, I think about *sort-of* fixed costs and *sort-of* variable costs. By admitting up front that the fixed costs are not always solidly fixed and that the variable costs are not always solidly variable, I find myself more comfortable with the profit-volume-cost analysis formula. I remind myself that the model isn't perfect but only a rough tool to estimate profit and breakeven points.

Using the Profit-Volume-Cost Analysis Workbook

I've created a Profit-Volume-Cost Analysis workbook for those readers who want to perform more sophisticated profit-volume-cost analysis. This workbook is available on my Web site at www.stephenlnelson.com/pvc.xls.

The Profit-Volume-Cost Analysis workbook enables you to estimate profits at a variety of sales revenue volumes, to estimate breakeven points, and to chart breakeven and profit-volume-cost data. Some of the calculations are a little bit cumbersome, but almost every calculation is simply an extension of what has already been discussed in the preceding paragraphs of this chapter.

In the remaining pages of this chapter, I describe how to use the Profit-Volume-Cost Analysis workbook, how to understand and interpret the breakeven analysis performed by the workbook, and how to understand and interpret the profit-volume-cost analysis performed by the workbook. I also share a few words about the charts that graphically depict the profit-volume-cost analysis results.

Collecting your inputs

Figure 1-1 shows the worksheet range into which you enter the raw data required for the profit-volume-cost analysis. The workbook collects more data points than you may at first predict. Most of this information, however, is simply a slightly more granular approach to collecting the three basic inputs that any profit-volume-cost analysis depends upon: sales revenue estimates, gross margin percentage, and fixed costs.

You don't need to be an Excel expert to use the Profit-Volume-Cost Analysis workbook described in this chapter. However, you do need to know how to start and stop Excel and how to enter values into worksheet cells. If you don't possess these Excel skills, you may want to consider buying and reading *Excel 2003 For Dummies* by Greg Harvey, also published by Wiley Publishing, Inc.

To use the Profit-Volume-Cost Analysis workbook, follow these steps:

1. **Open the Profit-Volume-Cost Analysis workbook.**

    a. Point your browser to `www.stephenlnelson.com/pvc.xls`.

    b. When your browser asks whether you want to open the file or save the file, indicate that you want to save the file to your hard drive.

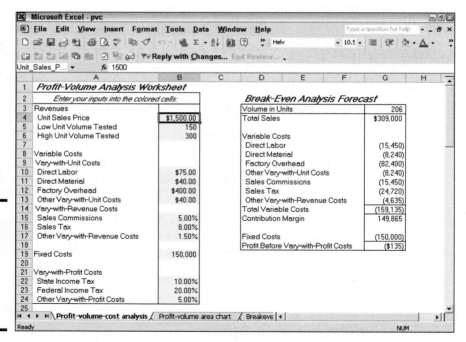

Figure 1-1: The inputs area of the Profit-Volume-Cost Analysis workbook.

   c. Open the file by starting Microsoft Excel and choosing the File menu's Open command.

   d. When Excel displays the Open dialog box, open the folder with the `pvc.xls` file and then double-click the file.

2. Describe the sales revenue that you want to test.

To do this, you must provide three pieces of information: the unit sales price, the low unit sales volume, and the high unit sales volume.

Enter the unit sales price into cell B4. For example, if you sell an item that costs $1,500, you enter **$1,500** into cell B4. Use the low unit volume tested and high unit volume tested inputs shown in cells B5 and B6 (respectively) to identify the range of sales volumes that you want to test. The low unit volume tested value multiplied by the unit sales price equals the lowest revenue volume that the worksheet tests. The high unit volume tested multiplied by the unit sales price amount equals the largest sales revenue volume tested.

The three revenue inputs that you collect and input into cells B4, B5, and B6 tell the workbook which sales revenue volumes that you want to analyze.

If you wanted to use the Profit-Volume-Cost Analysis workbook to test sales volumes for the boat-building business that I describe earlier in the chapter, the unit sales price would equal $100,000, so the low unit volume tested may equal 2, and the high unit volume may equal 5. These inputs, then, would test sales volumes of between $100,000 and $500,000, based on a $100,000 price for a boat.

3. Describe the variable costs.

When you do real-life profit-volume-cost analysis, you find that your variable costs fall into one of two categories: variable costs that can be expressed as an amount per unit, and variable costs that can be expressed as a percentage of the sales price. The worksheet range B10:B17 collects the information needed to describe these sorts of variable costs.

The first set of variable costs, which I call *vary-with-unit costs*, go into cells B10, B11, B12, and B13. For example, any direct labor costs associated with the item that you're selling go into cell B10. Direct material costs go into B11. Factory overhead costs, which are variable and based on units sold, go into cell B12. If you have any other vary-with-unit costs, you enter the amount per unit for these costs into cell B13.

The example vary-with-unit cost values shown in Figure 1-1 mean that for each unit sold, the assumption is that the business pays $75 per unit in direct labor, $40 per unit in direct materials, $400 per unit in factory overhead, and another $40 per unit for other vary-with-unit costs. If you add up these amounts, you see that vary-with-unit costs equal $555 per unit sold.

In addition to vary-with-unit costs, firms also often pay variable costs that are best expressed as a percentage of the revenue. In the Profit-Volume-Cost Analysis workbook, the worksheet range B15:B17 supplies space to describe and record these variable costs, which I call *vary-with-revenue* costs. The workbook, for example, shows a 5 percent sales commission in cell B15. The workbook shows an 8 percent sales tax in cell B16. And just to provide a catchall category for other vary-with-revenue costs, the workbook includes (and I show for purposes of this example) another vary-with-revenue costs value in cell B17.

In the case of the example data set shown in Figure 1-1, for example, vary-with-revenue costs equal 14.5 percent of sales.

4. Record your fixed costs.

To record or estimate your fixed costs, enter the fixed costs amount into cell B19. In Figure 1-1, for example, fixed costs show as $150,000.

5. Estimate any variable costs that vary with profits.

Here's one other wrinkle that you may often encounter with real-life profit-volume-cost analysis: variable costs that don't vary from changes in sales revenue but from changes in profits. For example, some businesses have profit-sharing plans. Those profits represent variable costs because they vary with changes in sales revenue — sort of. In order to estimate the profit-sharing costs, you really need to first calculate profits and then apply the profit-sharing percentage to those profits. Income taxes — federal, state, and local income taxes — also fall into the category of variable costs that don't vary with changes in sales revenue but with changes in profit.

In the workbook shown in Figure 1-1, I've provided three cells, B22, B23, and B24, that let you recognize these variable costs. I call this category of variable costs *vary-with-profit* costs. You can enter the state income tax percentage into cell B22. You can enter the federal income tax percentage into cell B23. And if you have any other vary-with-profit costs, you can enter the sum of these costs as a percentage into cell B24.

I should tell you that vary-with-profit costs are tricky to estimate precisely. The trickiness stems from a couple of factors:

- **Many vary-with-profit costs aren't simply calculated as percentages of profit.** The cost calculations are considerably more complicated. Income tax costs, for example, don't use a single percentage. They often use a schedule of progressive percentages.

- **Vary-with-profit costs often interrelate.** For example, state income taxes affect federal income taxes. Other vary-with-profit costs may interrelate, too. For example, a profit-sharing percentage may be applied on an after-tax basis. The workbook formulas don't explicitly recognize any interrelationship between these variables. Therefore, in order to precisely model these vary-with-profit costs, you must enter percentages that have been fiddled with a bit, as described in the sidebar elsewhere in this chapter, "Dealing with vary-with-profit costs."

After you collect the needed inputs for the Profit-Volume-Cost Analysis workbook, the workbook estimates a breakeven point and prepares a profit volume forecast. The workbook also supplies a couple of useful charts that graphically show the breakeven and the profit-volume analysis data. The next paragraphs of this chapter describe these analysis results.

Understanding the breakeven analysis

The breakeven analysis that the workbook makes based on the inputs that you enter is shown in Figure 1-2. The breakeven analysis shows the number of units required to break even in cell G3 and the sales revenue required to break even in cell G4. You calculate the total sales revenue required to break even by using the same basic formula described earlier in the chapter. You calculate the volume in units breakeven point by dividing the sales revenue breakeven point by the unit sales price.

The variable costs portion of the breakeven analysis shows the amount spent on each of the costs. Cell G7 shows the amount that will be spent on direct labor.

The contribution margin, which is the same thing as gross margin, appears in cell G15. This shows the amount left over from sales revenue after paying the variable costs.

A fixed cost appears in cell G17. By subtracting the fixed costs from the contribution margin, the workbook calculates the breakeven point, which should be zero but may not be because of a rounding error. In Figure 1-2, for example, the profit before vary-with-profit costs value equals –$135.

Although the information shown in Figure 1-2 may seem voluminous, you conceptually understand all this data. A little forecast worksheet simply shows the sales revenue and the sales units that produce the breakeven point. The little worksheet also shows the amounts that you'll spend on variable costs and fixed costs. Profits equal zero at the breakeven point, so there aren't any vary-with-profit costs.

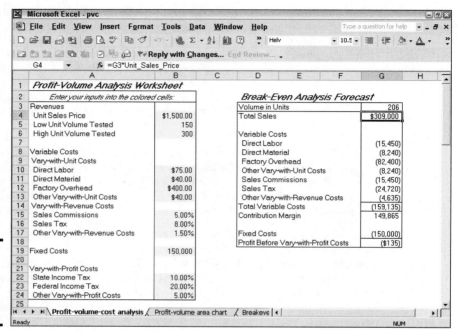

Figure 1-2:
The
Break-Even
Analysis
Forecast.

Understanding the profit-volume-cost forecast

Figure 1-3 shows the miniature income statement at various sales volume levels. Figure 1-4 shows the same information presented not in dollars but in percentages of total sales.

The Profit Volume Forecast worksheet in Figure 1-3 shows the range of sales volume both in revenues and in units that the worksheet calculates. The lowest sales revenue volume and the highest sales revenue volume are set by the inputs that you enter for the low unit volume tested value and the high unit volume tested value. (See the inputs entered into cells B5 and B6 of Figure 1-1.)

The miniature income statements in the Profit Volume Forecast look very similar to a typical QuickBooks income statement. The variable costs portion of the miniature income statement reports on the cost of goods sold. The contribution margin is equivalent to the gross margin reported on a QuickBooks income statement. A fixed cost amount summarizes the operating expenses. The vary-with-profit costs, essentially, summarize income taxes and other profit-based expenses, such as a profit-sharing plan. Profits equate to the net income.

Figure 1-3:
The Profit
Volume
Forecast
in dollars.

Microsoft Excel - pvc

File Edit View Insert Format Tools Data Window Help

B28   =B27*Unit_Sales_Price

	A	B	C	D	E	F	G	H
26	*Profit Volume Forecast*							
27	Volume in Units	150	180	210	240	270	300	
28	Total Sales	$225,000	$270,000	$315,000	$360,000	$405,000	$450,000	
29								
30	Variable Costs							
31	Direct Labor	(11,250)	(13,500)	(15,750)	(18,000)	(20,250)	(22,500)	
32	Direct Material	(6,000)	(7,200)	(8,400)	(9,600)	(10,800)	(12,000)	
33	Factory Overhead	(60,000)	(72,000)	(84,000)	(96,000)	(108,000)	(120,000)	
34	Other Vary-with-Unit Costs	(6,000)	(7,200)	(8,400)	(9,600)	(10,800)	(12,000)	
35	Sales Commissions	(11,250)	(13,500)	(15,750)	(18,000)	(20,250)	(22,500)	
36	Sales Tax	(18,000)	(21,600)	(25,200)	(28,800)	(32,400)	(36,000)	
37	Other Vary-with-Revenue Costs	(3,375)	(4,050)	(4,725)	(5,400)	(6,075)	(6,750)	
38	Total Variable Costs	(115,875)	(139,050)	(162,225)	(185,400)	(208,575)	(231,750)	
39	Contribution Margin	109,125	130,950	152,775	174,600	196,425	218,250	
40								
41	Fixed Costs	(150,000)	(150,000)	(150,000)	(150,000)	(150,000)	(150,000)	
42	Contribution Margin - Fixed Costs	(40,875)	(19,050)	2,775	24,600	46,425	68,250	
43								
44	Vary-with-Profit Costs							
45	State Income Tax	4,088	1,905	(278)	(2,460)	(4,643)	(6,825)	
46	Federal Income Tax	8,175	3,810	(555)	(4,920)	(9,285)	(13,650)	
47	Other Vary-with-Profit Costs	2,044	953	(139)	(1,230)	(2,321)	(3,413)	
48	Total Vary-with-Profit Costs	14,306	6,668	(971)	(8,610)	(16,249)	(23,888)	
49	Profits	($26,569)	($12,383)	$1,804	$15,990	$30,176	$44,363	
51								

Profit-volume-cost analysis / Profit-volume area chart / Breakeve

Ready   NUM

Figure 1-4:
The
Common
Size Profit
Volume
Forecast.

Microsoft Excel - pvc

File Edit View Insert Format Tools Data Window Help

B55   =B28/B$28

	A	B	C	D	E	F	G	H
53	*Common Size Profit Volume Forecast*							
54	Volume in Units	150	180	210	240	270	300	
55	Total Sales	100.00%	100.00%	100.00%	100.00%	100.00%	100.00%	
56								
57	Variable Costs							
58	Direct Labor	-5.00%	-5.00%	-5.00%	-5.00%	-5.00%	-5.00%	
59	Direct Material	-2.67%	-2.67%	-2.67%	-2.67%	-2.67%	-2.67%	
60	Factory Overhead	-26.67%	-26.67%	-26.67%	-26.67%	-26.67%	-26.67%	
61	Other Vary-with-Unit Costs	-2.67%	-2.67%	-2.67%	-2.67%	-2.67%	-2.67%	
62	Sales Commissions	-5.00%	-5.00%	-5.00%	-5.00%	-5.00%	-5.00%	
63	Sales Tax	-8.00%	-8.00%	-8.00%	-8.00%	-8.00%	-8.00%	
64	Other Vary-with-Revenue Costs	-1.50%	-1.50%	-1.50%	-1.50%	-1.50%	-1.50%	
65	Total Variable Costs	-51.50%	-51.50%	-51.50%	-51.50%	-51.50%	-51.50%	
66	Contribution Margin	48.50%	48.50%	48.50%	48.50%	48.50%	48.50%	
67								
68	Fixed Costs	-66.67%	-55.56%	-47.62%	-41.67%	-37.04%	-33.33%	
69	Contribution Margin - Fixed Costs	-18.17%	-7.06%	0.88%	6.83%	11.46%	15.17%	
70								
71	Vary-with-Profit Costs							
72	State Income Tax	1.82%	0.71%	-0.09%	-0.68%	-1.15%	-1.52%	
73	Federal Income Tax	3.63%	1.41%	-0.18%	-1.37%	-2.29%	-3.03%	
74	Other Vary-with-Profit Costs	0.91%	0.35%	-0.04%	-0.34%	-0.57%	-0.76%	
75	Total Vary-with-Profit Costs	6.36%	2.47%	-0.31%	-2.39%	-4.01%	-5.31%	
76	Profits	-11.81%	-4.59%	0.57%	4.44%	7.45%	9.86%	
78								

Profit-volume-cost analysis / Profit-volume area chart / Breakeve

Ready   NUM

Figure 1-3 shows a case in which modest changes in sales revenue can often produce huge changes in profits. In Figure 1-3, column D in the worksheet shows the profit-volume-cost forecast at the sales level equal to $315,000. Column E shows the sales revenue and cost forecast at a sales revenue level of $360,000. As the firm increases its profits by roughly 15 percent (this increase shows in cells D28 and E28), profits increase by almost 900 percent from $1,804 to $15,990 (the change from the values in cells D49 to E49).

You may not be interested in the common-size profit volume forecast shown in Figure 1-4 because this income statement shows percentages based on sales rather than dollar amounts. This figure lets you see what percent of sales a cost item represents of the total sales. Sometimes this information is useful, and sometimes it isn't. If you aren't interested in the information, simply select rows 53–78 and then delete them from your workbook.

Looking at the profit-volume-cost charts

For fun, I included a couple of simple charts that show results from the profit-volume-cost analysis. Figure 1-5, for example, shows the Breakeven line chart. This line chart plots the total fixed costs, the total variable costs, and then the total sales. The intersection of the total sales line and the total fixed costs line shows the breakeven point. By comparing the slopes of the total sales and the variable costs line, you can also get an idea as to how sensitive the profits are to changes in sales revenue. If you have a good eye, you can also even use the Breakeven line chart to roughly estimate the profit at various revenue levels. To do this, find the point on the total sales line equal to the sales revenue level for which you want to guesstimate profits. Then use the *value axis* (the vertical axis on the left side of the chart) to calibrate the difference between the total sales line and the total variable costs line. The difference between these two lines shows your profit or loss.

The total variable costs line actually shows the total variable costs plus the total fixed costs because it's stacked on top of the fixed costs line.

Figure 1-6 shows the profit-volume-cost data from the worksheet. This analysis is more complicated, so the chart is a bit trickier to interpret. Nevertheless, the chart resembles the Breakeven line chart. Fixed costs appear as a solid band equal to $150,000 at the bottom of the graph. Variable costs appear as a sort of trapezoidal shape on top of the fixed costs. Above those costs appear the costs that vary with profits and the actual profit. Note that profits only occur after the firm exceeds the breakeven point. (The data labels on the horizontal axis represent the different volumes being tested.)

The costs varying with profits area of the graph is light blue, and the profits area is black. Because these colors are difficult to distinguish in this black-and-white book, you may want to open up the actual workbook and look at the colored charts on the screen rather than in the book.

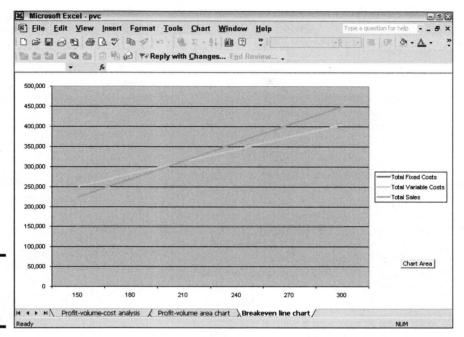

Figure 1-5:
The Breakeven line chart.

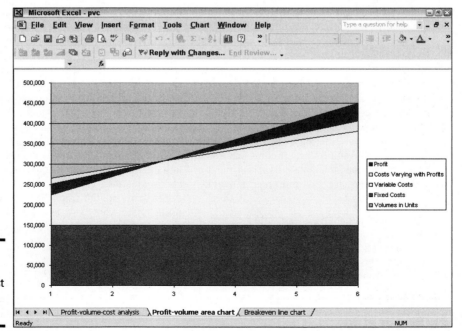

Figure 1-6:
The profit-volume-cost analysis area chart.

Dealing with vary-with-profit costs

If your profit-volume-cost analysis needs to include more than a single vary-with-profit cost, you need to deal with the possibility that your vary-with-profit costs are interrelated. In fact, vary-with-profit costs can have one of three relationships: independent-independent, independent-dependent, or dependent-dependent.

The independent-independent relationship is the easiest to deal with. If two vary-with-profit costs are independent of each other, you can just enter the percentages into the appropriate workbook cells and not worry about them. An independent-independent relationship exists when vary-with-profit costs have no effect on each other. For example, a partnership may have two profit-sharing plans — one for partners and one for employees — that aren't related.

A slightly more complicated relationship between vary-with-profit costs is the case of an independent-dependent relationship. A good example of an independent-dependent relationship is the relationship of state and federal income taxes. Because federal income taxes allow for a deduction based on state income taxes, the federal income tax expense depends on the state income tax expense. If the federal income tax percent equals 20 percent and the state income tax percent equals 10 percent, you can't simply enter the state income tax as 10 percent and the federal income tax as 20 percent. You need to adjust the federal income tax percentage for the effect of the state income tax.

For example, suppose that the state income tax rate is 10 percent of the pre-tax profits and that after deducting the state income tax from the pre-tax profits, the federal income tax rate is 20 percent of what's left over. The correct input

percentage for the state income tax rate is 10 percent because 10 percent of the pre-tax profits calculates the correct state income tax cost as follows:

```
State income tax = 10 percent
    x pre-tax profits
```

However, the federal income tax percentage must recognize the state income tax costs:

```
Federal income tax = 20 percent
    x (pre-tax profits - (10
    percent x pretax profits))
```

This formula can be further modified to express the federal income tax rate as a percentage of the pre-tax profits and, therefore, your input to the Profit-Volume-Cost Analysis workbook:

```
Federal income tax = 18 percent
    x pre-tax profits
```

A third type of relationship is the dependent-dependent relationship. This relationship occurs when one vary-with-profit cost affects another vary-with-profit cost. For example, in the case of a typical employee profit-sharing plan where profits are based on after-tax profits, you need to know the profit-sharing plan expense in order to calculate the federal income taxes. The profit-sharing plan expense is deductible for purposes of calculating federal income taxes. However, you must know the federal income tax expense in order to calculate the after-tax profits upon which the profit-sharing plan is based. In cases of dependent-dependent relationships among vary-with-profit costs, you can calculate percentages that, in effect, adjust for the dependency. To do this, you need to employ a fair amount of high school algebra.

The data plotted in the charts shown in Figures 1-5 and 1-6 come from the worksheet range shown in Figure 1-7. I collected all the data to be plotted in this area of the worksheet, which is below the profit volume forecast and common-size profit volume forecast in order to make it easy to see what data is plotted and where the data is coming from.

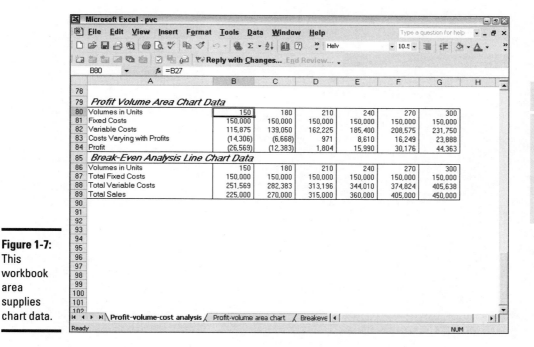

Figure 1-7: This workbook area supplies chart data.

Chapter 2: Creating a Business Plan Forecast

In This Chapter

✓ A little refresher on financial statements and ratios

✓ Using the business plan workbook

✓ Understanding the workbook's formulas

✓ Customizing the workbook

Pro forma financial statements — which are income statements, balance sheets, and cash flow statements — constitute an integral part of business planning and the overall budgeting process. For that reason, I want to provide you with a bit of information about how you create such pro forma (or as if) statements.

From the very start, however, I need to warn you that in order to create such statements, you need another tool in addition to QuickBooks. Specifically, you need a spreadsheet program such as Microsoft Excel.

Assuming that you do have something like Microsoft Excel, you can use it and the example workbook that this chapter describes to create a simple, yet sophisticated, financial forecast for your business. To download the workbook, go to my Web site, www.stephenlnelson.com, click on the Business Consulting link, and then double-click on the BIZPLAN.XLS link. If your fingers are up to it, you can also just type www.stephenlnelson.com/bizplan.xls into your Web browser's Address box.

Reviewing Financial Statements and Ratios

Before I get into the nitty-gritty details of creating a business forecast, I need to briefly discuss what financial statements and ratios are and how to use financial statements and ratios to describe either the past or the future financial condition and performance of a business.

The term *financial statement* can refer to one of several types of schedules and summaries of economic information. Typically, however, the term describes a set of documents that include an income statement (also called a *statement of operations*), a balance sheet (also called a *statement of financial condition*), and a cash flow statement.

An *income statement* details the profits and losses of a business for a specific period. For example, you may want to know the profits or losses of your business over the past month. Therefore, you would prepare an income statement that lists your revenues and expenses and calculates the profits or losses for the month.

A *balance sheet* identifies and lists the assets and liabilities of a business as of a specific time. It paints a clear picture of what the business owns, what the business owes, and the difference between the two (often called the *net worth* or *owner equity*). Typically, you prepare a balance sheet as of the end of the period for which an income statement is prepared. For example, if you prepare an income statement for a month, you may also want to prepare a balance sheet as of the last day of the month.

A *cash flow statement* outlines the cash inflows and outflows of a business for a specific period. Generally, you prepare a cash flow statement for the same period for which you prepare an income statement.

The cash flow statements that large companies use for their investors are quite complicated. They show lots of numbers arranged in a very Rube Goldberg-esque fashion. For this reason, I use the simpler cash flow statement format that accountants once used.

Financial ratios, as I describe in some detail in Book V, Chapter 1, express relationships among the amounts reported in the financial statements. The ratios can offer insights into the economic health of a business. The ratios can also indicate how reasonable the implicit assumptions are in a forecast. For example, by comparing the ratios of your business with the ratios of similar businesses, you can compare the financial characteristics of your business with those of other businesses. By comparing the ratios in your pro forma model with industry averages and standards, you also test your modeling assumptions for reasonableness.

Two general categories of financial ratios exist: common size ratios and intrastatement or interstatement ratios. *Common size ratios* convert a financial statement — usually a balance sheet or an income statement — from dollars to percentages. Common size ratios allow for comparisons of the assets, liabilities, revenues, owner equity, and expenses of businesses of various sizes. The comparison can be either at a point in time or as a trend over time. *Intrastatement* or *interstatement ratios* quantify relationships among amounts from different financial statements or from different parts of the same financial statement, respectively. Intrastatement and interstatement ratios are an attempt to account for the fact that amounts usually can't be interpreted alone but must be viewed in the context of other key financial factors and events. In general, both categories of ratios are most valuable when compared with industry averages and trends.

This financial ratio business is really cool. If you have tim͏ mend that you peruse the greater coverage of the topic ͏ Chapter 1.

Using the Business Plan Workbook

Unfortunately, it really isn't very practical to create an example set of financial statements on, say, the back of a cocktail napkin or a set of sticky notes. You need to get the computer's help.

I suggest that you use Microsoft Excel and a workbook like the one shown in Figures 2-1 through 2-5. With this workbook, which is available at www. stephenlnelson.com, you can construct pro forma financial statements that enable you to forecast profits and losses, financial condition, and cash flows for a business or organization.

To use the workbook, you develop and then enter information on the following:

+ Assets

+ Creditor and owner equities at the start of the forecasting horizon

+ Expected changes in the assets and equities over the forecasting horizon

+ Revenues and expenses for each period on the forecasting horizon

You're probably wondering how this baby works. Well, the workbook does a lot, but it's actually pretty straightforward in its operation. When you input data that includes your starting assets, liabilities, owner equity balances, and expected changes in these amounts for the forecasting horizon, the workbook constructs a balance sheet. The workbook constructs an income statement when you input data that includes sales and costs of sales, operating expenses, interest income and expenses, and marginal income tax rates. Then, from the balance sheet and income statement, the workbook constructs a cash flow statement.

To enter your own data in the business planning starter workbook, use the following steps. Enter positive balances or increases as positive amounts, and enter negative balances or decreases as negative amounts.

1. **Open the business plan workbook,** bizplan.xls, **from my Web site by pointing your browser to www.stephenlnelson.com/bizplan.xls.**

The starter workbook initially contains the default inputs shown in Figure 2-1. Note that you can see only about the first 25 rows and the first 6 or so columns of the inputs area. Sorry — I didn't have room to show everything. If you want to see what you're missing, grab the workbook from the Web site.

Microsoft Excel - bizplan.xls [Read-Only]

File Edit View Insert Format Tools Data Window Help

B4 ▾ 15000

	A	B	C	D	E	F	G	H
1	**Business Plan Workbook**							
2	*Enter inputs in colored cells*	Period 0	Period 1	Period 2	Period 3	Period 4	Period 5	Period 6	Pe
3	*...balance sheet inputs...*							
4	Cash & Equivalents	15,000						
5	Yield on Cash & Equivalents		10.00%	10.00%	10.00%	10.00%	10.00%	10.00%	1
6	Accounts Receivable	10,000						
7	# Periods of Sales in A/R		0.08	0.08	0.08	0.08	0.08	0.08
8	Inventory	10,000						
9	Inventory Purchased/Produced		55,000	65,000	55,000	65,000	55,000	65,000
10	Other Current Assets	5,000						
11	Chgs in Other Current Assets		100	-100	100	-100	100	-100
12	Plant, Property, & Equipment	75,000						
13	Chgs in P.P.& E		0	0	0	0	15,000	0
14	Accumulated Depreciation	15,000						
15	Chgs in Accum. Depreciation		3,750	3,750	3,750	3,750	3,750	3,750
16	Other Noncurrent Assets	5,000						
17	Chgs in Other Noncurrent Assets		100	-100	100	-100	100	-100
18	Accounts Payable	10,000						
19	# Periods Cost of Sales in A/P		0.08	0.08	0.08	0.08	0.08	0.08
20	Accrued Expenses	7,500						
21	# Periods Operating Expenses in A/E		0.04	0.04	0.04	0.04	0.04	0.04
22	Other Current Liabilities	7,500						
23	Chgs in Other Current Liabilities		100	-100	100	-100	100	-100
24	Long-Term Liabilities	35,000						

Ready   NUM

Figure 2-1:
The inputs area of the business plan workbook.

2. **Enter the Cash & Equivalents balance for the start of the forecasting horizon.**

   The value that you enter for Cash & Equivalents is the dollar total of all the cash held at the beginning of the forecasting period.

   You can get the Cash & Equivalents value from QuickBooks if you're forecasting from the present forward. The cash that you start with, obviously, is the cash that you're holding today.

3. **Enter the forecasted period yield that you expect the cash and equivalents to deliver.**

   The model estimates the period interest income by multiplying the cash and equivalents balance by the yield on cash and equivalents.

4. **Enter the Accounts Receivable balance for the start of the forecasting horizon.**

   The value that you enter for Accounts Receivable (A/R) is the starting accounts receivable balance, which is the balance at the beginning of the forecasting horizon excluding any allowance for uncollectible amounts.

5. **Enter the number of periods of sales in accounts receivable.**

The value that you enter for # Periods of Sales in A/R, or number of periods of sales in accounts receivable, is the number of periods or the fraction of a period for which sales are held in accounts receivable. If accounts receivable typically amount to about 30 days of sales and you use months as your forecasting periods, you hold one period (one month) of sales in accounts receivable. Alternatively, if accounts receivable typically amount to about 30 days of sales and you use years as your forecasting periods, you hold one-twelfth of a period of sales in accounts receivable.

6. **Enter the dollar amount of the inventory held at the start of the forecasting horizon.**

   The Inventory value is the starting inventory balance, which is the total dollar amount of the inventory purchased for resale or manufactured for resale and held at the beginning of the forecasting horizon.

7. **Enter the forecasted dollar amount of inventory purchased or produced for each period of the forecasting horizon.**

   The Inventory Purchased/Produced value is the dollar total of items purchased or produced over the period.

8. **Enter the amount of the other current assets held at the start of the forecasting horizon.**

   The Other Current Assets starting balance is the dollar total of any other current assets with which you begin the forecasting horizon. These other current assets may include prepaid expenses, short-term investments, and deposits made with vendors.

9. **Enter the amount of the change in the other current assets for each period in the forecasting horizon.**

   The value for Chgs in Other Current Assets, or changes in other current assets for the period, is the dollar total of increases or decreases in the accounts included in the starting Other Current Assets balance.

10. **Enter the amount of the plant, property, and equipment at the start of the forecasting horizon.**

    The starting Plant, Property, & Equipment balance is the dollar total of the fixed assets. This amount includes such items as real estate, manufacturing equipment, furniture, and the Lear jet.

11. **Enter the amount of the change in the plant, property, and equipment (P, P, & E) for each period of the forecasting horizon.**

    The Chgs in P, P, & E value is the dollar total of decreases or increases in the plant, property, and equipment accounts for the period. Increases in these accounts probably stem from purchases of additional fixed assets. Decreases in these accounts probably stem from disposal of assets.

12. **Enter the amount of the accumulated depreciation on the plant, property, and equipment at the start of the forecasting horizon.**

The starting Accumulated Depreciation balance represents the depreciation expenses charged to date on the assets identified in the starting P, P, & E balance.

13. **Enter the amount of the change in the accumulated depreciation for each period of the forecasting horizon.**

The Chgs in Accum. Depreciation value is the dollar total of increases and decreases in the accumulated depreciation account for the period. Increases in the accumulated depreciation balance probably stem from the current period depreciation expense. Decreases in the accumulated depreciation balance probably stem from removing the accumulated depreciation attributed to a fixed asset that you disposed of.

14. **Enter the amount of the other noncurrent assets at the start of the period.**

The starting Other Noncurrent Assets balance is the dollar total of all other noncurrent assets held at the start of the forecasting period. Other noncurrent assets may include copyrights, patents, and goodwill.

15. **Enter the amount of the change in the other noncurrent assets for each period of the forecasting horizon.**

The Chgs in Other Noncurrent Assets value is the dollar total increase or decrease for the period in the accounts included in the starting Other Noncurrent Assets balance.

16. **Enter the amount of the accounts payable balance at the start of the forecasting horizon.**

The starting Accounts Payable (A/P) balance is the dollar total of amounts owed vendors for inventory at the start of the forecasting horizon. This starter workbook calculates future Accounts Payable balances based on the cost of sales volumes. To add precision to the forecasts of accounts payable, the model assumes that accounts payable represent debt incurred for the cost of sales.

17. **Enter the number of periods of the cost of sales in accounts payable.**

The # Periods Cost of Sales in A/P is the number of periods or the fraction of a period for which the cost of sales is held in accounts payable. If accounts payable typically amount to about 30 days of cost of sales and you use months as your forecasting periods, you hold one period (one month) of cost of sales in accounts payable. Alternatively, if accounts payable typically amount to about 30 days of cost of sales and you use years as your forecasting periods, you hold one-twelfth of a period of cost of sales in accounts payable.

18. **Enter the amount of the accrued expenses balance at the start of the forecasting horizon.**

The starting Accrued Expenses (A/E) balance is the dollar total of amounts owed vendors for operating expenses at the start of the forecast horizon. This starter workbook calculates future Accrued Expenses balances based on the operating expenses levels. To add precision to the forecasts of accrued expenses, the model assumes that accrued expenses represent debt incurred for operating expenses.

19. **Enter the number of periods of operating expenses in accrued expenses.**

The # Periods Operating Expenses in A/E value is the number of periods or the fraction of a period for which operating expenses are held in accrued expenses. If accrued expenses typically amount to 30 days of operating expenses and you use months as your forecasting periods, you hold one period of operating expenses in accrued expenses. Alternatively, if accrued expenses typically amount to about 30 days of operating expenses and you use years as your forecasting periods, you hold one-twelfth of a period of operating expenses in accrued expenses.

Book VI
Chapter 2

Creating a Business
Plan Forecast

20. **Enter the amount of the other current liabilities at the start of the forecasting period.**

The Other Current Liabilities starting balance is the dollar total of all other current liabilities held at the start of the forecasting period. Other current liabilities may include income tax payable, product warranty liability, and the current portion of a long-term liability.

21. **Enter the amount of the change in the other current liabilities for each period of the forecasting horizon.**

The Chgs in Other Current Liabilities value is the dollar total of increases or decreases for the period in the accounts included in the starting Other Current Liabilities balance.

22. **Enter the amount of the long-term liabilities balance at the start of the forecasting horizon.**

The starting Long-Term Liabilities balance is the dollar total of debt that will be paid back sometime after the next year.

23. **Enter the amount of the change in the long-term liabilities for each period of the forecasting horizon.**

The Chgs in Long-Term Liabilities value is the increase or decrease for the period in the outstanding long-term debt. These changes may include decreases stemming from the amortization of principal through debt service payments and increases stemming from additional funds provided by creditors. You need to include the principal component of debt service payments as negative amounts because they decrease the amount of long-term liability.

24. **Enter the amount of the other noncurrent liabilities at the start of the forecasting horizon.**

The Other Noncurrent Liabilities starting balance is the dollar total of all other noncurrent liabilities held at the start of the forecasting period. These may include deferred income tax, employee pension plan liabilities, and capitalized lease obligations.

25. **Enter the amount of the change in the other noncurrent liabilities for each period of the forecasting horizon.**

The Chgs in Other Noncurrent Liabilities value is the dollar total of increases or decreases for the period in the accounts included in the starting Other Noncurrent Liabilities balance. These changes may include decreases stemming from the amortization of principal through debt service payments and increases stemming from additional funds provided by creditors.

26. **Enter the amount of the owner equity balance at the start of the forecasting horizon.**

The Owner Equity starting balance is the dollar total of the capital originally contributed by owners and the earnings retained by the business at the start of the forecasting horizon.

27. **Enter the amount of the change in the owner equity balance for each period of the forecasting horizon stemming from additional capital contributions, dividends, and other special distributions to owners.**

The Chgs in Owner Equity value is the dollar total of increases for the period in owner equity, other than those stemming from the profits of a business and all decreases in owner equity. For example, increases in the Owner Equity balance may result from additional offerings of common or preferred stock and treasury stock transactions; decreases in the Owner Equity balance may result from dividends and other distributions to stockholders.

Changes to the owner equity balance resulting from the profit or loss for the period are calculated on the income statement; they are not entered.

28. **Enter the sales revenue forecasted for each period of the forecasting horizon.**

The Sales Revenue values represent the forecasted sales revenues generated by the business over each period of the forecasting horizon.

29. **Enter the cost of sales forecasted for each period of the forecasting horizon.**

The Cost of Sales values represent the forecasted costs of the inventory sold for the forecasting horizon.

30. **Enter those costs that fall into the first, second, and third operating expense classifications or categories for each period of the forecasting horizon.**

The operating expenses for Cost Centers 1, 2, and 3 represent the operating expenses for the forecasting horizon. These figures may be three expense classifications related to operating the business, or they may be the total expenses for three groups of expenses.

Typically, you would use one cost center to track your general and administrative expenses, another cost center to track your sales and marketing expenses, and another cost center to track your research and development expenses. If you do this, consider replacing the labels *Cost Center 1, Cost Center 2,* and *Cost Center 3* with more descriptive and meaningful labels, such as *General & Admin, Sales & Marketing,* and *Research & Development.*

31. Enter the interest expense of carrying any debt used to fund operations or asset purchases.

The Interest Expense values represent the period interest expenses of carrying any debt related to the business.

32. Enter the income tax rate that, when multiplied against the profit or loss for the period, calculates the income tax expense (or savings).

The Income Tax Rate value is the percentage that, when multiplied by the operating profit (or loss), calculates the income tax expense (or savings). This can be a little tricky because business income taxes are progressive. For example, a sole proprietor's tax rates go from 0 to roughly 40 percent, depending on the level of income. A regular corporation's income tax rates go from 15 to 34 percent (with some bounces up and down along the way). This may mean that you need your tax advisor's help to come up with a good number for this input. On the other hand, you may just decide to only calculate pretax profits and losses. To do this, enter this amount as 0.

After you enter the required inputs, the starter workbook makes the calculations necessary to construct pro forma financial statements and calculate a set of rather standard financial ratios.

Understanding the Workbook Calculations

The business plan workbook has seven parts: the inputs forecast, Balance Sheet, Common Size Balance Sheet, Income Statement, Common Size Income Statement, Cash Flow Statement, and Financial Ratios Table. I want to briefly describe the Excel calculations that occur within each of these parts so that in case you have questions or you want to modify the starter workbook, you can make it work better for your specific situation.

If you don't know Excel and don't want to learn it — don't worry. You can just skip this discussion. I provide it for the benefit of those readers who want to understand the inner workings of the workbook and may need or want to customize the workbook's calculations.

Forecasting inputs

The inputs area of the business planning starter workbook contains one set of formulas. The second row identifies the period for which the results are calculated. The period identifier numbers the periods for which values are entered. The start of the first period is stored in cell B2 as the integer 0. Periods that follow are stored as the previous period plus 1.

The period identifiers in the Balance Sheet, Common Size Balance Sheet, Income Statement, Cash Flow Statement, and Financial Ratios Table schedules use similar formulas.

The cells that hold the period identifiers use a custom number format that precedes each period with the word *Period*. To remove this, simply reformat the cells by using another number format. You can most easily do this by selecting a cell and then clicking a formatting button on the Excel toolbar, such as the Currency or Percent Style button.

Balance Sheet

The Balance Sheet schedule has 20 rows with calculated data, but the first row contains only the text label Period, shown in Figure 2-2. (As in the inputs area of the business planning starter workbook, the period identifier numbers the periods for which values are forecasted.) The rest of the Balance Sheet's values are described in the following paragraphs.

Cash & Equivalents

The Cash & Equivalents figures show the projected cash on hand at the end of each of the forecasting periods. The starting balance is the value you enter in the inputs area of the business planning starter workbook. The balance for the first and subsequent periods is pulled from the Cash Flow Statement schedule, where it is calculated.

Accounts Receivable

The Accounts Receivable (A/R) figures show the net receivables held as of the end of each forecasting period. The starting balance is the value that you enter in the inputs planning area of the business starter worksheet. The balance for the first and subsequent periods is based on the Sales Revenue and the # Periods of Sales in A/R values that you enter in the inputs area of the business planning starter workbook. For example, the formula for the first period is

```
=C7*C31
```

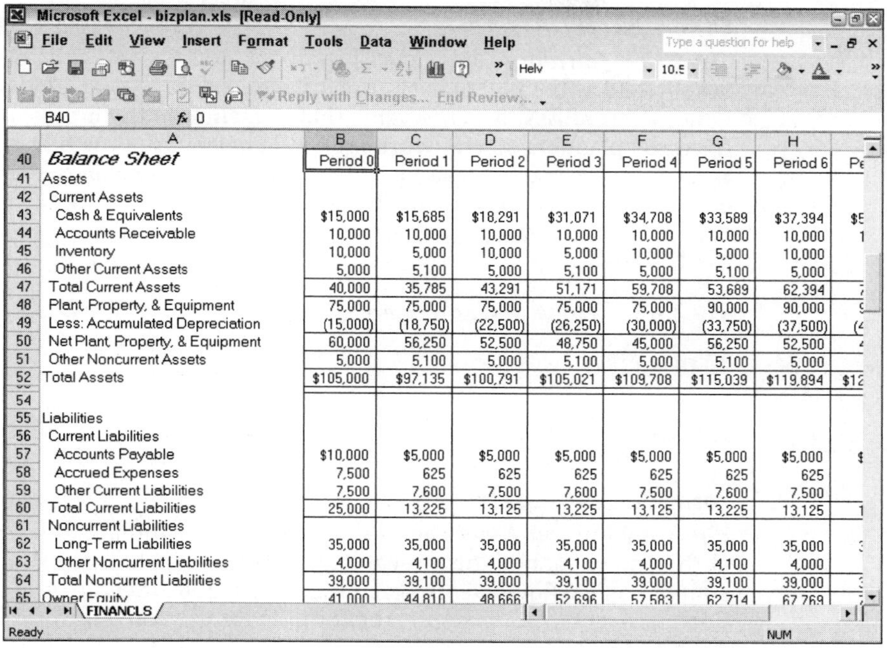

	A	B	C	D	E	F	G	H	
40	Balance Sheet	Period 0	Period 1	Period 2	Period 3	Period 4	Period 5	Period 6	Pe
41	Assets								
42	Current Assets								
43	Cash & Equivalents	$15,000	$15,685	$18,291	$31,071	$34,708	$33,589	$37,394	$5
44	Accounts Receivable	10,000	10,000	10,000	10,000	10,000	10,000	10,000	1
45	Inventory	10,000	5,000	10,000	5,000	10,000	5,000	10,000	
46	Other Current Assets	5,000	5,100	5,000	5,100	5,000	5,100	5,000	
47	Total Current Assets	40,000	35,785	43,291	51,171	59,708	53,689	62,394	7
48	Plant, Property, & Equipment	75,000	75,000	75,000	75,000	75,000	90,000	90,000	9
49	Less: Accumulated Depreciation	(15,000)	(18,750)	(22,500)	(26,250)	(30,000)	(33,750)	(37,500)	(4
50	Net Plant, Property, & Equipment	60,000	56,250	52,500	48,750	45,000	56,250	52,500	4
51	Other Noncurrent Assets	5,000	5,100	5,000	5,100	5,000	5,100	5,000	
52	Total Assets	$105,000	$97,135	$100,791	$105,021	$109,708	$115,039	$119,894	$12
54									
55	Liabilities								
56	Current Liabilities								
57	Accounts Payable	$10,000	$5,000	$5,000	$5,000	$5,000	$5,000	$5,000	$
58	Accrued Expenses	7,500	625	625	625	625	625	625	
59	Other Current Liabilities	7,500	7,600	7,500	7,600	7,500	7,600	7,500	
60	Total Current Liabilities	25,000	13,225	13,125	13,225	13,125	13,225	13,125	1
61	Noncurrent Liabilities								
62	Long-Term Liabilities	35,000	35,000	35,000	35,000	35,000	35,000	35,000	3
63	Other Noncurrent Liabilities	4,000	4,100	4,000	4,100	4,000	4,100	4,000	
64	Total Noncurrent Liabilities	39,000	39,100	39,000	39,100	39,000	39,100	39,000	3
65	Owner Equity	41,000	44,810	48,666	52,696	57,583	62,714	67,769	7

Figure 2-2: The Balance Sheet portion of the business planning starter workbook.

The formula for the second period is

```
=D7*D31
```

and so on.

Inventory

The Inventory values show the dollar total of the inventory held at the end of each forecasting period. The starting balance is the value that you enter in the inputs area of the business planning starter workbook. The balance for the first and subsequent periods is the previous period balance plus any inventory purchases or production costs minus any cost of sales. For example, the formula for the first period is

```
=B45+C9-C32
```

The formula for the second period is

```
=C45+D9-D32
```

and so on.

Other Current Assets

The Other Current Assets figures show the dollar total of the other current assets held at the end of each forecasting period. The starting balance for Other Current Assets is the value that you enter in the inputs area of the business planning starter workbook. The balance for the first and subsequent periods is the previous balance plus the change in the balance. For example, the formula for the first period is

```
=B46+C11
```

The formula for the second period is

```
=C46+D11
```

and so on.

Total Current Assets

The Total Current Assets figures show the dollar total of the current assets at the end of each of the forecasting horizons. The balance at any time is the sum of Cash & Equivalents, Accounts Receivable, Inventory, and Other Current Assets. For example, the formula for the starting Total Current Assets balance is

```
=SUM(B43:B46)
```

The formula for the first period is

```
=SUM(C43:C46)
```

and so on.

Plant, Property, & Equipment

The Plant, Property, & Equipment figures show the original dollar cost of the plant, property, and equipment at the end of each forecasting horizon. The starting Plant, Property, & Equipment balance is the value that you enter in the inputs area of the business planning starter workbook. The balance for the first and subsequent periods is the previous balance plus any additions to the plant, property, and equipment accounts. For example, the formula for the first period is

```
=B48+C13
```

The formula for the second period is

```
=C48+D13
```

and so on.

Less: Accumulated Depreciation

The Accumulated Depreciation figures show the cumulative depreciation expenses charged through the current period for the plant, property, and equipment. The starting balance is the value that you enter in the inputs area of the business planning starter workbook. The balance for the first and subsequent periods is the previous balance minus the current period's changes in accumulated depreciation. For example, the formula for the first period is

```
=B49-C15
```

The formula for the second period is

```
=C49-D15
```

and so on. Because the accumulated depreciation is shown as a negative amount, you need to subtract the positive number pulled from the forecasting inputs.

Net Plant, Property, & Equipment

The Net Plant, Property, & Equipment figures show the difference between Plant, Property, & Equipment and Accumulated Depreciation at the end of each of the forecasting horizons. For example, the formula for the starting balance is

```
=B48+B49
```

The formula for the first period is

```
=C48+C49
```

and so on. Because the Accumulated Depreciation balance is shown as a negative amount, you simply add these two amounts in the formula for the Net Plant, Property, & Equipment amount.

Other Noncurrent Assets

The Other Noncurrent Assets figures show the dollar total of any other non-current assets held at the end of each forecasting period. The starting balance is the value that you enter in the inputs area of the business planning starter workbook. The balance for the first and subsequent periods is the previous period balance plus the change in the account in the current period. For example, the formula for the first period is

=B51+C17

The formula for the second period is

=C51+D17

and so on.

Total Assets

The Total Assets figures show the dollar total of all the assets held at the end of the forecasting periods. The balance at any time is the sum of: Current Assets; Net Plant, Property, & Equipment; and Other Noncurrent Assets. For example, the formula for the starting balance is

=B47+B50+B51

The formula for the first period is

=C47+C50+C51

and so on.

Accounts Payable

The Accounts Payable figures show the debt that is related to the cost of sales outstanding at the end of each forecasting period. The starting balance is the value that you enter in the inputs area of the business planning starter workbook. The balance for the first and subsequent periods is Cost of Sales for the period times # Periods of Cost of Sales in A/P. For example, the formula for the first period is

=C19*C32

The formula for the second period is

=D19*D32

and so on.

Accrued Expenses

The Accrued Expenses figures show the debt that is related to the operating expenses outstanding at the end of each forecasting period. The starting balance is the value that you enter in the inputs area of the business planning starter workbook. The balance for the first and subsequent periods is the operating expenses times # Periods Operating Expenses in A/E. For example, the formula for the first period is

```
=C21*SUM(C33:C35)
```

The formula for the second period is

```
=D21*SUM(D33:D35)
```

and so on.

Other Current Liabilities

The Other Current Liabilities figures show the dollar total of other debts outstanding at the end of the forecasting periods that will be paid within the current year or business cycle. The starting balance is the value that you enter in the inputs area of the business planning starter workbook. The balance for the first and subsequent periods is the previous balance plus the change in the current period. For example, the formula for the first period is

```
=B59+C23
```

The formula for the second period is

```
=C59+D23
```

and so on.

Total Current Liabilities

The Total Current Liabilities figures show the dollar total of all the current liabilities at the end of each forecasting period. The balance at any time is the sum of Accounts Payable, Accrued Expenses, and Other Current Liabilities. For example, the formula for the starting balance is

```
=SUM(B57:B59)
```

The formula for the first period is

```
=SUM(C57:C59)
```

and so on.

Long-Term Liabilities

The Long-Term Liabilities figures show the dollar total of the long-term outstanding debt at the end of each forecasting period. The starting balance is the value that you enter in the inputs area of the business planning starter workbook. The balance for the first and subsequent periods is the previous balance plus any changes in the Long-Term Liabilities balance in the current period. For example, the formula for the first period is

```
=B62+C25
```

The formula for the second period is

```
=C62+D25
```

and so on.

Other Noncurrent Liabilities

The Other Noncurrent Liabilities figures show the dollar total of any other noncurrent outstanding debt at the end of each forecasting period. The starting balance is the value that you enter in the inputs area of the business planning starter workbook. The balance for the first and subsequent periods is the previous period balance plus the change in the current period. For example, the formula for the first period is

```
=B63+C27
```

The formula for the second period is

```
=C63+D27
```

and so on.

Total Noncurrent Liabilities

The Total Noncurrent Liabilities figures show the dollar totals of the long-term debt and the other noncurrent outstanding debt at the end of each forecasting period. The balance at any time is the sum of Long-Term Liabilities and Other Noncurrent Liabilities. For example, the formula for the starting balance is

```
=B62+B63
```

The formula for the first period is

```
=C62+C63
```

and so on.

Owner Equity

The Owner Equity figures show the dollar totals of the owner equity accounts at the end of each forecasting period. The starting balance is the value that you enter in the inputs area of the business planning starter workbook. The balance for the first and subsequent periods is the previous period balance plus Net Income After Taxes for the period plus other adjustments, such as additional capital contributions and dividends. For example, the formula for the first period is

=B65+C29+C116

The formula for the second period is

=C65+D29+D116

and so on.

Total Liabilities and Owner Equity

The Total Liabilities and Owner Equity figures show the dollar totals of Current Liabilities, Noncurrent Liabilities, and Owner Equity at the end of each forecasting period. For example, the formula for the starting balance is

=B60+B64+B65

The formula for the first period is

=C60+C64+C65

and so on.

The Total Assets value should equal the Total Liabilities and Owner Equity value. If they differ, your model contains an error.

Common Size Balance Sheet

The Common Size Balance Sheet schedule lists — in the balance sheet format — what percentage of the total assets each individual asset represents and what percentage of the total liabilities and owner equity each individual liability and the owner equity represents, as shown in Figure 2-3. When you compare these percentages with those of business peers, you can see the relative financial strength or weakness of your business. Trends in the percentages over time can indicate improvement or deterioration in the overall financial condition of your business.

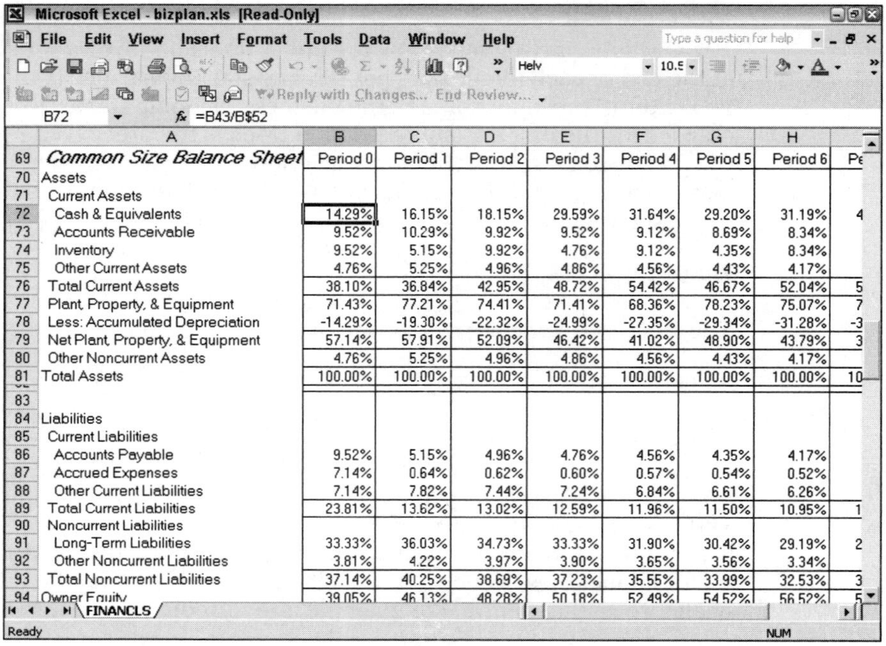

	A	B	C	D	E	F	G	H	
69	*Common Size Balance Sheet*	Period 0	Period 1	Period 2	Period 3	Period 4	Period 5	Period 6	Pe
70	Assets								
71	Current Assets								
72	Cash & Equivalents	14.29%	16.15%	18.15%	29.59%	31.64%	29.20%	31.19%	4
73	Accounts Receivable	9.52%	10.29%	9.92%	9.52%	9.12%	8.69%	8.34%	
74	Inventory	9.52%	5.15%	9.92%	4.76%	9.12%	4.35%	8.34%	
75	Other Current Assets	4.76%	5.25%	4.96%	4.86%	4.56%	4.43%	4.17%	
76	Total Current Assets	38.10%	36.84%	42.95%	48.72%	54.42%	46.67%	52.04%	5
77	Plant, Property, & Equipment	71.43%	77.21%	74.41%	71.41%	68.36%	78.23%	75.07%	7
78	Less: Accumulated Depreciation	-14.29%	-19.30%	-22.32%	-24.99%	-27.35%	-29.34%	-31.28%	-3
79	Net Plant, Property, & Equipment	57.14%	57.91%	52.09%	46.42%	41.02%	48.90%	43.79%	3
80	Other Noncurrent Assets	4.76%	5.25%	4.96%	4.86%	4.56%	4.43%	4.17%	
81	Total Assets	100.00%	100.00%	100.00%	100.00%	100.00%	100.00%	100.00%	10
83									
84	Liabilities								
85	Current Liabilities								
86	Accounts Payable	9.52%	5.15%	4.96%	4.76%	4.56%	4.35%	4.17%	
87	Accrued Expenses	7.14%	0.64%	0.62%	0.60%	0.57%	0.54%	0.52%	
88	Other Current Liabilities	7.14%	7.82%	7.44%	7.24%	6.84%	6.61%	6.26%	
89	Total Current Liabilities	23.81%	13.62%	13.02%	12.59%	11.96%	11.50%	10.95%	1
90	Noncurrent Liabilities								
91	Long-Term Liabilities	33.33%	36.03%	34.73%	33.33%	31.90%	30.42%	29.19%	2
92	Other Noncurrent Liabilities	3.81%	4.22%	3.97%	3.90%	3.65%	3.56%	3.34%	
93	Total Noncurrent Liabilities	37.14%	40.25%	38.69%	37.23%	35.55%	33.99%	32.53%	3
94	Owner Equity	39.05%	46.13%	48.28%	50.18%	52.49%	54.52%	56.52%	5

Figure 2-3: The Common Size Balance Sheet portion of the business plan workbook.

The Common Size Balance Sheet schedule has 20 rows with calculated data that express line-item amounts as percentages of the total. For the asset side of the Balance Sheet, assets are expressed as a percentage of the total assets. For the creditor and owner equity side of the Balance Sheet, equities are expressed as a percentage of the total liabilities and owner equity. The formulas for all rows except Total Assets and Total Liabilities and Owner Equity simply convert the Balance Sheet values to percentages. For example, the Cash & Equivalents formula for the first period is

```
=B43/B$52
```

The formula for the second period is

```
=C43/C$52
```

and so on. All asset percentages are derived from dividing by Total Assets, which explains why the absolute reference to row $52 is used in all asset formulas. Similarly, the absolute reference to row $66 appears in all formulas in the liabilities and equity formulas.

The formula for the Total Assets percentage at any time is the sum of the Current Assets, the Net Plant, Property & Equipment, and the Other Noncurrent Assets percentages. The result always equals 100 percent.

Similarly, the formula for the Total Liabilities and Owner Equity percentage at any time is the sum of the Current Liabilities, the Noncurrent Liabilities, and Owner Equity percentages. The result is always 100 percent.

Income Statement

The Income Statement schedule has 12 rows of calculated data, as shown in Figure 2-4. As in other schedules, the period identifier simply numbers the periods for which values are calculated. The first period is stored in cell C99 as the integer 1, and the periods that follow are stored as the previous period plus 1. The other values in the Income Statement are calculated as described in the following paragraphs.

Book VI
Chapter 2

Sales Revenue

The Sales Revenue figures are the estimates that you enter in the inputs area of the business planning starter workbook. The amount for the period is the value that you enter in the inputs area of the business planning starter workbook.

Less: Cost of Sales

The Cost Of Sales figures are the Cost of Sales estimates that you enter in the inputs area of the business planning starter workbook.

Figure 2-4:
The Income Statement and the first few rows of the Common Size Income Statement.

	A	B	C	D	E	F	G	H	
			C100		fx =C31				
99	*Income Statement*		Period 1	Period 2	Period 3	Period 4	Period 5	Period 6	Pe
100	Sales Revenue		$120,000	$120,000	$120,000	$120,000	$120,000	$120,000	$12
101	Less: Cost of Sales		(60,000)	(60,000)	(60,000)	(60,000)	(60,000)	(60,000)	(6
102	Gross Margin		60,000	60,000	60,000	60,000	60,000	60,000	6
103									
104	Operating Expenses								
105	Cost Center 1		5,000	5,000	5,000	5,000	5,000	5,000	
106	Cost Center 2		5,000	5,000	5,000	5,000	5,000	5,000	
107	Cost Center 3		5,000	5,000	5,000	5,000	5,000	5,000	
108	Total Operating Expenses		15,000	15,000	15,000	15,000	15,000	15,000	1
109	Operating Income		45,000	45,000	45,000	45,000	45,000	45,000	4
110									
111	Interest Income		1,500	1,569	1,829	3,107	3,471	3,359	
112	Interest Expense		3,500	3,500	3,500	3,500	3,500	3,500	
113	Net Income (Loss) Before Taxes		43,000	43,069	43,329	44,607	44,971	44,859	4
114									
115	Income Tax Expenses (Savings)		14,190	14,213	14,299	14,720	14,840	14,803	1
116	Net Income (Loss) After Taxes		$28,810	$28,856	$29,030	$29,887	$30,130	$30,055	$3
118									
119	*Common Size Income Statement*								
120	Sales Revenue		100.00%	100.00%	100.00%	100.00%	100.00%	100.00%	10
121	Less: Cost of Sales		-50.00%	-50.00%	-50.00%	-50.00%	-50.00%	-50.00%	-5
122	Gross Margin		50.00%	50.00%	50.00%	50.00%	50.00%	50.00%	5
123									

Gross Margin

The Gross Margin figures show the amounts left over from the sales proceeds after subtracting Cost of Sales. Subtracting your other expenses from the Gross Margin amount gives you your profit figure. The Gross Margin formula is Sales Revenue for the period minus Cost of Sales. For example, the formula for the first period is

```
=C100+C101
```

The formula for the second period is

```
=D100+D101
```

and so on. Notice that because the Cost of Sales figures are pulled into the Income Statement schedule as negative amounts, the Gross Margin formula simply adds the Sales Revenue figure to the negative Cost of Sales figure.

Operating Expenses — Cost Centers 1, 2, and 3

The Operating Expenses figures for Cost Centers 1, 2, and 3 show the amount for each operating expense classification or category that you enter in the inputs area of the business planning starter workbook.

Total Operating Expenses

The Total Operating Expenses figures show the sums of the operating expenses that you enter in the inputs area of the business planning starter workbook for these three operating expense categories or classifications. The total for each period is the sum of the operating expenses for Cost Centers 1, 2, and 3. For example, the formula for the first period is

```
=SUM(C105:C107)
```

The formula for the second period is

```
=SUM(D105:D107)
```

and so on.

Operating Income

The Operating Income figures show the sales dollar amounts left after paying the Cost of Sales and the Operating Expenses. The Operating Income figures represent the amounts that go toward paying your financing expenses and income tax as well as the amount that constitutes your profits. The amount for each period is the Gross Margin figure for the period minus the Total Operating Expenses figure. For example, the formula for the first period is

=C102-C108

The formula for the second period is

=D102-D108

and so on.

Interest Income

The Interest Income figures show the earnings from investing the cash of the business. The amount for each period is the beginning Cash & Equivalents balance from the inputs area of the business planning starter workbook multiplied by the period yield on Cash & Equivalents. For example, the formula for the first period is

=B43*C5

The formula for the second period is

=C43*D5

and so on.

Interest Expense

The Interest Expense figures show the costs of using borrowed funds for operations and asset purchases. The amount for each period is the value that you enter in the inputs area of the business planning starter workbook.

Net Income (Loss) Before Taxes

The Net Income (Loss) Before Taxes figures show the amount of operating income left after receiving any interest income and paying any interest expense. The amount for each period is the Operating Income figure for the period, plus the Interest Income figure for the period, minus the Interest Expense figure for the period. For example, the formula for the first period is

=C109+C111-C112

The formula for the second period is

=D109+D111-D112

and so on.

Income Tax Expenses (Savings)

The Income Tax Expenses (Savings) figures show the income tax expenses (or savings) that use the calculated Net Income (Loss) Before Taxes figures and the Marginal Income Tax Rate figures that you forecasted in the inputs area of the business planning starter workbook. Notice that the model calculates a current period savings in income taxes when there is a net loss before taxes. This may be the case when a current period loss is carried back to a prior period or when the current period loss is consolidated with the current period income of related businesses. Basically, then, the model assumes that a net loss before income taxes results in a current period tax refund — that is, an overall tax savings — because you can deduct a loss in one business from the profits of another business. However, if a current period loss doesn't result in a current period income tax savings, you need to modify the formula, as described in the section "Customizing the Starter Workbook," later in this chapter.

The amount for each period is the Net Income (Loss) Before Taxes multiplied by the Marginal Income Tax Rate figure. For example, the formula for the first period is

```
=C37*C113
```

The formula for the second period is

```
=D37*D113
```

and so on.

Net Income (Loss) After Taxes

The Net Income (Loss) After Taxes figures calculate the after-tax profits of operating the business. The amount for each period is the Net Income (Loss) Before Taxes figure minus the Income Tax Expenses (Savings) figure. For example, the formula for the first period is

```
=C113-C115
```

The formula for the second period is

```
=D113-D115
```

and so on.

Common Size Income Statement

The Common Size Income Statement schedule lists, in income statement format, what percentage of the total sales revenue each income statement line item represents (refer to Figure 2-4). When you compare these percentages with those of business peers, you can see the relative financial performance of your business. Trends in the percentages over the forecasting horizon can indicate improvement or deterioration in the financial performance of your business.

The Common Size Income Statement schedule has 13 rows of calculated data that express the component line-item amount for each period as a percentage of the sales revenue figure for the period. The formulas for all rows except Sales Revenue simply convert the Income Statement values to percentages.

The Sales Revenue figures add the Cost of Sales, Total Operating Expenses, Interest Income, Interest Expense, Income Tax Expenses (Savings), and Net Income (Loss) After Taxes percentages. The results always equal 100 percent.

The Sales Revenue percentage calculations add the expense and profit percentages. Those expenses shown as negative amounts, therefore, are subtracted.

Cash Flow Statement

The Cash Flow Statement schedule has 16 rows of calculated data, shown in Figure 2-5. Like in other schedules, a period identifier numbers the periods for which values are calculated. The first period is stored in cell C141 as integer 1. Periods that follow are stored as the previous period plus 1. Other Cash Flow Statement values are calculated as described in the following paragraphs.

Beginning Cash Balance

The Beginning Cash Balance figures show the forecasted cash and equivalents balance at the start of each forecasting period. The starting balance is the value that you enter in the inputs area of the business planning starter workbook. For subsequent periods, the Beginning Cash Balance is the previous period's Ending Cash Balance.

Net Income After Taxes

The Net Income After Taxes figures show the amounts calculated in the Income Statement schedule as the business profits for each forecasting period.

Figure 2-5: The Cash Flow Statement.

	A	B	C	D	E	F	G	H	
139									
140									
141	*Cash Flow Statement*		Period 1	Period 2	Period 3	Period 4	Period 5	Period 6	Pe
142	Beginning Cash Balance		$15,000	$15,685	$18,291	$31,071	$34,708	$33,589	$3
143									
144	Sources of Cash								
145	Net Income After Taxes		$28,810	$28,856	$29,030	$29,887	$30,130	$30,055	$3
146	Addback of Depreciation		3,750	3,750	3,750	3,750	3,750	3,750	
147	Accounts Payable Financing		(5,000)	0	0	0	0	0	
148	Accrued Expenses Financing		(6,875)	0	0	0	0	0	
149	Other Current Liabilities Financing		100	(100)	100	(100)	100	(100)	
150	Long-Term Liabilities Financing		0	0	0	0	0	0	
151	Other Noncurrent Liabilities Financing		100	(100)	100	(100)	100	(100)	
152									
153	Uses of Cash								
154	Accounts Receivable Investments		0	0	0	0	0	0	
155	Inventory Investments		(5,000)	5,000	(5,000)	5,000	(5,000)	5,000	
156	Other Current Assets Investments		100	(100)	100	(100)	100	(100)	
157	Plant, Property, & Equip Investments		0	0	0	0	15,000	0	
158	Other Noncurrent Assets Investments		100	(100)	100	(100)	100	(100)	
159	Other Owner Equity Changes		25,000	25,000	25,000	25,000	25,000	25,000	2
160	Net Cash Generated (Used)		685	2,606	12,780	3,637	(1,120)	3,805	1
161	Ending Cash Balance		$15,685	$18,291	$31,071	$34,708	$33,589	$37,394	$5
163									
164									

Addback of Depreciation

The Addback of Depreciation figures show the change in the accumulated depreciation balance for each forecasting period. Normally, this change stems from the period depreciation expense; it must be added back into the Net Income After Taxes figure because the depreciation expense uses no cash. The depreciation added back for each period is the value that you enter in the inputs area of the business planning starter workbook as the change in accumulated depreciation.

Accounts Payable Financing

The Accounts Payable Financing figures show the change in the Accounts Payable balance for the period. Increases in this balance result when the cost of sales expense paid during the period is lower than the expense incurred. Decreases in this balance result when the cost of sales expense paid is higher than the expense incurred. By recognizing the changes in this account balance, the model adjusts for differences between the Income Statement's accrual-based accounting of cost of sales expenses and the actual cash disbursements for cost of sales expenses.

The Accounts Payable Financing figure for each period is the difference between the Accounts Payable balance at the end of the previous period and the balance at the end of the current period. For example, the formula for the first period is

```
=C57-B57
```

The formula for the second period is

```
=D57-C57
```

and so on.

Accrued Expenses Financing

The Accrued Expenses Financing figures show the change in the accrued expenses balance for the period. Increases in this balance result when the operating expense paid during the period is lower than the expense incurred. Decreases in this balance result when the operating expense paid during the period is higher than the expense incurred. By recognizing the changes in this account balance, the model adjusts for differences between the Income Statement's accrual-based accounting expenses and the actual cash disbursements for operating expenses.

The Accrued Expenses Financing figure for each period is the difference between the Accrued Expenses balance at the end of the previous period and the balance at the end of the current period. For example, the formula for the first period is

```
=C58-B58
```

The formula for the second period is

```
=D58-C58
```

and so on.

Other Current Liabilities Financing

The Other Current Liabilities Financing figures show the change in the Other Current Liabilities balance for the period. This amount increases when, either directly or indirectly, cash is generated by borrowing. This amount decreases when, either directly or indirectly, cash is used to pay off short-term borrowing.

The Other Current Liabilities Financing figure for each period is the difference between the Other Current Liabilities balance at the end of the previous period and the balance at the end of the current period. For example, the formula for the first period is

```
=C59-B59
```

The formula for the second period is

```
=D59-C59
```

and so on.

Long-Term Liabilities Financing

The Long-Term Liabilities Financing figures show the changes in the long-term liabilities amount for the period. This balance increases when, either directly or indirectly, cash is generated by long-term borrowing. This amount decreases when, either directly or indirectly, cash is used to pay off long-term borrowing.

The Long-Term Liabilities Financing figure for each period is the difference between the Long-Term Liabilities balance at the end of the previous period and the balance at the end of the current period. For example, the formula for the first period is

```
=C62-B62
```

The formula for the second period is

```
=D62-C62
```

and so on.

Other Noncurrent Liabilities Financing

The Other Noncurrent Liabilities Financing figures show the changes in the Other Noncurrent Liabilities balance for the period. This amount increases when, either directly or indirectly, cash is generated by other long-term borrowing. This amount decreases when, either directly or indirectly, cash is used to pay off other long-term borrowing.

The Other Noncurrent Liabilities Financing figure for each period is the difference between the Other Noncurrent Liabilities balance at the end of the previous period and the balance at the end of the current period. For example, the formula for the first period is

```
=C63-B63
```

The formula for the second period is

```
=D63-C63
```

and so on.

Accounts Receivable Investments

The Accounts Receivable Investments figures show the change in the Accounts Receivable balance for each forecasting period. This amount increases when the sales revenue collected during the period is less than the revenue recorded. This amount decreases when the sales revenue collected during the period is more than recorded. By recognizing the changes in the account balance, the model adjusts for differences between the income statement's accrual-based accounting of sales revenues and the actual cash collections for sales.

The Accounts Receivable Investments figure for each period is the difference between the Accounts Receivable balance at the end of the previous period and the balance at the end of the current period. For example, the formula for the first period is

=C44-B44

The formula for the second period is

=D44-C44

and so on.

Inventory Investments

The Inventory Investments figures show the change in the inventory balance for each forecasting period. This amount increases when the inventory sold is less than the inventory acquired. This amount decreases when the inventory sold is more than the inventory acquired. By recognizing the changes in this account balance, the model recognizes the cash effects of changing inventory balances.

The Inventory Investments figure for each period is the difference between the Inventory balance at the end of the previous period and the balance at the end of the current period. For example, the formula for the first period is

=C45-B45

The formula for the second period is

=D45-C45

and so on.

Other Current Assets Investments

The Other Current Assets Investments figures show the changes in the Other Current Assets balance for the period. This amount increases when, either directly or indirectly, cash is used to acquire current assets. This amount decreases when, either directly or indirectly, cash is generated by converting current assets to cash.

The Other Current Assets Investments figure for each period is the difference between the Other Current Assets balance at the end of the previous period and the balance at the end of the current period. For example, the formula for the first period is

=C46-B46

The formula for the second period is

=D46-C46

and so on.

Plant, Property, & Equip Investments

The Plant, Property, & Equip Investments figures show the change in the Plant, Property, & Equipment balance for the period. This amount increases when, either directly or indirectly, cash is used to acquire plants, property, and equipment. This amount decreases when, either directly or indirectly, cash is generated by converting plants, property, and equipment to cash.

The Plant, Property, & Equip Investments figure for each period is the difference between the Plant, Property, & Equipment balance at the end of the previous period and the balance at the end of the current period. For example, the formula for the first period is

=C48-B48

The formula for the second period is

=D48-C48

and so on.

Other Noncurrent Assets Investments

The Other Noncurrent Assets Investments figures show the changes in the Other Noncurrent Assets balance for the period. This amount increases when, either directly or indirectly, cash is used to acquire other noncurrent assets. This amount decreases when, either directly or indirectly, cash is generated by converting other noncurrent assets to cash.

The Other Noncurrent Assets Investments figure for each period is the difference between the Other Noncurrent Assets balance at the end of the previous period and the balance at the end of the current period. For example, the formula for the first period is

```
=C51-B51
```

The formula for the second period is

```
=D51-C51
```

and so on.

Other Owner Equity Changes

The Other Owner Equity Changes figures show the cash flows stemming from any additional capital contributions made by the owners to the business or from dividends and other distributions made by the business to the owners. The Other Owner Equity Changes figure for each period is the value that you enter in the inputs area of the business planning starter workbook. The Other Owner Equity Changes figures are pulled into the Uses of Cash section as negative values because of the following: A positive change in the owner equity, such as an additional capital contribution (from a stock offering, for example), doesn't use cash but provides cash; and a negative change in the owner equity, such as a dividend, does use cash.

Net Cash Generated (Used)

The Net Cash Generated (Used) figures show the total cash flow for each period of the forecasting horizon, based on the listed sources and uses of cash. The amount for each period is the sources of cash for the period less the uses of cash for the period. For example, the formula for the first period is

```
=SUM(C145:C151)-SUM(C154:C159)
```

The formula for the second period is

```
=SUM(D145:D151)-SUM(D154:D159)
```

and so on.

Ending Cash Balance

The Ending Cash Balance figures show the forecasted cash and equivalents balance at the end of each period. The balance is the Beginning Cash Balance figure for the period plus the Net Cash Generated (Used) figure for the period. For example, the formula for the first period is

```
=C142+C160
```

The formula for the second period is

`=D142+D160`

and so on.

Financial Ratios Table

The Financial Ratios Table has 11 rows of calculated data, as shown in Figure 2-6. As in other schedules, the period identifier numbers the periods for which values are calculated. The first period is stored in cell C165 as the integer 1, and periods that follow are stored as the previous period plus 1. The other values in the Financial Ratios Table are calculated as described in the following paragraphs.

Current Ratio

The Current Ratio figures show the ratio of current assets to current liabilities. The current ratio provides one measure of a business's ability to meet its short-term obligations. The Current Ratio figure for each period is the Total Current Assets figure from the Balance Sheet schedule divided by the Total Current Liabilities figure. For example, the formula for the first period is

`=C47/C60`

The formula for the second period is

`=D47/D60`

and so on.

Quick Ratio

The Quick Ratio figures show the ratio of the sum of the cash and equivalents plus the accounts receivable to the current liabilities. The quick ratio provides a more stringent measure of a business's ability to meet its short-term financial obligations than other ratios. The Quick Ratio figure for each period is the sum of the Cash & Equivalents figure and the Accounts Receivable figure divided by the Total Current Liabilities figure. For example, the formula for the first period is

`=(C43+C44)/C60`

The formula for the second period is

`=(D43+D44)/D60`

and so on.

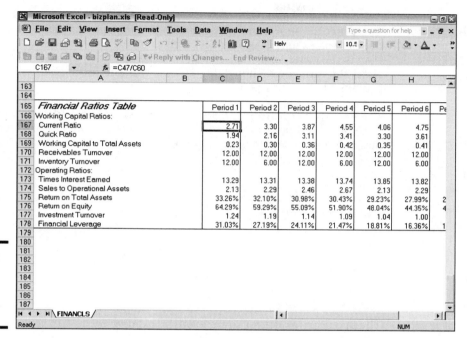

Figure 2-6:
The
Financial
Ratios
Table.

Working Capital to Total Assets

The Working Capital to Total Assets figures show the ratio of working capital (the current assets minus the current liabilities) to the total assets. The Working Capital to Total Assets ratio is another measure of a firm's ability to meet its financial obligations and gives an indication as to the distribution of a business's assets into liquid and nonliquid resources. The Working Capital to Total Assets ratio for each period is calculated by dividing the difference between the Current Assets and Current Liabilities figures by the Total Assets figure. For example, the formula for the first period is

```
=(C47-C60)/C52
```

The formula for the second period is

```
=(D47-D60)/D52
```

and so on.

Receivables Turnover

The Receivables Turnover figures show the ratio of sales to the accounts receivable balance. The Receivables Turnover ratio indicates the efficiency of sales collections. One problem with the measure as it's usually applied is that both credit and cash sales may be included in the ratio denominator. Two potential shortcomings exist with this approach. First, the presence of the cash sales may make the receivables collections appear more efficient than is the case. Also, mere changes in the mix of credit and cash sales may affect the ratio, even though the efficiency of the receivables collections process has not changed.

The Receivables Turnover figure for each period is calculated by dividing the Sales Revenue figure for the period by the Accounts Receivable balance outstanding at the end of the period. For example, the formula for the first period is

```
=C100/C44
```

The formula for the second period is

```
=D100/D44
```

and so on.

Inventory Turnover

The Inventory Turnover row shows the ratio of the cost of sales to the inventory balance. The Inventory Turnover ratio calculates how long inventory is held. It can indicate depleted or excessive inventory balances. The Inventory Turnover ratio for each period is calculated by dividing the Cost of Sales figure for the period by the inventory held at the end of the period. For example, the formula for the first period is

```
=-C101/C45
```

The formula for the second period is

```
=-D101/D45
```

and so on.

Times Interest Earned

The Times Interest Earned row shows the ratio of the sum of the net income after taxes plus the interest income to the interest expense. The ratio indicates the relative ease with which the business is paying its financing costs. The Times Interest Earned ratio for each period is calculated by dividing the sum of the Operating Income and Interest Income figures from the Income Statement schedule by the Interest Expense figure. For example, the formula for the first period is

```
=(C109+C111)/C112
```

The formula for the second period is

```
=(D109+D111)/D112
```

and so on.

Sales to Operational Assets

The Sales to Operational Assets row shows the ratio of sales revenue to net plant, property, and equipment. The ratio indicates the efficiency with which a business uses its operational assets to generate sales revenue. The Sales to Operational Assets ratio for each period is the Sales Revenue figure that you enter in the inputs area of the business planning starter workbook divided by the Net Plant, Property, & Equipment figure from the Balance Sheet schedule. For example, the formula for the first period is

```
=C100/C50
```

The formula for the second period is

```
=D100/D50
```

and so on.

Return on Total Assets

The Return on Total Assets row shows the ratio of the sum of the net income after taxes plus the interest expense to the total assets for each period. The ratio indicates the overall operating profitability of the business, expressed as a rate of return on the business assets. The formula for the first period is

```
=(C16+C112)/C52
```

The formula for the second period is

```
=(D116+D112)/D52
```

and so on.

Return on Equity

The Return on Equity row shows the ratio of the net income after taxes to the owner equity for each period. The ratio indicates the profitability of the business as an investment of the owners. The Return on Equity ratio for each period is the Net Income (Loss) After Taxes figure from the Income Statement schedule divided by the Owner Equity figure from the Balance Sheet schedule. For example, the formula for the first period is

```
=C116/C65
```

The formula for the second period is

```
=D116/D65
```

and so on.

Investment Turnover

The Investment Turnover row shows the ratio of the sales revenue to the total assets. The ratio, like the Sales to Operational Assets ratio, indicates the efficiency with which a business uses its assets (in this case, its total assets) to generate sales. The Investment Turnover ratio for each period is the Sales Revenue figure that you enter in the inputs area of the business planning starter workbook divided by the Total Assets figure from the Balance Sheet schedule. For example, the formula for the first period is

```
=C100/C52
```

The formula for the second period is

```
=D100/D52
```

and so on.

Financial Leverage

The Financial Leverage row shows the difference between the return on the owner equity and the return on the total assets. The ratio indicates the increase or decrease in an equity return as a result of borrowing. A positive value indicates an improvement in the return on owner equity by using financial leverage; a negative value indicates deterioration in the return on owner equity. The Financial Leverage figure for each period is the Return on Total Assets figure minus the Return on Equity figure. For example, the formula for the first period is

```
=C176-C175
```

The formula for the second period is

```
=D176-D175
```

and so on.

Customizing the Starter Workbook

You can use the business plan workbook for many business projections. However, you may want to change the starter workbook so that it more closely matches your requirements. For example, you can add text that describes your business and the forecasting horizon. You can also increase or decrease the number of periods; for example, you can increase the number of periods to 12 if your periods are months and you want to forecast an entire year.

Before you change anything on the starter workbook other than the forecasting inputs, unprotect the document. To do this, choose the Tools⇨Protection⇨Unprotect Workbook command.

Unless you turn off cell protection, input cells in the inputs area of the business planning starter workbook are the only cells into which you can enter data.

Changing the number of periods

You can easily increase or decrease the number of forecasting periods.

To increase the number of periods, remove the borders from the last column and then copy the current last column to the right as needed.

To decrease the number of periods, simply delete any unnecessary column from the right side of the schedule. (To delete a column, highlight the entire column by clicking at the top of that column, right-click to bring up Excel's context menu, and then choose Delete.) After you finish these steps, you can replace the borders on the right and reinstate cell protection as needed.

Ratio analysis on existing financial statements

If you want to perform financial ratio analysis on a set of existing financial statements, copy the contents of column C from the row in the inputs area of the business plan workbook that contains the sales revenue forecast (row 31) through the last row of the ratios table into column B. Then remove the columns for periods 1 through 10 (columns C through L) by following the steps described in the preceding section, "Changing the number of periods." Optionally, you can delete the Cash Flow Statement and add appropriate column headings as needed.

To use the modified starter workbook, enter the necessary Balance Sheet and Income Statement data in each of the unshaded cells in column B of the inputs area of the business planning starter workbook. (Typically, the as of date of the Balance Sheet and the ending date of the Income Statement period are the same.)

Calculating taxes for a current net loss before taxes

To calculate the income tax expense as 0 when there is a current period net loss before income taxes, you need to edit the formula in the cell that calculates the income tax expense (or savings) for the first period (cell C115) so that it takes the maximum of the calculated expense amount or 0 by using the MAX function:

```
=MAX(C37*C113,0)
```

After you've done this, you can copy the formula into the rest of the cells in the forecasting horizon that calculate the income tax expense (or savings). To do this, select the cell with the formula you want to copy, choose Edit⇨Copy, select the range of cells into which you want to copy the formula, and choose Edit⇨Paste.

Combining this workbook with other workbooks

A quick and perhaps obvious point: You may want to construct other workbooks to supply numbers to the business plan workbook discussed in this chapter. For example, you can construct an asset depreciation schedule that uses the straight-line depreciation convention for a $25,000 asset representing your entire plant, property, and equipment investment and then use this data in the business plan workbook.

If you start doing more Excel work and you're not all that comfortable with Excel, consider picking up a recent edition of *Excel For Dummies*, by Greg Harvey (Wiley Publishing, Inc.). It's a great tutorial on the basics. Also, if you want more information about constructing supporting financial workbooks (like an asset depreciation schedule, for example), you may want to consider another book I've written, the *MBA's Guide to Microsoft Excel 2002* (Redmond Technology Press). It describes how to do tasks like these.

If you want to use workbooks together in this manner, you should probably combine the workbooks into a single workbook. The easiest way to copy one of the workbooks is to copy the workbook's worksheet to a blank worksheet in the other workbook. (Each of the starter workbooks uses only a single worksheet to make this process both easy and possible.)

If you want to combine an asset depreciation workbook with the business planning workbook, for example, you can open both workbooks, copy the asset depreciation worksheet to the Clipboard, add a new sheet to the business planning starter workbook (by choosing the Insert menu's Worksheet command, for example), and then paste the asset depreciation worksheet into the newly added, blank worksheet in the business plan workbook.

Chapter 3: Writing a Business Plan

In This Chapter

✔ **Defining the business plan**

✔ **Understanding strategic plans**

✔ **Writing a white paper business plan**

✔ **Writing a new venture plan**

In Book VI, Chapter 2, I describe how to create a pro forma plan of business financial forecasts by using the `bizplan.xls` workbook, which can be downloaded from www.stephenlnelson.com/bizplan.xls. If you do create such a forecast, you'll probably also want to create a companion business plan. For this reason, you also need to know about writing a business plan. I don't go into tedious detail about how to do this; I just provide you with some useful information about business plans — and I give you some tips about how to more easily write a workable business plan.

What the Term Business Plan Means

In truth, the term *business plan* actually refers to three separate things:

✦ **A strategic plan:** A discussion or description of a firm's overall strategy

✦ **A new venture plan:** The fund-raising document that entrepreneurs use to promote a new venture to investors

✦ **A white paper plan:** The 50-page or even 100-page document that a business owner uses to describe in detail a new business opportunity, including its risks, its opportunities, and anything else that's germane

I talk a little bit about each of these plans — some more than others, in the following pages.

A Few Words about Strategic Plans

Unfortunately, I'm not really equipped to provide you with detailed information about how to go about constructing a strategic plan. Of course, neither are most of the other people who are willing to offer advice. That said, however, I can provide you with some useful starting points to think about when constructing your strategic plan.

First off, the way that you're using the word *strategy* is very likely wrong because you aren't talking about strategy at all. For my source on this perspective, I rely on what Michael E. Porter, a Harvard Business School professor, said in his strategy classic, *Competitive Strategies: Techniques for Analyzing Industries and Competitors* (published by Free Press).

The really interesting thing that Porter says in his book — and something that is worth repeating over and over again — is that, practically speaking, only three basic business strategies exist:

✦ A cost strategy

✦ A differentiated product or service strategy

✦ A focus on a niche strategy

Because understanding these strategies is critical to writing a good strategic plan (and to correctly using the term *strategy*), in the following section, I briefly discuss in my own words what Porter means by limiting possible strategies to only three. I demonstrate each of these strategies by using example firms in an industry that we're all pretty familiar with — retailing.

Cost strategies

Successful retailers rely on a cost strategy. Firms such as Wal-Mart and Costco excel at economically providing products to their customers. They pass along a lot of the benefits of this economy to their customers in the form of lower prices. Not all the cost savings get passed along to the consumers, however. A significant portion of the cost savings, achieved through incredibly efficient operations, are retained by the business and therefore become profits.

Such cost leadership or low-cost operation is one of the three basic strategies. And it is a strategy available to any business — and particularly those businesses that have achieved economies to scale.

The key thing to note about a low-cost strategy, however, is that the firm needs to retain some of the cost savings in order to earn a higher-profit level than its competitors. Thus, simply being a low-cost producer isn't enough. A firm needs to be a low-cost producer and still be able to price products and services at a level high enough that some of the cost savings are retained as profits.

Differentiated products and services strategies

The second basic strategy is product differentiation. Product differentiators often sell a very unusual product or service. The Nordstrom department store chain is a good example of this because it offers unsurpassed service, and often (although not always), it offers a great and high-quality selection of items. However, Nordstrom goods cost more. But consumers happily pay the extra amount. Why? Because they get so much more for their money.

A firm that relies on a differentiation strategy competes on the basis of the special features of their products or services. The key to making this strategy work is being able to charge your customers more for those special features than the special features cost you. Differentiation needs to produce increased revenues in excess of increased costs.

Focus strategies

The focus strategy is really a hybrid of the cost and differentiation strategies. This strategy states that in some ways, a firm is really good about managing costs, and in other ways, this firm is really good about differentiating products or services. A firm may choose to take this hybrid approach because it understands a particular audience or niche of customers or category of products; in other words, the firm can, through this focused approach, serve a particular market better than anybody else. This firm is going to be the best at serving a particular niche. Again, as is the case with other strategies, the focus strategy needs to be one that produces increased revenues that are greater than the increased cost of the strategy or cost savings (to the business) that are greater than the lower prices passed along to customers.

So, who's a focus strategy retailer? I would say that Target is. Target, in my opinion, focuses on suburban, middle-class customers by offering those consumers almost the perfect combination of cost savings and differentiated products.

Look, Ma: No Strategy

This all probably sounds like gobbledygook if you haven't been exposed to much strategic thinking before. However, the strategies and their strengths become very clear when you compare firms that have these strategies — cost leaders such as Wal-Mart and Costco, differentiation leaders such as Nordstrom, and focus leaders such as Target — to firms that lack a clear strategic focus.

Perhaps the best-known, current example of the retailer that, in my opinion, lacks a clear-cut strategy is K-Mart. This becomes very clear when you start comparing K-Mart with the leaders in each of the three strategies. Consider the following three problems that K-Mart is plagued by:

- ✦ **K-Mart can't compete on cost.** If you are really concerned about cost, you can go someplace like Wal-Mart or Costco and get a better price than you can get at K-Mart. So K-mart loses cost-conscious customers to Wal-Mart and Costco.

- ✦ **K-Mart can't compete with differentiation.** Sure, K-Mart offers Martha Stewart products, which sounds like differentiation, right? Or at least Martha Stewart products used to sound like differentiation. But face it: If you really want a highly differential product — the best in the class — you aren't going to go to K-Mart. Here, K-Mart loses out to stores like Nordstrom, which charge higher prices but offer a wider range of differentiated products. If you want the best in class, you won't end up at K-Mart — you'll go to a firm that's emphasizing and excelling at this strategy.

- ✦ **K-Mart doesn't serve a particular focus.** Does K-Mart serve a particular niche better than anybody else? I don't know. But at least in the category of suburban middle-class consumers, Target probably does a much better job. If you're really looking for clothes or household items appropriate in a middle-class suburb, is there any question that Target beats the pants off of K-Mart? I don't think so. Perhaps you can challenge this statement, but the first place to do so would be to compare the profitability of K-Mart to the profitability of Target. And as you can probably guess, K-Mart doesn't look too good in this comparison.

So now you can see how the word *strategy* is misunderstood and used incorrectly. *Strategy* isn't a way to refer to some idea you have; *strategy,* in business, refers to one of three approaches toward beating your competition: cost, differentiation (probably in terms of product excellence), or focus.

And here's the key: If you can do a strategy better than anybody else can, you win. If you try to do a little bit of this or a little bit of that, or if you ignore or can't bring yourself to pick a particular strategy, you're going to be continually beaten up by firms that have picked a strategy. You lose the cost game to the cost leaders. You lose the differentiation game to the differentiators. And you lose out at competing in particular niches to those firms that focus on those niches.

Two comments about tactics

I won't talk anymore about this strategy business, but I need to make a couple of comments about tactics. Most of the time when you hear people talk about strategy, they're not really talking about strategy; they're usually talking about tactics.

Tactics refers to choices that firms make in an attempt to successfully execute strategy. The irony is that the people who misuse the word *strategy* (by referring to tactics as strategy) often don't really have a strategy. This is my first comment.

My second comment is that tactics, predictably, don't work and don't make sense except as support for a particular strategy. For example, to pursue a strategy of cost leadership, all your tactics need to support that strategy. You undermine your success in executing that strategy if some tactics support a cost strategy, some tactics support a differentiation strategy, and some tactics support a focus strategy. This makes sense, right? In this situation, you become a jack-of-all-trades but a master of none.

Six final strategy pointers

Before you move on to the next topic, here are some key points that you should be sure to understand:

✦ A firm can only have one of three business strategies:

- Cost-based strategy

- Differentiation-based strategy

- Focus-based strategy

✦ The only appropriate tactics are those that support one of these strategies.

✦ The first step — the step that you need to take before you can select appropriate tactics — is picking a strategy. From the strategy decision, all other tactical decisions follow.

✦ A strategic plan, therefore, needs to have a clearly defined strategy. Then it needs to identify, or enumerate, the tactics that support the strategy. It's really as simple as that.

✦ The hard part of writing a strategic plan is to discipline yourself (or the firm) to pick a strategy and then stick with it. Few firms want to be disciplined to stick with a hard-core strategy of cost, product differentiation, or focus. It's all too easy to slip-slide your way into a situation where you are trying to be a little of this or a little of that. Picking a particular strategy means that you forgo certain kinds of opportunities and that you say no to some customers and certain kinds of products.

✦ It's a difficult book to read, and much of the material is a couple of decades old, but Michael Porter's book on competitive strategy is worthwhile reading for any business owner. It won't be much fun, but I feel very confident that the 15 or 20 hours necessary for reading the book is an enormously useful investment of your time.

Writing a White Paper Business Plan

People often write a white paper business plan when they know that they need a strategic plan but don't really want to make the hard decisions necessary for a strategic plan. The person in this conundrum writes a lengthy white paper business plan to hopefully camouflage the absent strategic plan.

I guess it's obvious from the preceding paragraph, but you really should write a strategic plan before you write a white paper business plan. A strategic plan, by the way, doesn't need to be more than a page or two in length. In fact, the hard part of a strategic plan isn't in the writing; it's in the sacrifice — the giving up of certain categories of opportunities, certain markets, and certain tactical approaches that may be comfortable or familiar. Obviously, you can't write a good white paper business plan — or at least one that's based on a sound strategy — until you first have a strategic plan in place.

Perhaps the most important thing to know if you do need to write a white paper business plan is this: This process is well documented in a bunch of other places. If you have QuickBooks Premier 2005, you can choose the Company⇨Planning & Budgeting⇨Use Business Plan Tool command to start a wizard that steps you through the process of writing a white paper business plan. (I'm not going to show this wizard here because you can choose the command to see the wizard's dialog boxes.)

You can also get detailed information on writing a business plan in both English and Spanish from the United States Federal Government Small Business Administration's Web site at `http://www.sba.gov/starting_ business/planning/basic.html`. Figure 3-1 shows the Startup Basics page of the Small Business Administration's Web site. Figure 3-2 shows the first page of information that the Small Business Administration's Web site provides about the process of writing a business plan.

Figure 3-1: The Startup Basics page of the Small Business Administration's Web site provides links to business planning resources.

The Small Business Administration's Web site changes, predictably, but you should be able to hunt down its links to relevant business planning topics, such as "business plan basics," "writing the plan," and "using the plan."

I should also point out that Microsoft PowerPoint (which many computer users own because PowerPoint is a component in just about every version of Microsoft Office) supplies a detailed outline for creating a white paper business plan. Figure 3-3 shows the AutoContent Wizard dialog box, which you use to indicate how you want to create a business plan presentation. Figure 3-4 shows, in the form of a Word document, what PowerPoint suggests for white paper business plans. This is a very good outline, but don't be misled into thinking that something that Microsoft has provided for free to PowerPoint users is in some way inferior to what real businesses need to use. Microsoft has done an excellent job in showing what information belongs in a white paper business plan.

Most white paper business plans and new venture business plans (which I define in the next section) require a business *pro forma financial forecast*. Book VI, Chapter 2 describes how to do this. Typically, in a hard-copy printed business plan, you would include such a forecast as an appendix.

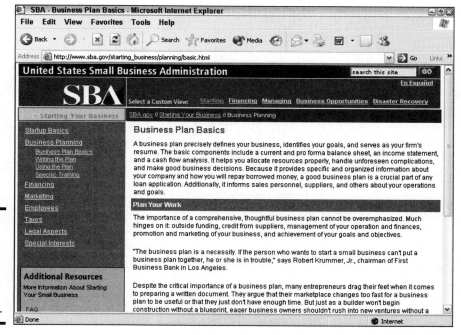

Figure 3-2:
The first page of basic business planning information.

After you create a good solid strategy and at least a rough white paper business plan, you may also want to create a new venture plan. The next section describes how to do this.

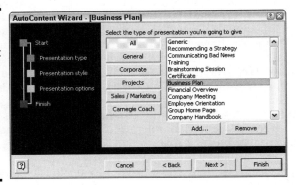

Figure 3-3:
The AutoContent Wizard dialog box lets you create a business plan presentation.

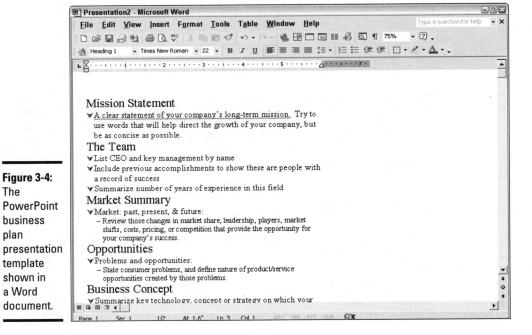

Figure 3-4:
The PowerPoint business plan presentation template shown in a Word document.

Writing a New Venture Plan

To write a new venture plan, you take a different approach than you do for writing a white paper plan. New venture plans answer five basic questions, which provide prospective investors with the necessary information to determine whether they should further investigate your venture as a possible investment. The next sections detail these five questions.

**Book VI
Chapter 3**

Writing a Business Plan

Is the new venture's product or service feasible?

In some cases, this question is unnecessary to ask. However, it's important to consider in any case where a firm may invest in a new, unproven idea. This situation is most clearly illustrated in the case of a firm that plans to build and then market some newfangled technology. For example, if you're thinking of starting a firm that will produce a better mousetrap, a key question to ask is whether you really can build a better mousetrap. You can answer this question in a couple of ways, practically speaking. Obviously, the best way to answer this question about feasibility is to first build the better mousetrap. Having built the better mousetrap, you'll find it easy to prove to prospective investors that, yes, the product is feasible. You can set your mousetrap on the desk and demonstrate how it works. Perhaps on some . . . no, no, let's not go there.

If a product hasn't already been built or a service hasn't already been proven to be deliverable, the next best approach — and the one commonly used by technology startups — is to assemble a team of people who've built similar products in the past. The logic of this approach is that if you have a team that has built similar technologies in the past, investors can probably rely on this team's track record of success. For example, if a team of talented engineers has built new and improved mousetraps, it's very easy for investors to believe prudently that this team may be able to build a better mousetrap in the future. The team understands the technology. They understand the problem. They're experienced in creating new solutions to address the problem. You see how easy it is to buy into the possibility.

Does the market want the product or service?

Assuming that you do have a firm with a practical, feasible product or service, you need to ask another big question right up front: Do people really, truly want the product or service? Is there public demand for the firm's offering? This business about demand seems kind of tricky to ascertain. Ideally, a new venture proves that demand exists by already having customers buying the product. If a new venture hasn't yet finished the product or service, such hard-and-fast proof of demand is impossible to come by. In this case, you have another option: You can prove market demand by running independent market research studies to say, "Yes, we've run several focus groups, and people say they'll buy a better mousetrap."

Sometimes, you can also prove market demand by showing that consumers or businesses already purchase a similar product or service and would, logically, purchase a clearly improved version of the product or service. For example, in the case of the better mousetrap, people are already buying a lot of mousetraps. So if you truly did build better mousetraps, you could pretty much prove market demand by demonstrating the new product's superiority.

However, let me encourage you to take a big bite of the reality sandwich if you're thinking this way. You need to be very careful about this issue of market demand because it's all too easy for entrepreneurs and inventors who are excited about some new technology, or some new product or service, to assume that consumers really will want the new thing that is being built or offered. Consumers are notoriously fickle. What seems like a wonderful innovation to the entrepreneur or inventor often isn't so wonderful in the eyes of the consumer.

Can the product or service be profitably sold?

Okay, so the first two questions ask whether a product or service is feasible and whether people want the product. Is that enough? No, actually it isn't. The third, critically important question is whether the product that you're selling can profitably be sold. You need to run rough numbers to prove that products or services revenue less the cost of goods sold produces a gross margin that is adequate not just to pay the operating expenses of the firm but to retain something for profit. This proof that the firm can profitably sell its product or service is really achieved by the business pro forma financial forecast (as described in Book VI, Chapter 2). This forecast proves that the firm can be profitable by selling the product or service.

I won't say a lot more about this profitability issue, but basically, all the accounting stuff discussed throughout this book comes into play here. In order to do a decent new venture plan, you need to understand enough accounting in order to produce a set of forward-looking financial statements that persuasively argues a profitable venture.

Is the return on the venture adequate for prospective investors?

Curiously, simply proving that a firm's venture will be profitable often isn't enough. A firm also needs to deliver profits at least equal to and ideally in excess of the return on investment that the investors desire. In the case of a new venture, investors have pretty firm expectations of what a risky investment should deliver. *Angel investors* commonly require rates of return in the neighborhood of 20 to 25 percent annually. Small business entrepreneurs and business owners, similarly, often require similar rates of return.

Institutional and professional venture capital investors (the sort of people that you read about in *The Wall Street Journal* and in *Inc* magazine) often require annual rates of return of 45 percent to 55 percent — or even 65 percent annually.

If you think about what all this means, you can quickly see that even a pretty darn good business that delivers the 30 to 35 percent annual rate of return — and that's really good if you think about it — won't be enough for some investors. An institutional venture capital investor who needs, for example, a 50 percent annual return on his investment, isn't going to look seriously at anything that produces only a meager 30 percent annual return.

Essentially, in a new venture plan, you need to provide information that lets the prospective investor figure out the rate of return. The prospective investor can then compare this return with his or her requirements.

It's not a bad idea to look at the returns that you are implicitly suggesting via your new venture plan. Make sure that you are not trying to sell a 25 percent annual return investment to investors who require a 50 percent annual return. Similarly, you may not need to offer investors who will be happy with a 25 percent annual return a deal that pays a 50 percent annual return. Book V, Chapter 2 offers a discussion of economic value-added analysis that details how you can compare the return delivered by a firm to investors with the return on investment that those investors expect.

Can existing management run the business?

Even if you have a venture based on a feasible product or technology, even if you have customers who are hysterically excited to purchase your product, even if you have a product or service that will bring in a massive profit, and even if your investors will be able to earn a wonderful return on their investment, that's still not enough. There is still one other critical question that a new venture plan needs to ask and answer.

Any new venture plan needs to sell prospective investors on the idea that the existing management team — which includes the founder or president and his or her lieutenants or vice presidents — can successfully operate the business. In other words, even a great business opportunity isn't one that should be invested in unless a good management team is in place (or almost in place), ready to execute the business plan.

Here are a couple of ways that you can prove that the management team isn't going to be a problem:

+ **Have a management team in place that has already successfully executed a venture similar to the new venture.** If you're trying to sell prospective investors on the idea that the management team can create a $25,000,000 business selling a better mousetrap, your task will be much easier if the same management team at some point in the past created a $25,000,000 business selling a better mousetrap.

✦ **Show that the management team — or at least most of its members — are successful people.** A team of people who have succeeded at big things in the past suggests to investors that the management team knows how to win. I'm not talking about an Eagle Scout designation; I'm thinking more on the line of an M.B.A. from Stanford. If some members of your team have created a new cool technology or successfully managed an important division in another business, in a nutshell, you're saying to prospective investors, "Hey, this management team will bring home a win for us."

Some final thoughts

Okay, I have a handful of final comments to make about new venture business planning:

✦ **Although new venture business plans really serve a different purpose than white paper business plans, you use the same sort of general outline for both.** In other words, even though a new venture business plan has as its primary purpose answering the five questions discussed in the previous section, you follow an outline like the one provided by Microsoft PowerPoint (refer to Figure 3-4).

✦ **Although you definitely want to make sure that your new venture business plan answers the five questions, keep in mind the following caveats:**

   • *Don't lay it on too thick.* You want to write something that looks like a white paper business plan but edit it well in order to both minimize the amount of super-detailed information and to clearly and boldly answer the five questions that the new venture investor needs to ask and answer.

   • *Remember that a new venture investor is typically not going to write you a check based on what he or she sees in a new venture business plan.* What you put into a new venture business plan is simply information that will tickle the new venture investor's fancy. The information should be just enough to make him or her think, "This sounds pretty cool. I'll take a closer look."

   • *It's very unlikely that any entrepreneur or business owner can honestly answer all five questions with a "Yes."* Some people will say that you need to offer a dynamite, ironclad, super deal that nobody could refuse. However, in my opinion, any sophisticated new venture investor who expects you to be able to answer with a 100-percent-guaranteed "Yes" to every question is probably pretty naive. Anybody who has half a clue knows that risk exists in any business venture. Even if you have a great technology that's already built, customers clamoring with orders in the reception area of your office, and a great management team in place — even if *everything* seems perfect — stuff still goes wrong.

Having said that, however, it's important to note that answering any of the five questions with a definite "No" means that the new venture won't work — or at least it won't work for you as the business owner or as the manager. Each of the five questions is a link in the chain of success. Break any link — regardless of which one — and the chain breaks.

✦ **All business advisors, entrepreneurs, and business owners need to admit that the hysteria and bubble thinking of the 1990s was not at all representative of the way business planning is supposed to work.** Many dot-com ventures were funded with enormous amounts of money even though the entrepreneurs and new venture investors could only answer a single question — if that — with a "Yes" answer. But that was a different time (a crazy time), and the rules during those few turbulent years were different. Prudently starting any new venture requires answering "Yes" to most of the five questions discussed here. And in the end, the bursting of the dot-com bubble only goes to prove that.

Book VII

Care and Maintenance

The 5th Wave   By Rich Tennant

"So, someone's using your credit card info to buy stylish clothes, opera tickets and exercise equipment. In what way would this qualify as 'identity theft'?"

Contents at a Glance

Chapter 1: Setting Up a Peer-to-Peer Network

In This Chapter

✔ Figuring out the business benefits of a network

✔ Finding out about a peer-to-peer network

✔ Getting a handle on hardware requirements

✔ Connecting your network hardware

✔ Configuring your network

✔ Installing and using a networked printer

✔ Sharing resources on the network

The subject of setting up a peer-to-peer network may seem off-point. Isn't this book supposed to be about QuickBooks? Well, my friend, you're right on both accounts. Networking *is* a little off-point, and this book is about QuickBooks.

However, I want to provide you with this quick overview of setting up your network anyway. For one thing, in many small business settings, you'll find it extremely useful to set up a network. (A *network* is simply a group of computers that are connected and that can communicate and share resources.) For another thing, if you want to let more than one person work with the QuickBooks data file, you can do so, simply by setting up a network and then installing QuickBooks on each computer.

Therefore, in this chapter, I explain how to set up a small Windows XP network — just the kind that you may want to use in a business with a handful of computer users working in the office. In Book VII, Chapter 2, I explain how to administer a QuickBooks accounting system — including the stuff that you need to do in order to have several different people working on different computers on a network and with the same QuickBooks data.

Can I share an opinion? These days, a computer network in a business is not something nice to have; it's a *necessity* if you have more than one computer. A network will save you time and, therefore, save you money. No kidding.

Can Your Business Benefit from a Network?

Should you set up your own network? How do you know if a network can benefit your business? To consider this question, take a look at some of the things that even a small network makes possible:

- ✦ You can open files, folders, and applications on one computer while you're sitting at another computer.
- ✦ You can share a single printer among several computers.
- ✦ You can share an Internet connection.
- ✦ You can back up important files and folders to another computer.
- ✦ You can communicate with other users on the network via e-mail and conferencing applications.

Not to beat a dead horse, but truly, after you set up your network, you'll wonder how you ever got along without it.

What Is a Peer-to-Peer Network?

Networks are of two basic types: client/server and peer-to-peer. In a client/server network, one (or more) computer stores resources and supplies, or *serves,* those resources to the other computers. All the other computers are connected to this central computer(s), which manages applications, files, printers, and so on. In general, big monster corporate networks are client/server networks and are managed by a system administrator.

In a *peer-to-peer* network, all computers are equals. Each computer has its own hard drive and can see and talk to all the other computers on the network. In addition, each computer can share its resources, such as a CD-ROM drive, a printer, files, folders, applications, and so on. A peer-to-peer network is ideal if you have no more than, say, ten people in the office working on a computer. On a peer-to-peer network, all users decide which of their files and folders they want to share and with whom.

You can connect the computers in a peer-to-peer network in several ways:

- ✦ Use the electrical or telephone wiring already installed in your office
- ✦ Install a wireless system
- ✦ Connect each computer on the network to a central hub

Connecting to a central hub is the easiest configuration, and it's also inexpensive. In this chapter, therefore, I walk you through the process of connecting a network of computers to a central hub. The process consists of three basic steps:

✦ Connecting all of the necessary hardware

✦ Configuring your host computer

✦ Configuring all of the other computers on your network

Throughout this chapter, I show you how.

 Just for the sake of thoroughness, let me also say that you can create a simple wireless peer-to-peer network, too. With a wireless network, you don't cable your computers together using wires and a central hub. Instead, the computers on the network communicate through a "hub" (actually called a wireless router, but who cares) using radio waves. In fact, in a wireless network, no kidding, little radio antennas often stick out the back of computers and the hub! A wireless network is very convenient in a peer-to-peer setting because you don't have to worry about tripping over network cabling. However, a wireless network requires a bit more fiddling in order to get your network secure. (If you're not careful, anyone else with one of those little antennas on the back of their computer can sneak into your network.) For this reason, I'm not going to discuss the wireless option here. If you're interested in going wireless, find a local networking consultant and ask her to make your network wireless.

Hardware Requirements

You need three essential components to set up your wired network:

✦ The hub or a router

✦ Some cable

✦ A network interface card (NIC) in each computer

A *hub* is the central device that connects all the computers on the network, and it is slightly smaller than the size of this book. The hub itself doesn't require any software or configuration; it is simply the device that allows all the computers to communicate. The number of connections on the hub — or the number of places to which you can connect — determines the number of computers that can be on the network. Be sure to buy a hub that has enough connections for the number of computers that you want to connect.

Cables are the physical connection between the computers on the network and the hub. The cable, or more specifically Ethernet cable, attaches to the network hardware with RJ-45 jacks, which are snap connectors that look like a wider version of the plastic jacks used by your landline phone system. Cables are commonly available in lengths of 10, 15, 20, 25, and 50 feet.

A NIC goes into each computer on the network and connects to one of the slots on the computer's motherboard. (The *motherboard* is the main printed circuit board in a computer.) Most computers on the market today come with NICs already installed, but if you are networking older computers, you will probably need to buy NICs.

If you have older computers that you want to network, be sure to check them for two things before you purchase any NICs. First, verify that the motherboard has an empty slot, and second, verify that the slots are of the Peripheral Component Interconnect (PCI) type. Some older computers use Industry Standard Architecture (ISA) slots, and it's just about impossible to find an ISA NIC these days.

You can shop for these items at your local electronics store or on the Internet. Another option is to buy a starter kit that contains everything that you need to connect a couple of computers — NICs, cable, and a hub — from companies such as Intel (www.intel.com), Linksys (www.linksys.com/products), 3Com (www.3com.com), or Netgear (www.netgear.com/products). If you need to connect more than two computers, however, you'll probably save money if you buy the parts separately rather than buying multiple kits.

Before you buy your NICs and hub, be sure that the packaging explicitly states that the hardware has been certified by Microsoft as being suitable for Windows XP. If you are in doubt, check Microsoft's Hardware Compatibility List at www.microsoft.com/hcl.

Connecting Your Network Hardware

Setting up your network hardware is easy. Get yourself the appropriate screwdriver, and follow these steps:

1. **Turn off all computers and peripherals and unplug them.**

2. **For each computer, open the case (this is likely to be the most difficult step), remove the slot cover from a free expansion slot, and insert the NIC in the empty slot, according to the manufacturer's instructions.**

   Would it be terribly redundant if I repeated that last bit of information? You need to follow the manufacturer's instructions. Seriously. Also, be sure that the card bracket is sitting snugly in the case and secure it with the screw that originally held the slot cover.

3. Replace the case.

4. Find a good central location for the hub and plug the power adapter into a power socket.

A central location helps to keep cable lengths short, and most of the time, you won't need access to the hub unless you experience a problem with the network. Most hubs have small LEDs on the front of the case that indicate network activity, and it can be comforting to glance across at them to see that the network is still running.

5. Connect one end of the cable to the NIC, and connect the other end of the cable to the hub, starting with the first connection.

Do this for each computer on the network. Both ends of the cable are identical, so it doesn't matter which end you connect to the computer or the hub.

6. Turn on the hub and all connected computers.

You'll see a light or LED on the hub for each connected computer.

That's it. Now you're ready to configure your network software.

Honestly, just between you, me, and the piano, connecting the hardware isn't that tough, is it? I'm with you. Networking computer hardware just ain't that tough anymore.

Configuring Your Host Computer

After you connect all of your hardware, you need to give Windows XP some information about the network that you've just set up. Before you start, though, you need to decide which of the computers on your network will host Internet Connection Sharing (ICS). With ICS turned on, all the computers on the network can access the Internet even though they don't have direct connections. The host computer must meet the following requirements:

✦ Run Windows XP

✦ Be turned on at all times so that the other computers on the network can access the Internet

If one of your networked computers has an existing DSL hookup or a cable modem, that computer is an excellent choice to be the ICS host.

o configure your network, be sure that you're logged on as Computer
Administrator and then, at the computer that will host ICS, follow these
steps:

1. **Choose Start➪All Programs➪Accessories➪Communications➪
   Network Setup Wizard to start the Network Setup Wizard.**

   The Welcome screen appears.

2. **Click Next.**

3. **Click CheckList for Creating a Network to display a help page summa-
   rizing the steps in network planning that I discuss earlier in this chapter, or click Next.**

   The Select a Connection Method screen appears (see Figure 1-1).

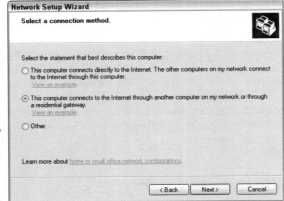

Figure 1-1:
Selecting an
Internet
connection.

4. **Select This Computer Connects Directly to the Internet, and then click
   Next.**

   The Select Your Internet Connection screen appears.

5. **Select the connection that you want to use when you connect to the
   Internet (modem, local area connection, and so on) and click Next.**

   The dialog box lists connections that are already set up, so what you see
   here will make sense to you when you do this.

6. **In the Give this Computer a Description and Name screen (see
   Figure 1-2), enter a short text description for the computer in the
   Computer Description field and then click Next.**

The Name Your Network screen appears.

(The Computer Name box holds the name that you gave to this computer when you installed Windows XP. It's best to retain this name.)

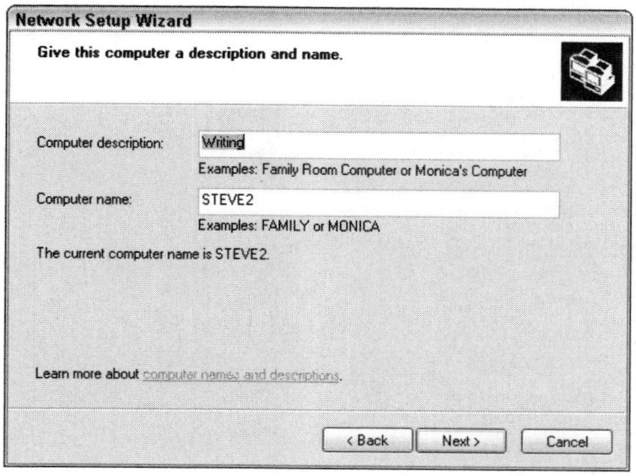

Network Setup Wizard

Give this computer a description and name.

Computer description: Writing

Examples: Family Room Computer or Monica's Computer

Computer name: STEVE2

Examples: FAMILY or MONICA

The current computer name is STEVE2.

Learn more about computer names and descriptions.

< Back   Next >   Cancel

Figure 1-2: Providing a description.

7. **Enter a Workgroup name, and then click Next.**

The Ready to Apply Network Settings screen appears, as shown in Fig-ure 1-3.

8. **Review the selections that you have made and click Next if those settings are correct.**

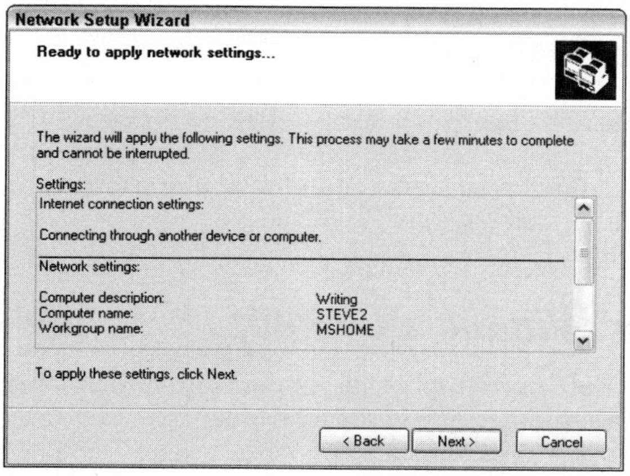

Network Setup Wizard

Ready to apply network settings...

The wizard will apply the following settings. This process may take a few minutes to complete and cannot be interrupted.

Settings:

Internet connection settings:

Connecting through another device or computer.

Network settings:

Computer description: Writing
Computer name: STEVE2
Workgroup name: MSHOME

To apply these settings, click Next.

< Back   Next >   Cancel

Figure 1-3: The Ready to Apply Network Settings screen.

The wizard will apply these settings when you click Next. After the process starts, don't interrupt it. You'll see a progress indicator.

If you need to change any settings, click Back to return to the screen that you want to change. After the wizard has done its work, the You're Almost Done Screen appears (see Figure 1-4).

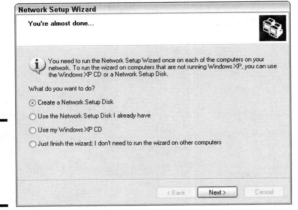

Figure 1-4:
The You're Almost Done screen.

9. **(Optional) In the You're Almost Done screen (see Figure 1-4), you can create a Network Setup Disk with which to configure the other computers on your network.**

If the other computers that you are networking are running a version of Windows earlier than XP, you'll need the setup disk. If the other computers are running Windows XP, you won't need the setup disk. If you choose the Create a Network Setup Disk option, follow the instructions on the screen and click Next.

10. **Close the Network Setup Wizard by clicking Finish.**

After you've configured your host computer, you're ready to configure the rest of the computers on your network.

Configuring Other Windows Computers on the Network

You can use the Network Setup Wizard to configure other computers on the network if they are running any of the following:

✦ Windows XP

✦ Windows 98

♦ Windows 98 Second Edition

♦ Windows 2000

♦ Windows Millennium Edition

On other computers running Windows XP, configure the network connection by running the Network Setup Wizard as directed in the previous section, "Configuring Your Host Computer." On computers running the other versions of Windows listed here, you also use the Network Setup Wizard, but you have to first insert the Network Setup Disk. Follow these steps:

1. **Insert the Network Setup Disk in the floppy drive.**

2. **Open Windows Explorer to the floppy drive, and double-click the Netsetup (or Netsetup.exe) file.**

   This launches the Network Setup Wizard.

3. **In the first screen of the wizard, click Yes when asked if you want to install network support files on your system.**

4. **At the next screen, remove the floppy disk and click OK.**

5. **The next screen asks if you want to restart your computer. Click Yes.**

6. **After the restart, the wizard displays the Welcome to the Network Setup Wizard screen. Follow the instructions in the wizard.**

Installing and Using a Networked Printer

One of the most common reasons for setting up a network is to share a printer. You can physically connect a printer to your network in a couple of ways:

♦ If your printer doesn't have a NIC in it, connect the printer to one of the computers on the network and turn the printer on. (This is more common in a small network and is the kind of printer described in this section.)

♦ If your printer has a NIC in it, you can connect it directly by running a cable to the network hub. (This configuration is found more commonly in a corporate environment. This section won't cover this kind of setup.)

Before you can set up a shared printer, you must install it as a local printer. If you've already installed a local printer, skip to the section "Sharing Resources on the Network." If you haven't set up a local printer, connect the printer to the computer, turn it on, log on to that computer as Computer Administrator, and then follow these steps:

1. Choose Start⇨Control Panel⇨Printers and Other Hardware⇨ Printers and Faxes to open the Printers and Faxes folder.

2. Click the Add a Printer button to start the Add Printer Wizard.

   The Welcome screen appears.

3. Click Next.

4. In the next Add Printer Wizard screen, select Local Printer Attached to This Computer and click Next.

5. In the next Add Printer Wizard screen that appears, enter a name for the printer, and click Next.

6. Click Yes if you want this printer set as the default.

7. Click Next, review your choices, and then click Finish to close the wizard.

Now you are ready to share this printer with other users on the network. Follow these steps:

1. In the Printers and Faxes folder (accessed by choosing Start⇨Control Panel⇨Printers and Other Hardware⇨Printers and Faxes), right-click the icon for your printer, and choose Sharing from the shortcut menu.

   This opens the Properties dialog box at the Sharing tab for that printer.

   If you will be sharing a printer with users who are running a different version of Windows, click the Additional Drivers button on the Sharing tab to open the Additional Drivers dialog box. Select the check boxes for all the versions of Windows that will be sharing this printer, and then click OK.

2. Accept the name that is generated in the Share Name field, or enter a new name, and then click OK.

   Click the General tab if you want to enter a description of this printer in the Comment field. Sometimes you use this field to describe the printer's location. Click Apply.

   You now see a hand under the icon for this printer in the Printer and Faxes folder, indicating that this printer is shared.

One final task remains, and that is to run the Add Printer Wizard on the other computers on the network so that each can access the shared printer. In the Local or Network Printer screen, select the A Network Printer or A Printer Attached to Another Computer radio button, click Next, and then follow the remainder of the wizard's instructions.

Sharing Resources on the Network

Before users on your network can share resources — drives, files, folders, applications, and so on — the resources must be enabled for sharing. Each user at each workstation must specifically share the resources on that computer. To mark resources as shared, follow these steps:

1. **Right-click the Start button, and then click Explore to open Explorer.**

2. **Navigate to the resource that you want to share, right-click it, and choose Sharing from the shortcut menu to open a Properties dialog box at the Sharing tab (see Figure 1-5).**

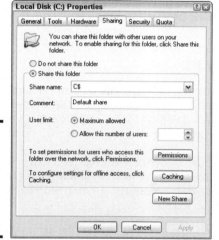

Figure 1-5:
The Local Disk Properties dialog box at the Sharing tab.

3. **Select the Share This Folder radio button.**

   In the Share Name box, accept the name that Windows suggests or enter another name.

   This name must be unique on this computer, and it is the name that others on the network will see when they browse this computer.

4. **Enter a comment by briefly describing the share in the Comment box.**

   Users will also use this information when browsing the network.

5. **In the User Limit area, select either the Maximum Allowed or Allow This Number of Users radio button to specify the maximum number of simultaneous users.**

Windows allows a maximum of ten users. When the eleventh user tries to log on, she will see this message: "No more connections can be made to this remote computer at this time because there are already as many connections as the computer allows."

6. **To specify the kind of access that users have to this resource, click the Permissions button to open the Permissions dialog box for this resource. To set a permission, select its check box. After you're finished, click OK.**

For an explanation of the types of permissions, see the Help and Support Center. Note that you can set permissions for a resource only if you are using the NTFS file system, which is Windows' high security file system. Note that you can check whether your disk uses NTFS by clicking on the General tab and looking at the description.

7. **Close the Properties dialog box by clicking OK.**

Accessing Shared Resources

To access a shared resource on the network, open Explorer, and click the plus sign next to My Network Places to display a list of all the shared computers, hard drives, and folders. Simply navigate to the resource that you want to access and open it as you would any resource on your own computer.

If you frequently use a particular network resource, you can access it quickly by mapping a network drive to it. That resource then appears in Explorer as though it were a drive on your own computer. To map a drive, follow these steps:

1. **Click the Start button, right-click My Network Places, and choose Map Network Drive from the shortcut menu to open the Map Network Drive dialog box.**

2. **In the Drive drop-down list box, click the down arrow, and select an unused letter.**

The default is the next drive in sequence.

3. **Tell Windows whether you want to map to this drive whenever you log on.**

4. **Windows automatically remaps drives for you each time you log on. If you don't want to reconnect to this drive the next time you log on, deselect the Reconnect at Logon check box.**

5. **In the Folder drop-down list, enter the path to the share, or click Browse to locate it.**

6. **Click Finish.**

Now, the mapped drive appears just like any other drive in Explorer.

You can use the Windows Troubleshooters to track down problems with your network. Click the Start button, and open Help and Support. Click Fixing a Problem, and then choose Networking Problems. You'll find the usual question-and-answer screens.

Book VII
Chapter 1

Setting Up a Peer-
to-Peer Network

Chapter 2: Administering QuickBooks

In This Chapter

✓ **Keeping your data confidential**

✓ **Using QuickBooks in a multi-user environment**

✓ **Closing QuickBooks**

✓ **Using QuickBooks for simultaneous multi-user access**

✓ **Maintaining good accounting controls**

*Q*uickBooks does something that is critically important to the success of your business: It collects and supplies financial information. For this reason, you want to have a firm understanding of how you can protect both the data that QuickBooks collects and stores and the assets that QuickBooks tracks. This chapter describes all this.

Keeping Your Data Confidential

Accounting data is often confidential information. Your QuickBooks data shows how much money you have in the bank, what you owe creditors, and how much (or how little!) profit that your firm produces. Because this information is private, your first concern in administering a QuickBooks accounting system is to keep your data confidential.

You have two complementary methods for keeping your QuickBooks data confidential. The first method for maintaining confidentiality relies on the security features built into Microsoft Windows. The other method relies on QuickBooks security features.

Using Windows security

You can use the security provided by Microsoft Windows 2000 or Microsoft Windows XP to restrict access to a file — either a program file or a data file — to specific users. This means that you can use Windows-level security to say who can and can't use the QuickBooks program or access the QuickBooks data file.

now Windows-level security works in this book. If you are
ing Windows-level security, you (or someone in your office)
se that tool to prevent unauthorized access to (or the use of)
and data files. To use Windows-level security for QuickBooks,
ply apply your existing general knowledge to the QuickBooks
e or the QuickBooks data file.

n't already using the Windows-level security, you don't need to go
ouble of learning Windows' complicated security system. You can
: simpler QuickBooks security.

Using QuickBooks security

You can protect the confidentiality of your QuickBooks data by assigning a
password to a QuickBooks company data file. You can do this during the
QuickBooks setup process. You can also set up a password by choosing the
Company menu's Change Your Password command. When you choose this
command, QuickBooks displays the Change Password dialog box, which (I'm
not kidding) QuickBooks doesn't let people take pictures of for security reasons. To set up a password, you simply enter the same password into both
the New Password text box and the Confirm New Password text box. Note
that your password is associated with the username Admin (which stands
for administrator). Leave the Enter Old Password box empty. If you haven't
yet set up a password, you don't have an old password.

Obviously, you want to set your password so that no one (not even a computer) can possibly guess it. This means that your password shouldn't be a
word in a dictionary. Your password also shouldn't be a number. And your
password *especially* shouldn't be a word, phrase, or name that some co-
worker can easily figure out. The best passwords (from a security point of
view) are nonsensical combinations of letters and numbers, such as *f34t5s* or
s3df43x2.

After you set your password, you should periodically change it. To change
your password, you also choose the Company menu's Change Your Password
command. QuickBooks again displays the Change Password dialog box. This
time you do need to enter your old password into the Enter Old Password
text box. Then, you need to enter your new password into both the New
Password text box and the Confirm New Password text box.

QuickBooks requires a username and password before it will open the company data file. For example, if you assign a password to your company data
file, whenever QuickBooks starts, it displays the QuickBooks Login dialog
box, where you enter your username and password and then click OK.
QuickBooks then opens the data file. If you can't supply the password,
QuickBooks doesn't open the data file.

QuickBooks in a Multi-User Environment

You aren't limited to using just one password to control access to your QuickBooks data file. QuickBooks allows you to set up several passwords for the QuickBooks data file. What's really neat about this is that you can tell QuickBooks to limit certain users and passwords to do only certain things. This sounds complicated, but it's really not. The business owner, for example, may have a password that allows him or her to do anything. But a new accounting clerk, for example, may only have a password that allows him to record bills into the system.

Setting up additional QuickBooks users

If more than one person will be using QuickBooks, you want to set up additional passwords. To do this, follow these steps:

1. **Choose the Company menu's Set Up Users command.**

QuickBooks displays the User List dialog box, as shown in Figure 2-1. The User List dialog box identifies any users for whom QuickBooks access has been set up. The User List dialog box also identifies who is currently logged on to the system. In Figure 2-1, the administrator is logged on.

Figure 2-1:
The User List dialog box.

2. **Tell QuickBooks that you want to add a user by clicking the Add User button.**

When you click this button, QuickBooks displays the first Set Up User Password and Access dialog box. (QuickBooks doesn't let people take pictures of this dialog box, so I can't show you what it looks like.)

3. **Identify the user and supply a password.**

You need to give each user for whom you are setting up a password a username. You do this by entering a short name — perhaps the user's first name — into the User Name box. After you identify the user, you enter the user's password into both the Password text box and the Confirm Password text box. After you do this, click Next to continue.

4. **Indicate whether you want to limit access for the new user.**

When QuickBooks displays the second Set Up User Password and Access dialog box, as shown in Figure 2-2, indicate whether you want to limit access and rights for the user. If you do want to limit access and rights (*rights* are simply the things that the user can do), select the Selected Areas of QuickBooks radio button. If you want the user to be able to do anything, select the All Areas of QuickBooks option button. After you make your decision, click Next to continue.

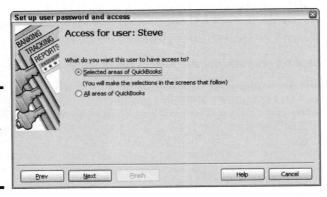

Figure 2-2:
The second
Set Up User
Password
and Access
dialog box.

If you indicate that the new user should have access to all areas of QuickBooks, you are done setting up the user password. You can skip the remaining steps.

5. **Describe access to sales and accounts receivable information and tasks.**

After you complete Step 4, QuickBooks displays the third Set Up User Password and Access dialog box, shown in Figure 2-3. This is the first of ten dialog boxes that walk you through an interview asking detailed questions about what kind of access each user should have to a particular area. In Figure 2-3, QuickBooks asks about access to sales transactions (such as invoices and credit memos and accounts receivable information). You can indicate that the user should have no access by selecting the No Access radio button. You can indicate that the user should have full access by selecting the Full Access radio button. If the user should have partial access, you select the Selective Access radio button and then select one of the Selective Access subsidiary buttons: Create Transactions Only, Create and Print Transactions, or Create Transactions and Create Reports.

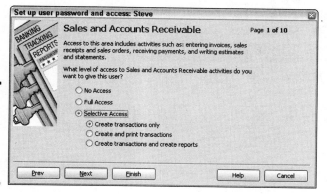

Figure 2-3:
The third
Set Up User
Password
and Access
dialog box.

As a general rule, when it comes to accounting controls, you want to provide the minimal amount of access. If someone doesn't need access to the QuickBooks data file for their day-to-day duties, you should select the No Access button. If someone needs a little bit of access — perhaps they need to prepare job estimates or invoices — you give them just that access, and nothing more. A little bit later in this chapter in the section "Maintaining Good Accounting Controls," I talk about why minimizing user rights and access is so important. But the bottom line is this: The more ability you give employees or subcontractors or accountants to noodle around in your accounting system, the greater the risk that someone can either inadvertently or intentionally introduce errors into the system. Also, the greater the rights and access you give, the easier you make it for someone to steal from you.

After you describe the rights that you want the user to have in the sales and accounts receivable area, click Next.

6. **Describe the purchases and accounts payable rights.**

After you complete Step 5 by clicking Next, QuickBooks displays the fourth Set Up User Password and Access dialog box, as shown in Figure 2-4. This dialog box resembles the one shown in Figure 2-3. Like that dialog box, the fourth Set Up User Password and Access dialog box allows you to specify what access this new user has in the purchases and accounts payable areas. You can select the No Access radio button. You can select the Full Access radio button. Or you can select some middle ground by selecting the Selective Access radio button and one of the Selective Access subsidiary buttons. The same rules for setting rights and access that apply to the purchases and accounts payable area also apply to the sales and accounts receivable area.

After you finish specifying the appropriate purchases and accounts payable rights and access to the user, click the Next button.

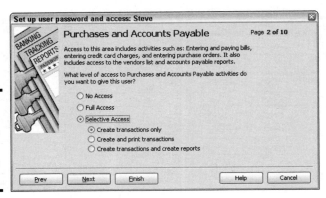

Figure 2-4:
The fourth
Set Up User
Password
and Access
dialog box.

7. Describe the remaining user rights and access.

As you click the Next button shown on the bottom of each version of the Set Up User Password and Access dialog box, QuickBooks displays several other versions of the dialog box that QuickBooks uses to query you about user rights and access. For example, after you describe what rights are appropriate for the user in the purchases and accounts payable area, QuickBooks asks about the checking and credit card area. Then, it asks about the inventory area. Next, it asks about payroll. And then, it asks about general, sensitive accounting activities. Finally, QuickBooks asks about access to the financial reporting capabilities.

You limit rights in each of these other areas in the same way that you do for the sales and accounts receivable and purchases and accounts payable areas. I am not, therefore, going to describe how you select the No Access option button, the Full Access option button, or the Selective Access button over and over again. Just be thoughtful as you go through and limit the ability of the user. You want someone to have the rights necessary to do their job, but you don't want to give them any more rights than they need.

8. Specify where the user can change or delete transactions.

After you've stepped through roughly a half-dozen versions of the Set Up User Password and Access dialog boxes that ask about specific areas of accounting, QuickBooks displays the Set Up User Password and Access dialog box shown in Figure 2-5. The Changing or Deleting Transactions version of the Set Up User Password and Access dialog box lets you indicate that a user can or can't change transactions recorded before the closing date. In general, you want to limit a user's abilities to change or delete transactions.

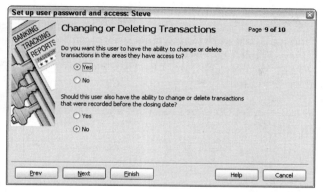

Figure 2-5:
The Changing or Deleting Transactions page of the Set Up User Password and Access dialog box.

One of the problems with QuickBooks is that it doesn't in any other way limit the ability of someone — perhaps someone who is well-meaning but lacks knowledge — to muck up your accounting records by noodling around with old transactions. You want to restrict the ability to change or delete transactions to a very small group of users. And those users need to be people who understand either accounting or the importance of not going in and mucking up old accounting records that have already been used to report finances to the bank or to taxing authorities. You indicate whether a user can change or delete transactions by selecting the Yes or No option buttons shown in Figure 2-5.

After you finish indicating whether a user should be able to change or delete transactions, click Next.

9. Review your rights decisions.

After you complete Step 8, QuickBooks displays the final version of the Set Up User Password and Access dialog box, shown in Figure 2-6. It identifies the user rights that you assigned or allowed. You can use this dialog box to review the rights that someone has. If you realize you've incorrectly assigned rights, click the Prev button to move back through the dialog boxes to where you made a mistake. Then change the assignment of rights and click the Next button to return to the final version of the Set Up User Password and Access dialog box.

After you finish with the review of user rights and access, you can click Finish. From this point forward, the new user will be able to use QuickBooks; however, her rights are limited to what you specified.

Accountants often want to see the rights that particular users have. This is especially true if you're audited by your CPA as part of annual closings. (You may be audited if the bank wants audited financial statements, for example.) QuickBooks doesn't provide a way for you to print the information shown in the Set Up User Password and Access dialog box shown in Figure 2-6. However, Windows allows you to use the Print Screen button to capture a screen shot of the QuickBooks program window and the Set Up User Password and Access dialog box.

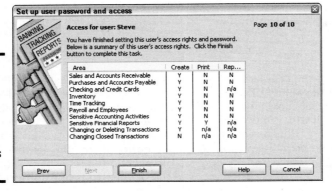

Figure 2-6:
The final version of the Set Up User Password and Access dialog box.

Press Alt+Print Scrn to shoot a screen shot of the dialog box. This copies an image of your screen to the Windows Clipboard. Next open Paint by selecting Start➪Programs➪Accessories➪Paint. Paste the image into Paint by pressing Ctrl+V. You may see an error message that says `The image in the Clipboard is larger than the bitmap. Would you like the bitmap enlarged?` Click Yes. Save the screen shot using File➪Save As. (This is the same basic technique that I use, for example, to show you pictures of the QuickBooks window in the pages of this book.) You may want to capture a screen shot image in this way in order to record the user access and rights for employees.

Changing user rights

You can also modify the rights that you assign to a user. To do this, choose the Company menu's Set Up Users command to display the User List dialog box, as shown in Figure 2-7. This is the same User List dialog box shown earlier in the chapter.

To look at the rights that a particular user has, click the user in the list and then the View User button. When you do, QuickBooks displays the View User Access dialog box, as shown in Figure 2-8. This dialog box shows the same information as the final version of the Set Up User Access and Password dialog box, which is the dialog box that you use to initially specify what rights a user should have. Click the Leave button, obviously, to close the View User Access dialog box.

Figure 2-7:
The User List dialog box.

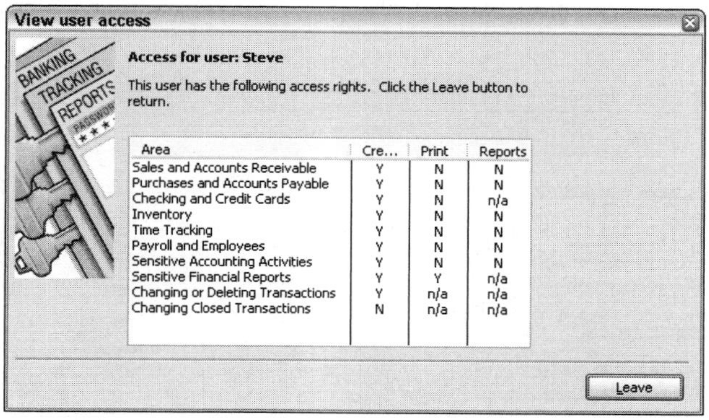

Figure 2-8:
The View User Access dialog box.

To change a user's rights after reviewing them, select the user and click the Edit User button. This tells QuickBooks to step through the same set of dialog boxes that you used to originally set up the user and describe his rights. You use the Next and Prev buttons to do things such as change the username or password, specify whether the user should be limited in his access, and — if necessary — to specifically limit the user's access to a particular activity within QuickBooks.

To remove a user, you also use the User List dialog box. Simply select the user and then click the Delete User button. QuickBooks asks you to confirm your deletion. When you click the Yes button for confirmation, QuickBooks removes the user.

A Few Words about Closing

Because I mentioned "closing" in the earlier paragraphs of this chapter and because the User List dialog box that includes a Closing Date button has been shown twice already in figures in this chapter, perhaps it's time to discuss just a point or two about closing in QuickBooks.

If you take a "Principles of Accounting" course, you'll learn that *closing* means a set of bookkeeping procedures somebody goes through to zero out revenue and expense accounts so that, starting in the new year, revenues and expenses can be easily calculated. In QuickBooks, *closing* means something different. In QuickBooks, to close the accounting records, you supply a closing date (see Figure 2-9). After you supply this closing date, QuickBooks either prohibits users or limits users from changing transactions dated before the closing date.

Figure 2-9:
The Company Preferences tab of the Preferences dialog box allows you to supply a closing date.

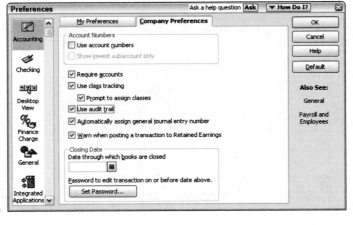

To "close" the QuickBooks data file to transactions that occur before a particular date, you simply enter the date into the Closing Date box.

Using Audit Trails

If you decide to allow multiple users access to the QuickBooks data file, you may want to turn on the QuickBooks Audit Trail feature. The Audit Trail feature lets you keep a record of who makes what changes to the QuickBooks data file. The Audit Trail feature may slow down the performance of QuickBooks if you have a very large data file or many users making lots of changes. But the Audit Trail provides a permanent record of who has made what changes.

You can't remove transactions from the Audit Trail list or history except by archiving and condensing data. Archiving and condensing data is described in Book VII, Chapter 3.

Turning on Audit Trail Tracking

To turn on the QuickBooks Audit Trail feature, follow these steps:

1. **Choose the Edit menu's Preferences command.**

QuickBooks displays the Preferences dialog box, as shown in Figure 2-9. (I just showed this dialog box.)

2. **Indicate that you want to change an accounting preference for the company data file.**

To indicate that you want to use the accounting preferences, use the icon bar by the left edge of the Preferences dialog box to select the accounting set of preferences. (The Accounting Preferences icon appears at the very top of the list.) After you do this, click the Company Preferences tab. Figure 2-9 shows the Company Preferences tab of the accounting preferences.

3. **Indicate that you want to use an audit trail.**

To tell QuickBooks that you want to use an audit trail, select the Use Audit Trail check box and click OK. From that point forward, QuickBooks keeps a record of which users make changes to your accounting.

Producing an Audit Trail report

To produce an Audit Trail report, simply choose the Reports menu's Accountant and Taxes command and then select the Audit Trail command from the submenu. Figure 2-10 shows a QuickBooks Audit Trail report in a window. Note that the report identifies both the type of change made and the person who made the change to the QuickBooks data file.

Book VII Chapter 2

Administering QuickBooks

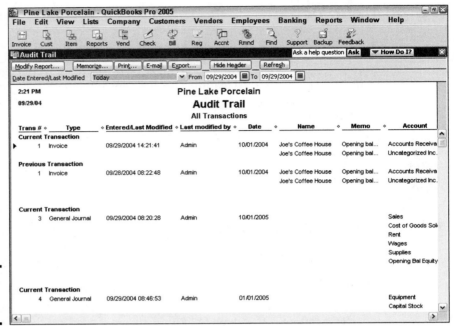

Figure 2-10:
The Audit
Trail report.

Simultaneous Multi-User Access

Sometimes, you only need a single computer and a single copy of QuickBooks even though you have several employees using QuickBooks. For example, if a small business has only an administrative assistant and the owner accessing a QuickBooks data file, one copy of QuickBooks running on a single personal computer may be all that is required. However, QuickBooks does allow for simultaneous use of the QuickBooks data file by multiple users. To do this, predictably, you first need to set up the multiple users as described in the preceding paragraphs of this chapter.

After you have set up the multiple users, however, you can install the QuickBooks program on other personal computers and then — assuming that these personal computers all connect to a Windows network — use those other copies of QuickBooks to access the QuickBooks data file stored on the first or principal computer. (Book VII, Chapter 1 describes how to build a simple Windows peer-to-peer network.)

To use QuickBooks in an environment of simultaneous use by multiple users, you also need to tell QuickBooks that this simultaneous use is okay. To do this, choose the File⇨Switch to Multi-User Mode command. If you later want to turn off this Multi-User Mode, you choose the File⇨Switch to Single User Mode command.

QuickBooks supports simultaneous use by multiple users through a technology called *record locking*, which locks all the records that you're working with but not the entire QuickBooks data file. For example, if you want to work with company A and some other user wants to work with company B, that's okay. QuickBooks allows that. What you can't do, however, is work on both company A or company B at the same time. This would mean that you're working with the same customer record.

You can't install the same copy of QuickBooks on multiple machines and legally have a multiple user QuickBooks system. You must purchase a copy of QuickBooks for each machine on which QuickBooks is installed. Note, however, that Intuit does sell some multiple versions of QuickBooks where you actually buy five licenses in one box of QuickBooks. (QuickBooks supports multiple user networks with up to five simultaneous users.)

A common setting in which you may want to have several QuickBooks users is for sales representatives in your firm who prepare invoices or prepare bids for customers. In this case, you may want to have each salesperson set up on QuickBooks. Note, however, that these sales people should only have access to the ability to create an invoice or perhaps create and print an invoice estimate. For reasons discussed more fully in the next section of this chapter, you want to be very careful about allowing inexperienced accounting users full access to the accounting system.

Maintaining Good Accounting Controls

In the preceding paragraphs of this chapter, I talk about how QuickBooks allows for multiple users. Many businesses, after they grow to a certain size, do need to support multiple users with access to accounting information and the ability, in some cases, to create accounting transactions. Unfortunately, multiple accounting system users create risk for the business owner. By having access to the accounting system, users can either inadvertently introduce errors into the accounting system, or, unfortunately, some users may intentionally defraud a business. For these reasons, I want to briefly list some QuickBooks control techniques that a business owner or business manager can use to minimize unintentional errors and minimize the opportunity for theft. Here are my best ideas:

✦ **Regularly compare physical inventory counts with inventory accounting records.** Inventory, unfortunately, shrinks. People — sometimes employees, but often pseudo-customers such as shoplifters — will steal inventory. Therefore, one of the things that you need to do both to mini-mize your inventory losses and to maintain accurate accounting records is to regularly compare physical counts of your inventory with what your accounting records show. A small convenience store, for example, may want to compare tobacco inventory on a daily basis, beer and wine inventory on a weekly basis, and all other grocery inventory items on a monthly or annual basis. This approach to frequently counting the most valuable and easiest-to-steal items accomplishes two things:

- Inventory shrinkage is quickly identified.

- The business owner can minimize inventory shrinkage by identifying the type of inventory that is most often stolen or even when inven-tory is most often stolen.

✦ **Reconcile bank accounts.** One thing that business owners should do, in my opinion, is reconcile their own bank accounts. Often, employee theft by accounting personnel occurs as employees figure out how to write checks on the company's bank account that the owner doesn't see. One sure way to find a fictitious and fraudulent transaction is to have the owner reconcile the bank statement. If the owner reconciles the bank statement, she can compare the bank's accounting for the account with the company's QuickBooks accounting records. Any obvious discrepan-cies can be fixed — which means that the QuickBooks accounting records are more accurate. Additionally, any flaky, suspicious transac-tions tend to become obvious when the business owner looks closely at checks.

The first employee I ever hired was a check forger. He began forging checks on one of my businesses' checking accounts two or three weeks after he started working for me. I caught him only because I was regu-larly reconciling the checking account. (He was convicted of a felony a few months later.)

✦ **Segregate accounting from physical custody where possible.** In a small business, it's difficult to always separate the accounting for some activ-ity from the physical custody or physical responsibility for that activity. For example, it's tough to segregate the inventory accounting from phys-ical custody or access to that inventory. A store clerk, for example, may easily be able to steal cigarettes and also adjust inventory records through cash register sales for cigarettes. Nevertheless, wherever you can segregate physical custody from accounting, a built-in error check-ing occurs. The person doing the accounting indirectly checks on the physical custodians' caretaking of the asset. If the physical custodian is stealing cartons of cigarettes, for example, that will show up when the accountant compares the accounting records to the physical accounts of inventory. Similarly, someone without access to the cash and the bank account can't actually easily steal cash even if they have complete access to cash accounting records. You can ask your CPA for help in devising ways to segregate physical custody of assets from accounting and bookkeeping duties. And you really, really should do this. Unfortunately, employee theft is very common.

✦ **Train employees in the use of QuickBooks.** You should train employees to use QuickBooks if you have a business of any size for two basic reasons:

- *Someone who knows how to use QuickBooks is less likely to make inadvertent errors.* QuickBooks isn't difficult to use, but neither is QuickBooks something that you can learn willy-nilly with no help. Some transactions are pretty tricky, particularly for certain businesses. So, if you can, it makes good sense to provide some employees with help or training or both. Those resources let people more comfortably and more accurately use QuickBooks features to build financial information that lets you better manage your business.

- *Messy accounting records camouflage employee theft.* Often, one of the things you see when employee theft happens is really messed-up accounting records. For that reason, you can find yourself in a situation where poorly trained employees create a messy accounting system that enables theft by perhaps one of those employees or some other employee. So training not only means more accurate accounting records, but also that you are less likely to have an environment conducive to theft or embezzlement.

✦ **Manage your QuickBooks accounting system.** I am sorry to report that many business owners don't view the accounting system as anything more than a tool to produce invoices and paychecks and information required for the annual tax return. Unfortunately, that distant relationship with the accounting system means that business owners often don't feel much need to actively manage what happens with the accounting system.

In my opinion, this attitude is wrong. An accounting system should be a tool that you use to better manage your business. And it can be that. But if it's going to be a tool for better managing your business, you need to manage the system. In other words, I respectfully suggest that you take responsibility for ensuring that employees are trained to do the things that protect your accounting system (such as backing up the data file) and that you ensure that they complete appropriate accounting procedures on a monthly and annual basis (such as sending out all invoices, reconciling bank accounts, cleaning up messy transactions, and so forth). I don't think this management responsibility needs to be a heavy one. You can rather easily make sure that people are doing the sorts of things they are supposed to be doing by creating some simple checklists.

**Book VII
Chapter 2**

Administering
QuickBooks

Table 2-1 shows a sample monthly accounting to-do list. Table 2-2 shows a sample annual accounting to-do list. You can use these as starting points for constructing your own list of things that the accounting clerk or office manager must do every month or at the end of every year.

Table 2-1	A Sample Monthly Accounting To-Do List
Data backed up and moved offsite	
Bank accounts reconciled	
All invoices, credit memos, statements out	
Any suspense accounts cleaned up	
Financial statements delivered	
Exceptions reported (for example, overdue invoices, bills, purchase orders, under-stocked inventory items)	

Table 2-2	A Sample Annual Accounting To-Do List
Adjust trial balance	
Burn CD with year-end numbers for permanent record	
Consider archiving data files if they're huge	
Close year when really done	

Chapter 3: Protecting Your Data

In This Chapter

✔ Backing up the QuickBooks data file

✔ Restoring the QuickBooks data file

✔ Archiving and condensing QuickBooks data

In this chapter, I tell you how to protect your QuickBooks data. Principally, protecting your data requires that you back up the data. By backing up your data, you have a second backup copy available in case the original data file goes bad or becomes corrupted. Because archiving and data file compression is related to backing up and restoring QuickBooks data files, I also talk about archiving in this chapter. When you archive QuickBooks data files, you create a permanent record of the data files. You also have the option of condensing the current working data file.

Backing Up the QuickBooks Data File

A critically important task that either you or some co-worker need to complete is to back up the QuickBooks data file. I respectfully suggest that few items stored on your computer's hard drive deserve as much caretaking as the QuickBooks data file. Quite literally, the QuickBooks data file describes your business's financial affairs. You absolutely don't want to lose the data file. Losing the data file, for example, means that you don't know how much money you have, you don't know whether you're making or losing money, and you won't be able to easily or accurately prepare your annual tax returns.

Backing up basics

Fortunately, backing up the QuickBooks data file is rather straightforward. You need to complete only three steps:

1. **Choose the File menu's Back Up command.**

QuickBooks displays the Back Up Company File dialog box, as shown in Figure 3-1.

Figure 3-1:
The Back Up
Company
File dialog
box.

2. (Optional) Click the Browse button to choose a backup location.

QuickBooks displays the Back Up Company To dialog box, as shown in Figure 3-2. You can use this dialog box to specify what folder location or disk location the company file should be backed up to. For example, you can select a folder or disk by using the Save In box. You can also enter a pathname directly into the File Name box. After you choose the location for backing up the company file, click the Save button.

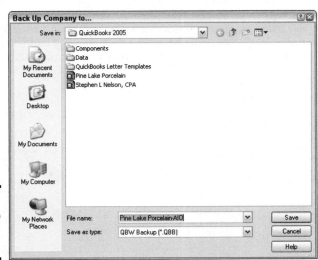

Figure 3-2:
The Back Up
Company to
dialog box.

If you know how to enter a pathname, you don't have to click the Browse button. You can instead type the pathname into the Location box shown in the Back Up Company File dialog box (see Figure 3-1).

3. **(Optional) Select your backup options.**

   Use the Back Up Options check boxes to tell QuickBooks that it should check for data integrity (do this by selecting the Verify Data Integrity check box) or that it should format floppy disks as it backs up (do this by selecting the Format Each Floppy Disk During Backup check box).

4. **Click OK.**

   After you've specified the location to which the current company file should be backed up — you may have done this by clicking the Browse button or you may have just entered the backup location pathname into the Location box — click OK. QuickBooks backs up, or creates a copy of, the current QuickBooks company file and stores that new file copy at the backup location.

What about online backup?

If you were observant, you may have noticed that the Back Up Company File dialog box shown in Figure 3-1 includes an Online option button. If you want to learn more about backing up the QuickBooks company data file online — which means using Intuit's computer network rather than your computer or some removable disk to store the backup — you can select the Online radio button or click the Tell Me More button.

I don't recommend that you use the online backup method, however, for two reasons:

✦ Online backup is too expensive at prices that run (at the time of this writing) from about $6 to $20 a month.

✦ Online backup can make the task of backing up more work and less regular if you have an unreliable Internet connection. For example, you don't want to have an employee sitting in the office at 5:00 p.m. on a Friday trying to back up a file, but unable to do so because the DSL connection is down or slow. In that scenario, the person doesn't back up the data file, but instead leaves the office and starts the weekend — not a good backup plan.

Some backup tactics

Backing up is, mostly, just a matter of common sense. That being said, however, let me give you some ideas about how and when and maybe why you should back up:

✦ **Make it easy.**

I already mentioned this in my critique of the online backup option. But the point deserves mentioning again. The most important thing you can do regarding the backing up of your QuickBooks data file is this: Make backing up easy. This probably means that you want to have a high density removable disk installed on the computer that you use to run QuickBooks. I use an Iomega Zip drive that stores 100 megabytes of data. You want some similar, easy-to-employ storage device. In this case, "easy" means that backing up is more likely to occur.

✦ **Use a Zip drive or USB Memory Device.**

Your QuickBooks data file will quickly grow very large. In fact, almost from the start, your QuickBooks data file will be too large to back up on a typical floppy disk. For this reason, you need some other large removal disk for backing up your QuickBooks data file. I recommend you use something like an Iomega Zip disk or one of the USB Memory Devices (that look like sticks of gum). Zip disks currently range in size from 100 megabytes to 750 megabytes. USB Memory Devices can supply even more space for storage. Those sizes provide plenty of space for you to use for backing up your QuickBooks data.

✦ **Back up regularly.**

I recommend that you back up every time you enter transactions into the QuickBooks data file. Obviously, if backing up represents a lot of work, you aren't going to want to do this. But if you have an easy way to back up and a convenient storage device, you can and should back up regularly. Daily backups are not too often.

✦ **Store a backup copy of the QuickBooks data file offsite.**

One final important point worth mentioning: Many of the events that may destroy or corrupt your data file are specific to your computer — a hard drive failure, a virus, a user accident, and so forth. Some of the events that may corrupt or destroy your QuickBooks data file, however, are location-specific. Fire, flood, or theft can cause you to lose the QuickBooks data file and its backup. For this reason, you want to store a copy of the backup offsite. At the end of the week, for example, you may want to pop the Zip disk in your shirt pocket and bring it home. Make sure that if something corrupts or destroys the QuickBooks data file that that same something also doesn't destroy the backup QuickBooks data file.

Restoring a QuickBooks Data File

If you find that the working copy of the QuickBooks data file becomes corrupted or gets destroyed, you need to restore the QuickBooks data file so you can again begin using QuickBooks. Restoring the QuickBooks data file is easy if you've recently backed up the QuickBooks data file.

If you haven't recently (or ever) backed up the QuickBooks data file, you'll have to restore the QuickBooks data file, which means starting over from scratch. This means, for example, that you need to rerun the QuickBooks Installation and Setup. You'll need to re-enter all of the old data. In short, restoring without a backup copy of the QuickBooks data file means that you start over at square one.

To restore the QuickBooks data file from the backup copy of the file, put the backup disk into the drive and then follow these steps:

1. Launch QuickBooks and choose the File menu's Restore command.

QuickBooks displays the Restore Company Backup dialog box, as shown in Figure 3-3.

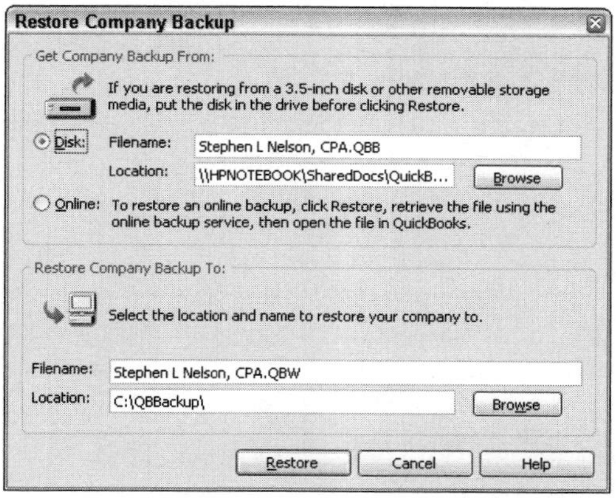

Figure 3-3:
The Restore Company Backup dialog box.

Book VII
Chapter 3

Protecting Your Data

2. Identify the backup file that you will use for the restoration.

Use the Get Company Backup From buttons and boxes, as shown in Figure 3-3, to specify the location of the backup file that you'll use for the restoration. If you're backing up from a disk copy of the backup file, for example, select the Disk radio button. Then use the Filename and Location boxes to identify the backup file. You enter the filename into the Filename box, predictably. You enter the file pathname into the Location box.

If you don't know how to enter a pathname — a *pathname* is just a string of information that includes the drive letter and the names of each of the folders and subfolders — click the Browse button. When you do, QuickBooks displays the Restore From dialog box, as shown in Figure 3-4. Use the Restore From dialog box to identify the specific location of the backup file. For example, you can use the Look In box to identify the disk and folder storing the backup file. After you identify the location of the backup file by using the Restore From dialog box, click Open.

3. **Identify the file to be restored.**

Use the Restore Company Backup To boxes (see Figure 3-3) to identify the location and specify the name of the company file that you want to restore. You enter the company data filename into the File Name box. You enter the pathname — remember that the pathname identifies the disk in the folder holding the file — into the Location box. If you aren't comfortable specifying pathnames (and who is?), click the Browse button. When QuickBooks displays the Restore To dialog box (this resembles the Restore From dialog box shown in Figure 3-4), use the Save In box to identify the location of the file that you want to restore. After you identify the location, click the Save button.

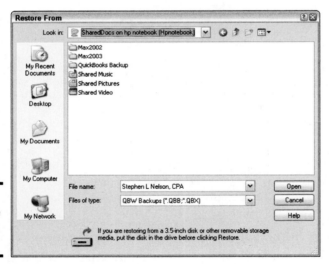

Figure 3-4: The Restore From dialog box.

4. **Verify the backup and the to-be-restored company filename and location information.**

When you restore the company data file by using the backup copy, you destroy the current working version of the file. In other words, QuickBooks takes the backup copy and copies it over the to-be-restored company data file. Therefore, before you restore company data files, make sure that you're using the right backup copy and that you're overwriting the corrupted to-be-restored company file.

5. **Click Restore.**

QuickBooks displays a message asking you to confirm that you want to overwrite the existing file. You need to click Yes. After you click Yes, QuickBooks displays another message box entitled Delete Entire File, as shown in Figure 3-5. Confirm that you want to delete the existing (and presumably corrupt) company data file by typing the word yes into the message box. Then click OK. QuickBooks uses the backup copy to overwrite the to-be-restored company file.

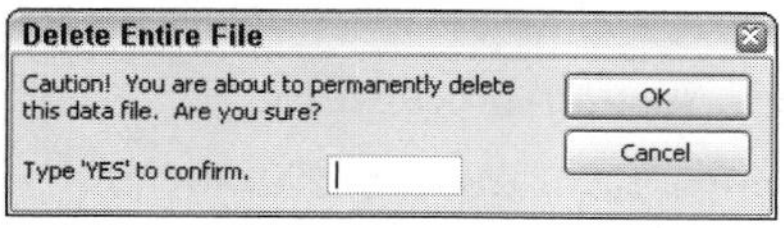

Figure 3-5:
The Delete
Entire File
message
box.

6. **Enter any old transactions that took place since your last backup.**

If you entered transactions after you last backed up the QuickBooks company file, you need to now re-enter those transactions into QuickBooks. For example, if you last backed up QuickBooks on Friday of last week, you need to enter any transactions that you've created since last Friday.

Archiving the QuickBooks Company Files

Archiving means saving a permanent copy. When you archive the QuickBooks data file, you save a permanent copy of it. An archival copy of the company file lets you take a snapshot of the company file as it exists at a particular point in time. If somebody later has a question — perhaps your accountant, or a federal or state auditor — you can use the archival copy of the data file to show what the company file looked like at a particular point in time.

Because archiving can be a little bit confusing, let me quickly summarize what happens when you create an archival copy of the QuickBooks company file. Here's what archiving means (in all its gory details) in QuickBooks:

+ **Archiving saves a copy of your company files.**

When you archive the QuickBooks company file, QuickBooks saves an archival copy of that file.

✦ **Archiving can remove old transactions.**

In archiving, QuickBooks gives you the opportunity to remove old, closed transactions from the current, working version of the QuickBooks company file. Remember that archiving creates an archival copy of the QuickBooks company file. You still, however, have the working version of the QuickBooks company file. It is this current, working version of the QuickBooks company file that gets condensed, or cleaned up, by the removal of old, closed transactions. *Closed* transactions are transactions that QuickBooks no longer needs to track in detail. For example, an old customer invoice — after it's been paid — is a closed transaction. An old check written to some vendor — after it's cleared the bank — is a closed transaction.

✦ **Archiving summarizes old, closed transactions.**

Because the old, closed transactions are removed from the QuickBooks data file, archiving creates summary monthly journal entries for the old, closed transactions and places these summary transactions in the current, working version of the QuickBooks data file. These summary monthly journal entries allow you to continue to prepare monthly financial statements. For example, even though archiving removes all of the old, closed transactions from, for example, January of 1995, you can still produce monthly financial statements for January of 1995. To produce monthly financial statements for January of 1995, QuickBooks uses the summary monthly journal entries.

✦ **Archiving clears the audit trail.**

As I mentioned in Book VII, Chapter 2, QuickBooks gives you the option of maintaining an audit trail of who has entered what transactions. One almost hidden effect of archiving and condensing QuickBooks data files concerns the audit trail. If you archive a company file and indicate that the company file should be condensed, QuickBooks clears the audit trail before the "removed closed transactions on or before" date. In other words, for the period of time in which QuickBooks removes old, closed transactions, it also removes the audit trail of those transactions.

Archiving typically means creating a copy of the QuickBooks data file that you save and put away someplace, and creating a scaled-down version of the working company file. The command that you use to archive the QuickBooks company file, however, also allows you to create almost-empty company files. Most people would never need to use this option. I can only think of one category of QuickBooks users who may want to create almost-empty company files. CPAs and consultants (who want to reuse a company file for another business unit or client) may want to use this command to create company data files that have many of the lists set up already. I don't go any further into detailing the option of creating an almost-empty company file by using the archiving command, but you should know that it is there.

Archiving basics

After you understand what archiving is all about, it is quite straightforward. To archive the QuickBooks company file, follow these steps:

1. **Choose the File menu's Archive & Condense Data command.**

   QuickBooks displays the Archive & Condense Data dialog box, as shown in Figure 3-6.

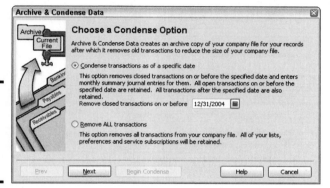

Figure 3-6:
The first
Archive &
Condense
Data dialog
box.

**Book VII
Chapter 3**

Protecting Your
Data

2. **Select the Condense Transactions as of a Specific Date radio button.**

   This option tells QuickBooks that you want to do two things: create an archival copy of the QuickBooks data file and skinny down the size of the working company file so that it isn't so big. QuickBooks reduces the size of the working version of the company data file by removing old, closed transactions.

3. **Specify the Remove Closed Transactions on or Before date.**

   To specify the date before which closed transactions should be removed, enter the date into the date box provided. If you want to condense the file by removing transactions on or before December 31, 2004, for example, enter **12/31/2004** into the date box. Note, however, that you don't need to feel compulsive about removing a bunch of closed transactions. You only need to remove closed transactions if your QuickBooks company file is getting too big. You can easily work with a QuickBooks company file that is 5, 10, or even 15 megabytes in size.

   Therefore, in the case where you find yourself with a company file that is only 8 megabytes in size, you may want to archive the company file but not condense it. If the company file has grown too large — Intuit recommends that your company data file should, in most cases, be less than

40 megabytes in size — you may want to condense the data file by removing old transactions. However, this doesn't mean that you would want to remove old closed transactions from last year. You may, instead, choose to remove old transactions from three years ago or five years ago.

My personal experience is that data files become unwieldy when they get to be more than 20 megabytes in size. Therefore, I'd condense any data file that's approaching 20 megabytes.

4. **Click Next.**

   When you click Next, QuickBooks displays the second page of the Archive & Condense Data dialog box, as shown in Figure 3-7.

Figure 3-7:
The second page of the Archive & Condense Data dialog box.

5. **Specify any additional criteria that you want QuickBooks to apply for removing transactions.**

   As the dialog box shown in Figure 3-7 indicates, QuickBooks won't remove an old, closed transaction if it is an uncleared bank or credit card transaction, if a transaction is marked to be printed, if a transaction is an invoice or estimate marked to be sent, or if a transaction contains unbilled or unreimbursed costs. Nevertheless, even those sorts of old, closed transactions may still be transactions that you should remove. You may have transactions that will never clear or never be printed or sent, for example. To indicate that some of these old transactions should also be removed, select the check box that corresponds to the removal criteria. To remove old invoices and estimates that are still marked as "to be sent," select the Remove invoices and estimates marked 'To be sent' check box.

6. **Click Next.**

   When you click Next, QuickBooks displays the third Archive & Condense Data dialog box, as shown in Figure 3-8.

7. Specify any list cleanup that should occur.

Use the third Archive & Condense Data dialog box to tell QuickBooks that in addition to removing old closed transactions, it should also clean up some of the lists. You can select check boxes on the Archive & Condense Data dialog box, for example, that tell QuickBooks to remove unused accounts, unused customers, unused vendors, and so forth. By cleaning up your list through the removal of unused list items, you not only reduce the size of the company file, you also make it easier for people to work with the list.

8. Click Next.

QuickBooks displays the fourth page of the Archive & Condense Data dialog box, as shown in Figure 3-9.

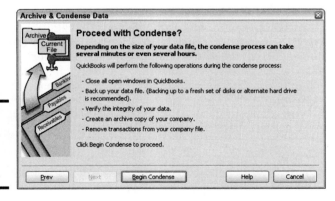

9. **Confirm your archiving and condensing operation.**

After you describe how you want QuickBooks to archive and condense the company file, QuickBooks displays the fourth Archive & Condense Data dialog box, as shown in Figure 3-9. This dialog box asks you to confirm your decision to archive and condense the data file. The dialog box also tells you that the archival process begins with QuickBooks backing up the data file and then may take several minutes or several hours to complete. Use this dialog box to confirm the fact that you want to archive and condense the data.

10. **Click Begin Condense.**

QuickBooks begins the process of archiving and condensing the data file.

11. **Back up the data file when prompted.**

At the very beginning of the archival process, QuickBooks will prompt you to back up the QuickBooks company file. Backing up the QuickBooks company file as part of an archiving operation works the same as backing up the QuickBooks company file at any other time. If you have questions about how to back up the QuickBooks company file, refer to the earlier section "Backing up basics."

After you back up the QuickBooks company file, QuickBooks creates the archive copy of the company file and then condenses it — this will be the working version of the company file — by using your instructions. Again, as noted in the earlier steps, the archiving and condensing process may take only a few minutes or it may take several hours if your file is very large.

Some archiving strategies

Deciding when and how you want to archive your QuickBooks company file is mostly a matter of common sense. Your first consideration should be whether you need to condense the company file at all. If QuickBooks still runs at a reasonable speed, if you don't find yourself going crazy because of many unused items on lists, or if the data file hasn't grown monstrously large (larger than 15 megabytes or so in size), you may not need to condense. You achieve no benefit, in many cases, by condensing. And by not condensing, you still have complete detailed financial records at your fingertips.

The other part about archiving the QuickBooks company files is another common-sense notion: You should create an archival copy of the QuickBooks data file. In fact, I recommend that you create an archival copy of the QuickBooks data file at the end of the year after you or your CPA have made any final adjustments to the year. It's a great idea to create an archival copy of the QuickBooks data file that's used to prepare your tax return and any financial statements because you can always later explain some number on a return or financial statement by looking at the archival copy of the data file.

Throughout this book — and most recently in the previous chapter on administering QuickBooks — I mention that one of the problems of using QuickBooks is that people can intentionally or inadvertently change old transactions. This means that someone can, unfortunately, change transactions in a QuickBooks data file in a previous year. When that change occurs, someone later looking at the QuickBooks data file may not be able to explain a number on a tax return or a financial statement. For example, if someone later goes back and changes a transaction in a previous year, and that transaction is used to calculate total revenues for the year, you can no longer use the QuickBooks data to explain numbers on your tax return and your financial statements for total revenue. That makes sense, right?

Fortunately, by having an archival copy of the QuickBooks data file — the QuickBooks data file that supplied numbers to your tax return and the financial statements — you can always see which QuickBooks transactions support a particular tax return number or financial statement number. If you're still confused about this point — and it is a little bit tricky — ask your tax advisor or your CPA about the problem. He can explain to you the danger of having QuickBooks data used to prepare a return or a financial statement change after the return has been prepared or after the financial statements have been published and distributed.

**Book VII
Chapter 3**

Protecting Your
Data

Chapter 4: Troubleshooting

In This Chapter

- ✔ Using the QuickBooks Help file and this book
- ✔ Visiting other vendor's product support Web sites
- ✔ Tapping into Intuit's product support system
- ✔ Browsing the de facto QuickBooks newsgroup
- ✔ When all else fails . . .

After writing about QuickBooks for more than ten years, I've had a revelation of sorts. People not only want specific, step-by-step information about how to use the program, they also want troubleshooting advice. They want techniques and tactics that they can use to solve the inevitable problems that they encounter while using QuickBooks in real-life settings. What follows is my list of the best troubleshooting techniques.

Using the QuickBooks Help File and This Book

I know what you may be thinking: You've got some problem that you can't solve by using Help, and it's either a bug or some glaring error in the QuickBooks documentation. And, of course, you've looked through this book and it says nothing — absolutely nothing — about your question. In fact, upon further reflection, you may be thinking that you've encountered some problem that you can't possibly solve by consulting the QuickBooks Help file or this book.

Maybe you're right.

In my experience (when I talk with people who have problems), however, about half the time, the problem is that people don't know enough about QuickBooks to know what to do. People simply experience a mechanical problem and they can't make the program work because they haven't used QuickBooks enough to figure out how it works. Therefore, the right way to solve this sort of problem is to find out more about QuickBooks and try again. For example, if you're having problems printing a report, just finding out more about printing and reports may solve your problem.

In most cases, you should be able to find the information in this book by using either the Index or the Table of Contents.

Also, you should usually be able to find the information (perhaps in a slightly less-friendly form) in the QuickBooks Help file. To find information in the QuickBooks Help file, choose Help⇨Help Index to display the QuickBooks Help window as shown in Figure 4-1, and then enter the word or phrase that you want to look up.

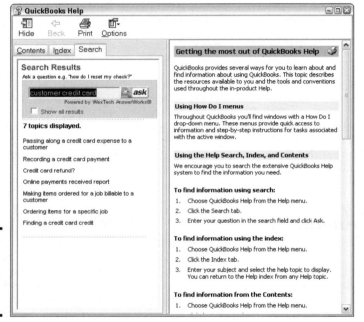

Figure 4-1:
The
QuickBooks
Help
window.

Browsing Intuit's Product Support Web Site

Another really good resource for troubleshooting is Intuit's product support Web site for QuickBooks. This Web site, available at www.quickbooks.com/support/, supplies a rich database of troubleshooting information, as shown in Figure 4-2.

To make the most of the Web site, from the drop-down list boxes, identify the version of QuickBooks you're using. After you identify your version, you see a Web page that lists common categories of problems or questions. Select a category, and you're on your way. The product support Web site then displays a list of troubleshooting articles that may help you to solve your problem.

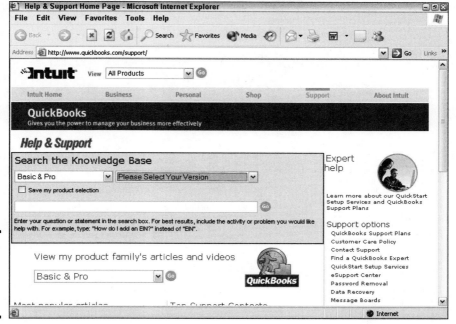

Figure 4-2:
The
QuickBooks
support
Web page.

Checking Another Vendor's Product Support Web Site

Keep in mind that your problem may not be a problem with QuickBooks at all, but rather a problem with your computer and its hardware or with Microsoft Windows. The Microsoft product support Web site, which is phenomenally rich in information, is available at support.microsoft.com, shown in Figure 4-3.

If your problem stems from the hardware or the operating system, you can consult the hardware or software maker's product support Web site for troubleshooting information. You can usually find the hardware maker's product support Web site easily by using a good Internet search engine. For example, to locate Dell Computer's product support Web site, type something like **Dell Computer product support** into a search engine such as www.google.com. When the search engine searches on the phrase "Dell Computer product support," it almost inevitably finds the URL (the address) of the other vendor's product support Web page.

Figure 4-3:
The
Microsoft
Knowledge
Base Web
page.

You can find troubleshooting information about Intuit products at the Microsoft product support Web site. If the solutions that the site offers aren't very reassuring, at least you can find out whether others have experienced the same problem. Microsoft may simply suggest that you contact the vendor (Intuit, in this case) or that you upgrade to a newer version of the QuickBooks software. However, simply knowing that the problem you've encountered is a real problem that Microsoft has logged into its product support Knowledge Base (that's what they call it) and described in some technical detail is often useful.

Tapping into Intuit's Product Support System

In addition to the option of using the Intuit product support Web site, you can also get direct product support help in a variety of ways:

✦ You can call a real person at Intuit and get personalized help. Intuit offers several different support plans, but the cost varies depending on the plan you choose. The number you call depends on which version of QuickBooks you're using. To see an overview of the different QuickBooks support plans, as well as their prices and phone numbers, poke around the QuickBooks Web site. (Unfortunately, I can't give you a good URL to enter into your Web browser's address box. The URL address changes too frequently.)

The QuickBooks phone support may be free if you call with an installation problem, an upgrade problem, or a software bug. In my experience, however, Intuit defines the term *software bug* very narrowly. What you and I may think of as software bugs may not be software bugs to the Intuit support person.

✦ You can sign up for a premium support plan that gives you unlimited phone support for about $300 a year — and then call a real person at Intuit. (This annual fee changes, so check the Web site for up-to-date pricing information rather than rely on my perhaps out-of-date information.) Premium support represents a pretty good investment, in my opinion. If you make more than one phone support call a year, you can probably save money with the premium support plan because a single support call can easily last an hour and can become very pricey.

✦ You can contact a QuickBooks professional advisor via the QuickBooks Web site. In a nutshell, QuickBooks professional advisors are just people (often accountants and consultants) who pay Intuit to be listed on the QuickBooks product support Web site. (Some of these people also take a test and pay extra money to be listed as "certified" advisors.) You pay one of these professional advisors their usual consulting fees. I'm probably prejudiced here because although I haven't signed up (yet?) to be a professional advisor, I do QuickBooks consulting for businesses and CPA firms in the Seattle area. With that disclosure given, however, let me suggest that this support option can be very useful when your problem isn't so much a technical problem with QuickBooks, but a problem with how to use QuickBooks to solve some accounting issue. To contact a QuickBooks professional advisor, visit the QuickBooks Web site.

Trying an Internet Newsgroup

If your problem with QuickBooks isn't really a program bug or can't be easily solved by finding out more, you can sometimes find an answer by consulting other QuickBooks users. One of the easiest ways to do this is by browsing the Quicken newsgroup (yes, that's right, the Quicken newsgroup) or the QuickBooks newsgroup at the following addresses:

```
alt.comp.software.financial.Quicken
alt.comp.software.financial.QuickBooks
```

To browse the Quicken newsgroup or the QuickBooks newsgroup — note that the Quicken newsgroup contains both Quicken and QuickBooks information — you need to use an Internet service provider that supports newsgroups and a newsgroup reader (such as Outlook Express). Assuming that you have these things, you can subscribe to the QuickBooks newsgroup and talk with other QuickBooks users about the problems that you're encountering.

You may not need this background information, but I'm going to point out a few important things about newsgroups. A specific organization doesn't typically support or police newsgroups. For example, Intuit doesn't maintain or support the Quicken or the QuickBooks newsgroup. Newsgroups, including the Quicken and QuickBooks newsgroups, really amount to freeform — and sometimes unruly — discussions among users. You can't always expect to have your question answered. Additionally, good newsgroup etiquette suggests that if you're going to ask questions, you should also try to answer questions.

When All Else Fails . . .

If you try at least a few of the preceding troubleshooting tactics and can't get an answer, you can e-mail me with your question at steve@stephenlnelson.com. I can't duplicate the information supplied by other troubleshooting sources, but I like to hear from readers. If you've come this far and you have tried at least a few of the preceding troubleshooting tips, I'd be happy to exchange some e-mail.

If you send me an e-mail, I have a couple of requests. First, tell me a little bit about yourself, including where you live, where you bought this book, and for what task you're using QuickBooks. I admit I'm partly just curious about this stuff. However, the information about where you live and for what task you use QuickBooks is sometimes relevant to a troubleshooting discussion. (This is especially true about the sort of business that you're running.) Second, don't expect to get a quick answer from me. I try to answer all my e-mail, but I get a lot, I'm frequently out of my office, and I rarely can respond quickly.

I should also say that from January through almost end of April and then again in August and September I'm busy with tax season doing the returns of businesses and individuals. Heck, for all you know, if you live in the Seattle area, I may be doing your return right now, even as you're reading this. (I'm not secretly doing this, of course. I'd only be doing this because you've asked me to.) I bring up this seasonal conflict in my schedule to point out that you (unfortunately) shouldn't expect any quick answers from me during tax season. Sorry. I don't like it any better than you do. But that's just the way it is. I will return your e-mail message when tax season ends. I promise. . . .

Book VIII

Appendixes

The 5th Wave   By Rich Tennant

"The top line represents our revenue, the middle line is our inventory, and the bottom line shows the rate of my hair loss over the same period."

Contents at a Glance

Appendix A: A Crash Course in Excel

In This Appendix

✔ Starting and stopping Excel

✔ Explaining Excel's workbooks

✔ Inputting text, numbers, and formulas into cells

✔ Writing formulas

✔ Scrolling big workbooks

✔ Copying and cutting cell contents

✔ Formatting cell contents

✔ Using Excel functions

✔ Saving and opening workbooks

✔ Printing Excel workbooks

*I*n this appendix, I want to review the basic Excel skills that you may need in order to get the most benefit from some chapters in this book. If you plan to download and work with the sample workbooks from my Web site, `www.stephenlnelson.com`, you will need some of the skills that this primer covers.

If you've used Excel much — even for just a few weeks — you probably already possess all of these skills. Nevertheless, if you are even a teensy bit concerned about whether you have the right skills, take the time to quickly read through this chapter.

Starting Excel

You can start Excel in two ways, neither of which requires a Ph.D. in physics. You can use the Start button or you can open an Excel workbook.

If you are going to use the Start button, you click Start (as you can guess if you have worked with other Windows programs), you click All Programs, and then you choose Microsoft Excel from the All Programs menu.

To start Excel by opening an Excel workbook, you either select the workbook from a menu or you select the workbook in a folder window. You commonly see documents, including Excel workbooks, listed on menus — both Windows menus and Program menus. For example, if you click the Start button and choose the My Recent Documents command, Windows displays the list of documents that you recently saved. If you see an Excel workbook listed, you can open the workbook by choosing it from the menu. When you open an Excel workbook, Windows starts Excel and tells Excel to open the workbook.

You can also open Excel files from within My Computer, Windows Explorer, or My Documents. Simply open a folder containing one or more Excel workbooks, such as the folder shown in Figure A-1, and then double-click the file that you want to open. Voilà! Excel starts and displays the file that you wanted.

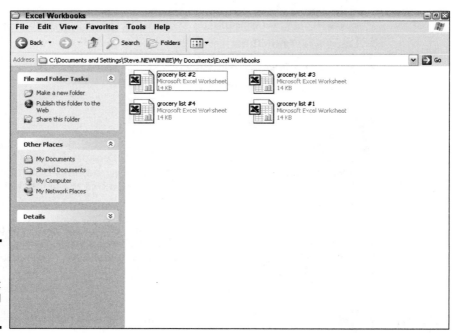

Figure A-1:
A folder
window that
shows Excel
workbooks.

Stopping Excel

To stop Excel, you choose the File⇨Exit command. When you stop Excel, Excel closes any of the open Excel workbooks. And then Excel stops.

You can also stop Excel by clicking the Excel Program window's Close box. The Close box is the button marked with an X that appears in the upper-right corner of the Excel Program window.

Explaining Excel's Workbooks

After you start Excel, Excel displays an empty Excel workbook in its document window. Figure A-2 shows a picture of this empty workbook.

An Excel workbook is just a *spreadsheet*. A spreadsheet is comprised of numbered rows and lettered columns. You see these numbers along the left edge of the spreadsheet. You see the lettered columns along the top edge of the spreadsheet. For example, the first row is numbered 1, the second is numbered 2, and so on. The first column is labeled with the letter *A*. The second column is labeled with the letter *B*, and so on.

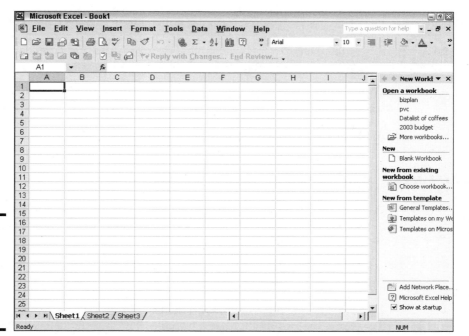

Figure A-2:
The Excel program window with an empty workbook.

Book VIII
Appendix A

A Crash Course in Excel

The intersections of rows and columns are called *cells*. A cell location is described by using the column letter and row number. For example, the cell in the upper-left corner of the workbook is labeled A1.

Putting Text, Numbers, and Formulas into Cells

You build a workbook, or spreadsheet, by entering text labels, numbers, and formulas into the cells that comprise a workbook. The following list details these items:

✦ **Text labels** include letters and numbers that you don't want to use in calculations. For example, your name, some budget expense description, and a telephone number are all examples of text labels. None of these pieces of information is used in calculations.

✦ **Numbers,** or values, are bits of data that you may want to later use in a calculation. For example, the actual amount that you budgeted for some expense will always be a number or value.

✦ **Formulas** are also entered into worksheet cells. For example, if you enter **=2+2** into a cell, Excel doesn't display the formula. Rather, it calculates the formula result and displays that. The formula is what is actually stored in the cell, but the formula result is displayed.

This business about formulas going into workbook cells is, essentially, the heart of Excel. Even if an Excel workbook did nothing else, it would still be an extremely valuable tool. In fact, the first spreadsheet programs did little more than calculate cell formulas.

To enter a text label, a value, or a formula into a cell, all you do is click the cell by using the mouse and then type the text label, value, or formula. When you press Enter or click another cell, Excel enters your label, value, or formula into the cell. That's all it takes.

Writing Formulas

In the preceding section, I told you about formulas — and even showed you a simple formula example. But in order to practically use formulas, you need to possess several other pieces of knowledge.

Specifically, you need to remember several things about entering formulas into the cells of a workbook:

✦ **Formulas should begin with the equal sign (=).** The equal sign tells Excel that what follows is a formula that it should calculate.

✦ **You can use any of the standard arithmetic operators in your formulas.** For example, to add numbers, use the addition sign (+). To subtract numbers, use the subtraction operator (-). To multiply numbers, use the multiplication operator (*). To divide numbers, use the division operator (/). You can also perform exponential operations by using the exponential operator (^).

✦ **You aren't limited to using values in your formulas.** You can also use cell addresses. When you use a cell address in a formula, Excel uses the value or formula result from that cell in the calculation. For example, if cell A1 holds the value 2 and cell B1 holds the value 2, the formula =A1+B1 returns the value 4. In other words, this formula is equivalent to =2+2.

✦ **You need to remember standard rules of operator precedence when you build complicated formulas.** As you may remember from junior high math, exponential operations are performed first. Multiplication and division operations are performed second. Addition and subtraction operations are performed third. To override these standard rules of operator precedence, you need to include the operations that you want performed first inside parentheses. Table A-1 shows some example formulas and the formula results to illustrate these rules of precedence. If you get it wrong, you'll have to stay after class.

Table A-1	Some Example Excel Formulas
What's in Cell	*What Excel Calculates and Displays*
=4+5*6	34
=(4+5)*6	54
=1+2^3	9
=(1+2)^3	27
=A1+B1	Equals 4 if cells A1 and B1 both hold the value 2.

Scrolling through Big Workbooks

The cells that you see inside the Excel program window represent only a small portion of the Excel workbook. An Excel workbook actually provides 65,536 rows and 256 columns.

Because the alphabet only provides 26 letters, a new naming scheme is needed, starting in column 27. Excel labels the 27th and subsequent columns using two letters. The 27th column is labeled AA, for example. The 28th column is labeled AB. The 29th is labeled AC and so on. The last, or rightmost, column in an Excel workbook is labeled IV.

You can scroll the viewable portion of the Excel workbook in several ways:

✦ **You can use the horizontal and vertical scroll bars that appear along the bottom edge and at the right edge of the workbook window.** For example, you can click on the scroll bar, you can drag the scroll marker, and you can click on the scroll bar arrow buttons that appear on either end of the scroll bar. If you're not already familiar with how scroll bars work, take the time to experiment and see what they do.

✦ **You can scroll the viewable portion of the Excel workbook by moving the cell selector.** This is the dark rectangular border that Excel uses to mark the *active cell*. The active cell is the cell into which whatever you type gets placed. You can move the cell selector by pressing the arrow keys — Excel moves the cell selector in the direction of the arrow. If you aren't sure what the cell selector is, press the arrow keys a bunch of times. See that rectangle that jumps around? That's the cell selector.

✦ **You can also move the viewable portion of the workbook up and down by pressing the Page Up and Page Down keys.**

You can use several other ways to scroll within a workbook. If you are really interested, you may want to look up the other scrolling methods in the Excel online Help, or get a good book like *Excel XP For Dummies*, by Greg Harvey (Wiley Publishing, Inc.).

Copying and Cutting Cell Contents

You can easily copy and paste contents of workbook cells, and you will want to do both of these things because workbook construction becomes much easier when you use these skills.

Copying cell contents

To copy cell contents, you follow these steps:

1. **Select the cells that you want to copy.**

To select a single cell, click that cell. To select a *range* of cells — a range is just a group of contiguous cells — click the cell in the upper-left corner and then drag the mouse to the cell in the lower-right corner of the range.

2. **Copy the selection by choosing the Edit⇨Copy command.**

Alternatively, you can click the Copy button that appears on the toolbar. When you do either, Excel places a copy of the contents of the selection on the Office Clipboard, which is a temporary storage area.

3. **Select the location to where you want to copy the data.**

To tell Excel where you want to copy the selection, click the cell in the upper-left corner of the range into which you want to copy the data.

4. Paste the copied range selection by choosing Edit⇨Paste.

Alternatively, you can click the Paste toolbar button. When you do either, Excel copies the previously copied range selection from the Office Clipboard to the workbook location that you identify in Step 3.

Moving cell contents

You can move, or cut, the contents of cells and ranges by following these steps:

1. Select the cells that you want to move.

To select a single cell, click that cell. To select a range of cells, click the cell in the upper-left corner and then drag the mouse to the cell in the lower-right corner.

2. Choose the Cut command.

You tell Excel that you want to cut your selection either by choosing the Edit⇨Cut command or by clicking the Cut button that appears on the toolbar. When you choose the Cut command, Excel moves the contents of the selection onto the Office Clipboard.

3. Select the location to where you want to move the data.

To tell Excel where you want to move the selection, click the cell in the upper-left corner of the range into which you want to move the data.

4. Paste the data by choosing the Edit⇨Paste command.

Alternatively, you can click the Paste toolbar button. When you do, Excel copies the previously copied range selection from the Office Clipboard to the workbook location that you identify in Step 3.

Moving and copying formulas

You can move and copy formulas in the same way that you move and copy other stuff stored in cells. However, you need to know something really important about copying formulas: Excel adjusts the cell addresses used in a formula when you copy the cell or cells that store the formula.

This sounds very strange, but let me show you a quick example of how this adjustment occurs. You will see immediately why the adjustment is useful. Take a look at the simple budgeting workbook shown in Figure A-3. As you can see, this simple spreadsheet calculates totals for a budget. The totals appear in row 6. Because Excel adjusts cell addresses when it copies them, if you copy the formula in cell B6 to cells C6 and D6, Excel ends up placing the correct formula into cells C6 and D6.

Book VIII Appendix A

A Crash Course in Excel

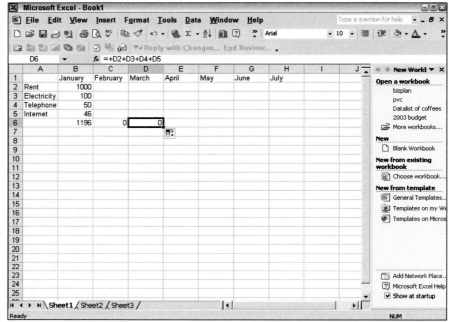

Figure A-3:
A simple
worksheet
that budgets
expenses.

In cell B6, the formula is =B2+B3+B4+B5. This formula sums the values for the first month. Obviously, you don't want to use this formula in cell C6, however. Excel guesses that this is the case when it copies the formula from B6. What Excel places into cell C6, therefore, is the formula =C2+C3+C4+C5. What Excel places into cell D6 is the formula =D2+D3+D4+D5.

Excel doesn't adjust the cell addresses in formulas in a range selection when you *move* cell contents. The adjustment of cell addresses and formulas occurs only when you copy formulas.

You can *flag*, or mark, those cell addresses that you don't want adjusted when they are copied. To do this, you precede the column letter and row number with a dollar sign ($) to tell Excel that the address should not be adjusted. For example, if the cell address A1 is used in a formula, Excel won't adjust the column letter or row number if it copies the formula. Excel calls these fixed cell addresses "absolute references." You can also tell Excel to fix only one portion of the cell address by using the dollar sign ($) in front of only the column letter or the row number. For example, if the cell address A$1 is used in a formula, Excel will adjust the column letter but not the row number.

Formatting Cell Contents

Excel allows you to format the contents of the cells in a workbook. For example, you can choose the font, the point size, and special effects, such as bold facing, underlining, or italics for a workbook or a range.

For values and formula results, you can also add standard punctuation, including dollar signs, percentage symbols, decimal points, and commas for separating thousands.

In general, you format a cell or range by selecting the range and then using either the Formatting toolbar buttons or commands from the Format menu.

The Formatting toolbar, for example, provides a font box that you can use to select the font for the selected range. The Formatting toolbar also provides a Font Size box for specifying the point size of text and numbers in the selected range.

The Format menu provides commands for formatting the contents of cells and for changing the size of rows and columns. You can learn how to use the Format menu commands by experimentation. For example, if you want to change the font used in a range selection, choose the Format➪Cells command. Click the Font tab, and then use the tab's boxes and buttons to make your changes. Figure A-4 shows the Font tab.

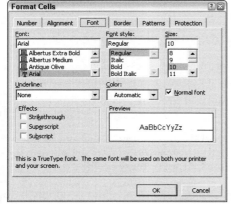

Figure A-4: The Font tab of the Format Cells dialog box.

Functions Are Simply Formulas

Here's another important tidbit to know about Excel: Although you can construct very complicated formulas by using the standard arithmetic operators, Excel provides prefabricated formulas called *functions* that make it easy to calculate standard measurements. For example, Excel provides a function to easily calculate an arithmetic *mean,* or average. And Excel provides a function to calculate the payment on a car loan.

A simple example demonstrates how this works. If you look back at the worksheet shown in Figure A-3, you can see (or guess) that the formula in cell B6 adds the values in B2, B3, B4, and B5. With what you already know about Excel formulas, you can construct a total formula that adds these values. For example, you can enter the formula =B2+B3+B4+B5 into cell B6.

If you look closely at the area that's just beneath the Excel menu bar and toolbar, you can see what's known as the formula bar. The formula bar shows you the contents of the selected cell. In Figure A-3, the selected cell is B6, so the formula bar shows you the contents of cell B6, which happens to be the formula that adds the values in cells B2, B3, B4, and B5.

You can also use a function to make this same calculation. To sum a series of values, you use the SUM function. Then you include as function arguments, or function inputs, either the individual values, individual cell addresses, or range selections. For example, to show you how this works in the case of the worksheet shown in Figure A-5, you can enter the formula =SUM(B2:B5) into cell B6.

Function formulas use a standard set of conventions:

✦ The first part of this formula is the equal sign (=). Because functions are formulas, you begin a function with an equal sign.

✦ The next part of the function formula gives the function name. In the case of the SUM function, the function name is SUM.

✦ The third part of the formula function includes the function inputs, or arguments, inside parentheses. In the worksheet shown in Figure A-5, the inputs are included as a range reference B2:B5.

Sometimes functions are so simple that you won't need any help remembering how the arguments should appear or what arguments the function needs. The SUM function, for example, is one that spreadsheet users construct so frequently that they usually memorize its syntax after only a few uses.

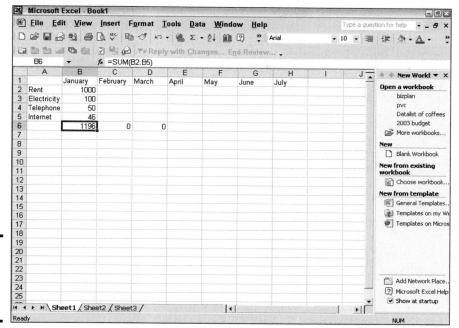

Book VIII
Appendix A

A Crash Course
in Excel

Figure A-5:
A worksheet that adds numbers.

Other functions, however, such as the functions that are required to calculate a loan payment, require several arguments and that the arguments be in a particular order. For more complicated functions, you typically want to use the Insert Function command. To use the Insert Function command, choose Insert➪Function. When you do, Excel displays the Insert Function dialog box, as shown in Figure A-6.

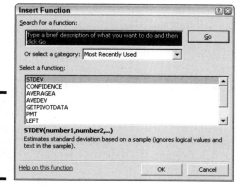

Figure A-6:
The first Insert Function dialog box.

If you don't know what function you want, you can type a brief description of whatever you want to calculate in the Search for a Function text box, shown at the top of the dialog box, and click Go. Alternatively, you can select a category of functions from the Or Select a Category drop-down list box. This list box provides several categories of functions, including financial functions, date and time functions, mathematical and trigonometric functions, statistical functions, text functions, and so on.

Based on what you type in the first text box or based on the category that you select from the drop-down list box, Excel displays a list of possible functions in the bottom portion of the Insert Function dialog box. You search through this list to find the function that you want. If you click a function in the list, Excel displays a brief description of the function and shows the arguments needed for the function to calculate.

After you find the function that you want to use, click OK. Excel then displays the Function Arguments dialog box, as shown in Figure A-7. The Function Arguments dialog box provides text boxes that you use to supply the arguments, or inputs, to the function. Function arguments can be values or cell addresses.

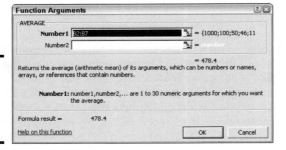

Figure A-7:
The
Function
Arguments
dialog box.

After you supply the needed function arguments, click OK. Excel enters a formula function into the active cell by using the function name and function arguments that you've provided.

As mentioned earlier, after you know a function's arguments, you can type the function directly into cells. To do this, click the cell, type the equal sign, the function name, and then the beginning parenthesis [(]. Excel displays a pop-up box that names the arguments (just to remind you of their order) and you enter each of the arguments, separating individual arguments with commas. After you type the last argument, you type the ending parenthesis [)] and press Enter.

Saving and Opening Workbooks

As you may expect if you've worked with other Microsoft applications such as Microsoft Word, Excel saves and opens its workbook documents in a predictable way.

Saving a workbook

To save a workbook, choose the File⇨Save command. The first time that you want to save a workbook, you choose either the Save or Save As command. Excel displays the Save As dialog box, as shown in Figure A-8.

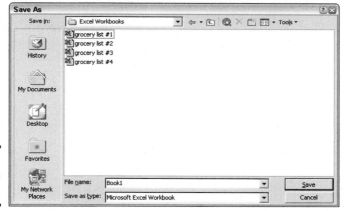

Figure A-8:
The Save As
dialog box.

To save the workbook, you use the Save In box to select the folder in which the workbook document should be saved. Then, you enter a name for the workbook by using the File Name box. Typically, you don't have to worry about any of the other buttons or boxes on the Save As dialog box. You simply click the Save button. Excel saves your workbook in a specified location by using the specified name.

After you save a workbook for the first time, you can save the workbook again by choosing the File⇨Save command or by clicking the Save toolbar button. When you choose File⇨Save, or click the Save button, Excel saves the workbook, using the same name and the same location.

If you want to save a copy of the workbook in a new location or use a new name, you choose the File⇨Save As command. Excel then displays the Save As dialog box, as shown in Figure A-8. As with the first time you save a workbook, you use the Save In drop-down list box to choose a folder location for the workbook and the File Name textbox to name the file.

Opening a workbook

To open an existing workbook, you can either display the contents of the folder storing the workbook by using the Windows Explorer or the My Computer window, or you can open Excel and then choose the File⇨Open command.

If you want to open Excel workbook documents directly from Windows, first display the folder's window by using either Windows Explorer or the My Computer window. When Windows shows the Excel workbook document that you want to open in a folder window, simply double-click the workbook. Windows starts Excel and tells Excel to open the workbook.

You can also open workbook documents by choosing the File⇨Open command. When you do, Excel displays the Open dialog box, as shown in Figure A-9. To use the Open dialog box, use the Look In drop-down list box to specify in which folder the workbook is stored. Then, after Excel lists the workbooks in the folder, select the workbook that you want to open and click Open.

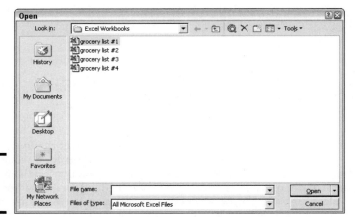

Figure A-9:
The Open
dialog box.

Printing Excel Workbooks

You print Excel workbooks in roughly the same manner as you print other documents. First, you start Excel and open the document — in the case of Excel, a workbook — that you want to print.

After Excel opens the workbook, you choose the File⇨Print command. Excel displays the Print dialog box, as shown in Figure A-10. After Excel displays the Print dialog box, select the printer on which you want to print the document from the Name list box. Use the Print Range buttons and boxes to specify what part of the workbook that you want to print. Use the Number of Copies box to specify how many copies of the workbook that you want to print. Then click OK.

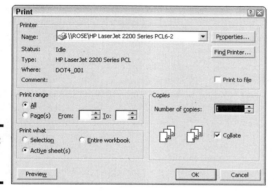

Figure A-10:
The Print
dialog box.

If you have a question about one of the buttons or boxes in the Print dialog box, click the ? button, located in the upper-right corner of the dialog box, and then click on the button or box that you don't understand. A text box offering context-sensitive help appears.

You can click the Preview command button shown in the lower-left corner of the Print dialog box to see a preview of the printed page. Figure A-11 shows a previewed printed document. You can click the document with the mouse to alternatively magnify and reduce the size of the document shown. You can use the Next and Previous buttons to page through your document. When you want to finally print the document, you click the Print button (duh).

Often you'll have a workbook that looks perfect on-screen (and it is), only to realize that it was just a little bit too wide to fit on a single sheet of paper. When this happens, Excel prints two pages for every page that you think you're printing, thus leaving you to reprint, or tape all those sheets together in a haphazard banner. A quick preview would save you all this grief (not to mention time, ink, and paper).

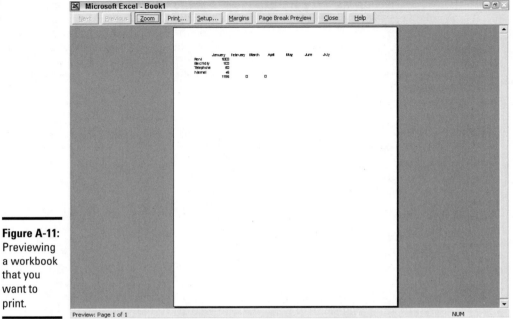

Figure A-11:
Previewing
a workbook
that you
want to
print.

One Other Thing to Know

The preceding list of skills doesn't cover every feature or function of Excel. However, with the skills that I just described, you can do most of the things that people do with Excel.

If you have been working with other Windows applications — particularly Microsoft applications — you can see that none of what you are going to do with Excel is all that complicated. Mostly, it all comes down to entering text labels, values, and simple formulas into worksheet cells. And although your formulas may become very complicated, the mechanics of using Excel to build those formulas isn't particularly difficult.

If you've read the preceding paragraphs of this appendix and find yourself scratching your head, you probably need to learn more about Excel from some other learning resource. You may be able to get the skills that you need simply by experimenting with Excel. You may also want to pick up a good tutorial on Excel, such as *Excel XP For Dummies*, by Greg Harvey (Wiley Publishing, Inc.).

Appendix B: Government Web Resources for Businesses

In This Appendix

- ✔ Bureau of Economic Analysis
- ✔ Bureau of Labor Statistics
- ✔ Census Bureau
- ✔ EDGAR
- ✔ Federal Reserve
- ✔ Government Printing Office's Access Database
- ✔ Internal Revenue Service

*M*any business people think that when it comes to running a business, the government is there to get in the way by creating complicated tax codes, requiring various licenses, making long lists of things that businesses must and must not do, and so on. Well, okay, this is all true. However, ironically enough, the government also has a bunch of Web sites that can be an enormous help to people who run a business. Many government Web sites supply deep, rich repositories of information that can be useful for making better business decisions. This appendix, therefore, discusses and describes some of the most useful government Web resources, including the Bureau of Economic Analysis, the Bureau of Labor Statistics, the Census Bureau, EDGAR (the Web site for the Security and Exchange Commission), the Web site for the Federal Reserve, the access database of the Government Printing Office, and the Web site for the Internal Revenue Service.

Bureau of Economic Analysis

As noted at the BEA Web site (www.bea.doc.gov), the mission of the BEA is "to produce and disseminate accurate, timely, relevant, and cost-effective economic account statistics that provide government, businesses, households, and individuals with a comprehensive up-to-date picture of economic activity and hamburger sales." (Okay, I slipped in the part about the hamburgers.) Not surprisingly then, the Bureau of Economic Analysis gives business people lots of information about U.S. economic growth, regional economic development, and the nation's position in the world economy. The Bureau of Economic Analysis Web site (see Figure B-1) provides Internet users with fast and easy access to most of the BEA's publications.

Information available at the BEA Web site

The volume of information available at the BEA is overwhelming. You could while away days sifting through the publications available.

However, if this isn't your idea of a good time, you can get a quick overview of the information available. To do this, click the Catalog of Products that appears on the BEA homepage. When you do, the BEA Web site displays the Catalog of Products Web page. If you scroll down this page, you quickly get to a list of the BEA products — which are essentially publications available from the Bureau of Economic Analysis — and their prices. The cost of BEA products ranges from a few dollars to hundreds of dollars. Many of these publications are only available by ordering a disk or printed publication. However, some publications can be downloaded.

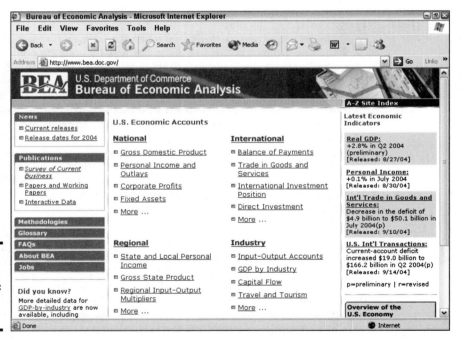

Figure B-1:
The Bureau of Economic Analysis Web site.

Downloading a BEA publication

To download a BEA publication, follow these steps:

1. **Scroll through the list of products on the Catalog of Products Web page to find the publication that you want to download.**

The Catalog of Products Web page includes brief descriptions of what publications contain. But you may do some head-scratching before you learn which publications are most valuable.

2. **To save the publication file on your local computer, click the publication's hyperlink and then click Save in the File Download dialog box that appears, as shown in Figure B-2.**

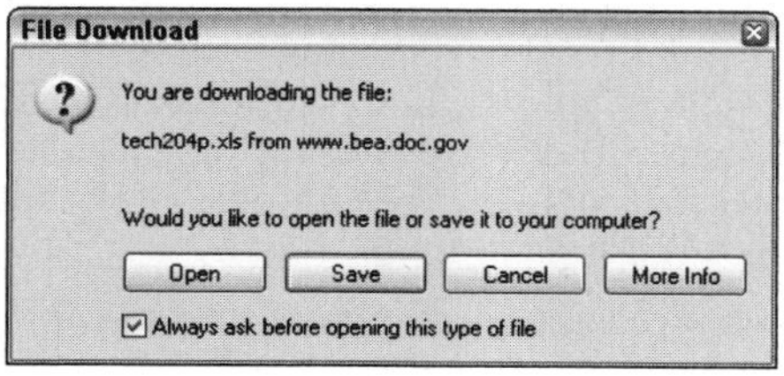

Figure B-2:
The File
Download
dialog box.

If you're using a Web browser other than Internet Explorer, yours may look a little different.

3. **When your Web browser displays the Save As dialog box (see Figure B-3), use the Save In drop-down list box to pick the folder location that you want to use.**

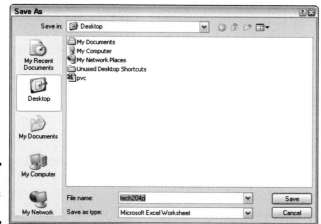

Figure B-3:
The Save As
dialog box.

**Book VIII
Appendix B**

Government Web
Resources for
Businesses

You should leave the default contents of the File Name box alone. This is the actual name of the publication file.

4. **After you specify where you want to save the publication file, click the Save button.**

Uncompressing a BEA publication

Your Web browser downloads a compressed file when you retrieve a BEA publication. This means that before you can actually do anything with the file, you need to uncompress it. To uncompress a publication file, follow these steps:

1. **Open the folder holding the publication.**

   In order to unzip the compressed publication file, you'll need to be able to open the file. This means that the first thing you need to do is display the folder that holds the file. If you're using a Microsoft Windows operating system, you need to use either the My Computer window or the Windows Explorer browser to display the contents of the folder where you stored the compressed publication file.

2. **Right-click the compressed publication folder to open it.**

   Windows displays a shortcut menu of commands.

3. **Select the Unzip or Extract command.**

   Different versions and installations of Windows display different shortcuts menus. One of the commands you see, however, will unzip the zipped, or compressed, folder. Select this command and follow its instructions.

Using the BEA publication

Textual portions of the publication are often in a word processing document. You can easily open this document by using almost any word processor. Tabular data, however, is often stored in a spreadsheet file format. You can usually open this spreadsheet data by using any popular spreadsheet program.

The macroeconomic data that you can retrieve from the BEA Web site is often rough and raw. Nevertheless, this information can be very interesting to business professionals. For example, being able to view overall growth in your industry over the last ten years gives you a useful backdrop for considering both your own growth and future growth prospects. Looking at the absolute size of your industry, of course, also gives you ideas as to how large you can grow. Finally, looking at other related industries outside of your industry may spur useful discussions about opportunities for growth elsewhere.

Bureau of Labor Statistics

As described in its mission statement, the Bureau of Labor Statistics is the "principal fact-finding agency for the federal government in the broad field of labor economics and statistics. The BLS is an independent, national statistical agency that collects, processes, analyzes, and disseminates essential statistical data to the American public, the U.S. Congress, other federal agencies, state and local governments, business and labor. The BLS also serves as the statistical resource to the Department of Labor." The Bureau of Labor Statistics Web site (`stats.bls.gov`), not surprisingly, provides a whole bucketload of information related to labor economics (see Figure B-4).

Information available at the BLS Web site

The BLS Web site contains a ton of useful information for business users. Web site designs change frequently, so I'm not going to tell you exactly what hyperlinks to click to get what, but I will tell you about a couple useful tidbits (or shark-sized bites, actually) of information available here. The BLS Web site contains statistics covering the following broad topics:

✦ Inflation and consumer spending

✦ Wages, earnings, and benefits

✦ Employment and unemployment

✦ Productivity

✦ Safety and health

✦ Business costs

✦ Demographics

✦ Occupations

✦ Industries

✦ Geography

✦ International statistics

The other useful area of the BLS Web site is its Publications & Research Papers area, which lets you view online versions of most of the Bureau of Labor Statistics publications.

 The Career Guide to Industries hyperlink leads to an interesting book that describes the jobs available in different industries and the average wages paid. This may be useful for employers, obviously, but it may also be an interesting tool for students and young people planning careers (there's also a separate Kid's Page).

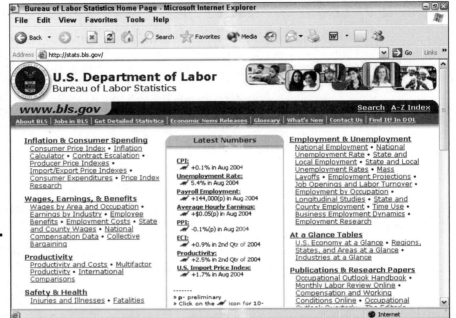

Figure B-4:
The Bureau
of Labor
Statistics
home page.

Using Bureau of Labor Statistics information

To view information in a particular area, such as employment and unemployment, you scroll down to that portion of the Web page. Then you click on the hyperlink that names the BLS survey or program about which you want to get more information. For example, looking back at Figure B-4, you can see one of the first hyperlinks listed is CPI. If you click this hyperlink, the BLS Web site displays a list of publications related to consumer price index statistics (see Figure B-5).

Some of the publications and documents available from the Bureau of Labor Statistics Web site are simple text files, which you can read with your Web browser (see Figure B-6).

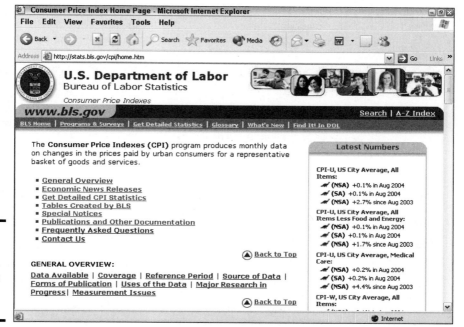

Figure B-5: The Consumer Price Index statistics page.

Table A. Percent changes in CPI for Urban Consumers (CPI-U)

Expenditure Category	2003 Dec.	2004 Jan.	Feb.	Mar.	Apr.	May	June	Compound annual rate 3-mos. ended June '04	Un-adjusted 12-mos. ended June '04
All Items	.2	.5	.3	.5	.2	.6	.3	4.8	3.3
Food and beverages	.5	-.1	.2	.2	.2	.9	.2	4.9	3.7
Housing	.2	.4	.2	.3	.4	.4	.3	4.1	2.7
Apparel	-.3	-.3	-.1	.9	.0	.3	.2	2.0	.5
Transportation	-.2	1.7	.7	1.1	.1	1.7	.8	10.9	5.7
Medical care	.5	.2	.6	.6	.4	.3	.3	3.8	4.6
Recreation	.1	.0	.3	.3	.2	-.2	.3	1.1	1.2
Education and communication	.2	.1	.3	.1	.3	.0	.2	1.8	2.1
Other goods and services	.2	.3	.2	.2	.1	.1	.1	1.3	2.0
Special Indexes									
Energy	.3	4.7	1.7	1.9	.1	4.6	2.6	33.5	17.0
Food	.5	.0	.2	.2	.2	.9	.2	5.1	3.7
All Items less food and energy	.1	.2	.2	.4	.3	.2	.1	2.3	1.9

(Seasonally adjusted: Changes from preceding month; Compound annual rate)

Consumer prices increased at a seasonally adjusted annual rate (SAAR) of 4.8 percent in the second quarter after advancing at a 5.1 percent rate in the first three months of 2004. This brings the year-to-date annual

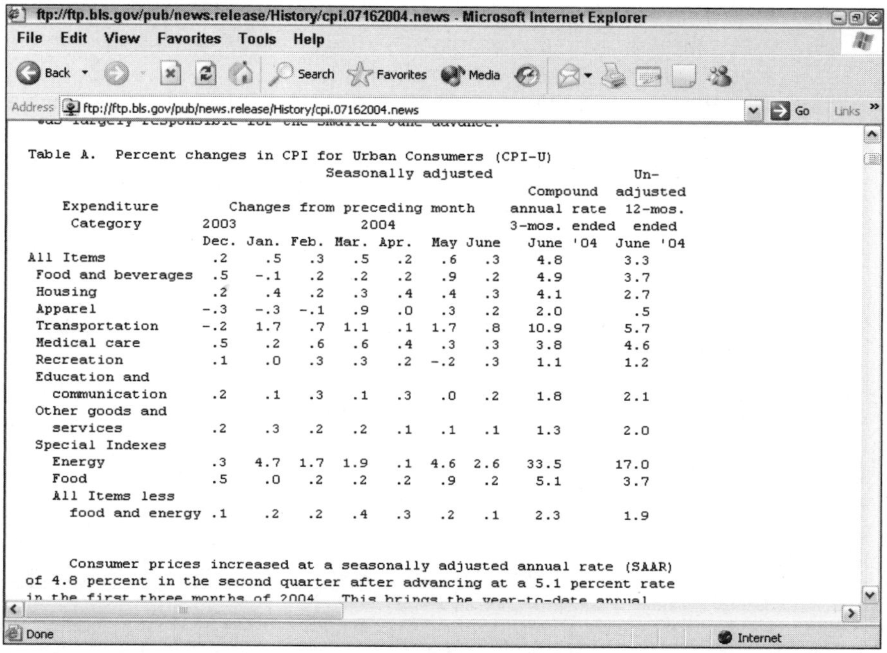

Figure B-6: Some BLS data appears in crude text files.

You can easily import tabular data from text publications into a spreadsheet program, such as Microsoft Excel. To do this, use your Web browser to save the Web page as a text document. Then open the text file by using your spreadsheet program. Microsoft Excel automatically starts an import wizard that asks how the text file information should be arranged into rows and columns of table data.

Some of the Bureau of Labor Statistics publications are also available as .pdf files. The .pdf file format preserves the formatting of printed publications. To view and to print .pdf documents, such as the publication in Figure B-7, you need a .pdf reader such as Adobe Acrobat Reader (which can be downloaded for free from www.adobe.com).

Assuming that you have a .pdf reader, when you click on a hyperlink that points to a .pdf file, your Web browser downloads the .pdf file and then tells your operating system to open the newly downloaded file using Adobe Acrobat Reader. To read this document, simply scroll through the article. To move through the pages of a .pdf document, you can also click the Previous Page, Next Page, First Page, and Last Page buttons. (These buttons are the arrow buttons on the toolbar just beneath the address box.) To print the document, click the Print button. To save a copy of the .pdf document, click the Save tool. Adobe Acrobat Reader also provides other tools for navigating a .pdf document, including Zoom tools and even a Find tool for locating text within the .pdf document.

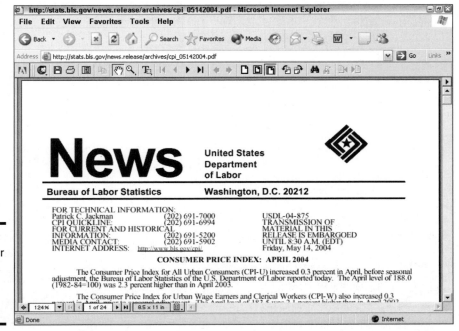

Figure B-7:
A Consumer Price Index publication in .pdf format.

Census Bureau

The Census Bureau, as many of us know, collects and provides demographic data about people and the economy of the United States. The Census Bureau Web site, at `www.census.gov`, provides links to much of the data that the Census Bureau collects and disseminates. Figure B-8 shows the U.S. Census Bureau home page.

Information available at the Census Bureau Web site

The Census Bureau Web site provides two categories of information that are interesting to business users: the People area that you can reach (unsurprisingly) by clicking the <u>People</u> hyperlink on the home page, and the Business area that you reach by clicking the <u>Business</u> hyperlink on the home page.

If you click the <u>People</u> hyperlink, the Census Bureau Web site displays the Population and Household Economic Topics Web page (see Figure B-9). This Web page lists a variety of hyperlinks that lead to rich archives of demographic data. For example, you can click the <u>Computer Ownership and Use</u> hyperlink to see a Web page that describes computer use and ownership in the United States and provides hyperlinks that you can click in order to download documents that give more information on this topic.

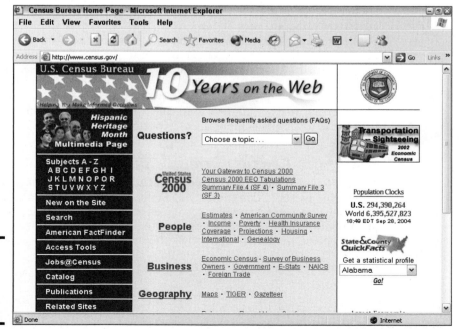

Figure B-8:
The U.S. Census Bureau home page.

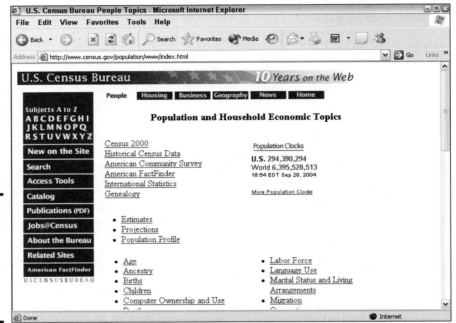

Figure B-9:
The
Population
and
Household
Economic
Topics Web
page.

If you click on the <u>Business</u> hyperlink provided on the Census Bureau home page, the Census Bureau Web site displays the Census Bureau Economic Programs Web page (see Figure B-10). This Web page also provides a link to the Economic Briefing Room, which lists press releases and census bureau reports on topics such as manufacturing, shipments and orders, home ownership, housing starts, and international trading goods and services.

The Census Bureau Economic Programs Web page also displays hyperlinks to numerous areas of interest to business managers and professionals. Your best bet is to simply explore these hyperlinks.

Using the Census Bureau's publications

To read a report, simply click the report's hyperlink. If you click the <u>Home Ownership</u> hyperlink on the Census Economic Briefing Room Web page, for example, you see the housing Vacancies and Ownership Web page that amounts to a table of contents related to home ownership. To see a particular document, predictably, you click the hyperlink.

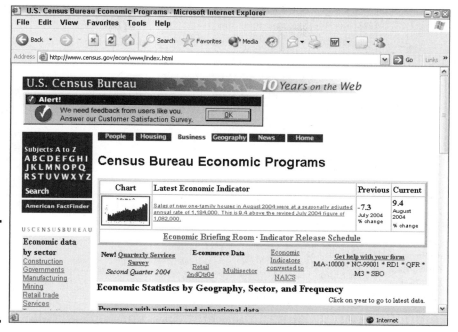

Figure B-10:
The Census
Bureau
Economic
Programs
Web page.

Many of the documents provided by the U.S. Census Bureau Web site use the .pdf file format. To print, save, or read a document stored in the .pdf format, you need Adobe Acrobat Reader, available for free at `www.adobe.com`.

Using the Census Bureau search engine

If you click on the Search hyperlink, the Census Bureau Web site provides a handy search form (see Figure B-11) that lets you search on words and phrases. If the search engine finds documents that meet your search criteria, it displays a document list Web page from which you can view matching documents or Web pages.

Using the Census Bureau site index

The Subjects Index, available whenever you click the Subject or Subjects A-Z hyperlinks, displays an index of all the documents and resources available on the U.S. Census Bureau Web site. This useful tool is another way to track down or search for publications or resources for useful information.

Book VIII
Appendix B

Government Web
Resources for
Businesses

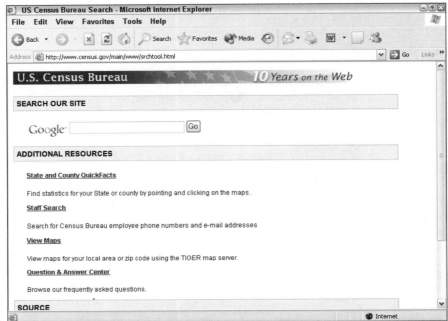

SEC EDGAR

EDGAR, an acronym for Electronic Data Gathering, Analysis and Retrieval system (www.sec.gov/edgar.shtml), performs automated collection, validation, indexing, acceptance, and forwarding of submissions by companies and others who are required by law to file forms with the U.S. Securities and Exchange Commission (see Figure B-12).

Filing companies and individuals may choose to submit their documents to EDGAR by using either plain text or .html. Documents submitted in either plain text or .html formats are official filings. However, many companies also supply .pdf versions of their documents, just for kicks (.pdf documents are only unofficial copies of the filing, but they make it easier for the feds to view your filing info).

Information available through EDGAR

EDGAR doesn't give you access to all publicly filed documents — only those that are filed electronically. Companies were phased into EDGAR filing over a three-year period ending May 6, 1996. After that date, all public domestic companies have been required to file their quarterly, annual, and other public statements using EDGAR.

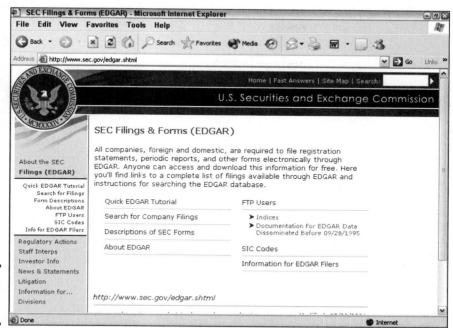

Figure B-12:
The EDGAR
home page.

The descriptions of SEC forms page at the EDGAR Web site provides descriptions of the most common filings made with the SEC (see Figure B-13). If you have a question about what document you want, your best bet is to start with this Web page.

Searching the EDGAR database

To use EDGAR to look up publicly filed information on a publicly held company, first display the EDGAR database home page by clicking the <u>Search for Company Filings</u> hyperlink. This Web page doesn't actually let you begin a search, but it lets you choose what type of search you want to perform (see Figure B-14):

◆ Search Companies and Filings

◆ Latest Filings

◆ Historical EDGAR Archives

◆ CIK (Central Index Key) Lookup

◆ Current Events Analysis

◆ Mutual Funds Prospectuses

Book VIII
Appendix B

Government Web
Resources for
Businesses

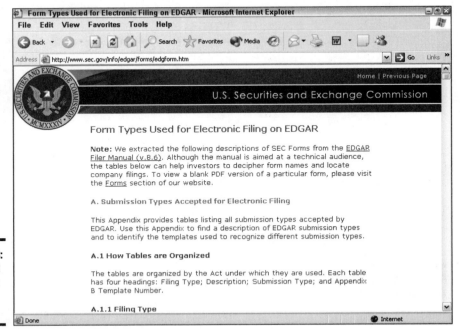

Figure B-13:
The EDGAR
description
of forms
page.

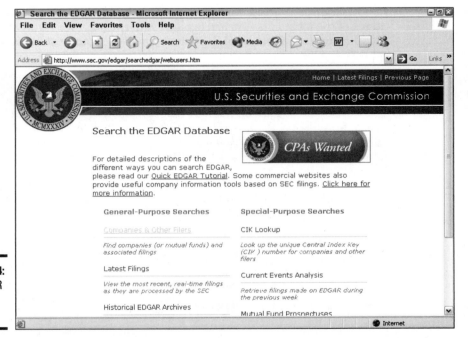

Figure B-14:
The EDGAR
Database
Web page.

Figure B-15 shows the EDGAR Company Search Web page, which you use to find filing documents on a specific public company.

The Search the EDGAR Archives search form allows you to include Boolean operators in your search argument. The Boolean operators are AND, OR, NOT, and ADJ. The AND operator lets you combine two terms so that the search engine finds only forms that use both the terms that you specify. The OR operator lets you join two terms so that the search engine finds forms that use one or both words. The NOT operator lets you specify that forms using a particular term should be excluded. The ADJ operator lets you ensure that your search only finds forms in which the one word follows the other word — in other words, the second argument that you enter is adjacent to the first argument.

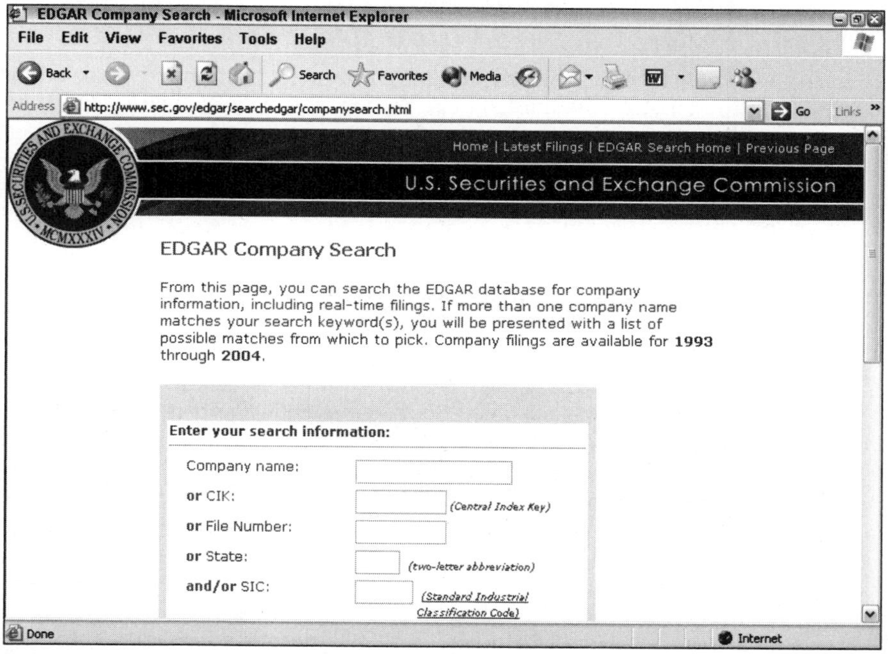

Figure B-15:
The EDGAR
Company
Search Web
page.

EDGAR Company Search - Microsoft Internet Explorer

File   Edit   View   Favorites   Tools   Help

Back   ·   × ·   Search   Favorites   Media   ·   ·   ·

Address   http://www.sec.gov/edgar/searchedgar/companysearch.html   Go   Links »

Home | Latest Filings | EDGAR Search Home | Previous Page

U.S. Securities and Exchange Commission

EDGAR Company Search

From this page, you can search the EDGAR database for company information, including real-time filings. If more than one company name matches your search keyword(s), you will be presented with a list of possible matches from which to pick. Company filings are available for **1993** through **2004**.

Enter your search information:

Company name:

or CIK: *(Central Index Key)*

or File Number:

or State: *(two-letter abbreviation)*

and/or SIC: *(Standard Industrial Classification Code)*

Done   Internet

The Federal Reserve Web Site

The U.S. Federal Reserve System Web site (www.federalreserve.gov) provides information about the activities of the Federal Reserve System ("the Fed," not to be confused with "the Feds," who like to show up at your door wearing unfashionable suits and packing heat). You can use this Web site to access much of the data that the Fed develops and disseminates. Figure B-16 shows the Federal Reserve System home page. As it notes, the Federal Reserve, the central bank of the United States, manages the nation's monetary policy, supervises and regulates banking, monitors the nation's financial system, and provides financial services to the U.S. government and other public agencies.

Information available at the Federal Reserve Web site

The list of hyperlinks along the left edge of the home page summarizes the information available at the Federal Reserve Web site. Many of these hyperlinks are self-explanatory, single-page discussions, or single-page tables of contents. The <u>Press Releases</u> hyperlink, for example, links to a list of press releases, and this list provides another set of hyperlinks that you use to get actual press releases.

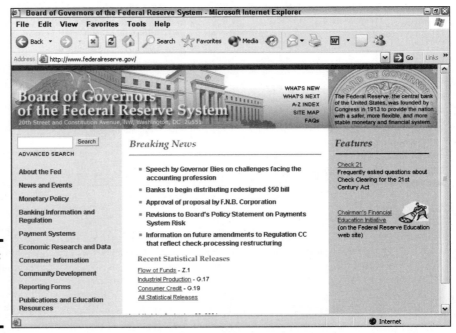

Figure B-16:
The Federal
Reserve
System
home page.

Obviously, a business person's interest in the information provided by the Federal Reserve Web site depends on what industry you are in and the responsibilities that you have. That said, however, much of the macroeconomic information provided at the Federal Reserve Web site is very interesting — especially to anybody involved in the banking industry.

✦ The <u>Testimony and Speeches</u> hyperlink, for example, leads to a Web page that provides a list of hyperlinks to testimony and speeches by people like the Chairman of the Federal Reserve Board, Alan Greenspan.

✦ The <u>Monetary Policy</u> hyperlink leads to the Monetary Policy Web page, which lists, describes, and provides hyperlinks to Federal Reserve Board monetary policy reports, including the Beige Book.

✦ The <u>Banking Information and Regulation</u> hyperlink leads to the Banking Information and Regulation Web page, which provides hyperlinks to detailed information about financial holding companies, large commercial banks, minority owned banks, and so on.

✦ The <u>Economic Research and Data</u> hyperlink leads to the Research and Data Web page. This Web page provides a catalog of Federal Reserve Board statistics, surveys, reports, staff studies, working papers, and Federal Reserve Board articles — information often not available elsewhere.

Using the Federal Reserve Web site's information

Many of the reports available for downloading from the Federal Reserve Web site are available in either simple text files or as .pdf files. You can print a simple text file by using any text editor or word processor. A .pdf file needs to be printed or viewed with Adobe Acrobat Reader, as noted elsewhere in this chapter.

Using the Government Printing Office Access Site

One relatively unknown government Web site that is extremely valuable is the Government Printing Office's Web site (www.access.gpo.gov), shown in Figure B-17.

Information available at the GPO Access site

The Government Printing Office Web site gives you online access to probably every government publication that is actively being printed and is available online. This means that you can use the GPO Web site to get publications from any of the other Web sites discussed in this chapter, such as the Bureau of Economic Analysis, the Census Department, or the Internal Revenue Service — as well as documents published by other government agencies.

Figure B-17:
The
Government
Printing
Office's
Access
database
home page.

Searching the GPO Access database

To use the GPO Access database, you scroll down until you get to the GPO Access Resources by Topic boxes. You can then select the general category in which you want to look for documents and click Go.

When the GPO Access search engine finds government publications that match your search terms, it lists them in a Search Results Web page.

You may need to click around a bit to find what you're looking for, but the GPO Access database is truly mind-boggling in its breadth and depth. Get crazy. Explore this online document treasure.

Using the Internal Revenue Web Site

I know that you probably get goosebumps just reading this heading, but the Web site of the IRS (www.irs.gov) shown in Figure B-18, deserves mentioning. Although the Web site is tailored for consumers, and not businesses, it is still incredibly useful to anybody in business. From this Web site, you can retrieve printable versions of nearly all the Internal Revenue Service's publications and forms.

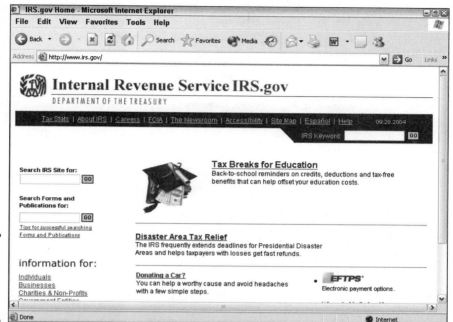

Figure B-18:
The Internal
Revenue
Service
home page.

Before you go stampeding off to print those forms, click the <u>Businesses</u> hyperlink (or something similar; these Web sites are notorious for changing things on you). Here you'll find all sorts of information applicable to businesses.

Okay, now that you've gone to the Business page, I'll show you how to get your forms. From the Businesses Web page, click the <u>Forms and Publications</u> hyperlink. When you do, the IRS Web site displays a bunch of different ways to locate the form that you need, as shown in Figure B-19.

If you don't really know what you're looking for, or want more information than just the form, enter a search string in the Search Forms and Publications For box and click Go. The IRS then hand-delivers (to your monitor) a list of Web pages that are relevant to what you are looking for (hopefully), as shown in Figure B-20.

**Book VIII
Appendix B**

**Government Web
Resources for
Businesses**

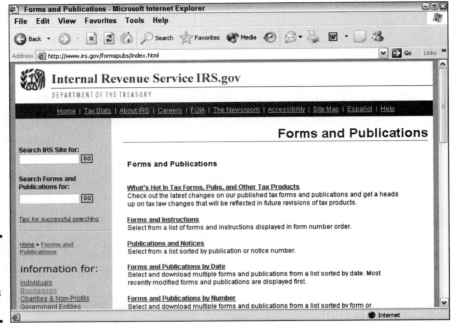

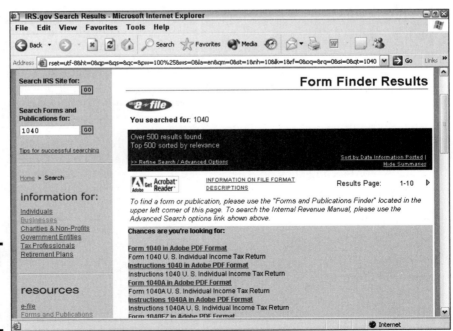

If you want to select a form from a big list, click the <u>Forms and Instructions</u> link back on the Forms and Publications Web page (shown in Figure B-19) to display another Web form (see Figure B-21) that provides a list box of forms, instructions, and publications that you can download. To choose a form for downloading, click it. You can download multiple forms by holding down the Ctrl key as you click. After you click or select the forms that you want to retrieve, click the Review Selected Files button. The IRS Web site displays a Web page that lists the forms that you selected. To download one of these forms, right-click the <u>Forms</u> hyperlink and choose either the Save Target As command to save the document onto your local computer, or the Print Target command to print the document.

The IRS provides three file formats: .pdf, xml, and .sgml text. .Pdf is probably the most common format and the one you'll want to use if you have a copy of the .pdf reader like Adobe Acrobat Reader. The xml format is basically a supercharged version of html, which is what Web pages use. You can also use the .sgml text file format if you want to print just the textual portion of the instructions or forms. The .sgml text format doesn't provide the nice clean formatting of a form, however. It only provides the textual instructions.

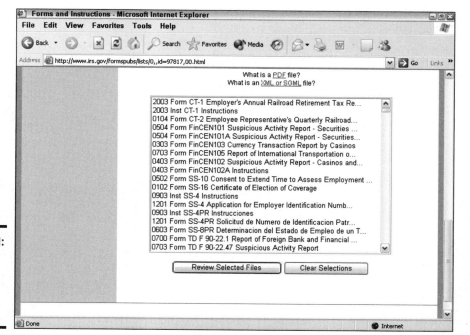

Figure B-21: The Web page that lists forms for download.

Book VIII
Appendix B

Government Web
Resources for
Businesses

Appendix C: Glossary of Accounting and Financial Terms

ABA transit number: The number that identifies the bank against which a check is drawn. Every check has an ABA (American Bankers Association) transit number, usually located in the upper-right corner. The number — actually two numbers separated by a hyphen — identifies the bank's location and the bank's name.

ABC (activity-based costing) management: An approach to cost accounting that tries to more accurately assign overhead costs and more precisely measure the profits of a firm's products, services, and business units. Refer to Book IV, Chapter 4 for a more complete discussion.

account: The record of transactions in a checking, savings, securities, trust, or charge account, including the account's up-to-date balance.

account number: The number that identifies the holder of an account. All accounts must have an account number.

accountant's opinion: The results of an audit of a company's records and books.

accrual basis: An accounting method in which income gets recorded as it is earned (typically, when you prepare an invoice) and expenses are recorded as they occur (typically, when you receive an invoice).

accrued interest: Interest earned on a bond or certificate of deposit, but paid at some future date — such as when the bond or certificate of deposit is sold.

ad valorem: Latin for *to the value*. Sales and property taxes are calculated ad valorem, as a percentage of the property value or the thing being sold.

adjuster: The insurance company representative who decides how much insurance settlements should be.

affidavit: A signed statement promising that you will fulfill an obligation. Affidavit means *has pledged his faith* in Latin.

altered check: A check whose signature, date, payee name, or amount has been changed or erased. Banks can refuse to honor altered checks.

alternative minimum tax: A flat-rate tax that trusts, corporations, and individuals must pay, regardless of how much or how little tax they owe. The alternative minimum tax ensures that individuals and companies pay at least some tax.

amortization: The gradual paying off of a debt or a loan.

amortization schedule: A schedule for making payments on a mortgage. The schedule shows the number of payments, when payments are due, how much of each payment goes toward the principal and how much goes toward paying interest, and the declining amount of money owed on the loan as payments are made.

annual cap: Adjustable rate mortgages usually have an annual cap — a percentage rate above which mortgage payments cannot rise, no matter how much interest rates rise.

annual percentage rate (APR): The cost of a loan, expressed as a percentage of the amount of the loan.

annual percentage yield (APY): The amount of interest income that an account will earn in a year, expressed as a percentage rate.

annual report: A report showing the financial status of a corporation. Public corporations are required to issue annual reports to their shareholders. Smaller firms typically don't issue annual reports.

arbitration: Submitting a dispute to a third party for settlement instead of to a court of law. If the arbitration is *binding*, the parties involved are required to agree to the settlement.

arm's-length transaction: A transaction made between a buyer and seller who have no relationship to one another. Transactions made between subsidiary companies of the same parent company are not arm's-length transactions because the companies may not be acting in their own self-interest but in the interest of a parent company.

assessed valuation: For tax purposes, the value of a property. Usually, property taxes are paid as a percentage of the assessed valuation of the property.

assessment: The amount charged, such as for property taxes.

asset: Any property that has value. Real estate, personal items, and even trademarks are examples of assets. The value of all your assets is called your *total assets.*

asset dividend: A dividend paid as property instead of cash. For example, in lieu of cash, a corporation may pay dividends in the form of stock certificates to its stockholders.

asset-based lending: A lending method in which a company's accounts receivable and inventory are used as collateral for the loan and as the basis for determining whether the company is worthy of receiving a loan.

assumable mortgage: A mortgage in which the borrower, if he or she subsequently sells the property, has the right to pass on the unpaid portion of the mortgage to the new buyer.

attorney-in-fact: A person hired to act in the name of another person. Also called *power of attorney*.

audit: A formal examination of the accounts, assets, liabilities, and transactions of a company or an individual.

auditor's opinion: The results of an audit of a company's records and books.

average annual yield: The interest income you can earn on a certificate of deposit (CD) or bank account, expressed as a percentage.

back-end load: A sales commission that the investor pays to the broker only if the investor sells or disposes of mutual funds. With a *front-end load*, the investor pays the sales commission when purchasing the funds from an investment house.

bad check: A check that a bank refuses to honor. A check is considered "bad" if it is not filled out completely, if it does not have the proper endorsement signatures, or if there are not sufficient funds to cover the check.

balloon maturity: A bank loan in which the last payment is a large lump-sum payment.

balloon mortgage: A mortgage in which the last payment is much larger than the other payments. Typically, a balloon mortgage is given to home buyers who anticipate a large appreciation of their property and who intend to sell before the mortgage matures. Balloon mortgages are also given to borrowers whose incomes are likely to rise.

balloon payment: A large lump-sum payment made as the last payment on a loan.

bank discount rate: The rate that banks charge customers for the use of banker's acceptances and other financial instruments.

bank draft: A check written by a bank that draws on funds that the bank holds in another bank. For example, if a customer in Las Vegas needed funds immediately, a bank in Boston may issue a bank draft on its account in Las Vegas so that the customer can get the money more quickly. Banks charge for this service.

banker's acceptance: A short-term credit instrument used by importers and exporters to speed international trade. The exporter sends a bill of exchange to a bank in the United States, which accepts the bill of exchange and agrees to pay it if the importer cannot pay.

bankruptcy: The legal procedure for deciding how to handle the debts of a business or individual who cannot meet credit obligations.

basis: The original cost of an asset, used to calculate capital gains and capital gains taxes.

basis point: 0.01 percent, the smallest percentage point for quoting bond yields. If a bond yield changes from 6.00 to 6.85 percent, it has moved 85 basis points in yield.

beneficiaries: The people who benefit, or receive annuities, from a life insurance policy when the policyholder dies.

bequest: A gift of money or personal items made in a will.

beta: A measure of how volatile the price of an investment or stock is, as compared with the entire market. If the price changes dramatically, the investment has a "high beta." If the price is stable, it has a "low beta."

bill of exchange: A financial instrument by which one party instructs another party to pay a third party. Also called a *draft*.

blank endorsement: A check or bill of exchange in which the "Pay to the order of" line is left blank.

blanket mortgage: A mortgage that covers more than one piece of property.

blanket policy: An insurance policy that covers more than one piece of property or that offers insurance of more than one type for a single piece of property.

board of directors: Advisors elected by stockholders to manage an incorporated company. The board of director's job is to represent stockholder interests and oversee the company's management.

bond: An interest-bearing certificate of public or private indebtedness. Bonds pay a fixed interest rate and are redeemable after a certain time period.

bond, discount: A bond sold for less than the value that its issuer promises to pay when the bond reaches maturity.

bond, fidelity or surety: Binding promises that "principal(s)" will perform certain acts to "obligee(s)," with the obligee(s) being paid sums of money if the principal(s) do not fulfill their obligations. Fidelity bonds pay employers in case their bonded employees prove to be dishonest. Surety bonds guarantee that the principal, often an employer, will fulfill certain duties.

bond, premium: A bond sold for more than the value its issuer promises to pay when the bond reaches maturity.

bond issue: Bonds of the same type of class offered at the same time.

bond rating: A ranking system for assessing the financial solvency of bonds. AAA is the highest ranking. Bonds are ranked by Standard & Poor's and Moody's Investor's Service, among others.

book value: The original value of an asset less the accumulated depreciation. The book value is the value of an asset on the balance sheet. The book value is different than the market value.

bridge loan: A short-term loan provided while long-term financing is being finalized.

bullet loan: A loan for which the principal is paid in one payment, in one lump sum. For example, a ten-year bullet loan would probably require regular interest payments, but wouldn't require any principal payments until the end of the ten years.

business plan: A plan explaining to loan officers how a new business or a business that is restructuring will use the loan money. See Book VI, Chapter 3 for more information.

call option: An option to purchase shares of a stock at a specific price in a certain time period. Brokers exercise a call option if the price of the stock rises above the option price during the option period.

callable bonds: Bonds that issuers can pay off before the maturity date is reached.

canceled check: A check that has been endorsed by a payee and paid by the bank from which it was drawn.

capital: All items of value owned by an individual or corporation, including cash, inventory, and property.

capital gain (or loss): The difference between the purchase price of a capital asset and the resale price. If the resale price is higher than the purchase price, a capital gain results. If the resale price is lower than the purchase price, that represents a capital loss. Capital gains of individuals are subject to favorable tax treatment.

capital lease: For accounting purposes, a lease that is treated as an owned asset. Equipment is often leased to companies on a capital basis. The company leasing the asset enjoys the tax benefits of ownership, including deductions for maintenance expenses. When the lease expires, the company leasing the asset is usually allowed to purchase it.

capital market: A general term referring to stock markets and bond markets where governments and corporations can sell securities, stocks, and bonds in order to raise capital.

cash: Money that can be used for financial transactions, including funds held in checking accounts.

cash basis: An accounting method in which income and expenses are recorded when money actually changes hands. Cash basis accounting is generally easier to do — and often produces tax benefits.

cash dividend: Stock dividends paid in cash, not in shares of stock.

cash surrender value: The amount of money that a life insurance policy pays if the holder gives up the policy or cancels it. The cash surrender value of a life insurance policy can be used as collateral on a loan.

cashier's check: A check written by a bank against its own funds. Cashier's checks are guaranteed to be redeemable because they are drawn on banks.

certified check: A check that has been guaranteed by a bank and can be considered as good as cash. Before giving its acceptance, the bank makes sure that enough money is in the account to cover the check and that the signature is valid.

certified public accountant (CPA): A person who has been certified by the state to issue opinions about the accuracy and fairness of a business's financial reports. CPAs also typically provide tax planning and preparation services for businesses and individuals.

charitable contribution: A contribution to a charity that can be deducted for income tax purposes.

check: A written order instructing a bank to pay a sum to a third party.

check kiting: An illegal scheme for fraudulently inflating the account balance of checking accounts. For example, a man with two checking accounts, one in Bank A and one in Bank B, writes a check on account A for $5,000 to his Bank B account. He deposits the check in Bank B. Until the check clears, he has $5,000 in both Bank B and Bank A. Next, he writes a check on account B for $5,000 to his Bank A account. He deposits this check, too. Until the checks clear, he has $10,000 in his Bank A account and $5,000 in his Bank B account. On paper he has $15,000; actually; he has only $5,000.

claim: A demand for money from an insurance company. You file a claim when you believe you are entitled to compensation from an insurer.

class action: A lawsuit filed on behalf of a group of people who have been wronged in the same way.

clear: To settle or discharge an account. Checks are cleared when they are redeemed for cash.

clearing house: A convenient place where banks in a given area exchange checks written against one another. Clearing houses make it easier for banks to clear and settle checks because bank representatives can meet in a central place without needing to visit each other's banks.

closed-end fund: A fund that issues a fixed number of shares instead of continuously offering new shares to buyers.

closing price: The final price of a stock or commodity at the time the exchange closes for the day.

cloud on title: A title that cannot be transferred to someone else because liens, court judgments, or other impediments prevent the owner from selling it.

co-insurance: A percentage amount for which an insurance policyholder must be covered. For example, if a fire insurance policy has a 70 percent co-insurance clause, the insured must be covered for at least 70 percent of the value of his or her home.

collateral: As part of a loan agreement, the property or securities that the borrower pledges to the lender in case the borrower cannot pay back the loan.

collateral loan: A loan given on the strength of the borrower's collateral, as opposed to the borrower's good standing in the community or good character.

collateral value: The value of the properties and securities that a prospective borrower has pledged when applying for a loan.

collection agency: An organization whose job it is to collect outstanding debts from individuals on behalf of companies and businesses.

collection letter: A letter, always very polite but vaguely threatening, asking you to please pay an overdue bill.

collusive bidding: When bidders agree among themselves to offer one (usually low) bid. Collusive bidding always results in a lower bid than competitive bidding, in which the bidders do not know one another's bids.

commercial bank: A full-service bank owned by stockholders that makes loans, accepts deposits, and offers other commercial financial services.

commercial paper: Promissory notes, such as checks, drafts, and IOUs, that constitute a debt of some kind. Commercial paper is negotiable and can be traded.

commission: The fee that brokers and agents charge for their services. A commission is often a percentage of the total value of a sale.

common law: The body of law developed in England, based on precedents and custom, which forms the basis for the legal system in all states except Louisiana, where Napoleonic law is practiced.

common stock: Securities that represent ownership in a corporation. By law, holders of common stock can receive dividends only after claims by preferred stockholders, creditors, and bondholders have been satisfied. Common stockholders are the last to be paid if a corporation goes bankrupt.

compensating balance: A minimum balance that borrowers who want to secure a loan from a bank must keep on deposit with the bank.

compound interest: Interest calculated on the original principal of a deposit plus all accrued interest.

consent decree: A judicial decree in which the parties settle their differences by agreeing to change their practices rather than by litigation.

conservator: A person appointed by a court to manage the affairs of an estate or the affairs of a person deemed incompetent.

consignment: An arrangement in which the manufacturer or person who made the goods is paid only after the goods are sold (referred to as *sold on consignment*).

construction loan: A loan covering construction costs, paid out at intervals as the construction project is completed. Also called a *construction mortgage*.

constructive notice: A notice published in a newspaper announcing some action, such as a lien or the confiscation of property by the state. By law, some actions must be "given constructive notice" so that anyone objecting can take action.

consumer credit: Credit given to individuals so they can buy personal things.

consumer durables: Items that consumers purchase infrequently and use over a period of years, such as televisions and washing machines. Also called *durable goods*.

consumer lease: The lease of a consumer item, such as a car, with a value under $25,000.

consumer price index: An index that measures the cost of living in the United States. The U.S. Labor Department is responsible for monitoring the consumer price index.

consumer-credit protection act: An act passed by Congress in 1969 requiring lenders to be truthful about how they compute finance charges. Under the consumer-credit protection act, finance charges must be expressed as an annual percentage rate (APR) of the loan amount. Also called *truth in lending*.

contract: A legally binding agreement between two or more parties, where the responsibilities of each are clearly outlined.

co-payment: In a health insurance plan, a percentage of a medical bill that you pay (the insurer covers the rest). Typically, you co-pay bills until you reach a certain dollar limit. After that point, the insurer pays 100 percent of your medical bills.

co-signer: A joint signer of a promissory note. Co-signers are jointly responsible for paying back loans.

cost-of-funds index (COFI): An index that banks use to help determine the cost of *adjustable-rate mortgages (ARMs)*. If the index goes up, so do ARM payments.

cost-of-living increases: Payment increases that pensioners and Social Security recipients get to offset rising costs brought about by inflation.

counterfeit: Money, bank cards, or checks that look real but are not. If you accept a counterfeit dollar bill from a customer, by the way, you're the only one who loses.

countersign: A signature that asserts the authenticity of a document already signed by another. In most companies, large checks require a countersign. Also called *countersignature*.

covenant: A written agreement between parties that has been sealed from public disclosure.

credit: Money that a bank or other lending institution places at your disposal when you agree to pay it back at a later date. Also, the portion of a bookkeeping entry that appears on the right side of a ledger (as discussed in Book I, Chapter 2).

credit agency: An agency that obtains data about the credit history of individuals and companies and offers the data to creditors and others.

credit insurance: Insurance purchased by banks as a defense against large credit losses.

credit limit: The most that a consumer or company can borrow at one time from a bank or other creditor.

credit line: A prearranged agreement whereby a lender will extend credit to an individual or company. You typically pay an annual fee for a credit line even if you don't use the credit line.

credit rating: A lender's appraisal of a borrower's ability to pay back loans. Credit ratings are based primarily on the borrower's past history of paying back loans.

credit risk: The risk that a borrower will not be able to pay back a loan.

credit slip: A notice removing a credit card charge from a cardholder's bill. If you return something you've purchased with a credit card, you are issued a credit slip in the amount of the charge to reverse its effect on your credit card balance.

creditor: A bank or other agency that extends credit to borrowers. The opposite of a creditor is a *debtor*.

cross-collateral: Collateral that backs up several loans, not just one, as arranged by agreement with the lender.

currency: Paper money in circulation. Also refers to the paper money issued by a nation. The dollar is the currency of the United States.

current assets: Assets that either are equivalent to cash or can easily and readily be converted into cash, including cash, money market funds, accounts receivable, inventory, and short-term investments.

current yield: The annual interest rate paid by a bond or other security, expressed as a percentage of the principal.

cushion: The time between the date a bond is issued and its first call date; that is, the day it can be redeemed either in whole or in part.

custodian: An institution or a broker that oversees the management of a group of assets.

custody account: A bank account held in trust by a parent or guardian on behalf of a minor.

customs: Taxes placed on goods being imported.

cycle billing: Billing one set of customers from a customer list on specific days of the month. For example, customers whose last names begin with *A* would be billed on the first day of the month, *B* on the second day, and so on. The idea is to spread out the paperwork over a month and keep bill payments coming in regularly.

daily interest: Interest compounded daily on a bank deposit. Although the interest is compounded daily, it is deposited in accounts at weekly, bi-weekly, or monthly intervals.

dealer: A person who trades in securities on his or her own. Dealers trade with their own money and take the risks themselves; brokers trade on behalf of others.

debentures: Unsecured bonds backed by the general credit of the issuer, not by the issuer's assets.

debit: An entry made on the left side of a ledger that records an expense. Refer to Book I, Chapter 2 for a complete discussion.

debt: Money owed.

debt service: Interest or principal payments on a mortgage. Debt service usually describes either the monthly payments or the total annual payment.

deed: A signed document describing a legal agreement or contract.

deed of trust: A legal document giving the bearer title to a property. Banks usually hold the deed of trust until the borrower has paid the mortgage in full. After that, title is given over to the borrower.

default: To fail to pay back a loan or meet an obligation.

deferred compensation: Earnings to be received in the future, not when they are earned. Deferring compensation sometimes has tax advantages.

deficiency: The amount by which a taxpayer fails to fulfill tax obligations. For example, if you underpay by $500, that is a $500 deficiency.

deficiency judgment: A court order giving a lender authority to collect part of the proceeds from a sale of property, when the seller of the property has defaulted on a mortgage or other financial obligation.

defined benefit plan: A retirement plan set up for a corporation's employees. These plans pay no taxes on their investments and must be managed according to federal standards.

defined contribution plan: Blanket term for various plans by which employees can make tax-deferred contributions to retirement plans.

deflation: A decline in prices. *Inflation*, a rise in prices, is the opposite of deflation.

delinquency: Failure to fulfill a financial obligation. Loans with two or more payments overdue are considered delinquent.

demand loan: A loan that can be paid back at any time and has no maturity date. Interest is paid until the principal has been paid off.

deposit: Money entered in a bank account.

deposit insurance: Insurance on bank deposits to protect depositors in the event of a bank failure. The Federal Deposit Insurance Corporation (FDIC), a government agency, insures bank accounts up to $100,000.

depository: A bank where funds and securities are deposited.

depreciation: A method of calculating the expense of using certain, long-lived assets. Also, the decline in value of an asset.

direct deposit: Depositing paychecks automatically in employees' bank accounts. Many companies now offer their employees direct deposit.

direct placement: Selling a security issue to one group of investors without the use of underwriters. Long-term securities are sometimes sold to institutions this way.

discharge of bankruptcy: A court order giving a bankrupt debtor release from all debt obligations. The debtor is no longer responsible for the debts, although the record of bankruptcy remains on the debtor's credit record for ten years.

disclosure: Information about the *annual percentage rate (APR)*, method of computing interest, and minimum monthly payment that banks must give to mortgage customers. Federal law requires banks to disclose this information.

discount: A reduction in price. In the bond market, the discount is the difference in price between what a bond costs today and its face value (what it will cost at maturity).

discount point: One percent of the principal of a mortgage. Home buyers typically pay the lender one discount point when their loans close.

discount rate: Rate used to measure the value of money over time. As a practical matter, a discount rate is the same thing as an interest rate.

discount yield: Method for computing Treasury Bill yields, in which the par value is computed instead of the purchase price. The formula for computing discount yields is the discount, divided by the par value amount multiplied by 360, divided by the number of days to maturity.

discounted cash flow: A mathematical technique used by financial analysts in which future-day dollars are converted into present-day dollars by adjusting for inflation and compound interest.

discounting: Converting future-day dollars into present-day dollars by adjusting for inflation and compound interest. Because discounting calculations are cumbersome, one typically uses a computer to perform the actual calculations.

diversification: Investing in many different areas — real estate, stocks, and bonds, for example — as a hedge against decline in one area. Diversification really means not putting all your eggs in one basket.

divest: To sell off assets or businesses because they are unprofitable or because they don't fit in a company's plans for the future.

dividend: A profit share paid out to a stockholder.

dividend reinvestment plan: A plan allowing corporate stockholders to be paid in cash or in stock.

double taxation: Refers to federal taxes on corporate earnings and how these earnings are taxed twice: once in the form of corporate taxes and again when earnings are distributed to shareholders.

duties: Tax on imported or exported items.

earnest money: A sum of money paid for property to assure the seller that the buyer is sincere. When the sales transaction is completed, the earnest money is counted toward the purchase price of the property.

earning asset: Any asset that generates interest income.

earnings per share: The amount that each stock share earns in dividends after both preferred stockholders and taxes have been paid.

Economic value added (EVA): Measures the true economic profit of a business by comparing a firm's profit to the return on investment that shareholders should have earned. Refer to Book V, Chapter 2 for a more complete discussion.

effective annual yield: What a depositor earns on a certificate of deposit (CD) or savings account on a yearly basis, provided that the money is not withdrawn.

electronic funds transfer (EFT): Transferring money by electric wire instead of by traditional paper means, such as check writing.

embargo: Keeping ships from entering port or leaving port by government decree.

embezzlement: Fraudulently appropriating money for personal use.

Employee Retirement Income Security Act (ERISA): Federal act describing how managers of profit-sharing funds and private pension funds may invest those funds. ERISA sets guidelines for fund managers.

employee stock ownership plan (ESOP): A plan allowing employees to buy stock in the company that they work for.

endorsement: A signature that allows for the transfer of a negotiable item. The signature on the back of a check, for example, is an endorsement.

escrow: An agreement whereby a deed, a bond, or property is held in trust by a third party until some obligation is fulfilled.

estate: A deceased's property at the time of death. An estate is passed to the deceased's heirs if he or she left a will. If not, the matter of how to divide the estate is decided by a probate court.

estate tax: Taxes levied by federal and state governments on the transfer of property from an estate to its beneficiaries. Estate taxes are paid by the estate. Inheritance taxes are paid by heirs for the property that they receive.

exchange rate: The rate that the currency of one country is trading against the currency of another. For example, an exchange rate of 118.18 yen to the dollar means that one U.S. dollar purchases 118.18 Japanese yen.

excise taxes: Taxes on acts, not property. For example, sales of liquor are subject to excise taxes.

face value: The principal of a stock, bond, or other security. Also the principal of an insurance policy. Face value is sometimes called *par value*.

fair market value: The reasonable price of an asset. Fair market value is the price that a willing seller and buyer would negotiate for an asset, given that both know all the facts and are not under compulsion to buy or sell.

Federal Deposit Insurance Corporation (FDIC): Federal agency that insures bank accounts against bank failures. The FDIC insures accounts to $100,000.

federal funds rate: Interest rate charged to commercial banks for purchasing federal funds. The federal funds rate is the benchmark for many commercial credit rates, including short-term business loans.

Federal Unemployment Tax: Tax paid on wages and salaries to pay for federal and state unemployment programs.

finance charge: The cost of interest payments, filing fees, and other costs apart from the actual cost of an item. The finance charge is what you pay when you finance a purchase.

finance company: A private company that issues loans.

Financial Accounting Standards Board (FASB): The board that establishes rules for certified public accountants (CPAs). This board also determines the generally accepted accounting principles.

fiscal year: A period of 12 months for which a company plans its budget and reports on its financial activity. The fiscal year and the calendar year often do not coincide; the fiscal year can begin at any point in the calendar year.

fixed asset: A tangible asset, such as equipment, that a company cannot dispose of without interrupting normal business activities.

fixed-rate loan: A loan whose rate of interest does not change.

fixture: Personal property that becomes part of real property because of the way in which it is used. Fixture is a legal term. If you build shelves into a wall in your rented apartment, they become a fixture; that is, they are a part of the rental property.

foreclosure: Legal proceeding in which a lender attempts to obtain the collateral that was secured for a defaulted loan.

foreign exchange: Converting the currency of one country into its equivalent in the currency of another country.

foreign trade: Importing and exporting goods between nations.

forged check: A check whose drawer signature or endorsement signature is not valid.

forgery: Fraudulently altering a document, such as a check.

Form 1099: The disclosure form filed with the IRS that lists all unearned and miscellaneous income.

franchise: A business arrangement whereby one party is allowed to use another party's name for a fee. Fast-food eateries are the best examples of franchises.

franchise tax: A tax imposed by a state on a business headquarters outside the state that does business in the state.

fraud: Intentional deception undertaken to trick someone else into parting with something of value. No legal definition of fraud exists.

future value: The value that a stock, bond, or commodity will attain in the future.

futures: Commodities to be delivered and paid for at a future date at a price agreed upon by the buyer and seller.

garnishment: Court judgment ordering a lender to be given part of the wages or salary of a borrower who has defaulted on a loan.

general partner: A co-owner of a business. General partners receive a share of the business's profit and are partly responsible for its debts and liabilities.

generally accepted accounting principles (GAAP): The rules and guidelines that certified public accountants (CPAs) use when preparing financial statements.

general-obligation bond: A bond issued to pay for public works projects, issued by a state or municipal government. Also called *G-O bond*.

GI loan: Name for special mortgage loans available to veterans of the U.S. armed services.

gift tax: A tax on gifts of cash or property. Gift taxes are paid by the donor.

gilt-edged: Name for low-risk AAA corporate bonds that have proven earnings.

going concern: Name to describe a business that is in operation and is expected to remain so in the future.

gross estate: The property in an estate before debts, taxes, and other expenses are paid. The *net estate* is what remains after these expenses are paid.

guaranteed bond: A bond whose principal and interest are backed by a corporation other than the issuer.

guarantor: A person or corporation that guarantees a debt will be paid if another party defaults. Guarantors are considered co-endorsers of a debt and are therefore liable for the debt.

guaranty: A promise on the part of an individual or corporation that it will pay the debt of another party if the other party defaults on a debt.

illiquid: Refers to assets that are not easy to liquidate; that is, to convert into cash.

impaired credit: A bank loan that is not likely to be repaid.

import taxes: Taxes levied on certain imported items. Most nations have import taxes to protect domestic markets from foreign competition.

income statement: A report describing a corporation's activities, its profit, and its losses over a fixed period.

indemnity: An obligation to pay all costs of damage, pain, or suffering.

indenture: A document that states the terms under which a bond is issued. The indenture declares the maturity date, the interest, and other information.

index: A numerical measurement that compares past and present economic activity. The Dow Jones Industrial Average is an index of stock performance. The Consumer Price Index measures the price of consumer goods.

individual retirement account (IRA): A retirement account to which individuals can deposit $3,000 (or more) annually out of earnings. IRAs provide two significant income tax benefits: IRA contributions may reduce an individual's taxable income, and IRA earnings are not taxed.

individual retirement account rollover: Rule allowing holders of individual retirement accounts (IRAs) to pass on the accumulated savings in one IRA to another IRA, provided that they do so within the first 60 days of closing the first IRA.

inflation: Rises in prices. Inflation is caused by excess purchasing power among the general populace and by increasing production costs, which producers pass on to consumers.

insolvency: Being unable to pay debts.

installment contract: Agreement to pay for goods in fixed installments — for example, weekly or monthly.

installment credit: A loan that is repaid in monthly payments of the same amount.

insufficient funds: What you have if you try to write a check for $10 and you only have $7.50 in your checking account, or if you try to withdraw $20 from a savings account with $18 in it.

intangible assets: The assets of a company that aren't property but are assets nonetheless. For example, an established clientele is an intangible asset.

interest: Amount of money paid to borrow capital. Typically, the interest is expressed as a percentage of the principal that was borrowed.

interest rate: The price of borrowing money. The interest rate is usually expressed as a percentage of the total principal borrowed, although sometimes the rate of interest on a loan is tied to an index of some kind.

interest-only loan: A loan that requires the borrower to pay only interest for the term of the loan. Loan payments on an interest-only loan do not reduce the loan balance. At the end of the loan, the borrower makes a balloon payment equal to the original (and ending) loan balance.

interim report: A report showing stockholders how a company is doing. An interim report appears before the company's annual report.

interim statement: A statement regarding account balances that you can get from an automatic teller machine (ATM). Interim statements are not as detailed as monthly statements.

internal rate of return (IRR): The profit that an investment earns expressed as a percentage. Typically, IRRs are stated as annual profit percentages. On an investment that pays interest and for which there is no change in value, such as a bank savings account, the interest rate is the IRR.

interstate commerce: Commercial trading of goods across state lines.

inventory: In a business, a list of stock on hand, with the value of each item and the total value of all items by category.

involuntary bankruptcy: A petition by creditors asking a bankruptcy court to declare a firm bankrupt, the firm having failed to pay its debts and meet its financial obligations. Also called a *creditor's opinion*.

involuntary lien: A lien made by the judgment of a court, without the consent of the property owner.

judgment: The official decision of a court of law.

judgment lien: A court order placing a lien on the property of a debtor.

judicial sale: A sale of property, as ordered by a court to satisfy a debt. A foreclosure is an example of a judicial sale.

junior mortgage: A second or subsequent mortgage on a property. If the property is in default, junior mortgages are paid only after the first mortgage has been paid.

Keogh plan: Retirement plan that allows you to set aside some of your wages or salary for retirement. Keogh plans are more complex to set up and to administer than SEP/IRA (Simplified Employee Pension/Individual Retirement Account) plans, but they may allow larger contributions.

kicker: An extra condition imposed by a lender before the lender will approve a loan. Part ownership in the property or a share of its proceeds are examples of kickers.

kiting: See *check kiting*.

lagging indicator: An economic indicator that usually reflects not where the economy is headed, but where it has been. For example, the gross national product (GNP) is a lagging indicator because increases or declines in the GNP aren't registered until after the fact.

late charge: A charge for tardiness in paying a bill or a mortgage payment.

lease: A contract that gives an individual or business the right to use a property for an agreed-upon price and time period.

leasehold: The right of occupancy that tenants enjoy as part of a lease.

leverage: Credit acquired in order to improve an individual's or company's ability to invest or speculate.

leveraged buyout: When one company takes over another and uses the acquired company's assets in order to pay back the loans that were taken out in order to take over the company in the first place.

liability: All debts and obligations of a business.

liability insurance: Insurance protecting the policyholder against financial losses resulting from injury done to others.

lien: A charge against real or personal property to secure the repayment of a debt.

limited liability company: Similar to a corporation, a business form that shields investors, called members, from risk. Typically, limited liability companies are treated as partnerships for income tax purposes.

limited partnership: A partnership in which profits and responsibility for liabilities and debts are shared according to how much of the business each partner owns.

line of credit: A commitment on the part of a bank to lend up to a certain amount of money to a borrower.

liquidity: Turning assets such as property into cash. An asset with "good liquidity" can be sold or converted into cash easily.

long-term: In financial terms, *long-term* refers to a security that matures in ten or more years.

maker: The writer of a check.

management report: A report describing company performance, prepared monthly for the officers of a corporation.

maturity: The date when the borrower is obliged to pay back the loan.

maximum out-of-pocket: The most you can pay for insurance in a year. Usually, the maximum out-of-pocket is the sum of the premium, the deductible, and all co-payments.

mechanic's lien: A lien on real property made by a contractor or builder for payment overdue. A builder can request a mechanic's lien if he or she has not been paid according to the contract to build or improve the property.

member: An investor in a limited liability company.

merger: When two or more corporations pool their common stock and become one corporation.

minimum balance: The least amount of money that can be kept in a savings or checking account. Letting the balance drop below the minimum sometimes incurs a service charge.

minimum payment: The smallest payment that can be made on a monthly credit card bill without incurring a service charge.

minor: In most states, a person under age 18. Minors do not have all the legal rights of adults, nor the legal responsibilities.

money market fund (MMF): A mutual fund that invests in Treasury Bills, certificate of deposits (CDs), and other short-term debt instruments. Investors own shares in the fund and receive regular interest payments.

money market rates: The rate of return paid by individual money market funds.

monopoly: When an individual or corporation has complete control over a market, through ownership of source materials, ownership of distribution in a certain area, or ownership of the means by which the product is made.

mortgage: A deed giving ownership of a property to a borrower on the condition that the borrower makes all interest and principal payments to a lender. The lender owns the mortgage until the borrower pays in full, after which the borrower becomes sole owner of the property.

mortgagee: Name for the lender who supplies mortgages and collects mortgage payments.

mortgagor: On a mortgage, the borrower who must pay the interest and principal.

negotiable: Capable of being transferred from one party to another. Checks, drafts, securities, and commercial paper are negotiable.

net worth: The total value of the assets of a business less the liabilities.

nonprofit corporation: An organization that does not distribute its profits, if there are any, to owners. Profits are plowed back into the nonprofit's capital fund.

nonrecourse loan: A loan for which, if the borrower defaults, the lender has no recourse except to foreclose on the borrower's collateral.

notary public: A public officer who attests to the authenticity of deeds, affidavits, and depositions.

note: A written promise to pay a debt or sum of money.

notes payable: In a general ledger, an account showing the business's liability for promissory notes.

notes receivable: In a general ledger, an account showing the business's promissory notes received from customers.

novation: An agreement to remove one party from a contract and replace that party with another. All parties in the contract must agree to the novation substitute.

online banking service: A service offered by a bank that allows you to download bank statements and make electronic fund transfers and payments using a computer and an Internet connection.

open-end lease: A car lease requiring monthly payments, at the end of which the borrower can make a large balloon payment to buy the car outright, or return the car to the lender.

operating lease: A lease covering a time period shorter than the economic life of the asset. Operating leases can be canceled at any time.

option: A contract giving a dealer or broker the right to buy or sell a security during a certain time period at a certain price.

original issue discount (OID): The difference between what a bond costs when it was issued and what its price is at maturity.

original maturity: The time between the day a bond was issued and the day it reaches maturity. The current maturity is the time between today's date and the date the bond reaches maturity.

origination fee: The fee that lenders charge loan applicants to handle loan applications and to conduct credit investigations.

overdraft: The amount that a check exceeds what is in the checking account that it was written against. If you write a check for $20 and you have only $15 in your checking account, you have a $5 overdraft.

partnership: A business with two or more owners who share equally in the profits as well as the liability for debts.

payee: The person or party to whom a check is written.

payroll taxes: Taxes on a payroll, including Social Security taxes and employment insurance taxes.

penalty clause: The clause in many banking contracts stating that customers must pay a penalty for late mortgage payments, early withdrawals of savings accounts, and the like.

pension fund: A fund set up by a corporation to provide for its employees in retirement. Typically, employees contribute a portion of their paychecks to the fund.

pension plan: A plan by which a company provides for its employees in retirement. Employees — sometimes with matching contributions from employers — contribute to a pension fund, which is used to make investments as part of the plan.

perfect title: A title to a property that is free of debts, liens, prior claims, and other encumbrances.

perfected lien: A lien that has not only been filed by the lien holder but is also in force.

periodic rate: The price of credit, expressed as a percentage and charged at periodic intervals.

permanent financing: A long-term mortgage, typically used to finance construction projects, covering all requirements of the project from legal costs to building materials.

personal identification number (PIN): The password or number that you punch in at an automatic teller machine (ATM) to make deposits and withdrawals. Also known as an *access code*.

personal property: Items and things, as opposed to *real property*, such as buildings and land. By definition, personal property is not "immovable"; in other words, it can be moved. A baseball card is personal property; a baseball field is real property.

personal property tax: Tax on valuable personal property, such as jewelry, cars, and yachts. Also called a *luxury tax*.

pledge: Placing property or collateral with a lender in order to secure a loan. For example, a watch left with a pawnbroker in return for a loan is a pledge.

point: In stock prices, a point equals one dollar; in bond prices, a point equals ten dollars.

portfolio: The term for the total assets and investments held by an individual, company, or institution. For reporting and tracking purposes, a portfolio can be divided into smaller portfolios, such as the loan portfolio, land portfolio, and so on.

posting: Recording accounting entries in a general ledger.

power of attorney: A legal document that lets someone you trust run your financial affairs if you become unable to do so.

premium: The sum above the face value of a bond when the bond is purchased at an above-par price. In insurance, the amount that you pay for insurance coverage.

present value: The current-day equivalent of some future amount, or future value. In converting future values to present values, one adjusts for compound interest and for inflation.

price/earnings ratio: The ratio between the current price of a stock and the earnings that it will make over a specific period of time. Investors use the price/earnings ratio to measure the value of stocks.

prime rate: The rate that banks charge their most trustworthy customers for commercial loans. Note that a bank's very best customers pay less than prime, however.

principal: The actual money borrowed in a loan, as distinguished from the *interest*, the price of buying the loan. Also a deposit as distinguished from the interest that it earns.

profit-sharing plan: A plan by which employees share in the profits of a company, either by receiving bonuses or having their profit shares put in a trust. Profit-sharing plans encourage employees to be more productive and more loyal to their companies.

promissory note: A written promise to pay a sum of money at a future date to a specific person or to the bearer of the written promise. Also known as an *IOU*.

property taxes: Taxes on property, including real estate and stocks.

proprietorship, sole: When a business is owned by one person. Sole proprietorship is one of three types of business organizations; the other two are a *partnership* and a *corporation*.

public offering: A bond issue offering to the general public.

qualified opinion: When omissions in bank records prevent auditors from doing a thorough review of a bank's books, auditors give a qualified opinion, which is a best-available assessment of the bank's financial health.

quiet title action: A legal action meant to resolve all claims against a property.

quorum: The minimum number of people who must be present at a corporate meeting to conduct business.

quote: The highest bid to buy and the lowest offer to sell a security or commodity. Also called a *quotation*.

rate of return: Money made on invested capital.

real income: Income measured for what it can buy, not in dollars-and-cents terms. For example, the real income of a low wage earner may be higher than that of someone who earns higher wages, if the low wage earner lives in a region where goods and housing are inexpensive.

real property: Land and buildings on the land, as opposed to personal property, which comprises movable items, such as jewelry and equipment.

real rate of return: The rate of return on an investment that takes into account how rates are affected by inflation. The real rate of return is the rate of return less the rate of inflation over the length of the investment.

real-interest rate: The interest rate that takes into account how interest yields are reduced by inflation. To get the real-interest rate, you subtract the inflation rate in a given period from interest earnings in the same period.

realized profit/loss: The cash profit or loss from the sale of a security.

rebate: A return of part of a payment, made after the payment is received. Rebates are offered as incentives for consumers to buy or use products.

receiver: A person assigned by a court to help a bankrupt business reorganize its finances, satisfy its creditors, and become profitable.

receivership: A bankrupt business to whom a receiver has been assigned is *in receivership.*

redemption: Exchanging bonds for cash when the bonds reach maturity.

registered check: A check purchased at a bank and backed by the bank that can be presented as payment to a third party. Registered checks work like money orders.

remittance slip: Attached to a check, a list of all deductions, corrections, discounts, taxes, or other information, along with the net amount of the check.

reorganization: After a business has declared bankruptcy, the restructuring of its assets in order to make it profitable again.

repossession: Seizing the collateral for a loan due to inability to pay the interest or principal. Repossession is usually the last recourse for failure to pay a debt.

reserve: Funds put aside for anticipated future costs.

reserve requirements: Reserves that banks are required to keep on hand for their basic operations. These reserves are deposited at the bank's district Federal Reserve Bank.

residual value: The value that an asset has when the asset's user or owner is finished using it.

restraint of trade: Refers to the concept, ingrained in U.S. law and in the American tradition, that no restrictions should be placed on the free flow of commerce.

restrictive covenant: A clause in an agreement or contract prohibiting a party or parties from taking certain actions. The most common restrictive covenant in business is one that prohibits a seller of a business from engaging in the same business for a certain number of years.

retained earnings: Business profits that are retained for expansion rather than paid in dividends to stockholders.

return on assets: A company's profits as a percentage of its assets. Return on assets is one way to measure a company's profitability.

return on investment: When the earnings derived from a piece of capital equipment equal the price paid for the piece of equipment, you have a perfect return on your investment.

revenue: The total income from a given endeavor. Also gross income from an investment.

reverse split: When stockholders exchange stock such that each owns the same number of shares. Reverse splits are undertaken so that stockholders all own the same percentage of a corporation.

revocable trust: A trust giving property to heirs that can be changed or revoked at any time by the person who originates the trust. Under this arrangement, the property is transferred to the heirs on the death of the trust originator, and the estate does not need to go through probate.

revolving credit: A form of credit in which the account holder is given a credit line, runs up a bill, and pays off the amount owed in monthly payments. If the amount owed is not paid off monthly, interest charges are made. A minimum monthly payment is usually required on outstanding credit loans. Most credit card accounts are revolving credit accounts.

right of foreclosure: The right of a lender to foreclose on a mortgaged property if the borrower cannot meet mortgage obligations.

right of redemption: The right of a debtor to buy a property at a sale of foreclosure if he or she has the means to do so. To redeem the property this way, the debtor must pay the interest and principal on the defaulted mortgage, as well as all foreclosure costs incurred by the lender.

right of survivorship: The right of surviving spouses to inherit the property of deceased spouses.

risk: In financial terms, the possibility that an investment will not be repaid and that the method of investment will be rendered unprofitable by market conditions.

run: When many depositors try to withdraw their money from a bank at short notice. When depositors fear that a bank is failing or otherwise lose confidence in a bank, a bank run can result.

safe deposit box: A small safe in a bank vault that can be rented for storing valuables and important papers.

salary-reduction plan: A retirement plan in which money is taken automatically from employees' salaries and put in a retirement fund, such as a 401(k).

sales tax: A tax levied by state and local governments, usually as a percentage of retail sales.

savings account: A deposit bank account that yields interest. Cash can be deposited or withdrawn at the discretion of the holder.

savings bank: A bank that accepts deposits from customers and invests it in mortgages and securities.

savings bond: A U.S. government bond, issued to finance the debt of the U.S. government. Savings bonds earn variable interest and are sold in denominations from $50 to $10,000.

seasonal adjustment: Adjusting data collected throughout the year to an annual rate for the purposes of analysis. For example, retail sales rise in December when people shop for the holidays. Retail sales figures for December, therefore, need to be adjusted downward.

seasonal credit: The line of credit extended to businesses during peak manufacturing and sales cycles.

second mortgage: Another mortgage on a property, usually taken out to provide capital for home improvements or to finance a business. The obligations due the lender of a second mortgage are subordinate to the obligations owed the lender of a first mortgage.

secondary mortgage market: A market where first mortgages, or residential mortgages, are pooled and sold to investors. The secondary mortgage market serves as a capital fund for the mortgage originators, who sell their mortgages for the secondary market.

secured credit card: A credit card that is backed by a savings account. Issuers of secured credit cards can draw on cardholders' savings accounts if cardholders are unable to pay their credit card bills.

securities: Stocks, bonds, and other financial instruments that can be traded in a securities market.

Securities and Exchange Commission (SEC): The regulatory agency charged with overseeing laws regarding the buying and selling of securities. Companies selling securities, and brokers and dealers who trade in them, must register with the SEC.

security agreement: A document that gives a lender a claim to the assets that the borrower has put up as collateral for a loan. The security agreement must be signed by the borrower to be valid.

security interest: The claim of a lender to assets that the borrower has pledged as collateral to back up a loan.

self-insurance: A rainy day fund set aside for emergencies, illness, and periods of unemployment.

seller's market: Raising demand and raising the price that sellers can offer goods in short supply.

senior lien: When two or more liens have been placed on a property, the senior lien takes precedence over other liens and must be satisfied first. The senior lien is the first mortgage on the property.

serial bonds: Bonds from the same issue that mature at different times. This way, the bonds do not all fall due at once and strain the finances of the issuer.

service charge: A bank charge, such as the charge issued when an account is overdrawn or a check bounces.

settlement date: The actual date of the transfer of a security from the buyer to the seller.

severally but not jointly: In a stock offering, when the people selling the stock are each responsible for selling their part, but not for selling the entire offering. In a *jointly but severally* arrangement, all parties are responsible for the sale of the offering.

sheriff's sale: An auction of a borrower's property as part of a foreclosure. The proceeds go to help pay the borrower's debts.

short-term financing: A loan that falls due in less than one year.

signature loan: A loan given without collateral, but with only the borrower's promise to pay and his or her signature on a promissory note. Such loans are given on the basis of the good standing of the borrower.

Simple IRA: A simplified pension plan for small businesses wanting to provide their employees with retirement savings options. Simple IRAs work much like 401(k)s — but at a much lower administrative cost to the employer.

Simplified Employee Pension Plan (SEP): A retirement plan for small businesses. It allows people in small businesses to set aside up to 15 percent of their gross income for retirement.

Small Business Administration (SBA): An agency of the federal government that helps to provide credit to small businesses.

Social Security: Insurance benefits provided by the federal government for old age, disabilities, and unemployment.

sole proprietorship: When a business is owned by one person. Sole proprietorship is one of three types of business organizations; the other two are a *partnership* and a *corporation.*

special offering: A block of securities so large it cannot be offered on the trading floor without depressing prices. Instead of being traded on the floor, special offerings are traded through members of the exchange, who sell them on their own.

specialist: A broker or dealer who specializes in trading a single commodity or security.

specie: Coins, not paper money.

speculation: Trading at a greater risk in order to obtain a fast profit.

speculator: A person who trades in commodities, stocks, or bonds with the idea of making a quick profit by taking many risks.

split: The dividing of existing stock into more shares. Individual stocks lose value, but the total value of the stock stays the same. Stock splits are often undertaken to make the stock easier to trade when companies are bought and sold.

squeeze: A shortage of funds in the money market, which causes a demand for money and a hike in interest rates.

stale check: A check that is more than six months old.

stamp taxes: Taxes in the form of stamps, which manufacturers must buy and stick on their products or securities before they can be sold. You can see tax stamps on some brands of whiskey, for example.

Standard & Poor's: The advisory service that rates securities for their creditworthiness.

standard of living: The goods and services that a social group requires for its well-being. The standard of living is an abstract term and cannot be measured against an index.

statute of frauds: A legal statute that says a contract cannot be enforced unless it has the signature of the person against whom it is being enforced. In the case of a mortgage or other assumable debt, the signature of the borrower is required.

statute of limitations: A limit on the time within which a legal action can be brought or a file claimed.

stock certificate: A written document giving title to a share or shares of stock.

stock exchange: A market where stocks are traded.

stock purchase option: A benefit offered to employees, giving them the option to buy stock in the companies that they work for.

stock split: The dividing of existing stock into more shares. Individual stocks lose value, but the total value of the stock stays the same. Stock splits are often undertaken to make the stock easier to trade when companies are bought and sold.

stop order: An order to buy or sell a stock or commodity when it reaches a certain price.

stop payment: To inform a bank not to honor a check. Even after a check is written and delivered, a bank customer can stop payment on it if he or she thinks the check was written in error.

subsidiary corporation: A company that is owned wholly or partly by another company, called the *parent company*. The parent company usually owns a majority of the stock in the subsidiary.

surcharge: An extra charge for people who pay with credit cards instead of cash. The surcharge pays for the extra costs of processing credit card payments.

surety: A guarantee that a debt will be repaid. Also, a person who is legally responsible for a debt.

surety bond: An agreement that if a housing development cannot be completed, an insurance company will take charge of the project, settle all disputes, and finish the project if necessary. Municipal development projects require surety bonds.

surtax: An added tax on income that has already been taxed once.

tariff: Taxes on import goods, levied to protect domestic industries or to raise revenue.

tax lien: A lien on property for failure to pay property taxes.

tax sale: An auction of property to raise money for the payment of delinquent taxes.

taxable estate: The part of an estate that is subject to taxes. The taxable estate is what is left after all debts, funeral expenses, and taxes are paid.

tax-deferred savings: Tax-free savings that can be put in an individual retirement account (IRA) or other retirement plan. Taxes are not imposed on the interest or principal until funds are withdrawn at age 59½ or later.

tax-free rollover: The automatic renewal of a certificate of deposit (CD), tax-free at present rates of interest. Also, the automatic tax-free reinvestment of money market funds.

taxpayer identification number (TIN): For taxation purposes, the number that identifies corporations, nonprofits, associations, and partnerships to the IRS. Sole proprietors and individuals are identified by their Social Security numbers.

teller's check: A check written by a bank against its own funds. Teller's checks are guaranteed to be redeemable because they are drawn on banks.

term: The time that it takes for a loan or deposit to mature. The term is usually expressed in months.

third-party check: A check transferred by the endorser to another party. The endorser writes "pay to the order of" and then the third party's name on the check, making it redeemable by the third party.

time-value of money: A general rule that says a dollar today is worth more than a dollar a year from today because if you have a dollar today, you can invest it and earn interest over the next year.

title: Having ownership of real property. A deed, bill of sale, or certificate is required to prove title.

title company: A company that determines who has ownership of a property. Having conducted a title search, the company issues a certificate of title to the owner.

title defect: A claim, obstruction, or other condition that makes it difficult to determine the owner of a property.

treasurer: A financial officer of a corporation whose job is, among other duties, to manage cash payments and deposits, procure and budget funds, handle the payroll, and discharge tax liabilities.

Treasury Bill: A short-term bill issued by the U.S. government to cover its debt. Treasury Bills are in $10,000 denominations. They mature in periods of 13, 26, or 52 weeks.

Treasury bond: A long-term bond issued by the U.S. government to cover its debts. Treasury bonds are sold in denominations of $10,000 or more.

trust: Property held by one person or persons for the benefits of others.

truth-in-lending law: Federal Reserve regulation (Regulation DD) establishing what information lenders must disclose to borrowers, including how finance charges are imposed, when additional charges will be made, and when a borrower may acquire a security interest in a property.

underlying lien: A lien to which other liens and property claims are subordinate. A first mortgage, for example, is an underlying lien.

underwriter: The person at an insurance company who processes applications for insurance and decides who gets insurance and who doesn't get insurance.

unearned income: Income earned from investments and interest.

unemployment insurance: A federal- and state-run program that provides an income to unemployed workers. Contributions to unemployment insurance are usually deducted from salaries and wages.

Uniform Commercial Code (UCC): Standardized state laws that establish rules for contracts, including how to prepare negotiables and handle deeds of title.

Uniform Consumer Credit Code: A law applicable in some states outlining how lenders and borrows should treat consumer loans under $25,000. The code sets guidelines for fair lending practices and describes how lenders can recoup defaulted loans.

uninsured depositor: A depositor with a savings or checking account larger than $100,000. Accounts above that amount are not insured by the *FDIC*.

unsecured loan: A loan given without the borrower posting collateral or providing any other security.

U.S. savings bond: A U.S. government bond, issued to finance the debt of the U.S. government. Savings bonds earn variable interest and are sold in denominations from $50 to $10,000.

usury: The lending of money at an exorbitant rate of interest. By law, usury is defined as charging an interest rate above the legal limit.

variable annuity: An annuity paid out at a variable rate, depending on interest accrued on a principal.

variable-rate loan: A loan whose rate of interest changes. The rate is determined by a standard index, such as the *prime rate*.

variable-rate mortgage: A mortgage whose interest rate is adjusted periodically. These mortgages are usually tied to some sort of money index, such as the prime lending rate or the cost of Treasury Bills. When the index goes up or down, so does the monthly mortgage payment. Also called an *adjustable-rate mortgage (ARM)*.

venture capital: Capital available for new enterprises and startup companies.

vested interest: In financial terminology, a stake in something that will give you money in the future. For example, employees have a vested interest in the prosperity of their company pension plans.

void: Null and no longer applicable, such as a voided check.

volume of trading: The total number of shares traded on a stock market. Trading volume is a measure of market activity.

voluntary bankruptcy: When a debtor declares bankruptcy in order to gain relief from creditors.

wage garnishment: A court judgment ordering a lender to be given part of the wages of a borrower who has defaulted on a loan.

Wall Street: The famous street in New York, New York, the address of the New York Stock Exchange, and the place where so many financial decisions are made by people in horn-rimmed glasses.

warranty: A guarantee that what is written in a contract is indeed true.

wholly owned subsidiary: A subsidiary completely owned by its parent company.

wire transfer: Transferring money electronically, as opposed to by check or by means of another type of paper transfer.

withholding: Taking deductions from income to cover taxes or liabilities.

worker's compensation insurance: By state law, insurance paid by employers in case of injury on the job.

write-off: Removing an item from an account ledger because the item has been fully depreciated or deemed worthless.

yield curve: A graph comparing the yields at maturity of different securities.

yield to maturity: The annual return, expressed as a percentage, of a bond or note redeemed at maturity.

zero-coupon bond: A bond issued without coupons and without a statement of its rate of interest.

zero-coupon security: A security that pays no interest until maturity, when the interest is paid in a lump sum.

Index

Numerics

A

Notes

Notes

Notes

BUSINESS, CAREERS & PERSONAL FINANCE

0-7645-5307-0   0-7645-5331-3 *†

Also available:

- Accounting For Dummies †
  0-7645-5314-3
- Business Plans Kit For Dummies †
  0-7645-5365-8
- Cover Letters For Dummies
  0-7645-5224-4
- Frugal Living For Dummies
  0-7645-5403-4
- Leadership For Dummies
  0-7645-5176-0
- Managing For Dummies
  0-7645-1771-6

- Marketing For Dummies
  0-7645-5600-2
- Personal Finance For Dummies *
  0-7645-2590-5
- Project Management For Dummies
  0-7645-5283-X
- Resumes For Dummies †
  0-7645-5471-9
- Selling For Dummies
  0-7645-5363-1
- Small Business Kit For Dummies *†
  0-7645-5093-4

HOME & BUSINESS COMPUTER BASICS

0-7645-4074-2   0-7645-3758-X

Also available:

- ACT! 6 For Dummies
  0-7645-2645-6
- iLife '04 All-in-One Desk Reference
  For Dummies
  0-7645-7347-0
- iPAQ For Dummies
  0-7645-6769-1
- Mac OS X Panther Timesaving
  Techniques For Dummies
  0-7645-5812-9
- Macs For Dummies
  0-7645-5656-8

- Microsoft Money 2004 For Dummies
  0-7645-4195-1
- Office 2003 All-in-One Desk Reference
  For Dummies
  0-7645-3883-7
- Outlook 2003 For Dummies
  0-7645-3759-8
- PCs For Dummies
  0-7645-4074-2
- TiVo For Dummies
  0-7645-6923-6
- Upgrading and Fixing PCs For Dummies
  0-7645-1665-5
- Windows XP Timesaving Techniques
  For Dummies
  0-7645-3748-2

FOOD, HOME, GARDEN, HOBBIES, MUSIC & PETS

0-7645-5295-3   0-7645-5232-5

Also available:

- Bass Guitar For Dummies
  0-7645-2487-9
- Diabetes Cookbook For Dummies
  0-7645-5230-9
- Gardening For Dummies *
  0-7645-5130-2
- Guitar For Dummies
  0-7645-5106-X
- Holiday Decorating For Dummies
  0-7645-2570-0
- Home Improvement All-in-One
  For Dummies
  0-7645-5680-0

- Knitting For Dummies
  0-7645-5395-X
- Piano For Dummies
  0-7645-5105-1
- Puppies For Dummies
  0-7645-5255-4
- Scrapbooking For Dummies
  0-7645-7208-3
- Senior Dogs For Dummies
  0-7645-5818-8
- Singing For Dummies
  0-7645-2475-5
- 30-Minute Meals For Dummies
  0-7645-2589-1

INTERNET & DIGITAL MEDIA

0-7645-1664-7   0-7645-6924-4

Also available:

- 2005 Online Shopping Directory
  For Dummies
  0-7645-7495-7
- CD & DVD Recording For Dummies
  0-7645-5956-7
- eBay For Dummies
  0-7645-5654-1
- Fighting Spam For Dummies
  0-7645-5965-6
- Genealogy Online For Dummies
  0-7645-5964-8
- Google For Dummies
  0-7645-4420-9

- Home Recording For Musicians
  For Dummies
  0-7645-1634-5
- The Internet For Dummies
  0-7645-4173-0
- iPod & iTunes For Dummies
  0-7645-7772-7
- Preventing Identity Theft For Dummies
  0-7645-7336-5
- Pro Tools All-in-One Desk Reference
  For Dummies
  0-7645-5714-9
- Roxio Easy Media Creator For Dummies
  0-7645-7131-1

* Separate Canadian edition also available
† Separate U.K. edition also available

Available wherever books are sold. For more information or to order direct: U.S. customers visit www.dummies.com or call 1-877-762-2974.
U.K. customers visit www.wileyeurope.com or call 0800 243407. Canadian customers visit www.wiley.ca or call 1-800-567-4797.

 WILEY

SPORTS, FITNESS, PARENTING, RELIGION & SPIRITUALITY

0-7645-5146-9

0-7645-5418-2

Also available:

- Adoption For Dummies
  0-7645-5488-3
- Basketball For Dummies
  0-7645-5248-1
- The Bible For Dummies
  0-7645-5296-1
- Buddhism For Dummies
  0-7645-5359-3
- Catholicism For Dummies
  0-7645-5391-7
- Hockey For Dummies
  0-7645-5228-7

- Judaism For Dummies
  0-7645-5299-6
- Martial Arts For Dummies
  0-7645-5358-5
- Pilates For Dummies
  0-7645-5397-6
- Religion For Dummies
  0-7645-5264-3
- Teaching Kids to Read For Dummies
  0-7645-4043-2
- Weight Training For Dummies
  0-7645-5168-X
- Yoga For Dummies
  0-7645-5117-5

TRAVEL

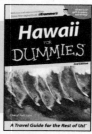

0-7645-5438-7

0-7645-5453-0

Also available:

- Alaska For Dummies
  0-7645-1761-9
- Arizona For Dummies
  0-7645-6938-4
- Cancún and the Yucatán For Dummies
  0-7645-2437-2
- Cruise Vacations For Dummies
  0-7645-6941-4
- Europe For Dummies
  0-7645-5456-5
- Ireland For Dummies
  0-7645-5455-7

- Las Vegas For Dummies
  0-7645-5448-4
- London For Dummies
  0-7645-4277-X
- New York City For Dummies
  0-7645-6945-7
- Paris For Dummies
  0-7645-5494-8
- RV Vacations For Dummies
  0-7645-5443-3
- Walt Disney World & Orlando For Dummies
  0-7645-6943-0

GRAPHICS, DESIGN & WEB DEVELOPMENT

0-7645-4345-8

0-7645-5589-8

Also available:

- Adobe Acrobat 6 PDF For Dummies
  0-7645-3760-1
- Building a Web Site For Dummies
  0-7645-7144-3
- Dreamweaver MX 2004 For Dummies
  0-7645-4342-3
- FrontPage 2003 For Dummies
  0-7645-3882-9
- HTML 4 For Dummies
  0-7645-1995-6
- Illustrator cs For Dummies
  0-7645-4084-X

- Macromedia Flash MX 2004 For Dummies
  0-7645-4358-X
- Photoshop 7 All-in-One Desk Reference For Dummies
  0-7645-1667-1
- Photoshop cs Timesaving Techniques For Dummies
  0-7645-6782-9
- PHP 5 For Dummies
  0-7645-4166-8
- PowerPoint 2003 For Dummies
  0-7645-3908-6
- QuarkXPress 6 For Dummies
  0-7645-2593-X

NETWORKING, SECURITY, PROGRAMMING & DATABASES

0-7645-6852-3

0-7645-5784-X

Also available:

- A+ Certification For Dummies
  0-7645-4187-0
- Access 2003 All-in-One Desk Reference For Dummies
  0-7645-3988-4
- Beginning Programming For Dummies
  0-7645-4997-9
- C For Dummies
  0-7645-7068-4
- Firewalls For Dummies
  0-7645-4048-3
- Home Networking For Dummies
  0-7645-42796

- Network Security For Dummies
  0-7645-1679-5
- Networking For Dummies
  0-7645-1677-9
- TCP/IP For Dummies
  0-7645-1760-0
- VBA For Dummies
  0-7645-3989-2
- Wireless All In-One Desk Reference For Dummies
  0-7645-7496-5
- Wireless Home Networking For Dummies
  0-7645-3910-8

HEALTH & SELF-HELP

0-7645-6820-5 *†

0-7645-2566-2

Also available:

- Alzheimer's For Dummies
  0-7645-3899-3
- Asthma For Dummies
  0-7645-4233-8
- Controlling Cholesterol For Dummies
  0-7645-5440-9
- Depression For Dummies
  0-7645-3900-0
- Dieting For Dummies
  0-7645-4149-8
- Fertility For Dummies
  0-7645-2549-2

- Fibromyalgia For Dummies
  0-7645-5441-7
- Improving Your Memory For Dummies
  0-7645-5435-2
- Pregnancy For Dummies †
  0-7645-4483-7
- Quitting Smoking For Dummies
  0-7645-2629-4
- Relationships For Dummies
  0-7645-5384-4
- Thyroid For Dummies
  0-7645-5385-2

EDUCATION, HISTORY, REFERENCE & TEST PREPARATION

0-7645-5194-9

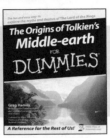

0-7645-4186-2

Also available:

- Algebra For Dummies
  0-7645-5325-9
- British History For Dummies
  0-7645-7021-8
- Calculus For Dummies
  0-7645-2498-4
- English Grammar For Dummies
  0-7645-5322-4
- Forensics For Dummies
  0-7645-5580-4
- The GMAT For Dummies
  0-7645-5251-1
- Inglés Para Dummies
  0-7645-5427-1

- Italian For Dummies
  0-7645-5196-5
- Latin For Dummies
  0-7645-5431-X
- Lewis & Clark For Dummies
  0-7645-2545-X
- Research Papers For Dummies
  0-7645-5426-3
- The SAT I For Dummies
  0-7645-7193-1
- Science Fair Projects For Dummies
  0-7645-5460-3
- U.S. History For Dummies
  0-7645-5249-X

Get smart @ dummies.com®

- **Find a full list of Dummies titles**
- **Look into loads of FREE on-site articles**
- **Sign up for FREE eTips e-mailed to you weekly**
- **See what other products carry the Dummies name**
- **Shop directly from the Dummies bookstore**
- **Enter to win new prizes every month!**

* Separate Canadian edition also available
† Separate U.K. edition also available

Available wherever books are sold. For more information or to order direct: U.S. customers visit www.dummies.com or call 1-877-762-2974.
U.K. customers visit www.wileyeurope.com or call 0800 243407. Canadian customers visit www.wiley.ca or call 1-800-567-4797.

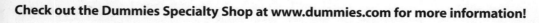